THE PASTORAL SERMONS OF
RONALD A. KNOX

THE
PASTORAL SERMONS
OF
RONALD A. KNOX

Edited, with an Introduction, by

PHILIP CARAMAN, S.J.

LONDON
BURNS & OATES

NIHIL OBSTAT: HUBERTUS RICHARDS, S.T.L., L.S.S.
CENSOR DEPUTATUS
IMPRIMATUR: E. MORROGH BERNARD
VICARIUS GENERALIS
WESTMONASTERII DIE X JANUARII MCMLX

The Nihil obstat and Imprimatur are a declaration that a book or pamphlet is considered to be free from doctrinal or moral error. It is not implied that those who have granted the Nihil obstat and Imprimatur agree with the contents, opinions or statements expressed.

First published March 1960
Reprinted October 1960

© Evelyn Waugh 1960

MADE AND PRINTED IN GREAT BRITAIN BY
THE DITCHLING PRESS LTD., SUSSEX
AND BOUND BY G. & J. KITCAT, LTD., LONDON, FOR
BURNS AND OATES LIMITED,
28 ASHLEY PLACE, LONDON, S.W.I.

Introduction

THIS collected edition of Mgr Ronald Knox's sermons is published in two volumes, entitled "Pastoral" and "Occasional". The division is exact and convenient, since the sermons fall naturally into these two groups, which happen also to be about equal in length.

In February 1959 Mr Evelyn Waugh, Mgr Knox's literary executor, placed in my hands all the typescripts of Mgr Knox's unpublished sermons and conferences as well as other miscellaneous papers. If Mgr Knox had been given time to work through these typescripts himself, it is likely that he would have continued his practice of gathering them into groups and publishing them at intervals of two or three years. This practice could have been continued; but it seemed that the time had come to attempt a complete collection of all Mgr Knox's sermons, both published and unpublished. Thanks to the co-operation of Mgr Knox's literary agent, Mr W. P. Watt, and his publishers, it was possible to undertake this work, which Mgr Knox's modesty would certainly have prevented in his own lifetime. This collection was all the more needed, because all the earlier books of sermons were, with one exception, long out of print. Moreover, there was never any doubt in my mind that the enduring value of the sermons more than merited a work on this scale.

Both in content and presentation all the unpublished sermons were as carefully polished as any Mgr Knox himself arranged for publication. Fortunately for his editor their effectiveness did not depend on the orator's arts or pulpit presence. Although, of course, all the sermons were written to be delivered, each is as compactly and incisively worked out as any chapter in his instructional or apologetical works: and each has the same restraint, refinement of diction and the painstaking search for the illuminating comparison. In the thousand pages that make up the two volumes there is much less repetition in thought and phrasing than in most theological works of the same dimensions. Nowhere do you find the preacher's inexact language or exaggerations that become distasteful as soon as they are exposed in print. Apart from annotation and arrangement there was no editing to be done to the text. All the sermons are printed exactly as they were written.

Only after I had read the sermons in this volume a second time, with the purpose of giving the references to Scriptural and other quotations, did I realize that this collection formed perhaps the most impressive body of pastoral teaching of our time. In scope and brilliance it appeared an achievement comparable only with Newman's Oxford sermons; yet more valuable because the idiom and message belonged to our own generation.

In the Introduction to the companion volume I have discussed Mgr Knox's style as a preacher. Here perhaps is the place to point to a few aspects of his teaching. Readers of Mr Evelyn Waugh's Life of Mgr Ronald Knox will not be surprised to notice that the largest single section of this book is devoted to the Eucharist. This is not due merely to the accident that from 1926 he was asked every year to preach at Maiden Lane on the feast of Corpus Christi: rather he agreed to the repeated request because, for him, the Eucharist was the central, inexhaustible and unifying mystery of his priestly life. It will be recalled that as an Anglican the Eucharist was the inspiration of his ministry; and that only when he began to be tormented with doubts about the validity of his priesthood did he take his first painful steps in the direction of Rome. "I never celebrate", he wrote at this time, "without wondering whether anything's happening"; and again, "I have to set my teeth to consecrate, and make my thanksgiving after communion or confession with a mental reservation."[1] The Catholic priesthood gave him the assurance that he was indeed offering the sacrifice of the New Testament; and the Mass became not merely the central act of his own life, but the unifying mystery of the people of God. It is striking how the social aspect of the Eucharist, a theme seldom developed by modern writers, recurs in many of these sermons, and each time in a different context. The same food, handed round like the bread in the miracle of the barley loaves, draws each man to his neighbour and makes each feel his human interdependence. Here, and in innumerable other places, Mgr Knox calls attention to precisely those things that Catholics forget, insisting always that the Eucharist is instituted as much for a social as for an individual purpose. If others receive Holy Communion at the same time as we do, it is not to save the priest trouble: it is a sacramental assertion of the bond of fellowship that unites all the faithful to Christ, and through him to one another.

This habit of thought on the Eucharist makes Mgr Knox quick to notice all the hints of the mysterious union of Christians in the Gospel narratives and parables. The wedding feast of Cana, for instance, has

---

[1] Evelyn Waugh, *Ronald Knox*, p. 145.

its lessons of union for the communicant as much as the feeding of the five thousand, and both, moreover, illustrate the need of our co-operation with God's grace. In both miracles our Lord leaves something to be done by his human assistants. "Give them to eat", he orders them in the one case; "Fill the waterpots", on the other occasion. "So in this most august sacrament", Mgr Knox concludes, "he does ask for co-operation; he does invite us to correspond by our own devotion with the grace we receive."

In this group of sermons there are many examples of the manner in which meditation on the Eucharist directed his reflections on certain theological or spiritual problems which are commonly considered in isolation from it. A striking example is the passage in the sermon entitled *Prope est Verbum*. Here Mgr Knox faces the problem that intermittently teases the Christian mind—how God can care individually for the souls he has made, for the thousands of our fellow human beings whom we see passing in crowds down the streets to their daily work with "faces hardened by money-getting, faces impudent with the affectation of vice, faces vacant with frivolity, faces lined with despair". It seems impossible that each of these faces can represent a human being for whom God cares as he cared for Zaccheus or Mary Magdalen. But it is the mystery of the Eucharist that allays the scruple, for the universality of its application makes it possible for us to imagine the universality of the divine love.

With much profit to himself the reader of these sermons can study the central place occupied by the Eucharist in Mgr Knox's spiritual life. The subject and its implications in our daily work is so well developed that the central portion of the book forms a most valuable and modern treatise on the Blessed Sacrament.

A study of this or any other section of the book shows the rare quality of Mgr Knox as a teacher. Through his own study of the Gospels he appreciated the basic characteristics of our Lord's own teaching method, and the didactic importance of the miracles and parables. Except in the instance of the multiplication of the loaves and fishes, the Gospels leave undeveloped the lessons our Lord himself drew from his miracles. Occasionally, as in the cure of the paralytic, they are briefly outlined; more often they are left unexplained. In these sermons Mgr Knox fulfils the traditional task of the true Christian teacher; he draws out to the full, for the spiritual instruction of his generation, the lessons of our Lord's actions and sayings. He knows that the parable is a device that no Christian teacher has been able to better; and as a student of Scripture he is able to employ both the fully developed and the suppressed parable with a skill that is perhaps not manifest at first reading, for his masterly treatment is partially concealed by the simplicity and freshness of his manner and the sureness of his interpretation.

However, this is more than a book of sermons. It can be considered a manual of meditation both for the layman and the priest. It contains instruction and material for self-examination. In the early series on the Sermon on the Mount his positive, and therefore most helpful, approach to the difficulties of the spiritual life is as manifest as in the later series on the Our Father. The direction is always away from the restrictive bonds of the commandments and towards the active charity which our Lord's discourse was designed to inspire in his followers, so that they might attain the inner freedom of spirit. The second sermon in this group is a good example of this approach. Mgr Knox is discussing lying. After observing that "men lie from selfishness, and women mostly from unselfishness", he continues: "Life is complicated and we work-a-day Christians mustn't expect too much of ourselves. But this I do say, that in proportion as a Christian lives a recollected life and tries to make our Lord his model, he will obtain a simplicity and lucidity of character which will have less and less need for untruth. He will live, not according to the caprice of the moment, but according to a plan; there will be less selfishness in his calculations, less partiality in his judgments. . . . His conversation will be more with our Lady and the saints, less with his exacting, distracting fellow citizens in this world below."

This is typical of Mgr Knox's balanced and realistic teaching. In the development of every subject that he handles, he is practical and sensible without making any concession to less than the highest ideal. Yet he tries to sketch a feasible plan for perfection from the teaching of our Lord which was directed, not to an élite, but to the multitude. He is always positive, whether his subject is swearing, lying, the taking of oaths or giving way to anger. No matter how matter-of-fact the subject of his instruction appears, he shows unfailingly how it is the same principle of active charity that our Lord is out to stress. And always there is the brilliant definition that brings home his point. Speaking of our Lord's emphasis on not measuring generosity or forgiveness in the scales, he says, with an alarming sense of realism, "The saint expects no more reward for attending lepers than you expect for looking after some relation of yours who should fall ill in the next street". Perhaps there is only one phrase that recurs in several sermons. It concerns God's care for each of us: with full awareness of what he is doing, he reiterates that "we are in the hands of God who made us and hates nothing that he has made".

It may not be an exaggeration to say that, at least in the spiritual interpretation of the Scriptures, Mgr Knox shows his finest qualities as a Biblical scholar in this volume of sermons. He is constantly posing questions that would occur only to a Scripture scholar, and he answers them with an honesty and originality that is always helpful. For instance, was St Joseph bound to appear at Bethlehem on a special day? If not, why did he choose a moment when our Lady's time was so close? No matter how baffling or obscure a remark of our Lord's may be, Mgr Knox is always ready to ask, "What does it all mean?" His answers are his own and are related to our daily lives. The sermon *Danger versus Safety* is an example. He explains satisfactorily our Lord's apparent equiparation of immodest glances with adultery, and then, typically, gives a precise and inspiring summary of all that is involved in the following of Christ—a summary that is illuminated by an original comparison which he sustains throughout the sermon.

There is rich material in this and in the companion volume for a profitable study of Mgr Knox's spiritual teaching. There are whole groups of sermons I have not even mentioned. This very inadequate comment is no more than an introduction.

These volumes are not intended to be a literary memorial to Mgr Ronald Knox. That is the last thing he would have wanted. The sermons have been collected with the conviction that they will perpetuate the influence of his teaching and extend it to many who were not touched by it in his lifetime.

The preparation of this and the companion volume has been an inspiring task. I am deeply grateful to Mr Evelyn Waugh both for the trust he has shown in me and for the constant help and advice he has given me. All who profit by these books owe him an enduring debt of gratitude for the conscientious and unselfish manner in which he has interpreted Mgr Knox's wishes and served his fame, to the immeasurable profit of the Catholic community.

A complete collection of Mgr Knox's sermons would have been impossible without the co-operation of his publishers. Mr T. F. Burns (Burns and Oates) and Mr Frank Sheed (Sheed and Ward) have allowed me to include all the sermons, both available and unavailable, first published by their respective houses. Most particularly am I grateful to the Earl of Wicklow, who, with the generosity one habitually expects and unfailingly receives from him, sacrificed for the sake of these books a small volume of unpublished sermons which he was in the course of preparing for the firm with which he is connected.

Mr W. P. Watt, Mgr Knox's literary agent, has assisted me in intricate negotiations, and has been ready always to answer my calls for advice.

In my absences from London, Fr James Walsh, S.J., has dealt with the correspondence arising from these books, and has discussed with me many problems of presentation. The work of typing has been done principally by Miss Marjory Courtney with the assistance of Lady Charlotte Chetwynd-Talbot, Mrs Barbara Downs, Mrs F. Whigham, and Mr Thomas Raworth. I am grateful for the prompt and expert help they have always given me.

It need hardly be said that I have made a nuisance of myself to many of Mgr Knox's friends, and to many parish priests throughout the country, by my persistent requests for information. I cannot acknowledge all of this help in detail, but I hope that none who have answered my enquiries will find their names missing from the following list: Lady Acton, Mrs Raymond Asquith, Mrs M. E. F. Averies, Canon Francis J. Bartlett, Mgr John M. T. Barton, D.D., Father Michael Benjamin, Father Bertrand, C.P., Sister M. Bonaventure Mackey, Father James Brodrick, S.J., Mother Mary Campion, Frederick W. Chambers, K.C.S.G., K.H.S., Father Casimir Chases, O.P., Mother Clare, S.A., Father Joseph Cleary, Lt.-Col. J. S. Close, O.B.E., Father Leslie Cole, Miss Dorothy Collins, Father T. Corbishley, S.J., Father Francis Courtney, S.J., Father John J. Coyne, Father Martin D'Arcy, S.J., Mr F. H. R. Dix, Mr Thomas Driberg, Canon Joseph Dunne, Mr Laurence Eyres, Brig. the Hon. Miles Fitzalan-Howard, M.C., Canon Charles B. Flood, the Right Rev. Thomas Edward Flynn, PH.D., Bishop of Lancaster, Dom James Forbes, O.S.B., Father Richard Foster, Mgr Laurance Goulder, Father Walter Gumbley, O.P., Dom Michael Hanbury, O.S.B., Mrs N. Hodges, Father Herbert Keldany, Father Bruce Kent, Father Nicholas Lambert, O.S.C., Miss E. Lander, Dom Peter Mann, O.S.B., Mgr Shaun Monaghan, D.C.L., Mr Alan S. Moffat, Father Kieran Mulvey, O.P., Father William Munster, Cong. Orat., Father William O'Brien, Father S. O'Sullivan, S.J., the Earl of Oxford and Asquith, Canon C. H. Parsons, Dom William Price, O.S.B., Father Peter Phillips, Canon Edmund Quinn, V.F., Mr Patrick Reynolds, Mr T. R. Rittner, Father Francis Roberts, S.J., Mr J. Riordan, Mr Hugh Ross Williamson, Mr W. John Sadler, Mrs K. Scott, Father Neil Smith, Canon John B. Shaw, John W. Silverlock, K.S.G., Father Peter Stonier, Father Clement Tigar, S.J., Father Wilfrid Tighe, Cong. Orat., Father James Thornton, Father

Ronald Torbet, o.p., Lt.-Col. J. D. Waters, c.b., d.s.o., Lt.-Col. Joseph Weld, o.b.e., j.p., Father Philip Whiteside, s.j., Mr Douglas Woodruff, Mr Wilfrid Woollen, k.s.g., Father Alfonso de Zulueta.

31 Farm Street, W.1.   Philip Caraman, s.j.

29th November 1959.

EDITOR'S NOTE

MY attention has been drawn to two passages which Mgr Knox, were he alive, would doubtless wish to clarify. In the sermon entitled *The Divine Sacrifice*, the phrase on p. 343, "the outward forms of bread and wine inhere in, are held together by, an underlying reality which is the very substance of his own body and blood", should be understood in a loose sense, and not with the precision which a theologian would give to the words. In the Eucharist, the appearances of bread and wine remain present, of course, without a substance *in* which they inhere.

The second passage occurs in the sermon entitled *Holy Saturday*, on p. 384, where strictly speaking a distinction should be made between the Limbo into which Christ descended *after* his death, and Purgatory. Mgr Knox's "fancy" should not be taken for a suggestion that our Lord passed through the state of Purgatory.

Contents

CONTENTS   xv

Page

24. Novum Pascha Novae Legis 306
25. The Great Supper 310
26. A Priest for Ever 315
27. Words of Life 320
28. The Hidden God 325
29. The Mirror of Conscience 330
30. Bread from Heaven 335
31. The Divine Sacrifice 339

VIII. *FEASTS AND SEASONS OF THE YEAR*

1. Advent 347
2. The Crowded Inn 350
3. The Birth of our Lord 354
4. "Ostende" 359
5. The Shepherds at the Crib . . . 361
6. The Effect of Christmas 364
7. The Divine Name 368
8. The Agony of our Lord 372
9. The Trial 378
10. Holy Saturday 383
11. The Guarded Tomb 386
12. The Risen Christ 392
13. The Corner-stone 395
14. The Triumph of Life 398
15. Belief 401
16. The Ascension 404
17. Pentecost 408
18. The Message of the Cenacle . . . 412
19. The Birth of the Church 416
20. The Heart of Christ 420
21. The Fire of Love 424
22. Saints Peter and Paul 429
23. The Fisherman 433
24. The Precious Blood: I 438
25. The Precious Blood: II 441
26. Mount Carmel 445
27. The Assumption 450
28. Christ the King 453
29. All Saints 458

I

OUR FATHER*

* This series of five sermons was preached in July and August, 1939.

B

I

THE FATHERHOOD OF GOD

Our Father, who art in heaven, hallowed be thy name.

I WANT, these five Sunday evenings, to attempt something which
bears the character of audacity, not because it has been attempted so
little but because it has been attempted so often before. If there are
fifty-five words in our language which are widely known—I am
afraid, not universally known—by heart, they are the fifty-five words
of the Lord's Prayer. They are treasured by thousands to whom the
Hail Mary is but a rigmarole, and the *Credo* a series of improbable
statements. Can we say anything about them which is interesting, or is
worth the saying? I do not think it is presumptuous to suggest that we
can. For, after all, human language is not a fixed thing; its shades of
meaning, its subtle associations, alter with the centuries; and a formula
of prayer, however simple, however familiar, will need re-interpreting
from time to time, if the richness of its content is not to be lost. Those
good gifts which we ask for when we pray come down to us from the
Father of lights;[1] we shall need light from him if we are to know what is
the value of those gifts, in what spirit that prayer ought to be uttered.

And perhaps more than usually just now, because more than
usually just now we look forward to a future which denies us certainty,
we look round us at a world which has forgotten the vocabulary of
peace. At such times, we are no longer content to shut ourselves up
in the circle of our immediate interests, in that familiar world, dominated by self, whose issues are so clear, whose lights and shadows are so
vivid to us. What *we* want and what will do *us* good, what changes of
fortune in the life of this or that friend will fit in best with the scheme
which *our* fancy has drawn out for his happiness—how easy it is to
make our prayers seem true and natural, as long as we confine ourselves
to simple themes like these! But when urgent anxieties about the
general welfare of the world in which we live crowd round us and
interrupt clamorously our times of prayer, then we begin to lose
confidence in our own powers of anticipating every event and finding
a solution to every problem; we are more conscious that the future is

[1] James I. 17.

in God's hands, not ours. And then, with a chastened reverence of approach, we come to our Lord as his disciples came to him long ago, and ask him, "Lord, teach us to pray". Let us follow that inimitable answer of his step by step, ready to learn and to listen for once.

"Our Father"—the first effort to make in our prayer must be to turn away from creatures and plunge ourselves into the Source of all existence. We must humble ourselves before God as our Father; without his creative activity this thing that prays would have no being. And yet, in creating us, he allowed something of himself to pass into us; he is our Father in that sense too. We are created in his image, although the resemblance be faint and the inferiority beyond calculation; more truly, more representatively in his image than the other creatures which share our world with us; we have intellects to know God, wills to love him, and so we are enabled to serve him by choice, not, like those others, by the inevitable law of our being; in calling him our Father, not simply our Creator, we claim, even as men, the privilege of sonship. How much more as Christians, incorporated by baptism into the mystical body of his Son, do we approach him with confidence; the Holy Spirit within us crying out to him, Abba, Father[1]—deep calling to deep under the troubled surface of our prayer! And then, as an earthly father does not merely give life to his children once for all, but continues to maintain life in them by supplying their daily needs, so the God who created us keeps us from moment to moment; showers down upon us, in the natural or in the supernatural order, the gifts by which we maintain ourselves in the order of his creation, the gifts by which we live.

Is that all fatherhood means? Why, no; fatherhood gives authority, demands the exercise of authority if it is to be fatherhood in the true sense. While the son's character is yet too wayward and inexperienced to let him choose for himself, decide for himself, the father must choose for him, decide for him; enforce those decisions, if necessary, by the use of correction. What son is there, whom the father does not chasten? So God, infinitely wiser, dictates our choice to us, recalls us by means of punishments if we set up our wills in obstinate resistance to his. Notice, that in all our Lord's teaching it is this side of fatherhood that he stresses least. He is more anxious we should love God for his goodness to us, than fear him for his punishments. The father of the prodigal son, so ready to grant even an unreasonable request, so anxious for the return of the ne'er-do-well, so prompt to forgive him, is to stand to us for a type of fatherhood. And yet, the other side of

[1] Romans 8. 15.

fatherhood is there: "Father, if it be possible, let this chalice pass; nevertheless, not my will, but thine"[1]—the sterner aspect of fatherhood is part of our Lord's teaching too. And in our age we are frightened of it; we fight shy of it.

You see, in our age filial piety is perhaps less taken for granted than in any age which went before us. I do not know whether the fault lies with the fathers, or with the sons, or with both; but it is certain there is a misunderstanding. Perhaps we need a new St John the Baptist, who will turn the hearts of the fathers to the children and the hearts of the children to their fathers. In any case, if you tell a young man or a young woman of our generation to think of God as a Father, they do not necessarily love him any the better for that. A smattering of psychology, imperfectly understood, assures them that it is quite natural to dislike one's parents, or one at least, if not both. How are we to recommend to them, then, as a model of all prayer the formula which begins with the words, *Our Father*? I think by pointing out to them that when we call God our Father we are not using metaphor; he is our Father in the full sense, not in some applied sense. When we call him a King, we mean that he is more of a king, not less of a king, than those earthly monarchs who share the title with him. Their sovereignty derives from his, not the other way round. So with fatherhood; it is from God, St Paul tells us, that all paternity in heaven and in earth is named.[2] It is he who is our Father in the full sense; who is the author, not the mere cause, of our being; from whom we inherit, not a few lineaments of our features or a few tricks of manner, but the whole form of our intellectual nature; who nourishes us, not by supplying this or that but by enabling us to be; who controls us and corrects us, not according to his pleasure like some earthly father but according to the appointed law of our own perfection. It is only where and as they fall short of that perfect type that earthly fathers forfeit, in some degree, their title to paternity. You must not wait till you can learn to understand your father before you learn to know God. It is by learning to know God that you will learn to understand your father.

There is something else. Our Lord does not begin his prayer with the plain word "Father", as we might expect; it is "our Father"; in the Greek, to be accurate, "Father of us". When we pray, we try to shut out the world; the thought of our fellow creatures, even of those who are bound to us by the closest of ties, even those in whose fortunes we are uniquely interested, serves to distract us and make our minds

[1] Matthew 26. 39.   [2] Ephesians 3. 15.

wander away from God. But before we say goodbye to the world like that, we have to remember and acknowledge our common sonship; we must not name the fatherhood of God without associating it with the brotherhood of man. On the very threshold of our prayer, we must offer ourselves to God as the ambassadors, if he will allow it, of all our struggling fellow mortals; of those who have no time, of those who have no taste for prayer; of those who forget through carelessness, or refuse through obstinacy, or fear through unworthiness, to make any approaches to him. When I pray, however much I am to be rapt and carried away by this intimacy with my Father, there must be a continual undercurrent in my prayer which reminds me that he is also *our* Father, the Father of us all.

"Our Father, who art in heaven"—is that addition meant to put us in our place? To remind us that he to whom we speak is very far away, separated from us beyond the furthest star, so that we must think ourselves fortunate if even some faint echo of our prayer wins its way through to him? St Teresa is not of that opinion. She boldly reminds us that God is everywhere, and suggests that the heaven in which we are to seek him is the silence of our own souls.[1] By a natural metaphor, to be sure, we lift up hands or eyes to heaven when we want to remind ourselves how far God's dignity surpasses ours, how independent he is of all those limitations and imperfections which encompass our own lives. But it is no more than a metaphor; the difference between what is divine and what is human cannot really be expressed in terms of space.

> Does the fish soar to find the ocean,
> The eagle swim to find the air,
> That we ask of the stars in motion,
> If they have rumour of thee there?[2]

No, the meaning of those words, "who art in heaven", is not that we should bring God down to our own level by trying to localize him in space. It is rather that we should raise ourselves nearer to God's level, by ridding ourselves, as far as may be, of those earthly attachments which embarrass our view. In the Old Testament, the God whose dwelling is in the heavens is contrasted with those gods of the heathen who have their sanctuaries on earth, tutelary deities of hill, wood and stream.[3] We have our own idols to distract us from worship, strong

---

[1] St Teresa of Avila, *Way of Perfection*, ch. xxviii (Allison Peers, *Complete Works*, 1946, vol. II, pp. 113 sq.).
[2] Francis Thompson, "The Kingdom of God".   [3] For example, Psalm 113.

affections, and prejudices, and solicitudes which bind our thoughts to earth. And we must begin our prayer by asking our Father *who is in heaven*, the God whose dignity removes him so infinitely above these petty preoccupations, to raise us too above them, and let us dwell with him, at least for some wretched interval of time, in the heavenly places, alone, unencumbered, attentive only to him.

Do we now pass on from the preliminaries of prayer to prayer itself? Rather, I think, though it is phrased in the form of a wish, we should regard that next clause, "hallowed be thy name", as an aspiration of our own hearts, not as a petition. The desire that God's name should be something hallowed, something kept apart and rescued from all unworthy associations—that is not so much a favour we would ask of him as an act of benevolence towards him on our part. It is a protestation from us, that the God to whom we pray is a God of such infinite holiness, that the very name by which he is known among men should be a word not spoken lightly, but full of mystery and of awe.

The name of a god—that is, to the mind of man in his more primitive stages, something tremendously important; you must get the name right if you are to get on the right side of your god. It all seems rather strange and superstitious to us; what is in a name, we ask?[1] A rose by any other name would smell as sweet, and if we believe in supernatural powers as affecting our destinies, surely they will not affect those destinies less or more because we use this title or that in addressing them? But we must be more imaginative than that, if we are to interpret the mind of our ancestors. A name, after all, in common human experience is something which gives power. We feel much more safe with a dog which is inclined to make unfriendly advances to us if we can call it by the name it is accustomed to hear. The schoolmaster, dealing with an unruly class, is in a better position to control it if he knows each boy by name. And any lover will tell you that there is magic in a name; that the sense of intimacy which comes when you are allowed to use a Christian name, or some special, privileged form of it, marks a definite stage in the growth of affection. Children and schoolboys are secretive, you will often find, about names; to give away your own Christian names or (curiously) those of your sisters was, at an early time of life, to expose yourself to being ragged. And so it is that with primitive peoples, to whom language itself is only a half-familiar instrument, names have a magic force, and none more so than the names which are applied to their tribal gods. We even hear of tribes which will not let the sacred name be mentioned at all, for fear

[1] *Romeo and Juliet*, Act II, Scene 2.

their enemies should hear of it and should learn to ingratiate themselves with the god himself by the use of it.

I suppose it was for that reason that the ancient Greeks and Romans would often address their gods in a long litany of alternative titles; would sometimes even offer to a particular god his choice of titles; "*matutine pater, seu Jane libentius audis*", that is, "O father of the morning, or Janus, if thou wouldest rather be called so". And I suspect that this was partly what our Lord had in mind when, asked by his apostles how they ought to pray, he warned them against the practices of the heathen. "When you pray" (he said to them), "do not use long rigmaroles, like the heathen, who think that the more words they use the more likely they are to gain audience"[1]—and so taught them this, his own prayer, instead. It was the tradition of the Jews that the very name of God was something almost too holy to be mentioned, certainly too holy to be written down. And in accordance with that tradition our Lord would have us, his disciples, begin our prayer with a kind of reverential silence. We do not even address him as God; we tell him instead that the word is too holy a word to be taken on our lips.

What is the meaning of that? Surely he would have us remind ourselves that the presence into which we enter when we pray is one of infinite majesty, to which words can do no justice; all the praises and aspirations we can offer are a kind of profanation; silence is the best tribute we can pay. We have not learned much about prayer until we have learned that an attitude of loving expectancy, of waiting upon God and allowing our souls to be overcome by the thought of his greatness, is the first preparation we need. We are to call him our Father, with child-like confidence in his love for us; but, having so addressed him, we are not to plunge straight into the business of petition, as if nothing could possibly be of more importance than the needs which we feel at the moment, as if nothing could possibly interest him except our petty concerns, our importunate anxieties. The citizens of that heaven in which he dwells cry "Holy, holy, holy" before him day and night; shall not we do well to tune our voices to that chorus of praise, before we dare to ask him for anything? Hallowed be his name; a hush must fall upon our hearts, a pause must be made in our tumultuous thoughts, before the right atmosphere can be established in which we, creatures of a day, can approach him who dwells in inaccessible light, the sovereign Ruler of Creation.

Our Father, who is in heaven, and we, his children, have so little of

[1] Matthew 6. 7.

heaven in our minds! That is the sublime paradox of prayer. He has
no need, it does him no good, that human voices should be raised to
him at all. His blessedness is such that all our praises, all our love, all
our congratulation can add nothing to it; when we worship God, we
are like men throwing stones endlessly into an abyss which eternity
could not suffice to fill. And yet he invites us to pray to him; he wants
us to come to him, not as strangers bringing their petitions to a King,
but as children running in to interrupt their Father, all begrimed as we
are with the dust of the world, and yet his children, with a right to his
audience. There should be a paradox on our side to match that paradox
on his. We should come to him, awe-struck with a consciousness that
only grows deeper with the years of the immeasurable gulf that lies
between us and him; yet at the same time unhesitatingly, knowing
that he wants us to be there, that he will not turn us away. St Peter,
after the miraculous draught of fishes, clung to our Lord's feet crying,
"Depart from me for I am a sinful man, O Lord";[1] he bids him depart,
but will not let him go. So we, at the very threshold of our prayer,
hang mid-way between doubt and confidence, doubt of ourselves,
and confidence in him. Hallowed be his name—silenced be every
thought, stifled be every affection, that is unworthy of his presence;
we will stop and take breath, as children do, before we open our hearts
to tell him of our needs.

2

THE KINGDOM OF GOD

Thy kingdom come; thy will be done.

WHAT do we mean when we say to God, "thy kingdom come"?
Make some attempt to put yourselves back into the mind of
our Lord's own contemporaries, and you will see that the words bear
a very obvious sense; only, that sense belongs to a world-picture which
is not ours, which is not to be reconciled with ours. At the time when
out Lord came, Jewish hopes were running high; not all the Jews by
any means, but a respectable number of them were waiting (so the

[1] Luke 5. 8.

phrase went) for the consolation of Israel. Many of the prophets had
spoken of a Messiah who was to come; and the prophet Daniel, more
definite than the others, had given indications by which the date of that
coming might be identified;[1] those indications pointed to what we
call the first century. The Messiah was to overcome the enemies of
Israel, who had so long kept the Jews in subjection, and was to set
up a kingdom of peace and righteousness in which the religion of
Israel would come to its own. Was it to be an earthly or a heavenly
kingdom? Opinion was perhaps divided; but it is probable that most
of our Lord's contemporaries thought of it as a kingdom set up on
earth, with the people of the Jews as a dominating world-power.
Then St John the Baptist appeared, and told his fellow countrymen
that the kingdom of heaven was at hand; urged them to repent, and to
purify themselves by baptism, so that they might be worthy to enter
into it. A great number of them had welcomed his message, and had
undergone this ceremony of initiation. Tell such people to pray that
God's kingdom might come, and it is not difficult to see what picture
would be in their minds. They would pray for a national deliverance
accompanied by a national regeneration; who would be slow, at
any time in the world's history, to pray for such an event? Men with
the outlook of which we have been speaking would accept it as the
most natural wish in the world.

As we know, a great deal of our Lord's teaching, and especially of
that part of it which was conveyed by parables, aimed at correcting this
false picture. But, so far as most of his followers were concerned, it
seems to have been a lesson slowly learnt. He had to explain to them
that the promises which were revealed to the prophets had reference
to two separate kingdoms; or, if you will, to a kingdom in two
separate senses. Complete regeneration of human nature, complete
triumph of justice over wrong, a reign of universal peace and universal
happiness, were not to be expected in the present world-order. All that
belonged to the future, would be realized when God should see fit to
set up a new heaven and a new earth, after the general resurrection of
mankind. In the meantime, the kingdom that had been foretold was
nothing other than what we mean by the Church on earth. It would
be a kingdom not confined to the Jews but open to their Gentile
neighbours as well. It would contain unworthy as well as worthy
members; not all those who boasted its privileges would in fact be
predestined to everlasting life. Sin and wrong and scandal would not
disappear, yet. And for how long, his hearers eagerly asked, would

[1] Daniel 9.

this temporary dispensation, this imperfect realization of God's kingdom on earth, continue? That was a question he never answered;
he would have his servants be watchful at all times. And this silence
of his meant—you can read it in the epistles to the Thessalonians, or in
the second epistle of St Peter—that the Christians of the first age lived,
for the most part, under an hourly anticipation of the last judgment
such as we, after all these centuries of waiting, find it difficult to
entertain.

To the Christians of the first centuries, then, the prayer "thy
kingdom come" was still a prayer easily intelligible, although they
had now learned to think of that kingdom as the experience of a risen
life, not as a mere vindication of God's justice under earthly conditions.
They were a persecuted sect, living in the midst of a world whose
corrupt manners and superstitious beliefs seemed to call, at every
moment, for a divine interference. They prayed that God's kingdom
might come, that the strain of all this waiting for deliverance might be
relieved, that the visible triumph of worldly power over spiritual
truth might be brought to an end, that the cruelty of their persecutors
might find its just reward. And there have been later periods in
history at which men's minds have returned to the same way of
looking at things. The time of the barbarian invasions, for example,
or the time of the Great Schism in the latter Middle Ages when it
seemed as if the Church had failed. There have been dark periods when
nothing seemed to go right, when misery and crime and degeneracy
seemed to go from bad to worse, so that no human solution remained
for the world's difficulties; and at such times it was felt that God could
not be long in coming now; the existing world-order stood self-
condemned, ripe for the charnel-house; new heavens and a new earth
were all that a disillusioned humanity could any longer hope for.
Let God's kingdom come; it was the only alternative to the Devil's.

But more generally, since the Christian religion first triumphed with
Constantine, religious thought has been occupied with the growth of
God's kingdom on earth. Fresh doors of opportunity continued to
open before the Church, fresh conquests remained to be consolidated,
fresh fields of knowledge to be assimilated; man's business, surely,
was not just to save his own soul—he had a work to do, a blow to strike
in God's cause; let heaven wait till earth had been evangelized. In recent
times, I think the devotion to the Sacred Heart had made the use of
such language more common; in our own day, the feast of Christ's
Kingship has canonized it and made it almost official. The mustard-
tree, destined to spread its branches everywhere, the leaven that must

needs energize in a formless and undisciplined world—these are the images that come naturally to our mind when we say, "thy kingdom come". So much evil—we will conquer it; so much ignorance—we will dispel it; so much apathy—we will revitalize it; the kingdom of God, surely, is something which grows between our hands.

Which is the right spirit in which to say the *Pater noster*? Today's events, perhaps, have contrived to set us wondering again. I think, if we could really learn to put God's glory first, and to see human effort for the insignificant thing it is, we should begin to understand that it doesn't much matter which attitude we adopt. God's kingdom here, God's kingdom hereafter—it is all one, which we pray about; the important thing is that we should be profoundly dissatisfied so long as the world around us remains indifferent, calculating, out of touch with God. The aspiration of this clause—for it is an aspiration rather than a prayer of petition—is that God should be all in all; that everything which offends his sight, whether in us or in human affairs at large, should be annihilated, winnowed away like chaff before the majesty of his presence. Intolerable that anything should be done which is not done in God and for God—that is to be the cry of our hearts. How long he will suffer the conflict to continue is no business of ours; it is in his hands. Enough for us that we should renounce in his presence, every time we come to him in prayer, the idleness or coward-ice which would allow us to acquiesce, while the world remains what it is.

If we desire the coming of God's kingdom among mankind in general, we shall desire it, naturally, in our own individual lives. Each individual Christian soul is a territory which awaits the advent of its Conqueror. And here again the same problem repeats itself; when I pray for the coming of God's kingdom in my own soul, ought I to mean that I want to die as soon as possible, and be with him? Or ought I to mean that I want space for the amendment of life; that I hope to be able to correct my faults and become altogether more worthy of heaven, before death overtakes me? The same problem, and surely it has the same solution. Whether we are to die soon or to live on is no business of ours, it is in God's hands. What is important is that we should be dissatisfied with ourselves, disown that rebelliousness of the human spirit which mars and defers God's reign in us. Let us live to amend our lives—let us die at once (so it be in his grace) and offend him no more by sinning—it is all one, if only he will assert his dominion, somehow, in us.

We approach God, then, as his vassals; we abdicate the puppet sovereignty which we appear to enjoy over our own fortunes, make over the kingship of them, as far as is possible for us, to him. And then we go further, we abdicate our wills; "thy will be done"—his will, not ours. Here is a curious point to reflect on. Our Lord Jesus Christ has given us two great models of prayer. One is the *Pater noster*; the other is his own prayer in Gethsemani. And whereas in Gethsemani he begins by asking his heavenly Father to deliver him from the hour of trial, and then adds, as if it were a kind of afterthought, "nevertheless not what I will, but what thou wilt", in the *Pater noster* it is the other way round, he directs us to put God's will in the forefront; it is our will, this time, that comes in as an afterthought, "Lead us not into temptation, but deliver us from evil", just as we are on the point of rising from our knees. It looks, doesn't it, as if he expected of us a higher degree of abnegation than he showed himself; what explanation are we to offer of that?

I suppose the answer to be this—that when he prayed in the garden our Lord wanted us to be able to recognize, without fail, the completeness of his humanity; he wanted to throw into relief the independence of his human will, lest we should be in doubt whether he had in fact a human will or no. But when we pray, there is no need to emphasize the independence of our human wills; no need, God knows, for that. So our Lord teaches us that before we begin to tell God what we want for ourselves, we should submit ourselves, from the very first, to what he wants for us. We are so apt to think of resignation to God's will as if it were a kind of second best; as if our first aim in life was to get what we want, and if we can't get that, we must derive a sort of gloomy satisfaction from reflecting that anyhow we have got what he wants. Could there be a more ridiculous perversion of the true order of our being? Imagine a human lover, a newly-married husband, perhaps, who should be continually saying to the woman of his choice, "Personally, I should prefer to spend the day doing this or that; I think it would be a good thing if we went to this or that place, had our meals at such and such times; but of course, if you have other ideas, I shall be quite content". Would it be possible to describe such a man as being in love? And can we be content with the state of our own souls, as long as we find ourselves, day after day, treating God like that— laying down the law to him, and then magnanimously granting him the liberty, if he wills, to disagree with us?

No, the clause "thy will be done" means something very much more than that. Divine love is meant to have the same effect on us as a strong human love has; it is meant to enthrone God instead of self as

the centre of our affections. And if we have done that, then we shall
want God's will in preference to our own; we shall want God's will
to be done, and nothing but God's will; and even where God's will
for us is precisely what we should have chosen for ourselves, we shall
want it because it is his will, not because it is ours. So our Lady, when
the angel reveals to her that she is to become the Mother of Christ,
does not break out at once into a *Magnificat* over the joy that has
befallen her; "be it done unto me according to thy word" is her first
thought; she welcomes that amazing message not for her own sake,
but for his. I don't mean to say that the ordinary Christian is like that;
that you and I are like that. Most of us have to confess that self-will,
disguised in a thousand subtle forms, is the regulating principle of our
whole natures. But our Lord is teaching us how we *ought* to pray;
and he is clearing the ground by teaching us to approach God in a
spirit worthy of Christians. We only achieve our business as Christians,
in proportion as God becomes in us that continual centre of reference
which self wants to be.

   "Thy will be done on earth, as it is in heaven"; does that mean that
God's will will be done on earth only if we pray for it, whereas it
will be done in heaven whether we want it or not? I suppose most of
us, in our childish efforts to construct the meaning of the *Pater noster*,
have had some imagination as that. But the truth is, God's will is
always done, whether in heaven or on earth; what need was there,
then, for the added clause? I think our Lord put it in because he
wanted us to see heaven as the diagram, the figure on the blackboard,
as it were, which shows us God's will working manifestly, unmistakably, whereas on earth it works secretly, under conditions of mystery,
so that we need faith to discern it. A bomb falls from the sky, and some
hundreds of human lives—a chance collection of human lives—are lost.
It all seems to us cruel and casual, a mass-production of calamity.
We cannot look behind the scenes, and find out for ourselves how it
was appropriate, how it worked in with God's scheme, that those
particular lives should be brought to an end just then. So it is with the
outward circumstances which affect our own fortunes; we cannot lay
a finger on the pulse of our own destiny, and decide for ourselves how
riches or poverty, health or disease, fitted in with the pattern that was
chosen for our lives. Our faith tells us that it is so; no sparrow falls to
the ground without our heavenly Father, and we are of more value
than many sparrows.[1] But we cannot see, must not expect to see,
the working of Providence. Our contemplation must be set on

[1] Matthew 10. 29.

heavenly things; there we shall find God's will mirrored in a calm surface, not disturbed and distorted by the accidents of mortality. God's will is being done—who can doubt it?—in heaven; and if we learn to see earth as a small thing in comparison with heaven we shall find no difficulty in believing that God's will is being done here, too.

There is a further reason why it is difficult for us to see God's will being done on earth; on earth the action of human wills, that rebel against his laws or mistake his purposes, appears to thwart his will, to put the machinery of his Providence out of gear. Once more, we know by faith that it is not so; the action of human wills, even of sinful human wills, does but in fact subserve his ends; he used the treachery of Judas as the lever of a world's redemption. And all the horrors we have lived through during the last three years are, in the same sense, part of his will. If we use the lesson aright, good will come out of all the evil, gain out of the loss. But we cannot see that happening; we fret and repine at the seeming triumph of human interests over his. All that will be a scandal to us, and a distraction to our prayer, until we have learned to familiarize ourselves with the thought of heaven— those myriads of blessed spirits, all willing freely the will of God, nothing but the will of God, eternally.

We have commented on twenty-four out of those fifty-five words which constitute our Lord's prayer; very nearly half, and still we have not reached any petition that is self-regarding, that makes provision for ourselves. Do we often observe that proportion between God's interests and ours, when we employ self-taught formulas of prayer? But he has given us our model, for all time. Let us not be in too great a hurry, when we pray, to introduce our needs, our ideas about what is best, to his divine consideration. Prayer is a conversation between us and God. And when you or I are talking to a human friend, it is not good manners to make ourselves the subject of the conversation all at once. Politeness demands that we should ask after our friend's health, ask what news he or she has had about husband or children or whatever it may be, before we start complaining about our cold, before we start relating our news. And surely our Lord wants us to observe the same rule, when we are privileged to converse with almighty God. His interests come first, the hallowing of his name, the coming of his kingdom, the doing of his will. Only then will we pass on to speak of what concerns us; infinitely privileged, that he should allow us to speak about it at all.

3

THE GIFTS OF GOD

Give us this day our daily bread.

I WAS pointing out, last week, that we had commented on nearly half the *Pater noster* without coming across, so far, anything in the nature of a petition. Nearly half of it consists of a majestic series of aspirations. We are to claim God's fatherhood, reminding ourselves of all the subtle associations which that word has; we are to measure something of the distance between his heavenly and our earthly being; we are to abjure and to wish away, whether in ourselves or in the world of men around us, all that spirit of rebellion which resists his sovereignty; we are to will his will, identify ourselves freely with it, putting away from our minds all instinct of self-regard. Hitherto we have not asked him for anything. And you may imagine the holy apostles, who had desired him to teach them how to pray, looking up at him with rather long faces; wondering whether, after all, he was going to sanction for them that deeply-rooted instinct which bids man go to God and talk to him about his own human needs.

After all, this notion of petitioning God for the things we want is very far from being self-evident. As our Lord himself points out, our heavenly Father knows what things it is we need. *Carior est illis homo quam sibi*—so the heathen poet wrote of his heathen gods: "they love man better than man loves himself". And when you consider that in his ordinary dealings with creation God observes regular laws, which operate independently of our human worthiness or unworthiness, makes his sun to shine upon the evil and the good, sends rain upon the just and upon the unjust;[1] when you consider that God is immutable in his purposes as in his own nature; when you consider that it really matters very little what happens to us in this world, so long as we learn to submit our wills to the divine will, you might easily imagine that there is not much room left in the scheme of things for prayer, if by prayer we mean asking God to satisfy our needs. "Teach us to pray, as John also taught his disciples"—perhaps the ascetic, with his desert food and his coat of camel's hair, had taught his disciples to pray for very little in this world; would our Lord go further, and tell them to pray for nothing at all? Their fears, if they thought that, were to be disappointed.

[1] Matthew 5. 45.

As he reaches the middle of his prayer, our Lord makes it quite clear that the instinct of humanity is right; God does want us to ask for the satisfaction of our needs. And, lest there should be any doubt about it, he takes a gross, physical need as typical of the rest. We might have supposed, I mean, that he who taught us not to be afraid of those who could kill the body, but only of one who could destroy both body and soul in hell, would observe the same distinction here; would teach us to ask, indeed, but only to ask what was profitable for our souls. The body—what does the body matter, after all, which lives and is important to us for so brief a time, which can be put out of gear, and fatally, by the smallest accident in its surroundings? Far better, when we take to our knees, to ask for benefits really worth having; for grace that will strengthen the immortal soul, nourish an indestructible life within us! But no, our Lord will not lend his authority to these extremes of ascetic doctrine. We are to ask for bread; for the gross, palpable comforts of this transitory world. All God's gifts are good, in the natural as well as in the supernatural order; it is only our misuse of them that can make them harmful to us. All of them good, and therefore in themselves a suitable subject for prayer. We are not to profess ourselves superior to all that sort of thing; we are not to tell ourselves, like the Manichees, that all matter is evil. Bread, give us bread—we are to come before God asking for health, for strength, for the enjoyment of every-day life, if he wills it.

At the same time, I think it is a point worth noticing that our Lord is telling us here to do something which most of us quite neglect to do, all the time. He is telling us to pray for things which are so simple and so easily come by that it is very easy to take them for granted.

Those of us who have lived through the Great War, and known what it was for England to be, as I think it was at one moment, within three weeks of starvation, those of us who have lived through the Strike of 1926, and wondered whether we were ever going to see a piece of coal in our coal-scuttles again, ought to have learnt—I wonder why we did not learn it better?—that even the simplest of God's gifts, those which we find waiting for us as a matter of course every morning, are God's *gifts*, a free present which we have no title to, no right to expect. Take the words in their most literal sense; I wonder how many of us have actually prayed to God for bread, and meant it? Perhaps in our younger days we prayed with some fervour about jam and cake, when these were not incidents of every day, but bread . . . you could not get up much excitement about that.

We need, I think, more simplicity of heart if we are to measure the extent of God's mercies to us. We need to be more like St Francis, who hailed the sun and moon as if they were a birthday present, the shade of the trees as if it were a surprise specially arranged for his benefit. We must be content with simple pleasures, before we can understand what it really means to ask God for our daily bread.

And I think he meant us to see that; he meant us to see that prayer is not intended to be a desperate remedy in moments of supreme emergency, but an affair of every day, the breath of the Christian life. We often come across some pious person who tells us a long story about how some object of value was lost, and prayer was offered to St Anthony, and sure enough it was found, somewhere where nobody would ever expect to have found it. And we say, of such people, what wonderful faith they have. But surely if we really had faith we should go about saying, "Yesterday I prayed for my daily bread, and, do you know, I got it". And I think our Lord means us to see that our prayer should be the measure of our wishes, and that our wishes should, at ordinary times, be on a simple and modest scale; that we ought to be content with the things we really need, not to be always destroying our peace of mind by sighing for the things we are not likely to get, for the things which, if we got them, very likely would not be good for us.

At least let us notice this, that we are to pray for our *daily* bread; for a fixed ration, designed for the immediate future.

It's true some scholars maintain, and I shouldn't wonder if they were right, that the true meaning of the phrase is "Give us this day our bread for tomorrow"; but, if so, that is only a technicality of the household; in remote parts of the country you would expect the baker to call overnight. Our Lord is not contradicting here, rather he is reinforcing here, his own principle that we should not take any thought for the morrow.

We are to ask him just for the ration of bread which will keep us going for the time being; we are not to be looking ahead and wondering where the day after tomorrow's bread is going to come from. Here at least this petition, which looks so simple and so encouraging at first sight, is meant to be a warning. Our prayers, as I say, are to be the measure of our wishes; and if our Lord does not want us to pray about next week's provisions, it is because he does not want us to think too much about next week's provisions. The birds of the air do not sow, or reap, or gather into barns, yet our heavenly Father feeds them;[1] and we are men of little faith if we do not trust him to feed us too; that is our Lord's teaching.

[1] Matthew 6. 26.

It is curious teaching, and embarrasses us sometimes, when we are anxious to urge on the young, or on the poor, the duty of thrift. Especially in these days, when Government departments are busy making arrangements to ensure that we shall all get our daily bread in case of a sudden emergency, it seems almost a mockery to stand up in church—we shall be doing it at the beginning of October—and listen to the gospel telling us we ought to be like the birds of the air, and make no provision for the morrow. I wonder those people who tell us it is wrong in all circumstances to go to war, because the Sermon on the Mount says we ought to love our enemies, do not equally object to the organization of a national food supply, because the Sermon on the Mount forbids us to be anxious about the future.

4

THE FORGIVENESS OF GOD

And forgive us our trespasses, as we forgive them that trespass against us.

WE all know how easy it is, and how misleading it is, to think of God's nature in terms of our own; to put ourselves in his place, or him in ours. We all know, for instance, how teasingly attractive at first sight, how blasphemous on closer examination, is the old Scottish epitaph:

> Here lie I, Martin Elginbrodd;
> Have mercy on my soul, Lord God—
> As I would do, gin I were God
> And thou were Martin Elginbrodd.

There is no parity of reasoning where an infinite distance in the scale of being is involved. Terms like "mercy" and "forgiveness" are terms which we borrow from our own human experience, and apply, not in their plain sense, but by analogy, to God's dealings with us. If that is so, how is it that our Lord would have us ask his heavenly Father to forgive us our trespasses as we forgive—just as we forgive, the Greek seems to imply—the trespasses of our fellow men?

It needs very little thought to convince us that such an interpretation of his words is unsatisfactory. Our forgiveness and God's—believe me, there is no comparison. We forgive capriciously; we find it easier to overlook an offence in one who is naturally attractive to us, in one whose dignity overawes us, in one from whom we have some expectation of profit. With God, there is no respect of persons;[1] we can plead no natural graces, no worth, no usefulness on our part when we throw ourselves on his mercy. We forgive idly, from an easy-going disposition which has little to do with any real goodness of heart; after all (we say to ourselves) it doesn't matter so very much, there's no great harm done. God cannot forgive like that; our offences against him clash with the order of creation. We forgive ignorantly; accepting excuses which are false, and so deceive us—excuses which we know to be false, yet win our pardon by appealing to our vanity. God cannot be deceived, cannot agree to accept falsehood as truth. How little light, then, does our experience throw on what forgiveness really means!

Or put it in a different way—would we like it, would it give us any confidence, if we supposed that God's forgiveness is like ours, is to be won on the same terms as ours? We forgive grudgingly: "Well", we say, "I suppose I must accept your explanation; but what has passed has given me a different view of your character, and things can never be quite the same again between us"—what if God forgave us like that? We forgive in proportion to the laceration which an offence has caused to our own feelings, not in proportion to the sorrow which is felt and is manifested by the offender; we make it up formally, perhaps, but weeks or years go by before the wrong done ceases to rankle—what if God forgave us like that? We forgive conditionally: "Very well", we say, "I will consent to overlook it for this once; but remember, if the same kind of thing happens again, it is the end; let that be understood"—what if God forgave us like that?

And yet there it is, at the very heart of our Lord's favourite prayer; somehow, it seems, there is an intimate relation between overlooking offences and having our offences overlooked; the two ideas are contained in a single clause, instead of coming up separately for our consideration; what are we to make of it?

The point is, surely, that the mention of the word "forgiveness" in the middle of this prayer—the prayer we say so often—ought to ring a bell in our minds, as it were, warning us of something we may perhaps have left undone. It ought to be a sudden flash, illuminating our consciences and enabling us, in an instant, to take stock of them; to make sure we are not concealing there the chief thing which God

[1] Acts 10. 34.

hates to see there, a grudge. And when we say "we forgive them that trespass against us", that phrase is not meant to state a fact, but to register a resolve. Forgivingness is not a state of mind which we find in ourselves, when this flash of enlightenment comes. It is a state of mind which we try to elicit in ourselves, there and then. We do not say to God, "forgive us our trespasses, a thing which we naturally never forget to do". We say to God, "forgive us our trespasses, a thing we are always forgetting to do, but now, Lord, it shall not be so any longer. Now, brought to our knees with the consciousness of our own guilt, we make an act of the will before thee; we resign in thy sight and at thy feet all the ill-will which we have borne, hitherto, towards our fellow men."

Our Lord has seen fit to illustrate the two central clauses of his own prayer by parables. "Give us this day our daily bread"—that reminds us of the man who finds that he has no bread in the house and knocks up a neighbour to ask if he can oblige him with a loaf.[1] The friend refuses; his house is locked, he says, and the children have all gone to bed and are asleep; he cannot get up and go down to the larder. So heaven seems, when our prayers are unanswered; God refusing to listen to us, and his saints deaf to our prayers. What is the moral of it? That we should go on praying; there is nothing else we can do but pray. "Forgive us our trespasses, as we forgive them that trespass against us"—that reminds us of the king whose servant owed him a large sum of money;[2] a debt which he was prepared to remit, but would remit no longer when he found that this same servant was being unmerciful towards a debtor, a fellow servant of his own. So heaven is, when we ask pardon for our sins. This time, there is no delay in the answering of our prayers; but this time, there is something that we *can* do—a condition is attached upon whose fulfilment, our Lord warns us, the grant of pardon depends. We cannot deserve our pardon by pardoning others. But we can suspend the action of God's mercy by our own unmercifulness. "As we forgive"—there is meaning, after all, in that "as"; sure enough, the two processes are connected.

God's forgiveness and ours—let us see, first, how one must inevitably fall short of the other. For one thing, in God the justice which condemns and the mercy which forgives are one; it is the same activity, mediated by a different set of circumstances. We do not understand how that can be so, but we know that it must be so; our pardon proceeds from the same source as our condemnation. We forgive because one mood in us has succeeded to another; a different spring in

[1] Luke 11. 5.   [2] Luke 7. 41.

our being has come into play. And again, when we offend God it does not matter whether we think of ourselves as having offered an affront to a person, or as having violated an eternal law; they are only two aspects of the same fact. But when we offend our neighbour, the essential malice of our action lies in the violation of a law, the law of charity; the person who undergoes the wrong has only an accidental, not an essential, connection with the wrong itself; he may condone the offence, and the guilt of it still lie on our souls. When my neighbour forgives me, something has happened to him; when God forgives me, something has happened to me. And again, when God forgives men, the advantage derived is all on one side. God is not the loser if we spurn his offer of pardon. Whereas if man forgives man, either side equally has lost an enemy. We cannot, for these and many other reasons, alter the whole situation by our human forgiveness, as it is altered by the divine.

And yet, in our measure, we are encouraged by this clause of the *Pater noster* to imitate the generosity with which God forgives. That generosity is portrayed for us, once for all, in another of our Lord's parables, that of the prodigal son.[1] Remember how the father, in that parable, goes out to meet the prodigal on his return. So it is with the divine forgiveness; God comes to meet us half-way—indeed, if he did not, we should never find the grace of repentance when once we had lost his friendship.

God comes out half-way to meet the sinner, but that is not all—he *runs* to meet him, if we may trust the parable; that is our Lord's way of drawing attention to the instantaneous effect which our act of contrition has; absolution follows it in the same breath. We know that, we expect that of God, although we have no conceivable right to expect it. But we, when we are offended, what a savage pleasure we often take in withholding our pardon for a time, even though we know that sooner or later we shall be bound to give way! What a petty instinct this is, on our part, to lick our lips over our injured dignity as long as possible, and then take credit to ourselves for clemency when at last we forgive! But, you see, that ought to be impossible. The next time we say the *Our Father*, the words ought to stick in our throats until we have resigned that sense of grievance, by a deliberate act of the will, into God's hands.

And once more, the parable teaches us how complete is the effect of God's pardon. The best robe, fresh shoes for the tired feet of the wanderer, the fatted calf killed in his honour, the ring put on his

[1] Luke 15. 7.

finger—everything is to be exactly as before. So it is when we experience absolution; there is a debt, to be sure, which remains to be paid, on this side of the grave or on the other, for the equilibrium of justice which we have disturbed. But we are forgiven absolutely, there and then; we are God's sons, God's friends, as surely as though we had never lost our baptismal innocence. If, then, the parallel is to hold between God's forgiveness and ours, our forgiveness should be absolute, like his. It is not enough that we should extend to the transgressor a formal, frigid hand of reconciliation, by way of avoiding a scene, or of keeping up appearances; we must forgive one another, our Lord says, from our hearts. As far as possible, the offence should be as if it had never been; only so shall we be the children of our Father who is in heaven.

I have said much about the second half of this clause; too little, perhaps, about the first. Let us notice this, quite briefly, that our Lord wants us to be constantly remembering our sins, every time we say our prayers. Those apostles of cheap optimism who have abounded in our day will commonly tell you that it is useless to waste your time in vain regrets over what you did wrong in the past; you should be looking ahead and making bright plans for the future. That, you see, is the exact opposite of our Lord's teaching. He does not want us to be exercised over the future; we are to ask each day for the bread which will be sufficient for that day, no more. He does want us to be exercised over the past; our old sins are to be a continual subject of conversation between us and him. Not that he wants to make us scrupulous or timorous about them, wondering whether in the past our contrition has been genuine, our confessions entire. Rather, he seems to take our sins as part of the day's work; we are sinners, we must not expect to be anything else. But we are to be sin-conscious, always. You will remember how St Mary Magdalen, during the last week of our Lord's life, anointed his feet at Bethany, exactly as she had anointed them, months before, when she came to him first with her story of misery, and he forgave her. To what purpose was this waste? Judas asks. But it was no waste; this anointing symbolizes her abiding penitence—she wants to reconstruct the scene of her conversion and live it all over again. Abiding penitence, that is what our Lord wants us to feel; not an hysterical outburst now and again, but a steady flow of sadness over our sins which will mingle with all the love and gratitude which our devotion offers to him. Forgive us our trespasses, forgive us our trespasses; we cannot say it too often.

I do not know whether any theologian has ever set himself to

answer the question: Did our Lady say the *Pater noster*? But I suppose
we are all inclined to imagine that she did. And if so, we might be
asked, how did she go on after "Give us this day our daily bread"?
There is no reason to doubt that she went on, "And forgive us our
trespasses". Herself immaculate, she was a member, and in some sense
she was the representative, of God's rebellious people; those Scribes
and Pharisees, so unforgiving, so much in need of forgiveness, were
her fellow countrymen. In that representative capacity she will have
prayed, while yet on earth, for the sins of mankind. Don't let us
forget, then, that we who need to pray for forgiveness on our own
behalf need not be, ought not to be, thinking only of ourselves. The
country we live in, the age we live in, have, God knows, great need
to do penance. It is to our Father, not to my Father, that I pray; it
is not only my trespasses, but our trespasses, that I will remember in
my prayer.

5

OUR DELIVERANCE

And lead us not into temptation, but deliver us from evil.

To the very end, the *Pater noster* preserves that curious character
we have already noticed, of being very simple on the surface, and
yet plunging us into deep waters of theological speculation the moment
we begin to look into it. In these concluding words, we come across
an actual problem of interpretation to which no certain answer can be
given; owing to an ambiguity in the Greek, it is not absolutely clear
whether we ask to be delivered from evil, or from the evil one, that is
the Devil. It may be said that that does not make much difference.
But what does make a difference, I think, as we repeat the prayer day
after day, is the question which is apt to present itself to our minds,
What is the evil I am asking to be delivered from? Am I simply saying
the same thing twice over, praying that I may not be led into temptation, but rather may be delivered from sin? Or are there two separate
petitions, one asking that I may not be led into temptation, but rather
may be delivered from sin? Or are there two separate petitions, one
asking that I may not be led into temptations which would be hurtful

to my soul, and the other that I may be delivered from the various
evils, pain, sickness, poverty, disappointment and so on, which
threaten my earthly happiness? We have not finished our exposition
of this greatest of all prayers until we have made some effort to discover
what our Lord's mind was about this.

Perhaps there is no word familiar to Christian piety which has
altered its meaning so much with the centuries as the word "temptation". At least, it has not exactly altered its meaning, but it has lost a
great deal of its early force. When we considered the clause, "thy
kingdom come", I suggested that we should do well to put ourselves
in the position of those who were listening to our Lord as he spoke;
that we should try to imagine what picture the phrase called up in their
minds. Perhaps it would be well if we did the same here. Did our
Lord's immediate audience understand by the word "temptation"
anything like what we understand by it? I don't think there is any
probability that they did. What do we mean by the term? I suppose
that the ordinary modern Christian, if he were asked to give an instance
of what he meant by a temptation, would say something like this:
"If I were very hard up for money, and somebody who was walking
in front of me in a lonely street dropped a pound note without realizing
that he had dropped it, then my duty would be to restore it to him, but
I should be tempted to put it in my pocket instead". Quite so, that
would be a very fair example. When we say we are tempted, we mean
that there is a bias in our corrupt nature which inclines us to gratify
the claims of our own appetite, our own self-interest, although we
know that in doing so we should be disobeying God's will.

But if you watch the usage of the word in the Bible, you will hardly
ever find it bears the sense we have been giving it. In the Old Testament,
the word scarcely occurs at all. In the New Testament, I think you can
say its normal meaning is rather what we call "a trial". We say that
some friend has had great trials to undergo, meaning that he has met
with suffering, and such suffering as was fitted to test his character—to
test his patience, is the main idea. Very often we forget about that part
of it, and simply say "My cook is a great trial", or something of that
kind. But this is to use words in a wrong sense; a trial means something
unpleasant which befalls us in such a way as to test our patience;
theologically speaking, it means something unpleasant which is
allowed to befall us in order that it may test our patience. And that is,
ordinarily, what is meant when you get the word "temptation" in the
New Testament; that and nothing else. When St Paul, for instance,
talks about the temptations which he encountered owing to the plots

which the Jews laid against him; or when St Peter or St James tells us
that we ought to rejoice when we meet with temptations, or when
St John in the Apocalypse writes of the hour of temptation which will
come to test every man on earth, you will see at once that they do not
refer to temptations in our sense; they refer to what we call trials.
And when our Lord himself bids his disciples in Gethsemani watch
and pray that they may not enter into temptation, he clearly means
they are to pray that the supreme test which he is about to undergo,
may not be a test for them also. "You", he says to them elsewhere
"are they who have been with me in my temptations",[1] who have
shared all the hardships and all the disappointments which have tested
and have proved my love for mankind.

I suppose, then, that there is little doubt what our Lord was understood to mean, by those who first heard him use the words, "Lead us
not into temptation". They were expecting the dawn of a Messianic
kingdom, the kingdom foretold by the prophets; but those same
prophets had warned them that it would only come at the end of a
period of great affliction, for God's people especially. "We must
through much tribulation enter into the kingdom of God"[2]—that was
the belief of the Jews in our Lord's time as it was the belief of the first
Christians. Nor was there any reason why our Lord should correct
these misgivings; for he knew well that his followers, a very short
time after his death, would be subjected to persecution everywhere;
knew that Jerusalem would be destroyed, in circumstances of unexampled horror, and that the Christians of Judaea would only save
themselves by flight from the invading Roman army. Looking forward, then, to a world in which his friends would have much tribulation; would be tested, tried in the fire, at the imminent risk of losing
their faith and denying his name, he taught them to pray "Lead us not
into temptation, but deliver us from evil". The two clauses offered a
single petition; they were to pray that they might escape, as far as
possible, the evils that were coming on their generation. And the first
clause was the explanation of the second; they were to hope for a way
of escape from these temporal evils, for fear that the temptation, the
trial, the test of their faith, might be too strong for them; for fear that
they should lose all, and involve themselves in eternal misery as the
result. Deliver us from evil lest by it we should be led into temptation
—that, I think, will have been the order in which these two petitions
will have been understood, by the minds of those who first used them.

Have they no meaning, so understood, for later ages? There have

[1] Luke 22. 28.   [2] Acts 14. 21.

been few periods of history at which the world has not moved among presentiments of evil, "Men swooning away for fear, and expectation of what shall come upon the earth".[1] They have not always interpreted these symptoms as the first Christians often did, mistaking them for signs of an approaching disillusion of the world-order. But they have felt the old landmarks slipping away from them, and recoiled in terror from the unimaginable prospect of what must follow, if things went from bad to worse. We have been living, these last few months —some of us much longer than that—in a state of eager anxiety, lest the bottom should fall out of our world, and strange forces be let loose which would replace its ordered structure by chaos. And although, as we saw, our Lord does not want us to indulge our imaginations in solicitous questionings about the future, he does mean us to pray, I think, quietly and steadily, for the averting of those evils which, for all our trust in his providence, we can yet see, as it were, out of the corner of our eyes. A new world war, more profound in its consequences than the last; a revolution on a world-wide scale; a general breakdown of that complicated economic system by which the modern world so precariously husbands its resources; with these and a score of other nightmares our busy publicists try to cheat us of our rest at nights. What attitude are we to adopt towards them, as we say the *Pater noster* before we go to bed?

We have prayed already for the coming of God's kingdom, for the fulfilment of his will rather than ours; we have tried to put things in their proper scale by reminding ourselves, by trying to make ourselves understand, that God's will is the only thing which matters, that our wills only find their true focus when they identify themselves with his. We have prayed for our daily bread, for the simple provision which will just last us out over the period of time which lies immediately beneath our eyes, leaving the further vista of the future shaded from us by his merciful hand. But, with all that, we cannot entirely dismiss from our view the agitations which crowd in upon us every time we catch sight of a newspaper or join in a discussion with our friends on public affairs. So we will pray about it, from God's point of view, as it were, not from ours. We will ask that the world may be delivered from such perils as imagination conjures up for us. But the chief motive which inspires us in doing so shall be, not the comfort or the convenience of ourselves and our friends, of the order or the nation to which we belong, but God's glory. It is because these world-catastrophes lead so many of our weak fellow mortals into temptation,

[1] Luke 21. 26.

put a strain upon their faith which it will not stand, that we want them not to happen. Lest the weaker brethren—and who knows, but we may ourselves be among their number?—should be tempted to despair, and to blaspheme God, and to fall away into a selfish material-ism which allows no place for him, we will pray for the world to be delivered from such general evils as it apprehends. We fear, not so much those evils in themselves, as the effects they are likely to bring.

It may be that before a year has passed over our heads public con-fidence will somehow have been restored, and we shall be facing the future with lighter hearts. If so, we shall not have the same reason for praying to be delivered from evil; the anticipation of it will be less close to our doors. Shall we, on that account, have the less reason to pray that we may not be led into temptation? Alas, no; the devil has more ways than one of working upon human inconstancy; temptation, for us, has more meanings than one, and we should do ill to forget it.

Those of us who can remember the atmosphere of the Great War can remember all the promises we made to ourselves and to one another that this lesson should never be forgotten; that, if God would give us peace again, his world should never slip back into its old habits of selfishness and indifference. God gave us peace, and prosperity came back with it; did England, did the world, profit by it? By delivering us from evil did he lead us out of temptation? Ask the recording angels; they would tell you, I fear, that our sins have never so cried for vengeance as in the days of our fullness, after the world had found peace.

Let us think once more of ourselves, and ask of ourselves individually whether prosperity is always good for us; whether our deliverance from evil always engages us to such gratitude as would make us rise superior to the temptations of the world, the flesh and the devil? The question is no sooner asked than answered; we know how seldom, when all goes well with us in this world, all goes well with our immortal souls. We need, then, a twofold construction for this final clause of the *Pater noster*. We are to pray that our weakness may be preserved from temptation, by whatever means. Deliver us, Lord, from evil, lest evil should bring us into temptation. Deliver us, Lord, from evil, unless thou seest that such evil is necessary for us, that no other remedy can save us from falling into temptation but suffering, but anxieties, but insecurity here.

Our Father, Father of all mankind, Father to whom we owe all our being, who dost preserve life in us at each moment, who dost correct and chasten us with a Father's love; hallowed be thy name, let us not dare to approach thee until we have put away from us the mean thoughts of earth; thy kingdom come, in us and in all thy creation, whether thou wilt soon put an end to this time of conflict and probation, or wilt prolong it until thou seest us more worthy to meet thy presence; thy will be done, rather than ours, and if ours, only because it is thine, although we cannot understand on earth why it was thy will, as we shall understand it one day in heaven; give us this day our daily bread; we are not afraid to ask thee for earthly benefits, only we will not ask for more than the needs of today, because we love to cast our care on thee, who dost feed us with the super-substantial bread of eternal life; forgive us our trespasses, our own individual sins, and all those sins of our fellow men for which thy immaculate Mother intercedes; and when thou forgivest, teach us to forgive our fellow men with a generosity which finds its model in thee; deliver us from evils that will be too strong a test for our imperfect faith, but not from those evils that will preserve us from the temptation to forget thee. Amen, O Lord, so be it as thou wilt; as thou hast taught us to pray, so pray our prayer in us, now and all the days of our life. Amen.

II

THE TEMPTATIONS OF CHRIST*

*This series of three sermons was preached in March and April, 1938.

I

STONES INTO BREAD

The tempter came and said to him, If thou be the Son of God, command that these stones be made bread. He answered and said, Man doth not live by bread alone, but by every word that proceedeth from the mouth of God.— Matthew 4. 3.

IT was part of the humiliation which our Lord took upon himself in his Incarnation that he would allow himself to be tempted by the Enemy of Souls. It is interesting to notice the resemblance there is between these temptations and those which continually assail his mystical body, the Church.

Temptation means testing; and it is easy to miss the point of the story, in great measure, if you lose sight of that. The Devil was testing our Lord; was conducting a series of experiments, in order to find out something he wanted to know. What he wanted to know was simply whether our Lord was or was not the Son of God; whether, therefore, the Devil's undisputed sway on earth was to be brought to an end. It was the devils, you will remember, who were the first to acclaim our Lord under a divine title; and he made them hold their peace, because he did not wish his secret to be let out in that way.[1] They did not, I think, know for certain who our Lord was, but they had guessed it; guessed it as the result of these experiments conducted in the wilderness; they were inconclusive experiments, as we shall see, but they pointed towards the truth which hell feared—that the conqueror of hell had come to earth in man's flesh.

"If thou be the Son of God"—the Devil did not really mean that. He meant, "If thou be the Son of Man". He who stands there in the wilderness is either Incarnate God or he is a man singularly favoured by heaven; his endurance of the forty days' fast is enough to show that. In either case he will have the power to turn stones into bread; or at least he will think that he has the power. If he is the Son of God, the suggestion will have no influence upon his will; it will fall off harmlessly, like a child's dart striking a stone wall. If he is only man, then it may be—you cannot be certain, but it may be—that he will succumb;

[1] Mark 1. 25.

will use his miraculous powers to relieve his own hunger; and the test will be conclusive. But what the Devil said was, "If thou be the Son of God"; not, I think, this time in a challenging tone, as if he doubted it (that comes later), but in a casual way, assuming it as if it were a matter of course. "You are hungry; it is a long distance to the nearest village; a voice from heaven has just assured you that you are the Son of God; would it not be simplest to provide for your needs by a miracle?"

Our Lord does not meet the challenge; he is content to wait until the occasion arises upon which he will feed five thousand hungry souls. He does not respond to the test; there is nothing in his answer to show whether he claims to be something of higher stature than man. For answer, he takes up the train of associated ideas which have lent the tempter's suggestion its force, and turns them inside out. The train of thought, surely, by which the Devil sought to work upon our Lord's mind, was, "Round, flat stones, looking like loaves of bread . . . Moses, fasting in the wilderness . . . Moses, giving bread to the people in the wilderness . . . those stones could be turned into bread, satisfying as manna to the Israelites." Our Lord replaces that by a fresh train of association; it runs, "Moses, fasting in the wilderness, why? To receive the Law . . . the Law, written on two tables of stone. . . . Flat stones in the wilderness, waiting to receive the new Law . . . for that, men's souls are hungering."[1] So he will retort the Devil's suggestion on its author by setting out, in a phrase drawn from the Old Testament but now for the first time made classical, the eternal contrast between the two elements in man; the beast-part, which hungers with the beasts; the angel-part, which lives, like the angels, on obedience to the divine will. *Non in solo pane*—there is work to be done; he has come to satisfy something higher than bodily cravings.

Neither of the two Evangelists who record the Temptation suggests even the possibility that any third person was present. It is a curious reflection, therefore, that we probably derive our whole account of the circumstances from our Lord himself. And if he was at pains to tell his disciples afterwards about a scene so very personal in character, it must have been, surely, because he wanted to give us an example to imitate; because he wanted our attitude in face of temptation to be the same, according to our measure, as his. Nor was he thinking only, I suspect, of those temptations which assail individual Christians as individuals. His Church, which is his mystical body, is united with him, as we know, in his prayer, in his ministry for souls, in his sufferings, in his glory. Is it too much to expect that she will be united with him in his

[1] Exodus 24.

temptations too? That the tempter will come to her and whisper, "If you are really divine in origin, show it by doing this or that"? A very little reflection will show that this is constantly her experience; not least in these days, when she enjoys a position of scarcely enviable prominence in a world so full of controversy and unrest.

Non in solo pane—our Lord, not merely in the hour of his temptation, but all through his ministry, was continually eager, in his great pity, to provide for the material wants of the multitude which flocked about him; to heal their sick, to relieve their distress. And always you find him thwarted in this ambition of his by their lack of faith; once, the sacred author goes so far as to say, "He could not do many miracles there, by reason of their unbelief".[1] Does that mean that the theandric[2] virtue which went out of him was limited in its effect by the disposition of the patient; that belief in his miraculous powers was actually a condition without which their exercise was impossible? To suggest that would be not only theologically intolerable, but inconsistent with the evidence at our disposal. When he cured the palsied man[3] in the house he was rewarding, not his faith, but the faith of those who carried him; when he was asked to heal the child of the Syrophenician woman, it was in the mother that he demanded faith, not in the daughter.[4] No, his miracles depended on antecedent faith, not in the sense that his power was limited, but in the sense that his mission was first to men's souls, to their bodies only incidentally. He had come, not to improve their material condition, but to awaken them to that belief in him which is the gate of eternal life.

The Church, a spiritual organization whose office is to train men's souls for heaven, has continually found herself under a charitable necessity of ministering temporal relief to her own children. The first resolution she ever took was that her clergy should be left to their prayers, undisturbed by financial anxieties; the first she ever took and, perhaps we ought to add, the last she has ever kept. All through St Paul's Epistles, if you read them attentively—for he shows an exquisite tact in dealing with the subject—he is constantly coming back to one great preoccupation—the collection for the poor saints at Jerusalem. And all through the centuries the Church has had to act in great measure as a nursing-mother to the faithful, not content to be merely their teacher in the faith; providing schools, hospitals, orphanages, tending the sick, relieving the poor, burying the dead; she has drawn a whole network of charitable institutions across the world,

---

[1] Matthew 15. 38.   [2] *Theandric:* pertaining both to God and man.
[3] Mark 2. 2.   [4] Mark 7. 26.

vying with one another in the service of men's bodies. And always, that is not the point. With the other Christianities there is a constant risk that their spiritual message will lose itself in philanthropic endeavour. The movement which began in an access of burning zeal for men's souls will have been replaced, a century or two later, by a vast organization, religious in name, but merely philanthropic in purpose. With the Catholic Church, so much older than these others, it has never been so. Her message is of the world beyond; on it her eyes are set; she tends, feeds, teaches her children distractedly, only that she may point them to heaven; she will not lose her soul in what the world calls charity.

2

THE PINNACLE OF THE TEMPLE

Then the devil took him up into the holy city, and set him upon the pointed roof of the temple, and said to him, If thou be the Son of God, cast thyself down; for it is written, That he shall give his angels charge concerning thee, and they shall bear thee up in their hands, lest perhaps thou dash thy foot against a stone. Jesus said to him, It is written again, Thou shalt not tempt the Lord thy God.—Matthew 4. 5.

OUR Lord stood on the pediment of the temple roof, with the accusing angel at his side; both watched the stream of people that swept to and fro beneath them. How fascinating it is, looking down from a height; how fascinating and how dangerous! More especially when you look down, as you can, for instance, from the great tower at Blackpool, on swarming thousands of human kind. You see them like ants, infinitely small and infinitely remote from you. You see them apparently swayed, all unreasoning, by blind natural forces; can there be free will in each unit of this undistinguished herd?

Some such appearance the streets of Jerusalem will have presented that day, watched alternately by the leer of Satanic malice and by the indulgent eyes of an all-embracing Love. Men swarming everywhere, buying and selling, haggling, gesticulating, begging, praying, cursing —what a panorama! Watch that Pharisee going up the temple steps to pray, proudly withdrawing the hem of his garment from the mob;

how ridiculous those airs of his look, from up here! Watch that publican, bound, it seems, on the same errand; what prayers can he be meaning to offer, this nervous little wreck of a man, this crouching rent-collector?[1]

And then, the temptation comes. Can nothing be done to awaken these souls, so bent on worldly aims, to eternal issues? Can nothing turn those earth-bound eyes heavenwards, startle and dazzle those dull hearts into faith? You could do it, urges the Tempter, strong in the power of your forty days' fast; you, in whom the spirit has already triumphed over the body. Suppose you were to take one step forward —a single step would do it—and let yourself fall? There would be a startled cry from beneath; hands would point, and all those eyes in the square beneath would be turned up, in a moment, to look. And then, a miracle; of course there would be a miracle! You are the Son of God, and God would not allow his own Son to be dashed to pieces by a fall. For his own honour, he would be bound to send his angels to bear you up. The crowds would find you uninjured; would learn to treat you as what you are, a messenger from heaven. Try it—why not? Can it be that you doubt God's providence, imagine that he could fail you?

We must not misunderstand our Lord's answer. "Thou shalt not tempt the Lord thy God"—most of us have made the mistake before now, I suppose, of imagining that our Lord in saying that, is claiming to be God, and is rebuking the Devil for subjecting him to temptation. That is not the sense at all; it does not mean "You, Satan, do wrong to tempt Jesus of Nazareth"; it means "I, Jesus of Nazareth, should do wrong to tempt the Lord my God". To tempt him—in what sense? To make trial of his love, to put his power to the test, by deliberately exposing myself to danger, and defying him to neglect me. We should trust God to rescue us, in his own time and in the way he sees best, from the difficulties which he has allowed to beset us. But, to court danger wantonly, and then expect Providence to save you from the effects of your own rashness, that is quite a different thing. That is to force his hand, to presume on his goodness. "Thou shalt not tempt the Lord thy God."

I have said that the temptations of our Lord are the temptations of his Church; that is, of her rulers, who are not immune from error in the decisions which they must sometimes make to meet the practical needs of the day. In the very earliest times, when the sword of persecution hung over her, the Church did make great demands, terrible demands, on the consciences of her subjects. She required them to

[1] Cf. Luke 18. 10.

confess their faith under the most infamous tortures; and if they failed at that test, she submitted them to a rigid ecclesiastical discipline at the very thought of which we, Christians of a softer age, must needs blush. But she did not tell them to go about publicly professing their faith, to hold their meetings in the market squares, to await, unmoved, the coming of the persecutor. Our Lord, himself, had given directions that, when persecuted in one city, Christians should flee to another,[1] and the right of avoiding persecution, where that was possible, was always recognized; some of the greatest and the boldest saints, St Athanasius for example, availed themselves of that liberty. There were heretics, the Donatist heretics, against whom St Augustine wrote, who held that it was the duty of a Christian to court death; and the more fanatical of them, we are told, would sometimes throw themselves down over precipices, as if, thereby, they established a claim to martyrdom. Against such extravagances the Church always made her protest; taught by her Master that we ought to pray not to be led into temptation, she would not put a harder yoke on her children than strict necessity demanded.

Often in history and, not least, in our own day, the Church has been rebuked for her want of spirit in allowing the world's injustices to go unchallenged, asked why she does not take a bolder line and interfere in secular quarrels, at whatever risk to her own popularity or influence. Those of us who are old enough to remember the Great War can remember how often we heard those reproaches on the lips of our fellow countrymen; here were all these Catholics in Austria and in Germany, fighting quite plainly (so it seemed to our friends), in an indefensible cause, making use of inhuman means to secure an unhallowed end. Why could not Pope Benedict the Fifteenth interfere, and bid them lay down their arms? Since the war, especially with the rise of the new tyrannies, frequent occasions have arisen upon which we Catholics have had to face this kind of criticism on the part of our well-meaning neighbours; they always assume that their own point of view is the only conceivable point of view which an honest man could take; and, doing the Holy Father the credit of believing him to be an honest man, they profess themselves pained and astonished at the pusillanimity which does not seek a direct issue, on purely moral grounds, with this dictator or that. We are not concerned, here, with the aberrations in our neighbours' opinions. We have only to consider the general principle why the Church is so slow, even when her own rights are concerned, to advise resistance to aggression; why she remains dumb,

[1] Matthew 10. 23.

sometimes, when there seems to be legitimate ground for protest. The Holy Father will sometimes intervene in the cause of humanity. It happened during the war, it happened the other day over the bombing of towns in Spain: but he does not threaten—why is that?

The argument against us, after all, is a formidable one. The Catholic Church rules, after all, over a vast empire of human souls, widely different in their national temper and outlook; she has a key, then, such as no other religion has, to the world-situation. She inspires a strong, a mysteriously strong, personal loyalty in her subjects; she has a hold, then—a lever to work by. And she claims, as no other religious body dares to claim, that her judgments are ratified in the world to come; if she told a body of Catholics, for example, to lay down their arms because their quarrel was unjust, she could excommunicate them if they disobeyed, make martyrs of them if they obeyed and suffered for it. Is she not in a unique position, where such interference is concerned?

Precisely; she is in a unique position, and because she is in a unique position she is reluctant to take advantage of it. Because her empire over souls is so vast, she knows that she retains some kind of hold, though it be a slight one, over many whose consciences are imperfectly formed; because they are such a Babel of nationalities, she knows that wide differences of tradition and outlook will divide them. Because she retains, in spite of everything, so powerful a hold over their affections, she shrinks from setting up in their minds a conflict of loyalties— Church against class, or religious against race—to confuse them and to hurry them into acting against their private conscience. Because her powers are so terrible, as holding the keys of the kingdom of heaven, she is more afraid of the consequences—to them—of alienation from her membership than some voluntary association of Christians, calling itself a Church, would be in the same circumstances.

It is time that we returned to the needs of the individual Christian life, and considered how the example of our Lord's second temptation bears upon them.

We tempt Providence when we go out of our way to expose ourselves to that which may be dangerous to faith or morals, when we lightly court the occasions of sin, and tell ourselves that it is all right; there can be no harm in it for us; there might be risk for others, but not for genuine Catholics, well-instructed Catholics like ourselves. And here, again, let us recall the fact that our Lord allowed himself to be tempted at the prime of life and on the threshold of his career, partly, at least, because he wanted to set an example to those who are in the same position. And I hope such people do not need to be reminded that it is a very confused and a very unsettled generation they have been born into. I will not say a generation worse altogether than those which went before it; it has its virtues as well as its vices. But it is a careless generation, which has grown up with very little attention to the advice of its elders and, to tell the truth, somewhat in reaction from them. It has discarded conventions without replacing them by principles; it is apt to mistake excitement for happiness, passion for love, and eccentricity for genius. And it is very easy for Catholics, much easier than they know, to be carried away on the tide of it.

"He that thinkest himself to stand", St Paul warns us, "let him take heed lest he fall."[1] He illustrates that by reminding us how the people of Israel, rescued from Egypt by their baptism in the Red Sea, houselled as it were with the manna which accompanied their pilgrimage through the desert, nevertheless fell away into idolatry. And we, he implies, baptized Christians though we are, sustained by the Christian sacraments as we are, is there no danger for us? "He that thinketh himself to stand, let him take heed lest he fall."

3

THE HIGH MOUNTAIN

Again, the devil took him up into a very high mountain, and showed him all the kingdoms of the world and the glory of them; and said to him, All these I will give thee, if thou wilt fall down and adore me. Then Jesus said to him, Begone, Satan; for it is written, Thou shalt adore the Lord thy God, and him only shalt thou serve.—Matthew 4. 8.

ST MATTHEW and St Luke, it is well known, give the three temptations of our Lord in a different order. I have adopted St Matthew's, because his account seems to imply more expressly that he has followed the order of time. It does not, in any case, make much difference whether the temptation to worship Satan assailed our Lord before or after the temptation to throw himself down from the pinnacle. For one is, if you come to think of it, the obverse of the other. Satan, let us

[1] i Corinthians 10. 12.

remind ourselves again, was putting our Lord to the test, uncertain whether he was God Incarnate, or only Man. But, if he was only Man, it did not follow that he might not think himself something greater than Man, after the divine testimony which accompanied his baptism. The Devil, then, will provide for either emergency. "If Jesus of Nazareth thinks he is only Man, with a whole faithless world to convince and convert, perhaps he will accept the offer of entering into an alliance with me. One way or the other, surely he will yield to my suggestions, unless indeed—unless indeed he is Incarnate God."

In this third temptation, you see, there is no question of "If thou be the Son of God"; that drops out altogether. Indeed, it has been suggested that the Devil in this passage is actually pretending to be the Son of God himself. That would explain the confidence with which he says, "All these things are delivered to me, and I give them to whom I will." And in that case our Lord's reply, "Get thee hence, Satan", has a special point. Our Lord addresses Satan by name, for the first time in the story, to show that he is not deceived; it is Christ unmasking Antichrist.

What was the high mountain to which our Lord was taken? I like to think it was Mount Carmel, our Lady's own hill; that would be a suitable setting for the incident. It looked down, landwards, over the plain of Esdraelon, which has been the battleground of East and West, from the days when Egypt and Babylon met there in conflict, in King Josias' reign, to the day when the Turkish armies retreated across it, at the end of the Great War. From Carmel, too, looking out seawards, you would catch sight of the huge grainships making their northward voyage across the Mediterranean. Whence do they come? From Egypt, the oldest civilization in history. Whither are they bound? For Rome, the latest civilization in history. All the kingdoms of the world, and the glory of them, in a moment of time.

It was a scene to stir a man's blood, to appeal to a man's imagination, if this had been only Man. If Jesus of Nazareth is only Man—that, surely, is the Devil's calculation—he is bound to hesitate, to parley with the temptation. "Look round you [he says], and read the history of the world's conquerors in epitome. Will you not be one of these? You come from a persecuted race, a race still suffering indignities under the oppression of a foreign invader. You have come to deliver your people; deliver them first from the tyranny of Rome. You have only to raise your standards, and the countryside will flock to them. You see that great camp yonder, which they call Legion? That camp you shall overrun and plunder; I will help you. You shall free your country, but that is not enough. You have come to reform the world; you must subdue it first, before you can reform it. With my aid, you shall follow up your victory here by a march on Europe; you shall challenge Rome itself. Think of him who now holds the reins of imperial power; a weakling, a voluptuary, who dares not show his face inside his own capital; such a man you shall overcome—Jesus shall replace Tiberius. Then, when from the shores of Britain to the deserts of Parthia a world obeys and deifies you, what a chance to effect the regeneration of the age! They are building temples, today, to the libertine Tiberius; tomorrow, Jesus of Nazareth shall have his temples instead."

Our Lord does not, in answering, give the obvious reason why the suggestion made to him is impossible; that would have been to fall into the Devil's trap, by revealing the secret of his own identity. Instead he takes his stand on ground which any man might take equally well—I cannot worship you, because worship belongs only to God. He does not question, what he very well might have questioned, whether Satan really has command over all the kingdoms of the world; does not discuss, as he very well might have discussed, whether a promise coming from such a quarter would be deserving of any confidence; does not even consider whether such a career of triumph as has been suggested would in truth be a benefit to humanity. There is a condition attached to the promise, and that condition is an impossible one. Satan wants him to do evil in order that good may come of it; that is asking God to deny his own Godhead.

The temptations of our Lord are the temptations of his Church. The Devil said to our Lord, "Since you are divine, why not fly in the face of Providence?" and in the next breath, "Since you are not divine but only human, why not acknowledge the fact by giving my claims the first place, and yours only the second?" History is scarred with the long record of that struggle between Church and State; we have only to think of St Thomas a Becket and St Thomas More in the annals of our own country. Again and again it would have been possible for the Church to make better terms for herself if she would have forgotten her divine origin, would have partitioned out human activity between God and Caesar, on the understanding that Caesar's claim came first, and God's second. Again and again she has been promised unlaborious success in her mission, on condition that she would hitch her star to the wagon of an earthly conqueror.

That temptation comes to her in a peculiar form and with a peculiar force today. For a century, nearly, she has been engaged in a long struggle, not of her own choosing, with the Left Wing parties in

European politics. Everywhere the politicians who have spoken loudest in the name of justice and of freedom have been the first to deny justice and freedom to their Catholic subjects. Of late, these Left Wing theories have taken exaggerated forms; and in the countries where their influence triumphed the Church has been exposed, as a matter of course, to bitter persecution. But in other countries a rival movement has showed its head; a spirit of Nationalism has taken up the challenge thrown down to it by Communism, and has beaten it by its own methods. Surely, you would be inclined to say, in these countries, at least, the Church will come into her own. The authoritarian States which recognize the menace of a common enemy will be drawn closer than ever to the Church, accord her unexampled privileges, that she may teach their citizens her own lesson of order and good citizenship. That is what we might have expected; but it is a matter of daily experience that such expectations were doomed to disappointment. Sometimes in these countries she lives on terms of precarious partnership; sometimes the new rulers of Europe combat her influence not less fiercely, not less openly, than Communism itself. What is the reason?

The reason is a direct conflict of ideals. The totalitarian State, whether its colour be of the Left or of the Right, has no room for any exercise of private freedom; has no room, therefore, for a Church which can dispute its claim over men's consciences. Especially where the younger generation is concerned; it is a straight issue whether the boys and girls of a country are to be Catholics first and citizens afterwards, or citizens first and Catholics afterwards. If that quarrel could be settled in a sense satisfactory to the totalitarian State, then doubtless it would be willing enough to make use of the Church as an engine of government, to grant her privileges on condition that she would be the mouthpiece of an inspired national policy. But such freedom would be bought at too dear a price. For the sake of peace, and to save her own subjects from unnecessary molestation, she does make the best terms she can, does everything to rebut the charge of unnecessary interference in politics. But she cannot sell her soul.

The temptations of our Lord are also the temptations of his servants individually. But the scale of them, naturally, is different; the Devil is not going to offer you and me all the kingdoms of the world. He knows his market; offers, like a good salesman, just as much as he thinks his customer will take. I suppose he thinks, with some justice, that most of us could be had for five thousand a year, and a great many of us for much less. Nor does he, to us, propose his conditions so openly; his offer comes to us wrapped up in all sorts of plausible shapes. But, if he sees the chance, he is not slow to point out to you and me how we could get the thing we want if we would be untrue to our better selves, and not infrequently if we would be untrue to our Catholic loyalties. And he is especially eager to put that kind of temptation in our way when we are young and just setting out on a career, as our Lord was. For he knows that at such a time of life the spur of ambition is strong, and the mind is less firm in its grasp of the supernatural.

There are all sorts of ways in which being a Catholic handicaps you, may handicap you at any rate, for worldly success. We are a Protestant country still, in the negative sense; and wherever there is a job to be got or an honour to be bestowed, there is a bias, although it may be a slight bias, against the Catholic candidate. Oh, I know, everybody is very broad-minded nowadays; but it is astonishing how broad-minded people will fight shy of giving employment or encouragement to a Catholic, for fear of coming across prejudice in somebody less broad-minded than themselves. But it isn't often that the prizes offered are so much worth having, it isn't often that the alternative of apostasy is so openly suggested as to make the prospect of a career dangerous to our faith. There is one special department of life, only one, in which the choice "God or Satan" is apt to be thrust upon us abruptly, hardly giving us time to think about it. And that is when man or woman begins to contemplate entering on the state of matrimony.

We English Catholics live, nowadays, in a mixed society. Home influence, for a number of reasons, does not count for as much as it did; we live our own lives, make our own friends. The plain intention of the Church, that a mixed marriage should be something exceptional, with special reasons to account for it, is almost universally ignored; young men and women are not going to be shepherded (they tell themselves) into making a suitable match; we have finished with that kind of thing. Very well, then; but remember the risks you run if your choice of a partner in life is going to be dictated to you by some sudden, violent attraction founded on passion, or even on sentiment. You may find that you have been betrayed into a position where you have to choose between resisting that attraction, at whatever cost to your feelings, or cutting yourself off, if not from the faith, at least from the life of the sacraments.

Pray God, that you may be spared such a temptation as that. But it may come, and it is well to remember what the author of *The Imitation of Christ* tells us: "Temptations do not make a man weak, but they show what stuff he is made of."[1] The Church loses, in these days, year by year, a steady proportion of souls through this drift into unfortunate marriage; but they are not, most of them, souls remarkable for their faith or their devotion; it is mostly among weak-kneed and careless Catholics that the harm is done. Make up your mind, then, if you are to walk safe in a world of temptation, that you will fortify yourself against the danger of it, while there is yet time, by faithfulness to prayer and the sacraments, by a practice of studying God's will for you and giving yourself to it, abandoning yourself into his hands. Then, whatever you meet in his creatures that seems to you adorable and worthy of worship will nevertheless be a lure you know how to resist, if you see that it is something contrary to his will. "Thou shalt worship the Lord thy God, and him only shalt thou serve"—that is not a mere negative precept, forbidding us to worship anything else, to serve anyone else. It bids us worship him who is infinite holiness, serve him who is infinite goodness, with the free choice of a Christian heart enlightened by faith and strengthened by sacramental life within us.

[1] Book I, ch. 12.

III

THE SERMON ON THE MOUNT*

*A series of sermons published in *The Cross* in 1927 and 1928.

FORGIVING—AND LOVING

You have heard that it hath been said, Thou shalt love thy neighbour, and hate thy enemy. But I say to you, Love your enemies, do good to them that hate you, and pray for them that persecute you and calumniate you. . . . For if you love them that love you, what reward shall you have? Do not even the publicans this? And if you salute your brethren only, what do you more? Do not also the heathens this?—Matthew 5. 43.

IF you read our Lord's words as a command that must be obeyed to the letter, as an obligation which binds upon your conscience under pain of some penalty, they can only involve you in scruples and disquiet. Does our Lord really command us to lose ourselves in admiration of a particular person's qualities, just because he happens to have done us a bad turn? Does he order us, on pain of his displeasure, to feel a violent attraction towards the people who do nothing but spurn our advances? Are we never to have time or money to spend on our relations, our benefactors, on the people who are fond of us, because we are so busy paying court to people who cannot bear the sight of us? Plainly, we are misinterpreting him if we suppose that he means our lives to be regulated on such principles as that. And, if you look at a book of moral theology, you will be appalled at the effect which is produced by the attempt to work out these verses into a system, a code of behaviour. You will be told that a Christian is bound, under pain of mortal sin, to accord to his enemy the common courtesies of life; not to refuse him recognition, for example, in public. Is that all that is meant by the Sermon on the Mount? Why, no, but that is all that moral theology can, in fairness, insist upon; that is all you will get out of the Sermon on the Mount if you insist on treating it as a piece of legislation, as a series of commands which must be obeyed.

The secret of our Lord's new law, as I have been trying to show you, is that it is not a series of commands which must be obeyed, but an active principle of charity which ought to make commands unnecessary for us. The quotation which he gives here from the Old Testament is not an exact quotation, it is rather an exposition of the text. The law said: Thou shalt love thy friend as thyself. It seems likely, from the context, that the word "friend" here was meant to indicate a fellow Jew, as opposed to the foreigner and the Gentile. And our Lord says: Surely this is very extraordinary, that there should have to be a law which *commands* a man to love his friends, obviously implying that he need be at no pains to love his enemies! Why should we need a law on such a point as that? To sympathize with your fellow countrymen, to be on chatting terms with your neighbours, to make little presents and perform little services for your friends—why, natural inclination is enough to make a man do all that! Do not even the publicans, for all their sordid minds and their grasping habits, go out of their way to do a good turn to a friend? Do not the Gentiles, with no law of Moses to guide them, pass kind words to one another? To do so much as that, it is not necessary to be a disciple of Moses, far less a disciple of the Sermon on the Mount!

I think our Lord means us to see that; means us to see that the love and kindness which we bestow on our friends is not, itself, the result of any law which enjoins such conduct, it comes quite natural to us, we do it from inclination. Now, the disciples of the Sermon on the Mount, he tells us in this passage, will be the children of their Father in heaven, who makes his sun rise upon the good and the bad, and rains upon the just and the unjust. The children of their Father, then they will imitate their Father. They will imitate the splendid promiscuousness of his generosity. They in their turn will show love and kindness, not measuring it out in the scales or feeling obliged by a law, but naturally, from inclination. Only they will not, like the Jews or the heathen, be moved to such expressions of affection only by men of their own kindred or men of their own race. All mankind will be their nation, every class of mankind will be their kindred. The saint will expect no more reward for attending lepers than you would expect for looking after some relation of yours who should fall ill in the next street. The saint will not feel that he has done something handsome in pardoning his would-be murderer, than you would feel you had done something handsome in accepting an apology from some friend you may have quarrelled with. Man's love for his friends, though it be enjoined by law, is not dictated to him by law; it springs from a natural inclination. And man's love for his enemies is not dictated to him by a law either; it springs from a supernatural inclination. That is the secret of the Sermon on the Mount.

It is a very common thing to find people really worried about their attitude in this matter. They say: "I know the Gospel tells us to forgive our enemies, but I can't do it". So-and-so has done them an injury, or, worse still, has done an injury to the one they loved, and the wound will not stop rankling. Of course, I pray for him (they will tell you), and when I meet him I do my best to be civil to him; and I try not to talk about him behind his back. In fact, I think I succeed more or less in *behaving* as if I'd forgiven him, but I haven't forgiven him, really; deep down in my heart there are the same smouldering fires of anger, and every time I think of the name, even in prayer, it only serves to fan those smouldering fires into a blaze. Now, what am I to do about it? Ought I to go to communion, when I still feel like this? Are my confessions really valid, when I tell myself I have forgiven, and tell the priest that I've forgiven, but feel sure all the time that I'm not speaking from my heart? Can our Lord really tell us to forgive our enemies? Doesn't he mean, simply, that we ought to behave as if we'd forgiven them?

Well, for purposes of moral theology, that's perfectly true. There can be no obligation to feel affected in a particular way towards our neighbour, if only because our affections do not come and go like that at the command of the will. The most that can be demanded of us as a matter of obligation is that we should bottle up our feelings of resentment; and the best test of whether we are doing that or not is the success with which we manage to conceal them. I don't think there's any reason to feel guilty about our resentment, if we're really doing our best to live it down. But there is, I think, reason to feel *humiliated*—humiliated, because we are so unlike the Sermon on the Mount. You see, our Lord doesn't tell us to forgive our enemies; nothing as simple as that; he tells us to *love* our enemies. You haven't done his whole will for you when you've stopped hating your enemies. He wants you to love them. And, of course, you don't; but, then, that's all part of a much bigger question. You say you don't love your enemies. I know; but do you love your grocer? Do you love the blind man at the corner of the road? Why, no; there are probably only only about two or three hundred people in the world of whom you could definitely say, "I like them". Of course, you don't love your enemies, if you haven't even learned to love strangers!

You see, that's where the saints differ from us in their attitude towards mankind. They really do love their fellow man as such; they feel the same thrill of pleasure when they see a man coming down the road which you and I feel when we see a friend coming down the road. Mankind is their kindred, the world is their parish. And, consequently, one who shows bitter enmity towards a saint, speaks evil of him, persecutes him, is to the saint simply a friend who is being tiresome;

it's a sort of tiff between lovers which is bound to blow over. I know the lives always tell us that the saints loved their enemies as being instruments of their own mortification; and I dare say that's true, but that's not all the truth. They didn't love them for being instruments, they loved them for being men.

I doubt if it is possible for a human being to love everybody in a completely impartial way. Our Lord himself loved St John especially; and surely our Lady claimed a unique place in the affections of his sacred heart. The trouble with us, mostly, is not that we spend too much love on our relations and friends, but that we haven't begun to love mankind in general at all. But that is what we ought to ask for, and hope for, as the result of trying to imitate our Lord—not a spiritless indifference to the hatred and ill-usage of our fellow men, but an all-embracing love of our fellow men so hardy, so boisterous, that no amount of insult, no amount of ingratitude, can conquer its irresistible optimism.

2

ARE WE LIARS?

You have heard that it was said to them of old, Thou shalt not forswear thyself: but thou shalt perform thy oaths to the Lord. But I say to you not to swear at all . . . but let your speech be: Yea, yea: No, no.—Matthew 5. 33, 34, 37.

I SUPPOSE if I were to write on the above text an article which dealt with profane swearing, and pointed out how the use of strong language by Christians is in itself something wrong, and, besides that, gives quite exaggerated scandal to those who hear us, you readers would take it all quite quietly. You would not point out that after all this is not what our Lord is talking about. If, in these words of the text, he had meant to talk to us about sins of the tongue, he would have taken a quite different starting point. He would have told us: "You have heard that it was said of them of old, Curseth be he that curseth father or mother. But I say to you, Curse not at all." But, you see, he is not talking about *cursing*. He is talking about *swearing*; and it is only by a modern abuse of language that we talk about swearing when we mean cursing. To swear means to take an oath that you will do such and such a thing, or that something you are asserting is true. Profane language does not come into the question at all.

What, then, you say, are the Quakers right? Does our Lord mean that taking an oath in a court of law, or taking an oath of allegiance to the King, is a wicked thing to do? Once again, you are on the wrong track. The Sermon on the Mount is not meant to tie us up with fresh obligations, fresh prohibitions. It is meant to inspire us with a principle of active charity which ought to make obligations and prohibitions unnecessary to us; which ought to make us do things through love for God, instead of abstaining from doing them through fear of his judgments. Our speech is to be Yea, yea, No, no—why? Not because that which is over and above is evil; he does not say that. He says that which is over and above these is *of* evil; the necessity for using an oath to make men believe our statements or trust our promises arises out of, is due to, a wrong attitude on our part altogether.

We are quite at liberty to take oaths when the law or some other important business requires it. But the taking of an oath ought to be a humiliating business to us, a dreadful second-best. It ought to make us sweat with pity for our fellow men, that the law should not be able to trust a man to tell the truth when his neighbour's life or liberty depends upon it, unless he is made to kiss the Bible first. What oaths mean, when you face the facts squarely, is this—that we men lie to one another so, cheat one another so, pervert the truth so much when we talk to one another, that it is assumed we shall tell lies unless we bind ourselves on pain of the divine vengeance to be as good as our word. What a satire it is on our human weakness, when we say casually in conversation: "I swear I won't tell a soul!" You *swear* you won't tell a soul. What need to swear? If you say: "I will not tell a soul", surely that would be enough? Surely a Christian's word should be as good as his bond?

It isn't true that all oaths are unnecessary; but it would be perfectly true that all oaths ought to be unnecessary—would be, if it wasn't that there are so many third-rate articles going about in the world. Think of a soldier having to take an oath of allegiance to the King! What a paradox, that a man who is just embracing the most gallant of all professions should have to pass his word that he will not betray his country! For the man who really means to be a soldier, really wants to be a soldier, the taking of an oath is a mere empty formality; it is not the oath, but loyalty to his country that will make him ready to die in her service. It is because there are, or might be, third-rate articles aspiring to the soldier's profession that the oath has to be exacted. The priest who is worth anything obeys his bishop, not because he has taken an oath to obey him, but because he knows that, in the last resort, the will of his superior is the voice of God for him. The witness who is worth anything tells the truth, not because he has sworn to tell the truth, but because he has an honest man's solicitude to see that justice is done. I expect some of you will remember a picture in *Punch* (I think it was) of a young and not well-instructed bridegroom being asked by the clergyman: "Wilt thou take this woman to wife?" and he replies: "A coom a' purpose!" To the lover, these legal solemnities seem quite superfluous; why take an oath to realize the wish of his heart?

There are special instances. What is the quality underlying them all, which (our Lord says) every disciple of the Sermon on the Mount ought to possess, so as to escape from legal obligation into the inner freedom of the spirit? It has two names; in matters of assertion, we call it sincerity; in matters of attention, we call it fidelity. Perjury was forbidden by the Jewish law. And the rabbis, the Jewish teachers, were very fertile in distinctions on the subject of perjury, which sort of oaths were really binding on conscience, and under how grave obligation they bound you. And the answer of the Sermon on the Mount is: Yes, but why should anyone want to commit perjury? Why should anybody be concerned to find out whether the oath he has taken is a binding oath or not? If you make a statement, it ought naturally to be a true statement, whether you swear to it or not. If you declare the intention of doing a thing, then, as a matter of course, you will do the thing, whether you have bound your conscience by oaths or not. The disciple of the Sermon on the Mount will (because he loves God) have a natural sincerity about him which will never trouble itself about perjury, because it will shrink from the mere suggestion of untruth.

That's very easily said; it isn't nearly so easily done. We Englishmen always say we tell the truth; but, you know, that's the worst lie of the lot. There's the propaganda instinct in all of us, whatever our nationality. How often do you describe an incident without putting some of your own colour into the telling of it? How often do you make an excuse—even a quite genuine excuse—without running it for a bit more than it's worth? How many people can do a stroke of business without a little bluffing? All men are liars—I'm afraid that's still true; and the women—well, you know, I think they do their share of it, too. Only we men lie mostly from selfishness, and women mostly from unselfishness, so they have the better of us there.

How many people we know who wouldn't tell a downright lie!
How few people we know, even among very pious people, who
always really tell the truth! Life is complicated, and we work-a-day
Christians mustn't expect too much of ourselves. But this I do say,
that in proportion as a Christian lives a recollected life and tries to
make our Lord his model, he will attain a simplicity and a lucidity of
character which will have less and less need for untruth. He will live,
not according to the caprice of the moment, but according to a plan;
there will be less selfishness in his calculations, less partiality in his
judgments; he will know himself better, because his examination of
conscience will be more careful and more determined. His conversation
will be more with our Lady and the saints, less with his exacting,
distracting fellow citizens in this world below. He will know the truth,
and the truth will make him free.

In so far as you approach that ideal, you will win a respect among
your neighbours that is not easily won. You will not be conscious of
that respect, you will not want to be conscious of it. But men will
take your Yea for yea, your No for no, without questioning your
facts, without exacting guarantees of your fidelity. The world, with all
its faults, knows an honest man.

3

ANGRY?

*You have heard that it was said to them of old, Thou shalt not kill. But I say
to you that whoever is angry with his brother shall be in danger of the
judgment.*—Matthew 5. 21.

O UR Lord Jesus Christ, who was at every moment of his life fully
conscious that he was the Son of God, and that he was, besides,
the Mediator appointed between God and men, saw fit to order the
circumstances of his earthly life that they should recall, now in this
detail, now in that, the history of his chosen people, the Jews. For he
was, as St Paul tells us, that true seed of Abraham to which the world
looked forward, and the fortunes of the Jewish race, as we read of them
in the Old Testament, were only the world's preparation for his
coming. Out of Egypt the people of Israel came, with Moses at their

head, to claim a promised inheritance. Out of Egypt our Lord came in
his Mother's arms to establish his everlasting reign in the hearts of men.
For forty years Israel tempted God in the wilderness; in that same wilderness for forty days our Lord was tempted by the Devil. It was on a
mountain-top, the meeting place of earth with heaven, that the first
imperfect law was delivered to Moses. It was on a mountain-top, too,
that our Lord delivered to his Apostles those laws of perfection which
we still call "The Sermon on the Mount".

Do not think, he said, that I am come to destroy the law. I am not
come to destroy, but to fulfil. Hitherto—St Paul tells us again—the
world has been like a schoolboy, who is kept under tutors and gover-
nors because he has not yet come of age. The schoolboy lives by rules,
which he is invited to obey for fear of consequences. It is not asked of
him that he should intelligently grasp or enthusiastically embrace the
spirit of these rules which are laid down for him; enough that he should
obey. Such was the principle of the Mosaic law; it threatened punishments, it held out promises of reward, but it did not explain itself or
seek to commend itself; justice was satisfied if its precepts were observed to the letter. Now all that is to be changed. When our Lord
Jesus Christ came on earth, mankind came of age. We Christians are
called, not to the bondage of desk and schoolroom, but to the glorious
liberty of the son in his father's house. The law by which we are to live
must be written, not on hard tablets of stone, external to ourselves,
rigid, lifeless, but in our own hearts, plastic to its influence and responsive to its spirit. It is for the schoolboy to be summoned by bells,
governed in his daily conduct by notices posted on a board. The man
must live by principles to which the mind lends its appreciation, the
heart its homage.

The fulfilment of the law does not mean, then, that the old law is
to be expanded by a series of codicils, as lifeless, as uninspiring as the
rest. It does not mean more commandments, it means commandments
of a different kind. And when our Lord goes on to say: "Unless your
justice abound more than that of the Scribes and Pharisees, you shall
not enter into the kingdom of heaven", he does not mean that we are
going to keep *more* rules than the Scribes and Pharisees did. He means,
that whereas their tradition and their training led them to carry out
God's commandments in the letter, it is for us to carry them out in the
spirit. It is for us to catch from the lips of our Master those eternal
principles of which the Old Law was only a rough, inadequate expression; to make those principles our own and to serve God, not by obeying them simply, but by living them.

At that point it is open to any unfriendly critic of the Catholic Church to say: "Yes, but why should you set yourselves up as superior to the Jews? You Catholics, with your elaborate Codex of Canon Law, your vast tomes of moral theology, your interminable rubrics of the Mass—surely you are enslaved to the letter every bit as much as the Jews were before Christ came? Much liberty the Gospel has brought you! Don't you spend labour and ink over determining exactly how great a sum constitutes a serious theft, exactly how much food a man may be allowed to eat on a fast day?" Well, I am afraid I have not time to enter into an apologetic argument here. For our present purpose it is enough to point out that moral theology is only necessary because Christians are not all good Christians: if they were, it would become a merely theoretical science. If we are followers of Christ, we Christians live not by laws but by the spirit of his Gospel. We do not spend our time calculating exactly how late we can be for Mass without missing it, or exactly how far we can go in saying unpleasant things about our neighbours without being guilty of the sin of detraction. Rather, the love of Christ constrains us; we would not, so far as in us lies, miss a single second of that short half-hour in which he gives us audience; our study is not to do our neighbour all the harm we can, but how to find in him, in spite of any natural dislike, the image of the Saviour who died for him and for us. Because the Catholic Church is so all-inclusive, unites so many different races, temperaments, stages of development, it is necessary for her to have codes and to legislate over details. But if you really want to find a good, practical text-book of moral theology for Catholics, I can tell you of quite a short one and quite a cheap one. It is called *The Imitation of Christ*.

Our Lord chose stupid people for his apostles, and he knew that his followers in later ages would be stupid people, like you and me. He was not content, therefore, to break out into short, enigmatic utterances, and leave us to interpret them for ourselves. He would give us instances, illustrations to show us the bearing of the principles which he was laying down. So, after telling us that our justice must abound more than the justice of the Scribes and Pharisees, he gives us twenty-eight verses of explanation as to how we are to make sure of this. And those twenty-eight verses are arranged in an ordered plan: they are divided into six separate sections; and at the beginning of each he says: "You have heard that it was said of them of old . . .", giving a quotation from the Old Testament; then he adds: "But I say to you", and gives us his own version of the same law, a version suited to the needs of those who want to be real Christians. He takes some old refrain from the Law of Moses, and sets it anew, writing celestial harmonies for it.

Let us examine another of these emphatic utterances of Christ this month. Our reflections will be very seasonable while Lent is yet with us.

"You have heard that it was said to them of old, Thou shalt not kill; and whosoever shall kill shall be in danger of the judgment. But I say to you that whosoever is angry with his brother shall be in danger of the judgment." That sounds terrible, doesn't it? That sounds, doesn't it, as if our Lord was fulminating from the Mount of the Beatitudes a law far more strict and far more searching than any precept of the decalogue. I can still remember how uncomfortable it used to make me when I was small to be told: "Whosoever shall say, Thou fool, shall be in danger of hell fire." Because I'm afraid I did sometimes call my brother a fool; and this text seemed to say that I'd done something quite as bad as if I'd murdered him. Are we really to understand our Lord as saying that under the New Dispensation every sin will be a mortal sin? If so, surely, the Gospel will bring no liberty to human consciences; rather the Christian life will be a life of servile terror for us all.

But, you see, our Lord only puts it in these legal terms as a kind of satire on the legalistic way in which the Jews regarded their religion; on the legalistic way in which you and I sometimes regard our religion, when we forget what Master it is we serve. The point is, not that an angry word is as culpable as a mortal blow, but that the source of either is a disposition of the human heart; and such a disposition as ought not to be found at all in the Christian heart, or if it finds a harbour there, should be harboured only for a moment. It is not always wrong to kill; it is not wrong to kill in war, or in self-defence. But it is always wrong to be angry; wrong, especially, to feel angry against a human being. And the real reason why Christians ought not to commit murder is not the fact that murder is against the Ten Commandments. Such motives as that ought to lie in the far background, the very horizon of their thoughts. The reason why Christians ought not to commit murder is that murder arises out of anger, and anger itself is something altogether out of the picture, if we really mean to be disciples of the Sermon on the Mount.

What did the priest say to us on Ash Wednesday? "Remember, O man, that thou art dust, and wilt return to dust." We have to be reminded of that; Almighty God does not have to be reminded of anything: "He remembers", says King David, "that we are dust." He remembers, therefore, the frailty of our nature; and he knows that we shall be angry in spite of ourselves, even with our Lord's own words ringing in our ears to prevent us. So he goes on to tell us the next best thing; if sudden irritation does get the better of us for a moment, and we say something we regret afterwards, we are to make it right as soon as possible. If you are offering your gift at the altar, and remember that your brother has some cause of offence against you, run back and be reconciled to him before you offer your gift. Do we remember that as often as we should, when we bring to the altar of the Christian sacrifice the poor gift of our unworthy devotion? We are careful to make our peace with God by confession; are we equally careful to make sure that we are at peace with our fellow men? That does not mean that we should always be going about apologizing to one another; a person who is always apologizing is very often a nuisance. But tell me, when you've "had words" with somebody, isn't there usually a chance, before the next time you go to confession, of saying some kind word, doing some trifling service, which will obliterate the memory of your quarrel without the need of referring to it? That is what Jesus Christ wants you to do. "Agree with thy adversary quickly, whilst thou art in the way with him."[1] You start a quarrel; how do you know that death will not intervene before it can be put right? And that means purgatory: "thou shalt not go out from thence until thou hast paid the last mite".[2] And our Lord does not want us to have any purgatory, he wants us to come straight to him. He wants us to be his children; and how can we be his children if we are not like our Father?

4

DANGER VERSUS SAFETY

You have heard that it was said to them of old, Thou shalt not commit adultery. But I say to you that whosoever shall look on a woman to lust after her hath already committed adultery with her in his heart.—Matthew 5. 27.

I WAS pointing out in a previous sermon that when our Lord says he has not come to destroy the law but to fulfil it, when he tells us that our justice must abound beyond the justice of the Scribes and Pharisees, he does not mean that we, as Christians, have got to observe a whole lot of additional regulations besides the Ten Commandments. He means

[1] Matthew 5. 25.   [2] Luke 12. 59.

that we Christians ought to have a law, written not on tables of stone, but on our inmost hearts; a principle of active charity which ought to supersede the necessity for commandments. We saw how that applied to the fifth commandment; and now we see it applied to the sixth.

Does our Lord mean that one immodest look is as culpable as a sin of adultery? No, that is not the point. The point is that the Christian who has the Sermon on the Mount written in his heart will never need to consider whether there is a law against adultery. His love for God will have shielded him from the spark which might have caused such a conflagration. He will never find himself threatened by the proximate occasions of sin, because he will have put away from him even the remote occasions of sin as inconsistent with the imitation of Christ.

Think of a ship outside the harbour at anchor. See how winds and tides drive it to and fro; how it is continually tugging at the chains that moor it. The strain is never eased for long; one faulty link, and at any moment the ship may drift out to sea. That is like a soul that is only moored by the Ten Commandments. Winds and tides of passion sweep it to and fro; restlessly, day by day, it tugs at the chain, only just safe, exposed, the moment something snaps, to the perils of the open sea. And now think of a ship riding at anchor in harbour. She is moored, yes, sure enough; but how lightly she tugs at her moorings! They have hardly any work to do, the strain is so slight. That is just an image of the soul that rides on the love of Jesus Christ. The sinful impulses which such a soul feels hardly make it tug at all on the chain that binds it to God's law. There is no strain on its loyalty, because it rides at rest.

The soul that only wants to keep the Commandments, wants to serve God without loving him, what a perpetual contradiction it makes of life! Its one effort is to avoid mortal sin—no more. Whatever passion it can indulge, whatever gratification it can give to its lower nature, short of mortal sin, it embraces, it greedily accepts. And this passion, like a tide, sweeps it onwards, until suddenly it comes up against the Ten Commandments with a jerk, like the ship tugging at the cable that moors her! It's bad for the cable, you know, that jerk. Well, the rope holds, thank God, and immediately the soul conceives some fresh passion, sails off in some fresh direction, according to the set of the tide it drifts by. Can a life like that be a life of freedom? Can a life like that be worthy of a Christian, called by baptism to partake in the divine Nature?

Christ calls us to freedom. The soul that has mastered the Sermon on the Mount is not exposed to the storms of passion, because it rests in his love. But remember, in this matter of modesty we have all to be afraid of ourselves; we have not the privilege of our Blessed Lady, to be free from concupiscence. And, consequently, even the soul that lives by the law of Love must continually be checking, by little acts of mortification, even the slightest impulse towards the passions that might sweep it away. "Whosoever shall look"—what a long distance it is, please God, between a careless look and an act of sin! Only a remote occasion, but even the remote occasions of sin are not for the soul that really loves Christ; they strike a false note, they are out of the picture. In all the lives of the saints you will not find one, however angelic his purity, who fancied that because he had been so long preserved from temptation he could take any risks even with the remote occasions of sin.

And that is why our Lord Jesus Christ reinforces this warning by a direction which seems, as you first read it, to be the hardest of all the paradoxical directions he gave us. "If thy right eye scandalize thee, pluck it out and cast it from thee; if thy right hand scandalize thee, cut it off and cast it from thee"[1]—what can all that mean? Are we called upon to make any sacrifice, however heroic, sooner than run the risk of the least temptation? Surely here at least we are under a sterner law than the Jewish people before us; surely here the law of Christ outdoes the thunders of Sinai! But no, that is not the point. The point is simply this: that a thing may be good in itself and useful in itself, and yet if for us it is an occasion of sin, we shall rule it out of our lives if we really love God. There may be some branch of study, some kind of reading, which is not in itself disgraceful, which is followed by others without danger; but if we see there is danger in it for us, then it must go. "If thy right eye scandalize thee, pluck it out." It may be a friendship which is perfectly pure and honourable in itself; which from some points of view, even, is good for us, braces us up and makes better men of us; others can cultivate such friendships without any danger to themselves, and yet, if we see there is danger in it for us, it must go. "If thy right hand scandalize thee, cut it off." Better an amputation, you see, than blood-poisoning.

But, you say, surely we are meant to develop our natures to the full? Surely the Christian vocation is not meant to warp and stunt a man's life, to dwarf his character and make him into a plaster saint of the sacristy? Mortification is all very well, if mortification means making some little sacrifice here and there of things that are not at all important. But mortification cannot mean that a man should cut a whole piece

[1] Matthew 5. 29-30.

out of his life, abandon great opportunities and solid happiness, for the sake of a scruple. How poor the world would be, if we all acted like that! I know; but it is not everyone who has your dangers; it is not everybody, therefore, who has to make your sacrifices. But if you do see that there is danger for you, do not make any mistake about what our Lord counsels. "It is better for thee to enter into life maimed or lame" . . . maimed or lame, he does seem to contemplate the possibility, does he not, that the Christian life will be an incomplete one in this direction or that? But then, you wish to enter heaven through the imitation of Jesus Christ. And when Jesus Christ entered heaven before you, his side was wounded, and his hands and feet were scarred.

Do you still say that the Sermon on the Mount is too exacting? Do you still find it difficult to believe that the yoke of Christ is sweet? That is because you do not consider this—that a sacrifice is hard to make, not according to the amount it costs, but according to the spirit in which you make it. Think of a young lover going out to buy a present, and then think of a man paying his income-tax—do you not see that it is the will which makes sacrifices easy or hard? The servile Christian, who would keep the Ten Commandments and no more, finds common morality a millstone round his neck. Love, says the author of the *Imitation*, feels not its burden, counts not its labour, attempts yet more than it can achieve. The Law given on Sinai speaks with the thunders of authority; the Sermon on the Mount, only with the whisper of Love.

5

THE FREEDOM OF BONDAGE: MARRIAGE UNMARRED AND UNMOURNED

And it hath been said, Whosoever shall put away his wife, let him give her a bill of divorce. But I say to you that whosoever shall put away his wife, apart from the question of fornication, maketh her to commit adultery and he that shall marry her that is put away committeth adultery.—Matthew 5. 31.

OUR Lord, as we have seen, came to fulfil the law, not by adding to it fresh precepts, or precepts still more rigorous, but by putting a new law in our hearts, positive instead of negative, an active principle of charity. In this article you may point to the above text and say that here at least we have come across an exception to the rule. For under the old Mosaic law the Jews were allowed, for a grave cause, to divorce their wives, and, if they would, to remarry. For us Christians, it is not so. The Church, here, has taken her Master's words literally, and though she allows legal separation, recognizes no possibility of dissolving the bond of matrimony. Is not our liberty the poorer, then, in this instance, for the Sermon on the Mount?

I have not space to discuss this subject at length. But I would emphasize two things. In the first place, the Church, as an organized institution, must necessarily have a flat rule about the nature of the marriage tie. She must either say that it can be dissolved, or that it cannot be dissolved; she cannot trim her sails, and parley, and make exceptions. Since it was necessary for her to have a rule, how could she adopt any other rule than that which she had heard from her Master's own lips? But, more than that—this was not the only occasion on which our Lord spoke to his disciples about divorce. On another occasion, when he was confronted with the fact that the Mosaic law allowed it, he replied: "It was owing to the hardness of your hearts that Moses gave you this commandment. But from the beginning it was not so. For this cause a man shall leave father and mother [he is quoting from a precept older than Moses here] and shall cleave to his wife, and they two shall be one flesh."[1] He tells us, then, that the permission of divorce to the ancient Jews was only a special dispensation from the natural law under which we were created. To forbid divorce altogether, as the Christian Church does, is not to add a new burden, hitherto unknown, to the conscience of mankind. It is to withdraw a privilege; and he who withdraws a privilege does not impose a fresh obligation.

But now, are we to suppose that in these three verses our Lord was simply laying down a principle of Canon Law? That in these three verses he departed from the principle which he observed all through the rest of the chapter—the principle, I mean, that, for the Christian soul, fear of the law ought to be replaced by the love of God? Surely not. Surely his words have a message still for us practising Christians, who loyally observe the rules of the Church about marriage and divorce. There is something he would say to us, if we only read between the lines and apply the spirit of his teaching to our present subject, which is going to make this age-long business of marriage and marriage duties easier, not harder, to us, the children of his New Covenant.

[1] Matthew 19. 5, 8.

What, then, does our Lord say about marriage to our own day—our own day, with its habit of speaking about marriage as if it were a kind of slavery, with its cheap jokes about matrimonial unhappiness, with its despairing efforts to find out a way in which a man and a woman can live peaceably in the same house? Surely he tells us, as before, that the only way in which you can make an obligation rest lightly on you is to turn an act of obedience into a labour of love. There is only one way to solve the problem of marriage as a vocation to which Almighty God calls us and asks us to undertake out of love for him. We Catholics have a touching habit of making the profession of a nun into a sort of parody of a wedding service: the preacher is expected to address the novice as if she were a bride just waiting for the nuptial blessing. One of these days, I would like to reverse that process, and preach a wedding sermon in which I should address the bride and bridegroom as two souls who were about to take their solemn vows in some enclosed order of religious. A little enclosed order of two, with an object of its own and a spirit of its own—the oldest of all the religious orders, because it was founded by Adam and Eve.

Tell me, when you meet an enclosed nun, do you expect to find her grumbling all the time about the loss of liberty which she experiences? About the strictness of her rule, the unreasonableness of her superiors, the uncongenial ways of her sisters? Surely, if you did find such a religious, you would say she was a very bad religious indeed. And why? Because, although she was conforming externally to all the rules of her order, she had no love for her order, no sympathy for its spirit, no generosity in the discharge of her duties. And yet, is not that very much the position of the married woman who finds her husband an infliction, her wifely duties a nuisance, her marriage vows a contract of slavery: who makes little secret of the fact when she is talking to her intimate friends; and who yet prides herself on her loyalty to the Catholic profession in not seeking ground for a divorce? It is we ourselves who make a slavery of marriage; Christ calls us to it, not as to a slavery, but as to a loving service undertaken for him.

What are the dispositions that make for a happy marriage? Physical health and beauty in man and woman? No; health may fail, and beauty may be marred. Common interests and tastes? No; tastes and interests may change as the years go on. A violent passion of love, the feeling that neither could live without the other, that each has found a soul's mate? Even that, though it be a gracious and a fortunate thing, is not enough; love is blind, they say, and it is a dangerous thing when the blind leads the blind to the altar. No; the disposition that makes for a happy marriage is the conviction in man and woman that God has called them to do something for him: to build up a Christian home, and, if he sees fit, a Christian family, by a common act of self-oblation, not to the other party, but to himself. That a Christian community is being founded, with that primary intention of all Christian communities, the sanctification of its members.

For every marriage, God has his own purpose, just as he had for the betrothal of our Lady and St Joseph. It is, before all else, to the fulfilment of that purpose that the bride and bridegroom devote themselves. And if, as too often happens, one partner fails to understand this duty, and plays the divine vocation false, that does not release the other partner from a duty that is owed to God. The wife or husband who really loves Jesus Christ will find, in the circumstances of an unhappy marriage, only fresh opportunities for proving and for strengthening that love. God knows it is hard, sometimes; God knows there are tragedies of fidelity in unhappy marriages which can rival the most severe mortification of the most strict religious, and are valued, I think, no less in eternity. But it takes two to wreck a home.

Under the Old Testament, Almighty God allowed divorce. But the Old Testament was itself only a temporary covenant; he allowed himself at last, wearied with the long history of their infidelities, to divorce his own chosen people. But the New Covenant which Christ made with his Church is irrevocable; and under that Covenant, the vow of marriage is irrevocable too. "Husbands, love your wives as Christ also loved the Church."[1] Has he never found reason of complaint in his Church—lukewarmness, divisions, scandals in high places? Yet his Covenant stands firm; and the Christian who is called upon to remain faithful to the marriage bond in spite of difficulties, in spite of estrangement, is only called upon, after all, to mirror the eternal fidelity of Christ.

[1] Ephesians 5. 25.

D

6

OUR RETALIATION

You have heard that it hath been said, An eye for an eye, and a tooth for a tooth. But I say to you not to resist evil, but if one strike thee on thy right cheek, turn to him also the other, and if a man will contend with thee in judgment and take away thy coat, let go thy cloak also, and whosoever will force thee one mile, go with him other two.—Matthew 5. 38.

THIS is, I suppose, the best known passage in the Sermon on the Mount; and, from the way some people talk, especially in the newspapers, you would think it was the only thing in the Sermon on the Mount. And you cannot have failed to notice that they often entertain very extraordinary ideas about what it means. There are quite a lot of sincere people going about who talk about "putting the Sermon on the Mount into practice", and when you ask them how they meant to do that, they will tell you, "Why, next time the country tries to go to war, we will all go on strike to prevent it". Failing, apparently, to see that if this passage forbids going to war, it equally forbids going on strike. Personally, I do not think it does either; but if it forbids either, it forbids both. If you take it literally, it forbids altogether any attempt to prevent injustice. Now, none of us, I hope, wants to deny that nations in their dealings with one another, and classes of men in their dealings with one another, ought to apply the spirit of the Sermon on the Mount a great deal more than they do. But it is no good talking as if the Sermon on the Mount had only to be taken literally to avoid all further possibility of social disagreement. It is not meant to be a social programme; it is a message, primarily, to the individual Christian soul.

And, as we were saying in previous sermons, the difference between the old law and the new law is that the old law issues a series of commandments which have got to be obeyed, whereas the new law instils into Man's heart a spirit of active charity which ought to make commandments unnecessary for him. The old law said: An eye for an eye, and a tooth for a tooth. When it said that, it did not order you to take revenge on your enemies; that would be absurd. It laid down the principle that if you *did* take revenge on your enemies, you were to observe a strict law of retaliation; you were to exact so much vengeance *and no more*. How much, you ask? Why, the precise equivalent of the wrong done to you. If a man struck you on the right cheek, you were to strike him on the right cheek, not on both. If he took away your coat, you could take away his coat, not his cloak, which was more valuable. If a man forced you to go a mile with him as his guide, perhaps, or to carry his luggage, you might force him to go a mile with you, but not two. You were not to charge interest, that was the point, when you inflicted retaliation.

Observe, then, that our Lord turns that principle exactly inside out. Instead of hitting back his assailant on both cheeks, the Christian will want to be hit on both cheeks himself. Instead of wanting to get a cloak in exchange for a coat, he will want to lose coat and cloak as well. Instead of wanting to drag the other man two miles in his own direction as compensation for having been dragged one, he will go three miles in the other man's direction altogether. The natural man wants to charge interest, the Christian's immediate thought is to throw in a bonus. That is our Lord's teaching about retaliation.

And what does it all mean? Why, it means this—that the Christian who has really drunk in the teaching of the Sermon on the Mount is thinking always, not how he can get something or how he can keep something which is his own, but how he can give something away. I think my favourite story among all the stories of the saints is one about the Polish saint, St John Cantius.[1] He was a seminary professor, and rather absent-minded, as seminary professors are apt to be. In his holidays, he was fond of going on pilgrimage to Rome or Jerusalem; and, for fear he should not get back in time for term, they always used to sew up some gold pieces in the lining of his cloak, in case he should run short of money. On one of these journeys he was set upon by robbers, who took away all the money they could find on him, and asked him if he had anything else. No, nothing else. So the robbers left him and had passed out of sight when St John suddenly remembered those gold pieces sewed in the lining of his coat. Here were these poor men obviously in need of money, and he had told them a lie! So the next thing the astonished robbers saw was the figure of the saint pounding down the road after them at full speed, shouting out: "Stop, stop, I find I've got some more after all". I am glad to say that they did not take it; indeed, they gave back what they had taken already. But that is what I call living by the spirit of the Sermon on the Mount.

Our Lord gives us three instances of how the real Christian will behave when he suffers injustice. When he is smitten on the cheek,

[1] Professor of Theology at the University of Cracow. He died there on 24 December 1473. His feast is kept on 20 October.

when his clothes are taken from him, when oppressors (no doubt he is thinking of Roman soldiers) force him to accompany them on a journey. Did it ever occur to you that our Lord himself gave us a model of patience with which we ought to behave in all three situations? He was smitten on the cheek in the high priest's judgment hall; and all he said was: "If I have spoken evil, bear witness concerning the evil; but if well, why dost thou smite me?"[1] He was forced by the soldiers to tread the long road to Calvary, bearing the heavy weight of his own cross; he was despoiled of his garments, the soldiers tearing some of them into portions, and casting lots for his coat, perhaps our Lady's own handiwork; and all he said was: "Father, forgive them, for they know not what they do". He suffered because he willed it; and the real Christian suffers because he wills it because suffering identifies his will with the will of the Master who suffered for him.

It is a mistake, then, to quibble over the language our Lord uses here, as if the literal sense of it were important. He says, for example, "Give to him who asks, and do not turn away from him who would borrow from you".[2] Well, as you know, the most deserving object of charity is often the person who does not ask for it; and the habitual borrower is often the person who, for his own sake, ought not to be entrusted with money. But that is not the point; the point is that the real Christian has a quite new attitude towards his own belongings. Our belongings are of various kinds. There is our dignity; most of us are fond of that; we do not like being hit in the face. There are material possessions, some of which we do not mind parting with, but we do like to have something we can call our own—the clothes we wear, for example. And there is our time, our leisure, our ease; we like to have that at our disposal, as far as necessary occupations allow it. Now, the true love of Christ kills in us the love of all these things. We cannot all of us join religious orders, in which we should have to make public and formal renunciation of our dignity, our possessions, our spare time. But the love of Christ, if it really takes hold of a man's heart, brings with it a spirit of detachment which makes him as indifferent to the loss of these things as if he had entered religion and signed them all away.

I am afraid that does not sound very much like us, does it? But that is the model after which we are striving, in our very inferior way. Shall we remember that, sometimes, when nature, still strong in our immortified hearts, makes us quick to resent an injustice? When an insult from a stranger humiliates us in public, shall we think of our

[1] John 18. 23.   [2] Matthew 5. 42.

Lord's cheek, red under the mark of his persecutor's hand? When we suffer a temporal loss through man's injustice, shall we think of our Lord praying for the soldiers as they threw dice for his cloak? When exacting superiors, or tiresome friends, make unreasonable demands on our time and energy, shall we think of our Lord on the road to Calvary, burdened with the instrument of his own death? I think we shall become rather more like Christians if we do.

7

"IN CRUCE SALUS!"

You therefore shall be perfect, as also your heavenly Father is perfect.—
Matthew 5. 48.

THAT text is the concluding verse of St Matthew's fifth chapter; it concludes, therefore, the long section of the Sermon on the Mount about the difference between the old law and the new, which I have been trying to explain. It sums up the doctrine of the whole chapter, and sums it up, at first sight, in a rather startling way. The old law said: Thou shalt be perfect before the Lord thy God. The new law says: You shall be perfect as also your heavenly Father is perfect. What, then, are we to set about in imitating the perfections of Almighty God? He is eternal; are we to imitate him in that? He is present everywhere; are we to imitate him in that? He is incomprehensible, immutable, impassible; are we to imitate him in that? You cannot draw up any list of the divine perfections which will not make you despair, from the outset, of being able to imitate them, at whatever distance, at least in this life. Nay, for the most part, so borrowed and derivative is all our knowledge of God, we only arrive at the concept of such perfections *per viam remotionis*: we say, for example, that God is wise, and then hastily add: But he is not wise in the same way in which human beings are said to be wise. Even of God's goodness we have to say that God is good, but his goodness is not like your goodness and mine. And here is our Lord saying that your goodness and mine must be like the goodness of Almighty God. Surely that is hard?

I think it will help us to understand what our Lord means, if we remember the passage which comes immediately before this text, the passage I was speaking about.[1] Our Lord tells us to love our enemies, that is, to love *all* men, including even our enemies. Why? In order that we may be the children of our Father in heaven, who makes his sun rise upon the good and bad, and sends rain upon the just and the unjust. We, if we are his children indeed, will naturally recall the image of his splendid generosity; of that utter impartiality with which he showers his blessings on good and bad alike. And not temporal blessings only; he sends his grace, too, in sufficient measure to save them if they would, even to those souls who will be lost, and whose perdition he already foresees. Why is that? Why does he do that? Because goodness is naturally diffusive of itself; it is like the light, which spreads itself everywhere in equal measure, except in so far as obstacles are interposed to withstand its influence. Put a shade over a lantern, and you do not extinguish its light; you only imprison it. The light is there all the time, beating as it were against the bars of its prison, and struggling to be free; ready to stream out without shock or effort the moment the obstacle is removed. So the mercy of God and the grace of God beat against the ingratitude of human hearts.

It is in this, then, that the true disciple of the Sermon on the Mount will imitate his heavenly Father—in the universality of his outlook. He will have lost, as far as it is possible for man to lose it, that spirit of self-seeking which is at the bottom of all our imperfections. The spirit, I mean, that makes us resent a wrong action not because it is wrong, but because it is wrong to *us*. The spirit that cannot admire human beauty without translating its admiration into desire. The spirit that prevents us making a plain statement of fact without importing into the picture the colours which our own prejudice dictates. The spirit that limits our benevolence completely, or almost completely, to our friends, our own kindred, our own party, instead of squandering it nobly upon mankind. In each of the instances we have been considering you will see that it is the spirit of private interest which makes you and me so unlike what the Sermon on the Mount wants us to be.

But, granted that this is the quality we would like to achieve, you may still say: How am I to imitate Almighty God in this? How can I make him my model, whose dealings with his creation are so mysterious? What practical help can I gain from contemplating the ineffable goodness of the Omnipotent, and moulding my own conduct —I, who am a man, subject to such frailty, so limited in my powers of judgment and my scope of action—in accordance with that transcendent example? I know so little of God, find it (naturally) so impossible

---

[1] See *supra*, p. 49, "Forgiving—and Loving".

to put myself in his position, that I can derive no profit from the comparison. If only we could see God as he is, of course it would be different; but can it mean anything to us, who see him only in a glass after a dark manner, here on our pilgrimage?

Yes, it is a genuine difficulty, but it is one that has been raised before. It occurred to somebody on Maundy Thursday, nearly 1,900 years ago. Philip then said to Jesus: "Lord, show us the Father, and it is enough for us". Jesus saith to him: "Have I been so long a time with you, and have you not known me? Philip, he that seeth me seeth the Father. How sayest thou, show us the Father?"[1] That is the answer to our difficulty: when we are told to imitate the goodness of the Eternal Father, we do not need to set before ourselves the idea of an unlimited Being, who created worlds, we know not why, gave man free will, we know not why, allowed man, we know not why, to increase and multiply on the earth, even when he had disobeyed the Divine Law and forfeited his eternal inheritance: we do not need to set such an idea before ourselves, and somehow puzzle out from that a principle for the regulation of our own lives. No, we have seen the goodness of the Father, which is the goodness, also, of the Eternal Word, translated for us, through the Incarnation, into the goodness of a human character, and mediated for us by the activities of a human will. He has seen the Father, who has read and meditated the life, Passion and death of our Lord Jesus Christ.

The Incarnation, you see, means all that; means that the Image of Eternal Godhead has been thrown onto the screen of time; that the mystery of his ineffable mercy has been translated for us into a language we can understand, the language of a perfect human life. And what is that shadow which God's goodness has thrown across the world? Listen to King David's description of it, and you will find out easily enough. "According to the height of the heaven above the earth, he had strengthened his mercy towards them that fear him. As far as the east is from the west, so far hath he removed our iniquities from us."[2] Two vast lines, one of them reaching from earth to heaven, the other from east to west. And where they meet, they throw a shadow onto the world; it is the shadow of a cross.

Yes, the cross stands there, an eternal contradiction; for it is God's goodness meeting with man's sin. You have seen, perhaps, the effect of drawing a violin bow across a resonant plate with a little sand in it? When the chord has died away, you will find it has left the sand in a symmetrical pattern at the bottom of the plate. Something

[1] John 14. 8-9.   [2] Psalm 102. 11-12.

in the same way we may conceive to ourselves the eternal meaning of the Crucifixion. For once, in the life of our Lord, a perfect chord of the heavenly music thrilled through our dusty world; and when it had ceased, it left a pattern behind it, the pattern of a cross.

And that pattern is the pattern of your life and mine. For in the life of a real Christian, divine grace crosses and contradicts the motions of our corrupt human nature, makes us love what nature shrinks from, hate what nature covets, destroys in us the self-seeking, the private interest, which else would dictate every action of our lives. You have heard people, perhaps, in defending some act of selfishness, say: "Well, after all, you've got to look after Number One". Number One, that means self. And the cross represents something quite simple; it represents the figure of one stretched out. The picture of the world which the Sermon on the Mount gives is not anything fantastic, believe me, or far-fetched. It is only a picture of the actual world, with self scratched out. This thought should be useful for the season of Lent, upon which we shall enter in a few weeks.

May the Passion of our Lord Jesus Christ, and the prayers of our Lady and the other saints that have stood beside his cross, win us the grace to follow their examples in this world of striving; that our justice may abound more than that of the Scribes and Pharisees, our anger and lust and covetousness be stilled, that we may also be the children of our Father, who is in heaven.

IV

THE MYSTERY OF THE KINGDOM*

* This series of twelve sermons was preached at the Church of Our Lady of Mount Carmel and St Simon Stock, Kensington, and was first published in *The Mystery of the Kingdom* (1928).

I

PARABLE

His disciples came and said to him, Why speakest thou to them in parables? Who answered and said to them, Because to you it is given to know the mysteries of the kingdom of heaven, but to them it is not given. Therefore do I speak to them in parables: because seeing they see not, and hearing they hear not, neither do they understand.—Matthew 13. 11.

IT is a curious thing that Catholic commentators on Holy Scripture are often regarded as superstitious and even insincere because they attach to the Bible a mystical meaning, beyond and behind the literal meaning which the words carry. And yet from this text it is perfectly certain that the most important of all the texts in Scripture, our Blessed Lord's own words to the multitude of the Jews, were deliberately spoken by him with an ulterior meaning underlying them. It would be quite natural to suppose that the Incarnate Revelation of Truth would announce a single message to all alike in plain, unmistakable language. It would be quite natural to suppose so, only as a matter of fact he did not, and has told us that he did not. After uttering the parable—surely a very simple one—of the sower sowing his seed, he goes out of his way to explain that he does not want all his audience to penetrate the full meaning of what he is talking about. That, surely, is something for us to think over.

What is all this talk of mysteries? What place has mystery in the self-revelation of God to man? If you have at all caught the spirit of the early Fathers and of the New Testament, you will know that it has a very considerable place. And there is one occurrence of the word in particular which deserves attention, in the third chapter of St Paul's Epistle to the Ephesians. "According to grace", he says, "the mystery has been made known to me, which in other generations was not known to the sons of men, as it is now revealed to his holy apostles and prophets in the Spirit, that the Gentiles should be fellow heirs and partakers of the same body, and co-partners of his promise in Christ Jesus."[1] There, you see, St Paul lets the mystery out—or, if not the whole mystery, at least the great central fact of it. The mystery of the

[1] Ephesians 3. 5-6.

kingdom of God, the secret which our Lord Jesus Christ whispered in the ears of his apostles, while he taught the crowds on the mountain-top or by the lake-side, was just this—that the Gentiles were to be admitted into the Church of God.

When St John the Baptist cried "The kingdom of heaven is at hand", he was delivering a message which was at once understood by those who heard it—or, rather, they thought they understood. "The kingdom of heaven? Really? At last, then, the Romans are going to be driven out of the holy places. At last a great national leader is to arise, who will crush the Gentiles under the feet of the chosen people, and for the space of a thousand years Jerusalem will be the centre of the world, and there will be no wars or famines or pestilences, but we shall all dwell together contentedly, with the Gentiles under our feet—at last, the kingdom of God!" That was the sort of picture which St John's words must have conjured up to their minds. They had read all about it in the book of Daniel; read about it, in more detail, in numerous works which owed their inspiration to Daniel, but which were never accepted by the Church as Scripture, and survive only as literary curiosities today. They were expecting a kingdom, but it was the wrong kind of kingdom. And because they had a wrong idea of what to expect, our Lord proceeds to educate them very carefully and tact-fully, by hints at first and by prophetic allegories, out of that wrong idea into the true idea of the Church he meant to institute. He knew that the chosen souls who were to accept his message would, under the direction of his apostles, learn to interpret the mystery aright; he knew that those whose pride was to prevent their accepting his message would see with blind eyes, hear with deaf ears, as the patient work of education went on. You must think of the Pharisees, as they listened to these simple lessons about the good Samaritan, or the prodigal son, or Dives and Lazarus, hanging on his words with an uneasy feeling that there was something behind it all, that underneath the plain moral lessons they heard there was a deeper meaning, a meaning which, if they could but catch it, was to their ears blasphemy, revolution, scandal only to be expiated by a cross. And when the plainest of all the parables was delivered, that of the wicked husbandmen, St Matthew tells us that they perceived he was speaking of them, and were only restrained from laying hands on him because they feared the multitude. At last the blinded eye saw, and the deaf ears heard, and the discovery of the great secret was the prelude to Gethsemani and to Calvary.

It is important to keep in mind this hidden meaning of the parables, for two reasons. The first reason is a mere question of apologetics.

If you come across people who have been priming themselves with Protestant theology of the more heretical type, or read in the newspapers the reviews of the critical works on the New Testament which are produced nowadays, it will not be long before you find somebody making the statement, as a simple matter of fact, a point on which modern critics are agreed, that our Lord when he was on earth had no intention of founding a Church. He expected—so they tell us to believe—that either during his lifetime or immediately after his death the world would come to an end. How could he, then, wish to found a Church? That is quite sound logic; if the premisses are true, then the conclusion follows. But on the other hand, if the conclusion proves to be false, the premisses fall to the ground with it. If our Lord *did* mean to found a Church, then it is nonsense to imagine that he expected, or allowed his disciples to expect, that the world was coming to an end as soon as he died. And as a matter of fact there is plenty of evidence in the Gospels which shows that he did mean to found a Church; but there is no evidence more cogent, and no evidence more neglected both by the opponents and by the defenders of orthodox Christianity, than the evidence which is afforded by the parables, if you take the trouble to interpret them. The Sadducee of today, like the Pharisee of our Lord's time, goes wrong because he skims lightly over the parables, and accepts their moral lessons without penetrating the theological mysteries which underlie them.

And there is a second reason. We shall not understand the theological import of our Lord's parables unless we remember that he was speaking to Jews, and Jews who were expecting to see a victorious Messias and a world-wide kingdom. We have to read them against a background of Jewish thought, which shows up their meaning just as a dark background will show up a picture that is but faintly coloured. All the time our Lord is correcting the Jewish habit of thought. The kingdom of God, says the Jew, will come suddenly and sensationally, with the visible triumph of God's people: no, says the parable of the mustard seed, it will grow from small beginnings, spread gradually through the nations: no, says the parable of the leaven, it will work silently and secretly, before the world is aware that it is at work. In the kingdom there will be nothing evil or unclean: no, say the parables, there will be tares among the wheat, useless dog-fish caught in the net. Solomon's Temple and Levi's priesthood will be the centre of a regenerated world: no, says the parable of the good Samaritan, the priest and the Levite have lost their chance, they passed by on the other side. But at least the kingdom will be for the Jews? No, say the parables, the invited guests have excused themselves, and the table has to be filled with strangers brought in from the highways and hedges; the wicked husbandmen have defrauded their employer and killed his servants, and the vineyard will be given to others. But even if the Gentiles are admitted, surely it will be the chosen people, fortified by so many promises, tested by so many tribulations, that will be the chief inheritors? No, say the parables, those who come to work at the eleventh hour will receive the same reward as those who bore the burden of the day and the heat; indeed, there will be more rejoicing in heaven over the prodigal son who has found his way back to God than over the elder brother who never departed from his service. But, anyhow, when once the kingdom is established, the Jews will flock into it? No, says the parable of Dives and Lazarus; they have Moses and the Prophets to guide them; they will be given no second chance of repentance. We shall find, I think, that the meaning of the parables becomes far clearer if we keep that background of polemic in view.

Seeing they see not, and hearing they hear not, neither do they understand—what a terrible irony there is in the situation of those Pharisees! The Messias has come, the kingdom is at hand; prophets and kings desired it long and died before the sight; these men have attained the privilege denied to their forefathers, to be the contemporaries on earth of the Son of God. He announces in a series of allegories the programme of his kingdom; and that is just what they want to hear him do. Want to hear it in order that they may trip him up in his talk and have material for accusing him and condemning him to death. They rub their eyes and cannot see; strain their ears and still cannot hear. "Now, what of that last parable? Surely we might make something out of that. . . . No, no, you can't go to the people with evidence of that sort. We must have proof, not vague insinuations and suspicions of double meaning." And all the time, under their very eyes, the death-warrant of the Old Covenant is being signed, in words which those faithful auditors, the apostles and disciples, will never forget. The Pharisees listen to the hated Prophet, and he says exactly what they want him to say, and yet God's providence shuts those vigilant eyes, stops those attentive ears, and, to them, the message is lost. What irony! Surely, even if it were a mere human story, our pulses would thrill to read it!

But it is far more thrilling than that, if we come to think of it; it concerns ourselves. Not that the Church which Christ founded is in the same danger as the Jewish Church, the danger of being found wanting, rejected, and superseded. Not that the Church of Christ can misinterpret the message entrusted to her, as the Pharisees misinterpreted the meaning of the old dispensation. We have our Lord's own word for it that the gates of hell cannot prevail against his Church, and that his Holy Spirit will guide us into all truth. But it is possible for Christians, as individuals, to fall into the same terrible fault as the Jewish nation; we too may watch and fail to see, we too may listen and yet neither hear nor understand. "Take heed how you hear",[1] our Lord warns us. It seems that hearing is not such a simple business as we had supposed; it depends on whether from the outset you are listening in the right spirit. Most of us know how easy it is to listen to a speech or look at a picture or read a book with a prejudice already formed in our minds against the author of it; how we deliberately miss his best points, pick out his weaknesses, impute fault where an unbiased mind would have found none. The spirit in which you approach your subject does make a difference; we are human beings, not thinking machines. And that is why, in matters affecting divine truth and our eternal salvation, we have a terrible duty of being honest with ourselves.

"But surely", you say, "you do not mean to condemn the Protestants? After all, they are in good faith." It is a curiously defective verb, "to be in good faith". It has a second and a third person, but no first person. You can say, "Thou art in good faith", "he is in good faith", "you are in good faith", "they are in good faith", but you can never say "I am in good faith", or "we are in good faith". For being in good faith implies that you are wrong, and if you admit that you are wrong and still do not change your opinion you are no longer in good faith.

Here is the Catholic Church brought to your door, a big affair, an impressive affair, whichever way you look at it. You can hardly doubt its continuity with the Church Christ founded. Say it has developed if you like, say it has become deformed if you like, but it alone among the tangled religious systems of our country—so tangled that it is often hard to know where this or that thread started—it alone raises the claim to continuity undisputed. The Christian religion has been proposed to you, a religion believed by significant numbers of seriously minded people; the issue between acceptance and rejection has become, for you, a matter of moral responsibility.

And you? "Oh, I have been to Catholic churches and I cannot say that I was much impressed." Yes, but what did you go for? Just to hear the music? Just to see a kind of pageant? Just to find out how these things were done? Seeing, you saw not; your eyes were focused on your own worldly schemes, your own transitory enjoyments; the

[1] Matthew 15. 10.

parable went over your head. "Oh, but I have read Catholic books, and the arguments always left me very much where I was." Yes, but in what spirit did you read them? Just to improve your mind? Just in idle curiosity? Just to see what flaws you could find in them, and scribble notes in the margin? Just to select the passages you already agreed with, and skip over the parts that were meant for you? Hearing, you heard not, neither did you understand; it was like a novel that we take up in a dentist's waiting-room; the sentences form themselves as ideas in the brain, but never group themselves into thought or impress themselves on the memory. "Well, if I am wrong", you say, "at least I am in good faith." God grant you may be. And yet our Lord had no such faithful attendants as his critics; no such careful listeners as the Pharisees who put him to death.

But, once we are inside the Church, does the duty of keeping our eyes and ears open no longer exist for us? The strict duty, yes; for in the Church we have an infallible interpreter of God's revelation, and we are secure within the confines of its teaching. But if, as Christians, we have any spirit of generosity which prompts us to make full use of our privileges, we shall still want to sit at the feet of our divine Master, and the spirit in which we hear or read his words will have a great deal to say in the matter of our soul's advancement. You have a friend, I dare say, whose house is full of beautiful things, whose library is stocked with the rarest and choicest editions, and yet he himself, perhaps because he has inherited, not collected them, seems to move quite unimpressed in the world of beauties you envy; the books are coated with dust, the pictures badly hung, and all the best things seem to be kept in some vast reception-room, swathed in dust-cloths and chilly from long disuse of the hearth. He is surprised, perhaps even impatient at your enthusiasm, and hurries you on to see the next of the two dozen things he really does value, and those, apparently, not for their intrinsic worth, but because some story hangs by them: this is an interesting heirloom, that came into his possession in a rather curious way, that watch went with him all through such and such a campaign—he seems to have eyes for nothing else. I sometimes feel that we Catholics are just a little like that in our use of the Bible. We have a score or so of good fighting texts at our fingers' ends, "Thou art Peter", "Whoso eateth my flesh", "What God hath joined", and so on. We learnt them from the Catechism, and it's useful to know them because we may want to use them at any time; they are regular landmarks in the history of controversy. And for the rest, the whole treasure-house of the Gospels is there at our elbow, and somehow we never seem to have more than a nodding acquaintance with it; it doesn't seem to have sunk in. Seeing, we see but dimly; hearing, we hear abstractedly, and only half understand.

2

THE INCARNATION

Which of these three, in thy opinion, was neighbour to him that fell among the robbers? But he said, He that showed mercy to him. And Jesus said to him, Go, and do thou in like manner.—Luke 10. 35.

THE parable of the good Samaritan has a moral significance so fruitful and so obvious—even if our Lord had not himself underlined it—that in apprehending it we might easily be supposed to have exhausted the whole lesson which the story is intended to convey. Yet it is the continuous tradition of Christian exegesis from very early times that the story has a further theological significance, and that the good Samaritan is also a type of our Lord himself. Nor should we be surprised at this twofold function of the utterance. It is part of our Lord's method that he enforces by example what he teaches by precept; he who blesses the poor, the meek, the mourner, the souls that hunger and thirst after justice, himself became poor, humbled himself, became a man of sorrows and acquainted with grief, thirsted upon the cross for our sakes. The practical moral of the story becomes more, not less important to us when we realize that the examples we are encouraged to follow is the example of our Redeemer.

According to the teaching of the Holy Fathers, the man who fell among robbers is human nature as it is left to us after the Fall, robbed of its supernatural gifts and wounded even in its natural faculties. For man in the state of innocence had endowments of two different kinds, those which were, so to speak, owed to his nature, as the proper complement of his being, and those which, being supernatural, were not owed to him, but granted him merely by the mercy of God. The robbers strip their victim of his clothes—that is to say, this second and supernatural class of endowments, which are no true part of our nature, is altogether removed from us by the Fall; but the process does not stop there, the man's own body is crippled by wounds—that is to say, even the natural endowments of humanity, though not done away by the Fall, are pitiably maimed and stunted by its effects. So maimed, so stunted, that we are no longer able by our own powers to retrieve the mischief; the wounds that are growing cold and stiff by the road-side also prevent the poor traveller from crawling away to find a physician; unless help comes from outside, there is no redress for the wrong and no hope of recovery.

And the priest and the Levite pass by. Why the priest and the Levite? If we supposed that this parable were merely a moral lesson, the choice of terms would be inexplicable. For it is always the Pharisees and lawyers that our Lord singles out as typical of that pride and blindness which preaches what it dares not practise; the priest and the Levite would be Sadducees, no friends to the Pharisee but his hated rivals. And it is actually a lawyer to whom this parable was first spoken; would our Lord have missed the opportunity of bringing the lesson home to him, as he might have done, by making a Pharisee and a lawyer pass by the wounded man and leave him unattended? Here it is that we have to remember the secret polemical purpose of the parable, to see it thrown into relief against the Jewish background of which I have spoken. The Jew looked forward to a kingdom of heaven in which Solomon's Temple would be the centre of a world-wide devotion, in which the ministry of the sons of Levi would be every-where recognized as the appointed meeting-ground between God and man. That impression, by a mere casual piece of colouring in the course of a moral apologue, our Lord is at pains to correct. The priest and the Levite are inadequate to the task which is demanded of them, the reconciliation of sinful humanity to an offended God. For centuries the sacrifices of the Old Covenant have continued, burnt-offerings and peace-offerings and sacrifices for sin—in vain. The blood of bulls and calves and rams has been shed at the brazen altar, and the doorposts and the vessels of the sanctuary have been sprinkled with it—in vain. And the censers clash and steam and the bells jangle and the jewels shine upon the sacred vestments as the high priest goes up into the holy of holies—in vain. Human nature still lies where it lay, hurt to the death and powerless to achieve its own recovery; no priest, no Levite can help here.

Who comes to aid the wounded man? Who but a Samaritan, a stranger and his enemy? For centuries the Jews have hated and despised the Samaritans, shut them out from their sacrifices and denied their claim to be children of Abraham. If anything, one would say that the Samaritans had a right to take vengeance, seeing his enemy thus delivered into his hands; at least there is no tie of blood, of friendship, or of gratitude that can impose on him the duty of bringing relief. And yet it is the Samaritan who comes to the wounded man's side. Who stoops to raise and restore human nature undone by Adam's fault? Who, but the very God whom that fault has offended, the God whom we have defied and set at nought, and tried, if it were only possible, to shut him altogether out of our lives and out of our thoughts? There was no claim man could make on God's mercy; through his own fault he had become God's enemy. "In this the love of God is made manifest, not that we love him, but that he first loved us . . . while we were yet sinners, Christ died for us."[1] The Samaritan expects no word of gratitude from the sufferer; nay, if he had but the strength, it is likely enough that the Jew would refuse the help that comes from such a quarter: so God, when he came to our rescue, did it with no view to any worthy return we could make for such benefits; helped us in spite of ourselves, overcame the peevish reluctance that bade him hold off and leave us in peace. Is not this a God worthy of love?

A certain Samaritan being on his journey. God did not send an angel or a man to succour us; he himself became for our sakes a *viator*, a traveller in this world of pilgrimage. The Jews looked forward to the coming of the Messias, they did not understand that the Messias was to be God made man. Yes, God is a stranger in the world his own hands made; he came to his world, and found only a stable for shelter, only cruel faces and hard looks, only jeers and misunderstanding. He dwelt in the world, as he would have us dwell in it; not as home, but as the way towards home, a foreign country where a man asks nothing better than to do his errand and be gone. What would have become of the poor Jew, if the Samaritan had chanced to stay at home? What would have become of our souls, if the Son of God had not set out upon his travels?

And going up to him, he bound up his wounds, pouring in oil and wine. Some wounds need the soothing oil, to allay the irritation, some need the bitter acid that stings, and heals while it stings, staunching the flow of blood; the wise Samaritan knows how to use both. So, too, the heavenly Physician is not content with the healing influence of the unction he bestowed upon our weak nature when he took it to himself; there is need, too, for the chalice of suffering, for the wine of his most precious blood. In the Incarnation we are made partakers of the divine nature, and it might have been supposed that as the result of it pain and

[1] I John 4. 10; Romans 5. 8-9.

sorrow would vanish from the world, and the primitive happiness of Paradise be restored to us: certainly the Jews must have imagined that in the kingdom of heaven all such disabilities of our fallen humanity would be done away. But the physician of souls knows better; knows that while sin persists, even though it be sin forgiven, there is salutary penance to be done, preaches pain to us, recommends it to us and hallows it, as he sheds his life-giving blood upon the cross.

The Samaritan sets his patient on his own beast to bring him to the inn; see once more how helpless the wounded man is, how he has to have everything done for him. Grace comes to us, not we to grace. And the inn where he is to make his recovery can be nothing else than the Church which Christ our Lord left behind him. The Church triumphant is the home to which we look forward; the Church militant is the inn, the temporary resting-place in which we find shelter from the storms of this travel-stained and transitory world. Three things above all we shall look for in the inn—refreshment, good company, and repose. What refreshment this inn of the Church gives us, as we feed upon the body and blood of Christ! What company, as we are knitted together in its holy fellowship with all God's chosen people in this world and beyond—our boon companions at the divine altar! What rest for sin-worn consciences, when scruples and doubts and fears are lulled by the murmur of absolution, and we can draw free, deep breath once more! We are all convalescents, recovering by degrees from the terrible blow sin dealt to us, building ourselves up and making the most of our time till the good Physician gives us our discharge and we are fit to travel safely home.

And the innkeeper—an inn would be a poor place without an inn-keeper. The innkeeper stands for St Peter and his successors. To them, as having the care of this inn, this convalescent home, his Church, he leaves the stipend that is to see us through our time there—bequeaths to us the inexhaustible treasure of his merits.

"*And whatsoever thou shalt spend over and above, I, at my return, will repay thee.*" It is not only his merits that aid us; the prayers and good deeds of all the saints are entrusted to the Church's keeping, with promise of repayment hereafter, and these, too, distributed to us by the prudent stewardship of Christ's Vicar, will help to heal the scars of our roadside encounter. We who once lay helpless, God's enemies, awake from the swoon of unbelief or misbelief to find ourselves his guests, provided for at his own expense, from the table his own hands have made ready!

A single parable, and such a simple one! And yet it did not take much digging beneath the surface to find the whole scheme of grace laid bare. Or, rather, there is one point over which the parable is not quite explicit: our Lord does not tell us here, formally at least, of the price our ransom was to cost—his own Passion and the shedding of his blood. He was still keeping the scandal of the cross in the background, lest even the most faithful of his hearers should be still unprepared for such an exercise of faith. It is only in the parable of the wicked husbandmen that this last point is cleared up.

And, meanwhile, we are left with that uncomfortable corollary: "Go, and do thou in like manner." The good Physician, it seems, has left behind him a school of medicine, in which those who would serve him must graduate. Sorrow and want and infirmity and sin are still with us, citizens of the heavenly kingdom though we be, and the law of charity binds us to relieve each other's necessities according to our power. The mercy of God shown to us in the Incarnation is to be the model for all our acts of human mercy.

What sort of answer was the lawyer expecting when he asked, "Who is my neighbour?" "The word *neighbour* for the purposes of this Act shall be understood to include all persons having a domicile or quasi-domicile within a radius of three hundred yards, or being within the third degree of consanguinity or the second degree of affinity, or otherwise entitled to consideration under subsection B of Schedule 2 of this Act." That was the sort of answer the lawyer wanted. What was the answer he got? Why, this: "Can you imagine a Jew left helpless by the roadside and then relieved with every attention, cared for with every solicitude, by a stranger, hated and despised, yes, a Samaritan? That will only give you a faint idea of man's helplessness before the Incarnation, of God's condescension and forgiveness in taking human nature upon him and reconciling the world to himself. Is it for you, the beneficiary for all time of that unique act of charity, to haggle over obligations and weigh out mercy with a balance? The world is your neighbour. Your enemy is your neighbour. The people who annoy you, bore you, rub you up the wrong way, are your neighbours. Whoever needs your help, however unworthy, however ungrateful, however unwilling, that man is your neighbour."

Now it's perfectly true, and sound theology, that there is an order of charity, and that there are claims on all of us which, merely by the law of nature, must come next after God's claim, to the exclusion of others. It would, for example, be wrong for a man to give so much in charity as to leave his family unprovided for; wrong for a woman to become so immersed, even in the most pious work, as to neglect her children. But do let us remember that charity—the charity with which Christ loved us—does not end at home.

The good Physician's task is not always to soothe; he pours in oil and wine. The avoidance of suffering is not man's chief business, nor is it the chief business of religion. Remember, Jesus Christ took our nature upon him, and then crucified it. Lest we should suppose that the kingdom of heaven on earth was to be a millennium from which all hurtful things are banished—so, perhaps, some of his hearers imagined—he ratifies his New Covenant from the very outset with the chalice of his precious blood spilt for man. And the measure of his sufferings, let us make no mistake about it, is to be filled up with human pain. There is a pain that kills and a pain that heals, and suffering comes to our lives for us to make use of it in which way we will. If we have learned in all our adversities, in sickness, in sorrow, in bereavement, in anxiety, in desolation, yes, even in doubts and scruples, to unite ourselves with his Passion, ours is the pain that heals: the more to suffer, the more to offer, that is the first principle of the Christian medicine.

And this has to be remembered not only in the ordering of our own lives, but (what is, to some good souls, far more difficult) in our dealings with others. The same charity which bids us at times bind up the broken heart, allay scruples, smooth over difficulties, compose quarrels, bids us at other times arouse the sinner to a sense of sin, check the thoughtless, disturb the false peace that sacrifices principle or condones wickedness. We must carry with us the wine that stings as well as the oil that soothes. Never, to spare your own feelings or to enhance your own reputation for kindness, shirk the celestial surgery when the wound cries for the knife.

He brought him to an inn, and took care of him. It was not enough for Christ to redeem us and then leave us to ourselves, not enough to turn the sinner back to himself, he pursues us and importunes us with his grace. Don't let us leave our good actions half finished. You have been of assistance in bringing a convert into the Church, for instance; do not drop him at the door and turn round as if to say, "Next, please". This is a tired soul, just beginning to find itself in a strange world; it may be, not without difficulty. It would be a poor doctor who should never call again when his patient had passed the crisis; it is a poor friend who loses interest before he ceases to be of use.

3

THE CHURCH AND THE WORLD

The kingdom of heaven is like unto treasure hidden in a field; which a man having found, hid it, and for joy thereof goeth and selleth all that he hath, and buyeth that field.—Matthew 13. 44.

THIS parable and the parable immediately following it—the pearl of great price—coming next to one another in this important chapter of St Matthew, are obviously to be taken in close connection. In either the emphasis is the same: the kingdom of heaven has a value which can be measured by the quantity of the sacrifice which is undergone in the securing of it; the pearl in itself is worth all the rest of the merchant's property; the field with the treasure in it is worth more than broad acres around it. And the ordinary explanation of these parables is one with which we are all familiar; namely, that when he speaks of the kingdom of heaven here our Lord means the inheritance of that kingdom to which the faithful soul attains. And he warns us that it is an inheritance which may cost much sacrifice in the winning, but that the sacrifice is more than worth while; what we give up in order to find that treasure, to possess that jewel, is nothing in comparison with it. That is the interpretation given, so far as I know, by all the Fathers and all the commentators, and God forbid that we should depart from it.

But it is perfectly possible that a single parable should have two meanings, and more especially when one of those meanings is of its own nature a mystery, a secret that explains itself only to the few, while it is lost upon a larger audience. Let us look at these parables again. Bend down, as it were, and see them in a different light; find in these passages, too, an underlying theological lesson. Suppose we take the kingdom of heaven to mean, quite literally, the Church, as it does in the other parables of this chapter; suppose the merchant, suppose the finder of the treasure were not man but God? That when he came to earth God saw the Christian Church as a prize to be worked for and won? "And the twelve gates were twelve pearls"[1]—twelve, like the tribes God chose for himself under the old dispensation, like the apostles whom our Lord chose for himself in the new. "He sold all that he had"—yes, "for you know the grace of our Lord Jesus Christ, that being rich he became poor for your sakes, that through his poverty

[1] Apocalypse 21. 21.

you might become rich".[1] "Christ loved the Church and delivered himself up for it, that he might present it to himself, a glorious Church, not having spot or wrinkle or any such thing"[2]—the jewel, polished and perfect; the buried gold shining once again in the sunlight, with the rust and mould that soiled it all purged away. If I am right, if there is anything in this way of looking at the two parables, then what our Lord wanted his disciples to understand here was that he came, not simply to reaffirm the Old Covenant with Israel, but to choose out from among mankind a Church of his own, bought with a price; a Church worthy of such an origin, worthy of the sufferings of the Son of God.

But that is not all; there's a terrible lesson still to come. The man who buys the field buys the field for the sake of the treasure; redeems all mankind in order that he may save—some. No, there is no truce with Jansenism: he bought the whole field, died for the sins of the whole world; yet it is not the whole world that his death will profit. In the unfathomable foreknowledge of Almighty God some souls shone out like gold, though they were still buried and sunk in earthly defilement—the souls that were to become his, and enjoy his presence eternally in heaven. For their sakes Jesus Christ made the world his own possession at the price of his precious blood: "Ask of me, and I will give thee the Gentiles for thy inheritance, and the utmost parts of the earth for thy possession."[3] And, having found the treasure, notice that the man hides it again; only he knows the secret of the *cache*. Only God foreknows the souls that are his; it is not for us to say this man is saved, or that lost. Only the shortest of the parables, only a single verse of the Gospel, and here is Calvin as well as Jansen refuted from the lips of Incarnate Truth.

That, then, is the immediate effect of our Redemption; our divine Lord has called to himself a Church. And he has called it out of a world. Church and world will in future be two correlative terms, the latter including the former, as the field includes the treasure, yet, in God's redemptive purpose, valued only for its sake. Meanwhile the centuries must run their course, and Church and world will be brought into mutual relation. What sort of relation? I do not mean conflicts or persecutions, which need a positive attitude on the part of the world to create them. But what will be the immediate effect of God's calling to himself a Church, from the point of view of the world out of which he calls it?

Two parables answer the question, both included by St Matthew in

---

[1] 2 Corinthians 8. 9.   [2] Ephesians 5. 25-27.   [3] Psalm 2. 8.

this same chapter. Pearl and treasure were inadequate illustrations to this extent, that they are both dead things: the treasure is as lifeless as the soil that hides it, while the pearl is actually the lifeless by-product of a living organism. In the parable of the leaven this deficiency is made good, and we see that the Church works in the world as an energy at work upon a mere mass, a disturbing agent which radiates an infectious influence. Elsewhere we find leaven used to illustrate the corruption which evil brings into a society or an institution. That metaphor is a natural one, but this is in truth more accurate, for it is really redemption that is the force, the energy, while the sinful world is the dead matter that can resist its influence, if it resists at all, not by movement but by mere inertia—"the evil is null, is naught, is silence implying sound".[1] The Church is like treasure hid in a field because the Church not the world, the treasure not the field, is the true object of the divine search; yet the Church is like leaven hid in meal because of its own nature it cannot remain inactive; it cannot exist in surroundings which it does not modify and transform.

But the Church is more than force; it is an organizing principle of life; hence the parable of the mustard seed. While the leaven radiates the mustard seed absorbs; it sucks in from the earth, the moisture, the very air that surrounds it, and the atoms of dead matter pass into a living organism; the world is not merely infected with energy, it yields up, however reluctantly, its tribute of souls to build up the body of the Church. The Church is divine in its origin, not merely in the sense that it is God who calls it, but in the more intimate sense that the seed from which it is sprung is the grain of wheat that fell into the ground and died—the human nature of our incarnate Saviour in which he suffered death upon the cross. But it is by his attraction to himself of human souls, sucked away from the dead world and vitalized by incorporation into his own body, that he enables his Church to multiply and increase.

The Jew thinks of the kingdom of heaven as a renovated world in which God will reign as a conqueror; the parable of the pearl teaches him to think of it as something for which God comes down to make a sacrifice. He thinks of it as a manifestation of glory in which, as Daniel foretold, the just will shine like the sun in the kingdom of their Father. Our Lord explains to his disciples, in the forty-third verse of this chapter, that Daniel's prophecy will only be fulfilled at the end of the world in the last judgment—"*Then* shall the just shine forth", an emphatic Then. And meanwhile? In the forty-fourth verse, he goes on

[1] Robert Browning, "Abt Vogler", stanza 9.

to compare the kingdom of heaven, the Church on earth, to treasure hidden away, treasure which will remain hidden, so far as man's prescience is concerned, till the end of time. The Jew thinks of the kingdom as a theocracy imposed on the world by force of arms from without; our Lord teaches, in the parable of the leaven, that it is, on the contrary, a hidden influence which by its own inherent energies is to transform the world from within. Finally, the Jew thinks of it as a sudden violent upheaval, a catastrophe of history; our Lord teaches that it will be a growth, gradual though it be rapid, akin in the method of its accomplishment to all that we know of organic growth in nature. There is an afternoon of busy thought for the Jewish theologian, if the Jewish theologian had had ears to hear, and a heart ready to understand.

And now let us put the light behind our parables, and throw them against the screen of history; blurred, perhaps, in their outlines, but surely not difficult to recognize. Like the leaven, the Church in history gives itself out to the world; like the tree, it absorbs from the world and assimilates what it absorbs. Not all the sophistries of Gibbon and his followers can blind the eye of the historian to the brute fact that the advent of Christianity is an epoch in the story of our planet; that, even if our faith be a dream, it is a dream that has been more profound in its influence than all the waking thoughts of the human imagination. Not all at once, not with violence and the sword, like the creed of the false prophet, but silently and secretly like the leaven, in a manner foreshadowed by the life-history of its own Founder when he came to earth.

> He comes, but not in regal splendour dressed,
> The jewelled diadem, the Tyrian vest;
> Not like a Prince, all-glorious from afar,
> Of hosts the captain, and the Lord of War—

a little Baby in a manger, a hunted criminal, a malefactor weighted with the instrument of his own punishment—so our Lord looked to the world; not otherwise did his Church look—does his Church look, to the scornful eye of the politicians that reject it. Christianity was the religion of slaves; it has abolished slavery. It was thrown to the lions in the amphitheatre; it has abolished the amphitheatre. Absolute monarchy, like a flustered giant, laboured to crush it; it has outlived absolute monarchy. Silently through the centuries the supernatural miracle has worked, like nature's miracle of fermentation.

And while she has spread her influence outwards, the Church has also drawn to herself, by the hidden spell of that heavenly seed once planted in the soil of our dead nature, the souls of such as would be saved. Not men of one temperament or one nationality, of one class or one set of interests, of one age or one stage of civilization. And those souls have been not fitted together merely, like the stones of a building, into one plan, but incorporated and grafted into a single stock, and made partakers of the organizing form of the whole. Art and learning and poetry and rhetoric, courage and prudence and the qualities that make one man the guide or the ruler of his fellows—the Church has absorbed into herself all types of human endurance and of human activity. The shadow of it covered the hills, and the branches thereof the cedars of God; it stretched forth its branches unto the sea, and its boughs unto the river. While the leaven worked, the mustard seed has grown.

And yet, if I ended there, you would accuse me, all too justly, of optimism. In the last three and a half centuries, to the external view at any rate, that process of leavening and of growth has been retarded, interrupted, checked, nay, reversed. In the Europe she once conquered the Church is, politically at least, an outweighed influence; now, as in France or Portugal, an ineffective majority; now, as in Germany or Holland, effective only as a minority; in our own country, a thing men can still pretend not to see. In the new worlds opened up at or since the time of European apostasy, she stands out less through her own impressiveness than from the insignificance of her rivals; in the lands of ancient superstition her progress is certain but wearisomely slow. What wonder that men look back to the greatness of the medieval Church, and pity themselves that they were born in a time when faith has grown cold? "Why hast thou broken down the hedge thereof, so that all they who pass by the way do pluck it? . . . We are become a reproach to our neighbours, a scorn and derision to them that are round about us. . . . How is the mistress of the Gentiles become as a widow, the princes of provinces made tributary! Weeping she hath wept in the night, and her tears are on her cheeks." Do not the very words used by God's ancient people when he seemed to have rescinded the covenant made with their fathers echo terribly in our ears, as if the New Covenant, too, might be set aside; as if the leaven had spent its force, the tree might be cumbering the ground, ripe for the axe and the charnel?

Nor is this all: is it not likely that amid all the forces, some evil, some misdirected, some merely distracting, which have been created or let loose in the last few years, we shall hear of further reverses, further apostasies? Some would even have us expect that civilization itself will be dethroned, and that a new age, rivalling if it does not repeat the barbarism of the past, will sweep away the laborious fabric of our history as if the Christian Church had never come to leaven it:

> Lo! thy dread empire, Chaos, is restored;
> Light dies before thy uncreating word;
> Thy hand, great Anarch, lets the curtain fall,
> And universal darkness buries all.[1]

Till the whole was leavened. . . . When it is grown up, it is greater than all herbs. . . . Are we to suppose that the words have come short of fulfilment? Or that they refer only to a stage in the course of history, a stage which is passing or has passed, to be succeeded by some new dispensation of God? We shall go wrong in our interpretation, as I think we often do go wrong in our estimates of where the Church stands, if we do not keep the two parables, the two relations of the Church to the world, distinct in our minds at this point. The Church is to leaven the world till the whole is leavened, but we have no means of knowing how complete, how effective, or how permanent an influence our Lord meant to suggest by those words. After all, was Europe ever really leavened? Is it certain that the world was conquered by the medieval Church, not merely caged? It is certain, at any rate, and our critics do not let us forget it, that even in the Middle Ages, and still more today, the world is not what it would be if the principles of the Sermon on the Mount had really become the governing principle in the lives of men or of nations. Nor is the Church to be blamed if the process was interrupted, if today her leavening influence has ceased to exert its old, silent pressure. For at the great apostasy of the sixteenth century, when so large a share of Europe was cut off from its old allegiance, the shock of the amputation drove the blood back to the heart; the whole strength of the Church was needed to repel the invasion of false doctrine and to secure her own position against attack. Her philosophers became controversialists, her theologians propagandists, her preachers missionaries. Men tell us that we are narrow-minded and cramped in our outlook, when their own heresies have forced us back upon the apologetic we had thought no longer necessary. They take offence at the gimcrack ornaments of our modern churches, while they themselves are giving sacred concerts in the old cathedrals. They exiled our priests for two hundred years, and then cast it in our teeth that we are a foreign invasion. God knows the leaven has still a work to do, in protecting the purity of marriage

[1] Alexander Pope, "The Dunciad", 653-6.

and the sanctity of family life, in vindicating the liberty of the citizen, in a score of ways besides. But we must not be blamed if that influence is a remote one. While Protestantism forces us to wage a defensive war, what marvel is it that we should have little influence upon the world's citizens?

But the tree—the body of Christian people that is to grow and multiply till the end of time? Let me remind you again that it is this function of the Church which is of eternal importance; the world is to pass, and the glory of it, but the Church only reaches its fulfilment when the world reaches its dissolution. The pearl is only the by-product of the oyster, but it is the oyster, not the pearl, that goes to the scrap-heap. The hidden treasure, the pearl of great price—of infinite price, surely, if God became man to die for it. Has God made a bad bargain? An easy question to ask, but have we any real standard by which to judge, any access to the statistics on which we could base our answer? Certainly it is true that in most European countries there are less Catholics in proportion to the total population than there were four hundred years since. But, once consider the Church not as an association of so many parishes, but as the seed-plot, the training-ground for the celestial citizenship—have we any means of assuring ourselves that the Church has dwindled, or even remained where it was? We are apt to think of the fewness of saints in the modern world, the world of the Little Flower and Gemma Galgani; but is it certain that the ages of the saints are the ages of faith, and not rather the ages when sins are many, and saints needed? I could mention a dozen saints whose names would be household words to most of you, who were all born out of the very throes of Europe's apostasy. Had the medieval world indeed such great advantages over us? Or is it not possible that Lourdes, the Sacred Heart devotion, frequent communion, and the other remedies devised for our days by an untiring Providence, are peopling heaven as it was never peopled before? I do not even suggest that we should try to answer that question. "Say not", the wise man warns us, "say not, What thinkest thou is the cause that former times were better than they are now? For this manner of question is foolish." Enough for us that the Lord knows them that are his, enough for us that, whether by many or by few, his eternal purpose is being brought to its accomplishment.

Meanwhile, the treasure is there as of old, if we will dig for it; the pearl is still offered for sale if we will pay the price asked—all that we have.

4

THE CHURCH A VISIBLE
INSTITUTION

Many are called, but few chosen.—Matthew 20. 16.

THIS solemn warning, twice repeated by our Lord at the end of two different parables, points to the Jewish background against which we ought to read this part of his preaching. In both clauses it gives the lie at least to popular ideas about the kingdom of God. For that kingdom, according to the view of his hearers, was to exist, at least primarily, for the sake of the Jewish race, a tiny minority among the peoples of the world: "many are called" is as much as to say, more are called than you think. On the other hand, allowance was seldom made in Jewish theology for a kingdom within which a further selection was to be made before the work of salvation was accomplished; "few are chosen", our Lord tells them—it will not be by mere right of birth and nationality that they will be able to claim an entrance. Many are called—not all the saved will be Jews. Few are chosen—not all the Jews will be saved. It is noticeable that these words, so open in their exposition of the truth, are used after two of the latest parables, spoken only a few days before the crucifixion. I do not think it is fanciful to see in such indications as this a progressive fullness of revelation about our Lord's public teaching.

But the words have theological importance for a controversy of far more recent times. For the word Ecclesia, which we translate "Church", means simply, by derivation, that which is called out. Applied first to the "congregation" of Israel under the Old Covenant, and as such a familiar word to our Lord's own contemporaries, it naturally was used to describe the body of his followers under the New Covenant. The many who are called, then, constitute the Church, the thing called out; and the fact that many are called but few chosen means that the Church is something other than the whole body of the redeemed. The Ecclesia is one thing, the Elect are another; and it was the capital mistake of early Protestantism that it never realized that.

Now, in two at least of his parables our Lord did definitely condemn the idea, which a too literal or too impatient interpretation of certain prophetic passages had made common among the Jews, that when the

Messias came to earth it would be the signal for a millennium, in which sin, and with it all the miseries which are consequences of or visitations upon sin, would have wholly disappeared. We have already seen that the kingdom of heaven, though world-wide in its invitation and world-wide in its influence, is to consist in itself only of a selection of souls called out of a sinful world. We are now to be taught that even within that Church, that selection, there will be evil mingled with good, until the day shall declare it, and the fires of a world's dissolution shall refine the tried gold of the celestial treasure.

Cockle sown in the field by an enemy's hand, while the good man of the house was asleep.[1] What? Did God sleep? We shall see, later, that when God is said to sleep in these parables of our Lord it means that he permits what is going forward without positively willing it. So our Lord himself slept while the storm raged round the little boat on the Lake of Genesareth, the apostles' boat that typified his Church, not that he was blind to the danger of the situation, but because he wished in that manner to test and to foster the faith of those around him. God, then, permitted what followed; and the Devil lost no time in sowing the bad seed; he made a traitor out of Judas within three years of his call to the ministry. We are in error if we speak of the uncorrupted Christianity of the primitive Church. There never was an uncorrupted Christianity; the cockle was there before the good seed had time to spring. And, springing up, it does so with healthy growth and clinging roots. It is one of the grim paradoxes of gardening, and has even passed into a proverb, that your weed thrives more stoutly and clings more closely than the flowers you cherish. Nor is it less showy than the good grain. Who has not seen a cornfield so thick with poppies that from some distant hillside he misnamed it a poppy-field? So in the Church, God's chosen seed-plot, the nursery of all sanctity, evil can strike deep roots in human souls, be their position in the Church never so exalted; can cling there with a desperate obstinacy, and can flaunt itself in such a way that the careless onlooker will see in the Church nothing but a tangled mass of foul growths. Be shocked, be grieved, be indignant at scandals in the Church, but if you are a disciple of our Lord's parables do not be surprised at it. The worst of it has been foretold.

A net cast into the sea, gathering together of all kind of fishes.[2] What? Did not God leave his Church the power of the keys? Did he not mean that by the exercise of that power the unworthy should be repelled from communion, expelled, if need be, for their contumacy

[1] Matthew 13. 25.   [2] Matthew 13. 47.

from the body of believers? How comes it that the meshes of the net are too fine to let out the worthless catch? We only know that it is so, that, still liable as we are to human error, we dare not judge one another's motives in matters of conscience, except where open contumacy makes the sinner clearly unworthy of participation in the privileges of the Church. But we know there are those in the net who will be brought to shore, yet be rejected there as unprofitable.

The lesson of these two parables is especially valuable, because they contradict not only the preconceived Jewish idea of what the kingdom of heaven would be like, but also the Protestant idea—the real Protestant idea—of what the Church ought to be like. Since the primary purpose of the Church is, as we have seen, the separation from the world of the souls that are to reach heaven, there is a constant tendency in Christian thought to restrict the title of Christian or Catholic to those who are, as far as human insight can judge, going forward on the way of salvation; to set up a sort of Church within the Church, consisting of "the saved", of those who combine spiritual gifts of a high order with a delusion. And the delusion is that because they are Christians, because they have believed in Christ with a saving faith, nothing can ever interrupt their progress; nay, nothing that they do can be really sinful, seeing that their consciences are now enlightened by the Holy Ghost. There must have been something of this feeling abroad among the early Christians at Corinth, since St Paul is forced to take up his master's parable and warn them that it is not enough for them to be Christians, any more than it is enough to start in a race: all run indeed, but one receiveth the prize,[1] and in the same way there may well be many called by the name of Christ who will not reach the prize of their high calling. The Israelites, he says, were all baptized in the Red Sea, all ate of the heavenly manna and drank of the spiritual rock, yet only a remnant of them attained to the land of promise. So in the New Covenant we Christians all escape from the bondage of sin through the waters of baptism, are all refreshed on our pilgrimage by the very body and blood of Christ, yet—the inference is not hard to draw. "He that thinketh himself to stand", St Paul concludes, "let him take heed lest he fall."

This dangerous tendency, with its accompanying delusion about the salvation of the individual concerned, occurs in different forms at different periods of Church history, but never more logically than in the system preached by Calvin and his followers in those parts of Europe where the Old Religion had been stamped out. The Calvinist

[1] 1 Corinthians 9. 24.

Church is in its whole idea a Church of Saints. To say that you belong to the Church, and to say that your soul is infallibly bound for heaven, is to say the same thing in two different ways. The world is therefore cut in halves by a terrible dichotomy: those who belong to "the Church", that is, those who feel an interior conviction that they are destined for heaven, can do no wrong, because they are in the grace of Christ; and—the others. For all the rest of the world every act, every word, every thought is unsanctified by grace and therefore sinful.

> I have God's warrant, could I blend
> All hideous sins, as in a cup,
> To drink the mingled venom up,
> Secure my nature will convert
> The draught to blossoming gladness fast,
> While sweet dews turn to the gourd's hurt
> And bloat, and while they bloat it, blast,
> As from the first its lot was cast. [1]

Not all Protestants have followed the ruthless logic of Calvin into his speculations about irresistible grace. But Protestantism, wherever the word has stood for a consistent body of thought, not for a mere loose series of half-truths and negations, is bound to follow him in his belief that the Church is simply the assembly of God's elect, that the holiness of the Church consists in the fact that every member of it is sanctified, that there will be no Christians in hell.

St Paul, as I have said, was at pains to warn his Corinthian converts against any approach to such an error. He tells us that you can be a member of the Church—and he is thinking of the Church as an institution, or why should he refer to her two chief sacraments?—and yet come short of grace and so fail to reach eternal life. That sounds very obvious to us, but do not make the mistake of thinking it has no theological importance. For the whole controversy about the true Church is not whether it is the Roman Catholic Church or the Greek Church or the Anglican Church or some other definite religious body. The real controversy is this: Is the true Church of Christ a visible or an invisible institution? Ninety per cent of the people who reject the Catholic Church reject it, not because they really believe in some other visible Church, but because they do not believe in a visible Church at all. Therefore it is of great importance to know whether St Paul taught, and of still greater importance to know whether our Lord taught, that the Church was visible, or that it was invisible. And if the

[1] Robert Browning, "Johannes Agricola in Meditation".

E

Church is invisible, if it is not a clearly defined body of people, boun
together here on earth by a common faith and common institution;
but merely a number of souls known only to God, who have reall
received with a lively faith the message of his kingdom, merely th
sum total of all the people in the world who are really Christians, the
. . . Why, then, there are no bad Christians, no cockle among th
wheat, no worthless fish in the net, no unsuccessful starters in the race o
Christian perfection, and St Paul's reference to the children of Israe
who were baptized in the Red Sea and ate the heavenly manna an
then failed to reach the land of promise is without point.

It may be objected that the field in which the cockle grows is th
world, not the Church—"the field is the world", our Lord himsel
says—and that the cockle growing among the wheat only means tha
Christians will have to live in the world among wicked people wh
are not Christians. But if so, why should wheat and cockle be so har
to separate? And in any case, what of the net? There, surely, if word
have any meaning, the sea stands for the world, and the net for th
Church, and there are bad fish in the net. Very well then, bad Christian;
members of the Church who will not reach heaven. Either reject thes
two parables and two whole chapters of Corinthians as spurious, o
else admit that the Church our Lord founded, the Church St Pau
preached, was a visible institution, with bad members as well as good
"Many are called, but few chosen", how solemnly our Lord says that
And what is the Church? The Ecclesia. And what does Ecclesia mea
by derivation? The thing that is called, not the thing that is chosen
"Many are called, but few chosen." To talk of the Church as a
invisible Church is to make Christ a deceiver.

St Paul, after describing the way in which the Israelites, after all th
spiritual privileges which had been conferred on them, were not foun
worthy, most of them, to enter into the promised rest, adds, "Where
fore he that thinketh himself to stand, let him take heed lest he fall".
He himself, he explains, apostle and preacher of the gospel as he is
takes the discipline for fear that he himself should fall from grace an
become a castaway. All of us who have become members of th
Church have duly entered ourselves for the great competition; call it
race, or a fight, which you will; it is quite another thing to ensure tha
we run prudently, fight effectively. It is, he says, a matter of training
he that striveth for the mastery refraineth himself from all thing;
"But", you say, "I have been baptized, redeemed with the blood o
my Saviour; he is not likely to leave his work unfinished in me."

[1] 1 Corinthians 10. 12.

That is what the Jews said, answers St Paul; they argued that because God had brought them out of Egypt and led them through the Red Sea, he was certain to bring them into the land of Canaan. Were they right? "But I am a regular communicant, fortified with the body and blood of Christ, who himself has said that whoso eateth of this bread shall live for ever." I know, answers St Paul, and that is what the Jews thought; they argued that it would not have been worth God's while to support them on their pilgrimage through the wilderness, opening the doors of heaven to rain down bread upon them, and bringing waters out of the rock, if he meant them all to die in the desert on the further side of Jordan. Were they right? The people who had been brought out of slavery in Egypt with miracles and catastrophes of nature turned their affections back, and pined for the old food, the old customs, the old false gods of their servitude. These things were written for our correction, upon whom the ends of the world are come: therefore, he that thinketh himself to stand, let him take heed lest he fall. Let us then learn correction, learn to refrain ourselves from all things, that by mortifying the senses, by self-imposed silence and solitude, by making a special campaign against some ruling passion of our lives, by insisting upon and if need be revising our rule of prayer, we may become worthy of the vocation by which we are called; we may be found pure grain fit for a King's garner, a prize safely landed at the feet of the Fisherman of souls.

By God's permissive will the cockle is allowed to grow up with the wheat in his Church; it his will, but not his wish. It is impossible that scandals should not come, but woe to him through whom they come! There is no single excuse so freely used by people who want to justify themselves in remaining outside the Church as the behaviour of some of us who are inside it. The fact that moral laxity, carelessness, and formalism could be pointed to in so many parts of Christian England was the rallying-cry of the apostasy through which England lost the faith. There is nothing more jealously watched or more bitterly criticized today by people who criticize religion than the behaviour of professed Christians. Fifty years ago, people did not pay very much attention to what we did; today, when the Catholic Church is the only considerable religious body that dares to claim an increasing and not a diminishing membership, we have a heavier responsibility. More and more, even in England, the Church becomes a city set on a hill, whose doings cannot be hid; more and more, it may be, it will fall to her to be the salt of the world in which she lives. The stronger the light beats on us, the more clearly outlined, motes though we be in the rays of it, do our lives appear in the public scrutiny. We do not want that scrutiny, so often pharisaical, to make hypocrites of us. But do let us take some care, not only about motives, as God sees them, but about the external appearances of our actions, lest they should be keeping back souls from God.

> Nor knowest thou what argument
> Thy life to thy neighbour's creed hath lent.[1]

Do not let us give the impression, as far as it is in our power to avoid it, that the infinite patience of our Mother the Church is habitually abused by her children, and that the gentleness of her rebukes is demoralizing—yes, Protestants will tell you that—to the consciences which she directs. A scandal carried further than a tale of sanctity; our Blessed Lady lived and died unknown, but all Jerusalem knew when Judas hanged himself.

5

THE RESPONSIBILITY OF MAN

For the earth that drinketh in the rain which cometh often upon it, and bringeth forth herbs meet for them by whom it is tilled, receiveth blessing from God; but that which bringeth forth thorns and briers is reprobate and very near unto a curse, whose end is to be burned.—Hebrews 6. 7.

IT was after proclaiming the parable of the sower that our Lord explained to his disciples his method of preaching, a method which was meant to enlighten his faithful hearers, while it left his critics and his calumniators in the dark. Why had such a simple and harmless parable to be explained to the apostles afterwards in secret? If you consider the background of Jewish expectation against which our Lord's preaching is thrown into relief, you will see that this parable, too, forms part of the revolutionary programme which foreshadowed the foundation of the new kingdom. The seed, according to St Mark, is the word, according to St Luke it is the word of God, but in St Matthew —and it is fairly certain that St Matthew wrote to convince the Jews, while the other Gospels were written chiefly for the Gentiles—in

---

[1] Ralph Waldo Emerson, "Each and All".

St Matthew it is the word of the kingdom. And, in Jewish thought, a word means a great deal more than a mere spoken word. The word of the Lord, all through the Old Testament, is practically a synonym for the divine power. The word of the kingdom is the life-giving secret, the energizing power, the motive force, which brings the kingdom into existence. And this word, this power, it seems, is to be ineffective in some places, effective in other places, but with a variation of degree. Well, what is there so revolutionary about that?

It is not necessary for us to inquire what one or two Jews here and there, with more learning or with better dispositions than the rest, may have anticipated about the kingdom of the Messias. But it is clear that the average Jew thought of the qualification for that kingdom as a mere matter of race; it was a case of "founder's kin"; if you were Abraham's seed, you participated in whatever happiness that kingdom brought with it; if not, it was no fault of yours, but you had no part in it. Whatever indirect advantages the Gentiles might derive from it, the kingdom was for the Jews. Remember the tremendous emphasis which Jewish thought has always laid on race. Ezechiel found it quite hard to persuade his countrymen that the individual soul would be judged on its own merits, not on those of its ancestors. It would not be surprising to the Jew that mere race should be a qualification for enjoying the happiness of the Messianic reign. And this notion of a seed being sown broadcast, and meeting with a different amount of response and bearing a different amount of fruit—what is it but an open challenge to current Jewish theology?

The Calvinist's idea of salvation is closely akin to the Jewish. The Calvinist thinks of salvation as something which comes to you, not indeed on the ground of race, but on grounds quite as arbitrary, and which is certain, absolutely certain, of attaining its object. Our salvation is effected without so much as the co-operation of our own wills. And on this head the Calvinist may derive considerable satisfaction from the parable of the cockle in the wheat. The soil, which is the human heart, is exactly the same all over the field; but in some places wheat is sown upon it by God, in other places cockle is sown upon it by the Devil. And what is sown, salvation or damnation, comes up by a merely natural law; the soil, the human heart, does not in any way modify the character of the crop produced; it acts automatically, supplying to the useless weeds the same nutritive force which it supplies to the genuine harvest. There is no blaming the soil for producing cockle, or praising it for producing wheat; it simply brings to birth what was sown in it. Could anything be clearer?

And having thus created me,
Thus rooted me, he bade me grow
Guiltless, for ever, like a tree
That buds and blooms, nor seeks to know
The law by which it prospers so:
Yes, yes, a tree which must ascend,
No poison-gourd foredoomed to stoop—

Here, it seems, are our Lord's own words justifying, by a quite simple allegory from nature, the very position which the Calvinist labours to defend.

And then, just when the Calvinist is triumphant, this parable of the sower throws out all his calculations. For in effect it is the exact opposite of the other parable. As before, the seed sown is the grace which brings us to God. As before, the soil on which it is sown is the human heart. But whereas in the other parable the soil was the same all over the field, in this parable it is the soil that is different. And whereas in the other parable it was the seed sown that differed, here it is the seed that is the same. The Pelagian tells you that grace has nothing to do with it; it is man's free will that decides his place in eternity. Confront him with the parable of the cockle, and show him that it is the seed sown, the grace God gives, that brings up the fruit of eternal life. The Calvinist tells you that free will has nothing to do with it; it is grace that does everything, in despite of ourselves. Confront him with the parable of the sower, and show him that wherever the seed fails it is the fault of the soil, not of the seed. If we attain heaven, we have to thank the divine Husbandman who sowed the seed in our hearts. If we miss heaven, we have to blame the hardness, or the shallowness, or the entanglement of our own souls for what we have lost. That is the teaching of Christ, that is the teaching of his Church.

It is doubtful whether our Lord means to tell us anything here about the position of those people to whom the Christian Gospel is not proposed at all; nor, we might add, about those people who are prevented by invincible ignorance from accepting it when it is proposed to them; you can see from his own interpretation of the parable that the qualities he is discussing are the qualities of the will. And yet the condemnation he utters is not only for bad Christians, but for a certain class of people who never become members of the Church at all. *When any one heareth the word of the kingdom and understandeth it not, this is he that received the seed by the wayside.*[1] We may console ourselves if

---

[1] Matthew 13. 19.

we like by the reflection that there is only one failure of this kind to every two of the other kind; still, it remains true that there is a hearing of the word and a failing to understand it. *The devil cometh and taketh the word out of their heart, lest believing they should be saved.*[1] There is such a thing as bad faith, and our Lord compares it here to the resistance which is offered to the husbandman's sowing by the hard, smooth crust of the wayside. The field-path, I suppose, that runs along the edge of the sown land. There is, as it were, an outer fringe round the Church of people who are only just outside it, yet, from some quality of hardness or dryness in themselves, fail from the outset to accept its message. Three kinds of hardness are apt to produce this effect: prejudice, conventionality, and insensibility.

Prejudice is not carelessness, it is something deliberate; it means refusing to investigate the claims of the Church because you dislike it, the will driving the intellect, and driving it in blinkers. Prejudice is a soil which is deliberately hardened as if with a steamroller, a sort of macadamization of the conscience, and it is a terrible thing. Only God's mercy knows whether or when it is excusable. Conventionality, the beaten track, the dusty field-path trodden down by generations of habit until it seems incapable of receiving any idea, is terribly common in our own country, but not so deliberate, and therefore, let us hope, not so culpable. There remains insensibility, the moral deadness and indifference which arises from a sinful habit of living, which has lost all the nobility of character that would respond to a heroic appeal, soil that has become caked and dusty through sheer lack of watering. Miracles of grace are sometimes worked in such hearts, but in itself this is the most dangerous hardening of all. It is not for us to judge where those conditions are present, but if and in so far as they are present there is human fault barring the way against the initial impact of grace; the seed never even sprouts. The Devil comes and takes away the seed—remember that the Devil is, by derivation, the slanderer, the accuser of the brethren. Having rejected the Church, these souls are willing to accept and to spread the calumnies that thwart her mission. Hard hearts, not broken hearts, are the world's tragedy.

The other two kinds of soil—the stony ground and the thorns—represent souls that have found their way into the Church. There is, of course, a class of convert whom we readily associate with the former description: there are not many of them, thank God, but most of us have heard of one or two. The good seed proves, after all, to have been committed to a very shallow layer of earth, and its early shooting was

[2] Luke 8. 12.

but evidence that it had never taken deep root: when the sun of persecution or of difficulty was up, it withered away. How impatient they were at the beginning, those souls, always wanting to hurry on their reception, saying, "Yes, yes", before the priest had time to explain the doctrine they were discussing! How they roped themselves with medals, in those days of first enthusiasm, and knew what Mass was being performed at which church next Sunday, and were in two minds about a religious vocation! And then the sun of temptation rose, and the blade that shot up so green in the pale light of early morning, under the shadow of the hedge, drooped and died in the glare of common day. We try to believe that they never really made the act of faith, and so never committed formal apostasy. But there are other souls whose case is even more disheartening—not converts this time. They learnt their religion in the nursery; the names of Jesus and Mary were almost the first words their stumbling utterance knew. They went to school, and made the faith infinitely attractive to all who watched them with that strange graciousness which boyhood or girlhood lends to Christian piety. And yet somehow the seed we sowed so anxiously never took root; and when they left school it seemed but a moment before the sun withered their promise, and—they fell away. I do not want to harrow you by suggesting that these exceptions are to be taken as the rule; but they were as our Lord warned us they would be, souls in whom the spade never dug deep, the root never struck firm.

And even when the heart has opened itself to receive the heavenly gift, and the seed has not lodged merely but taken root in it, there is danger still. We do not wear our faith upon our sleeve for daws to peck at; no casual assault of temptation against perseverance in the faith will dislodge us now. We have become acclimatized to the sun of the world's criticism; we have stood the test and, thank God, survived it. But we have still our lives to live; and those lives will not be—for we are human still—a peaceful and uninterrupted growth in the ways of the spirit. There will be cross-currents and side-issues in our progress; we have to make our way in the world, and times are hard; we expect, and are justified in expecting, relaxations and recreations that have their centre in this present life. And there are claims upon us more unselfish than these; we cannot isolate ourselves from family, from acquaintance and friendship, from society of some kind, and that means that worldly anxieties can never wholly leave us. "And that which fell among thorns are they who have heard and, going their way"—not turning their backs on what they have heard, but going quietly about their business—"are choked with the cares and riches and pleasures of this life, and yield no fruit." Cares and riches and pleasures—just the three things we decided we could not get away from. Worries can crowd out, riches can stale, pleasures can drown the life of the spirit. As Catholics, we are right to join in political and social activities; we are leaven as well as mustard seed. But it is possible for social, for political, even for religious activities to absorb so much of our concentration that our own souls become locked in the entanglement, and a scanty and struggling growth is all we have to show for the seed committed to us, in danger, perhaps, of being stifled altogether. And if our unselfish enthusiasms carry this peril with them, how much more the pursuit of money, how much more the dallying with our pleasures?

All habits grow, and the ill weed is likely to grow the fastest. We must not expect that because the seed of grace in us starts fair, side by side with the small beginnings of avarice or self-indulgence, it will come to its own untended. We do need mortification, whether it be the internal or external, to cut back and disentangle those clinging roots of habit. Mortification is not only meant for advanced souls, for them to reap merit by it; it is for imperfect souls too, who, so little conscious of it, are yielding more from day to day to the choking grip of the habits they are forming. Good soil whose crop has run to seed —on how many of this world's successes will that be the heavenly verdict!

And the good seed—thirtyfold, sixtyfold, a hundredfold? We will leave that aside for the present; it will be our subject when we are treating of a later parable. At present, let it be enough to remind ourselves of our dangers. If we are outside the Church, the danger that, in that mysterious background of motive which lies behind the conduct of our lives, there may be some strain of hardness in us which needs to be recognized and perhaps to be overcome before we can be properly receptive to the message of him who calls us. The danger, if we are in nominal, external communion with the Church, that we may still have failed to make its meaning our own, still be ill-prepared to face the midday heats which will test the vitality of our faith. The danger, even if we have a real, living religion as Catholics, that we may at the same time be encouraging habits in ourselves which are capable of choking and strangling the true seed, the one harvest that will be ours in eternity.

EX

6

THE PATIENCE OF GOD

He said to the dresser of his vineyard: Behold, for these three years I come seeking fruit on this fig-tree and I find none. Cut it down therefore. Why cumbereth it the ground?—Luke 13. 7.

W E have seen that, in spite of the pains our Blessed Lord took to heal the wounds of our fallen nature, there will always remain, according to his own prophecy, bad members, unsatisfactory members, of the Church which he coveted and bought for himself with his precious blood. And we have seen that although he knows this, he will not allow us to make an excuse of the divine foreknowledge, as if that necessitated our sins: the individual soul is responsible for the scandals it creates in the Church, however much those scandals are allowed for in the divine Architect's plan. And now we come to the further question: What are the conditions—we can hardly ask to know the explanation—of the divine patience in face of human sin? How is it that God sees men sinning and foresees that they will never abandon their sins and gain an entrance into the kingdom of heaven, yet does not interfere to vindicate his own law, put an end at once to the human life that is being so misused, that can only do harm to its surroundings? And there is a complementary question to be asked from man's side: What are the conditions of our tenure? How far can we afford to neglect the calls and inspirations of the Holy Spirit? When is it, and how is it, that we are given a second chance?

It is in itself a large subject, containing deep mysteries of theology, and practical lessons of the utmost moral importance. Further, it is a subject to which our Lord's teaching continually recurs.

Let us begin with the parable of the seed growing secretly, because the allegory in it is closely akin to the allegories we have been considering hitherto. *So is the kingdom of God, as if a man should cast seed into the earth, and should sleep and rise, night and day, and the seed should spring and grow up whilst he knoweth not. And when the fruit is brought forth, immediately he putteth in the sickle, because the harvest is come.*[1] If we take the kingdom of God as meaning the end of the world and the final judgment, we shall have to identify the kingdom with the harvest. But if, in accordance to the principle we have hitherto followed,

[1] Mark 4. 26-28.

we regard the kingdom of God as another name for the Church, then the kingdom of God, the period of the Church's warfare, is here being compared to the whole period between seed-time and harvest. Remember once more what sort of kingdom it was that the Jews were expecting—an open manifestation of God's power; a theophany in which God would respond to the age-long cry of his servants, "Arise, Lord, why sleepest thou? Awake, and be not absent from us for ever!"[1] He would raise up in Juda a national hero, or something more than a mere hero, a triumph visibly over the heathen. In this millennium that was coming, men would at last learn, to their comfort or to their cost, that there is a God who controls human destinies, and watches over the welfare of his servants.

Instead of which, God sleeps. Our Lord tells us so in this parable; God sleeps. Twice in the parables we are told that God sleeps, and twice that he goes off on a journey into a far country. We know, of course, that God, though he dwells in the inaccessible light, is nevertheless present at all times to all his creatures, and that nothing which passes in the whole of space and the whole of existence can be outside his knowledge and his notice. The idea we have here, then, is a metaphorical one; but it was a metaphor which our Lord's hearers would readily understand. When the prophet Elias was mocking the priests of Baal because their God would not help them, he said, "Cry with a louder voice, for perhaps he is on a journey, or perhaps he is asleep, and must be awaked."[2] A God who is asleep or on a journey means a God who behaves as if he took no interest in the welfare of his servants, left them entirely to themselves. And so it is in many passages of the Psalms like the one I quoted just now, "Arise, Lord, why sleepest thou? Awake, and be not absent from us for ever." The Jews, then, think of the kingdom as the time when God will awake from sleep. Our Lord tells them that the kingdom will be as if God awoke only to sow fresh seed in his field, and then slept again. The husbandman in the parable rises from sleep each day; that may mean that God will from time to time interfere providentially in the world's history; but in general our lesson is that God will still leave us to ourselves, still allow each man to act in his own way unrebuked, without thereby sanctioning or approving his action. So it will go on until the harvest. The harvest, as before, is the end of the world, and our Lord here as elsewhere refuses to give his audience any hint as to when that will be.

But, for his Jewish hearers, the patience of God is a subject of immense importance—far more importance than they realize. They

---

[1] Psalm 43. 23.   [2] 3 Kings 18. 27.

themselves, the chosen people, are on their trial. And, quite a short time, it seems, before his Passion, our Lord opens their eyes to their position almost in so many words. I mean, of course, in the parable of the wicked husbandmen.[1] This time, the human agents concerned are not compared to the blades that spring up and become ripe for harvest, but to the cultivators of the crop. He calls it a vineyard here, using a symbol that could hardly fail to be recognized. Had not David complained that the vine God brought out of Egypt, his chosen people, was now laid waste, so that the passers-by plucked off its grapes? Had not Isaias sung, in the name of the God who spoke by him, a song concerning his vineyard—the vineyard that was so carefully planted and fenced in, with tower to guard it and wine-press to receive the fruits of it—the vineyard that was expected to bring forth grapes, and only brought forth wild grapes? That passage must have sprung to the minds of our Lord's hearers. And when he went on to mention the hedge and the tower and the wine-press there could be no further doubt about it: "Listen! He is talking about us! At last, with no pretence of concealment, he is talking about us!" And the servants who had been stoned and beaten and cast out of the vineyard, who could they be but the old prophets, the prophets whose tombs the Pharisees built so eagerly, yet not without some twinges of conscience about the attitude of their fathers who had been the prophets' murderers? Chance after chance was given you, our Lord tells them, message after message was sent to turn you back from your sinful ways, and this was the use you made of your opportunities! They could hardly deny the argument, but where was it leading to?

Therefore, having yet one son, most dear to him, he also sent him unto them last of all, saying, "They will reverence my son".[2] What does he mean? Just for a moment the listeners are taken aback, and then it dawns on them what the words involve. Oh, they understand then what the new Prophet claimed to be. And what did they do about it? They crucified him. "Because he made himself the Son of God"—it was this parable of the wicked husbandmen that formed the case of his accusers at his trial. The parable says, "You Jews have again and again been given a fresh chance, and every time you have shown yourselves unworthy of it. Now is the supreme test; now you must decide what to do with the Son of God." And they crucified him. Was ever a nation given fairer warning? Did ever murderers act so completely with their eyes open? But, remember, that was not all the parable. That he made himself the Son of God was the charge preferred against him, but

[1] Luke 20. 9-16.   [2] Luke. 20 13.

there was further motive for their hatred in the words with which our Lord concluded: *He will come and destroy those husbandmen, and will give the vineyard to others.* To others! To Gentiles! What has Nicodemus, what has Joseph of Arimathaea to say in defence of that? Away with him, away with him, crucify him!

We must be thoughtless indeed if we fail to recognize in the history of his dealings with his chosen people the unutterable patience of God. First one prophet then another called, trained, sent on his errand; first one calamity then another brought upon the rebellious land; first one deliverance and then another wrought when deliverance seemed impossible: and always the people return to their sins and forget their covenant. And now at last the sands have run dry. There shall be one more mission; and the emissary this time is eternal God himself. It is kill or cure: Israel is at the crisis of its long hesitation: *surely they will reverence my Son.* But no; you can see from the very beginning of our Lord's ministry which way the decision is to be. Seeing they see not, and hearing they hear not, neither do they understand. Why is that? Surely it is not hard to see. With each fresh rejection of God's messengers the habit of rebellion has grown deeper into the Jewish heart; act after act of apostasy has moulded their character until it is ready for the greatest apostasy of all. It is never too late for repentance. The Jews might have welcomed as a people the chance so many individual Jews welcomed, to repent and return to God; but, from the habit their history had formed in them, it was all but certain that they would fail at the test.

And that, surely, is God's way with sinners under the new dispensation too. His patience seems infinite; again and again he gives them the chance of retrieving the past, nor, as each motion of grace is refused, does the succeeding one become fainter or weaker. On the contrary, if you consider how the Jews' last chance was also their best chance, since almighty God came down from heaven to bring them back to himself, you may even find reason for supposing that, the further the sinner strays, the more powerful are the motions of grace that woo him back again. But God does not interfere with the composition of our natures, and the composition of our natures is such that our good habits and our bad habits alike grow in response to every act which exercises them. You pass easily from one venial sin to another: each time, the habitual grace that is at work in you resists, and you overpower its resistance. The grace does not lessen as the weeks go by, but the habit that is impressing itself on your character becomes more deeply engraved with each succeeding failure. The first messenger to the vineyard is beaten by the husbandmen, the second wounded, the third killed. And then, at last, comes the crucial temptation, a temptation to mortal sin; and with it comes grace, we know that, grace sufficient to resist it; a stronger impulse of grace than we have yet known. But the habit is there, the facility for going in the wrong direction, and how often habit conquers! Transfer all that process to the case of a soul that has already lost first grace by mortal sin, fallen back on the merciful promptings of actual grace as its only protection against temptation, disobeys, again and again, that prompting. Its last chance comes at the hour of death; the habit of impenitence has grown; the last temptation, that to final impenitence, lies before it. Who shall say what tides of grace flow into that heart, what prayers the Mother of Sorrows offers for its conversion? But the habit is there. . . . From an ill end, from the power of the devil, deliver us, O Lord.

There is another parable whose main thesis is closely allied to that of the husbandmen, the parable of the fig-tree. The fig-tree, after all its careful tending and the anxious expectations of its owner, remains fruitless. Cut it down, he says: why cumbereth it the ground?[1] And it adds terribly to the point of this parable, in which the fig-tree clearly represents the Jewish nation, that our Lord, as you will remember, did actually cause a fig-tree outside Jerusalem to wither away when he found no fruit on it, as if in testimony against the people which had rejected him. But notice that here we have a new character, the gardener. He withstands the owner's suggestion, and urges that the tree should be allowed to stand one year more, till he has digged it about and dunged it; till he has made every effort that could be made to restore its fruitfulness. I think there can be little doubt that this gardener is our Lord in his sacred humanity, pleading to his Father for the people of the Old Covenant. What effort did he spare to effect that purpose? What avenue of repentance did he not open to his rebellious subjects? And he pleaded for them to the last: "Abba, Father, all things are possible to thee; remove this chalice from me." Was there no thought there for Judas, no thought there for his persecutors, whose torches even now glimmered among the trees in the distance?—surely the gardener of the parable is the Gardener who watched in Gethsemani.

If St Luke's arrangement of events is at all significant, this parable was spoken immediately after the question raised about the Galileans, whose blood Pilate mingled with their sacrifices, and the eighteen men

[1] Luke 13. 6-7.

upon whom the tower fell in Siloe.[1] Was it to be supposed that these people were especially sinful, to deserve such a fate? Our Lord answers no, and adds, "Except you do penance, you shall all likewise perish". It is not the bodily death that matters, it is the dispositions of the soul that meets it; and the sinner who, given time for repentance, fails to use the opportunity, is no better off than if he had been thus suddenly plunged into eternity. And then comes the parable of the fig-tree, warning us that there is a limit to the long-suffering patience of almighty God. But it seems, from what we hear of the gardener, that there is room for intercession to prolong the date of the divine tolerance. That is a point surely of some importance. Can it be that our prayers avail to win for the sinner a space in which to repent?

They can. Two other parables, little known and perhaps less understood, throw some light on the difficulty we all feel at times as to how human prayer can alter the purposes—so it appears—of eternal God. The importunate friend managed to borrow the loaves he asked for, although the householder was already abed, merely by his importunity.[2] The poor widow succeeded by the same means in securing redress for her son's wrongs even at the hands of an unjust judge.[3] Why, we ask, should God be compared to a rather unwilling and unneighbourly friend; why, above all, to an unjust judge who neither feared God nor regarded man? The answer, I think, is what we are looking for: in both these parables importunity secures something which the nature of the circumstances does not seem to warrant. Does not that mean that our prayers are really allowed to alter the course of events into something other than might have been expected? God foresaw from all eternity the offering of those prayers; there is no real change, then, in the divine purpose, but our prayers have done something. Importunity has prevailed.

We ought to remember that theological truth when we consider the parable of the fig-tree. Not only the Gardener, who is our Lord himself, can intercede for sinners; we, too, through his merits can help to prolong the patience of God. Think of us, if you like, as children who have been allowed, each of us, a tiny little patch of the great garden to cultivate, a few souls here and there for whom our prayers are allowed to win grace. Read the lives of those chosen souls that lived very close to God, such lives as St Catherine's of Siena, or Gemma Galgani's, and see how they wrestled with God, you would almost say bullied him, to effect the conversion of the most hardened sinners. Our prayers, God knows, must have little weight in comparison, but

[1] Luke 13. 4.   [2] Luke 11. 5-10.   [3] Luke 18. 2-5.

they have *some* weight. You look round at the world, and see sin unpunished and virtue unrewarded, and you would think that God slept, took no responsibility for the harvest of what he has sown; but we know better. He does not, as a rule, interfere with us by outward evidence of his power and clear advertisements of our peril; but within stubborn human hearts, the hearts that despite his messengers and crucify the Son of God afresh, the merciful influence of his grace is still working; still ready to work, if we will intercede for it.

7

PROBATION

But God said to him, Thou fool, this night do they require thy soul of thee.— Luke 12. 20.

So much for the patience of God, his terrifying mercy. He does not cut us down at once as soon as we have consented to sin, but waits to give us space for repentance, sends us warnings to correct, and grace to counteract the sinful habits we have formed, allows the intercessions of others to prevail in putting off the evil day, and finally, when by our own fault we have succumbed to the supreme temptation, rejected the supreme offer of renewal, abandons us and leaves us to go to our own place. All that means that our lives here are granted us under particular conditions of tenure, which we are accustomed to call probation. God acts, you might almost say, like a father or mother who deliberately leaves a child alone for a while to see how it will behave; we are on our good behaviour, we are being put to the test. Not that God needs any experimental test to probe our characters or to read our destiny; he knows, has known from all eternity, the dispositions and the future of every soul he has created. Man's earthly career is not a test God needs for his information, but objectively it is a test. We are put here to declare by our conduct where it is that we want to spend eternity.

The parable of the ten virgins[1] is very different from those we have hitherto been considering. In the first place, because it has nothing to

[1] Matthew 25. 1-12.

do with the issue between Jew and Gentile, with Jewish expectations about the Kingdom. In the second place, although, as St Gregory suggests, the kingdom of heaven here must be the Church militant, not the Church triumphant, yet the interest of the parable certainly centres round the final judgment. Our Lord has been asked privately by his disciples what will be the sign of his second coming, and he has answered them in a way which clearly means—whatever else his much-disputed words do mean—that it is of the very nature of that coming to be sudden and unexpected, and therefore it is no good asking him for precise information, which it would be contrary to his divine purpose to bestow. Then he illustrates this by the comparison of servants, waiting for their master's return from a journey, some of them watchfully and faithfully, some of them in a spirit of carelessness and disobedience, as if taking advantage of his absence. His sudden return is compared to the sudden return of the Son of Man to revisit the world in which he has left us to work out our probation.[1]

And then follows this very difficult parable. I say difficult, because there are at least three theories of its interpretation, all of them backed by the names of great doctors. We have not time to consider them all, and I must content myself with saying that I am understanding the parable here, in its broad outlines, as it was understood by St Chrysostom or St Gregory. The ten virgins represent the Church, or the Church as it will be at the time of the last judgment; virginity being used here to imply merely the special dedication to God which Christians, as such, are bound to profess. And the lamps which all the ten carry represent the illumination we receive in baptism, which is frequently alluded to in St Paul's Epistles, the same illumination which is also symbolized by the paschal candle and by the lighted candle which is given to the sponsor in the baptismal ceremony. And the bridegroom tarried, did not come as soon as he was expected. How often, in the history of the Church, men have looked for the second coming of Christ as something immediately imminent, and have been disappointed! Without giving his disciples any assurance that might lead to lack of watchfulness on their part, our Lord thus gently indicates that the time of his tarrying, of the Church's waiting will be relatively long. And the effect is that all ten virgins, wise as well as foolish, slumber and sleep. The sleep is simply carrying out the idea on which our Lord has laid such emphasis in the preceding chapter, that the advent will be sudden as the advent of a thief in the night; we shall, please God, be prepared for it, but we shall not be expecting it. Their eyes have been

[1] Mark 13. 34-37.

long strained, looking down the road through the darkness for the bridegroom's coming; it is no fault of theirs that they become drowsy and fall asleep.

And when he comes, they all spring up to meet him. Now, surely, the just will shine like the sun in the kingdom of their Father; and, for every lamp there, a tongue of fire will shoot up, that the bride and bridegroom may pass through an avenue of illumination. But no, something has gone wrong, some precaution has been neglected. On one side the flare is only momentary; the dry wicks sputter, the flame flickers, smoulders, and dies down. And they have no oil in their vessels, those virgins. What is to be done? Well, at least they have lamps, at least they have wicks, can they not borrow the accessory they need from the other virgins' store? No; their expectations have been too sanguine; there is not enough to go round. And if they go away now to buy oil, they will miss the wedding-feast and find the door shut in their faces.

The bridegroom to whom they are dedicated, the bridegroom for whom they carry those baptismal lamps, greets them with the words: "Amen I say to you, I know you not". St Matthew alone has preserved this parable for us, but there is a passage in the thirteenth chapter of St Luke which is clearly to be regarded as a kind of pendant to it. "But when the master of the house shall be gone in and shall shut the door, you shall begin to stand without and knock . . . and he shall say to you: I know you not whence you are. Then you shall begin to say: We have eaten and drunk in thy presence, and thou hast taught in our streets. And he shall say to you: I know you not whence you are. Depart from me, all ye workers of iniquity." The Church has familiarized us with our Lord's sacred presence, she has taught us her saving doctrines, but—that is not everything. What was wrong, then, with the five foolish virgins? They had the lamp of baptism, they had the wick of faith, all beautifully trimmed; they lacked the oil to feed it with—charity, the gift of sanctifying grace. Some people ask why faith should matter at all as long as we do God's will. They might as well ask why an oil lamp should not burn without a wick. Here we are dealing with people who have kept faith and lost charity, and expect their lamps to burn just as brightly without the mysterious unction of habitual grace. And Christ says, "I know you not". He denies them before the angels, as they, in their actions, have denied him before men. What is to be done? They turn to others in their need, to Mary and the saints; but it is too late; even those merits, even Mary's merits, cannot supply them with the oil of charity. And the door was shut.

None of them were expecting the last judgment, but some, and only some, were ready for it. The lesson is the same for all of us, though God should see fit to take us to himself by the ordinary visitation of bodily death. He does not reveal to most of us what he sometimes reveals to his saints, the day or the hour of that visitation; it will come upon us without much warning; it is as if we slumbered and slept while the bridegroom tarries. That is part of our probation. It will find some of us ready to spring up and greet their Lord, but only those who are in a state of habitual grace, who have bought for themselves the oil of charity before it is too late. When once the terrible moment of decision has passed, not all the prayers of Paradise will avail us: as the tree falls it will lie. "That, as he believed and hoped in thee", so run the words of the burial prayer. It is right that we should commend the faithful in a special way to the mercy of the God in whose presence they have eaten and drunk, who has taught in their streets; but it is possible to have kept the faith, to know where to turn in hours of spiritual need, and yet to find the door shut and the sentence pronounced, *I know not whence you are.*

The parable of Dives and Lazarus gives us the same warning under a different figure. Clearly, as St Gregory points out, Dives and Lazarus are representatives of the Jew and the Gentile:[1] Dives enjoys his good things, the privileges of the Old Covenant, and is unwilling to share them with the Gentile, the beggar at his gate. His purple and fine linen are the pride and hypocrisy, the outward seeming of piety, which brought upon the Jewish race as a whole, and upon some Jews as individuals, their rejection. It is otherwise with Lazarus, who lies there full of sores; it is the external appearance which is the worst part about him—the open sores are in truth less deadly than the hidden wounds which rankle under the Pharisee's purple. And the beggar dies, and is carried to Abraham's bosom. Why Abraham's bosom? "Many shall come from the east and the west, and shall sit down with Abraham and Isaac and Jacob in the kingdom of God." That is why. The vineyard, as we have heard, is to be given over to other husbandmen; it is the despised Gentiles who will prove to be the true children of Abraham. And the children of the kingdom will be cast out. Dives, the Jewish race, so highly privileged and so little worthy of its privileges, will be the beggar this time, and his prayers will be unavailing, not because of any want of charity upon Lazarus' part, but because Dives has banished himself beyond the reach of belief. Nor, as a race, will the Jewish race ever learn from its failures. *If they hear not Moses and the prophets, neither*

[1] Luke 16. 19-31.

will they believe if one rose again from the dead. The Jews have had their chance, their probation is over now, and the punishment for their neglect of the warnings already given them will be to be left in their blindness. And, indeed, one did rise from the dead, and still the Jews would not understand.

If this parable applies allegorically to the probation of the Jewish race, it applies with even more strictness to our probation as individuals. It belongs to this life only. As the foolish virgins could not borrow oil from the wise, as Dives could not secure relief in hell even from the charitable offices of Lazarus, so the soul that has passed out of the body unforgiven will be able to derive no benefit from the suffrages of the Church or of the saints. *Between us and you there is fixed a great chaos,* the unbridged gulf that lies between eternal happiness and eternal misery.

There is another warning, another assurance, which comes to us from this parable. Dives asks that Lazarus may be sent to his five brethren, to tell them, what Dives himself now knows to his cost, the conditions of our life here and our life beyond; if one went to them from the dead, he says, they will do penance. And the answer is, that they have already Moses and the prophets; they have every chance of repenting if they will; a special dispensation from heaven would not alter their decision. Every one of us has sufficient grace given him, sufficient to enable him to do penance if he would. And yet we find it so hard to believe that! We think of the sinners who have been converted by coming in contact with the great saints, and seeing miracles done by them; or we think of the instances in which God has pulled up a sinner and drawn him to penance by some providence that struck across his life; and how we wish that that particular sinner, in whom we are so interested, could be given the same chance of restoration! And the answer is, *They have Moses and the prophets:* the sinner has sufficient grace, and greater graces still would not be efficacious, where their present grace fails from lack of co-operation. We are given a whole lifetime for our probation: so many years, so many weeks, so many days; it will be useless to complain that we were not given more. And we were given the graces we needed, the admonitions proper to God's call upon our lives; there, too, it will be useless to complain that more was not given us. At the final judgment we shall know that.

It is an uncomfortable thought that in both these two parables the people who meet with rejection deserve it simply by carelessness. The foolish virgins clearly did not know, when they started out, that their stock of oil had run so low; they thought they were in as good a position as their neighbours. And we are not told of any specially grave sin that Dives committed; pride, hypocrisy, self-satisfaction, the leaven of the Pharisees, brought him to the pass we know of. His purple had blinded his eyes to his spiritual needs, while Lazarus' running sores were enough to keep him in mind of his spiritual infirmities. It is not enough simply to know, as a theological proposition, that we are on our probation here; we have to apply that knowledge and live in the light of it. There are so many other things to be done in the world, so many echoes that deafen us, that we are apt to forget the first principle of our probation, which is this: that the most important moment of our lives, the moment around which all the rest of our life ought to be grouped as its centre and its climax, is the moment when we leave it.

Our Lord has called our attention to that in a story which is ordinarily described as a parable, though in fact it is not a parable at all, the story of the rich fool. It is not really a parable, I say, because it is of the essence of a parable that it draws a certain comparison, or at least a certain proportion between an external fact and a spiritual truth; here we have no comparison, only a warning in the form of an anecdote. Unless, indeed, the rich fool is yet another type of the Jewish people, with the shadow of the destruction of Jerusalem hanging over it. He has had a good year, and as he sits over his fire and sips his glass of wine he thinks whether he would not be well advised to put some more of the profits back into the business. He will pull down his barns and build greater, so that next year he may hold up some of the harvest till prices rise, instead of having to sell it off because he cannot store it. For the moment it will involve some pinching and management, this policy of expansion; for the moment he will have to deny himself a few luxuries: but afterwards! When the enhanced prices tell on the market! Then he will really be able to retire from the business and begin to live. And then the whisper comes to him, *Thou fool! This night do they require thy soul of thee.* All those years he has worked like an evangelist, pinched himself like a contemplative, simply for what it will mean in his old age—and that old age is never coming. If he had bethought himself of spiritual riches; if in the life of the soul he had shown that energy in hoarding all his resources, not resting content with one victory achieved, but labouring to make it the foundation of fresh victories to come, he might have welcomed the message, or at least bowed to his fate.

The real commercial equivalent of our life on earth is not so much pleasure, so much fame, so much love from those around us, so much attractiveness to our neighbours, but so much done for God. We are on our trial; there is a term to our effort, a limit to our opportunity. And the time is short and the end sudden. Blessed are those servants whom the Lord, when he cometh, shall find watching.

8

REPROBATION

I say to you that many shall come from the east and the west, and shall sit down with Abraham and Isaac and Jacob in the kingdom of heaven: but the children of the kingdom shall be cast out into the exterior darkness.—Matthew 8. 11.

I HAVE already suggested that, as time went on and as the shadow of his Passion drew nearer, our Lord used less economy in his announcements about the coming of the kingdom, explained his meaning more openly, so that even the blindness of his enemies and his critics could no longer fail to penetrate its secret. This is particularly so in the matter with which we are here concerned, the rejection of the Jewish race; their removal as a race from the position of honour and of responsibility to which God had called them when he made them the guardians of his oracles. The parable of the wicked husbandmen, that of the two sons, that of the labourers in the vineyard, were all part of the final phase in our Lord's teaching. And, if we are to follow St Matthew's order, so also is the parable of the wedding-feast. I do not see any reason to doubt that it is the same parable as that recorded in the fourteenth chapter of St Luke (the Great Supper); and, therefore, if we had only St Luke to guide us, we might have supposed that it came a good deal earlier in the course of our Lord's ministry. But since in St Luke it follows immediately on two other quite unconnected sayings about being bidden to a feast, it is surely probable that St Luke, here as often, is grouping his matter by subjects rather than by the order of time. I think we may take it, then, that by the time he speaks these words our Lord is beginning to make an almost open announcement of his programme, no longer concerned to baffle the watchfulness of his opponents, or to give them an excuse for their blindness, now that his last hours on earth are approaching.

It is a very human parable, this. There are two stages in the process of calling the guests to the feast. They are *invited* first of all, presumably without definite notice of date, and we must suppose, therefore, that they accept. That is clear, I think, from St Luke's account; the invitation is one thing, the calling another. The guests, then, did what we often do: they accepted the invitation when it was provisionally issued, and then, when the actual notice of date came round, repented of their acceptance and retracted it. And each—it is a human touch—has a different excuse; each, no doubt, is prepared to criticize scornfully the excuses offered by the others.

There can be no doubt, I suppose, that this first part of the parable refers primarily to the Jews. God has made a covenant with their fore-fathers by which they are to be his people and he is to be their God; that is the accepted invitation, which binds him in faithfulness to summon them first into the kingdom of his Son, binds them in faithfulness to respond with alacrity to the summons. First of all he sends round a sort of reminder, *he sent his servants to call them that were invited, and they would not come*; already the chosen people have repented of their acceptance. That is when God sent his prophets to school the Jews into suitable dispositions for receiving the final revelation, and they showed themselves unwilling scholars. And now the beeves and the fatlings are killed, and all is ready—the time has come when, in the inscrutable providence of God, it has been ordained that the old offerings of the Levitical covenant should be abolished, when the Old Law would be superseded by that ineffable marriage between things human and things divine, the Incarnation. And the invited guests, the Jews, refuse point-blank. They too have got their excuses, and a whole crop of different excuses. The people who rejected and crucified our Lord were not all Pharisees. There were the Pharisees, with their blind traditional interpretations of the law, their hatred of everything Gentile—they could not accept Christ, because he encouraged the Gentiles, and ate with publicans and sinners. There were also the Zealots, the National Party, who were ready to support our Lord only up to the time when they discovered that his kingdom was not of this world, his warfare not against the Roman oppressor. And there were the Sadducees, who conformed to all they knew of pagan culture and held liberal views about Scripture and the Law; and to them (to Caiphas, for instance) our Lord is a political menace. And each thinks the others' excuses inadequate. The Pharisee and the Sadducee think the Zealot a fanatic; the Pharisee and the Zealot think the Sadducee worldly; the Sadducee and the Zealot think the Pharisee an obscurantist; but, fanatics or worldlings or obscurantists, they all crucify Christ.

And, St Matthew adds, they laid hands on the servants who brought the message and put them to death: the messengers this time are our Lord himself and his apostles, whom the Jews persecuted. And the king sent his armies and destroyed those murderers and burnt their city—Jerusalem was destroyed by the Romans only a year or two after the martyrdom of St Peter and St Paul. There is the Jewish background to the picture.

And it has a lesson for many people today; I mean, of course, for those to whom the claim of the Catholic Church has been fully proposed, so that their refusal of the invitation is culpable. That, surely, is guaranteed to us by the mention of the first, preliminary invitation which is accepted, but with an acceptance which is afterwards cancelled; we are dealing here with people who are definitely acting with their eyes open. And yet, of course, they have their own excuses. One has family reasons, one is too young to decide yet, one too old to make a move now, one has no time to think it out, one has not the brains to go into the historical questions—but they are all rejecting the call of Christ's Church. And they laugh at one another's reasons for not being Catholics. "If I believed what A does about the Pope I would go tomorrow." "If I could believe in eternal punishment, like B, I would never dream of staying where I am." And, worse than that, sometimes, "If I were as young as C, as free from family ties as D, as simple-minded and uneducated as E, as little connected with Anglicanism by my early training as F, I would not think twice about it." If only some power would give them the gift to their own excuses as others see them, as they themselves see the excuses of others!

The Jews had rejected their God; God rejects his people. Those empty places at the marriage-feast must be filled somehow, and the servants are sent out, first into the streets and lanes of the city, then into the the highways and hedges, to bring in the poor and the feeble and the blind and the lame. There are, I suppose, two separate stages there, representing two separate stages in the preaching of the apostles; they went first to the proselytes of Judaism, and then, fired especially by St Paul's example, to these Gentiles that knew not God. They are poor, the Gentiles, like Lazarus at Dives' gate; feeble, like children, tossed to and fro and carried about by every wind of doctrine; blind, for they sit in darkness and the shadow of death, groping about after God if haply they may feel after him and find him; lame, because nature without grace is lame, but the time is coming when the lame man shall leap as a hart. The Jews have so long been accustomed to being the sole beneficiaries of God's covenant with man that it seems incredible to them now that God should be able to do without them. But he can. "I say to you that God is able out of these stones to raise up children to Abraham."[1] "Many shall come from the east and the west, and the children of the kingdom shall be cast out."[2] The same free grace that could separate Israel from all the nations of the earth could, when Israel proved unworthy, draw together from among all the nations of the earth, a new people, chartered with a new covenant, to fill the places of those surly guests, those disobedient sons, those neglectful husbandmen.

That fatal error on the part of the Jews has been repeated only too often in the history of nations. The emperors of Constantinople used to think that their support was essential to the Church. And there was a king once, who was given the title of Defender of the Faith. . . . And the French kings would fain be protectors of their own Church; and Gallicanism arose and died. Next to thinking that you can do without God the most dangerous mistake you can make is thinking that God cannot do without you. Individuals, too, can fall into it and have fallen into it; have imagined that their particular style of apologetic, their particular theories about the right relations between Church and world, their methods of devotion or of evangelization, are the only ones that can save the Church now; hugging that illusion, they are deaf to the appeals of other Catholics, no less anxious to get something done, but more cautious in their choice of weapons; and there is excommunication, and defiance, and apostasy. Take warning, all you without the Church who still shirk the eternal issue, from the men whose false consciences shut them out from the kingdom of Christ when it was first preached. Take warning, all you within the Church who would pose as her indispensable bulwarks, from the fate of the chosen people whose pride dared God to show that he could do without them: could, by other means, bring his unswerving purpose to its fulfilment.

But there is a further warning; a fresh rejection, this time within the confines of the kingdom, amid the gaiety and the splendour of the wedding-feast itself. The man without a wedding-garment was expected to have a wedding-garment; clearly from the whole context he is being blamed for neglecting some precaution which he might quite easily have taken. I cannot understand how it is that some commentators explain this marriage-feast as representing the eternal happiness of heaven. For there nothing unclean can come, nor anything that maketh a lie; God's judgments are not as man's judgments, that

[1] Matthew 3. 9.   [2] Luke 13. 29.

they should be reversed. The marriage-feast in our present parable is simply the Church, which bestows upon all its members the spiritual delights that flow from the hypostatic union of Manhood and Godhead in our Lord. But, as we know, in order to partake of those delights, it is necessary to be clothed in the wedding-garment of charity. The wedding-garment here is simply what the oil was in the parable of the virgins, sanctifying grace. Here are all the guests, sitting like olive branches about the Church's table—wild olive branches, as St Paul reminds us, that have been grafted into the stock of the good olive tree, when they were incorporated, at the summons of free grace, into the mystical body of Christ. All alike, you would think, have been destined to make full proof of the mercy of their divine benefactor.

But they are not really all alike. There is one man there who has not taken the trouble to come properly prepared. So in the Church, so in the Church's most solemn acts of worship, so at the very altar, there may be one who knows himself unworthy. His sins are hidden from all other human view; his fellow guests do not suspect or at least dare not question him. And then the king comes by, passing slowly down between the tables to see that his company have all they want. It is a terrible moment for the poor intruder, who tries to hide himself from observation as much as possible, lest the king should see anything amiss. "And when they heard the voice of the Lord God walking in Paradise at the afternoon air, Adam and his wife hid themselves from the face of the Lord God, amidst the trees of Paradise."[1] It is the same God that comes now. Comes, not in the terrors of the second advent, but veiled under the species of the blessed Eucharist, to give himself to the Church's children as their feast. *Judex crederis esse venturus* —yes, he will come; but does he not come among us now, all unseen, in the holy Eucharist, judging already the hearts of those that receive him?

There is one difficulty that has been raised by commentators which it would be well to consider in conclusion. Why is there only one man rejected among the whole company? And why, as if in flat contradiction to that, does our Lord add, "For many are called, but few chosen"? Does he wish us to understand that many will be saved, or few? I do not believe that the difficulty is a real one. The phrase "Many are called but few chosen" belongs properly to the case of those who reject the Church, the Ecclesia, not to those inside it. And if we compare the occurrence here with its occurrence at the end of the labourers in the vineyard, it becomes plain that it is to the first half of the parable

[1] Genesis 3. 8.

rather than the second that it refers. And if you ask why there was only one man without the wedding-garment, I would suggest that those words were spoken directly to one man among our Lord's audience, Judas Iscariot, who also betrayed him. Christ will give him one more warning yet, before he crowns his treason by a sin of sacrilegious communion. I do not think, therefore, that we can conclude anything from that about the number of the souls that will be rejected. Nor, on the other hand, do I think that there is any real information on this subject given in the words "few are chosen". "Many" and "few" are surely used here as meaning simply "a large number" and "a smaller number"; if you put it in modern mathematical language, it would be "n are called but $n-x$ are chosen". It is part of our probation that God will neither give excuse for carelessness nor temptation to despair by revealing to us the proportion between souls saved and souls lost.

9

REMISSION OF SINS

There shall be joy in heaven upon one sinner that doth penance, more than upon ninety-nine just who need not penance.—Luke 15. 7.

THE parable of the wedding-feast[1] is very closely allied with that of the prodigal son. But the wedding-feast might give us a false impression, a false scale of values, if it stood by itself. For it seems as if God's invitation to the Gentiles to come into his Church was issued only as an afterthought, because the Jews were found unworthy, just as the king bids the poor from the streets and the highways to come in only when he finds that the guests first invited have decided to cancel their acceptance. Is that a right way of looking at it? Was the inclusion of the Gentiles in the Church an afterthought, as it were, a second best, a desperate expedient to save an impossible situation? Such a conception would be unworthy at once of the divine prescience and of the divine omnipotence. We look about for some other parable to fill out the picture, to correct the imperfect impression, and we find it in what

[1] Matthew 22. 1-14.

is, with the good Samaritan, probably a favourite parable to most people, the story of the prodigal son.

The story itself is so familiar and told in such detail that there is little need to follow it in detail. Let us just remember the stages of it. First, the prodigal wastes all his substance, till he begins to be in want; he is living on a bare margin of income. Then, as if ill-luck dogged him, there is a great famine in the land he has made his home: he loses whatever means of livelihood he had, and comes down to a menial occupation. He is so poor now that he envies the very swine their food. Then he "returns to himself", and reflects that in his father's house he would fare better than this, though he were only a servant. He arises and goes to his father, asks for a servant's post and a servant's hire, and is given instead the first robe and the ring and shoes for his feet, and the fatted calf is killed in his honour. The elder brother comes in and protests; he has never been made much of in this way, although his behaviour has always shown those very good qualities his brother's lacked. And the answer is, "It was fit that we should make merry and be glad, for this thy brother was dead and is come to life again; he was lost and is found".

It is not likely that this was one of the parables in which our Lord's Jewish critics saw any hidden meaning. And modern authors have doubted whether this is one of the parables that refers to the issue between Jew and Gentile at all. It is, however, enough for me to quote the authority of St Jerome, St Augustine, and St Bernard when I say that to me it seems lucidly obvious that the elder son here is the Jewish people, and the younger son represents the Gentiles. Now, suppose some acute Jewish hearer to have been present, and to have realized, as he listened to the parable, that there was that hidden meaning behind it. One point must have struck him from the first with a sense of utter bewilderment and surprise, considering the historical tradition he had been brought up in.

It is a characteristic of our northern fairy-stories that it is always the youngest son who comes off best. It is always his business to set out and look for the two elder brothers and set them free from their enchantment, by finding the appropriate talisman that can help him to accomplish his quest. The two elder brothers, in all our northern stories, are the ne'er-do-weels; it is the youngest who carries off the princess. That is not so, as far as I know, in other mythologies; I can think of no instance in which the Greek legends thus reverse the principle of primogeniture. But Hebrew history, as the Scriptures have preserved it to us, corroborates entirely this guess, this instinct of us northerners; here again the youngest son comes to his own. Isaac is the child of promise, not Ishmael; Jacob, not Esau. Joseph has the dominion over his ten elder brothers, and when he brings his sons to be blessed by Jacob, Jacob deliberately blesses Ephraim first, although he is the younger, in spite of the father's protests. And we all know the story of David, the last of eleven sons, yet chosen out of them all to be king; Solomon, too, is preferred to his elder brother Adonias. St Paul explains it for us in his Epistle to the Romans.[1] God chooses the younger son so as to show that his election is of free grace, and not as of right. Now, imagine that Jewish listener when he hears our Lord speak of the man with two sons. Does he not at once leap to the conclusion that the younger son represents the chosen people? And then the parable goes on, and he realizes as it goes on that it is the other way round. History is reversed; it is Israel who is the elder brother, the Gentiles who are the younger brother this time. Yes, here is something to make him think.

The father in this parable is almighty God. And he is represented, I think we may say without hesitation, as an over-indulgent parent. Just as our Lord compares his Father to an unjust judge in order to emphasize the need of prayer, so he will compare him to a fond father in order to give us some idea of the depths there are in the divine mercy. And the two sons are Jew and Gentile. The Gentile also is called a son, because of what he will be in the kingdom of grace, although before that he has become, through the Fall, a child of wrath. After all, he is God's creature. And while the elder brother, the Jew, stays at home in the service of God, establishing as it were a right to his promised mercies, the Gentile sows his wild oats—makes bad use of the natural gifts and of whatever actual graces God bestows upon him, wanders far from the knowledge and the thought of God, lives carelessly on the very brink of hell. And then, even in that godless world to which the Gentile has banished himself, a famine arises. Pagan civilization, after a long period of civil wars and of brutal proscriptions, finds itself bankrupt. And the prodigal son begins to be in want; learns from his humiliation to crave for spiritual gifts; his very vices have grown stale and colourless. He was fain to fill his belly, and no man gave unto him. We met that phrase before. Lazarus at the rich man's gate desired to be filled with the crumbs, and no one did give him. Can we doubt that the two parables refer to the same situation? The Gentiles *have* begun to be conscious of their bankruptcy in our Lord's time; their poets will tell you of an age turned upside down, in which they have already

[1] Romans, ch. 9.

expiated enough the sins of their ancestors; that they are worse than their forefathers, and still on the downgrade; that there can be no escape from their misery unless they set sail for some fabulous Islands of the Blessed, where a Golden Age will be restored to them. Oh yes, they know their failure. God grant that a later generation, no less conscious of its need, may find the remedy by which alone that need can be satisfied!

And grace comes, and brings the Gentile world back to its Creator. No sacrifices are demanded of them, such as they might have expected; they are to rank side by side with the children of the covenant; "they shall return as strangers, they shall remain as sons". Nay, a better portion has been reserved for them than was ever given to their elder brother under the old dispensation; as at Cana, the best is reserved till now. And they began to be merry.

And, meanwhile, what of the elder son? Perhaps because this parable was spoken earlier in our Lord's ministry, before the Jews had forfeited their chance; perhaps because, after all, Jew as well as Gentile was to enter the Church—our Lady and the apostles were Jews—the position of the chosen people is not represented here as it was in the other parables. We hear nothing of their refusals of grace, their stoning of the prophets. Christ is content to take their own point of view, and represent them as sons who have been faithful in all things: he will put the best interpretation upon their formal, external attachment to the religion of their fathers. Jew and Gentile are invited to the same feast; only, will the Jew be willing? The elder brother calls one of the servants —St Paul, perhaps—and asks him what all the feasting means, and hears that it is in honour of the Gentile world redeemed. Will he consent to come in? He must pocket his pride, forget his exclusiveness, ask no questions about merit now that it is the hour of grace. But if he will, then the family is to be reunited; there will be neither Jew nor Greek, bond nor free.

And the theological principle is clearly the same as that expressed in the two similitudes that come immediately before this: the lost sheep and the lost piece of silver. "There shall be joy in heaven upon one sinner that doth penance, more than upon ninety-nine just who need not penance." That, surely, is a curious point of view. Are we to suppose that our Lord is giving countenance here to the illusion of those Protestants who will tell you that the forgiven sinner is a finer character than the soul that has kept its first innocence; that Mary Magdalen should claim higher honours than Mary the Mother of God? From a multitude of New Testament evidence we know that it cannot be so. The just persons who appear to have no need of penance are those who, to their own anxious peril, regard themselves as justified by their own merits. But there is no need to labour this point here; we shall meet it again in discussing the parable of the Pharisee and the Publican, and the conditions requisite for penance. It is Jew against Gentile, works against grace. A higher critic might easily suspect these parables of having been influenced by the teaching of St Paul.

Meanwhile, the moral application of the parable is too plain to need exposition, too beautiful to need commendation. Yes, the unhappy soul has sinned; has started out with great graces, forestalling, as it were, by a single draft on the Treasury of the divine Mercy all the supernatural aid it could expect in a lifetime. There is nothing more, surely, that it can expect, if it fails to make good this time. And yet the old habits cling; and, as it has abused lesser graces before, so now it abuses these greater privileges; it wanders far from the memory of God, throws away its chances, courts the occasions of sin. You have known some such soul, perhaps—some habitual sinner to whom God has given a fresh start, set him on his feet again, by a signal act of mercy, it may be, by conversion to the true Church. And all that has been wasted, and the soul has gone back to the riotous living and the pigsty. And then some breath of grace pursues it: the echo of a prayer, the thought of death, a word heard at random, just when the bankruptcy of its worldly pleasures has cast it back upon itself.

> "Ah must—
> Designer Infinite!
> Ah must thou char the wood ere thou canst limn with it?
> My freshness spent its wavering flower i' the dust,
> And now my heart is as a broken fount,
> Wherein tear-drippings stagnate, spilt down ever
> From the dank thoughts that shiver
> Upon the sighful branches of my mind.
> Now of that long pursuit
> Comes on, at hand, the bruit;
> That voice is round me like a bursting sea:
> And is thy earth so marred,
> Shattered in shard on shard?
> Lo, all things fly thee, for thou fliest me!"

I will arise and go to my father, and will say to him, Father, I have sinned against heaven and before thee; I am not worthy to be called thy son; make me as one of thy hired servants. As a hired servant the

¹ Francis Thompson, "The Hound of Heaven".

soul enters the confessional; as a son it comes forth. The white robe of charity restored, shoes upon our feet to walk the world's ways bravely once again; the ring of absolution that marks us sons in our Father's house, affiances us to God! Oh, mercy not to be measured by any standard of human mercy, for our judgments are at fault, and our indulgence blind, and our forgiveness grudging. Oh, happiness not to be compared with any human happiness, for our satisfaction is but momentary, and our loves grow old, and our delights wither and decay. *O felix culpa, quae talem ac tantum meruit habere Redemptorem; quae tantam ac talem meruit habere Redemptionem!* There may be scornful eyes that watch us, bitter tongues that complain of so much charity wasted on the ne'er-do-weel, prophesy fresh falls and keep the record of our sins indelible; but it is our Father's forgiveness, not theirs, we come to cry for, as it was his Majesty, not their self-righteousness our sins offended. Go to other religions and they will promise you sin condoned, sin discounted, sin explained away: only as Christians do we understand, only in the confessional do we experience that divine contradiction, sin forgiven.

10

GRACE AND GOOD WORKS

Jesus said to them, Amen I say to you that the publicans and the harlots shall go into the kingdom of God before you.—Matthew 21. 31.

Two parables, one recorded only by St Matthew, the other only by St Luke, seem designed to act as pendants to that of the prodigal son. The story of the two sons, from which the above words are taken, naturally recalls to us the elder and the younger brother which we have just been considering. And the story of the Pharisee and the publican is associated in most of our minds with that same contrast between pride and self-abasement, between respectability and heart-felt penitence, which emerges also from the conversation after the prodigal's return. And the general drift of both stories is the same—it is not necessarily the people you expect to join the Church who do join the Church, not necessarily the people who had the best chance of reaching heaven who do reach heaven. But there is also a very important difference between them; in fact, it seems natural to suppose that our Lord meant them to be complementary, balancing each other, as I shall try to point out. Let us take the better-known story, that of the Pharisee and the publican, first.

We must notice this about the Pharisee's account of himself; it was not untrue or exaggerated, and it was a good account to be able to give. He really was not extortionate or unjust, really had more notion of self-respect than the publican, and did practise his religion. He fasted twice in the week; he gave tithes of all he possessed. And I make no doubt that the publican was a bad man. He fawned on the rich people and bullied the poor people, and fleeced both; and when he put his head round the corner of an alley all the children ran away from him shouting "Here comes the rent!" And the extraordinary thing is that we don't find anything put down here about his good resolutions for the future. St Matthew, when he was called, forsook all his gains and followed Christ. Zacchaeus, when he was converted, gave half of his goods to the poor and offered fourfold restitution for every sin he had committed against justice. This publican says nothing of the kind. He simply goes on beating his breast, bowing towards the earth, and repeating "God be merciful to me a sinner". And yet he goes to his house justified rather than the Pharisee—and all because of an attitude of mind. The one is good and knows it, the other is bad and knows it; and it is not what they are that makes the difference, but their knowledge of what they are. A strange story.

Knowing what we do of our Lord's attitude towards the Pharisees generally and towards the publicans generally, we can hardly doubt that the two men represent whole classes of men; the Pharisee standing for the Jews, and especially the strict Jews; the publican for the Gentiles, or all those who, whether Jews or Gentiles, had nothing to hope for from the promises of the Old Covenant as the views of our Lord's day understood them. Like the elder brother, like the Pharisee, the Jew has been, at least since the Captivity, faithful to what he knew of God's calling for him; only, self-centredness has turned to self-consciousness, and self-consciousness to self-congratulation; and self-congratulation has crystallized itself in its most odious form, contempt of his neighbour. Like the prodigal, like the publican, the Gentile has made the most of this world, has given himself over, as if by deliberate calculation, to the pursuit of sin; only, godlessness has turned to the craving for God, and the craving for God has turned to God-fearingness, and God-fearingness has taken its most salutary form, the contrite and the humble heart that men may despise, but not God. Now, remember,

F

the prodigal's elder brother was not cast out into the exterior darkness; and our Lord does not say that the Pharisee left the temple with *no* answer to his prayer: only there was *more* joy in heaven upon one sinner that did penance, only the publican was justified *rather* than the Pharisee. It's the sinner that finds it *easier* to believe and to be saved—that is all.

Does our Lord, then, give countenance to antinomianism? Does he treat salvation as if it depended entirely upon an attitude of mind, and our actions made no difference one way or the other? I suppose it was for fear that corollary should be drawn that our Lord saw fit to give us the other parable—that of the two sons. A very simple story it is: each is asked to go into the vineyard; one says "I will not", but afterwards is moved with repentance and goes; the other says "I go, sir", and does not go after all.[1]

The application of this parable is decided, not only by the fact that it comes immediately before the wicked husbandmen, but by the words with which our Lord sums up: *Amen I say to you that the publicans and the harlots shall go into the kingdom of God before you. For John came to you in the way of justice, and you did not believe him, but the publicans and the harlots believed him: but you, seeing it, did not even afterwards repent, that you might believe him.*[2] This is one of the final parables; it is spoken to those Jews who have had their chance and missed it, failed in their probation. The Jewish race is pledged to watch for the coming of the Christ, and to receive him when he comes; he came to his own, and his own did not receive him; the publicans and the harlots, either Gentiles, or Jews who had utterly lost caste, repented and went into the kingdom. The vineyard, as we shall have occasion to notice later, is the Church of Christ, and the Church of Christ viewed as the theatre of hard work and painful striving. The other parables might have made our Lord's hearers suppose that anybody entirely lacking in merit, like the men from the streets and the highways—anybody sufficiently disreputable, like the publican—was sure to find admission into the kingdom of God, where all would be feasting and making merry, like the prodigal's home-coming feast. Now we see that that is not so; that would be a caricature of the whole doctrine of grace. Jew and Gentile alike are called upon to undertake a laborious, it may be an heroic task; it is the free consent of their wills that is asked, and it is by free acceptance and free refusal that they seal their own destinies. And the kingdom into which they are called is not to be a kingdom of rest and reward, but a kingdom of striving and of meriting.

[1] Matthew 21. 28-31.   [2] Matthew 21. 31-32.

These two parables, then, are a pair; their subject is the same, but they are to complement and correct each other. People will tell you that repentance is merely a feeling, and in itself valueless; at best sentimental, at worst hypocritical; the morality of our actions is our only title to the Christian name and the Christian dignity. Show them the parable of the Pharisee and the publican, and prove to them that they are wrong; point out that the man who had no merits to show for his past life, but could only beat on the breast and cry God mercy, went to his house justified rather than the other; the other with his strictness of moral observance, his generosity, his mortifications. And show them that the justification here was not dependent on good resolutions or promises to turn over a new leaf; there is no word of resolutions or of promises: it is the mere attitude of the heart that is the passport to divine mercy.

And here the Calvinist sees his chance. "Precisely", he says, "but you Catholics do not teach that." The meaning of the story is as plain as it could possibly be. There is the Pharisee, full of good works, really an excellent man, but only an excellent reprobate, if you understand what I mean. None of these good deeds will avail him.

> Priest, doctor, hermit, monk grown white
> With prayer, the broken-hearted nun,
> The martyr, the wan acolyte,
> The incense-swinging child—undone
> Before God fashioned star or sun![1]

The man who is justified is the wretched sinner, not by any merits of his own, for he has none; not by any good resolutions he makes, for we hear of none: grace, as if to advertise us of its own independence from all human worthiness, singles out this pitiable creature, who by his faith in the divine mercy has become a child of God.

And again we have to say no. The man who exalts himself is abased, and the man who humbles himself is exalted, to be sure. But that is not all. There were two sons who were told to go and work in a vineyard, and which of them was it that did his Father's will? Not the one who said "I go, sir", the one who came to church and sang hymns and then went off and forgot all about it; but the one who, with no protest or parade of religion, took off his coat and got to work on those vinepoles. Catholic theology will have the whole truth, not stray bits of it, however neat and tidy you can make your theology by making it one-sided. It is the cause of a great many misrepresentations of our

Robert Browning, "Johannes Agricola in Meditation".

religion by outsiders that they only see half of what we believe, and that's the half they do not agree with.

In this matter of contrition for sin, how many pious people there are who will tell you that the Romish Church teaches its children to go to confession and elicit some kind of regret for the past, and then sends them away thinking they are absolved, and they go and do just the same things again. They will tell you all about the criminals who have been Catholics, and the people who are no better than they should be who are Catholics, and the statistics of crime or of vice in Catholic countries. And they will tell you of women on the streets who go to confession—sometimes; and the tongues will cluck and the teaspoons click and a picture will come to your mind, not a real picture, only a picture in a story—a respectable gentleman standing by a pillar in the temple, counting up on his fingers the list of his good deeds in the past fortnight; and, standing afar off—for we must not, if it can be avoided, distract the quality at their prayers—a bowed figure that beats its breast, not daring to lift its eyes heavenwards, only the sob that comes to its lips doing duty for an act of worship—"God, be merciful to me a sinner! God, be merciful to me a sinner!"

Our Lord sat at meat with the publicans and the harlots. Had all the publicans thrown in their lot with Zacchaeus, bestowed half their goods on the poor; had all risen with Matthew and left even the remote occasion of their sins behind them? Or were there some who still plied the old trade, still now and again, as they thought of their tattered clothes and of hungry mouths to feed at home, palmed off a false stater on a traveller in a hurry? Had all the harlots made St Mary Magdalen's venture of sanctity, taken the veil of contemplation and devoted their lives to penance? Or were there some whom weakness still betrayed, passion still overcame at unawares, who had to bring fresh tears, fresh gifts of ointment, and pour them at his feet? "All the world is gone after him", men said; had that world no unfortunates?

And then move on, and you will hear, perhaps, an exactly opposite criticism passed on the Catholic religion. You will be told that it exacts too high a standard of conduct, expects obedience to its commands where human nature is too weak to receive and to execute them. You will hear that continence is impossible, that divorce is a necessity for our society, that men's consciences are their own and you cannot bully them into compliance with artificial standards of behaviour. Or you will hear that we set too high a value on mortification, on penances, on external acts of devotion; making of Christianity a rule of life instead of a character, a hurdle-race with sins for obstacles instead of a close walk with God. You will hear that we are unpractical people, who pay so much attention to our religious duties that the age passes us by and we leave no mark on it: Catholicism, they say, drains the life-blood of a nation by its untimely insistence on the claims of the other world. And we have to answer again with a parable. We only know one thing for certain about this mysterious many-sided world on the shores of which we were cast up at our birth, that God is our Father, that he has planted a vineyard, and told us to go and work in it. Yes, it looks ugly enough now, rows and rows of poles with strings running in between, but that was what he told us to do, and we suppose there must be something behind it all. We do believe that man cannot be called upon to undertake what grace cannot enable him to fulfil. We do believe that external acts done for God's sake, even if in this world they are fruitless, will earn his commendation. We do believe that the first duty of Catholics is to make heaven populous. And the lip-service which merely applauds pious sentiments and likes a dash of religion about its newspaper articles, but does not alter the lives and the hearts of those who make their tribute of it, is, to us, a grudging and an unfilial apology for doing our Father's will.

One word I have still left out in the parable of the two sons. We must not forget the full formula of the Father's demand: "Son, go work *today* in my vineyard." While it is called today, while the impulse of grace is yet warm within us, while the powers that may fail us at any moment still answer our bidding, the opportunities that may at any moment be withdrawn still invite us, let us give the summons its effect. We have been churlish, perhaps, in our attitude towards the first call of grace; the love of ease, and the self-conceit which bids us choose our own plans, has made us hesitate and set the call aside. We must not expect that God will ask twice if we have so refused him. The memory of his call should be enough for us, the mere echo of a familiar tone. There is commendation for faithful service; there are rewards: we must deal with those two points yet before we think we have exhausted the mystery of the kingdom.

I I

INEQUALITY OF MERIT

I say to you that to every one that hath shall be given, and he shall abound:
and from him that hath not, even that which he hath shall be taken from him.
—Luke 19. 26.

THE parable of the talents in St Matthew and the parable of the pounds in St Luke are at once tantalizingly alike and significantly different. Commentators are much disagreed as to whether they are the same parable or no. Possibly both views are right. We learn from St Luke that, immediately after his interview with Zacchaeus and immediately before his triumphal ride into Jerusalem, our Lord put forward, apparently in the presence of the whole multitude, the parable of the pounds. We learn from St Matthew that some time after his triumphal ride into Jerusalem the disciples came to our Lord privately and asked him about the signs of his kingdom and of his coming again in judgment. After replying to them, our Lord continued his discourse to them with the parable of the ten virgins, and then with the parable of the talents. It may have been that the apostles, here as elsewhere, had been slow in appreciating the meaning of the story, and had asked him to repeat it for their benefit, which he did with slight alterations, suited to their more advanced grade in the school of divine instruction, unsuited (because confusing) to the minds of the multitude who thronged round him on the Jericho road.

Let us take the public version, St Luke's version, first, with its interpretation, and then go on to consider the modifications introduced in the second and more private version of it. The original utterance was inspired, St Luke tells us, first by the fact that they were drawing near to Jerusalem, secondarily because they, the multitude at large, expected the kingdom of God to appear immediately. Even as Christ spoke they were tearing down palm branches to strew the road before him, under the impression that they were to witness some sudden theophany. The story he tells is this: A nobleman went to a far country to receive a kingdom; his fellow citizens, who hated him, sent a message after him to say that he was not to rule over them. Meanwhile, he had given to each of his ten servants a pound to trade with against his return. When he returned he found that at least two had prospered, gaining an added ten pounds and an added five pounds respectively. Seven of them we do not hear about. But there was one who had buried his pound in a napkin—the heel of an old stocking, we should say—and made nothing on it. Why was that? He explains that it was because he knew his master was a hard man, taking up what he laid not down and reaping what he did not sow. Now, where is the logic of that? Why does that knowledge explain his behaviour? You would have thought it would make him all the more particular to do good business with his pound, instead of putting it away.

But we must remember those fellow citizens who hated the nobleman. The servants knew all about that; and the wicked servant attributes this unpopularity of his master to his stern, exacting methods. Very well, then, his argument is this: "I knew you were a hard man, taking more than was your due; knew that in consequence your neighbours were conspiring to get rid of you, and so I thought your pound would be safer buried in a stocking than if it were put into securities, where any day your enemies might manage to confiscate it as property forfeited by a revolution. I really meant it for the best." That is his excuse—an excuse which is not accepted.

Because he was nigh to Jerusalem, and because they thought that the kingdom of God should immediately appear. The nobleman goes to a far country; does not return, St Matthew tells us, for a long time. The object of his absence is to receive a kingdom. We have seen already that the absence in a far country means that God—in this case Christ himself—leaves us as it were to ourselves, does not interfere to arrest our foolish or sinful actions. Why? In order that he may test us; we are in a state of probation. The kingdom of God, in the sense in which the Jews expect it, is still very far off; Christ will absent himself for a long time before he comes to claim it. Meanwhile, the kingdom which is really imminent, the kingdom of the Church militant, will not be a glorious theophany but a period of waiting, while God still hides his hand and his faithful servants are left to make the most of their time by adding to the graces already given to them; in other words, meriting. The parable, then, is meant to revise the impression of his audience that the kingdom is immediately to appear. And it is suggested by our Lord's proximity to Jerusalem—its *citizens* hated him. Those wicked citizens who sent an embassage to say, "We will not have this man to reign over us", are in the first place the Jews who rejected him, in the second place those who, whatever their race and whatever their period in history, follow that fatal example.

What sort of testimonial was it that Christ our Lord took away with him when he left our earth? Why, this: that he had lived thirty-three years among the people who, more than any other people in the world, might have been expected to take an understanding and a sympathetic view of his claims, and that at the end of it they had crucified him. "We will not have this man to reign over us." That is the cry that follows him as he returns to his Father's throne to ask for the empire of the world, and it comes from his own fellow citizens. Now, what is to be the effect of that comment upon his own trusted servants? You find the answer in this parable. One of them, more timid than the rest, half-listens to these blasphemous criticisms. Of course, he does not in the least agree with them, but there is that point of view —that Christ is a hard taskmaster, expecting too much of his followers, and then claiming, when they have done all, that they shall pronounce themselves unprofitable servants. Of course he will scrupulously guard the grace that is entrusted to him, but he will not expose it to any risks. To speculate with it might mean losing it all; far safer to hide it away somewhere, and bring it out undiminished at his master's return.

So terrible an enemy is worldly respect to heavenly merit. He had the same chance as all the others, this slothful servant; the same graces were given him, and he could have increased them just as they did. That is the law of the celestial usury: that by turning your graces to good account you deserve fresh graces for the future. But how shy we are of doing it! It is painfully true that small things do matter; and it is in small things that we are always missing the opportunities which grace offers to us. The life of the Little Flower might have been given to our age merely to bring that lesson home; you feel that she was a miser with her grace. We must take care, no doubt, not to become scrupulous. But it is possible to waste so many gifts, to lose so many opportunities, that we become like the man who kept his pound in a stocking. Never a prayer more than what precept demands of us, never a sacrifice made but what sheer justice involves. And the end of it all? Remember the story of the man who had no wedding-garment, remember that we are being judged all the time. The moment comes when God tests us, to see what profit we have made by our graces, and there is nothing to show for it. "Take away the pound from him, and give it to him that hath ten pounds." The grace we kept, but misused by merely keeping, is withdrawn from us, and the divine Economist makes a better investment with it. From him that hath not, even that which he hath shall be taken from him. Be discreet by all means in this spiritual commerce, but do not simply play for safety; we need not gamble, perhaps, but we can all invest.

In St Luke's version, as I have said, each servant starts with the same deposit. But St Matthew does not seem to have heard this. It may be that when the words were spoken he was with Zacchaeus, helping him out, as himself a convert publican, with the business of making restitution. It may be that he was one of the two disciples who had been sent on ahead to unloose the ass for the triumphal entry into Jerusalem. Anyhow, he seems only to know another account, that given privately to the disciples, and in this there are only three servants mentioned, and, though the rest of the story is the same, each has a different amount entrusted to him. The minutiae of the doctrine of merit are not for the crowd by the wayside, but the apostles must be scribes instructed in the kingdom of heaven. It is true in a sense that all start with the same opportunities of grace; in the sense that every one of us has the grace given him that is suited to the particular vocation God has for him. This meaning is indicated even by a phrase in St Matthew: the lord gives his servants a different number of talents "each according to his ability"—viewed relatively, in relation to the needs of each, the quantity is in every case the same at starting. So a school-master might be said to give the same help to all his class if he gave each boy the help which his standard of intellect demanded. But, viewed absolutely, it is quite certain that grace is given to different souls in different measures. Fill a cask, and fill a cup; each is full, but not each holds the same quantity. And the grace of our Lady far exceeds that given to any other because her capacity for it and her need for it were beyond all other need, all other capacity. If your neighbour has received five talents, and you only two, there is no ground for envy: God has a different call for him; it is enough for you to make the most of what you have. If your neighbour has received two talents and you only one, that is no excuse for you to neglect your small opportunities. That you will do at your own deadly peril. Remember the momentous arithmetic of the celestial treasury: $5 + 5 = 10$, $2 + 2 = 4$, but $1 + 0 = 0$.

So much, then, we can learn from our Lord's own parables about the doctrine of merit: that there is that in human action which can earn his "Well done"; that it consists in a right use of the graces he himself vouchsafes to us; that such grace is given to all in varying measures, if we look at the quantity concerned, in the same measure, if we take into consideration the different vocation he has for each; that to neglect altogether the divine gifts of which we have the usufruct is to challenge him to withdraw what was only committed, not made over to us. What, then, are we to make of his command that when we have done all we are to own ourselves unprofitable servants? For we do do

FX

something, even if that something is very little. The answer, surely, is this, that the merits he won for us by his life and death as Man so infinitely exceed, and are so entirely the source of, all human merit—for our Lady herself received her unique privilege by the foreseen merits of her Son's Passion—that it is only by a sort of legal fiction that our merits can be imputed to us at all. We are all convicts in the debtors' prison, and the grace that is given us to trade with is so much pocket-money which, bankrupts as we are, we are allowed to write down on the credit side. To convince ourselves of our bankruptcy we have only to look at two other parables—the unjust steward[1] and the unmerciful servant.[2]

The unjust steward is often a source of difficulty, I think, only because we misconceive the nature of the transaction which passes between him and his master's debtors. Surely he is a steward in the sense in which the servants in the parable of the talents are stewards; that is, he has taken charge of the money and is responsible for it, and whatever is remitted to the debtors is so much out of pocket, not to the master, but to the steward himself. One owes a hundred, and is told to write down fifty; another owes a hundred, and is told to write down eighty—at the steward's expense. The moral, in fact, is the same as that of the unmerciful servant: we have all had so much remitted to us that it is the least we can do to be easy creditors ourselves. The unjust steward is commended as having done wisely, for the children of this world are in their generation wiser than the children of light: the policy which dictates itself to the business man in his generation, that is in matters of earthly finance, is the right policy for us to adopt in matters which concern the heavenly usury. And the unmerciful servant is condemned because he fails to mete out to others the treatment he would desire to receive, and indeed has received, himself.

Who is the unjust steward? Not the Jews, not the wicked, not the worldlings. He is you and I and every one of us; we are all, as children of Adam, unfaithful servants who have been detected in our delinquency. By rights, if legal right is to be pressed, we have forfeited every claim. We have earthly riches—the unrighteous mammon—still in our possession, and it is out of that that we must strive to gain ourselves a good reward in the day of necessity, by giving alms generously to those who are in need. Those for whom the request is made have no claim on you—no; it was not you who brought them to this pass—no; they themselves in all probability have been the cause of their present misfortunes—quite true. All that can be said, and yet—is there no

---

[1] Luke 16. 1-12.   [2] Matthew 18. 23-35.

account *you* shrink to see audited, are there no books in which *you* are written down a defaulter? Not in those comfortable ledgers on your writing-table, but in a book which God sees now, which we shall all see one day, the record of human actions and human sins. You too have no claim on the mercy of that all-just Creditor; you too have been the cause of all your own shortcomings; God is not responsible for your misuse of his gifts. If you would find mercy in that hour, will it not be wise—even with the common wisdom of the worldling —to establish a precedent for generosity, by largess, made while there is yet time, of the perishable goods of earth?

The parable of the unmerciful servant gives a slightly different turn to the same consideration. Here it is not a question of bestowing alms, but of forgiving injuries you have sustained. Is it always the most strict, the most God-fearing people that are most at home in God's own character of the master that forgives? Isn't there, rather, a temptation to let the thought of our own spiritual progress aggravate the case against the defendant? "What have I done", you will hear people say, "that I should be cursed with so worthless a son, with a friend who makes such return for my confidence?" What have you done? Why, you have merited the eternal torments of hell! Let him who now asks for your forgiveness, or, too shy perhaps or too thoughtless to ask, yet needs your forgiveness, serve you for an image of your own soul as it kneels to God for pardon of the sins conscience brings home to you, as it kneels not, so blind are we, for pardon of the sins false conscience hides from you. We are all in the same case, all bankrupts, all beggars; it is not our merits that will meet the claims at the end of it.

12

EQUALITY OF REWARD

Jesus said to him, Amen, I say to thee, this day thou shalt be with me in Paradise.—Luke 23. 43.

WE have been trying not to imitate the enemies and the critics of our Lord, but, though he spoke to us in parables, to receive his message with eyes that saw, and ears that heard, and hearts that understood. We saw, under the figure of the Samaritan, how he himself

came to raise fallen man, his enemy, bound up his wounds, and gave
him a Church to be his inn upon the roads of his pilgrimage. We saw
how, for the sake of that Church, the coveted jewel, he was ready to
strip himself of the majesty of his Godhead; how, at the greatest price
that has ever been paid, he bought that field which is the world for the
sake of that hidden treasure which is the Church. Yet the Church was
not an inert, lifeless thing, but an energy that permeated the world
like leaven, that sucked in from the world, as a tree sucks in nourishment from its surroundings, the souls of men. It caught them as with a
net, but it cast its net wide, so that there were worthless ones among the
catch; or, if you will, worthless grain among the wheat—in any case,
practising Christians who will be rejected at the judgment. But the
rejection will not be the fault of the seed sown, the grace which is the
beginning of all supernatural life; but the fault of the varying soils to
which it was committed, the hard or shallow or preoccupied hearts of
those that harboured it.

Such, then, was to be the kingdom, far different from anything the
Jews hitherto imagined; secret, not manifest, in its results; gradual, not
sudden, in its development; promiscuous, not finally selected, in its
membership. What, then, is its relation to the old Jewish Church?
Why has God bound up his earthly worship, for all these centuries,
with the fortunes of a single race, if nothing is to come of it? The answer
is: that God's patience lasts very long; that though his unfaithful vine-
dressers have spurned and persecuted and killed his messengers the
prophets, they will not be finally rejected and superseded till they have
been judged by the last crucial test, and crowned their apostasy by the
murder of his own Son. Even now he, like a patient gardener, is asking
that the tree may be allowed one more chance before it is cut down.
And we saw that God is equally patient with our sins, as we go from
bad to worse; but that there is a limit to that patience, and that it is a
Christian duty to importune God, as if he were an unjust judge or a
churlish neighbour, so that the limit of his patience may be prolonged,
and obstinate sinners given space for repentance. For, under the New
Covenant, Man is still on his probation; God seems to sleep while the
seed grows up and ripens for the harvest; but, once the doom is
pronounced, once soul and body are parted, there is no second chance
for the soul that was found unprovided with the oil of sanctifying
grace; nor will there be any opportunity to complain that our grace
was insufficient, any more than for the Jews who neglected to hear
Moses and the prophets. To prepare ourselves for that dreadful hour is
man's business in the world, not to labour for profits here which he

may never live to enjoy. We, poor and blind and helpless, have been called into the kingdom to replace the ungrateful Jews who refused the invitation; but for us, too, there is rejection, if at the moment when God tests us we are found to lack the wedding-garment of charity.

Jew and Gentile will be found side by side in the kingdom; for God loves the prodigal son that repents, and it is not for us to be indignant at the mercy thus shown to the unworthy. It is not for those who Pharisaically trust in their own righteousness, but for the sinner who dares not for shame lift up his eyes to heaven, that the divine treasury is rich with pardon. Not that such shame-faced contrition is the whole of our duty; it was the Gentiles who withdrew their refusal to labour in the vineyard, not the Jews who cancelled their acceptance of the command, that showed the true penitence. Forgiven, we must labour to increase our grace by meriting more through right use of the grace given us, putting back the heavenly coin into circulation, not burying it away. Yet always, because we are forgiven, we must remember that we are unprofitable servants; must give generously of our earthly goods, as we hope to have our misuse of the heavenly goods condoned; must show mercy to our brethren as we ask mercy of an offended God.

There only remains, I think, one of our Lord's parables—if we restrict our use of the word so as to include only his formal parables—which we have not yet considered. The story of the labourers in the vineyard is at once simple in itself and obvious in its primary interpretation. It follows, I think we ought to notice, immediately on St Peter's question, "Behold, we have left all things and followed thee, what therefore shall we have?"[1] After assuring him that neither he and his fellow apostles, nor any faithful follower of the same Master, will fail to reap his reward a hundredfold, our Lord adds, "And many that are last shall be first, and the first last",[2] and then without any break (it is only an accident that the chapter ends here) goes on to tell a story. A man went out to hire day-labourers for his vineyard. Early in the morning, and again at nine, and at midday, and at three o'clock, he finds the labour he wants; and finally, as late as five, he goes out—I suppose the business was urgent—and gets some casual labourers, who had been standing about in the market-place as only casual labourers can; and with these as with all the others he makes the arrangement that he is to pay them a penny a day.

And, as we should expect, when pay-time comes round there is trouble. What, these unskilled hands drawing a penny each for a couple of hours' employment, and we who have been at it all through the heat

[1] Matthew 19 27.   [2] Matthew 19. 30.

of the day are not to have any bonus? Yet the master of the house is surely justified in pointing out that if he likes to pay a fancy price to the eleventh-hour men it is nobody's business but his own. Here there is only one primary interpretation which will fit: namely, that the idle folk who come in at the eleventh hour are the Gentiles, who, with no preceding merits, have been called into the kingdom as if by an afterthought, while the others who had "laboured like men for working-days" are the Jews who for so many centuries have kept alive the true worship of God. And the answer given to the malcontents by the master of the house means this—that the call to membership of the new kingdom and to the consequent rewards is so entirely a matter of privilege, there is so little question of prescriptive right in it, even for those who have endured persecution and captivity for God's honour, that there is no room for jealousy or for questioning. The Jew has already learned that he will have to share the kingdom with the despised Gentile, to honour with the best grace he can the prodigal brother's home-coming feast: he now learns further that his position in the kingdom and the reward which follows upon it will not differ at all from the Gentile's position in the Church or the Gentile's reward in heaven. The eleventh hour is the coming of Christ; pay-time is the final judgment.

Now, it would naturally be attractive to transfer the moral to our own position as Catholics, and especially as Catholics in England. Some of us are converts, eleventh-hour men who have been called in by grace at the last moment: there are others in whose families the faith has never been lost through the whole era of the persecutions. But, as I have said before, I think our Lord means us to apply his parables, however much topical value they had for the people of his own day in their allusion to the controversy between Jew and Gentile, not to nations or to bodies of people, but to the dealings of God with the individual Christian soul. And there, too, our parable is not without its lesson, and the lesson is, I take it, one of broader application.

The working-day, surely, is man's life on earth. Some turn early to God; their childhood is passed under sheltered influences, and they grow up from the first staunch Catholics; as Catholics they meet, and fight, and triumph over temptation, and never think to excuse their falls with the plea of conscience ill-informed. Others learn for the first time to take their religion seriously as the result of a retreat before they leave school: others sow their wild oats, and return to their religion when they have tasted the bitterness of sin, or when some good influence, the influence, in many lives, of a good woman, has brought them back to God. Others, when the full strength of manhood or womanhood is past, and the remainder of life is seen as a slow declining towards the grave, betake themselves late, but not too late, to the meditation of eternity, and labour to make what amends they can for lukewarmness and lip-service in the past. And there are others— thank God for it—whom grace calls back when there is only just time, before the fatal separation of soul from body. How often one hears of condemned criminals making a good end! May it not be that others, no less sinful, but not found out by Society in their misdoings, have the same chance given them, though their end be suddener and their time for preparation shorter? We hear of them, of course, when there is time for a priest to come and receive the last whispered confession; but there are so many cases of conditional absolution, so many cases in which no priest could be found in time, and yet we hoped that there was a perfect, act of contrition. . . . Let us not outline any such pro-gramme for our own last moments; that would be playing with grace: but there are death-bed conversions.

And of course, over such death-bed conversions, the world sees fit to make merry, and to reflect what a pleasant affair the Catholic religion must be. Do as you like all your life, indulge your passions as you will, and then . . . seventeen words mumbled by a priest, and all is well; you are safe for eternity. Well, these labourers of the eleventh hour have a patron, the good thief who was crucified beside our Lord. He had made a mess of his life; he had his fling, while others bore the burden of the day and the heats; while the apostles, and Judas as one of the apostles, were toiling and suffering to win souls for Christ: he had no merits that we know of to set against his record, unless the story of his encounter with our Lady and St Joseph be true. It only needed one anguished look towards his fellow crucified, one word in detestation of sin and another in hope of pardon, and he earned the reassurance you and I dare not hope to earn when our time comes: "Amen I say to thee, this day thou shalt be with me in Paradise".[1] And the Catholic Church clings to its faith in that promise, welcomes, and boasts of, the theological anomaly it involves; boasts of it in the words of the greatest of French preachers: "Today! What promptitude! With me! What company! In Paradise! What repose!"

There is, surely, a double message in the parable; it offers hope to the idlers, and a warning to the toilers. So many years spent, and what has our life been but a loitering in the market-place? You have, perhaps, passed such loiterers in the streets with mixed feelings of pity and

[1] Luke 23. 43.

contempt, marked how they seemed to converse but rarely, puffed at empty pipes, gazed vacantly at the stream of busy life that passed them by; and you have wondered how existence could be tolerable with so little of apparent purpose. And yet, look at your own record as you would look at it if you were told that the story of it was to close tomorrow: how much of it has more value for eternity than if your lot had been cast at the street corner? So much of misdirected effort, of aimless drifting, of unreflective self-indulgence, of unworthy solicitude! And then remember that when Christ our Lord came to earth he came not only to the souls that awaited and welcomed his advent, but to those who, till then, had lived without the thought of God: remember that as he hung upon the cross he had words not only for those two who watched him so faithfully, but for the unwilling spectator of the Passion who had come out to die defiantly, with no anxiety for his soul's case, yet, on the impulse of a moment, yielded to the pursuit of those nailed feet, the beckoning of those motionless hands. It is not too late to devote what remains of life, though it be but the spent ashes of a life, to all outward seeming, in service of God's vineyard. That service will not be reckoned by length of days, but by the whole-heartedness of the final surrender. "Because no man hath hired us"—no man? Here is an employer who values the evening as if it were the morning sacrifice; let the lifting up of your hands be your evening sacrifice now. "Son, go and work today in my vineyard"—it is never too soon. "Today thou shalt be with me in Paradise"—it is never too late.

And for those who have toiled and suffered under the fierce suns of noon there is a warning. If we press the parable too literally, we shall have to suppose, in the first place, that some of the souls ransomed at the final judgment will be resentful at the ransom of others; and in the second place, that all souls in heaven will receive an equal share of glory. We know that we shall not all be equal in glory; the equality, as we have seen already, lies in this, that each soul is fulfilled to its full extent with the delights of God's house. And we know that there can be no murmuring or envying in that manifestation of the sons of God. We shall, I imagine, have no time to say "Who could have thought of seeing you there?" We shall be too engrossed in the reflection, "Who would have thought of seeing me here?" That part of the parable, then, is suitable rather to our earthly conditions. It is quite a real subject of heart-burnings, the envy of another's spiritual good: we realize all the time how foolish such envying is, but we go on doing it. Here are you who have been a daily communicant all these years, living in the fear of God, practising meditation; the whole of your past years seem a vista of first Fridays, and yet your prayers are so cold, so dull, so destitute of spiritual consolation! And there is So-and-so, yesterday's convert, with a past which charity forbids you to contemplate, overwhelmed with sweetness and tenderness and every sort of sensible devotion. Must not there be some flaw here in the divine economy? Well, you have your answer. Is it not lawful for God to do what he wills with his own? Must you frown because he smiles, criticize because he lavishes his rewards? His grace is free, else what would be your soul's position? His grace is free; how then should your unworthiness limit it?

See then the infinite variety of God's holy Church; the thousand facets that sparkle from that heavenly jewel! She is the inn of our rest and refreshment, and yet the vineyard of our labours; the leaven that gives out its energies to the world, yet the tree that makes the world's energies its own; the treasure which a God could covet, yet a prize some part of which is worthless; the seed-plot of a heavenly harvest, yet a crop in part unfertile; a marriage-feast, yet a vigil in expectation of the bridegroom's coming; the home of the prodigal, and yet a trading firm, jealously and warily investing its supernatural capital. See how grace follows us from the beginning of the story to the end; spares, finds, heals, restores, nourishes, perfects, crowns us. See how man is called, is tested, falls, is rejected, is recalled, is forgiven, merits, achieves. Hear, if you will, attentively, faithfully, fruitfully; hear, if you will, incredulously, scornfully, with hostility; but do not say that Christ our Lord left us with nothing but a string of moral maxims or a series of devotional considerations, do not pretend that no theology comes from Galilee: in secret he has said nothing. The claim he made for himself and for his Church was enough to make the Jews crucify him; we, too, if we will only listen, must either crucify or adore.

V

THE HARVEST OF THE CROSS*

* This series of five sermons was preached at the Church of St Charles Borromeo, Ogle Street, London, and was first published in *The Mystery of the Kingdom* (1928).

I
THE WAYSIDE

Behold, the sower went forth to sow. And whilst he soweth, some fell by the wayside, and the birds of the air came and ate them up.—Matthew 13. 3.

WHAT is the seed sown? The word of God. Who is he that sows it? The Word of God. And as he sows it, he hangs upon a cross. But we have nailed his feet, so that he cannot go forth. You have nailed his feet, but you cannot interrupt his progress. We have nailed his hands, so that they are powerless to move. You have nailed his hands, but still the life-giving seed falls at his command. You thought it was but dead wood, that tree of the cross, hard and bare and leafless, that you set up for a king's resting-place, but still it puts forth its shoots, roses of Christian charity, and in all the history of the Church, in all history, there is no meritorious action but drew its life from the sap of that tree, the precious blood of Jesus Christ. *Unless the grain of wheat falling into the ground die, itself remaineth alone, but if it die, it bringeth forth much fruit;*[1] that is the sower's own prophecy about the harvest of the cross.

The seed is sown everywhere, and everywhere the same seed. What thought is there more terrible than this, that Christ died for all the sins of the whole world? For the sins of the unbelievers who rejected him, for the sins of the heathen who never heard of him, for that last, irrevocable sin, the impenitent death-bed—Christ died for its remission. The seed falls everywhere, everywhere with the same possibility and promise of life; it is the soil that differs, and in proportion as it rejects or receives will belie or assure to itself the promise of a harvest to come. "For the earth that drinketh in the rain which cometh oft upon it and bringeth forth herbs meet for them by whom it is tilled, receiveth blessing from God, but that which bringeth forth thorns and briers is reprobate and very near unto a curse, whose end is to be burnt."[2]

> Sumunt boni, sumunt mali,
> Sorte tamen inaequali,
> Vitae vel interitus:
> Mors est malis, vita bonis,
> Vide, paris sumptionis
> Quam sit dispar exitus!

[1] John 12. 24-25.   [2] Hebrews 6. 7-8.

There was no spectator at the death on Calvary, however casual, however insignificant, that did not carry away in his heart the seed of life or of death. There has been and will be no human creature who, when the last sheaf is bound and the last load garnered, will not be found to have accepted or refused that seed of life, and in accepting or refusing it signed the warrant of its own eternal destiny.

The seed is all alike; and to the heart's soil there is only a single choice, to harbour it or to frustrate its purpose; but not one single attitude on the part of those in whom it misses its aim, not one single measure in which it fructifies amid the varying dispositions of those who receive it. In this parable our Lord himself has illustrated those differences, and has himself interpreted for us his illustration. The seed, he says, may fall on the hard wayside, which never gives it harbourage; or it may penetrate a shallow layer of earth, enough to bury it but not enough to protect it from the sun's heat; or it may strike deep root, yet be strangled at its birth by the thorns that grow up along with it. And in the good ground where it finds response, the amount of response will differ in quantity, and the richness of the crop differ in the same proportion. Let us watch how the seed falls from the crucified Sower into the hearts of those who witnessed or contributed to his death, and, arguing from them to the case of our own souls, learn to watch the heavenly seed-time, to dread the everlasting harvest.

Some fell by the wayside, on that hard crust that forms itself over a field-path, trodden down by men's feet and unvisited by the plough. It might as well have fallen in the sea; it will be food for the birds before night. These are the souls who present to the heavenly seed a hard crust of indifference or of initial prejudice on which it makes no impression. Such souls there were among the watchers by the cross; people who had come to Calvary inspired by no feeling of love or of hatred towards the crucified, but merely in the way of business: the soldiers—Roman soldiers we call them, but they may perfectly well have been Britons—who had been sent to carry out a common act of execution, staled to them, and robbed at once of horror and of pity by the frequency of its occurrence. The best you could make out of such an order was a half-hour of brutal sport, and then there was nothing for it but to play dice for the dying man's clothes, to while away the dull hours of waiting. Such a soul, too, there was among the authorities who sent our Lord to his execution—Pontius Pilate, the Roman governor, to whom the whole business was hateful merely as to one who hated a scene; the fierce excitement of these Jews about their unimportant religious differences jarred on his Roman gravity. In other provinces, where Greek culture had been properly diffused, it was easy enough to popularize the worship of a dead emperor, not greatly distinguished in life for the more rigid virtues; and the smug, municipal religion which that worship created was a useful asset in encouraging the theory of Roman supremacy by divine right. Here, in this God-forsaken corner of the earth to which his unkind fates had sent him, he not only had to be tactful about the ceremonies of his own religion, but must needs be called in to adjudicate the claims of these Jewish impostors among themselves. What a life for a man who had started with good chances, and promised himself in his daydreams a victorious campaign against the legions of Parthia!

The immediate agents who were responsible for our Lord's Passion were not blinded by hate or thirsting for blood; they were simply *blasés*. They were like the hard path across the fields, the beaten track that by long habit has lost the receptive faculty with which nature had once endowed it. The habit of cruelty and callousness in the soldiers, the habit of cynicism and unscrupulousness in Pilate were not created but merely discovered when they were put to the test by the delivery of the hunted malefactor into their hands. The callousness, the indifference, was an obstacle to conversion which their own past fault had introduced into their souls. To be sure of that, you have only to look at the case of the centurion, who, for all the coarse-grained nature that years of campaigning had given him, was yet receptive enough to realize and, tradition informs us, to retrieve his monstrous error before night fell upon the tragedy. He, too, had the Roman toughness of fibre; he, too, had developed that insensibility to the feelings of others which marks the conquering race; he, too, had learnt life in a hard school, from brutal teachers. We must not think of him as an elegant young officer in the Guards; the man was just a regimental sergeant-major; he had just the same excuse of environment as the rest of them; yet he only, so far as we know, learnt the meaning of that sacrifice at which he had been the unwilling acolyte.

And Pilate, too, had his chance. It is easy to see in the Gospel story where he begins to be impressed, begins to wonder, begins to think it might be worth while to investigate the truth, and then just, only just, decides that it is too much trouble. "Truth? What is that?" he says, as if excusing himself to his own conscience, and hurries from the judgment hall. So many conflicting systems of philosophy, so many hopeless efforts of man's poor bewildered mind to solve the riddle of his existence: and shall I stop to listen to one of them? Oh yes, Pilate failed at the test, but only just; and there must have been times in the life of St Augustine when he came very near to making the same confession of failure. "What I have written, I have written"—the weak man's refusal to reconsider his action: and I have no doubt that when he went home to his wife he silenced her with "What I have done, I have done". Can any soul that lives in the fear of God read Pilate's story and not tremble for its own salvation? Truly as the Lord liveth, and thy soul liveth, there is but one step between me and death.

God forbid that when we look round at our friends who are outside the Church, and often seem unresponsive to any whisper of its claims, we should attribute to all of these, or even to a large part of them, this attitude of culpable indifference which we have seen in Pilate and in the men who executed Pilate's orders. God himself alone, in his unfathomable wisdom, can read the secrets of those hearts, and know how large a part the accidents of birth and environment have played in keeping away from them the consciousness of their Christian vocation. But there is, surely, terrible reason to fear for some; for those who, disregarding what lights they have, harden by long habit of disuse or misuse their faculty for the appreciation of spiritual issues, and wilfully debauch their intellects by incuriosity, uneasy at first, but more acquiescent as time goes on, about the whole meaning and purpose of life. Like Pilate, they do not hate the Church, but, like Pilate, they are weary of controversy; like Pilate, they evade the issue with a shrug of the shoulders. "Truth? What is that?" they ask, and, running away from the intellectual encounter, leave vacant the judgment-seat of their immortal minds. They are excellent companions, these people. They put very little strain upon our spiritual powers, administer no rebuke to our own careless habits of living. They plunge themselves into their own amusements, prepared to live and let live. How we would like to believe that "butterflies may dread extinction", that those fellow creatures of ours, so gracious in all that is human, so lacking, apparently, in all apparatus for spiritual activities, so attractive even in their conventional prejudices, would, at death, simply cease to be!

> . . . merely born to bloom and drop,
> Here on earth they had their fruitage; mirth and folly were the crop;
> What of soul was left, I wonder, when the kissing had to stop? [1]

But we know it is not so. We know that every one of those souls must appear before its Maker to give account of its own works; that on these patches of earth, so hardened, so stamped into unresponsive

---

[1] Robert Browning, "A Toccata of Galuppi's", xiv.

barrenness, the seed that sprang from the cross has been cast for their acceptance; and where is the fruit?

Nor is it the only malady of today that men's intellects are hardened, as Pilate's was, by long indifference to truth until it is difficult for them to receive any impression; hearts are hardened, too, like the hearts of the soldiers at the crucifixion. And here it is that the warning of the seed by the wayside comes home to us, too, professing Christians; we have received first grace, and our minds have rested content in the intellectual satisfaction which God's Revelation brings with it: we have found the answer to the question, What is truth? But are we pressing our Lord's parable too far if we remind ourselves that the constant treading of feet which turns the soft ground into a footpath may be just as fatal to the seed if it occurs after, not before, that seed has fallen into the furrow? That when the seed is newly sown it needs but little trampling from stray cattle or from boys who go birds'-nesting to expose it anew, on hard ground this time? Our Lord tells us that the seed which fell by the wayside represents the souls that hear the word of the kingdom and do not understand it—does he mean by the word "understand" a merely intellectual appreciation? Is it not, rather, certain that for any fruitful understanding of the word the heart must be engaged as well as the intellect, that the will and the affections, no less than the intellect, must be receptive if the Devil is not to come and take the seed away from our souls?

Surely you must have met them, those souls that are within the unity of the Catholic faith, yet, for all purposes of spiritual growth, seem as hard as the beaten wayside, as callous as the soldiers that played dice under the shadow of the cross. Some of them are living in a state of mortal sin; some, not yet, but they seem only to be waiting for the temptation to come their way. The spiritual needs of their neighbours never touch those souls, nor the dishonour done to our Lord and his saints by those who blaspheme them, nor the crimes men do and the wrongs men suffer in the world around them. The solemnities of the Church pass them by; she mourns to them in Lent, and they do not weep; she pipes to them at Easter, and their hearts never dance to the melody. The conversion of other souls to God never excites their hopes, nor rejoices their ears, nor shames their lethargy. You can talk to them about priests they know, countries they have visited, churches they have worshipped in, never about the Church, or the faith, or the things of God. Playing dice under the cross, in all contentment; what if the shadow of it lies on them lightly? After all, they are playing a game.

Remember, there is one other spectator of the Passion, case-hardened as they; even better placed, perhaps, but not with their advantages. The impenitent thief—is he really made of different stuff from the soldiers? is he not rather the unfortunate one whom Society has found out and cold-shouldered? It was hardly more than an accident that determined his decision to take to thieving instead of joining the colours: he too has played dice, only—the throw has gone against him. See how the hardness of the soil reacts in him on the stimulus of the divine sowing! Not even his own torments, rake and harrow his physical frame as they will, can prepare a ground in that heart; not even the sight of his innocent fellow sufferer can elicit the tears of compassion which might have watered and softened it; already, as his body writhes in agony, the rigour of spiritual death numbs the faculties of his soul. Is there a reason in nature for these hard hearts? There is, surely; it needs only a natural development to cake and crumble the soil, if it be not ploughed and harrowed and watered under the influence of the grace we have so often slighted, so seldom turned to account.

2

STONY GROUND

And other some fell upon stony ground, where they had not much earth; and they sprung up immediately, because they had no deepness of earth. And when the sun was up they were scorched; and because they had not root, they withered away.—Matthew 13. 5.

To the people of whom we have been speaking, to Pilate and his soldiers, seed-time and harvest are one; they are no sooner faced with the claim of Christ than they reject it. And the cause of it is the bad preparation of the soil beforehand; unploughed, unwatered, it offers from the first an impervious surface to the heavenly seed. We have now to consider a different class of people, those in whom the seed finds a lodgment but, alas! an insufficient one. They are not confronted for the first time, at the crucifixion, with the message of the kingdom, they have had ample opportunity, these three years past, of studying it. To them, then, the cross is not the sowing of the seed, but the scandal which causes the seed to fail of its effect. To these, the cross is what we should expect it to be, an *experimentum crucis*, a crucial test. The Jews, for example. They have heard our Lord, welcomed him, acclaimed him; we have now to see what their acclamations were worth.

Something evidently happened, something which the Gospel story does not explicitly describe, between the time when the Pharisees did not dare to lay hands on our Lord because they feared the people, and the time when the people, with the Pharisees at their head, stood round the judgment-seat and shouted "Crucify him, crucify him". And the simplest explanation of that change is obviously this: that the people who regarded our Lord as a great prophet; the people who thronged his path as he entered Jerusalem and welcomed him as a king, had not really understood, had not really digested the purport of his message. They were not prepared, as they would have been prepared if his teaching had really penetrated their hearts, to acclaim him as the Son of God. In the course of the Holy Week, either something in his own teaching made clear what was not clear to them before, that he "made himself the Son of God"; or else, as has been ingeniously suggested, the secret had been given away by one of the few people who really knew what our Lord claimed to be, one of the apostles. In that case, you see, the matter of Judas' treachery was the matter of Peter's confession —*Thou art Christ, the Son of the living God.*[1] What Peter had confessed, Judas had betrayed. Before our Lord was brought to trial the principal witness had disappeared; Judas had hanged himself. But he had done his work all too well; the people were by now convinced that the prophet of Nazareth was no national liberator but an impostor who claimed divine honours, and all their hosannas had turned into *Crucifigite*. Something like that seems necessary as an explanation.

And a crowd will always act like a crowd, under the same law that governs the rise and fall of prices on the Stock Exchange. Once it began to be whispered that the new prophet had gone too far, and that his popularity was on the wane, the crowd began to turn against him. On Palm Sunday, how promising a harvest those souls appeared! On Good Friday, the blades that sprouted thus prematurely lie withered and dead. Some of these fickle supporters, I suppose, were our Lord's own countrymen, Galileans who had come up for the feast; enthusiasts, no doubt, as the Galileans generally were, for an insurrection against the Romans. So long as our Lord could be taken for a political agitator he had no keener supporters than these; here, they say to themselves,

[1] Matthew 16. 6.

is a patriot, and a local patriot, the champion of our own countryside. How a crowd will always rally to a local champion! Not distinguishing very clearly what his message is or what platform he adopts, but merely intent on voting for their own man. In some such flush of excitement these Galileans had cried Hosanna, had stripped off their coats and thrown down palm branches along the triumphal route; at home, in Galilee, the prophet might have little honour; here, in Jerusalem, with all these southern Jews about, they must stick by one another. Hurrah for the Son of David! And now? The boldest of them, it seems, have deserted their prophet; the more weak-kneed are joining in the cries of derision that are hurled against the crucified. You see that silent, unprotesting figure that stands adoring beneath the cross? These men have known her for forty years and more, and they are crucifying her Son.

And there are others who have been more recently attracted to the new movement; not Galileans, these, but Jews of Judaea, who never heard of our Lord at all until three years ago, when he began his active ministry. They have written themselves down his adherents, caught by some momentary enthusiasm. One had no higher motive than the experience of feeding on the loaves and fishes; it seemed to him worth following a cult which had such concrete possibilities. Another was genuinely impressed by the miracles as evidences of a supernatural power, yet never stopped to ask himself what was involved by adhesion to the cause of such a wonder-worker; he never sat down and counted the cost. One was arrested by the earnestness of our Lord's speech, the cleverness of his repartees, has heard the message, but not understood it and made it his own. Another was genuinely caught, heart and head, by the gracious words he listened to; but since then he has been a good deal discouraged by the opposition of his family—our Lord warned him that it would be so, warned him that it was not worth putting his hand to the plough if he meant to look back afterwards; but somehow he never realized at the time how persistent or how effective family opposition could be. Another went back after his conversion to bury his father; and now the father is dead, and he has a stake in the country, and is beginning to reconsider his youthful enthusiasms. Another never heard our Lord himself, but joined the movement because he was so impressed by the preaching of one of the apostles; and now, it seems, this apostle has himself deserted the movement and laid information against his Master, and it is a little difficult to know what to do. In all of them the seed has taken root, but ah, in how shallow a depth of earth! And now the sun of persecution is up; its pitiless rays glare down upon the over-hasty growth; will it stand the test? Or will it fail at the crucial experiment?

The Galileans of our Lord's time have their analogue in all too many Catholics of today, born Catholics, who have been to a Christian school and learnt their faith as naturally and as unquestioningly as they learnt their multiplication table. Their religion was part of the air they breathed, part of the patriotic tradition which invested their school, part of the intimacy which was the bond of their school friendships. They knew no better way of securing a fine day for the match, or of passing in an examination, or of getting out of a scrape, than a prayer to the Madonna in the ante-chapel, a candle if you were hard put to it. I am not criticizing Catholic education; it is the most beautiful thing on earth. But you cannot do everything by teaching, whether in a day-school or in a boarding-school; and there are those, be your education as perfect as you will, who only receive the good seed in a shallow soil. It is wonderful so far as it goes; it blossoms out into a hundred attractive pieties. But it has not stood the test yet. When it springs up beyond the shelter of the hedgerow that protected its early growth, when it becomes exposed to the sun-glare of the unbelieving and unregenerate world, then begins, not persecution exactly, but a withering influence that will test to the utmost the depth to which that early teaching has sunk in. The wicked old world, with its raised eye-brow for the miraculous, its shrugged shoulder for indecency and immorality, will do its best to parch and stale the fresh flowers we saw so gratefully, prayed over so anxiously. And because it had no root, it withered away.

So much for the Galileans, brought up from birth within easy reach of the sacred home at Nazareth. And the Jews will represent converts to the faith; not insincere converts, but such as have thrown themselves into the Church without ever counting the cost of it, and now begin to feel doubtful. Some did it for temporal convenience as much as anything—a Catholic marriage or the favour of a Catholic patron. Some had come to realize suddenly that the Church was a vast organization, or were impressed by a significant providence in the life of a friend. Some were carried off their feet by a sermon or a book. Some were not prepared to face the disapproval and disappointment of their family or their circle—the world does still hate Catholicism. Some have increased in their own sense of importance, and begin to think that youth has betrayed them into a false step. Some—God forgive us!— are converts of priests who go wrong. In a thousand ways it may happen that the world looks different when the sun is up and the rocks are almost cracking in the glare of it, from what it did in the pure, pale light of dawn. Thank God it does not often, but it does sometimes happen that the faith of a convert proves ill-grounded and withers away. Somehow the test comes—a question of forbidden marriage, as likely as not, and the priest who received the convert is told (usually without truth) that he ought to have made things clearer than he did; and there is misery, and scandal, and another soul that put its hand to the plough has turned back.

But there is another case behind the scenes all the time; not quite a Galilean, and not quite a Jew, yet no stranger to the message of the kingdom. King Herod did not seek an interview with our Lord as a matter of business; it was nothing to him whether the Pretender were crucified or merely discredited. *He was desirous*, St Luke tells us, *of a long time to see him, because he had heard so many things of him, and he hoped to see some sign wrought by him. And he questioned him in many words. But he answered him nothing.*[1] He had heard the word of the kingdom— as soon as most people—from St John the Baptist; and he had received it in a curious way, quarrelling with the great Forerunner when he protested at his immoralities, and then keeping him at his side, half as a prisoner, half as a kind of court chaplain. Probably he had very little idea what he meant to do with him, until that unfortunate evening when the wine had heated his blood, and, his maudlin generosity triumphing over his maudlin regrets, he gave orders for the execution of his formidable captive. And Herod was not likely to have difficulties about the faith; he was actually the first person who believed in the Resurrection. When he heard of the fame of our Lord, he said at once, "This is John the Baptist, whom I beheaded; he has risen from the dead"—what difficulty in that? Was there no parallel for such an occurrence in the old mythologies? Herod is, I take it, the cultured dabbler, who is far too broad-minded to dismiss the claims of the new Prophet on any ground of superstitious prejudice; he would not be at all surprised if there's more in it than you think. Here's a new movement; already he has been disappointed once when he hoped for an interview; now his chance has come; he will go into the whole subject. *And he questioned him in many words. But he answered him nothing.*

It is not difficult to recognize in Herod a type of that curious class of people whom you can only call honorary members of the Catholic Church. They have never been received, and do not mean to be, but when they do go to church it is always to a Catholic church. They know all sorts of odd points of moral and devotional theology better

[1] Luke 23. 8-9.

than the ordinary Catholic; they turn up their noses at the mention of Protestantism; if you meet them at dinner it is quite a shock to be told by your hostess afterwards that they are not Catholics. But they are not Catholics; they are only cultured dabblers. I do not know whether it is quite true to say that the heavenly seed has taken any root at all in these people. They have no depth of earth, in fact, you can hardly call it earth at all, but there is a patch of mud there which has produced a bastard growth, like the barley you will sometimes find growing on a window-sill. Anyhow, they are not serious, and the crucial test comes to them when something strikes across their lives which forces them to be serious; a bad illness, or a severe bereavement, or a strong gust of passion; and the illness takes them to Christian Science, or the bereavement to Spiritualism, or the gust of passion blows them away altogether, but there is another seat empty at the eleven o'clock Mass. What appearance of religion they had has gone the way it came; if you meet them again and talk to them about Catholicism you will hear that they went into it a good deal at one time.

Shallowness? You despise it in everyone else; in everything else, except your religion. You would admit, in any other connection, that if a thing is worth doing at all it is worth doing thoroughly. How mysterious that over the one thing which, if it matters at all, matters supremely, you should be content to take chances, to acquiesce in a low level! There is no reward laid up, when the time comes for the harvest, for early promise, for the fair show you made when the morning dew was still fresh upon the first bloom of faith; it is for the root that has felt and faced the scorching suns of mid-day that the heavenly garners are opened.

3

AMONG THORNS

And others fell among thorns, and the thorns grew up and choked them.—
Matthew 13. 7.

THE failure of the good seed in the characters we have hitherto been considering was due to something negative, to a defect on the part of the soil to which it was committed. In the first case there was earth, but it was earth trodden down and hardened, which had lost its proper faculty of receptiveness; it was earth, but it was not really soil. In the second case the earth was there, and was soft as earth should be, but there was not enough of it: it was only a thin covering spread over useless stones. In the first case the character of the soil was unreceptive, in the second case it was unretentive; but always there was something lacking. In the soil of which our Lord goes on to speak in this verse there is nothing lacking, and the seed has all the effect which you could expect it to have, but its fruitage is spoilt, this time, by the presence of something else side by side with the crop, which develops to its destruction. It fell among thorns. Its right to grow in that piece of ground was disputed by other claimants, self-sown and therefore as it were natural to the soil, but not necessarily, at the beginning, more deeply rooted than it. The two crops grow up side by side, and the baser of them, more rapid in its growth or more exacting in its claims, strangles the pure seed.

Notice that our Lord says "the thorns *grew up* and choked it"; there was not, then, when the seed first fell, any particular disparity, any unfair odds against the good seed. He does not mean that the word of the kingdom sometimes makes its way into a soul where the thorns —worldly cares, pleasures, the love of riches—are already so firmly established that from the first the Gospel has no chance. The seeds of those cares, those pleasures, that covetousness, are already present; the germs are there, but only the germs. In the field, nature takes its course, and the strongest growth predominates, if man does not interfere to prevent it; in the soul—for we are free agents—it will depend (under grace) on the encouragement we give to the good seed, the discouragement we give to the useless weeds, how the issues of the battle will go.

And Judas Iscariot, who also betrayed him.[1] So ends the list of the twelve apostles, as if from the first, from the very moment of his call, he was at least in heart a traitor, but I doubt if we are meant to conclude so; it is only, I think, by way of distinguishing him from St Jude that the description is added. The germs of his downfall are there already, in the sense that if you could see into his character you could already tell what his temptations will be, but you cannot tell how the temptations will be met. The source of his temptations is, surely, also the source of his usefulness; he is the treasurer of the new movement, the organizing man of the party. We might be surprised to find that St Matthew, with his experience as a tax-gatherer, was not appointed to this post. But, after all, it may very well be that Judas had been bred in the same trade: his native town of

[1] Matthew 10. 4.

Carioth was close to one of the large main roads to the south, and on the very edge of the desert, just where you would expect a customs house to be. Anyhow, he starts with the same gifts as St Matthew—the same gifts, and the same temptations. He has the knack, and is proud of having the knack, of the ideal procurator; he is the man for making both ends meet. Our Lord and our Lady had some money between them, no doubt, St Joseph's savings; and it is likely enough that the apostles each made their contribution to a common fund. And Judas, the efficient man, is naturally put in charge of it.

At first, I suppose, all goes well. He takes to his duties lovingly, and if at times he finds himself over-absorbed in the detail of them, he consoles himself by reflecting that it is all for the glory of God and for the Master's honour. Here and there he wrinkles his brow over a phrase in a sermon: *Lay not up to yourselves treasures on earth. Be not solicitous, therefore, saying, What shall we eat? or What shall we drink? or Wherewith shall we be clothed? Be not therefore solicitous for tomorrow: for the morrow will be solicitous for itself.*[1] "Yes, it is all very well, that sort of thing, but . . . well, it takes all sorts to make a world. No doubt the Master is talking in a slightly exaggerated way to drive his lesson home. . . . In any case, it cannot apply to me; my solicitude is not for my own needs, but for the needs of others, the needs of the Master himself." And so it goes on, until after a time he begins to allow himself little liberties, not altogether sharing the hard, ascetic life which the rest of the party lead; as procurator, he has to keep up his strength. . . . And then the little liberties grow into perquisites, and the perquisites into temporary loans, and the temporary loans into defalcations. He has realized by now that the Master never audits the accounts. *He was a thief, and had the purse, and carried the things that were put therein.*[2] Did it ever occur to you what a terrible irony there is about that sentence? Judas falsifying the accounts, and congratulating himself, while he half-pitied his Master, on the want of business instinct that left those accounts unaudited? And all the time, that Master is omniscient God; not only knows about those petty thefts, but sees in the still unrevealed future the result they will lead to—the thirty pieces of silver, the traitor's kiss in the Garden, the suicide's end. We have a grim phrase about giving a man rope to hang himself with; have you ever thought how hideously that phrase applies to our Lord's dealings with the traitor? Omniscient God, omnipotent God, all-merciful God. . . .

What was the climax? There is nothing definite in the Bible about it, nor any tradition as far as I know, but there is something, surely, to be

[1] Matthew 6. 19, 25, 34.   [2] John 12. 6.

G

said for the construction which they put upon it in the Passion Play at Oberammergau. When Mary Magdalen pours the ointment over her Saviour's feet, all Judas' business instinct, which makes the hoarding of money a fixed idea with him, is shocked at the act; still more shocked when our Lord signifies his approval. His faith in the unworldly, unbusinesslike Prophet is now strained to breaking-point, and —it breaks. It has been a thankless task, serving a Master who will never look to his own interests; he will go elsewhere, somewhere where people realize the value of money. And he goes off and drives his bargain—what a bargain! Thirty pieces of silver as blood-money for handing over the Redeemer of the world!

For two years past Judas has lived with a false conscience. The petty thefts have gone on, and still day by day he has greeted our Lord with "Hail, Master!" and a smiling face—it was not the evil inspiration of a moment that turned Judas into a hypocrite. But to him, too, the crucial test comes, the touchstone of the character that has formed itself in him. This time, the crucial test is not the crucifixion; nor is it even the moment when he agreed to betray his Master, perhaps hardly knowing what he did; nor even the moment of his betrayal, for it was, humanly speaking, too late for him to draw back then. The moment of decision came, for him, at the last supper. Again and again the Master who has hitherto seemed so blind, so unsuspecting, drops those terrible hints that seem to argue knowledge of his most secret movements: *Woe unto that man by whom the Son of Man is betrayed.*[1] *You are not all clean; One of you shall betray me.*[2] And then the sacrament of the New Covenant is instituted, and it is Judas' last chance. Now or never he must throw himself at his Lord's feet, and confess all, and be forgiven! But no, the hardened conscience goes through with it; he receives the saving host to his condemnation, receives the sop which is the special pledge of charity, and with the sop Satan enters into him, and he hurries out into the night. The cares of the world and the love of riches had so strangled the good seed that no root survived even of penitence; he went out into the night, and night went out with him.

Our Lord chose Judas, knowing him to be the traitor; he did not choose him to be the traitor. He had a vocation for him, if he would, to preach the Gospel before kings and princes, to suffer stripes and imprisonment in his Master's name, to die a martyr's death, and be raised to the altars of the Church, if he would. Take up any chapter of the Gospel that records our Lord's teaching, and before you have read half-way through it you will come across some saying, some parable,

[1] Matthew 26.24.   [2] John 13.10, 21.

that ought to have shown Judas which way he was going, ought to have warned him that the cares and the avarice which were strangling his vocation must be cut back in good time. Only because he left the thorns unchecked, the good seed untended, was it his destiny to sow a field of blood to reap a harvest of eternal death.

The deceitfulness of riches, so our Lord calls it in the parable; the stealth with which they strengthen, from year to year, their hold on our lives; the deadly power they have of warping our judgment, the false conscience they so often create in us! The love of money, we are told, is the root of all evil; and certainly the New Testament is full of that warning—Judas and Simon Magus, and Ananias and Sapphira. I know it sounds very unpractical to suggest that we ought to be on our guard against covetousness; I suppose it is less mentioned in confessions than any other of the deadly sins, but—does the fact that so few of us are conscious of its influence necessarily mean that it is not dangerous? May it not be just the other way? I do not mean that any of us are likely to commit a fault like Judas'; God preserve us all from the temptation to it. But money does mean something in our lives, and either having a little more money or having a little less money than is just suited to your needs brings with it a danger, the danger that you should lose the singleness of eye which, our Lord tells us, illuminates the whole body. Even if it is not our own finances we are anxious over, but the finances we have to manage, it is wonderful how the mere breath of money can mar the freshness of human character.

But it is not only the deceitfulness of riches; it is the care of this world, and, St Luke adds, the pleasures of this life. The world we are all moving in, the life we are all living. The thorns are not something foreign to the soil; thorns and briers have grown up naturally in our hearts, as well as in the world about us, since Adam fell. Cares and pleasures do come more natural to us—it is as sound theology as it is sound common sense—than the claims of religion. We think with horror of the double life Judas must have lived all those years, a thief and a miser in the service of the Prophet that had not where to lay his head. But have we really to look farther than our own souls to find the key to his psychology? In theory we sanctify our pleasures by offering them to God; in theory we cast our care upon him and submit it to his will. But in practice, are we not conscious of a dual control in our souls, two principles fighting for the mastery? The echoes, the anticipations of our worries and our enjoyments pursue us into the moments we think we are dedicating to the service of God—for all the world like Judas, listening to the Sermon on the Mount and fingering his keys.

Please God, we are only like Judas in his early stages. But it may give us cause to pray more earnestly, *Lead us not into temptation*.

There is one other character in the New Testament who, like Judas, impresses the serious reader with a profound discomfort. He is only mentioned twice, and we know practically nothing about him, but what we do hear is enough to make us shudder. In the last chapter of St Paul's Epistle to the Colossians you read: *Luke, the most dear physician, saluteth you, and Demas*. And in the last chapter of his Second Epistle to St Timothy you read: *Demas hath left me, loving this present world . . . only Luke is with me*. His name is not mentioned in the Acts. I suppose that St Luke left it out after what happened. I imagine St Luke and Demas as friends, class-mates, you might say, in the seminary. They have followed the apostle of the Gentiles to Rome, not to share his imprisonment, but to attend to his wants and comfort him in his hours of enforced idleness. And the legal process drags on, and there is no question for the present of preaching the Gospel. Demas finds himself unoccupied. We do not know what it was that produced the change in him; not necessarily any disgraceful, not necessarily any mercenary motive. But somehow he suddenly falls in love—that is, if anything, the emphasis of the Greek words—suddenly falls in love with the present world. His visits to the prison grow fewer and fewer, some outside interest has gripped him and holds him in its grip. And then one day the visits cease altogether, and St Paul, tried hard already by outward circumstance, learns what it is to be deserted by a friend. He rejoiced, as we know, to fill up that which was lacking of the sufferings of Christ; he lived to suffer, even as his Master, betrayal by a friend on the eve of his Passion. Only Luke is with me: Demas has been carried away on the stream of the world's interests, and passes out of sight.

Please God, the seed of the Gospel did not fall on us in vain; we gave it a lodgment, grace overcoming the stubborn hardness of our nature. And receiving it, we did not receive it lightly, with the shallow enthusiasm that springs up for a moment and withers away; with all our daily faults, we do take our religion seriously. But we are not out of danger yet. Secular interests, however unselfish, however enlightened, may dispute with the heavenly seed the right to dominate our lives. Habits of self-indulgence which subtly enervate our spiritual resources, drain the sap out of our religion. *I passed by the field of the slothful man, and the vineyard of the foolish man, and behold it was all filled with nettles, and thorns had covered the face thereof.*[1] I do not mean that

[1] Proverbs 24. 30-31.

you ought to neglect your business or your mission in this present
world, or that, such is our weakness, you could afford to dispense with
relaxations and innocent pleasures. But do, sometimes, take stock of
your position; make sure that other interests do not wholly engross
and absorb your spiritual energies, cutting down unreasonably the
time, interfering unseasonably with the attention, which you owe to
the things of God; make sure that your pleasures are not becoming an
idol, to be schemed for, looked forward to, lived for, instead of
recreations that you simply take, and take with gratitude, as they come.
Examine yourself to find, not the sin you most often commit, but the
thing in your life which counts for most next to your religion, the
thing which is more likely than anything else to count for even more
than your religion. And then imagine to yourself what would happen
if a strong temptation came across your path in that very matter.
You are always thinking about money—what would happen if you
suddenly lost all you had, or if you had the opportunity to increase
your possessions unjustly? You are anxious about health—what would
you do if you became a permanent invalid? You are promoting some
good work—what attitude would you adopt if legitimate authority
were suddenly to suppress the object of your devotion? Imagine the
worst that could happen, and then tell God that, happen what may,
he comes first.

4

THIRTYFOLD

They that sow in tears shall reap in joy: going, they went and wept, casting
their seeds, but coming they shall come with joyfulness, carrying their sheaves.
—Psalm 125. 5.

IN the parable of the sower our Lord does not mark any interval
between the seed which fails altogether and the seed which comes up
with increase. Here, as in the parable of the talents,[1] it would seem that
he does not recognize the possibility of standing still in the Christian
life: the servant who restores his talent whole but without any interest
is written down as worthless; the seed either produces no harvest at all

[1] Matthew 25. 14-30.

or produces a harvest in excess of what was sown. The careless Christian would do well to reflect on this, if he is in the habit of supposing that he is likely to attain heaven by fulfilling the bare minimum of his obligations and doing no more. It is theologically possible, but our Lord does not seem to think it likely.

We pass on straight, then, from lamentable failure to glorious triumph, from complete barrenness to generous growth, from the arch-apostate to the prince of the apostles. We do not hear that any of our Lord's disciples were actually present at his crucifixion except his blessed Mother and the holy women. Yet to his friends as to his enemies the occasion of his death was a test; the seed sown would bear fruit in accordance with the preparation bestowed on the soil of their hearts. And, at first sight, how disastrously the disciples react upon the test! You would say that in them, too, and in St Peter particularly, we had a most clear instance of the seed falling on stony ground, and so first sprouting up prematurely, then withering away under the sun of temptation. Only waiting to see whether our Lord would deliver himself by some miracle from the hands of his captors, they have taken to their heels and run for it. That is, I suppose, the explanation of why they waited so long and then fled so suddenly; witnesses of his wonderful works, they never imagined that he would be taken until they saw him submitting himself meekly to the will of the chief priests. Then, with a sudden panic fear that their Master's power is at an end, they leave his side and escape into the darkness. And they meet at a rendezvous, the same upper room, no doubt, where they had made their communion a few hours before. There they are: St Thomas, the dogged cynic, who had tried to dissuade our Lord from going to Judaea, and then with a shrug of his shoulders, had said "Let us also go, that we may die with him"[1]—there he is, in hiding. And St James, who had wanted to call down fire on the Samaritans—he never tried to call down fire on our Lord's persecutors—St James, who had boasted that he was able to drink of our Lord's chalice and be baptized with his baptism—there he is, in hiding. There they all are, ashamed of meeting one another's looks, and wondering what to do next, or who is to take the lead—why, no, they are not all there; there is a face missing: what has become of St Peter? Of course, he was the first to swear—but remember, they had all sworn—not to leave our Lord in any extremity; he, it seems, must have been as good as his word—perhaps when the trial is over they will get news of him.

And meanwhile, huddled up by the fire in the high priest's house,

[1] John 11. 16.

not daring to look up for fear he should be recognized as the dangerous fellow with the sword, not daring to speak for fear his north-country accent should betray him, sits the hero of their imagination. Already he has had two narrow escapes, and came out of them with some sacrifice of dignity, of consistency—yes, it must be admitted, of truth-fulness. Is it wise to run further risk of discovery, now that he knows his own weakness and the peril he is in? He can do just as much good, see what is going on just as well, if he goes and waits in the shadow of the porch. But—it is very cold outside, and they have left him in peace nearly an hour how, and the fatal inaction, inability to make a decisive move, that dogs most of us at times, keeps him chained to his seat. And then the dreaded thing happens; someone asks a question; he has to answer; he just fails to avoid the little barbarism of speech that marks him for a Galilean; angry with himself, angry with his questioner, he blusters and tries to brazen it out with an oath. The sudden crow of a cock startles him, and as he looks up he catches his Master's eye turned towards him from the other end of the hall, who shall say with what reproach, what warning, what pity in its glance? *And going out he wept bitterly.*[1]

I know it is fashionable to make the most of St Peter's sin. We seldom mention the attitude of the other apostles, who had taken the same oath of loyalty to our Lord, and deserted him from the first, who never denied him with St Peter because they had not courage to face St Peter's temptation. And we exaggerate the deliberateness of the fault. There was a great deal of heroic courage mixed up with the rashness which brought St Peter into his danger, and the first two denials were made on the spur of the moment—it is very hard to tell the truth when we are given no time to think. He did let himself in for it gradually, just like ourselves, first courting the occasion of sin, the pleasant, warm fireside, then equivocating ("I cannot understand what you say", was his first answer, perhaps with the pretence that he was deaf), then lying, then forswearing himself. And, anyhow, he wept bitterly. He felt, it may well be, more poignantly than the other apostles the baseness of his desertion, and those tears were the rain that made the good seed spring up thirtyfold. Let us not criticize St Peter overmuch.

Still, none of them have come out of it very well: ought we not to say, if only in justice to the other characters we have been considering, that they have failed at the test? *Therefore have I chosen you, that you should bear much fruit*[2]—where is the harvest now? The answer to that question seems to lie in a verse of the Psalms which refers, as the

[1] Matthew 26. 75.   [2] John 15. 16.

preceding verse shows, to God's saints. "Their infirmities were multiplied, therefore they made haste."[1] All through the Gospels the infirmities of the apostles are unsparingly brought to our notice. Only a schoolteacher can realize what a faculty there is in human nature for getting a thing perfectly right forty-nine times and making a hopeless blunder over the fiftieth. The disciples have drunk in eagerly, one would suppose, their Master's teaching, and what is the effect of it all? "Blessed are the meek", he tells them, and they propose to call down fire from heaven upon his enemies. "Sit not in the highest place when thou art bidden to a feast"—and again and again they quarrel as to who shall be the greatest. "He who will come after me, let him take up his cross and follow me", and they try to prevent him going into danger. And finally, although at least three times he has carefully explained to them the circumstances of his coming Passion, they are so surprised by his attitude of resignation that they forsake him and flee. He has trained them so carefully, so gently for this last test, and they have all failed at it!

Their infirmities were multiplied—this is their crowning infirmity. Therefore they make haste—it was the direct result of it, that from that moment their rapid strides in sanctity began. Calvary was a test for the apostles, but a different kind of test from that applied to Pilate, or to the Jews, or to the traitor. It was not the last momentous decision in which failure means rejection; it was the salutary test by which, before it was too late, they could learn their own shortcomings. Ill-success in some examination which is not of final importance is often the best way of finding out your own ignorance. Cowardice in face of persecution was, in this case, the surest proof the apostles could have of their own weakness, their own need of grace. God bestows his blessing, the *Imitation* tells us, where he finds vessels empty to receive it. *We are able, Although all shall be scandalized in thee, yet not I; Although I should die together with thee I will not deny thee*[2]—that was not the spirit which could welcome and draw down upon itself supernatural assistance. It was only after the humiliation of Good Friday, after the penitential tears and the experience of forgiveness, that the disciples learned, as it seems, all in a moment, the fortitude which enabled them to stand against kings and princes and to carry their Master's name to the utmost ends of the earth. Satan, our Lord told them, had desired to have St Peter that he might sift him as wheat, and God allowed it; allowed him to blow away the chaff, the bluster and the brag and the self-confidence, that were the last obstacles to his sanctity; but the good

---

[1] Psalm 15. 4.   [2] Mark 14. 30.

seed remained, ready to be ground in the mill of persecution and give life to the body of the Church.

There are few souls, I suppose, that have not felt at some time the humiliation of defeat. We thought we had counted the cost, prepared ourselves for the worst that could happen, worked ourselves up to an unshakable resolution. We had practised with our swords, slashing about in front of the looking-glass, as it were, and felt that we knew all the strokes. And then we went out and did manfully, and found ourselves following our Master in his Passion, albeit at a distance; it may be, where others failed. Come what might, we would not lose sight of him. And then, astonished at our own courage, we began to play with fire: we allowed ourselves some little indulgence—what if it were a remote occasion of sin? We had faced worse, and come out of it unharmed. And then we began to parley with temptation, and failed, somehow, to give it a straight answer. And then suddenly, without giving us time to remember all our good resolutions and our admirable array of motives to the contrary, Satan made a violent assault on us, and we consented. And still we would not be warned, and, partly with the feeling that it did not matter much now, partly ashamed to draw back from a position once adopted, we remained where we were exposed to the temptation, and this time the consent was deliberate, final, inexcusable. Only then did we awake, as the cock-crow awakes a man from sleep, from the lethargy of a disordered conscience; only then did we see, in a single glimpse, the face of Christ suffering for our sins. And, please God, we wrenched ourselves free, and the night we fled into opened up to us the flood-gates of contrition.

Satan had desired to have us, that he might sift us as wheat, in the hope that the rude blasts of temptation might sweep us away altogether, the grain with the chaff. But if we had the humility to accept and to profit by our warning, he was doing God's work. We trusted, not to the fervour of our contrition, but to the healing grace of the sacrament of penance, to fortify us against the next attack. And now, what is the harvest we are to derive from our failure? For we are meant to reap a harvest even from failure. God never leaves us without sufficient grace to resist a temptation, but where he foresees that we shall succumb he so directs his providence as to form a loving plot for our further advancement, if we will. There are, I think, three principal graces we can receive, three principal qualities we can develop, so as to fertilize the soil of our hearts from the mouldering remains of sin. If we think of the apostles emerging from their ordeal with ten times the strength they had before in each of those three directions, then we shall

GX

understand how they reaped thirtyfold from the harvest of the cross.

First, then, from all such failures we are clearly meant to derive a fuller humility and sense of our dependence upon God. *Amen, amen I say to thee*, our Lord told St Peter after the Resurrection, *when thou wast younger thou didst gird thyself and walk where thou wouldst. But when thou shalt be old, thou shalt stretch forth thy hands, and another shall gird thee and lead thee whither thou wouldst not. This he said, signifying by what death he should glorify God.*[1] But surely it was also a forecast of St Peter's life. Till now, he had always been the first to gird himself for action and go where his impetuous nature bids him; over the waves of the lake, into battle against his Master's captors, into the judgment-hall. But in those three days he grows up. Do we not always think of St Peter in the Gospels, for all the grey beard the pictures give him, as a young man? Do not we always think of St Peter in the Acts of the Apostles as an old man, who, even apart from his position, derives authority from his reverend years? What has happened? It is not that he has lost energy or forcefulness or courage; not that he has become content to direct and let others act for him. No, the secret of the change is that he has learned the true source of his strength; no longer rushes into the conflict where legions of angels fear to tread, content rather to stretch out his hands in prayer and let the impulse of the Holy Spirit move him along in accordance with the divine will. If we learn that from our defeat we shall have learned something.

And if we come to recognize our dependence upon grace that recognition will bring with it a second quality, prudence in avoiding the occasions of sin. Grace does not come automatically at our bidding but is supplied to us in pure mercy by God himself, not in the measure we expect, but in the measure his eternal purpose demands. That is the danger of presuming on grace. Though you have resisted the appeal of temptation under the influence of the same occasion a thousand times, if it was grace that gave you the victory, what emboldens you to demand as a right that which came to you always as a free gift? We shall cease, then, to court temptation, to walk heedlessly into the occasions of sin, as we used to before failure came to admonish us. We all know the old legend about St Peter at the end of his life being induced by the prayers of the faithful to go away into hiding when persecution was raging at Rome, and what followed.

> *Lo, on the darkness broke a wandering ray,*
> *A vision flashed along the Appian way.*
> *Divinely in the pagan night it shone,*

[1] John 21. 18-19.

A mournful Face, a Figure hurrying on,
Though haggard and dishevelled, frail and worn,
A King, of David's lineage, crowned with thorn.
"Lord, whither farest?" Peter, wondering, cried.
"To Rome", said Christ, "to be re-crucified."
Into the night the vision ebbed like breath,
And Peter turned, and rushed on Rome and death.

We wonder, perhaps, that the boldest of the apostles should ever have felt any hesitation at such a crisis. But is it not possible that, mindful of that night of fear, those faces by the fireside, in the unforgettable past, he would not presume on grace being given him to face his persecutors, until he was quite certain that it was God's will he should be exposed to the test? I like to think that, if the story be true, humility shone out in Peter's flight no less than heroism in his return.

And the third grace is the most obvious of all, though the world at large often fails to recognize it. God would always save us, if we would, from falling into sin; but, once we have fallen, the penitence those very sins occasion is in itself acceptable to God. Penitence is not merely a redressing of the balance; it has a value of its own in God's sight. The saints have hoarded up, you might almost say, the memory of their sins, as matter for contrition, and (since he loves much to whom much is forgiven) for love. Sorrow for our sins, however far we have been enabled by God's grace to leave them behind, is a virtue which, so far as I know, only Christianity encourages; certainly it is one which no Christian should ever neglect.

5

SIXTYFOLD AND A HUNDREDFOLD

As the rain and the snow come down from heaven, and return no more thither, but soak the earth and water it, and make it to spring, and give seed to the sower and bread to the eater, so shall my word be.—Isaias 55. 10.

WE have watched the divine Sower casting abroad the seed of his kingdom as he hangs on Calvary. And we have seen something of the harvest which that seed-time produces in accordance with the varying nature of the soil on to which the good grain fell. It fell on the hard wayside, on hearts trodden down and unreceptive; sometimes from cynical indifference to truth, as with Pilate, sometimes through brutal insensibility to all the higher feelings, as with the soldiers and the impenitent thief. It fell among stony ground, where it had not much depth of earth; into shallow, fickle, frivolous hearts, where it sprung up at once with great display of fruitfulness, but withered away all too soon when it had to face the glaring rays of the sun—the temptations of the world. That effect was found both among souls within the Church, as among the Galileans and Jews who hailed Christ on Palm Sunday and crucified him on Good Friday, and also among souls just outside the Church, the Herods, the enlightened, patronizing intellects that seem so near Christian truth and are yet so far from it. It fell among thorns, the love of money or the world's cares or the world's pleasures; and so, though it had taken deep root at the beginning, it was choked and strangled in its growth: the root of bitterness sprang up, and there was no harvest there, only Judas' reaping, a reaping of blood. It fell on good ground, where it found a genuine lodgment; and to these souls, as to Peter and the other apostles when they deserted their Master, the scandal of the cross fertilized the seed, instead of destroying it, and it came up thirtyfold. And now we are left with the best soil of all, which is to bring forth fruit a hundredfold; and that, surely, we shall find in the hearts of the three faithful watchers by the cross; our Lady and St John and St Mary Magdalen.

It is worth noticing that, to each of these five classes of soul, the crucifixion represents a different stage in the preparing of the grain. To Pilate and his soldiers it was seed-time; the Christian religion had never been proposed to them in any way before, and it was left to the previous preparation of the soil to determine whether they would accept or reject the message now for the first time brought to them. And it would seem that they refused, all except the centurion—here, then, is the grain frustrated in the act of sowing. To Herod and the Jews and the Galileans the faith has already been proposed, and they have welcomed it after their fashion: the crucifixion is the sun of persecution which is to test the hardiness of the growth, and the test is all too searching—here we have the grain frustrated in the shooting. To Judas, it is the final test, the reaping of the field; and it proves that the thorns have cramped and strangled the growth, so that whatever grains have come up are not worth the gathering; the grain is frustrated in its harvesting. To St Peter and the apostles the crucifixion is again a test, but it is a test which sifts wheat from chaff and purges away nothing but what is useless; the grain is perfected in the winnowing. To these last three beside the cross there is no further need of the winnowing-fan; they have been tested enough; they are ripe for martyrdom, and martyrdom comes, though it be of the soul, not of the body, as they stand and watch the Passion; the grain is perfected in the grinding.

And these three have a special privilege at the Resurrection. I think we may say that these three, more than anyone besides, were expecting it to happen. St Mary Magdalen had surely some instinct that strange things were afoot, or why was she in such a hurry to run to the sepulchre and fulfil what you would have said to be Martha's office, the embalming of the sacred body? True, the sight of the empty tomb took her by surprise, and she did not understand at first, but she must have been prepared for something unusual. St John, as we know from the Gospel, permitted himself the intellectual satisfaction of making sure that the tomb was indeed empty, but he would not go in; the mere sight of the linen clothes was enough to corroborate his expectations. And our Lady does not seem to have gone at all—was that because she did not care? Unless you are prepared to accept so monstrous an alternative, her absence, and the absence of any reference in the Gospels to that first meeting with her risen Son, can surely be explained only by one suggestion—she must have believed already.

And these three, more than any other characters, I suppose, in the New Testament, represent to us the contemplative life. The Magdalen, who after her conversion chose the better part that should not be taken from her—should not be taken from her when even Thomas doubted and even Peter was afraid—contemplation, that finds its natural home at the foot of our Saviour's cross. And St John, who leaned on our Lord's breast at supper, and drank from that fountain the secrets of the divine love; St John, whom our Lord would have tarry till he came, not going out to meet, in some far corner of the Gentile world, the image of his Master's Passion, but growing old in the service of his Church and abiding his love. And what need to speak of her whose love of solitude and silence is proved for us, not only by the little the Gospels tell of her, but still more by what they do not tell, so that in most of our Lord's life-history her name is scarcely more than an echo and a fragrance? She, the pattern and the patroness of all who embrace the contemplative life, she too is here, and all Calvary is eloquent with the throbbing of her unspoken prayer. For these contemplatives, this is to be the hour of their Passion; let us watch them for a moment, one by one.

St Mary Magdalen has passed, long since, through the way of purgation. Her sin was great, but it was all washed away in the hot tears that fell on our Lord's feet in the supper-chamber. Many sins are forgiven her, because she loved much: such is the testimony our Lord himself bears her, and to herself he ratifies the promise, *Thy sins are forgiven thee.*[1] No need, then, so far as concerns the perfectness of her contrition, to weep further, and yet on Calvary she weeps still, her own sins and his sufferings melting together in the crucible of her burning love. Be she a thousand times forgiven, those dead memories shall not cease to provide her with matter for penitence so long as the past cannot be unmade. She will have them bear a hundredfold the acceptable fruit of contrition.

> Heavens thy fair eyes be,
> Heavens of ever-falling stars;
> 'Tis seed-time still with thee,
> And stars thou sowest, whose harvest dares
> Promise the earth to countershine
> Whatever makes Heaven's forehead fine.[2]

To others the crucifixion was a test of character, to her an opportunity of love; what better place than at her Lord's feet, what better time than in the hour of his Passion, to rend her heart once again and yet once again with those sighs of love, those sobs of repentance? *Lord, if thou hadst been here, my brother had not died*[3]—so she told him when he came to visit Lazarus; and now Lazarus is raised to life, and he who came to raise him has, in doing so, come to meet his own death; is that thought, perhaps, an image to her of the part her own sins have played in demanding the sacrifice that secured her ransom?

And St John has advanced too far in the science of the divine love to feel doubts or ask for explanations. But he is here as a witness, the only witness who will set his memories on record at first hand. It will be for him to hand down to us, over and above the cries of the Passion, those whispered words, not spoken to the multitude around, *Woman, behold thy son . . . Behold thy mother . . . I thirst . . . It is consummated.*[4] Still, then, it is he who is the recipient of our Lord's secrets, as at the last supper. And not only spoken secrets; but the whole meaning of that sacrifice it was for him to unravel: not with anxious speculations of the human reason, but, since love will only be expressed in its own terms, in terms of love. St Mary Magdalen is the mourner, St John the learner. The fruit he will derive a hundredfold is not so much the outpouring of his affections as the illumination of his mind, which is to

---

[1] Luke 7. 48.   [2] Richard Crashaw, "The Weeper", Stanza 2.
[3] John 11. 21.
          [4] John 19. 26-30.

hand on to us, and to all time, the lesson of the Passion. We know that his testimony is true—what hours of celestial contemplation, more revealing in its utterance than the speculations of all the philosophers, must have been needed before St John felt that he could deserve that commendation from his disciples! The seed is the word of God; ripened long since in this loving heart, it has been ground in the mill of that heart-rending experience to become the bread of life to our souls.

And of our Lady—who shall say what thoughts were hers? If you need proof that a mystery faces you here, consider the various representations that are made, both in art and in writing, of her feelings. Now you will see her bathed in tears, now gazing in rapt adoration, now betraying no sign of her emotion. One book will tell you that she wept for her Son, another that she wept not for him but for our sins, another that she did not weep at all; and then the hymn tells you that her face was bedewed with tears, but her heart unmoved as adamant. I do not attempt to say what picture comes nearest to the right idea in this matter. But surely our instinct is this: that she was certainly not sorrowing, as men sorrow without hope, for she believed in her Son's Resurrection; that all the physical pains she endured were, through the power of sympathy, reproduced in her heart; and further, that she knew the meaning of the scene that was being enacted, realized its relation to human sin and the redemption of the human race. Does not the true grandeur of her compassion lie in the complete union between her will and his? In the fact that, in imitation of him, she steeled her will against the anguish his anguish communicated to her, in order that her will might communicate and co-operate with his will in the work of our redemption? As you may see the figure of the crucified now bent in agony, now calm and stately, according to the artist's impression—and neither impression is false—so you may paint tears on Mary's cheeks if you will, or see her standing there motionless and emotionless, for she is one with him.

> Before her eyes,
> Her and the whole world's joys
> Hanging all torn she sees, and in his woes
> And pains, her pangs and throes;
> Each wound of his, from every part,
> All, more at home in her one heart. . . .
> While with a faithful, mutual flood
> Her eyes bleed tears, his wounds weep blood.[1]

[1] Richard Crawshaw, "Sancta Maria Dolorum", Stanzas 1 and 2.

From him she derives the martyrdom of her affections, to him she offers the sacrifice of her will.

I have represented St Mary Magdalen as the type of our affections, St John of our minds, the blessed Virgin of our wills, a hierarchy of saints corresponding to the hierarchy of our faculties. And all alike are reaping a hundredfold from their participation in the sufferings of the divine Redeemer. Let us see if we can follow them, and garner a few gleanings, though they be but poor handfuls, from the rich harvest they are reaping there.

The crucified hangs there to quicken our affections. It is easy to decry the value of the affections in prayer; to say that their exercise in such matters may border dangerously on hysteria, that the ease with which they are excited is often no more than a matter of temperament, the practical effect of them on our lives often weak and evanescent. That is all true, and the spiritual authors do not fail to warn us against a religion which does not advance beyond emotionalism, barren at best, and at worst dangerous to our nerves, even to our sanity. But it is a cowardly exaggeration of that warning to suppose that, as the soul proceeds higher in the scale of prayer, the affections cease to play any part in its spiritual activities. Read the history of the saints, and you will find chapter after chapter which, taken by itself, would represent them as the victims of their emotions.

The crucified hangs there to answer the questionings of our intellect. What is the meaning, what is the value of pain? Why does man have to endure it? Or, granted that, why is its distribution among men so unequal, disproportionate to the merits of the souls affected by it? I do not say that the crucifix provides us with a complete answer that must carry conviction to the mind of any sceptic who may have posed us with difficulties at a street corner. But I do say that in so far as our meditations deal faithfully, though in a humble and reverent spirit, with the doctrine of God made Man, sinless yet suffering for sins; in so far as we honestly propose to ourselves the questions we all know so well—Who hangs here? Doing what? By what means? At what moment of time? In what manner? For what purpose?—in so far as we beg the grace of the Holy Spirit to enlighten our dull minds and to lift the veil from the mystery, we shall come away from our meditation of the Passion both firmer in our faith and more reconciled to the pains and the sorrows that the sons of Adam are called upon to suffer—suffer them in such company as that.

The crucified hangs there to confirm the purpose of our wills. Two activities of the will we need continually in our Christian course, resolution to undertake what we see God wants us to undertake, resignation in enduring whatever—not asking our permission or leaving room for our cowardice to assert itself—he tells us to endure. In the meditation of the Passion we find the pattern of resolution and of resignation combined in each single act. Christ resigns himself to his sufferings, to the tremors of the flesh, the lashes of his persecutors, the buffeting, the crown of thorns, the way of the cross, the nails that fasten him there. And at the same moment he is resolved upon all this for the redemption of his creatures; it is his will that lays the cross on his shoulders, his will that chains him there a prisoner, when all the angel armies wait but a word to spring to his deliverance. And if we can learn from Mary something of the secret by which at that dark hour she made her will all his, it will be no transient upheaval of the emotions, no mere enlargement of the horizon of our speculative intellect, but a true determination of the will to action and to endurance that we shall carry away with us as we turn to go down the hill, back into the dust of the city and the world that has crucified its God.

It fell by the wayside—please God, not here. It fell upon stony ground—God pardon us that it should be so, but there is still time to break up the clods and water the parched earth. It fell among thorns—we know the peril, and confess ourselves hourly pensioners upon the divine grace; but, grace helping us, we will not allow those thorns free scope to thwart the progress of the good seed. It sprang up thirtyfold; we have sinned, but our very sins, if we will but make use of them, will enable us to mount higher and to go further. It brought forth a hundredfold; may all those chosen friends of God, in whose lives we read the story of that glorious increase, intercede for us their poor brethren, that we too may know, some day, the joy of reaping, and appear not all empty-handed at the harvest that is to come.

VI

THE CROSS OF CHRIST*

* A series of sermons preached on Wednesdays during Lent, and later published in
The Cross, July to December, 1928.

I

THE TRAVESTY OF TRUTH

In all things let us exhibit ourselves as the ministers of God, . . . by evil report and good report, as deceivers, and yet true; as unknown and yet known, as dying and behold we live, as chastised and not killed, as sorrowful, yet always rejoicing, as needy, yet enriching many, as having nothing and possessing all things.—2 Corinthians 6. 4.

THIS passage of St Paul, which is read out to us every year on the first Sunday of Lent, is apt to strike upon our ears as a series of vaguely encouraging sentiments, without leaving any clear impression behind as to the argument which runs through it. We are to recommend ourselves publicly—that is the force of the word—as the ministers of God in a variety of ways; first of all as the victims of manifold tribulations, in labours, in watching, in fastings; next, by a series of reactions in our own character, in chastity, in long-suffering, in sweetness, and so on; and finally by evil report and good report, that is, as labouring under a set of misrepresentations which happen to be the exact opposite of the facts; we shall be called deceivers when we tell the truth, we shall be accounted beggars when in reality we are in possession of spiritual riches such as the world never dreams of, and so on. Now, why is it that St Paul takes it for granted that the servant of God can be recognized first by the sufferings he undergoes, next by the perfections of his own character, and last by the misunderstanding which he encounters? Why does all that go without saying?

I believe there is only one way to make sense of the argument, and that is to suppose that St Paul was doing here what he doesn't often do —was using the word "God" simply as the equivalent of the word "Christ". In all things let us recommend ourselves as the servants of Christ—see how that simplifies the whole argument. Our Lord himself had said, "The servant is not greater than his master; if they have persecuted me, they will also persecute you".[1] We recommend ourselves as the servants of Christ when we are like Christ; first, when we suffer all manner of tribulations, as Christ did; next, when we suffer them in that spirit of patience and sweetness in which Christ

[1] John 15. 20.

suffered them; and last of all when in spite of that we are assailed, as our Lord was assailed, with criticisms which are the exact opposite of the truth. I want to take those accusations under six different headings on these six Wednesdays, and try to show you, first of all how our Lord incurred those accusations, next, how his Church incurs those accusations, and last, how we ourselves are likely to, and ought to, incur those accusations, in proportion as we live up to the model set us by our divine Master.

As deceivers, and yet true—that means that the Christian, like Christ, will be called a deceiver by those around him precisely in proportion as he loves the truth, and wishes to spread it. When our Lord stood before Pilate he warned him, "Everyone who is of the truth heareth my voice"; and Pilate answered "What is truth?"[1] Next day, the Jews who had demanded his crucifixion stood at the same judgment-seat, and referred to our Lord as "this deceiver".[2] There was really no other description they could give. Only three comments were possible on that career. One is this. His friends went out to lay hands on him, for they said, "He is become mad". Another is this, "Nay, but he deceiveth the people". And the third is, "Thou art Christ, the Son of the living God". Blinded by their prejudice, the Jews could not conceive this last as a possible solution. Nor would they disregard our Lord as a harmless madman; they feared the people. Necessary, then, to write him down as a deceiver; as one who, for some obscure purposes of his own, was deliberately misleading the people; laying claim to fantastic powers and backing up his assertion by an appeal to the magical arts. Notice two points about that. In the first place, they never even pretended to discover any motive which such a man could have in putting forward these claims. Again and again he had refused to aspire to any political power; he lived, and died, a poor man; what incentive, then, could he have had for setting out on a career of deceit? And the other point is this—the people who crucified our Lord as a deceiver didn't themselves believe in truth. Pilate openly admitted it; the Jews showed it by their conduct. They condemned our Lord on the charge that he claimed to be the Son of God, and then accused him before Pilate because he said he was the king of the Jews. And these were the men who called their victim a deceiver!

The Catholic Church, again and again in her history, has undergone persecution or incurred angry criticism for precisely the same reason. She alone, in a world which had lost its sense of truth and contented itself with shams in which it half believed, asserted the claims of an

[1] John 18. 37-38.   [2] Matthew 17. 63.

absolute, because a revealed truth. And the world's reply has been to call her a deceiver. In the last days of paganism, when the old heathen gods had lost all their prestige, and their altars still smoked only in deference to a historic sentiment or a political convention, Christians were found asserting that there was one God. They did not suggest it as a possible solution; they did not introduce it as an interesting speculation; they asserted it as a fact. And the answer was, The Christians to the lions! And today, when the world has become so fuddled with its own philosophies that men cannot be sure whether two and two really make four, whether black is not really white under another aspect, they all agree on one thing—that the Catholic religion can't be true. They will tell you one moment that it is impossible to discover whether truth exists, and the next moment that the Catholic religion is certainly false—such is their logic. The Catholic religion must obviously be a deception, because it claims to know what is true.

You and I, as Catholics—there's no getting out of it—have got to labour under that imputation; of course we are liars, all Catholics are. If a Catholic writes a book in defence of his religion, it is at once discounted because he is a Catholic; naturally he writes like that, Catholics always do. If he is a priest, it is because he is paid to; if he is a layman, it is because he is made to; but of course, he can't really mean it. Why on earth the world supposes that we go on repeating to one another and to the general public a series of statements in which we do not believe ourselves, I for one could never discover. It must, surely, be some monstrous perversion of the intellect which enables three hundred millions of people to recite a common creed Sunday by Sunday and wink at one another at they do so!

And the reason of that is that we believe in absolute truth. The world has got so accustomed to half-beliefs that it is afraid to look absolute truth in the face—it would be like staring at the sun. It can imagine a man dying for a sentiment, such as loyalty, or for a point of honour, such as the good name of a woman; it cannot imagine a man dying for a mere affirmation, such as the affirmation that the eternal Word is of one substance, not merely of like substance, with the Father, or that the blessed Virgin is the Mother of God. Meanwhile—that is the irony of it —truth, even abstract truth, does matter to us, and matters enormously. We cannot be content, like the casual Englishman, with a vague aspiration towards something higher than ourselves, we know not what. We cannot be content, like the average Protestant, with repeating to ourselves that certain spiritual ideas, certain avenues of approach towards the unseen, have been helpful to the Christians of other ages, and therefore may well have an abiding value for us too. We are committed to a creed. The Catholic religion is very much more than a creed; it is a life, a warfare, a loyalty, a romance. But it is a creed too; and the assertion of it involves us in an intellectual responsibility. Man's intellect is part of himself, and must be represented, consequently, in the scheme of his salvation.

Let us learn this, then, first, from St Paul's admonition; that we, whom the world thinks liars, have on the contrary the duty of being true, of living by a series of intellectual affirmations. We ought not simply to draw a blank cheque upon our own powers of credulity, telling ourselves that we believe everything the Church teaches without having much idea what she does teach. We ought to be instructed in Christian doctrine according to the general level of our intelligence; we ought, in these days, to know something about the attacks which are being made upon our faith from outside, and the refutation of them. We shall get no credit for it; we shall still be called liars. But we can put up with that, when we remember that the eternal Wisdom of the Father came down to earth and was hailed as a deceiver. If only they knew what it means to be a Catholic! God grant that they may come to know.

2

THE CHARM OF OUR OBSCURITY

As unknown, and yet known.—2 Corinthians 6. 8.

I SHOULD like to point out how each of these random criticisms, which were directed long ago against the early Church, were verified or rather were falsified, in the life of our blessed Lord himself, in the life of his Church, and in our own lives today, so long as we are faithful in following him. I say verified, or rather falsified; for indeed St Paul reminds his converts that as a matter of fact each of these criticisms is misdirected; each is the precise opposite of the truth. As unknown—yes, in the world's eyes; as well known, if the world only knew!

It was one of the principal charges brought against our Lord by his enemies—their principal motive, probably, for rejecting him—that he was an unknown man, that he was the son of a carpenter's wife; that he had never graduated in any school of rabbinical learning. Could any good thing come out of a provincial place like Nazareth? Could it come, in any case, out of a carpenter's shop? Hath any one of the rulers believed in him (they asked), or of the Pharisees? He did not move in the world of political influence, or of fashionable thought. He had a following, of course, among the vulgar; but who was he, after all? A nobody. As unknown, and yet known—do you ask how our Lord was known? "As the Father knoweth me, I also know the Father."[1] He, who to the world's eyes seemed friendless, without influence, without honour, had been from all eternity, was then, as he would be to all eternity, the unique object of his heavenly Father's loving regard, knowing and known with an intimacy of which all our earthly knowledge is but a shadow. "No man knoweth the Son but the Father, neither doth anyone know the Father but the Son"; himself the medium and the term of all knowledge, the unknown God lived on earth an unknown man.

Nor is there any reason to doubt that his Church, during the first century and more of its existence, was discredited in the world's eyes by the humble origin and insignificant status of its adherents. Now and then we come across a name in the records of early Christianity which suggests the conversion of some member of a noble family; but for the most part, clearly it was a religion of slaves and freedmen. At Rome they met together in underground passages under the pretence that they were a sort of burial club such as poor men cultivated. The stories that were believed of them were the kind of stories which the fashionable world repeats only about men whom it has never met in real life. "Not many wise according to the flesh, not many mighty, not many noble"[2]—such was St Paul's own estimate of the flourishing Church at Corinth. The influence of the Christian faith makes no ripple on the surface of politics, of social life, of public institutions, during those first ages of the Church. St Paul, then, comforts his friends in their obscurity by the reflection that, like their Master, they are unknown yet known —unknown to men, known to God.

It is, I fancy, a piece of current Christian language which has fallen out of use, to describe a Christian as a known man. Yet it is a word frequent on St Paul's lips. "I am the Good Shepherd", our Lord had said, "and I know mine, and mine know me"[3]—the intimacy is

---

[1] John 10. 15.   [2] 1 Corinthians 1. 26.   [3] John 10. 14.

mutual. St Paul catches up the phrase; in heaven, he says, "I shall know even as I am known"; "the Lord knoweth them that are his"; "if any man love God, the same is known by him"; "after that you have known God, or rather are known by God"[1]—you see how readily the idea springs to his mind. You have felt what it is, sometimes, in a company of strangers, when you are suffering from that sense of loneliness which only a crowd can give, to come across a familiar face, though it be only that of a casual acquaintance? So it is with the Christian; wherever he is, there is Somebody there who knows him.

Now, it would be very easy to draw, as I drew last Wednesday, a parallel between the position of the early Church in its heathen surroundings and our position as Catholics in England today.[2] It would be very easy to point out that we Catholics are all the time outnumbered and overshadowed by the representatives of another creed; that we are not merely a minority in the nation, but a minority whose doings arouse little interest and whose claims command little attention; that we are comparatively ill represented in the press and on public bodies; that, in many ranks of society, you still lose caste by becoming a Catholic; that it is possible for people who are determined not to have anything to do with us to pretend that we do not exist. But I don't want to emphasize here that comparative obscurity of the Catholic body in England, for several reasons. Partly because, after all, it is only due to an accident of history. Partly because it is not as noticeable now as it was half a century ago, and indeed becomes less noticeable every day. But chiefly because such complaints do not reach to the heart of the matter. The point is not that in this age or in that, in this country or in that, the Catholic world is a small and a comparatively provincial world. The point is that it is the instinct of the Catholic genius at its highest to court obscurity, to shun publicity, and, if it can do so without prejudice to the salvation of souls, to live and to die unknown.

This Catholic instinct of humility is a quite different thing from the modesty which forbids us to boast of our own performances, to push ourselves forward in conversation, which makes us deprecate our own importance and defer to other people as more worthy of consideration than ourselves. That modesty is a natural quality, a gracious thing, in youth especially. But the source of it is only a mixture of embarrassment and good breeding; it has no real kinship with that hunger for self-obliteration which drove the saints to take refuge from the world

[1] 1 Corinthians 13. 12; 2 Timothy 2. 19; 1 Corinthians 8. 3; Galatians 4. 9.
[2] This sermon was preached in 1928.

in deserts or on lonely hillsides, which empties the ballroom to fill the cloister. Read through all the files of all the French newspapers from the year 1873 to the year 1897, and I doubt if you will come across a single reference to the name of Mary Frances Theresa Martin. Yet, of all her contemporaries, who is so much on men's lips today as the Little Flower? She hid from us, and we never knew her; never heard of her name till she had already placarded heaven with the record of her virtues and her charities. And so it has been even with the busiest, even with the most active of the saints. They were jealous of the least impurity of intention with which publicity might tarnish the offering they made to God. Their Father saw them in secret; why should anybody know, why should anybody want to know, save he?

With this form of obscurity the world does not tax us, in theory. In theory, although it cannot see why people should want to shut themselves up in monasteries and convents, it has become broad-minded enough, or vague-minded enough, to reflect that after all there is no accounting for tastes; perhaps the cloistered life suits some temperaments. I say, in theory; but when the concrete case arises, when beauty, and charm, and social gifts disappear for ever behind the jealous bars of the grille, then the old criticism does break out, the old catch-words are still repeated. She might have done so much good in other ways, she had such a useful life before her; was it not rather selfish, even if she did feel drawn to it, to hide away such talents where they can be of no use? So the world round us talks; and sometimes, in the concrete case, it finds half-hearted Catholics to agree with it.

I will not speak this morning of the justification of the monastic idea in general; we shall meet with that when we consider the other criticisms which this passage of St Paul refers to. But let us make no mistake about this; in the pattern of Christian life, whether you study it in the hidden years at Nazareth, or in the history of the saints, or in the ideals of the religious orders, the love of obscurity, of waiting upon God alone and letting the world go its own way without you, is an integral part of sanctity. And imperfect Christians like ourselves must not altogether forget that lesson amid the clash of other voices; we must have a hidden life if we are to cultivate the familiar friendship of almighty God. What greater consolation than to be certain, however little the world knows or understands us, of being known to him? What more terrible formula of rejection than that with which he threatens the impenitent, "Amen I say to you, I know you not"?[1]

[1] Matthew 25. 12.

3

JOY IN SORROW

As sorrowful, yet always rejoicing.—2 Corinthians 6. 10.

I AM taking the liberty of altering, for the purpose of these sermons, the order in which St Paul treats these reproaches, these criticisms, which were brought in his day against the Church. As I explained before, I want to show how they apply not only to the life of the Christian but to the life of Christ. And if we are thinking of their application to the life of Christ, it will be natural to consider the words "as chastised and not killed" in Passion Week, to consider the words "as dying, and behold we live" in Holy Week. Today, then, we are to consider the words "as sorrowful, yet always rejoicing".

The Man of Sorrows—so we call our Lord, and so we think of him. How, indeed, he could be sorrowful who enjoyed at every moment of his life that vision which is the happiness of the Blessed in heaven, is a mystery we shall never understand on this side of the grave. Yet, if you look at it from a different point of view, the difficulty is all the other way; the difficulty is to imagine how a single ray of light-heartedness could visit such a life as his. Remember, he saw the existence of sin in those around him, understood the meaning of sin, realized the horror of sin, as only Incarnate God could. And at the same time, he was perfect Man, with all man's capacity for tears. Think of the great saints, and how they have wept and agonized over the sinful lives of those around them; what, then, must have been his tragedy, who hated sin more and was more conscious of its existence even than they? More than that—our human sorrows are lightened, even when we do not realize it, by hope; when things are darkest, we still hope that the sinner will be converted, that the tragedy will be avoided. That pathetic consolation of our poor mortality was not to be found in Christ; he knew all that lay before him. He chose Judas for his friend, although he knew Judas would betray him. He laboured to convert the Jews, his fellow countrymen; yet he knew that they would reject him and deliver him up to be crucified. What comfort, then, was his, in the days of his mortality? How could he be otherwise than sorrowful, with such dark clouds hanging over the horizon of his career?

And yet there is one passage, only one, where the Gospel, only one Gospel, tells us, "In that hour Jesus rejoiced in the spirit".[1] Jesus looked round about on them with anger—yes, he had that generous human sentiment of indignation which revolts from man's cruelty and man's hypocrisy. He marvelled—yes, he shared that human astonishment which we all feel, sometimes, over the blindness of our fellow creatures. Jesus wept—yes, he would experience that human weakness which can find relief in tears. But "Jesus rejoiced"—that, surely, is the most astonishing proof of his full humanity. He, who in his divine nature could suffer no diminution of his eternal blessedness, he who as man possessed the beatific vision, condescended nevertheless to feel and to be refreshed by a human sentiment of joy.

In that hour Jesus rejoiced in the spirit, and said, "I thank thee, O Father, Lord of heaven and earth, because thou hast hidden these things from the wise and prudent, and hast revealed them to little ones. Even so, Father, for so it hath seemed good in thy sight."[2] He rejoices, not because everybody is prepared to receive his message; no, some will reject, will persecute, will crucify him. No, he rejoices because the right people will receive his message, the simple, the child-like, the humble. He sees its intrinsic worth proved by the reactions of human souls upon its preaching—the Pharisees who stand aloof, the publicans and sinners who flock to hear. He is testing and dividing men's hearts as God wills that they should be tested and divided, and because God's will is being done, he rejoices. And then he goes on to invite us to share in his rejoicing; "Come to me, all you that labour and are burdened, and I will refresh you."[3] You labour and are burdened with all the tragedies of mortality, yet who so deeply, who so intimately, as I? "Come to me, then, and I will refresh you"; the Man of Sorrows will communicate to you his human sentiment of joy.

The Church of Christ has always borne in the world's eyes, but especially during the first centuries of its existence, the reputation of a gloomy and a kill-joy institution, so oppressed with the realization of human sinfulness, with the dangers which beset man in his path towards salvation, that she has no time to smile through her tears. Why else these solitudes and mortifications of her holiest disciples, these orgies of penance, these feverish anticipations of a judgment to come?

Perhaps this penitential atmosphere was more marked in the first centuries than it was in the Middle Ages, than it is in our own day. Mr Chesterton has suggested somewhere that all through the late empire and the Dark Ages Christendom was doing penance, making

---

[1] Luke 10. 21.   [2] *Ibid.*   [3] Matthew 11. 28.

atonement for the foul sins of the heathen world that went before it; only in the medieval world, the world of St Francis, did it begin to show a child-like appreciation of the beauties and the joys with which God has endowed this our perishable world. But remember, there is one season of the year at which the Church returns to her origins, at which her whole liturgy tends to return to a more primitive model. It is the season of Lent, when the different Masses for each fresh day recall to us those solemn processions by which our forefathers in the city of Rome sought to avert the anger of an offended God. In Lent the Christian fast is proclaimed, the solemnities of the marriage rite are forbidden, the organs are hushed, *alleluia* is sung no more. Yet next Sunday—Mid-Lent or Refreshment Sunday, as we call it—the Mass begins with the word *Laetare*, "Rejoice"; the organs sound again, flowers reappear on the altars, the sober purple of the priestly vestments loses a shade of its mournfulness. Even in the middle of that season during which she bids us lament, the Church, for a moment, encourages us to rejoice.

She would remind us, surely, that we Christians are the followers of Christ, and as he, the Man of Sorrows, could rejoice in spirit, so we his servants, must be sorrowful yet always rejoicing. There is a joy which is mere thoughtlessness, the world's privilege; you may be light-hearted because you are hard-hearted, because the sorrows of others and the sins of others strike no responsive chord in your being. But there is also a sorrow which is mere melancholy; which finds in suffering only material for pessimism, which finds in sin only the occasion for disgust. Not such is the sorrow, not such the joy, of God's saints. They have felt, with a sensitiveness of which you and I can only form a dim idea, man's impiety towards God, man's cruelty towards his fellow man, and have pitied, too, all the suffering they saw around them, itself the fruit and the expiation of sin. They have wept and scourged themselves, and spent long nights in an agony of prayer. Yet they have rejoiced, too, because they saw, as we do not see clearly, the beautiful and harmonious working of God's will for men, the perfect-ness of his dealings, the justification of his revealed message. The senti-ments of pity, of horror, of indignation which were provoked in them had no power to dislodge from their hearts that abiding happiness which comes only from a perfect conformity to God's will. They shared the seven sorrows of our blessed Lady, but they shared her joys too. They agonized with their Master, yet, even while they agonized, they rejoiced with him.

In proportion as we are good Christians, the world will find us dull dogs, a little removed from its insensate pursuit of pleasures, a little obsessed with thoughts of death and of judgment, a little sceptical about its facile optimisms. But, again in proportion as we are good Christians, this seriousness of character will not reflect itself in empty brooding on the wickedness of the world, will not make us morbid, self-centred, disillusioned. Rather, we shall find that Christian sorrow and Christian joy have their roots nearer together than we fancied; that the desire for God's will to be done perfectly in us and in all creatures, which *is* the Christian religion, bears a double fruit of sadness and of gladness. For so it must be, until our earthly Lent is over, and we rejoice for ever in the triumph of the eternal Easter-tide.

4

THE WEALTH OF OUR POVERTY

As beggars, yet enriching many; as having nothing, and possessing all things.
—2 Corinthians 6. 10.

It is a peculiar circumstance that, with all the details which have been left to us about our Lord's life, we do not know how he provided the money which went to meet his daily needs. It is certain that he and his disciples had a common fund; no doubt the basis of it was derived from the savings which our Lady and St Joseph had made in the sacred home at Nazareth; we do not know whether those savings were supplemented by the alms of charitable people. But, when he sent out his apostles on their preliminary tour of preaching, our Lord directed that they should take no money in their purses; he seems to have assumed that they would live on charity, and it is probable that his own position was not much different. If you come to think of it, we never hear of his having money to spend. And I suppose there can be little doubt that a good deal of the contempt which his adversaries felt for him, a good deal of the security with which they proceeded against him, was due to the fact that his clothes, his haunts, his habits, his atmosphere were not those of a rich man, or of one accustomed to move in rich society.

We tend to forget all that, because to us the Gospel story is irradiated with all the associations left by nineteen centuries of Christendom. Christian art, perhaps with a justifiable instinct, has eliminated from the picture of our Lord's life all the circumstances which we commonly associate with poverty. In the most realistic representations, you will never see a speck of dirt on the figure of an apostle, any tear or darn in his clothes. And yet, if you come to think of it, it is fairly certain that from the outside that sacred company must have looked like a crowd of poor men, and travellers at that. Think of Palm Sunday, for example—how impressive to our minds is the idea of our Lord's triumphal entry (so we call it) into Jerusalem! But what must it really have been like to those who saw it? A tired man riding on an ass, with a bodyguard of fishermen and working people, dusty old coats strewn in the way among the palm-branches, a rabble of unwashed pilgrims shouting "Hosanna"—giving every opportunity for ridicule and satire which you might find today in some local demonstration of the unemployed. That was what Palm Sunday looked like; and it was fitting that it should.

I say, it was fitting that it should, because after all the event which was taking place was such that no degree of human ceremony or pomp could even begin to do it justice. Almighty God coming to his own favourite city to be crucified—would the situation have been more adequately treated if those palm-branches had been replaced by rose-petals, if those garments had been of silk and of velvet, if those Hosannas had been repeated by choirs of professional singers? Why no; all the elaborate achievements of the human genius could never have done justice to such a situation as this. Our Lord, being rich, for our sakes became poor; to save us, he left heaven for earth; how could gold or jewels or purple have made a home for incarnate Godhead here?

If our Lord was content to be a poor man, his Church, in its very beginnings, was not merely a Church of poor men, it was a Church of beggars. There are two words for "poor" in Greek, one expressing honourable, the other dishonourable poverty. The word which expresses honourable poverty occurs in the New Testament exactly once; the word which expresses dishonourable poverty occurs thirty-four times. It is a word which gives you, by its derivation, the picture of a man who crouches at the street corner and says, "Give us a copper, mister". If ever there was a beggar, it was St Paul. You talk about the clergy always wanting money, but it is extraordinary how large a part of St Paul's writings refer directly to the Sunday collections. And I suppose it is probable that St Paul was criticized—whether by discontented Christians or by people outside the Church—for the persistent way in which he raised funds from his Gentile converts to supply the needs of the Church at Jerusalem. And his answer was perfectly simple; "if we have sown unto you spiritual things, is it a great matter if we reap your carnal things?"[1] He did not care if people represented his errand as an organized effort to raise money for some starving Jews at Jerusalem. For the message which he brought contained such spiritual riches that it was quite absurd to weigh any earthly possessions in the scale against them. We look poor, yes; but in reality we are the administrators of a huge spiritual largesse. We seem to have nothing, yet in reality we possess everything, because we possess Christ.

It would be easy to reflect that the Catholic Church in our own day, in our own country especially, enjoys the reputation of being a poor and a beggarly Church. Men taunt us, often enough, with the gimcrack ornaments of our churches, and the tawdriness of their appearance; people will tell you how offensive it is to them, and how disturbing to their devotion, to have a plate presented to them and be expected to pay for admission, as it were, at the doors of a Catholic church. It would be easy to dwell on that subject, and to examine why it is that the Catholic Church in our own country is still predominantly a Church of the poor, why it is that we cannot always enter into aesthetic competition with our heavily-endowed neighbours. But that, once more, would be to lose ourselves in merely local considerations, and to miss the heart of the subject. The point is that it is the instinct of our religion at its best not merely to distrust money, as the root of all evil, not merely to despise money, as something perishable and indifferent, but actually to love poverty, to preach poverty, to undertake voluntary poverty even when there is plenty of money to be had.

Look at St Francis' love of poverty—we think of it as somehow characteristic of St Francis, but in truth it was a characteristic which he shared with many great saints. To him poverty, which most of us regard as a negative thing and an abstraction, was our Lady Poverty, was a person and a playmate, nay, the bride of the religious. Poverty has appealed to the saints in a multitude of ways. For one thing, the absence of earthly possessions means the absence of worldly solicitudes, and oh, what a difference that makes! For another thing, the necessity of begging for your bread is a salutary form of humiliation. And again, the fact of not knowing where your next meal is to come from gives you a clear sense, very much to be desired but not easily attainable, of man's continual dependence upon the providence of almighty God.

[1] I Corinthians 9. 11.

H

But behind all that there is a deeper reason why the saints loved poverty—because they were following our Lord Jesus Christ. Being rich, for our sakes he became poor; if he stripped himself, on earth, of all the glory and the privileges that belonged to a divine person, was it too much that they should strip themselves of those perishable goods by which one man is distinguished from his fellows?

Some few of us are called to a life of holy poverty; all of us are called to a life of detachment. And in order to achieve that detachment from worldly goods which belongs to our Christian profession, we must learn to realize the true scale of values. We are poor, we Catholics; it is easy for people to keep out of our way and pretend that they do not see us. Yet we make many rich; in those ugly, angular convents you see—a cross on a gable, a name on a door-plate, easily overlooked—what lives have been spent in a pure activity of prayer! And we share that beneficent influence. There are financiers inside those secluding walls who deal in a currency the world does not dream of putting into circulation, by whispered prayers and unuttered aspiration, that golden stream of grace that floats our souls' enterprises, when we think that our own credit is carrying us through. One bank looks very much like another from the outside; you cannot tell from the front windows whether it is doing good business. One religion looks very much like another from the outside; we cannot see yet what is happening behind the counters. But it is to us that our Lord, by impoverishing himself, has left the true capital to trade with.

5

THE TRIUMPH OF SUFFERING

As chastised, and not killed.—2 Corinthians 6. 9.

HERE is one more point over which the Church, and the individual Christian, will mirror the life of Christ. As he was constantly the object of hatred and of murderous plots, so his Church was from the first, has been at all times, assaulted by enemies from without; so too the individual Christian, in so far as he tries to live up to his vocation, is never given more than a brief rest from his trials. Yet as our Lord delivered himself, more than once, out of his enemies' hands, so he delivers his Church; so he will deliver us—he has promised it, and his promise cannot fail.

Our Lord came to earth resolved to live until he had completed the thirty-three years of full manhood, and then to die. But all through his life he chose the career of a hunted and persecuted victim. Those who followed him must realize that the cause which they made their own was an unpopular and a proscribed cause, that every success it achieved would strengthen the determination of its enemies to repress it. Even in his infancy, you must remember, even before he had issued one challenge or made one protest against the corruptions of his age, our Lord's life was sought by King Herod, and only saved by the flight of our Lady and St Joseph into Egypt. At the very beginning of his ministry, when he had preached in the synagogue at his own village of Nazareth, his fellow countrymen took him out to the brow of the hill in order to cast him down, and it was only by a miraculous disappearance that he escaped from their malice.[1] More than once, as his teaching became better known and better understood, the Jews of Judaea took up stones to cast at him.[2] Quite a short time, it seems, before the crucifixion he retired into the northern country that was outside the soil of Palestine, or into those cities east of the Jordan where the Jewish law was not observed—an exile from the country which he came to save. He would know, and his followers should know, even from the first, what it was to be hedged about by a conspiracy of repression—Herod fearing him, the Jewish leaders hating him, his own Galilean neighbours quick to take offence at anything he said. From the first, Christians must learn what it meant to be unpopular.

As chastised, that is, as continually persecuted and repressed, yet not killed—for the comfort of his servants in after times, our Lord would show that he had power to lay down his life at a moment, and in circumstances, of his own choosing; till then, the malice of his enemies was baffled by the watchful care of divine providence. In the midst of continual dangers, his constant word to his disciples is "Fear not". And I suppose the greatest practical demonstration he gave them of that lesson was the stilling of the storm on the lake. The wind howled about them as they laboured in rowing; the huge trough of the waves on which they rose and fell threatened at any instant to engulf them; and he—he was asleep. "Master", they cried as they awoke him, "Master, doth it not concern thee that we perish?"[3] And he, before he will speak the word that restores calm to the troubled elements, rebukes

---

[1] Luke 4. 29.   [2] John 8. 59; 10. 31.   [3] Mark 4. 38.

them for their faithlessness, "Why are you fearful, O ye of little faith?" Should they not have known that while they carried such a passenger as himself, wind and wave had no power to harm them? Could they not learn that every danger which could surround them, while they were in such company, was powerless to hurt them, whether it arose from senseless nature or from the rage of their fellow men? Was it not possible for a fatherly providence to chastise them, without making them fancy that it had deserted them?

They needed that lesson, not many years after their Master had been taken from their side. Although the pagan empire was slow to take alarm over the rise of the Christian religion, there is scarcely a chapter in the Acts of the Apostles that does not show you the new sect everywhere persecuted, everywhere spoken against. To be sure, all new movements are greeted with opposition; that is only human nature. But was ever a movement so persistently disowned, so ruthlessly repressed, as the Christian Church was during the first three centuries of her existence? And, ever since that time, although she has had respite here and there, respite now and again, she has been constantly assailed by her enemies either within or without. After the pagan persecutions, the heresies; after the heresies the barbarian inroads, after the barbarians the Mahomedans, after the Mahomedans the heretics again; then the great apostasy of the sixteenth century, then the horrors of the French revolution. Again and again the Church, like the apostles on the Lake of Galilee, has been tempted to cry out in despair, "Master, doth it not concern thee that we perish?" And still, in answer to such doubts, the same reproof comes from him, "Why are you fearful, O ye of little faith?" Again and again through the centuries the Catholic Church has seemed to be at the point of dissolution; again and again the divine protection has rescued the lost cause from perishing, and has enabled her to draw fresh strength from the lesson of her sufferings. For nineteen centuries men have been trying to repress the Catholic Church, and she emerges from the persecution chastised but not killed.

Some of us have to suffer as Catholics, simply because we are Catholics—petty persecution, it may be, in the home, or perhaps even some loss of worldly prospects. But that is merely a question of our individual circumstances; it is one way in which almighty God may allow us to be chastised, but it is not the only way. If you read through the long list of St Paul's mortifications,[1] or "infirmities", as he calls them, by which he vindicates his title to apostleship, you will find that

[1] 2 Corinthians 11.

whereas some of them are due to persecution from without, many of them refer merely to the incidental discomforts—cold, sleeplessness, shipwreck, and so on—which were incidental to a busy life like his. These mortifications, then, made him out as the servant of Christ, not because they prove the bitterness of the opposition which his preaching arouses, but simply because they *are* mortifications. "Whom the Lord loves, he chastises", he tells us, and again, "If you are without chastisement, whereof all are partakers, then are you no true sons".[1] In a word, suffering of some kind is the badge of the Christian profession, the accolade of the Christian knighthood. Suffering, to be sure, is the common lot of mortality, but Christians—I mean good Christians—will suffer more than their neighbours, because they are less indulgent to themselves, less sparing of their personal comfort, more sensitive to the needs of others. And they have, too, a warfare to fight against spiritual enemies, all the more painful because they are really in earnest about it, because they really care.

As chastised, and not killed. Servants of Christ, we must embrace, with sublime confidence, his assurance that not one hair of our heads can fall to the ground without the will of our heavenly Father.[2] The providence that watched over our Lord in his helpless infancy, the providence which he trusted so utterly amidst the dangers which surrounded him, has watched over his Church all through the ages, will watch over us when all hope seems lost and all prayers unanswered. The eternal God is our refuge, and underneath are the everlasting arms.

6

UNDYING DEATH

As dying, and behold we live.—2 Corinthians 6. 9.

I WAS saying last Wednesday that our Lord came to earth resolved to lay down his life at a moment, and in circumstances, of his own choosing. Yet the time which he set before himself for accomplishing his mission was a very short one: we speak of his ministry as having lasted for three years, but it was only for the inside of three years.

[1] Hebrews 12. 6-8.   [2] Matthew 19. 30.

And during that short space he was to give the Jewish people full opportunity to accept if they would, to reject if they would, the momentous message with which he was charged. It is not wonderful, then, that all through his ministry there is a sense of hurry, of urgency, of something to be done which will not allow of postponement. "I must work the works of him that sent me, while it is day; the night cometh, when no man can work. I do cures today and tomorrow, and the third day I am made perfect. My meat is to do the will of him that sent me, and to finish his work."[1] There is no time to waste in his life, because the shadow of an early death hangs over it. When he made the world, he worked for six days and rested the seventh. When he came to redeem the world, he must perform his marvellous works even on the sabbath; there could be no space, no interval for rest until he rested in the tomb.

He lived, in fact, the life of a dying man—an artist who sees the end coming, and must at all costs accomplish his masterpiece before it is too late. Those intervals of rest and leisure which we all value so highly have no place in the dying life. We all know what the world says about a career of feverish activity spent in preaching and in mission work; "It can't last", people say, "he can't go on keeping it up at that pace; he will wear himself out". That is what his enemies must have felt about our Lord; that, I fancy, was the reason why they did not take steps earlier on to put him to death. The followers of the movement were nobodies, a set of peasants and artisans; there was only one man who counted in it, and he was a man who had not where to lay his head; he denied himself food and sleep, he was constantly wearing himself out by exhausting contact with the crowd. Moreover, he was mad—he must be mad, there could be no other explanation of his behaviour. Let the movement alone (they would say to one another) and see what becomes of it; it is a mushroom growth, which appeared yesterday and will disappear tomorrow. For the author of it and the organizer of it is a doomed man, a dying man. . . .

"As dying, and behold we live"—he, who thus moved about the world with the sentence of death written on his brow, hastened over the work he had to do because the time allotted to him was so short, was eternal God. When he sat, spent and exhausted, by the road-side in Samaria, he was reigning then and there in heaven, the tireless source of all energy, the timeless source of all being. He lived, not as men live, with an existence that depends from moment to moment upon the thousand accidents of mortality, but with an independent, necessary

[1] John 9. 4; Luke 13. 32; John 4. 34.

existence, the Lord of life and death, the creator of time itself. Even when their baffled malice could brook delay no longer, and they hurried him to the death which they had prophesied for him, he was not dead but lived. His body lay in the winding-sheet; his soul entered that place of waiting where the Father expected its coming; but body and soul alike, even then, were indissolubly united to the Person of the divine Word. "I am he that liveth, and was dead, and behold, I am alive for ever and ever."[1]

And from the first, the Church which our Lord left behind him must have seemed a dying sect. Not merely because its leaders were unimportant people, not merely because its funds were low, not merely because it seemed destined to attract towards itself the hatred of human kind. It was, to the world's eyes, a race which was committing race-suicide. It is quite clear, I think, that in that dawn of Christianity, probably right up to the destruction of Jerusalem, Christians were expecting daily, almost hourly, the return of their Master in judgment. Not merely in the way in which you and I expect it, as an event which must happen some time and may happen any time, but with constant expectation, sometimes even with impatience. Both St Paul and St Peter, in their epistles, are at pains to satisfy the curiosity of their converts as to why the second coming has not happened yet. And, in the shadow of that expectation, they lived as men live to whom the world and all worldly ties are passing and ephemeral things, hardly to be thought of. "This therefore I say, brethren, that the time is short; it remaineth that those who have wives be as if they had none, and they that buy as though they possessed not, and they that use this world, as if they used it not to the full."[2] From the very first, the ideal of virginity was the natural thing among Christians; it seemed as if they did not care to help in populating the world. A dying sect (men must have said), a handful of fanatics whose own principles guarantee their speedy extinction.

And all the time, this dying Church was in fact bringing life to the dying world of paganism, was to put new vigour into its failing energies, rescue it from those consequences of physical degradation with which its own vices threatened it. "As dying, and behold we live." The years rolled on, and Jerusalem fell, and still, it seemed, judgment was to be delayed, and the Church must nerve herself for fresh centuries of activity. Just as the Jews had become alarmed, and put Christ to death when they saw that our Lord's influence did not burn itself out like a sudden flame, so the pagans became alarmed when the

[1] Apocalypse 1. 18.   [2] 1 Corinthians 7. 29, 30.

Christian Church, in spite of its other-worldly principles, grew and became vigorous instead of dwindling to its extinction. So persecution arose; for two centuries, with only slight intervals, the Roman Empire tried to extirpate Christianity. And the Church, which had thriven upon her ideal of virginity, throve upon her ideal of martyrdom. She drew fresh life from every wound, and at last, after those two centuries, her vitality proved irresistible, and she strangled, like ivy, the tree of paganism whence she had sprung. And still, all down the centuries, the Church has shown that magnificent disregard for her own preservation; she has hated life in order to find it. The most valued and the most treasured among her children, men and women devoted to religion, have died without offspring; even her ordinary workaday priests are pledged to a life of celibacy—and yet the Catholic type is perpetuated, the Catholic body grows and flourishes. When persecution arises, she defies all maxims of prudence, and plunges the most devoted of her servants into a hopeless struggle, which leads to nothing but their imprisonment and death. And still, on the ruin of those types, fresh edifices of faith have been built up, fresh ramparts to defend her from her assailants. "As dying"—a hundred times the world has prophesied our imminent dissolution—"as dying, and behold we live."

The lesson of all that for the individual Christian is a simple but a hard lesson. In the words of the *Imitation of Christ*, we have to live a dying life.[1] A life from which the thought of our death-bed is never wholly absent, giving us a contempt for the hollowness of worldly things, giving us a sense of urgency and haste, because our time is so short. "Ye are dead" (St Paul tells us), "and your life is hidden with Christ in God."[2] As the children of Israel passed to their deliverance through the dark waters of the Red Sea, so Christ, our Leader, delivered us by passing, on Good Friday, through the dark gates of the tomb. In baptism, we have all mystically achieved that ordeal by water, we have all been mystically identified with Christ's death—buried with him (St Paul says again) in baptism. "As dying, and behold we live"; it is only in proportion as we are dead to the world that we live to him.

> As Christ upon the Cross in death reclined,
> Into his Father's arms his parting soul resigned,
> So now herself my soul would freely give
> Into his sacred charge to whom all spirits live;
> So now beneath his eye would calmly rest
> Without a wish or thought abiding in the breast;
> Save that his Will be done, what e'er betide,
> Dead to herself, and dead in him to all beside.

[1] Book I, ch. 23.   [2] Colossians 3.3.

VII

THE EUCHARIST*

* The first twenty-six sermons in this section were preached at Maiden Lane, London, on the Feast of Corpus Christi, between the years 1926 and 1956, and the first twenty were first published in *The Window in The Wall* (1956).

HX

I

THE WINDOW IN THE WALL

And now he is standing on the other side of this very wall; now he is looking through each window in turn, peering through every chink. I can hear my true love calling to me, Rise up, rise up quickly, dear heart, so gentle, so beautiful, rise up and come with me.—Canticles 2. 9.

Set in the middle of the Old Testament, in striking contrast to those collections of dry aphorisms which come before and after it, the Canticle of Canticles occupies a position unique in sacred literature. In form it is a drama, in literary inspiration it is a love poem, such as might have graced any anthology in any language; it has, in its literal acceptation, no connection with theology from beginning to end. It is the story, apparently, of a young bride carried away to the harem of King Solomon, yet true to her lover, who comes and calls to her, rescues her from her gilded bondage, and takes her back to freedom and to her country home. And that book, as we all know, is a kind of palimpsest, in which the saints of every age have read between the lines, and found there the appropriate language in which to express their love for God, God's love for them. No part of the Old Testament gives rise more easily to outraged astonishment, to pharisaical scandal, when it comes into the hands of the profane: that *this* should be reckoned as sacred literature! No part of the Old Testament, I suppose, has more endeared itself to the greatest friends of Christ; they would have spared all the rest to save this.

In the passage from which I have taken my text, the voice of the country lover makes itself heard, all of a sudden, amid the distractions of Solomon's court. He stands close to the wall of the harem, and whispers through the window. The voice of the beloved—everywhere, in the mystical interpretation of the poem, the voice of the beloved is understood of Christ speaking to the faithful soul. And that voice at the window brings to my own mind a fancy which I have often had, which I suppose many of us have had before now, in looking at the sacred Host enthroned in the monstrance. The fancy, I mean, that the glittering disc of whiteness which we see ocupying that round opening is not reflecting the light of the candles in front of it, but is penetrated with a light of its own, a light not of this world, shining through it from behind, as if through a window, outdazzling gold and candle-flame with a more intense radiance. Such a visual impression you may have just for a moment, then you reflect that it is only an illusion; and then on further thought you question, Is it an illusion? Is it not rather the truth, but a truth hidden from our eyes, that the Host in the monstrance, or rather those accidents of it which make themselves known to our senses, are a kind of window through which a heavenly light streams into our world; a window giving access on a spiritual world outside our human experience?

Behold, he stands behind "our wall"; the wall of our corrupt nature, which shuts us off from breathing, as man breathed in the days of his innocency, the airs of heaven; the wall of sense, which cheats us when we try even to imagine eternity; the wall of immortified affection, which shuts us in with creatures and allows them to dominate our desires; the wall of pride, which makes us feel, except when death or tragedy is very close to us, so independent and self-sufficient. Our wall—we raised it against God, not he against us; we raised it, when Adam sinned, and when each of us took up again, by deliberate choice, that legacy of sinfulness in his own life. And through that wall the Incarnation and the Passion of Jesus Christ have made a great window; St Paul tells us so; "he made both one, breaking down the wall that was a barrier between us",[1] as the temple veil was torn in two on the day when he suffered. He "made both one"; made our world of sin and sight and sense one with the spiritual world; made a breach in our citadel, let light into our prison.

Not for a moment, amid the confusion of an historical situation; the window is there for all time, if we would only recognize it. He himself, in his risen and glorified body, is the window between the two worlds. As the window belongs both to the room inside and to the open air outside, so his glorified body belongs at once to time and to eternity; belongs to time, because he took it upon himself, when he was born in time of his blessed Mother, belongs to eternity, because it is now transfigured with the light of glory which is part of our future inheritance. That glory is something human eyes cannot bear to see; when Moses had talked with God on Mount Sinai, he came back with his face shining, so that he had to put a veil over it lest the people's eyes should dazzle when they beheld him; and if he, who was only

[1] Ephesians 2. 14.

God's ambassador, who had only spoken with God in the darkness, was so illuminated by it, what of him who is himself God, whose human nature has been caught up into the Abyss of all being? When he rose from the dead, and still for forty days walked about our earth, that glory was hidden from mortal eyes by a special dispensation. And now, now that he reigns in heaven, he will make himself manifest on earth still; but his glory will be veiled, more jealously than ever, as he confronts, now, the gaze of the sinner and the doubter, as he gives himself into the hands of the unworthy.

We all know what veil it is that covers him now; it is the mystery which occupies our thoughts this morning. In this mystery of transubstantiation, he has broken into the very heart of nature, and has separated from one another in reality two elements which we find it difficult to separate even in thought, the inner substance of things from those outward manifestations of it which make it known to our senses. Burn all the candles you will in front of it, call to your aid all the resources of science, and flood it with a light stronger than human eyes can bear to look upon, still that white disc will be nothing better than a dark veil, hiding the ineffable light of glory which shines in and through the substance of Christ's ascended body. A veil, that is what we look at, a curtain drawn over the window, as you may curtain the windows of a sick-room, because the patient's eyes are not strong enough to face the full glare of daylight. But behind that curtain, all the time, is the window which lets our world communicate with the world of the supernatural. As the angels ascended and descended on Jacob's ladder, so here our prayers go out into the unseen, so here grace comes flooding through, like a rushing mighty wind, into the stagnant air of our earthly experience.

And at the window, behind the wall of partition that is a wall of partition no longer, stands the Beloved himself, calling us out into the open; calling us away from the ointments and the spikenard of Solomon's court, that stupefy and enchain our senses, to the gardens and the vineyards, to the fields and the villages, to the pure airs of eternity. Arise (he says), make haste and come. Come away from the blind pursuit of creatures, from all the plans your busy brain evolves for your present and future pleasures, from the frivolous distractions it clings to. Come away from the pettiness and the meanness of your everyday life, from the grudges, the jealousies, the unhealed enmities that set your imagination throbbing. Come away from the cares and solicitudes about the morrow that seem so urgent, your heavy anxieties about the world's future and your own, so short either of them and so uncertain. Come away into the wilderness of prayer, where my love will follow you and my hand hold you; learn to live, with the innermost part of your soul, with all your secret aspirations, with all the centre of your hopes and cares, in that supernatural world which can be yours now, which must be yours hereafter.

Not that he calls us, yet, away from the body, from its claims and its necessities; that call will come in his own time. Nor yet that the occupations, and the amusements of this life, his creatures, given us for our use, are to be despised and set aside as something evil. Rather, as a beam of sunlight coming through the window lights up and makes visible the tiny motes of dust that fill the air, so those who live closest to him find, in the creatures round about them, a fresh charm and a fresh meaning, which the jaded palate of worldliness was too dull to detect. But he wants our hearts; *ut inter mundanas varietates ibi fixa sint corda ubi vera sunt gaudia*[1]—our hearts must be there fixed, where are pure joys, before we can begin to see earth in its right perspective. We must be weaned away from earth first; and the means by which he does that is holy communion. That is the medicine which enables the enfeebled soul to look steadily at the divine light, to breathe deeply of the unfamiliar air.

I wonder, is that why some of us are so frightened of holy communion, because we still cling so to the world of sense? It is certain that Catholics are most apt to neglect communion just when they most need it; in the spring-time of youth, when the blood is hot, and the passions strong, and ambition dominates us. Why is that, unless that we are more wedded, when we are young, to the desires that perish? I wonder, is that why so many of us who go often to communion find that it makes, apparently, little difference to us; that we are still as full of bad habits as we were ten or fifteen years ago, that our lives, if anything, compare unfavourably with the lives of others, who have not our opportunities for going to communion frequently? Is it perhaps because, all the time, we are shrinking from the act of confidence which would throw the whole burden of our lives on our Lord; do not want holy communion to have its proper effect on us, which is to make the joys and distractions of this world have less meaning and less appeal for us? We must not expect him to work the marvels of his grace in us, if we oppose its action through the stubbornness of our own wills, still clinging to self and to sense.

Meanwhile, it is certain that as life goes on he reminds us, more and more, how transitory it is and how unsatisfactory, by taking from us

[1] Collect for the fourth Sunday after Easter.

the supports which allowed our hearts to rest in this world. Our friends are taken from us by death; and if we would reach them now we must pierce beyond the veil; must live in Christ if we are to be one, consciously, with those who sleep in him. May God have mercy on their souls, and grant them light in their place of waiting; and may he grant us, who have adored him today beneath the veil of his sacramental presence, grace to hear his voice, and obey his call, and live with him in heavenly places, until he calls us, too, to himself, and makes us glad at last with the beauty of his unveiled presence.

2

THE CITY OF PEACE[1]

Jerusalem is built like a city which is one in fellowship.—Psalm 121. 3.

A CITY which is one in fellowship—a city isolated by its position from the rest of the world, and therefore dependent for its very existence on the mutual good-will of its inhabitants. Palestine lies, as we know —we were never more conscious of it than today—across one of the great strategic highways of the world. It is on the direct route between Egypt and Northern Asia; and its plain of Megiddo was consequently a place where the armies of opposing empires were always meeting in conflict. We shall hear of it again, for it is the valley of Armageddon. But Jerusalem itself stands remote among the hills, as if to let the rumours of world-history pass it by. Let Samaria enjoy the rich cultivation of the plains, and feel every passing tide of conflict between North and South; Jerusalem, safe on its lonely peaks, was to look down on this pageant of history undisturbed. The world was to sweep round its feet, leaving it alone and unconquered through the centuries. Meanwhile, its inhabitants, so cut off from commerce with their kind, were to be bound together by strong ties of civic unity; it was to be the city of peace, its very name announced that. A grand destiny, partly but imperfectly fulfilled.

Is it fanciful of us to detect in this providential accident of sacred

[1] This sermon was preached early in the Second World War.

geography, a type, a symbol, of that institution which, more than anything else, represents and secures for us Christian people the supernatural unity by which and in which we live; I mean, the institution of the Holy Eucharist? The Christian altar, like the temple at Jerusalem, is the rallying-point of God's people. Here, as there, heaven touches earth, yet remains uncontaminated by its contact. Christ is not moved when the sacrament is moved, is not broken when the sacrament is broken; so close does he come to our experience of daily life, so remote does he remain from it. And one of the chief influences he exerts, one of the chief ends he attains, by that nearness of his, is to draw us, his children, closer together. It is the sacrament of peace, as Jerusalem was the city of peace; through it we are one in fellowship. We speak of Christians as united in a single communion, of one Christian body as being in communion with, or out of communion with, another; that is no accident, no abuse of language. The whole notion of Christian solidarity grows out of, and is centred in, the common participation of a common table. As the many grains of wheat are ground together into one loaf, as the many grapes are pressed together in one cup, so we, being many, are one in Christ. How could we be one with Christ, without becoming one in Christ? I could quote a hundred phrases from the liturgy which insist on this doctrine, now so little remembered, or at least so much disregarded. But it will be sufficient to refer you to the liturgy of today's feast, the Corpus Christi feast. Look at the secret prayer which the priest will be saying in your name a few minutes from now; what does it say? "Grant, Lord, to thy Church the gifts of unity and peace, which are mystically betokened by these gifts we are offering to thee."[1] Unity and peace—even the unconsecrated elements, the Church tells us, are meant to be symbolical of that.

Under the old dispensation, you see, the yearly sacrifice of the Passover was the signal for the reunion of all faithful Jews at a common centre. "His parents went up every year to Jerusalem"—every year, our Lady and St Joseph had the opportunity of meeting Zachary and Elizabeth; they had no difficulty in keeping alive the gracious bond of family affection. So it was with all the pious Jews of their time; it was like the diocesan pilgrimage to Lourdes on a grand scale. When the new covenant superseded the old, it was the daily sacrifice of the Mass, instead of the yearly sacrifice of the Passover, that became the rallying-point of God's people. The primitive Church in Jerusalem broke bread from day to day from house to house; visibly and consciously they were a single family. And when the Gospel spread to different centres all

---

[1] Secret Prayer for the feast of Corpus Christi.

over the Mediterranean world, each local church prepared itself for the celebration of the divine mysteries with an *agape*, a love-feast, at which rich and poor sat down together; you may read in the first epistle to the Corinthians how deeply distressed St Paul was by any behaviour on the part of Christians which threatened to obscure the significance of that common act. And although the Church, scattered over three continents, could no longer muster all her membership within four walls, it was felt from the first that every Christian was mystically united to all other Christians by his participation in the mysteries. That is why St Ignatius, early in the second century, speaks of the Roman Church as presiding over the *agape*, the communion of all faithful Christians everywhere. That is why each local church would write up, on tablets over the altar, the names of neighbouring bishops, so as to be one with them in prayer. The Church throughout the world was the new people of God, and its Jerusalem, its stronghold of peace, was not any local centre; it was in a common meal that they found themselves mystically united to one another.

That supernatural unity is still laid up for us, if we would only realize it, in the tabernacle. Christian people, however much separated by long distances of land or sea, meet together in full force, by a mystical reunion, whenever and wherever the bread is broken, and the cup blessed. We do well to remember that notion in times like these. War is a sword; it brings division into our lives. It severs nation from nation; at the moment we have less opportunity of exchanging ideas with our fellow Catholics on the continent of Europe than at any time within living memory. But when we communicate, you and I, we sit at a common table with them, we are united, even with our enemies, by a bond of mystical fellowship. Families, everywhere, are being split up; here, young men and women have been called away to distant centres in the service of their country; there, children have been separated from their parents, to ensure their safety in times of peril. Increasing difficulty of communication, whether across the seas or within our own island, is underlining the difficulty; how seldom, comparatively, can we meet old friends now, how difficult it is to arrange a reunion of families at Christmas time, or of friends for social enjoyment! A sense of isolation is creeping over us, of old ties broken and old associations forgotten; we cling to everything that will unite us to one another. And shall we not cling, above all, to the sacrament which provides us with a real opportunity of making ourselves one with those we love? Bitterest of all, at such times, death comes close to us and breaks up our circles of family and of friendship; but death itself cannot dissever the bond of Christian unity which joins us to our dead. We remember God's servants and handmaids who have gone before us, outstripped us in the race for eternity; who now sleep in the sleep of peace, while we must watch still in the watchfulness of war. And remembering them, we are still one with them; not by sentimental make-believe, but in a real fellowship, closer and more enduring, could we but realize it, than all the bonds of earth.

On that altar, Christ is present; is present in space, though not under the conditions of space. And wherever the words of consecration are pronounced, a hundred miles from here, a thousand miles from here, Christ is present in the same way. Is that a different Christ? No, the same Christ, present here and equally present a thousand miles away. Is it possible to doubt that we are near to those we love, when we and they are equally near to Christ, equally present to both of us? And if that is true, even when we kneel before the tabernacle, does it not become more startlingly, more significantly true when we and they partake together, whatever leagues of distance intervene, of this body and blood, given to us in holy communion? Equally united to the same Christ, are not we and they united together, more closely in fact than if we could see one another's faces, hear one another's voices, sitting in the same room? And did we complain that we are *separated* from those we love? It is our fault or theirs if we are.

War has sundered the nations—yes, it can interrupt the exchange of commerce, of ideas, of diplomatic courtesies. It cannot interrupt the current of sacramental fellowship which unites us with all Christians, even with our enemies, when we and they partake of the same heavenly banquet. Only an unworthy reception, on their side or on ours, can interrupt that. The bread and wine which the priest will be offering a moment from now are gifts of unity and of peace, making us one with all our fellow Catholics, in Poland, in France, yes, in Italy and Germany too. Years may have to elapse before the external conditions of free intercourse are re-established between us. But by the greatest of all titles, as children round our Father's table, we are already at one. The Blessed Sacrament, the Jerusalem of our souls, stands apart from and above all the ebb and flow of world-politics, its citizenship a common fellowship between us and those who are estranged from us, those who at the moment are our enemies. Our friends yesterday, our friends tomorrow—in the timeless existence to which that altar introduces us, they are our friends today.

War has divided families, and circles of familiar acquaintance—yes, it can interpose distance between us and those we love, make it difficult, sometimes, to obtain news of them, to exchange our good offices with theirs. It cannot interpose a barrier between us and them, so long as both draw near to the source of all real unity, the heart of Jesus Christ. In the hour when this sacrament was first instituted, not all the apostles were equally close to their Master in space; only to St John was it given to rest his head on his Friend's bosom. But all alike were united to their Master and to one another—all except one, separated from his Master, separated from his fellow apostles, by the estranging influence of unrepented sin. In absence from our homes, in perilous places, in prison it may be, or in exile, we are still united, all of us, unless that same barrier should intervene.

War divides men's souls from their bodies; and in doing so, divides us, irreparably, it seems, from those we love. And, this time, we can no longer console ourselves with the reflection that we and they, in spite of distance, can meet at one altar and share one meal. For them, the use of sacramental means has come to an end, with the body itself, and whatever grace visits them now must clothe itself in other forms than those to which we are accustomed. And yet the Church clings, obstinately, to the instinct which tells her that they, too, are somehow partakers of the altar; no Mass is complete unless they, too, are remembered. An empty place at table, yes, and an empty chair by the fireside, but not an empty place at the communion rail—that sacrament which unites the living unites too, somehow, the living with the dead. Union with Christ is given to each of us in accordance with the needs of his state. To us, living men who live by bread, he comes under the form of bread; to those others, who belong to a world of spirits, he must impart himself in other ways. He makes them one with himself, none the less surely for that; it is only our imaginations that are at fault if we find it difficult to remember that they, too, are with us; if we could see things with their eyes, should we not find them, perhaps, closer than ever to our side? Neither life nor death nor any other creature can separate us from the love of Christ; in that love, we are all one; without it, we should be crying to one another helplessly in the dark. May he draw us all nearer together by drawing us, continually, nearer to himself.

3

HIRED SERVANTS

How many hired servants there are in my father's house, who have more bread than they can eat, and here am I perishing with hunger.—Luke 15. 17.

WE all know the parable of the prodigal son nearly by heart; we can all see for ourselves how accurately it delineates the experiences of the penitent sinner; many of us find it linked, by a sad chain of memories, to the history of our own lives. You see him, the prodigal, receiving a patrimony from his father without gratitude, taking it as a matter of course; and you consider how little we value, commonly, our patrimony of divine grace until we come to lose it. You see him starting off for a far country, just turning to wave farewell at the end of the drive, as he slaps the new cheque-book in his pocket; and you consider how lightly, how carelessly we Christians will march off into the midst of spiritual dangers. You see him wasting his money in riotous living, and caught unawares by the great famine for which he had made no provision; you consider how we men waste our capital of grace through neglect, until at last the occasion of sin finds us out, and we fall without a struggle. You see him sunk in the pig-sty's degradation, and then visited by a gracious touch of home-sickness; rousing himself suddenly, and squaring his shoulders for the humiliating journey to his father's house; you consider how grace uses our human instability of mind to make us grow weary of our sins, drives us back to God, who is our heart's rest. You see the father running out to meet the prodigal, forgiving him, restoring him to favour, making a feast in his honour; you consider how God loves to forgive, how prompt is his pardon, and how full, and how effective; how in absolution that which was dead comes to life again, that which was lost is found.

All *that* we remember, the main structure of the story; I am not sure that we always give sufficient attention to the details, the exquisite touches with which this epic of the human heart is etched in. Here is one, apparently very unimportant, which will give us enough material for a whole sermon this morning, and dispose us for the better celebration of today's feast. What was the train of thought which produced, at last, repentance in the prodigal? What was the loophole by which grace shone into the prison of his soul? He is in the fields, feeding swine; anybody who has done that, knows how the spectacle absorbs the onlooker—this hurrying, jostling pageant of animal life has something of the grandeur of a water-fall; the whole world seems to be full of eating, as you watch. It does not take any long stretch of the imagination for the poor prodigal to be brought to a sense of his own condition, half-starved in this strange country where only man goes wanting, and the beasts have their fill. Those husks we read of were used, are still used, for human food. But the bucket has been overturned now; there will be no crumbs left for the prodigal. So hungry; he has never known before what it was to work for hire.

For hire—and yet, to be a paid workman is not always to be underpaid. He thinks of the men who used to work on his father's estate; as a little boy he used to watch them, fascinated, when they sat down under a hedge and undid those mysterious pudding-basins, tied up in coloured handkerchiefs, they carried their meals in. *They* never seemed to be hungry; there was no hoarding scraps about *them*; he can remember picking up some of the bread they had left lying about and feeding the ducks with it. So his mind runs on; associations of memory assert themselves easily in a brain weakened by want of food. Are they still at work, he wonders, laying that piece of road, mending that hedge? And then suddenly, the contrast forces itself upon his mind; "How many hired servants of my father have more bread than they want, and here am I, dying of hunger!" Here, among strangers; here, miserably employed; here, when there was never any need for me to have left my home. "I will arise, and will go to my father, and say to him, Father, I have sinned." One train of thought has led from the swill-tub to the prodigal's return.

So much for the parable; and now, what of the interpretation of the parable? What is this hunger for food which only becomes articulate at the sight of beasts feeding, and then expresses itself in a hunger for home? It is the hunger of the immortal soul for God; he has made us for himself, and our hearts cannot rest until they find rest in him. The soul that has plunged into vicious habits, and seems so deeply sunk in them, now, that there is no chance of a recovery, still finds itself dissatisfied with the brief enjoyments, the narrow horizons, of earth. It looks round it at the pig-sty that has become its world; conceives a distaste and a contempt for the sinners who share that world, no better than a herd of swine, foot in trough, grunting and scrambling; was man born for this? And then, on a rebound, the half-repentant mind turns away from the beast-world that surrounds it to the angel-world from which it came out, and which must for ever be its goal; "How many of my father's servants". . . was not that service, after all, perfect freedom? "And I, here, perish with hunger"; here, far from the thought of God, here, environed with corruption; here, where nothing but my own pride and obstinacy stands between me and my home. "I will arise, and go to my father, and say, I have sinned."

With us Catholics, brought up to the life of the sacraments, this longing for God makes itself felt more, expresses itself best, in hunger for our souls' bread, the Holy Eucharist. This supernatural food has become, as it were, our natural food; without it we languish. Oh, we may be rare communicants, we may be indevout communicants, and not feel the loss; but once we cut ourselves off from it altogether, the hunger is there; faint, perhaps, perilously faint, but unmistakable. God knows how many souls there are all round us who are living, year after year, a maimed life; smothering, all the time, a secret bitterness that gnaws at the heart—because they have drifted away from their communions, and know that they cannot really do without them. With some of them, sin has turned into an inveterate habit; they shrink from the confessional, because they no longer feel that they have the power to shake it off. Some have married without the sanction of the Church, and are deprived of the sacraments while they persist in an attitude of rebellion. With some, faith itself has grown numb; they say they do not believe the doctrine of the Holy Eucharist is true, and yet, not believing it true, they wish it were true, so that they might go back to their starting-point, regain the home and the table they have lost.

Now, when the touch of grace comes, effectively, to those souls, as God grant it may, they will be in the prodigal's position. They will turn aside disgustedly from the flat and shallow consolations of the world they live in; they will remember the ease, and the contentment, and the confidence of living in their Father's home; and their eyes will turn enviously towards what, towards whom? Towards you and me.

God forgive us, towards you and me. "How many hired servants of my father"—we are those hired servants; privileged with a privilege they only can estimate who stand far off and perish with hunger. The hired servants have more bread than they can eat, more bread than they know what to do with. It is the word used of those fragments that were taken up after the feeding of the five thousand. Your communions and mine, what are they like? What sense do they show of the privilege we enjoy, of the possibilities that are open to us? How casual is the preparation that earns them for us, the thanksgiving that crowns them for us! How ready we are to forgo them, on some slight excuse of health or work; how little they mean to us, an hour after they have happened! Should not we do well, perhaps, to take the prodigal's

words on our lips, but to read them the other way round? "How many
sons there are, sons of my Father, outside their Father's house, perishing
with hunger; and I here have more than I can eat, have more of sacramental grace offered me than I know what to do with!'

Hired servants of my father—is it, perhaps, because we are *hired*
servants of God that we make so little of our opportunities? These
others, who have rebelled against him, betrayed by passion, who have
fallen away from him, discouraged by human weakness—how often
they are really sons, though sons in exile! How often there is a generosity about their failings, which is lacking to our virtues! If they come
back to him, when they come back to him, they will be the Magdalens,
the Augustines, the great penitents, and therefore the great Christians.
What a tragedy that they, who might serve him so well, have wandered
away from him; that we, who have stayed at home like the stay-at-
home elder brother, should be so second-rate!

We act like hired servants, if we take pains to do no more for God
than bare duty demands of us, jealously watching, as it were, the terms
of our contract with him. The priest gets up and goes back to the
sacristy, and we are on our feet before he can reach the door. We act
like hired servants, if we think of our communions only as they affect
ourselves. "I go once a month", you say, "and really I don't seem to
need more than that; there is very little to mention, as a rule, when
confession-time comes round." Is that all the body and blood of Christ
means to you, a kind of talisman to keep down the number of your
sins? Or you say, "I'm not unhappy about my communions; because
when I make them and just after I've made them I always have such a
wonderful sense of peace, of consolation." Is that all the body and blood
of Christ means to you, a kind of spiritual treat you can indulge in
now and again? When we go to communion, you and I, we should
aim at nothing less than making the life of Jesus Christ ours; immolat-
ing ourselves to God, annihilating ourselves before God, in him and
through him and in union with his sacrifice, so that we can say, "It is
no longer I that live; it is Christ lives in me."[1] Until we aim at that, the
bread of our Master's house is being wasted on us; we are hired
servants, asking, and receiving, nothing better than a pittance for our
livelihood.

Oh, if we could only realize that the Holy Eucharist is *panis fortium*,
the bread of the strong! That it is meant to energize us and vitalize us,
not merely to discipline and to soothe us! Let us pray our blessed Lady
and all the saints of the Blessed Sacrament to win for us, in these times

[1] Galatians 2.20.

that are so difficult, and that are going to be so difficult, so dark for the future of religion, more generosity in our dealings with God, more boldness and imaginativeness in the graces we ask from him. "Father, give me the portion of the inheritance that falls to me"—are we justified in thinking of that as an impudent request? Or was the prodigal right in asking for his patrimony, and only wrong in the use he made of it? The elder son, who asked for nothing, gave nothing, did nothing. . . . May the grace of this holy feast be new life, new energy, new adventurousness to us all.

4

WHERE GOD LIVES

Daily I must listen to the taunt, Where is thy God now?—Psalm 41. 4.
Tell me, my true love, where is now thy pasture-ground, where now is thy resting-place under the noon's heat?—Canticle 1. 6.
They said to him, Where dost thou live? He said to them, Come and see; so they went and saw where he lived, and they stayed with him all the rest of the day, from about the tenth hour onwards.—John 1. 38.

IF it may be said with reverence, what a bad story-teller is St John! His gospel is a series of fragments—infinitely precious fragments, but fragments nevertheless—preserved from the hoarded memories of a very old man, who follows his own train of thought, as old men will, not stopping to consider what details it is that his hearers want to know. Nobody, you might say, would have been a worse journalist. He just recalls for us those unforgettable hours when he and St Andrew paid an afternoon call on our blessed Lord in his own lodging-place, and put the sun to rest as they sat talking with him. On that memory his mind reposes, and he tells us no more—what manner of habitation it was, whether our Lord was staying with friends, or with his Mother, or quite alone, what his habits of life were, all the things we want to know. Our Lord lodged with Zacchaeus, he lodged with Martha and Mary; otherwise the gospels tell us little about the entertainment earth gave to Jesus of Nazareth, the man who had nowhere to lay his head. For once, we think we are to hear more, and we go away disappointed.

And yet St John himself had felt just that curiosity, long before. What a natural instinct it is, when we meet somebody casually whose personality impresses itself on us, dominates us, to want to see more of him, and to want to see him in his own setting, against his own background, where he lives! The pictures on the walls, the books that lie on the shelves, the very knick-knacks on the mantelpiece will have something, surely, to tell us about him; they will make a frame for his personality, and we shall feel that we know him better. So it is with the bride in the Canticles—in those voluptuous airs of King Solomon's harem, her lover is out of place, he does not fit into the picture; let her see him among his flocks in the still, midday countryside, and she will know him as he is. So it was with St John and St Andrew; they know our Lord only as passer-by in the crowded ways; they follow as if to track him down to his lodging, and he divines their purpose, and invites them to pass the rest of the day there. What kind of picture are we to form of it? Possible, no doubt, that when Nicodemus came to see our Lord by night he found him in some rich dwelling where a devout host made everything comfortable for him. But I think we are more inclined to imagine the scene of that sacred hospitality as a more makeshift affair; a deserted house, perhaps, with the windows half boarded up; a straw mattress in a corner and not much else in the way of furniture; or just a cave in the cliffs, beyond Jordan. And this is the Prince who has come to suffer for his people; this is the palace which suffices for his earthly needs! Such was the kind of picture, I imagine, that conjured itself up in the memory of the old apostle, and he did not tell us about it; why should he? After all, it is what we should expect.

At the same time, I think St John will have read in that old question of his, "Master, where dost thou live?" the echo of a much older question which has been tormenting humanity since man's eyes were first troubled with a human soul. King David complains of those enemies who mocked at his misfortunes by asking him, "Where is thy God?" And we, because the age in which we live is impatient of old formulas, because the set of its mind is against the supernatural, share, often enough, that confusion and hesitation of his. "Where is your God?" they ask us. "Men of science have swept the heavens with their telescopes, and they have not found him. They have peered with their microscopes into the very heart of being, and they have brought us no word of him. Does he dwell in infinite space? But we are not sure, any longer, that space itself is infinite. Where is he, that we may worship him? Where is he, that we may reproach him for all the unhappiness that he allows to mar his creation?"

These questions of theirs, though it be only at the back of our minds, disconcert us; we know that they are foolish, based on a wrong apprehension of what it is that spirit means, and how it is related to matter. But for all that the imagination, tied down as it is to the world of space and of sense, will not be satisfied by the answers which commend themselves to the reason. We demand that, somehow, we should be allowed to locate the presence of God as concentrated and focused in one particular spot. "Master," we cry, "*where* dost thou live?" We know, of course, that he is everywhere, that he cannot be confined in space, we still we ask for evidences of his presence, and would trace the influence of it, if we might, *here* rather than *here*. When a storm of wind howls about our ears with unaccustomed fury, we catch an echo, as it were, of his omnipotence; when a sunset paints the sky with unwonted richness of colour, it seems like a mirror, however imperfect, of his uncreated beauty. But the illusion only lasts for a moment; when we think about it, we realize that this is a trick of the fancy; we are isolating an experience and making something divine of it; God is not in fact any nearer to us—how could he be nearer to us?—in the storm than in calm, in the cool of evening than under the brazen sky of noon. God is everywhere, but he is not here or there, that we should find him here or there more than anywhere else.

Has he done nothing, then, to make it easier for us to find him? Why yes, surely; in the mystery of his Incarnation, so full of his condescension, this is perhaps the greatest condescension of all—that he who is without limit should be limited, as Incarnate, to one position in space. When Moses drew near to the burning bush, when Elias heard from his cave a whisper of the divine voice, God manifested his presence in a special way, but that was all. When our Lady bent over the crib at Bethlehem, God was *there*. It was not necessary for her to say "Where is thy pasture ground, where now is thy resting-place?"— he lay in her arms, he fed at her breast. It was no use for the scornful unbeliever to challenge St John or St Andrew with the old question, "Where is thy God?"—those first apostles could say, and did say, "Come and see". For thirty-three years of human history it was possible to say, "There is God! Look, where he feeds, with publicans and sinners! Look, where he lies, asleep in the forepart of a ship which the waves threaten with destruction!"

Yes, for thirty-three years: but afterwards? We can make our pilgrimage to the holy places, pass along the roads which were once trodden by divine feet, mount the hill on which our Lord suffered, worship, perhaps, at his very tomb. But it is all a story of yesterday;

what use is it (we complain) that God should draw near to us in space, if he does not also draw near to us in time? It is not enough that *our* God should make himself present to *us*; why does not *my* God make himself present to *me*?

As we know, God has foreseen that complaint of ours, and has condescended to make provision for it. Everything else about the Blessed Sacrament may be obscure to us; we do not see our Lord as he is, we cannot fathom the mystery of that change which is effected in the consecrated elements, we have no clue to the manner in which holy communion imparts its virtue to our souls. But one thing we can say, without bewilderment or ambiguity—God is here. Like those two disciples when they heard St John the Baptist acclaim the Lamb of God, who should take away the sins of the world, we, taught by the Church that all salvation is to be found in Christ, are eager to know more of him, to see him in the most representative light possible, to catch a glimpse of him in the setting, in the surroundings which most truly manifest his character. "Master", we ask him, "where dost thou live?" And he points to the tabernacle with the invitation, "Come and see."

Let us look at Jesus Christ in his home, in the tabernacle, and see how those surroundings fit him, illustrate his dealings with us. First he dwells in a very public place. The lodging in which the two disciples found our Lord was in the wilderness, perhaps, beyond Jordan; but it was a place of coming and going, for all Jewry went forth to John, we are told, to be baptized by him. Our Lord was near the centre of things, then; and so he is today; in the heart of the greatest city in the world, you can find him without difficulty. So great is his desire to be of use to us that he throws himself in our way, makes himself cheap by familiarity. He is not afraid of irreverence, so long as he can be there when we want him. When they ask us where our God is, we do not have to map out the route of some far pilgrimage in foreign parts; he is close by, at the end of the next street. "O thou whom my soul loves"—we should do ill not to love him, when he makes himself so accessible as that.

Yet he lives there very quietly, a prince in incognito. He walked beyond Jordan for all the world to see; but it was the tenth hour when he invited the two disciples to follow him; it was an evening interview; and it was under cover of night that he talked to Nicodemus. Easy to find out where our Lord dwells; but if we would converse with him, be intimate with him, it must be in the obscurity of faith—the veil of the sacramental species hides him from our sight. He demands something of us after all; we must make a venture of faith in order to find him. So accessible to all, and yet such depths of intimacy for those who will take the trouble to cultivate his friendship!

And when he makes the tabernacle his home he dwells among us very humbly, in great simplicity. St John tells us nothing, as we were complaining just now, about the hospitality he and St Andrew enjoyed that evening. But everything we know about our Lord's life and our Lord's attitude makes us feel certain that it was only a mean lodging to which he brought them; I picture him as stooping low, and warning them to stoop in their turn, as they entered the door of it. So in the tabernacle he lives a life of utter humility. Oh, we try to make the best of it with gold and marble and precious silk; but he has chosen simple things, common things, to be the hiding-place of his majesty. And as he has stooped, so we must stoop if we are to keep our appointment with him in his favourite meeting-place. We must come to him in abject consciousness of our own unworthiness. For, see, there is something more he wants to tell us about the lodging he has chosen on earth.

Master, where dost thou live? Come and see, he answers—and bids us look into ourselves, into our own souls. It is there that he has chosen his lodging; there, amid all those tainted ambitions and unholy desires, there, in the heart of our warped nature, he dwells in us, and we what we are! Show me where is thy resting-place—heaven knows we need a guide to assure us of it, before we would dare to guess that he is content to dwell *here*.

> If by chance thou e'er shalt doubt
>   Where to turn in search of me,
> Seek not all the world about;
> Only this can find me out—
>   Thou must seek myself in thee.
>
> In the mansion of thy mind
>   Is my dwelling-place; and more
> There I wander, unconfined,
> Knocking loud if e'er I find
>   In thy thought a closèd door.

A door closed, to him? Not here, Lord, not in these hearts; come, take possession of them, and make them more worthy to be thy home.

5

GIVING OF THANKS[1]

Not one has come back to give God the praise, except this stranger.—
Luke 17. 18.

THOSE words form the conclusion of a very simple and telling incident in our Lord's life. Ten lepers, isolated by their common calamity from the rest of their kind, cried out to him from a distance asking to be cured. He sent them off to show themselves to the priests, as the law of Moses ordained that a leper should, when there was any doubt about his condition. And as they went, they were cleansed. One of them, it seems, was doubly an untouchable. He was not only a leper, but a Samaritan, hated and distrusted by the Jews among whom he lived, tolerated only by those nine others who were smitten with the same disease. And he, finding himself cured, had other thoughts than to go off at once to the priests and obtain a certificate of his cure. He must go back, and find his benefactor, to cast himself at his feet in gratitude. It was done, and he received the welcome none ever failed to receive from Jesus of Nazareth. But there was a touch of sadness about the words in which it was extended to him. "Were not all ten made clean? And the other nine, where are they? Not one has come back to give God the praise, except this stranger." Ten cured, and only one grateful. Nine spoilt children of God's chosen race, cured of their leprosy, and taking it as a matter of course!

I am mentioning this incident for a curious reason; I think it is the only occasion on which you can quote our Lord as insisting on the duty of gratitude. If you look through St Paul's epistles, you will find it dwelt on almost wearisomely; thirty or forty times in the course of them we are reminded that we must, all the time, be giving thanks to God. Yet you will find no phrase expressing gratitude in the Our Father. What will account for this strange difference between the teaching of St Paul and the teaching of his Master? Why, I think you can say this—that our Lord, because he was God, would not be for ever demanding from his creatures the thanks they owed to him. In our common experience, who is it that excites our dislike almost as much as the ungrateful man? Surely the benefactor who is always harping on his benefits and demanding gratitude. So, with that

[1] Preached during the advance of the allied armies through Italy.

infinite courtesy of his, our Lord would not go about saying, "Be grateful; whatever you do, remember to be grateful". He would leave us to find out *that*, at least, for ourselves; he would trust poor, wounded human nature to retain at least that grace, if it had nothing else left to it—the grace of gratitude.

I have said that St Paul is constantly recurring to this thought; let us not forget to notice that the word he uses for gratitude is *eucharistia*. And when, as often happens, he couples the notion with that of prayer, when he says, for example, to the Philippians, "make your requests known to God, praying and beseeching him, and giving him thanks as well",[1] it is not by any means clear that he is not referring, at least by implication, to the sacrament of Holy Eucharist. For this, it is certain, is one of the earliest titles by which that greatest of all sacraments was known to Christian thought. "By prayer and supplication, together with the offering of the Holy Eucharist, let your petitions be known unto God"—that gives the sentence, it must be admitted, a more familiar turn. But, always, the notion of gratitude is there. And rightly so, naturally so; for this sacrament is by its very title, in its very origin, a sacrament of thanksgiving.

How often did our Lord himself publicly offer thanks to God? Only three times, as far as our records enlighten us. He gave thanks to God at those two great miracles, the feeding of the five thousand and the raising of Lazarus. And he gave thanks to God once more when he was about to perform the greatest of all his miracles; when he stood there in the cenacle, on the night on which he was betrayed, ready to turn the substance of bread and wine into that of his adorable body and blood. In all three gospels that record the scene, and equally in the account of which St Paul gives us, that detail is prominent; he gave thanks, and broke the bread; he gave thanks, and bade them drink of the cup. Even now the chief priests are making ready for his arrest, and he knows it. Even now the traitor is sitting with him at table, and he knows it. But the thought which fills the heart of our divine Lord at that first Mass of Christendom is an overwhelming impulse of gratitude.

How strange, that when you read the ordinary kind of instruction you get about the Mass, so little is said about this primitive, this dominating aspect of it! You will be told that in the Mass we offer praise to God; that is implied in all sacrifice. You will be told that in the Mass we offer reparation for our sins; we are not likely to forget that. You will be told that in the Mass we offer petition for our own

[1] Philippians 4. 6.

needs and the needs of all Christians, living and dead; the very urgency of those needs is clamorous in our minds, threatens, almost, to be a distraction. But how little they insist that at the Holy Eucharist we ought to be giving thanks to God, because that is what the word "Eucharist" means!

It is not the liturgy that is at fault. For, if you will examine the familiar words of it, you will find that everywhere praise and thanksgiving are inextricably mingled. When we praise God, we think of what he is in himself, high above us, infinitely greater than we are, wholly independent of us. But in the same breath we thank him for what he is to *us*, what he does for *us*. "We praise thee, we bless thee, we adore thee, we glorify thee, we give thanks to thee in the greatness of thy glory." So, in the *Gloria*, we dispose ourselves for sacrifice; and when the sacrifice proper begins, we allow ourselves, for the moment, to forget even the duty of praising God, so overwhelmed are we by the thought of his benefits to us. "Let us give thanks to the Lord our God. . . . It is fitting, it is right so to do. . . . Indeed it is fitting, it is right, it is to be expected of us, it is our hope of salvation, that always and everywhere we should give thee thanks." For every mystery of our faith, from our Lady's child-bearing to the expectation of the faithful dead, it is always thanks we offer to God, just here. And when we reach the solemn moment of consecration, the liturgy does not forget to echo the overtones of Maundy Thursday. "Lifting up his hands to thee, his almighty Father, he gave thanks and blessed, and broke." "Taking this glorious cup into his holy and worshipful hands, he gave thanks to thee again, and blessed, and gave." Even when he communicates, the priest has to keep the same thought in mind. He has already received the sacred host, and you would expect him to drink the precious blood immediately afterwards. But no, a kind of scruple seems to occur to him, and make him hesitate. "What can I do for the Lord", he asks himself, "*in return* for all that he has done for me?" He will make sure, before he completes the sacrifice, that it is a sacrifice of thanksgiving from first to last.

The reason for that is not far to seek. In the Mass, helpless man is trying to hide away, to compensate for, the utter worthlessness of his own aspirations towards God, by uniting them to the perfect aspirations of the God–Man here offered up in sacrifice. Sinful creatures, we have neither the status nor the capacity to make any worthy oblation. We *want* to praise God, but what do our earth-bound minds know of his greatness? And what is our praise worth? No, we will leave it to Jesus Christ; he shall praise God for us. We want forgiveness, but what title have we to obtain it? We will burden the divine victim with the weight of our sins; he shall lay them at our Father's feet for us, and be told that they are forgiven. We want so many graces and favours, for ourselves and for others; but do we know what is best, for ourselves or for them? And if we did, have we the effrontery to make any demands before the throne we have so often rebelled against? No, we will put it all in our Lord's hands, make him our plenipotentiary and let him act for us, win for us just the graces and the favours he wants us to have.

And so it is with our thanksgiving. We might have been inclined to suggest that here, at least, we could trust ourselves to do our duty unaided. Surely the very consciousness of our own inadequacy, which makes us so eager to find an intermediary with God, should have the effect of enhancing our gratitude; that he should have mercies to spare for people like us, gifts to bestow on people like us! But no; once more we are not competent even to thank God as he deserves to be thanked. How little we know, really, of what he does for us! How often we may have been within an ace of death, and we none the wiser! How often we have been preserved from the temptation that might have proved too strong for us, and we never knew that it was there! Even if we knew how good he has been to us, have we the apparatus for feeling, still more for showing, the gratitude which that goodness deserves? You have seen, before now, a present given to a child which is only just beginning to speak; how it will gaze at the toy with obvious pleasure, but never once look up into the eyes of the person who gave it, as if there were any connection between giver and gift. You know how the mother has to elicit a decent appearance of gratitude from her child, while she herself, really, has to do all the thanking there is to be done. . . . If we could see the Holy Eucharist at work, as the angels see it, I wonder if that isn't the light in which we should see our gratitude, and Christ's?

Thanksgiving, then, must be added to praise, reparation and intercession as an integral part of the Christian sacrifice, as one of its chief ends. And among these four ends it takes the second place. Praise comes first, because we praise God in himself without any thought of our own interest. Thanksgiving next—it comes before reparation for our sins, because, sinful creatures though we are, we are creatures before we are sinners; it comes before intercession, because justice demands that we should thank God for what he has done for us before we ask him to do more. God wants us to ask for his favours. But he wants us first to assure him of our loving gratitude for the past. Many of you will know, at least by seeing reproductions of it, Michelangelo's picture of the creation of Adam, in the Sistine Chapel at Rome. You will remember that recumbent figure, stretching out one hand, at the full length of the arm, towards the Creator, as if in acknowledgment of its utter dependence, its creaturely reliance, on him. That attitude, that eucharistic attitude, should be at the roots of all our devotion to almighty God. It should be in our thoughts at all times; it should be in our thoughts especially when we assist at holy Mass, or when we see, throned above the altar, that body which is our victim in the holy Mass. And when, from time to time, the consciousness of some great mercy strikes across our lives, it should intensify this eucharistic attitude in us, turn us into living flames of thankfulness; *Dignum et justum est*, we should cry out, uniting our voices with those of the blessed angels in heaven, "It is fitting and right, almighty, eternal God, that we should always and everywhere give thanks to thee."

When we say a Mass of thanksgiving, we say the Mass of Trinity Sunday. And, this Trinity Sunday, a great load of anxiety has been lifted from the minds of civilized people all over the world. It was not merely that Rome passed, overnight, into the hands of the Allied Powers, though that in itself was matter enough for gratitude. It was the first capital of a European nation that has been won by our arms. And there is finality about the very name of Rome; those of us who remember the last war could not help being reminded of a similar omen, when General Allenby's troops captured Jerusalem in September, 1918. But there was more in it than that. If Rome, the capital of all our fortunes, was to be won, could it be won, standing? Or would we see pictures of it lying in the dust, like the Abbey of Monte Cassino? In that city, isolated from the ambitions, but not from the perils that surrounded him, lived the ruler of a great spiritual empire, the personification of a great spiritual ideal. Was he to see the city he loved wrecked, amid the wreck of the world he loved? We know the answer. Rome stands; and Adam, on the ceiling of the Sistine Chapel, stretches out his hand towards the Creator, unharmed as when Michelangelo drew him, more than four hundred years ago.

J

6

AS YOUR SERVANT

Blessed are those servants, whom their master will find watching when he comes; I promise you, he will gird himself, and make them sit down to meat, and minister to them.—Luke 12. 43.

How old-fashioned the setting of our Lord's parables look to us nowadays! We have forgotten even what it was to stay in a large house with half a dozen servants to look after it; and our Lord is speaking of slaves. A slave did not expect much; our Lord has given us elsewhere what was obviously a familiar picture of a farm servant coming in from a hard day's work, and being told to wait on his master before he got a meal himself. Here, he is giving us what is obviously an unfamiliar picture, that of a master waiting on his servants.

The Master waiting on his servants—as if to assure his disciples that the Holy Eucharist was a foretaste of heaven, we know what our Lord did. At the last supper he knelt down and washed their feet. And when he came to St Peter—last of all, I suppose; that seems to have been the spirit of the occasion—St Peter made the obvious protest, "Lord, is it for *thee* to wash *my* feet?" The disciples, you will remember, had just been having a discussion among themselves, which should be the greatest. It seems an inappropriate moment, but St Luke assures us that it was so. And our Lord solved the difficulty by asking them, "Tell me, which is the greater, the man who sits at table, or the man who serves him? Surely the man who sits at table, yet I am here among you as your servant."[1] Then he suits the action to the word; girds himself like a slave and kneels with a basin at their feet. Oh yes, Peter is to be the greatest among them; but when he achieves that position, it will not be long before he realizes what it involves; to be the chief Christian is to be *servus servorum Dei*, slave of the slaves of God.

Our Lord does not say, "Look at me, watch what I am doing at this moment; see how, when need arises, I can abase myself." He says, "I am here among you as your servant"—it is not a mere momentary gesture; what he says of himself is true all the time. I am here among you, here on earth, among you men; there would be no point in God becoming Man, unless he who was fashioned in the likeness of men

[1] Luke 22. 27.

went further, and took upon himself the form of a slave. The whole process of the Incarnation, if you come to think of it, is a topsy-turvy kind of arrangement; it is God doing something for the sake of man, when man only exists for the sake of God.

He came to earth, and lived for the sake of us men. Oh, to be sure, the first motive in every action of his was to please his heavenly Father; "I must do the will of him who sent me."[1] But that general resolve does not exclude the influence of ordinary human motives, "I am sorry for the multitude, because they have nothing to eat."[2] It wouldn't be true of our Lord to say that he never did anything for his own comfort or content. He did sit down and rest by Jacob's well; he did go to sleep in the boat when he was tired out; he did steal away onto the mountain side by himself, when everybody was looking for him and he could get no time for prayer. Even more noticeably, he did allow other people to do things for him, and accepted their good offices with gratitude; he let the Magdalen anoint him, and Simon help to carry his cross, and at the last moment of his life he, who had been nursed at a human mother's breast, would slake his thirst with a little wine, accepting the rough charity of his executioner. But the whole nature of his career marks it out for what we are accustomed to call it—a ministry. The long lines of eager suppliants, demanding health, repulsive in their very importunity; the burning glare of publicity, without a platform, without an orator's privileges, so that every foolish criticism must be weighed and answered; the complete condescension to the ordinary man's level, so that every chance comer can pluck you by the sleeve, instead of waiting in an ante-room to gain admission—all *that*, as anybody will tell you who has had, even in a small way, an experience of the limelight, means a constant drain on the vitality, a constant sense of virtue having gone out of you, which makes a man the victim of his audience. And then there were the apostles—honest, warm-hearted men, but, until he had finished with them, how slow and stupid! A schoolmaster, if he is a good schoolmaster, must needs be a servant, and almost a drudge; in that drudgery, how much of our Lord's earthly life was spent!

Propter nos homines—if that was true of his life on earth as Man, it is equally true of the sacramental life which continues it. Why do we not have those words written up over every tabernacle? Here is God, if we may dare to put it in that way, at the beck and call of us men. Oh, it is true that in all the sacraments you have a direct impact of God's power on human lives. It's only because we are so incorrigibly spoilt that we

[1] John 6. 38.   [2] Mark 8. 2.

will think of the sacraments as if they were laid on, and nothing remained for us to do except turn a tap. No, God is present in all his sacraments, if we like to think of it in that way. But, as if to cure us of our stupidity, he would honour us by a special kind of presence in the Blessed Sacrament of the altar. Our Lord should be present as Man, for the sake of us men; putting himself at our disposal whenever we wanted him, making himself available for every purpose for which we want him, like a servant who says to his master, "Here I am; what do you want of me?"

Putting himself at our disposal—what a lot of difference there is between the servant who is always there and the old lady who will come in sometimes to oblige! If our Lord consented to be present once a year, at one particular altar in the world, what a condescension it would be! And here he is, always at our elbow. Making himself available—how grateful we are to the servant who is ready to take on unaccustomed duties in an emergency, instead of saying "That isn't my place!" And our Lord is ready to meet all our needs, chime in with all our moods, from the day of our first communion to the day when we receive him in Viaticum. Always waiting there in silence, not pressing his services upon us, but ready if we want him. What a poor idea we form of the man who passes over a service without gratitude, because a fellow man has rendered it so unobtrusively! And yet we go on from day to day, forgetting the unobtrusive service of a God.

See how he stoops, when he comes to a child in its first communion! The priest himself must stoop, almost ridiculously, to reach the tiny figure that has to stand upright if he is to reach it at all. And this posture of the priest, which itself, somehow, brings tears to the eye, is but the outward image of the unbelievable condescension involved on the part of his divine Master. Can we really believe that he had this sort of thing in mind when he instituted the Holy Eucharist? It is meant to be the bread of the strong, the day's rations for the campaigner in life's battle; a child like this, not yet capable (it is to be supposed) of sinning mortally, does not take the strain of conflict, does not need, therefore, supernatural refreshment. St Paul tells us that the communicant eats and drinks unworthily, if he does not recognize the Lord's body for what it is—can this child of five years old really grasp anything about eucharistic doctrine, beyond the fact that what he is receiving now is mysteriously different from his everyday food? Are we not presuming too much on the condescension of the Incarnate, when we throw open his mysteries to such under-developed spirituality as this?

So men thought, so even Catholics thought, till yesterday; and God had to raise up a saint to show us that we were wrong; had to raise him up, under the title of Pius the Tenth, to the throne of Peter, before we could realize that we were wrong. "It is not for thee to know *now* what I am doing, but thou wilt understand it afterwards";[1] so our Lord spoke when Peter was bewildered by the condescension of Maundy Thursday, and the lesson was not fully learned for eighteen centuries. But we *ought* to have known; had not this same divine Master said, "Let the children be, do not keep them back from me; the kingdom of heaven belongs to such as these"?[2] Evil as we are, we know well enough how to give our children what is good for them; if a child falls sick, we all turn hospital nurse; if a child is in danger, we compete for the honour of rescuing it; and should our Lord care less for children than we? *Propter nos homines*, for us human beings, children as well as men; the more he stoops, the better he is pleased.

See how he stoops, when he comes to a dying man in holy Viaticum! Those poor wandering wits, that cannot string a coherent sentence together to take leave of us, who knew him so well—have they really enough powers of concentration left to be called properly alive? The trembling fingers move as if to make the sign of the cross, but is that more than a kind of automatic gesture? Is it really directed by the tired brain? Absolution, yes, to be sure, on the chance that there is still time for a change of heart so momentous; extreme unction, oil knows how to consecrate even lifeless things. But, the Holy Eucharist—to receive that, we must surely be at our best! Is it kind in us to demand effort, perhaps to awaken scruples, in the soul that is so nearly cut loose from its last anchorage? But, even as we hesitate, a gracious Figure brushes us aside, still bent on his errand of mercy; "The child is not dead, she is asleep. . . . Our friend Lazarus is at rest now; I am going there to awake him."[3] *Propter nos homines*; the dying man can do so little for himself; because he cannot come to our Lord, our Lord comes to him.

"Why then, if I have washed your feet, I who am the Master and the Lord, you in your turn ought to wash one another's feet." When next we find ourselves refusing service to a fellow man, let us remember who it was that came to us this morning, and woke us from our sleep, and asked what orders we had for him.

---

[1] John 7. 13.   [2] Matthew 19. 14.   [3] John 11. 11.

7

THE GLEANER

Listen, my daughter, Booz said to Ruth; do not look for any other field to glean in.—Ruth 2. 8.

MAY I remind you—it is well for us to be reminded sometimes about the less read parts of Holy Scripture—of the story told in the book of Ruth?

Noemi, a woman of Bethlehem, went to live in the land of Moab. Her husband died there, leaving two sons; these married Moabite wives, and died also, leaving, it seems, no children. Noemi then returned to the land of Juda, accompanied by her two daughters-in-law; she pressed them to go back to their own kindred, and one of them, Orpha, at last consented, but Ruth stuck close to her mother-in-law. "I mean to go where thou goest, and dwell where thou dwellest; thy people shall be my people, thy God my God; whatever earth closes over thee when thou diest shall be my place of death and burial. Due meed of punishment the Lord give me, and more than due, if aught but death part thee and me."[1]

They came to Bethlehem, then, together. They were poor, and Ruth went out to glean in a rich man's field—she was allowed, for charity, to follow behind the reapers and pick up the stray handsful of corn they had left behind them. Without knowing it, she followed the reapers in a field which belonged to Booz, who was her own kinsman. He, recognizing her, encouraged her to remain with his reapers, "Daughter, do not go to glean in any other field"; and he gave secret directions to his own servants, telling them to leave generous store for her to gather as she followed them. At last they made themselves known to each other, and Booz claimed her hand in marriage. And so it was that Ruth, the woman of Moab, became the ancestress of St Joseph, of our blessed Lady, and, according to the flesh, of our Lord Jesus Christ himself.

A remote story of days long dead, touching in its simplicity, a favourite subject for the painter and for the poet—but what has it all to do with us? What message has it for us, children of a less lovable age? I never realized how plain was the symbolism of it until I came

[1] Ruth 1. 16-17.

across a chapter in an old-fashioned book of meditations from the French, headed "The Field of the Holy Eucharist".

After all, do they differ so much from ourselves, those two daughters-in-law of the exiled Jewess Noemi? Do they not represent two different types of soul, the soul which chooses and the soul which forsakes the world, the soul which is false and the soul which is true to its super-natural loyalties? The memory of a dead husband, what power has it to chain the affections, to spoil the life of a woman still young and still beautiful, as Orpha was, or Ruth? Yet Ruth was loyal to the country of her adoption, the country she had never seen; an Israelite by marriage, she would become an Israelite by choice. "Whither thou goest, I will go; thy people shall be my people, and thy God my God." So the faithful soul hears two voices, the flattering accents of the world at its elbow, the distant call of its unseen, because supernatural, home. Will it throw in its lot with the Christian Church, its mother by adoption, or will it go back to the world which claims it by right of natural kinship? The Church does not make it easy for us; she makes exacting demands of us, she tests our loyalty. "Go back", she says, "unless you are prepared to throw in your lot with mine for better or worse." And the faithful soul still answers, "Due meed of punishment the Lord give me, and more than due, if aught but death part thee and me".

And so she brings us to Bethlehem, to the house of bread. She brings us to the altar, where he who is our kinsman by right of his Incarnation, he who would espouse our souls to himself through divine charity, hides himself from us and bids us glean what we may in the field of the Holy Eucharist. His field, for who bought it, who sowed it, who culti-vated it, if not he? He bought it by his Incarnation; being rich, he became poor for our sakes; he sold all that he had, and bought that field. He sowed it, by his death; "A grain of wheat must fall into the ground and die, or else it remains nothing more than a grain of wheat; but if it dies, then it yields rich fruit";[1] his own sacred body was the seed, committed to the tomb that it might live with a new life. He cultivated the field by all the merits of his life and Passion; it was watered by the tears which he shed over Jerusalem, by his sweat in Gethsemani, by the blood of his scourging. And as, by a miracle of nature, one seed multiplies itself, till the harvest far exceed the measure of those grain from which it sprang, so from that one sacred body, that was sown in tears by the rock-tomb on Calvary, sprang a harvest world-wide, incalculable, inexhaustible, the harvest of the holy

[1] John 12. 24-25.

Eucharist; millions of Hosts in thousands of tabernacles all over the world. The harvest which was sown in tears on Maundy Thursday is reaped with joy on Corpus Christi. That is what the feast of Corpus Christi is, our spiritual harvest home. Pentecost, for the Jews, was a harvest festival, and we, when we have kept our Pentecost, carry in triumph through field and hedgerow that consecrated sheaf which is the harvest of Calvary. See how they shine today, those myriad Hosts of the world, in the sun of Eastertide, swayed as if by the wind of Pentecost.

In that field of the Holy Eucharist you and I are gleaners. Gleaners—why not reapers? Would that we were reapers; but look into your heart, and ask whether gleaning is not the true description for those poor, half-hearted crumbs of devotion which you and I carry away with us from God's altar. Imagine what Ruth must have felt as she watched the servants of Booz, lifting great armfuls of the wheat and binding them together, while she herself might only pick up, here and there, a stray wisp or two dropped from careless hands. How sadly she must have followed them with her eyes, she, no better than a super-numerary and a hanger-on! So you and I, when we read the lives of the saints, follow, with a wistful regret that tries not to be envy, the account of those spiritual privileges they received when they came to the altar. St Philip Neri, with his daily hours of ecstasy. . . . The Little Flower at her first communion. "Jesus asked nothing of me, and claimed no sacrifice. That day our meeting was more than simple recognition, it was perfect union. We were no longer two; Thérèse had disappeared like a drop of water lost in the immensity of the ocean"—her first communion; and have you and I, after so many years spent in fre-quenting the sacraments, had an experience to match that?

Yes, it is the saints who reap; you and I are only gleaners in their track. You come into church, and, just for a moment or two, the coolness and the retirement of it compose your mind for holy thoughts; you begin to pray. And then, at the most improbable tangent of thought, by the most grotesque association of ideas, your attention wanders to some detail of your daily life, some anxiety that troubles you, some pleasure you forecast, some ambition you cherish . . . why, here is the Gospel being said already, and no prayers yet! A fresh effort, a little more recollection, and then some oddity of manner about the priest, some eccentricity in your neighbour's deportment, carries you off again into profitless speculations; it is only the bell ringing for the consecration that brings you back, with a shock, to the sense of where you are, what you are doing. "My Lord and my God!"

In five minutes from now, you are to receive him, your God and your all, into the hospitality of this distracted soul. Well it is done somehow; and some affections of love and gratitude spring, as if unbidden, from the heart; and then all at once you find yourself fidgeting, your eyes straying to take a peep at your watch, and so you leave the church again. My daughter, my daughter, where hast thou gleaned today?

Would it not be better, you ask yourself sometimes, to give up the idea of frequent communion? Without abandoning your religious duties to transfer your inmost loyalties elsewhere; to fix your ambitions, as others do, on worldlier objects? There are other fields, oh yes, which promise some kind of satisfaction besides the field of the Holy Eucharist; the pursuit of power, or of human wisdom, or of riches, or of pleasure—would you not be better employed over one of these? It is so hard to be always doing a thing, and always doing it badly. And then it is that the Celestial Husbandman says to you, "Daughter, do not go to glean in any other field". Wherever we turn, whatever field of activity we choose for ourselves, you and I will only be gleaners still. Are we ambitious? Then see how few posts there are in the world by which ambition can really be gratified; others will reap the reward, we shall only be allowed to glean as best we may in their track. Do we desire knowledge, would we wrest from Nature yet more of her secrets? Then see, how many have been in the field before us; how they have swept it bare, and only left to us a few undistinguished avenues of research. Or would we fall back on the vulgar pursuit of riches? Here, too, we are too late in the field; others have been beforehand with us, have scraped up all the prizes, and left only the gleanings of their harvest for us who follow them. Would we live for mere pleasures? Why, this is a more pathetic fallacy than the rest! For who that ever asked for pleasure, ever devoted his life to pleasure, found that he could fill his bosom with its grudging sheaves? No, pleasures themselves are only the stray pickings of life to be gleaned by the wayside; there is no satisfying yourself with them. Daughter, do not go to glean, for thou canst do no more than glean, in any other field but mine!

Booz, when he saw that Ruth was following with his reapers, gave them special directions concerning her. "They were to put no hindrance in her way, though she were to go reaping in their company; and of set purpose they were to drop some of the handfuls they gathered, and leave them there for her to glean."[1] What other householder would so have instructed his servants? And who but our blessed Lord would have

[1] Ruth 2. 15-16.

left to us, his indevout worshippers, gleanings so rich from his all-sufficing harvest? Those wayward thoughts of ours, those wandering prayers—what sort of blessing could we expect that they would call down from above? We are not worthy of the least of his mercies, and he gives us—himself! In that Host which was carried round St Peter's this morning, with princes of the Church for its escort, with multitudes adoring on every side, there was not more of Christ than in the Host which this morning the priest laid upon your tongue. In the Host with which Soeur Thérèse was given her first communion there was not more of Christ than in the Host which you receive, week by week, day by day. It is not his generosity that is wanting, if we glean so little from his harvest; it is ours.

Glean on, then, faithful soul, in the field of Jesus Christ. He has sent us, he himself says, to reap that whereon we bestowed no labour; he ploughed, he sowed, he cultivated that harvest which he bids us gather day by day; no root of grace has ever sprouted since the hour of his crucifixion which has not owed, to that momentous act of charity, its origin and its value. It was the curse of fallen man that he should eat bread in the sweat of his brow; nor has our redemption lifted from us, so far as our natural needs are concerned, the weight of that sentence; we must labour, must suffer, must be anxious still. But the supernatural grace which the redemption won for us comes to us all unsought, all unbought, thrusts itself upon us, lies scattered in our way. And, above all, the grace of the Holy Eucharist, no transient influence of the divine mercy, but God himself, is lavished upon us with reckless bounty; we have but to stoop to gather it, and it is ours! What, glean in any other field, when the heavenly manna, the bread of angels, offers itself to our taste?

With happy significance, this church of Corpus Christi lies close to one of the busiest thoroughfares of the world's greatest city. Day in, day out, to and fro, these pavements are trodden by the hurrying foot-steps of men and women going forth to earn their daily bread. Towering hotels offer to the traveller, at fantastic prices, a night's lodging. And here, thrust into their midst, a Catholic church, the depository and the namesake of a treasure greater than any merit of man could earn, preaches its dumb message of refreshment and repose. "It is but lost labour that ye rise up so early, and so late take rest, and eat the bread of carefulness, for so he giveth his beloved sleep." Ruth, when her long day of gleaning was over, lay down at the feet of Booz, her protector; and when morning came he awoke, and claimed her for himself. So we, when the day's burden and its heats are done, will lay ourselves down at the feet of him whom we adore in this most august sacrament; and we shall awake to see his face in the clear air of morning, and be united with him for evermore.

8

PEACE IN OURSELVES[1]

That they too may be one in us, as thou, Father, art in me, and I in thee.— John 17. 21.

OUR Lord, on the eve of his Passion, quoted the words, "I will smite the shepherd, and the sheep shall be scattered".[2] The prospect of being deserted by his apostles in the hour of danger does not fill him with a sense of loneliness; he is well prepared to face, alone, the false verdict, and the mockery, and the shame of crucifixion. The tragedy is rather that these friends of his, who for three years past have been united in so close a bond of companionship, because they were his friends, are to lose that centre of common loyalty, and be scattered every man to his own. The compact little society will become a rabble of self-contained units, each fending for itself; the link that bound them together will have gone. Somehow, we do not know why, man is born for fellowship, and the breaking-up of any human circle demands its tribute of tears. By way of fortifying their human hearts, fortifying, perhaps, his own human heart against the strain of this parting, our Lord prays such a prayer as no merely human leader would have ventured to conceive. He prays that the disciples may be one with that very unity which binds together the three persons of the Godhead itself.

And we, year by year, recall to ourselves that prayer of his by celebrating two feasts in close conjunction. The Thursday after Trinity Sunday is for us what you might call Unity Thursday; we keep the festival of Corpus Christi, and in doing so we cast our minds back to the upper room and the first Eucharist, when our Lord incorporated his friends into a society by incorporating them into himself. Always the liturgy remembers what we, who use the liturgy, are so prone to

---

[1] This sermon was written just after the end of hostilities in Europe.
[2] Matthew 26. 31.

forget—that the Holy Eucharist is a sacrament of unity. When the consecration takes place, what happens? The substance of the bread and wine is withdrawn from them; the accidents remain. And yet, in our ordinary experience, it is the substance and the substance alone which lends any natural thing its unity. Shape and size and colour and smell and the resistance which it offers to the touch come together in a single principle of unity, the substance; it is the linch-pin which holds them all in place. Take away the linch-pin, and the wheel flies off. Take away the substance, and, by a miracle, so stupendous that our minds can hardly conceive it, the accidents do not fall apart; they remain there to be the garment and the vehicle of a quite different and a far greater substance, that of our Lord's own body and blood. His word upholds them; the same word which prayed, at the last supper, that the apostles might remain one; might remain one, even when their Master, the focus of loyalty by which their fellowship maintained itself, was taken away. The unity which unites three persons in one Godhead, the unity which preserves in being a set of accidents which have lost their substance—that is the unity we Christians pray for, and claim as our own when we gather round our Father's table at the Holy Eucharist.

Again and again you will find the language of the sacred liturgy dominated by this idea of oneness in Christ; a supernatural oneness which triumphs over every disparity, every separation. That is, I think, the idea which underlies one of the most beautiful, and at the same time one of the most obscure, petitions which we make during Lent; when we ask almighty God *ut congregata restaures, et restaurata conserves*,[1] "that thou wouldst bring together and mend, mend and for ever preserve, what now lies broken". Bring together and mend, mend and for ever preserve, what now lies broken—is it possible not to feel like that about the cruel divisions introduced into the world, into states, into families by these six years of war? So many millions of men torn away from their homes; and of these a great number, even now, unable to go home because circumstances have changed at home, and they find themselves outlaws. So many nations torn by bitter internal feuds, that will hardly be healed in our lifetime. And the world in general so weary of war, and yet so far from the very elements of harmony, so ignorant of the very alphabet of peace! "That thou wouldst bring together and mend, mend and for ever preserve, what now lies broken"—do we not need that prayer, when we see the mortar of civilization cracking all around us?

Congregata restaures, et restaurata conserves; the Church, knowing

---

[1] *Oratio super Populum* for the third Thursday of Lent.

well what we are, members of a fallen race, does not simply ask God to keep us in our present position, and leave it at that. She knows that *that* will not do, we are scattered all over the place, like broken pieces of china, and we have got to be put together again before we can be worth preserving. No, we must not be so miserably small-minded in our prayers as to tell God that we want him to keep the world just as it is, a mass of quarrels and seething discontents, if only we can have five or ten years of peace before hostilities start again. We must ask him to gather up the broken pieces of our world and cement them together again in some kind of world order, based on real justice, to give Europe statesmen who will keep their word and will grant freedom to their fellow countrymen, before we can ask him to keep things as they are.

But there is more behind it. If we will be honest with ourselves, we shall admit that the war has brought disharmony into your life and mine; we are not at peace in ourselves. Most of us are much busier than we used to be; in days when labour is short, we have more things to do; in days when the necessities of life are harder to come by, we have more things to think about. The great cruelties, the great injustices we read about in the newspapers rankle in our minds, and turn the milk of human kindness bitter within us. We shrink from the novel experiment of building a new world on the ruins of the old; we are sad at the disappearance of old landmarks, uneasy at the changes in our familiar habits of life. Travel is more difficult and more wearisome; we find it hard to make contact with old friends, even when we are little divided from them by distance. All *that* sets up a restlessness in our minds which perhaps is good for us in a way; it may save us from falling too much into a rut and taking life too easily. But it does not make the business of our souls a more encouraging task. For that, we need tranquillity, recollection; how are we to think about God or eternity, with daily needs and worldly preoccupations and public cares so weighing on our minds? The thought of God seems to get crowded out; our own sins get overlooked—they are so petty, compared with the needs of a distracted world, the perils of an uncertain future. While the war was still close to us, and danger seemed imminent, we could fix our minds on the common effort, forget the future and everything that was not part of our own immediate job. Now, the strain has relaxed, but our thoughts are still over-occupied. They rattle through your head as the rosary-beads rattle between your fingers; you feel as if you were not one person, but a mass of whirling fantasies, of disconnected trains of speculation.

Not one person, but a mass of fantasies—haven't we got back again to the need for unity? Aren't we conscious, once again, of the need for praying that almighty God will bring together and mend, mend and for ever preserve, what now lies broken? Haven't we got to be at peace within ourselves before we can bring any peace to the world in which we live? Instead of that, we lose our heads, take counsel of the prejudice that is uppermost, and make hasty decisions. We get irritable, and give way to depressions and despairs. How are we going to introduce any singleness of purpose into our lives, any recollection and repose into our thoughts?

You will learn to integrate yourself, pull yourself together, in the way we are speaking of, precisely in proportion as you manage to get more closely in touch, and more intimately in touch, with the eucharistic life of our blessed Lord. The Blessed Sacrament is the sacrament of unity; and when you receive it, it does not merely produce in you more charity towards your neighbour, more loyalty towards the Church, more unselfishness in your human attachments. It makes you more at unity with yourself; it catches up your life into a rhythm that echoes the heavenly music. Strange if it were not so; as we have seen, this presence which comes to you in holy communion comes to you veiled under the accidents of bread and wine, accidents which have now no substance to support them; it reigns amidst chaos, and will it not reign amidst the chaos of your heart? It comes to you, since our Lord's prayer could not go unanswered, full of that unifying love which is the bond of the blessed Trinity, and will it not bring unity into your scattered thoughts, your conflicting ambitions?

Only, there is something to be done on our side. The wheat must be ground into bread, the wine must be pressed out of the grape, before we can give our Lord the opportunity to work his miracle of transubstantiation. The offertory first, man stretching out his hands to God; then the consecration, God accepting and transforming man's gift. We must come to meet him, come to meet him early in the morning, when sleep has smoothed away for us the memories of yesterday, and no cares have yet assailed us to disturb the equilibrium of our lives. We must hand over the direction of our lives to him, if we are to know what it means to live an ordered life, heart-whole and mind-whole in a world like ours. Then we can go to communion.

9

THE MASS AND THE RITUAL

As Christ comes into the world, he says, No sacrifice, no offering was thy demand; thou hast endowed me, instead, with a body.—Heb. 10. 5.

I SUPPOSE any impartial observer, comparing the religious ceremonies of the Jews with ours, would be struck by this fact—that the Jews expressed their religion in sacrifices, and we in sacraments. And he would notice this, that whereas sacrifice means the destruction of the body—the body of a bull or a goat or a lamb, substituted by a kind of legal fiction to redeem the body of the man who offers it—our Christian sacraments do not mean the destruction of the body at all. They mean, rather, the consecration of our bodies to God, with the understanding that such consecration symbolizes, and effects, a consecration of our souls as well. God in Christ has abolished the old, destructive sacrifices; he has prepared for us instead a redeemed body in which and through which the sanctification of our souls can take place. The body is washed, and the soul is made clean; the body is anointed, and the soul is strengthened; a little circle of gold is put round one finger, or the hands are tied with a plain strip of linen, and the soul enters, thereupon, into a new state of life.

Consider how, at the three most solemn moments of his career, the ordinary Christian comes before God to receive the sacramental grace which those moments require, and can take upon his lips, without irreverence, the very words which our Lord himself uses in the greatest of all his sacraments, *Hoc est corpus meum*—This is my body.

The infant presents itself before God at the font with the words, *Hoc est corpus meum*, this is my body. What other words can it use? There is no other thought of which it can be directly conscious. The troubled eyes, looking out on a world altogether strange to it, are already beginning to isolate one set of phenomena from the rest, those white things, its own hands and feet. If one of those white things comes in contact with the edge of the cradle, feeling results, feeling that communicates itself to the mind; somehow, then, these white things are part of itself. The first judgment we are capable of making is simply the identification of the body as something belonging to us; *hoc est corpus meum*. Soul is there, to be sure, as well as body, in the newly born infant; but the soul has not yet found its own means of expression, has not yet begun to grasp life by experience; it is dumb, inarticulate, has not reached the knowledge of itself. The body is something that has already begun to be known; that, then, must be offered to God, and that is enough; God will cleanse and sanctify this new soul, enable it to partake of eternal life, through the body which he has prepared for it.

Man and woman present themselves before the altar to dedicate their lives in mutual fidelity; and once again it is the body that is uppermost in our thoughts. *Hoc est corpus meum*, the bridegroom says to the bride; with my body I thee worship. For here it is, in the fullness of its powers, that body which was carried, years before, tiny and helpless to the font. It is strong enough to work, now, and to make a livelihood for itself; and not for itself only, but for a household. It is strong enough to defend others besides itself against attack. And it is capable now, if God so wills, of continuing its kind, of begetting fresh life. With all these powers the bridegroom does worship to the bride; yet these are only the symbol of that love whose true sphere is in the soul. And the bride in her turn puts out her finger to receive the ring; *hoc est corpus meum*, she seems to say, here is my body, for you to hold it prisoner; yet her soul goes out with it. As they offer the bodies he has prepared for them to him and to one another, God finds his opportunity to breathe sacramental grace into their souls.

And once again, at the last scene of all, when a man lies on his death-bed, it is through his body that sacramental grace comes to heal him. His body is closer to him than ever; he is conscious of little except its labouring breath, its fevered pulses—this body of which he must take leave so soon, this body which now means so little. *Hoc est corpus meum*, he says, this is my body, still mine for a little, before it returns to its parent earth. This is my body, in which I have taken such pride, to which I have devoted so much attention, in which and through which I have sinned. This is my body; come, holy oil, and anoint it—these eyes that have seen and coveted what was unlawful, these ears that have been open to evil communications, these lips that have lied, detracted, blasphemed, these hands and feet that have been the ministers of my wicked passions. This is my body, which will soon be cold clay, now giving access to my soul, for the last time, through the gateways of sense; let these last sense-impressions of mine be all of holy things; seal them, holy oil, and shut them against the echoes of earth. So God's grace comes to him, for the last time, through his body, and his soul is healed.

We Christians, then, can offer our bodies to God, a reasonable, living sacrifice; but only for one reason. Only because God himself was made flesh, took upon himself a passible body like ours, offered it at every moment of his life to his heavenly Father, was born in it, laboured in it, suffered in it, died in it. He wore that body in its state of infancy, humiliated, annihilated for our sakes. . . . This is my body, for you, my mother, to feed and tend; this is my body, for you, my foster-father, to support and protect. He wore it in its state of maturity, espoused to poverty and hardship for our sakes; . . . This is my body, life-giving and life-bringing, stinted of food and sleep, travelling mile upon mile over weary roads, to claim that Church which is my destined bride. He wore it in its state of death, drained of sweat and blood for our sakes; . . . This is my body, so torn with scourges and buffeting that it can scarcely be recognized; for you, with the nails, to crucify; for you, with the spear, to pierce; for you, Joseph, to bury; for you, Magdalen, to embalm. *Hoc est corpus meum*, the body of a man, belonging to me, who am God; here it is, helpless; here it is, overspent; here it is, pale in death.

And in the greatest, the most wonderful of all his sacraments, once again we remind ourselves, "No sacrifice, no offering was thy demand; thou hast endowed me with a body instead". Only this time it is not our body, but his. In that daily miracle of his love, he wants to give us grace for the soul's needs, as in the hour of birth, or of marriage, or of death; but this time it is he who says, *Hoc est corpus meum*; and, so saying, he shows himself again in those three states of his Incarnation. Every communion we make is a birth, a marriage, and a death.

As those words are pronounced, he comes silently into the priest's hands, as he came to Bethlehem; "he shall come down like rain into a fleece of wool"[1] the Psalm tells us; so he came, and so he comes. When last you went to communion, what were the dispositions of your heart as the bell tinkled in the sanctuary? Were you waiting for him, like the shepherds of Bethlehem; were you keeping watch, as they were, keeping watch over your thoughts, as they over their flocks, so that you were ready for his coming? Or was your heart like the wayside inn, too full of other guests to give a thought to his miraculous birth? When we make our preparation for communion, there should be a silence as of midnight in our hearts; not a feverish activity of aspirations and petitions, but an interior silence that banishes from the mind the busy echoes of its daily preoccupations; those plans we were forming, those grudges we were nursing, those anxieties we

[1] Psalm 71. 6.

were harbouring, those fears we were encouraging—well, perhaps it is too much to ask that we should banish them altogether, but they should be hushed, as men's footsteps are hushed outside the door of a sick-room. It is in the silence of the heart that we shall hear that whisper, *Hoc est corpus meum*, and know that Christ is born.

But if our Lord's presence in the Holy Eucharist means a birth, it also means a marriage; the moment at which we receive the Blessed Sacrament is the moment at which he plights his love to us in a supreme manner, making us one with himself. *Hoc est corpus meum*—it is the voice of the bridegroom in the Canticles, standing behind the wall, and bidding his beloved come away into the fields and the villages, rousing us from the heavy sleep of our neglect. When we receive holy communion, it is well enough if we find ourselves in the dispositions of Martha, eagerly entertaining our divine guest with prayers for this and that; for the graces we covet, strength to resist temptations, the needs of the Church or of our friends. But, just at that moment, it is surely better still if we find ourselves in the dispositions of Mary Magdalen, sitting at his feet and hearing his word; sitting at his feet, in a humility which makes us forget self, hearing his word, in a raptness of attention which makes us forget all besides. Just in that moment, we want to be all for him, *dilectus meus mihi, et ego illi*; that is the good part, surely, which shall not be taken away from us.

And finally, our Lord's presence in the Holy Eucharist means a death. Not only in the sense that somehow, mysteriously, he who was immolated once for all on Calvary makes fresh offering of his death every time we celebrate the holy mysteries; but in this sense too, that his sacramental presence in our bodies at least is a transitory one; it is withdrawn from us when he has given us the opportunity to profit by it as we should. And at our Lord's tomb, as at our Lord's cradle, there were two classes of watchers. The soldiers had been set there to watch, and they fell asleep. While they slept, Mary Magdalen and the other holy women were on their way to embalm the body with spices. And when our mortal bodies share the privilege of the holy sepulchre, to receive into them the body of Christ, which are we more like—the soldiers who went to sleep, or the women who could not rest till they had embalmed his memory? When we make our thanksgiving after communion, we ought to hoard up those precious moments as if they were some precious liquid, ointment of right spikenard, that we must guard jealously even as we run, for fear that a drop of them should be wasted. Ten minutes, it may be, is all we can spare when Mass is ended, but those ten minutes, if they are well used, will suffice to grant us the privilege Mary Magdalen had, of hearing him call us by our own name, of calling him by his.

This is my body, born for you at Bethlehem, and between the priest's hands. This is my body, spent with labours for my bride the Church, made one with my faithful in this sacrament. This is my body, forgotten and remembered in death, forgotten or remembered, every day, by the souls it has visited and nourished.

10

THE BEST MAN

He must become more and more, I must become less and less.—John 3. 30.

I THINK I am right in saying that the feast of Corpus Christi falls, this year, on the latest date at which it can possibly fall, the 24th of June. And, so falling, by a curious coincidence, it clashes with, and supersedes, the only very great feast which Corpus Christi ever does supersede—the Nativity of St John the Baptist. To be sure, we do not let him fall out of the calendar altogether; we celebrate him tomorrow. But, for once, the great forerunner comes lagging behind his Master.

I do not think there is any saint you can imagine accepting that situation with a better grace than St John the Baptist. He was born, if we may dare to say so, to be the odd man out. Our Lord himself tells us that. Poor John, he says, the greatest man ever born of woman, and yet he is less than the least of you people here, because the kingdom of heaven is for you, not for him. He takes rank with the heroes of the Old Testament, who lived in hope and never saw their hopes realized; prophets and kings desired it long, and died before the sight. Everybody is rushing the barriers, Tom, Dick, and Harry swarming into the kingdom of heaven, the violent take it by force, and he, John, is left outside. Remember, St John wasn't dead when our Lord said that; he was only in prison. But St John was not destined, that is the point, to see the world's salvation achieved.

And St John realized that, felt that. The crowds which used to come and demand baptism from him had thinned down into a mere trickle; and his disciples complained that this new prophet, Jesus of Nazareth had stolen his thunder, had borrowed his methods, and was eclipsing him. And St John replied in the words I quoted to you just now, "He must become more and more; I must become less and less." It was his fate, he said, to be like the best man at the wedding; all the interest centred in another, all the acclamations reserved for another; and he must stand by—jealous? Out of humour? No, "rejoicing at hearing the bridegroom's voice". He had learned the trick of standing on one side, and making way for Jesus Christ.

That is why, today, I am proposing St John to you as one of the saints of the Blessed Sacrament. He never lived to kneel at the last supper and receive the body of Christ from the hands of Christ himself. He never lived to wait with our Lady and the apostles, and see the Holy Spirit which descended upon Christ at the Jordan descend upon Christ's Church in the cenacle. But he has left us one golden phrase, which should never be far from our minds when we are waiting for our blessed Lord to come to us in holy communion; "he must become more and more; I must become less and less".

If you look at the last verse of the first chapter of St Luke, you will find the words, "the child grew"; that refers to St John. If you look a little lower down, in the fortieth verse of the next chapter, you will find the same words again, "the child grew"; this time, they refer to our Lord. Take those two verses together, and you have the whole biography of St John. Outwardly, St John grew up; inwardly, in his soul, he never grew up—it was the Christ-child, his cousin, that grew up within him. "Some fell upon good ground, and these sprouted and grew, and yielded a harvest"—there, in the parable of the sower, you have the explanation. The sower sows the word, and the word of God, we are told, came upon John in the wilderness. The word of God, the grain of wheat which falls into the ground and dies, that it may bring forth much fruit, was sown in the heart of St John; and what grew up was not St John; it was the word of God, Jesus Christ.

The seed sown, what a splendid parable that is of the influence of divine grace in human hearts, and how unsparingly the New Testament makes use of it! Go out into the country at this time of year, and look at some piece of ground that has only been recently reclaimed for tillage, in these days when every acre is of value. What do you find there? A sea of green; catching the eye, as the sea does, with its waves of light and shadow, when the breeze goes rippling over its surface. But it is all one uniform surface; nothing, you would say, but green blades everywhere, each bowed by the growing burden of the ear that is forming on it. Then, go up closer and look down underneath the crop. What do you find now? Nettles, thistles, docks, bracken, brambles, ragged robin, willow-herb, a network of wild undergrowth. These were the native masters of the soil, till the farmer, the other day, buried in it this mysterious treasure of good grain. It has been a struggle for domination, it is a struggle still, between those old, rugged native growths, and the patient intruder. A struggle, which of them shall enjoy the richness of the soil beneath; a struggle, which of them shall grow higher and shut out the sun's light from the other. And the crop which man intruded there has won.

That is an image of your soul and mine. Or rather, would God that it were! It is the image of a soul in which divine grace has the upper hand; the soul of a saint, or something next door to a saint. The Psalmist represents almighty God as saying to our Lord, *Dominare in medio inimicorum tuorum*, "Dominate amongst thy enemies".[1] And that should be our prayer, every time our Lord comes to us in holy communion; we want him to dominate in our souls, in the midst of his enemies—our souls are so full of his enemies, pride, covetousness, resentment, self-indulgence, ready to dispute every inch of territory with him. We are fallen creatures; thorns and briers spring up not only in the ground which was cursed for our sakes, but in the fertile depths of our own souls, of which it is the image. Grace comes as an intruder, to struggle for the mastery in hostile surroundings. And the most sanctified of human souls is no better than that cornfield we were considering just now; look under the surface, and all the human passions are still there underneath, got down but not fully eradicated. God help us, what of your soul and mine?

He must become more and more, I must become less and less. Rooted deep in our nature, mysteriously prolific, spreading out in a network of subtle ramifications, lies the instinct of self-assertion. You see it in its crudest form in children, that desire to show off, to be thought important, which is sometimes so irritating, sometimes so amusing. School days come, and school-masters combine with school friends to weed out this obvious defect. But they haven't really weeded it out, they've only driven it underground. It is rooted in us none the less firmly—perhaps we ought to say, all the more firmly—because we are compelled by the conventions of society to cover it up and pretend it is not there. But we know that it is there; how few people there are that can take it well, even outwardly, when their advice is not asked for, or is asked for and not taken; when they are passed over in the filling up of a vacancy and somebody else is put in instead; when

[1] Psalm 109. 2.

some professional rival achieves fame, in the very department where they hoped to achieve fame themselves! Even outwardly; and when we come to look inside, each of us into his own heart, how much deeper it lies, often, than the world knows, that bitter feeling of ill-usage we have when our self-importance is wounded! Don't let's be too despondent about it, if we find such feelings are often with us; they are common enough, God knows, in the life of any moderately good Christian. But they are perhaps the surest sign which could be given us, that we are not saints.

And one of the reasons, surely, why our Lord comes to us in holy communion is to make us more Christ-assertive, and therefore less self-assertive, as life goes on. The two qualities, you see, cannot really exist together; or perhaps we ought to say that they can exist together, but they cannot flourish side by side. In your corn-field, the bracken will win here, the wheat there, but one will always get the better of the other. So it is with us; he must become more and more, I must become less and less; you can be sure that Christ is not yet dominating among his enemies, if that instinct of self-assertiveness is still strong. That "I" which is so covetous of petty superiorities; that "I" which infects even our prayer, even our virtues, making us want to be pure so that we may feel pure, be humble so that we may be free to criticize the pride of others, be mortified so that we can congratulate ourselves on being mortified, instead of simply wanting God's will to be done in us, and in everybody else. The "I" which takes all its losses and disappointments so badly, asking why *this* should have passed others by, and have been reserved for *me*.

Shall we try to humble ourselves occasionally, get some idea of the little progress *we* have made, by thinking about today's saint, St John the Baptist? When the priest holds up the sacred Host before giving us communion, it is from St John the Baptist that he quotes. "Look, this is the Lamb of God; this is he who takes away the sins of the world!"[1] And when St John said that, he knew that he was directing the attention of his disciples towards another Teacher; that he would lose them, that he would lose, gradually, all his popularity, all his chance of getting a hearing, as the result of this competition; and he didn't mind. Shut out from the kingdom of heaven, like a child flattening its nose against a shop-window when it has no money to buy the coveted things that are set out there; and he didn't mind. He must become more and more, I must become less and less; less of me, so that there may be more of him.

[1] John I. 29.

Do we sometimes find it difficult to stir our imaginations with the thought of holy men who died long ago? Then let me, for a moment, evoke a more recent memory. Some of you will have known, most of you will have heard—he has often stood in this pulpit—the great Dominican whom death has just removed from us, Father Vincent McNabb. When he delivered his memorable panegyric on Father Bede Jarrett, he took a text which refers to St John the Baptist, "He was a burning and a shining light."[1] Let me suggest to you this for *his* epitaph, "He must become more and more, I must become less and less." Here was a man whose very eccentricities were due to his absorption in the Christ he preached. People often felt inclined to say to him, "You are forgetting yourself, Father"; and they would have been right—he always did forget himself. His was a voice crying in the wilderness, crying out, in Hyde Park, to a London which would not listen; in these last few weeks, through his mortal ailment, that voice became a whisper, scarcely audible, but he went on. He must become less and less; but we knew that Christ was becoming more and more in him, all through those last heroic days. May his soul find, beyond the grave, the rest it never asked for here; may his gracious influence still haunt, in the troubled times that are coming, his familiar walks, the streets he knew and the city he loved so well.

I I

SELF-EXAMINATION[2]

My judgment is judgment indeed; it is not I alone, my Father who sent me is with me.—John 8. 16.

IT is always interesting to speculate what historians will be saying, a hundred years hence, about the period in which you are living. What will they be saying about us, what figure shall we cut in the estimation of posterity, living in this uneasy twilight of 1946, an uncertain twilight, whether of dusk or dawn? One thing they will say, I fancy, of which for the most part we are quite unconscious. This will be regarded as the age of the great judicial trials. On a scale unexampled

[1] John 5. 35.
[2] This sermon was preached at the time of the Nuremberg trials.

in history, judgment is being passed on men who, till yesterday, felt that they were above the law; felt, too often, that considerations of human justice need not apply to their actions. Today, their lives are in jeopardy, all over the continent of Europe, and in the remote islands of the eastern sea.

It would be an excess of charity to pretend that all these legal proceedings, everywhere, are being conducted with legal fairness. The consciences of English people are only committed to seeing justice done in a limited number of them. And I think we can derive great comfort from the criticisms which foolish people are making, in the newspapers especially, about the slowness and elaborateness of the procedure on which we, more than any other nation in the world, obstinately insist. It is easy for the cynic to point out that in spite of it all we shall probably be accused, in a hundred years' time, of having taken vengeance on our enemies with a hypocritical show of impartiality. It is easy to object that there is no instance in history where a man tried by his enemies has had, indisputably, a fair trial. We can afford to neglect such criticisms. We are not concerned to put ourselves right in the eyes of posterity. We are concerned, when we pass judgment on our fellow creatures, to put ourselves right in the eyes of almighty God.

When we judge, remember, we are usurping the privilege of God himself. When we judge our enemies, how shall we make certain that we are not blinded by prejudice? The evidence cannot be too laboriously compiled, the pleadings cannot be examined too scrupulously here. The man who judges a fellow creature on earth stands his own trial, in doing so, before the tribunal of eternal justice; not less so the nation which judges the crimes of another nation. We, as we give just or unjust verdict, as we impose deserved or undeserved sentence, at this hour, are claiming for ourselves, or forfeiting, the divine approval.

It was this contrast between human justice and divine to which our Lord was drawing attention when he used the words from which I have taken my text. "You", he says to the Jews, "set yourselves up to judge after your earthly fashion; I do not set myself up to judge anybody. And what if I should judge? My judgment is judgment indeed; it is not I alone, my Father who sent me is with me."[1] The opinions which his contemporaries formed about Jesus of Nazareth were utterly worthless; dictated to them by prejudice, by injured vanity, by jealous hatred of a life spent in doing good. The opinions which Jesus of Nazareth formed about his contemporaries were so many decrees

[1] John 8. 15-16.

registered in eternity. The Father was with him; he saw with the eyes of that infallible wisdom. The Father was with him; he made allowances with the clemency of that inexhaustible love. The Father was with him; he pronounced sentence with all the terrors of that irresistible power. Every perspective seen by the eyes of the Incarnate was true; he was himself the truth.

Why does he say, "I do not set myself up to judge anybody"? Is not this the same Jesus of Nazareth, who promised that he would come again to judge the living and the dead? Yes, but he was not judging them yet. You see, it was not necessary. He has only to come and live amongst us men, and we men, at the mere neighbourhood of him, pass judgment on ourselves. We accept or reject him, and thereby betray ourselves as the kind of men we are; no more is needed for our condemnation or acquittal. That is, in a sense, the whole message of St John's Gospel. "Rejection" (he says) "lies in this, that when the light came into the world men preferred darkness to light; preferred it, because their doings were evil." All those dark secrets of the human conscience, on which our limited human knowledge finds it so difficult to pass judgment, gave themselves away when the light came into the world; it is an automatic process, the dispelling of darkness by light. And our Lord could tell us quite truly, that he had come to save the world, not to pass sentence on it. But the people who rejected him thereby passed sentence on themselves.

After all, you see, when we talk about having to undergo judgment when we are dead, we are only using a kind of metaphor, a kind of analogy. God's judgments are not like ours; he does not have to find out the truth, he knows it already. There is no citing of witnesses, no discussion of arguments for and against; when we die, we are judged already—our own lives, our own dispositions, mark us down already for the doom that is to be ours in eternity. When man judges man, the accused knows whether he is innocent or guilty; it is for the judge to find out. When God judges man, the judge knows the truth already; it is the accused that has to learn it. Our judgment will be the exhibition to ourselves, and later to humanity at large, of our own record; in the sight of God, that record is already plain to view.

We are often encouraged to think seriously about the hour of death, and to remind ourselves that our judgment will immediately follow it. That is, no doubt, a salutary exercise of piety, but familiarity has staled it for us, and we sometimes find that it does not affect our lives as it ought to. We think of our lives as a record folded over and put into an envelope and pigeon-holed somewhere in a kind of celestial clearing office, where they will lie, till the moment of our death, unread. Then, to be sure, the envelope will be opened, and eternal justice will take a look at its contents. But by then, so much may have happened; that pious old age we look forward to, that edifying death-bed! It seems such a long distance away. I wonder if we shouldn't do well sometimes to remember that, in a sense, our judgment is happening *now*. You are wondering whether you will or will not decide to go to confession, and renounce, in your act of contrition, some darling sin. And God is already sitting in judgment on you; picture, if you will, the black cap as lying on the desk in front of him. Picture him as saying, "This shall be the test. If this creature of mine cannot do so much for me, this very little I ask of him, then he is no use; nothing can ever be made of him, nothing will ever pierce that conscience of his, it is hardened beyond remedy." The judgment is set, and the books are opened; I am calling down upon myself, here and now, a verdict which will take its effect in eternity.

"What a curious sermon", you are saying, "for Corpus Christi Day! We might have been given something less depressing to think about, on this day of all days, than death and judgment." Yes, but I can't help it; it's in this morning's epistle; it's all over this morning's epistle. "It is the Lord's death you are heralding, whenever you eat this bread and drink this cup, until he comes; and therefore, if anyone eats this bread or drinks this cup of the Lord unworthily, he will be held to account for the Lord's body and blood. A man must examine himself first, and then eat of that bread and drink of that cup; he is eating and drinking damnation to himself if he eats and drinks unworthily, not recognizing the Lord's body for what it is."[1] The Christian who partakes of this gift without concerning himself to ask whether he is in a fit state to receive it becomes the accomplice of Pontius Pilate, judging and misjudging Christ. By not recognizing that virgin-born body for what it is, he associates himself with the crime which crucified it. Whatever else the Church wants us to have in mind when we keep the Corpus Christi feast, it is certain that she means us to spare a thought for the dangers of sacrilegious communion. She comes back to the subject again, you see, in the *Lauda Sion*:

> The good, the guilty share therein,
> With sure increase of grace or sin,
> The ghostly life, or ghostly death:

she wants us to be quite certain where we stand. And we stand in the dock.

[1] 1 Corinthians 11. 27-29.

Our blessed Lord, in his divine nature, is present to us at all times, is close to us at all times. Yet, to allow for the weakness of our own imaginations, he likes us to think of him, doesn't he, as coming to pay us a visit now and again. "My Father and I will come to him",[1] he says; and again, comparing himself still more vividly to some earthly guest, "Behold, I stand at the door and knock."[2] It is our fault, remember, if that visit proves to be a surprise visit. He does not come to us in the manner of a suspicious policeman, or a prying school-master, to see what we are up to. No, he who came into the world to save it, not to pass sentence on it, comes to us still not to find out what is wrong with us, but eager for our good. Only, when he comes and knocks at the door, if that knock is followed by scuffling, and silence, and the door does not open, it means that all is not well within. We were not ready for him; we were taken off our guard. And, found in that posture, we have proclaimed ourselves guilty men. It is not he, it is we ourselves, that have passed the sentence of our condemnation.

As the rays of the sun, whose heat is present everywhere, are caught and focused in a single point by the lens of a burning-glass, so our Lord will have these celestial visitations of his focused for us, crystallized and concentrated for us under the forms of outward things, when he comes to us through his sacred humanity in the Holy Eucharist. Here at least we cannot complain that he takes us by surprise. He is so utterly condescending, in this sacrament of his humiliation, that he will visit us at a time of our own choosing, will leave it to us to invite him when we want him to come. His knock at the door shall be gentler than ever; there can be no excuse, surely, for haste or confusion within. And yet . . . is it always so? We so easily get wrapped up in our own petty concerns, get carried away by our own foolish trains of thought, that most of us know what it is to hear the bell ring at the *Domine non sum dignus*, and be awoken from our daydreams by the sudden intrusion of that supreme reality.

That only happens at the surface level of consciousness. We ought not, I think, to worry about it a great deal when we find ourselves, day after day or week after week, incapable (I don't think that is putting it too strongly) of concentrating our thoughts on what we are doing when we go to communion until the very last moment. This habit of wool-gathering is a weakness in us, not a crime; and it is certainly wrong to argue, "It seems impossible for me to receive holy communion with anything like recollectedness, therefore I shall go to communion less often." We shall do far better to communicate often, and to go on

[1] John 14. 23.   [2] Apocalypse 3. 20.

apologizing to our Lord for this persistent absent-mindedness of ours, which is so far from representing our real attitude. No, what St Paul wants us to be careful about is something different; "a man must examine himself first"—we have got to dig down below that surface level, and lay bare our secret infidelities. Those grudges against our neighbour which we forget all the time, but forget about them because they are buried so deep; those obstinate attachments to deliberate venial sin, perhaps only needing opportunity, perhaps only needing more enterprise, to turn them into something worse—those are the real marks of disrespect we show when our Lord comes to visit us. And we shall continue to show those marks of disrespect, until we learn to do what St Paul tells us we ought to be doing all the time, examine ourselves. Oh, we do that, every now and again, when we go to confession; but do we really dig deep enough? The gracious influence which comes to us in the Holy Eucharist ought to fill the soul to its depths. But, at those depths, it encounters infidelities, reluctances, a half-hearted attitude towards eternity; an unspiritual habit of mind, which challenges and resists it.

We have to welcome our Lord in holy communion, not only as the friend who comes to visit us, not only as the physician who comes to heal us, but as the auditor (if I may put it as prosaically as that) who comes to put our accounts straight for us. How wonderful if the first voice which greets us after death should be heard saying, "His sins? That is all right; we have been into all that before"!

12

THE THING THAT MATTERS

It is through him, then, that we must offer to God a continual sacrifice of praise.—Hebrews 13. 15.

I WAS preaching last Sunday down at Exeter, to commemorate a sad and much-forgotten event in English history. Four hundred years ago an order went out from the Government in London that the Latin Mass should be discontinued, and a new, English service-book should be used in all churches and chapels of the realm. It was the signal for a rising among the men of the Western counties, who took up arms in defence of the old religion; and the Government had to call in German and Italian mercenaries before the rebellion was stamped out in blood.

Not for the first time I found myself wondering why it was that this particular piece of provocation, the English service-book, should have been the signal for an outbreak. After all, the people of England had put up with a good deal already. The rights of the Holy See had been repudiated, and for fifteen years the whole country had been in schism. The monasteries, so intimately bound up with the religious life of the Middle Ages, had been dissolved and lay in ruins. Gangs of hooligans, with royal encouragement, went about everywhere breaking down the statues of our Lady and the saints, defacing even the pictures in our churches. But when all that had been done, one line still remained which you must not overstep, on pain of driving the common folk into violent insurrection; you must not touch the Mass.

It was not open provocation, only the thin end of the wedge, in 1549. The new service-book, modelled much more closely on our Catholic liturgy than anything the Church of England has had since, was perhaps meant to be a compromise; more probably, to be a first instalment of change. The communion service, "commonly called the Mass", had a recognizable Canon, offered prayer for the dead, commemorated our blessed Lady and the saints. But already the men of the West saw what was coming, and turned out with the rude armour of country folk crying, "We will not receive the new service, because it is but like a Christmas game." There was plenty of fine English prose about it, but it lacked reality. It was not the Mass.

In a curious way, when they made that protest, the insurgents defined an issue, marked out an arena of conflict, for three centuries ahead. Within a lifetime, the word "Mass" came to have an abominable sound in English ears; it belonged to the jargon of a discredited underworld. To say Mass became high treason; if you described a person as going to Mass, you meant that he was a Popish recusant. And the stigma has persisted right up to our own times; at the beginning of this century, an epigrammatic statesman could still arouse prejudice against us by declaring, "It is the Mass that matters". And we caught up the slogan, and made it our own; it is the Mass that matters, that is what we *must* get people to understand.

What was clear, I think, to the men of the West country, was that the Government wanted to abolish the Holy Eucharist as a sacrifice, while retaining holy communion as one of the sacraments. And they demanded roundly that Mass should be said "without any persons communicating with the priest". I'm afraid we have to admit it, our forefathers in the later Middle Ages did not use the sacraments as faithfully as they might have done, as they should have done; a bad tradition had grown up. That was why the Council of Trent expressed a wish that "at each Mass the faithful who are present should communicate"; for all the world as if they shared the opinions of the Reformers. But the emphasis was entirely different. The Fathers of Trent were determined to honour the sacrament of holy communion; the Reformers were concerned to discredit the doctrine of the eucharistic sacrifice. They weren't hardy enough to deny it, but they meant to obscure it, to soft-pedal it, until gradually it fell into oblivion.

The men who died at Exeter in 1549 saw through that intention of the Government, and were determined to force the issue. They had grown up in an England where Christ was offered day by day at a thousand altars for the living and the dead; this new England, in which the Lord's Supper would be administered once a week if there was enough demand for it among the parishioners, was something they had no use for. And that remained, as I say, for three centuries the whole pattern of English religion; on one side there were the old-fashioned people, a majority at first, then a dwindling minority, who held by the Mass; on the other side a confused body of Anglicans and sectaries who sang psalms, listened to sermons, and every now and then, if they were pious folk and were feeling pious, partook of the Lord's Supper.

Have I spoilt the feast for you by talking so much about history by recalling "old, unhappy, far-off things and battles of long ago"? Forgive me, but I think we do well to remember these lost causes of a bygone age, if only so as to remind ourselves of the eternal thing they stood for. I do not mean, heaven forbid, that you and I should bear a grudge against our non-Catholic neighbours, as if they were responsible for the loss sustained by English religion four centuries back. No, but the truth ever shines brighter by contrast, and we shall understand our own faith better if we understand the meaning, however dimly realized, that underlay the protest of the West country people so long ago. We shall see the doctrine of the holy Mass as a thing worth living for, if we can see why it was, in their day, a thing worth dying for.

What is it exactly that the old-fashioned Protestant misses as he kneels at the communion-rails? To be sure, he finds there nothing of the miraculous; he has lost sight of what is our chief motive for admiration and gratitude; if the doctrine of transubstantiation is proposed to him, he dismisses it at once as a piece of medieval superstition. His theology, then, is hopelessly attenuated, but I am not thinking so much about theology, just now. I am thinking of his devotional attitude; and his devotional attitude is not, perhaps, so unlike ours as this theology would lead you to expect. He does, after all, hope to receive supernatural grace. The reception of it, he would tell you, depends entirely on the faith which he brings to the exercise; if faith were lacking, he would receive nothing, because there would be nothing to receive. Once more, he is wrong; but since he does in fact approach in a spirit of faith, the embarrassment does not arise. He hopes to receive sacramental grace, and there is something more; he probably believes that our Lord is present in a special way, communicating himself mysteriously to the soul of the worshipper. About the manner of that presence he can tell you nothing; he avoids the question, and, if you press him, takes refuge in metaphors. But, left to himself, he approaches with awe, none the less real, none the less comforting, because the object of it remains undefined. "Christ's was the word that spake it; he took the bread and brake it, and what his word doth make it, that I believe and take it"—the lines are attributed to Queen Elizabeth, and if she was really the author of them, I think most of us will be inclined to blame her for shirking an issue which it was her duty to face. But if they are quoted by somebody born outside the Church, somebody who has no head for theology, I do not know why such a person may not have made, according to his lights, a good spiritual communion.

His devotional life is impoverished, rather, for *this* reason—that his communion service has nothing of Mass about it. It has been a mere service of consecration, in which lifeless things were set apart to be the pledge of *his* salvation, to bring a special grace to *his* soul. As water in baptism, so here bread and wine, were hallowed only for the satisfaction of a human need; Christ became present, in whatever sense Christ did become present, only so as to be made one with him. There was no transaction external to himself, in which and for the purpose of which Christ would have become present, even if there had been nobody to communicate. There was no sacrifice.

We of the old faith, instinctively, approach the mystery of Holy Eucharist from the other end. For us, holy communion, important as it is, awe-inspiring as it is, figures as something secondary in intention to the Mass itself; a gracious corollary, a stupendous after-effect, which unites us in a special way with the thing done. For us the immediate, dazzling truth is that here and all over the world Christ, in the person of the priest, is offering Christ under the forms of bread and wine in perfect sacrifice to the eternal Father. If I am worthy, if I am willing, he gives himself to me; but, worthy or no, willing or no, he gives himself for me, as for all mankind, his brothers; on earth, as in heaven, he is our High Priest and representative. All that vision, familiar to the Middle Ages, faded from the eyes of English folk when German and Italian troops raised the siege of Exeter.

I have used the word "impoverishment"; when they abolished the Mass, the Government of that day robbed the English people no less really, and far more importantly, than when they took away the common lands which had been free to all in the time of the monasteries. The thoughts of the Christian were turned fatally in upon himself: "What effect is this sacrament going to produce in me? How am I to get rid of my sins? How can I be certain that I am, here and now, in the grace of Christ? Can I feel his love, here and now, at work in me? Am I predestined to a happy eternity?"—and so on. And the result of that was scruples, and religious melancholy, and despair, and a reaction which made men turn away from the whole Christian idea. You see, a man who enjoys bodily health is not always thinking about whether he is well or not, and a Christian who enjoys spiritual health is not always thinking about whether he is saved or not. I don't mean that he doesn't want to be saved, I don't mean that he is prepared to neglect his salvation; but his first concern is not that, it is something other. His first concern is that God should be worthily worshipped, for the sake of his own glory. And we Catholics have the assurance that that is being done, whenever we go into a church and find a priest saying Mass. The priest may be somebody for whom we have little respect, somebody who does not strike us as an exact follower of his Master's rule; God forgive us, how few of us priests are anything like that! No, but he is a priest, and in him we see the hand of Christ invisibly extended; Christ is here, offering himself to the Father, and through him not you or I but all mankind is pouring out its helpless, stammering accents of worship. God's glory first, the Paternoster said, and the Victim broken; and *then* we can gather round the altar rails, and make the sacrifice, by communicating with it, more than ever our own.

It's the Mass that matters. No need to follow the theologians into their nice disquisitions about the exact meaning of sacrifice, the exact sense in which the Mass is a sacrifice, the exact moment at which the sacrifice takes place. All *that* we can take as read; enough that the Catholic religion points us to an altar and bids us fall down in worship. To us, and to our brethren still separated from us, may God restore his ancient mercies; now, when so many other lights are put out, may England, as in happier days, bear integral witness to his truth.

13

REAL BREAD

Who will come and get him food, no price to be paid?—Isaias 55.1.

THERE is a curious point about our Lord's teaching, or at any rate about that more intimate, more characteristic teaching preserved for us in the Gospel of St John, which we sometimes fail to notice because we are so accustomed, nowadays, to the use of metaphor in common speech. I mean this point—that our Lord does not simply compare heavenly things with earthly by way of illustration, does not simply say, for example, "You see that vine? Well, that vine will give you some idea of the unity of the Church." Rather, he treats all the earthly things with which we are familiar in this world of sense as if they were mere shadows, mere inferior copies of the reality which awaits us in heaven. He starts, if we may say so, at the other end; not at the earthly end which is more familiar to us ordinary human beings, but at the heavenly end which is more familiar to the incarnate Son of God.

So it is when he talks to the Samaritan woman;" If thou knewest what it is God gives, and who it is that is saying to thee, Give me drink, it would have been for thee to ask him instead, and he would have given thee living water."[1] By "living water" he does not mean fresh water or running water, as the woman supposes. He means that all the water you can find in this world of sense, the purest, the freshest to be had anywhere, is only dead water; the real water, the real living water, is something which does not belong to the world of sense at all. We shall never know what water really means until we have the direct experience of that reality of grace of which water is only a pale image. So with the vine; the vines you may see growing on some hill-side in France are not real vines, he tells us, they are only a sort of imitation. We shall never understand the mystery of organic growth, of that principle in nature whereby a tree or a plant goes on producing fresh shoots according to its kind, until we know, as not even the saints can know it on earth, the nature of that bond which unites all Christian people with their divine Head, and through him with one another. And so it is, he tells us, with the very bread we eat; the simplest,

[1] John 4. 10.

K

most primitive fact of human life—so much so that the old poets used to describe the human race as "men that live by bread". The true bread, the living bread, is not the common bread which we eat. The common bread which we eat is only a sham, a copy, an image of that true bread which came down from heaven. And if we ask what is the true bread which came down from heaven, he has given us the answer: "I myself am the living bread; the man who eats my flesh and drinks my blood enjoys eternal life."[1] You see, we are so materialistic, our minds are so chained to the things of sense, that we imagine our Lord as instituting the Blessed Sacrament with bread and wine as the remote matter of it because bread and wine reminded him of that grace which he intended the Blessed Sacrament to bestow. But, if you come to think of it, it was just the other way about. When he created the world, he gave common bread and wine for our use in order that we might understand what the Blessed Sacrament was when it came to be instituted. He did not design the sacred Host to be something like bread. He designed bread to be something like the sacred Host.

Always, it is the things which affect us outwardly and impress themselves on our senses that are the shams, the imaginaries; reality belongs to the things of the spirit. All the din and clatter of the streets, all the great factories which dominate our landscape, are only echoes and shadows if you think of them for a moment in the light of eternity; the reality is in here, is there above the altar, is that part of it which our eyes cannot see and our senses cannot distinguish. The motto on Cardinal Newman's tomb ought to be the funeral motto of every Catholic, *Ex umbris et imaginibus in veritatem*, Out of shadows and appearances into the truth. When death brings us into another world, the experience will not be that of one who falls asleep and dreams, but that of one who wakes from a dream into the full light of day. Here, we are so surrounded by the things of sense that we take them for the full reality. Only sometimes we have a glimpse which corrects that wrong perspective. And above all, when we see the Blessed Sacrament enthroned, we should look up towards that white disc which shines in the monstrance as towards a chink through which, just for a moment, the light of the other world shines through.

There are periods, there are moments in history, which seem to men living at the time to show up the world for the transient, fleeting thing it is. Wars or famines or pestilence have depopulated countries, and have left the survivors uncertain of their prospects, uncertain of life itself; the energies of human nature seem to have used themselves

[1] John 6. 55.

up, and it feels as if the forces of inanimate nature, too, were threatened with dissolution. At such times, men have often turned to their religion with more ardour, have separated themselves from the world and gone to live as hermits or in the cloister, reminded at last that we have here no abiding city. You will catch the echoes of that feeling in the sermons of St Gregory in the sixth century, in the rhythm of Bernard of Morlaix in the twelfth. It is not an illusion people get at such times that the world is transitory. Rather at such times they lose the illusion that the world is permanent. They realize more than at other times what is true at all times, that the whole of this visible creation is but a thin plank between us and eternity.

Now here is an extraordinary thing—that *we* live in times when, perhaps more than ever before, we ought to see through the hollowness of the material things around us, and yet, so far have we travelled from the age of faith, we love the things of the world more than ever, clasp them more than ever, as we see them ready to disappear from us. Anybody who knows anything knows that our country is in a bad way, and that other countries, when you come to look at them, are not much better off than ourselves. Unemployment is the difficulty which most readily leaps to the eye, but unemployment is only a symptom of some hidden and mysterious disease which has come upon an over-civilized world. A trade depression, we say, a slump in the world market; but does anybody really know what is happening? Does anybody really know how soon we may be involved in the miseries of wholesale bankruptcy? Our comfortable world of prosperity, inherited from our Victorian ancestors, is threatening to tumble about our ears; and we smile nervously and hope for the best.

And here is what makes it still more extraordinary—we do not owe our present troubles to any of the common forces of nature, to a world-wide drought, to torrential rains, to any pestilence among mankind or blight among the crops. Something that is happening in the unreal world of high finance is having its effects, devastating effects, upon the real world—or so we think it—in which men must earn their bread or starve if they cannot come by it. Imagine some visitant from the past who should come to earth nowadays and hear of our modern distresses. So much poverty, he would say, so much uncertainty about the very means of livelihood—I suppose you must have had bad harvests, and there is not enough corn to go round? And we should have to tell him that it is just the opposite; that whole stocks of grain are being destroyed for fear that corn should be too plentiful, and therefore too cheap!

You see, we are caught up in the wheels of our own economic system. The fields of wheat flourish, there is corn and wine and oil in abundance, there is treasure still locked in the bosom of earth; and yet through our own laws of supply and demand, laws which have no root in nature, but depend simply upon our human actions, the whole world is at a standstill! Did we not say well that this world in which we live is a world of shadows? When forces that have no existence outside our own wills can threaten society with destruction?

And the effect of all that on us? Is it to drive us nearer to God, to make us disgusted with the insufficiency of this world? I am afraid it is very difficult to avoid the impression that it is all the other way; that we try to forget our solicitudes by drowning ourselves in pleasures and amusements, by getting all that we can out of today, when tomorrow has so little to offer. If the investments that call for our savings are insecure, very well, we will not save; if hard work earns so little, we will give up to leisure the hours that were meant for work. That is not the moral God means us to draw. He means us to realize, when our labour is ill-paid, that all labour is ill-paid which is crowned with earthly rewards; he means us to understand, when money is hard to come by and hard to keep, that all treasure is wasted when it is laid up on earth. Do not labour for the meat which perishes, he tells us; lay up for yourselves treasure in heaven.

Without money and without price. . . . Lord, give us always this bread. That is his invitation; that should be our response. His temporal gifts he will lavish at one time, withhold from us at another; that is because they do not really matter; they only refer to the needs of this life, such a short one. Your fathers, he says to the Jews, did eat manna and are dead; more highly privileged, you would think, than any nation on the earth, they were kept alive from day to day with supplies of food miraculously maintained and miraculously multiplied. And the upshot of it? They went the way of all flesh at last; they passed over the horizon, and the slopes of the wilderness grew white with manna no more. Does he not, perhaps, say the same to us? Your fathers did eat manna and are dead; in the times of national prosperity, I gave them such abundance as no other nation has known; their fleets peopled the seas, their workshops rang with industry, and it profited them for the time, but . . . they are dead. Scarcity or prosperity, it is all one now. But with his eternal gifts it is not so. Lord, evermore give us this bread; to every generation of Christian people alike he offers the unlaborious dole that is to strengthen them for their spiritual journey, his flesh and his blood in the sacrament of Holy Eucharist. Shall we not learn to value it, we, to whom the value of earthly commodities has grown so small?

If thou knewest the gift of God!—if we could only find some standard, but there is no standard, which would compare earthly things with heavenly; if we could only measure, but there are no terms in which to measure, what it is that we miss when we go to communion seldom, grudgingly, and indevoutly. No, you cannot estimate the value of such a gift by any human standard, and least of all by a standard we are accustomed to use in daily life, the standard of rarity. We confuse value with price; we think that because a thing is difficult to come by it is worth a great deal, that because the opportunities of enjoying a thing are rare, no such opportunity should be lost. God forgive us, we despise his graces because he has made them so cheap for us; the heavenly bread which is offered us without money and without price we put down, for that reason, as not worth having! That is not the law of the divine economy. All the graces bestowed on our blessed Lady and the saints, all the visions and the ecstasies and the power of working miracles, are not to be compared in value with what he gives us in holy communion; for that is himself. This gift, which is himself, is not for the few, but for everybody. *O res mirabilis, manducat Dominum pauper, servus et humilis:* we are all paupers in his sight, all slaves, all creatures of earth, and he will make no distinctions between us. He only asks that we should purge our consciences of mortal sin, and so come to him, asking him to bring just what he wants to give us, just what he knows that we need. "I am he who bade this be done; I will supply what is lacking to thee; come, and receive me."

14

THIS MASS AND THE MASS[1]

Eastward then he faced, measured a thousand paces, and led me across a stream that reached my ankles. Another thousand, and when I crossed the stream it reached my knees; another thousand, and it was up to my waist; another thousand, and now it had become a torrent I might not cross any longer. Mark it well, son of man, said he.—Ezechiel 47. 3-6.

THE prophet Ezechiel, during the exile in Babylon, had a vision in which he saw the temple precincts rebuilt; not on the old scale,

[1] This sermon was preached during the Holy Year.

but according to divine specifications; a plan which as a matter of history was never realized. Very painstakingly, an angel with a measuring rod in his hand conducts the prophet all round the sacred enclosure, till our heads swim as we read it in the effort to retain some picture of it in our minds. Then, suddenly, at the end of it all, he catches sight of a trickle of water, flowing out eastwards from the threshold of the temple itself. A trickle at first, but (as we have seen) it grows deeper; flows eastwards still, out into the desert, into the Dead Sea and beyond it, cleansing those waters by its passage. "Wherever it flows, there shall be teeming life again . . . and on either bank of the stream fruit-trees shall grow of every kind; never leaf lost, never fruit cast; month after month they shall yield a fresh crop, watered by that sanctuary stream; fruit for man's eating, and medicinal leaves."[1]

The Church, as we know, has borrowed that allegory for her use in Easter-tide; it shall be the type for her, of that new life which springs from our Lord's Resurrection; and all through Easter-tide, instead of the *Asperges* before Mass, we have the *Vidi aquam* of Ezechiel's vision.[2] Shall we turn that allegory into a type of something not very different, the blessings which flow from the Holy Eucharist? You can see for yourselves that it would be possible, if we had time, to draw out the parallel in detail. But I thought, just for this evening, we would confine ourselves to one aspect of the picture; I mean the contrast between the tiny stream that flows out at the temple doors, and the great river into which it broadens out all at once. The holy Mass is something so intimate, we are so snug within the four walls of a church, cut off from the noisy coming and going of humanity. And yet, if we allow ourselves to think about it for a moment, how the echoes of it, the ripples of it, fill the world!

So intimate, surrounded by all the furniture of piety which suggests nothing but holy thoughts; the hushed voice of the priest, his restrained gestures; the little mementoes I keep in my prayer-book, mortuary cards and a few favourite devotions; how nice to be alone for a little! And when I go to communion, how everything conspires to make it a private encounter with our blessed Lord—his body given for *me*, as if there were nobody else, preserving *my* soul, as if that were the only thing that mattered! Even we priests, who ought to know better, are tempted to cultivate this atmosphere of friendly isolation; we talk about "my Mass". *My* Mass—how "mine"? How could the holy Mass belong to anybody? But there it is; for this one half-hour in the day we are guaranteed against interruption from other people, their

[1] Ezechiel 47. 12.   [2] Ezechiel, ch. 47.

troubles, their grievances, their sins; with the words *Introibo ad altare Dei* we have gone behind a curtain and fenced the world off from us; we are shut in with a limited sphere of familiar action, symbolical gestures are the cushion of our thoughts; the server is there, ready to hand us the next thing we want, our *Dominus vobiscum* sets up the expected echo of response. *Solus cum solo*, at last we are alone with God; we who ought always to be alone with him, yet somehow manage to forget him, because we are so busy in his service.

If a priest were wrecked, all by himself, on a desert island, and by some incalculable chance had all the requisites for Mass ready to hand, I suppose he would be justified in saying Mass, day after day, without even a server to share in the exercise. And still, day after day, he would find himself interceding not only for himself but *pro omnibus circum-stantibus*, for all the people standing round; he would turn and bid them ask acceptance for this sacrifice, his sacrifice and theirs; he would ask God to remember, together with his own, the intentions of the by-standers; and all the while there would be no answer to his Mass except the lapping of the waves and the cry of sea-gulls. I wonder if he wouldn't be impressed, merely by this ironical contrast, with the fact which ought to impress us whenever we go to Mass, but all too seldom does; that the Mass is essentially a corporate affair, a family affair, in which the priest is meant to stand out against a background of faithful laity; in which the laity ought to have the sense of sharing God's mercies with all the people round them, even with the woman who has taken their favourite seat, even with the man who looks as if he had come to rob the poor-box? The Mass is not just me worshipping; I am part of a crowd, the crowd of *circumstantes*, who are making, by their concerted action, a joint offering to almighty God.

If only people heard Mass at their own parish churches, I think we might realize that more clearly than we do. In a small country congre-gation, where the people are all neighbours and mostly related to one another, you do sometimes get the sense of the Mass as it ought to be, a family affair. One of the antiphons for Corpus Christi day tells us that the children of the Church ought to be like sturdy olive branches round the Lord's table, a reminiscence from that beautiful psalm which gives you such a glimpse of harmonious family life. The priest is the father of his congregation; not only in the sense that he adopts them at the font, not only in the sense that he corrects their faults in the confessional; he is the bread-winner, welcoming his children and dividing up their portions to them. A family meal is not meant to be like a *cafeteria*, where you sit reading your newspaper and glaring at the other people;

it is a common feast of unity, everybody conscious of a common relationship to their father and to one another. And when we go to Mass, although we don't need to be looking round and seeing what other people are wearing or wondering why they are late, we ought to be generally conscious of our fellow worshippers as forming part of a unity, in which unity we and they as a family are approaching almighty God.

That is our first step, then, out into the stream of the prophet's vision. The Mass is not just that shallow trickle—you can hardly call it more—of your own pious thoughts, your own aspirations to be made one with Christ. It is already a mountain torrent, swirling round your knees and bidding you be careful not to lose your footing. But is that all? No, absent friends come into the picture too. The priest is not allowed to offer the sacrifice merely for himself and for the congregation. He tells God that he is offering it for the bystanders themselves and also for their intentions on behalf of other people, *pro se suisque omnibus*. The people who are too old or too ill to go to Mass, the people who are too busy to go to Mass, even the people who could perfectly well go to Mass but for some reason don't go to Mass, all form part of the shadow family that is gathered round the Lord's table. When you begin to remember *that*, to remember that you are charged with the weight of everybody else's special intentions as well as your own, you do begin to take the strain; you are like St Christopher crossing the stream, with the holy Child feeling more and more of a weight on his back. Or, to stick more closely to our original metaphor, you find that the stream is flowing waist-high, breast-high; you are a mere struggling unit in the tide of intercession. The Mass is no longer your Mass, as you fondly thought of it; the church is crowded to suffocation with all the people who might be there, you and they all struggling to get to heaven together, helping one another on. There's no end to it.

But there is worse yet to come. The priest doesn't simply recall before God the needs of the people who are there in church, and the needs of the people they are interested in; you suddenly find that this Mass, your Mass, is being offered for all faithful people, all over the world. And with that, the stream has grown so full that it carries you away altogether, quite out of your depth. The walls of the church seem to enlarge, the altar, instead of being a few feet away, becomes a mere speck in the distance; it isn't *a* church any longer, it's *the* Church, the holy Catholic Church, that bounds your horizon, and what is happening there is not *a* Mass, it's *the* Mass, the one sacrifice that is going on all over the world, of which this Mass, your Mass, is only the pin-point, focused at a particular moment of time, within a particular determination of space. Your family worship is not merely that of the parish; it's the worship of the whole Christian family, and you are there with the Hottentots and the Laplanders, children of the same family, met round the same table. More distant presences come to mind; our Lady and the saints and the faithful departed. But even without them, how vast a thing our family worship is seen to be!

And the Father of that common family? We name him in the Mass; our Father, Pius. Do not think that the Holy Year is merely a device for increasing the tourist traffic; do not think that the intentions of the Church in proclaiming it are sufficiently realized when millions of people are transported, by mere locomotion in space, to a particular built-up area called Rome. No, the journey which pilgrims take there is meant to be simply an attestation of loyalty; loyalty to the person of the Holy Father, and in his person to the whole idea of Catholic unity. Go to Rome this year merely to see the sights, and your visit is laudable enough, but you have missed the spirit of the occasion; it was love, not curiosity, that was meant to draw you. And if, for whatever reason, you have decided not to go to Rome this year, that does not mean the Holy Year has no meaning and no message for you. So many millions of Catholics in the world that cannot be present at the Confessio; not one of them but can take part in the Holy Year by letting his heart go out to the Father of Christendom. Every time you go to Mass, when the priest's voice dies away into silence after the *Sanctus*, that is your cue. Offer, in union with the priest, your own prayers for our Father Pius, father of the whole family, and his intentions.

The Pope's intentions, how lightly those words fall on the ear, like a mere rigmarole, a mere formula! Have you ever thought what it would be like to be the Holy Father, to take, for a single day, for a single hour, the strain of his world-wide office? When you pray for the Pope's intentions at Mass, take your stand beside him in imagination, the man on whom we Christians, millions of us, have laid the burden of our common solicitudes. Plunge yourself, for a moment, in that full tide of prayer which is the prayer of the Church universal; then, if you will, scramble up the bank again, and return to the intimacy, the solitude of the Mass you are offering, just you and a few friends about you, nothing else to distract your thoughts from God. Your own prayer will ring truer, strike deeper, if just for a moment you have faced the glare, and felt the burden.

KX

15

THE PATTERN OF HIS DEATH

So it is the Lord's death that you are heralding, whenever you eat this bread and drink this cup, until he comes.—1 Corinthians 11. 26.

THE theology of St Paul has not come down to us in the shape of carefully thought out catechetical instructions. It tumbles out of him at haphazard, by a series of providential accidents, when he is not meaning to talk about theology, but is devoting himself to the practical needs of the moment. It is to a providential accident that we owe his wonderful chapter on the Holy Eucharist, which is the basis of so much that we know, so much that we believe, about the sacrament of the altar. St Paul did not set out to extend the knowledge, or to confirm the faith, of the Corinthian church on that subject. No, it all comes out incidentally, when he is trying to correct certain abuses which had sprung up among those very half-baked converts of his in a rather easy-going seaport town. In those days the Christians used to meet for a common meal, which served as a preface to the celebration of the divine mysteries. And the meal was meant to be a share-out; everybody, rich or poor, brought what he could and divided it with his brethren. But at Corinth the richer and the more leisured folk used to come early, before the rest, and get through the good things they had brought, in agreeable solitude. It was turning into a boisterous convivial party, their preparation for holy Mass, and St Paul, in recalling them to a sense of decency, points out among other things that their merriment is ill-suited to an occasion which must, in some sense, be an occasion of mourning. You cannot receive communion without associating yourself with a death. You are heralding the *death* of Jesus Christ, until he comes again.

Until he comes—when he used those words, what kind of perspective opened out, do you suppose, before St Paul's imaginative view? I think, if you had asked him, his guess would have been that it could not be very long now before his Master returned in glory. Everywhere, in that Mediterranean world he knew, the gospel had sprung up overnight, like the mustard-plant in the parable; everywhere the defences of the old gods were beginning to crumble, as they had crumbled at Corinth. There was as yet no persecution, except what was raised by Jewish incredulity; and could that incredulity last? At the moment, indeed, there was a veil over the hearts of his fellow countrymen, which mysteriously made them blind to the truth, while the Gentiles outstripped them in the race for salvation. But surely it could not be long before the Jewish people accepted the gospel; theirs were the promises, for them in the first instance Christ had died; and, day by day, whenever the Christian mysteries were celebrated, that death was heralded anew—surely it must avail them? Then, when Jew and Gentile alike had had their chance—in a few years, why not?—the skies would open, and the living Christ would come down, to judge the world which the dying Christ had ransomed.

Whatever be the truth about that, however little St Paul may have guessed that there was a long panorama of history still awaiting mankind, of this at least we can be certain, that the Spirit who spoke through St Paul bade him write those words for our comfort, so far removed in time, living in a world so altered. Till he comes—age after age must pass, and still the Church must suffer a hundred deaths as she heralded, with a kind of despairing confidence, the death of the Master who still did not return. At dead of night she would herald it, in the long subterranean passages that run mysteriously beneath the outskirts of Rome; slaves and patricians met together under the pretence that they were a burial club, among pagan tombs, pagan altars. In secret rooms of old country-houses she would herald it, in remote fastnesses of the hills, when our fathers were persecuted, and priests put to death, for love of the Mass and of the old ways. In foul prisons and concentration camps she would herald it, where some handful of deported Catholics had managed to collect the bare essentials for a valid sacrifice. And still he would not return.

What did St Paul mean, when he told us that in receiving holy communion we are heralding the Lord's death? When we kneel before the relics of some martyr, of Oliver Plunkett at Drogheda or John Southworth at Westminster Cathedral, we are, in a sense, heralding his death. We are reminding ourselves, and the same time we are acknowledging before the world, that this man's death was more worth while than any other kind of death; that the suffering which it cost him was the supreme proof of his loyalty, was a title to glory. In recognition of that, we venerate and salute with our lips those mortal remains of his from which death parted him, which he has left behind to us as a trophy of his victory. The saint himself is not here, or not here more than anywhere else; the bones we touch were once part of him, will be part of him once more at the General Resurrection; we do not doubt that (under God's providence) a grace and an influence still clings to them which may bring us help in our needs. The saint is alive, but in heaven; all we have got here is a dead body. No matter; it is the man's death we are heralding, and it is appropriate that we should do that by putting ourselves in contact with that dumb part of him which itself recalls the manner of his dying.

Is that what St Paul means? Does he imply that we receive, in holy communion, the dead body of Jesus Christ? It would be a very ill-instructed Catholic who would accept such a conclusion. On the contrary, what you and I receive in holy communion is precisely the risen body, the living body of Jesus Christ. If our hearts burn within us as we come away from the altar, it is because we, like the two disciples on the Emmaus road, have been offering hospitality to the risen Christ, though hidden under a form in which we could not recognize him. The risen body, which could defy the laws of nature, has passed into us, so that we may be energized by its supernatural power. The risen body, which went up to heaven in the sight of the apostles, has passed into us, so as to plant in us the seed of immortality. It is the risen body of Christ that reigns there over the altar; how should it be his dead body? There is no such thing; there never has been any such thing except during the brief interval between the first Good Friday afternoon and Easter morning. When we venerate the relics of a saint, we see him there, but in death. When we venerate Christ on the altar, he lives there, but lives unseen.

How is it then that St Paul tells us we are heralding the death of Christ when we communicate? St Paul of all men, who of all men was most conscious of Christ's death as a transaction done and finished with, a door shut and slammed on the past? St Paul, who wrote "Christ, now he is risen from the dead, cannot die any more";[1] St Paul, who wrote "Even if we used to think of Christ in a human fashion, we do so no longer"[2]—why does he tell us that we are heralding the death of Christ when we communicate, instead of saying the life of Christ, the Resurrection of Christ? We should find it hard to understand his attitude, if we had not the Christian tradition to fill up the gaps in his thought. Christian tradition teaches us that the Holy Eucharist does not merely consist in the consecration of the elements and their reception by the faithful; it is something more, it is a sacrifice. And because it is a sacrifice it involves, somehow, the death of a victim, and the application of that death to our needs. What is heralded in these mysteries is Christ dying, not Christ dead.

Christ dying—oh, to be sure, as a matter of history, Christ could only

[1] Romans 6. 9.   [2] 2 Corinthians 5. 16.

die once; it is given to men to die once for all, and he was Man. And you may say if you will that the sacrifice of the Mass is only the echo, only the ripple, set up day after day, century after century, by the sacrifice made once for all on the cross. An echo, a ripple, those are pleasing and perhaps helpful metaphors, but they are only metaphors; the sacrifice of the Mass is a mystery, and perhaps its relation to the sacrifice on the cross is the most mysterious thing about it. Only this is certain, that the victim who is there presented to the eternal Father for our sakes is the dying Christ; it is in that posture that he pleaded, and pleads, for our salvation, atoned, and atones, for the sins of the world. We herald that death in the holy Mass, not as something which happened long ago, but as something which is mystically renewed whenever the words of consecration are uttered. From the moment of his death on Calvary until the time when he comes again in glory, the dying Christ is continually at work, is continually available. It is in this posture of death that he pleads for us, when the Mass is offered. And it is in this posture of death that he comes to you and me when he comes to us, the living Christ, in holy communion. "This is my body which is being given for you . . . this is my blood which is being shed for you"; so he spoke to his apostles when his death still lay in the future, so he speaks to us now that his death lies in the past.

What wonder if the Church, heralding his death from day to day, has caught something of this, his victim character? That life-cycle which he underwent in the natural body he took from our blessed Lady, he undergoes anew in his mystical body, which is the Church. St Paul knew that, from the moment when he fell dazzled on the Damascus road, and heard a voice saying to him, "Saul, Saul, why dost thou persecute me?" He rejoiced in his own sufferings, because they helped to "pay off the debt which the afflictions of Christ leave still to be paid, for the sake of his body, which is the Church".[1] How often, nowadays, men tell us in a half-pitying, half-contemptuous tone that we belong to a dying religion! Let us accept the omen, let us boast of the accusation; we are, we always have been, a dying religion. From the first, we went underground in the catacombs; again and again we have been forced to our knees, fought a losing battle all down the centuries; do they think it is any news to us that the world is our enemy; persecutes us as it persecuted our Master? Today as yesterday, she is content to herald his death until he comes.

And you and I, how do we come into the picture? Surely when we

[1] Colossians 1. 24.

go to communion, we ought to reflect among other things, "This is his body which is being given for me; this is his blood which is being shed for me—after all this lapse of time, he still comes to me in the posture of a victim. And he wants to impress something of himself on me; I am to be the wax, he the signet-ring. Something, then, of the victim he wants to see in me; does not the *Imitation* say it is up to every Christian to lead a dying life ?[1] Not for me, perhaps, to enter very deeply into the dispositions of my crucified Saviour, but . . . to be rather more humble, when I am thwarted; rather more resigned, when things go wrong with me; rather less anxious to make a chart of my own spiritual progress, more ready to let him do in me what he wants to do, without letting me know about it! If I could only die a little, to the world, to my wishes, to myself; be patient, and wait for his coming, content to herald his death by dying with him!"

16

THE CHALLENGE

This is my body, on your behalf.—1 Corinthians 11. 24.

THE Christian liturgy seems to have grown up at haphazard, on no principle, every age leaving some mark on its development until it was crystallized four centuries ago. All the more strange, and (perhaps we may say) all the more obviously providential, that the phrases and the ceremonies of the Mass—antiquated, you would think, not designed by men of our world, or for the needs of our day —should so often exactly hit off our spiritual mood, say exactly the thing we wanted to say! There are moments, aren't there, in the Mass at which you catch your breath in surprise over what seems to be —what would be, in any human document—superb dramatic skill.

One of those moments is when the priest, having absolved the communicants, turns round with the sacred Host, and doesn't give it to them. They must be kept waiting, while he says three times the *Domine non sum dignus*. He treats them as if they were children, impatient for

----

[1] *Imitation of Christ*, Book II, ch. 12, 14.

some treat which has been promised them, and needing to be taught patience by finding, just for a little, that the treat is held back. We thought we had prepared ourselves for holy communion so carefully —examining our consciences, perhaps going to confession, saying a lot of prayers and making a lot of acts, as the book told us to, and here we are at last at the altar rails, all ready; but no, it seems we were not ready. Lord, I am not worthy, Lord, I am not worthy, Lord, I am not worthy, even now. And perhaps during that tantalizing interval while the priest holds out to our view, but still will not give us, the bread of life, we do well to imagine that it is not the priest who is speaking in our name, it is our Lord himself speaking to us, asking us for a welcome, and at the same time warning us what that welcome involves.

Curiously, no one can tell us with certainty what words our Lord used when he, the first Christian priest, stood there in the cenacle offering his own flesh to his disciples. "This is my body on your behalf"—I am quoting from the earliest account we have of the scene, given us by St Paul in his first letter to the Corinthians; I am quoting it in the form in which it has been preserved by our oldest manuscripts. "My body on your behalf"—the phrase was a mysterious one, and it was natural that copyists should try to fill it out and make sense of it, some writing "my body which is being broken for you", and others, "my body which is to be given up for you". But it looks as if our Lord simply said "my body on your behalf", not tying it down to the moment at which he spoke, nor to the foreseen moment of his betrayal. It was, indeed, when it was broken on the cross that the body of Christ became most evidently and most significantly ours. But all his life— that, I think, is what he wants us to see—all his life, from the moment when that body was formed in the womb of his virgin Mother, it existed on our behalf. *Propter nos homines*, for the sake of us men he came down from heaven, and took upon himself the outward fashion of a man; and this body of his was not merely to be the victim of our redemption; it was to be the means and the model of our sanctification from first to last.

This is my body (he says) on your behalf. God is all spirit; man is matter and spirit, but the bodily part of him is all matter. And therefore, when God becomes man, it would not be so extraordinary that he should take upon himself a human soul, which, after all, is spirit; but a body! This is the low-water-mark of our Lord's condescension; the abiding trophy, therefore, of his achievement. By taking a human body at all how utterly did he, who was pure spirit, dispossess himself! But that was not enough; it should be fashioned and grown as our human bodies are fashioned and grow; it should be a prisoner in the womb, it should have the inarticulate needs of childhood. All that experience it went through, this body of mine which you see in the hands of my priest; it was dressed in rough clothes, nourished with the simple necessities which are not denied to the poor. And you, who would receive it, you, who would be made one with it—are you ready to be made like me in my humiliation? Are you ready to be made one with me in poverty, enduring privations, content with the company of simple folk? Are you ready to be made one with me in my helplessness, accepting, with no murmur of pride, the good offices of your fellow men? Are you ready to be made one with me in the darkness of the womb, clinging to me by faith, when you can see nothing but night around you? That is what it means, if I come to you.

This is my body (he says) on your behalf. The body which he took upon himself when he became incarnate for our sakes was, as we have seen, the body of his humiliation; its movements, restricted by space and time, were a poor vehicle, in themselves, for the activities of the Eternal. And yet—so transfigured is everything by the touch of the Divine—this weak body became the accomplice of the wonders our Lord performed on earth. That hand, a hand like yours or mine, had only to touch the sick and they were cured; a glance from that eye could strike his persecutors to the ground; that voice had only to speak a word of invitation, and the dead man came out from four days' sojourn in the tomb. *Theandric* action, we call it, when all that is most human in the Incarnate is associated with the achievements that are most divine. And we, as we look up and see the priest holding out that body towards us, are comforted by the assurance that its powers are not exhausted; no ailment of our souls, no blindness, no feebleness, which cannot be healed by its contact. Yes, but that body, when it laboured for us on earth, was not sustained by any native strength beyond human strength, yours or mine; it was weary, as yours or mine might be, when he rested it by Jacob's well. Only the sanctified will which was in command of it could make it bear up under those long journeyings, against the constant strain of the multitudes thronging round it. "Virtue has gone out of me", he said; each miracle took its toll of that frail human organism. He never spared it; and we are so sparing with our bodies; give in so easily to their slightest murmur of complaint! Are you ready (he asks us) to be made one with me in my constant defiance of fatigue, to pray, to work, to face new situations, resolute and unflagging, as I did? That is what it means, if I come to you.

This is my body (he says) on your behalf. Most of all, when it was betrayed, when it was broken for our sakes; when it exchanged activity for passivity. How hard that is! And that is what the Passion meant, almighty God letting things happen to him. He let them hurry him away, bound and helpless, from Gethsemani to the council-chamber, from the council-chamber to the praetorium, from the praetorium to the cross. He let them nail him to the cross, those feet which tired on the roads of Galilee idle now, that hand which had so often reversed our human tragedies motionless. It was as if he wanted us to see that the greatest act of all his life was what he did when he seemed powerless to do anything. Tied hand and foot, he could still pardon, and absolve, and love. And now he rests motionless in the hands of his priest, carried this way and that at the discretion of human wills, but still pardoning, still absolving, still loving. We cannot fail to recognize, we cannot afford to ignore, this third challenge which our Lord's body throws down to us. Suffering is our common lot; it awaits all of us sooner or later, some of us in forms that may be acute and prolonged. And what makes it more than ever hard to bear is the feeling of help-lessness; we have not willed this, it has been forced on us, and pride offers no consolation. To let ourselves suffer, only because it is his will; to let ourselves suffer, perhaps, as he did, from the neglect and the cruelty and the contempt of our fellow men—that is the chief, and perhaps the hardest thing he asks of us. But he does ask it of us. That is what it means, if I come to you.

I have been suggesting that when the priest, just before communion, says the threefold *Domine non sum dignus* in your name, you should imagine our Lord himself as holding back, keeping you waiting for a little, so as to test your dispositions. He often did that, didn't he, before consenting to perform a miracle; he told the Syrophenician woman, "It is not right to take the children's bread and throw it to the dogs." He told St Martha, "Thy brother will rise again." Even to our Lady he said, "My time has not come yet." But, when I speak of testing our dispositions, do I mean that he looks into our hearts and expects to find his own likeness already there? Must we already be humble with a humility like his, already be unwearied in his service, already be perfectly resigned to all the sufferings which may befall us, or be told that we are not fit to receive him? If I meant that, if I meant that holy communion is a privilege reserved, at least commonly, for an *élite* of almost perfect souls, then I should be falling back into the error of the Jansenists, and I should be wronging the memory of that great Pope who has just been raised to the altars of the Church. For whatever else

St Pius the Tenth is remembered, he will be remembered for having thrown open the gates of the sanctuary to hesitating and struggling souls; to the unworthy who know themselves to be unworthy.

No, the dispositions I am speaking of are not those which qualify us to receive holy communion; we go to holy communion in order that those dispositions may be formed in us. Only, we must *want* them to be formed in us. The trouble, you know, about you and me is not that we aren't saints, but that we don't want to be saints. Lord, I am not worthy, because I am not humble; but I do want to be humble. Lord, I am not worthy, because I am backward and slothful in your service; but I hate my backwardness, I hate my sloth. Lord, I am not worthy, because I am a bad sufferer; but how I wish it were otherwise! Let it be otherwise, Lord; speak the word only, and thy servant shall be healed.

17

A BETTER COUNTRY[1]

We have an everlasting city, but not here.—Hebrews 13. 14.

WHAT a chilling experience it is to stand, as we stand today, on the morrow of a great occasion! Two days ago, only two days ago, the thing was happening; history was shaping itself under our view. And on a scale, I suppose, hitherto unparalleled; no human being has ever been watched by so many eyes simultaneously as Queen Elizabeth was on Tuesday morning. Oh, to be sure, our modern vulgarity had done its best to ruin the sacredness of it; there was a wealth of false sentiment, and of hysterical propaganda. But behind all that, behind all the masquerade and the publicity, you felt a perfectly genuine reaction of popular enthusiasm; each of us looked at his neighbour's face, and saw his own embarrassed loyalty reflected there. For one brief hour, a world torn by dissension stood agreed; all alike would do homage to a young woman, born to accept homage with a kind of natural grace. The streets which are so familiar to us, in which we jostle our way through a meaningless crowd of unrelated humanity, had turned overnight into a river-bed, through which a dazzling stream of pomp

[1] This sermon was preached in the week of her Majesty's Coronation.

went by; and we shouted and waved like school-children, all our anxieties, all our grievances, momentarily forgotten. Time stood still, and the care-lined features of this modern age were rejuvenated by the experience.

Only two days ago; and now it is all over, and we are fain to distract ourselves with the fireworks. The decorations hang limply, waiting to be taken down; we look at them half-ashamed, like a schoolboy confronted with the toys of childhood. All our pomp of yesterday is one with Nineve and Tyre—the gaping crowds still eddy to and fro in the streets of London, but with a sense of anti-climax. After all, the Queen we crowned two days ago wields no powers she did not wield, commands no loyalty she did not command, before the ceremony took place. We are back where we were, just as anxious as before over yesterday's problems; can the world's peace be kept? How is our trade balance going to recover? What is to be the next step in Korea, in Egypt, in South Africa, all the world over? We have awoken from a dream of chivalry to the hard facts of real life. But it is not simply that the thing has come to an end, and we are sorry it could not last. We look back on our great moment, and somehow find it unsatisfying. What lies at the root of our disillusionment?

One ceremony our English Coronation lacks, for all its splendid history; a ceremony which takes place, as far as I know, only at the crowning of a Pope, I mean, when a bundle of tow is burned in his presence, to the accompaniment of those famous words—nobody knows where they come from, who invented them—*sic transit gloria mundi*, "So passes the glory of this world." Man was born for eternity, and every experience of his, when he comes to look at it afterwards, is found to be unsatisfying, not simply because it was impermanent, but because all the while it was imperfect. The crown which we set on the royal forehead is only, after all, a collection of mineral products, prized because there are not more of them. And the Queen herself, though she rightly claims the obedience and the homage of her subjects, is only a human creature like ourselves; she eats and drinks and catches cold and feels bored like the rest of us. When we crown her, we crown her as the symbol of the divine authority, of which she is the representative on earth; and we would crown her, if we could, not with mineral deposits, but with the imperishable glories of heaven. If we are haunted by a sense of unreality about Tuesday's proceedings, it is not that we regret what we have done. It is only that all our earthly experiences are, of their very nature, unsatisfying, and this, the most splendid experience of our lives, is unsatisfying like the rest—so dazzling to the eye, so challenging to the imagination, and yet, like all the things of time, it has eluded us, and is gone!

Man is born for eternity, and the horizons of a fallen world are too little for him. Always he tries, and fails, to express himself fully in his earthly surroundings, like some noble beast in captivity, that grows accustomed to its prison bars, yet never ceases to chafe at them. The lover feels, in his first flush of happiness, as if his love was something immortal, indestructible, only to see his romance fade into commonplace. The artist hails the inspiration that has come to him as something almost divine; once it has been committed to paper or to canvas, it no longer contents him. Always we are striving after the unattainable, and achieving the imperfect. Man—fallen man—is a misfit, an exile from his true country. It is that note of exile which has imposed itself, from the first ages, on the language of the Christian Church. We cry to our heavenly Queen as "poor *banished* children of Eve." "After this our *exile*", we say, "show unto us the blessed fruit of thy womb." It was St Peter himself who gave us the cue for it, "Beloved, I call you to be like strangers and exiles." It was a familiar metaphor, God knows, to his fellow countrymen. The whole history of the Jewish race has been a history of exile; exile in Egypt, exile in the wilderness, exile in Babylon; and their whole literature is permeated with a sense of homesickness to which we, Christian people, have given a new meaning. "What, should we sing the Lord's song in a strange land?"—to the Jew, all the world was exile, away from Jerusalem; for us, there is no home except the new Jerusalem, and we shall not find it in this world. We have an everlasting city, but not here.

Does that mean that we are bad patriots, bad citizens of the British Commonwealth? God forbid that it should; God forbid that we should rake up memories of the past. For us, the institution of kingship is all the more real and all the more valuable because it is derived from, and symbolizes, the supreme power of almighty God; and in the same way the sentiment of patriotism is all the more real and all the more valuable because it is derived from, and symbolizes, that yearning love with which we look towards our heavenly country. Only, when we have witnessed all the pageantry of this last week, witnessed the homage that is paid by a multitude of nations, even in these dark days, to the historic continuity of the British crown, we must be pardoned if our afterthoughts bring with them something of melancholy. How should we not be reminded of that Jerusalem which is our true home, eternal in the heavens, whose gates stand ever open, while the nations flock into it with their honour and their praise? Citizens by right, we are not yet citizens in fact; we are only exiles, only displaced persons, in this world of sense and time. We are only strangers, with our faces set towards home.

If we are on a journey, we must have provisions. And the language of the liturgy leaves us in no doubt what those provisions are. *Esca viatorum*, the food of travellers, *per tuas semitas duc nos quo tendimus*, bring us, by thy own path, to our journey's end; *ecce panis angelorum factus cibus viatorum*, behold the bread of angels, sent to pilgrims in their banishment! *Qui vitam sine termino nobis donet in patria*, so may we pass eternity, poor exiles, on our native shore! The Holy Eucharist is our *viaticum*, our allowance of food at every stage in our travels; it is only by a gracious technicality that we reserve the name for that iron ration which will strengthen us for the last stage of all. Day by day and week by week, this is our appropriate nourishment. Not that the divine resourcefulness could not find other means of sustaining us. The prophet Elias went a journey of forty days through the wilderness in the strength given him by a single meal; and wherever there are faithful souls deprived, through no fault of their own, of sacramental opportunities, we do not doubt that God will provide them with all the graces they need. But normally it is the Holy Eucharist that will bring us to our journey's end, the day's food for the day's march, the heavenly manna we need, God knows we need it, on this parched earth.

The day's food for the day's march—shall we take comfort sometimes, from that thought, when we are disheartened over the miserably small effect which this heavenly nourishment seems to have on our lives? We are thinking of the Blessed Sacrament, you see, under another metaphor when we feel thus discouraged. We are thinking of it as the medicine which is meant to cure the disease of our souls; and more than that, to strengthen them, give them fuller, more robust health. And instead, our petty faults seem to go on unchecked, the meanness, the selfishness, the touchiness of our natures—how is it that they do not yield to treatment? Instead, our spiritual health seems to languish; we have no appetite for heavenly things, no energy for carrying out God's will even when we see it clearly enough—how is it that we still lack vigour, refreshed morning after morning with the bread of the strong? It is natural, it is right that we should sometimes ask ourselves these questions, but I think it is a mistake to be always feeling one's own pulse, always watching one's own symptoms. Let us be content, instead, to think of the Blessed Sacrament not as the medicine but as the food of our souls; acting on us, as material food does, without our knowing it, yet all the time sufficing for the day's needs, carrying us along on our journey, though we seem to make such a weary business of it, dragging foot after foot. The invalid who refuses food because it has so little relish for him becomes a worse invalid yet.

The food of pilgrims—shall we make use of those words to read ourselves, now and again, a different lesson? True enough, it is possible to fall into scruple by watching our own spiritual development too eagerly. But it is also possible to fall into carelessness by not watching our own spiritual development at all. Marching food is meant for the march, and you must have stretched your muscles if you are to enjoy it; how dull picnic fare tastes, if you are weather-bound, and compelled to eat in your arm-chair! "Your loins must be girt", our Lord says; we must be *bona-fide* pilgrims if we are to find our proper food in the Holy Eucharist. And it is so easy to forget, amid the distractions of the wayside, the country of our dreams.

Hard enough, even in days gone by, to draw the mind away from the things of earth, and let them rest on the unseen things that are eternal. Always the gossip of your neighbours filled the ear; always the busy pageant of life displayed itself to the eye. And what of our age, when you may turn a switch, and listen endlessly to the jarring voices of a discordant world? Our age, when the eye can rest on a thousand images, good, bad, and indifferent, which are no better than shadows, yet the shadows of things seen? Of that everlasting city no sound, no sight can reach us. There, over the altar, our King is enthroned, but hidden under symbols, and in silence. And yet so close to us; closer than hands or feet.

18

JESUS MY FRIEND

Iron sharpens iron, and friend shapes friend.—Proverbs 27. 17.

IF you come to think of it, a priest who celebrates his jubilee has stood at the altar about 9,000 times. Supposing him just fifty years old, he was a boy of eight when Pius X gave us daily communion as a target for the ordinary faithful layman to aspire to. So he has probably made some fifteen thousand communions in his life; and there are many of the faithful laity who don't lag far behind. What a terrifying thought it is that the good Shepherd should have fed us so often with his own hand, and here are we still straying; that the good Physician should so often have asked, "Well, how are we this morning?", and we are still so weak!

Less discouragingly, let us think this evening of our eucharistic Lord as a Friend, a personal Friend. That title, after all, he claimed at the last supper, "I have called you my friends"; using, probably, a Hebrew word which throws into relief the reciprocity of human friendship, and thereby raising his apostles to a kind of equality with himself. A shepherd has so many sheep to look after, the doctor has so many calls to make; your friend, when he comes to see you, is at liberty, is at your disposal; he has "just dropped in". And our Lord wants each of us to think of him in that way; nor do we deceive ourselves if we think of him in that way. Infinite power, infinite goodness, makes itself infinitely available. Go to communion in some little country church, where you find yourself alone at the altar rails, or go to midnight Mass at Westminster Cathedral, and get sucked into the interminable queue which is slowly moving eastwards—it makes no difference. In either case the sacred Host which you are destined to receive contains the whole of Christ, all meant for you. "Is my friend there?" he is saying; waiting for you, like the person who comes to meet you at a crowded terminus, looking out for that particular trick of walking, that particular way of holding yourself, which will single you out at a distance.

Our friends—how they change, don't they? Those chance meetings on the Underground, when you sit chatting to someone who was your bosom friend years ago, and find yourself with very little to say except "Wonder what's become of old So-and-so" and hoping that there will be enough old So-and-so's to last out till Charing Cross! And even with the friendships we make later in life, founded not on accidental association, but on a real community of tastes and interests, how seldom they last a lifetime, or anything like a lifetime! Destiny shuffles our partners for us; one friend or the other gets a different job, goes to live somewhere else; it may only mean changing from one suburb to another, but how easily we make an excuse of distance! More and more as we grow older, we find that the people we see most of are recent acquaintances, not (perhaps) very congenial to us, but chance has thrown them in our way. And meanwhile the people we used to know so well, for whom we once entertained such warm feelings, are now remembered by a card at Christmas, if we can succeed in finding the address. How good we are at making friends, when we are young; how bad at keeping them! How eagerly, as we grow older, we treasure up the friendships that are left to us, like beasts that creep together for warmth!

There is no difficulty of that kind with the Friend who makes himself known to us in the Blessed Sacrament; he is always at hand, always available. Do not complain that his friendship always feels unreal to you, feels impersonal to you, because he is hidden under sacramental veils. After all, what a sense of intimacy we derive simply from a friend's handwriting in a letter! It is only by a trick of memory that we associate it with his or her personality, and yet how near it brings us, this veil of handwriting! Even when you are sitting talking to a friend, you are not really talking *to* him; your mouth is talking to his ear, his mouth to yours; the play of expression on his features is nothing more than a twitching of muscles. Face and voice are only veils that hide the real person from you, and yet how easily you see behind those veils! And if we had faith, the sacramental veils under which our Lord comes to us would be lifting and parting all the while; we should get a much greater sense of nearness to him, under the token of eating bread, than we get when we are talking to a friend under token of watching the muscles of his face. Go about the world as you will, change your home as often as you will, in the nearest Catholic church your Friend is always there, and day by day he is at home to you.

It is not only distance that estranges us from our earthly friends. After all, how little we really *know* of one another! You meet a person for the first time, and you are charmed by some trick of manner, or you find some common topic of conversation which interests you, and you go home saying to yourself that it is really a great piece of luck to have met somebody who is so absolutely cut out for you. And yet it may take only a few weeks of further intercourse for each to discover a want of sympathy for the other's point of view, some tiresome mannerism that gets on one's nerves, and the friendship fades away into a bare acquaintance. We are changing, too, all the time, ever so little; habits grow upon us, new interests grip us; how easy it is even after years of friendship to find that the other person is not quite what you thought he was—or is it that you are not quite what you thought you were? Anyhow, an illusion has faded. But the Friend who comes to you in the Holy Eucharist is the same yesterday, today and for ever; and as better knowledge brings more intimacy, you can find nothing there but what will make his qualities more lovable. Or again, you may fall upon evil times, when poverty, or some suspicion cast on your character, lowers your standing in the world. Friends may desert you then; or, more likely, you will wrongly suspect them of deserting you, or you will shun their company because you think they are trying to patronize you. There is no need for such fears, there is no need for such pride, about our friendship with Jesus Christ. "Zacchaeus, come down, for today I must abide at thy house"; it is all arranged, the despised publican is to be our Lord's host. And he will invite himself in as our guest too, even when we despise ourselves, even when the world despises us. What a Friend to have, changeless himself, and never minding how much we change!

Always the same warmth of welcome from him, whatever coldness there has been on our part. Each day he makes good our wastage of yesterday, like a patient grown-up helping a child with its toys. Each day he offers us the whole of himself, infinite possibilities of sanctification, knowing that we shall make so little of them! And this strange condescension of his has been repeated so often that it has ceased to surprise us; hardly ever, apart from rare moments of recollection, engages our gratitude. Most of us have had the same experience with some unselfish friend—God be thanked for all such—who always gave much and asked little. The help, the sympathy, the little attentions we get from such a friend become a normal part of our daily lives, like the sun rising in the morning; we take them for granted. Then, perhaps, the friend is removed from us by death, and we remember with a sudden shock, "I shall never get those flowers from the country again!" or something of that sort. The friendship of our Lord in the Holy Eucharist is all the more easily forgotten, because the benefits which he bestows upon us are in the order of grace; we are not aware of them, we cannot count and check them. Sometimes, to be sure, there is an overflow of them into our feelings, but as a rule that is only something transient, and quite certainly it is something to which we ought not to attach a great deal of importance; one day we are all gratitude after communion, all floods of tears, and the next we are all dry and hard— what does it matter? All those feelings of our are a mere echo, a mere by-product of divine grace; they are no more to be confused with grace itself than the humming of the wheels are to be confused with the work the machine is doing. The growth of grace in us through holy communion is something as secret, as silent, as the restoration of tissues which natural food brings to our bodies. Only over a long space of time, as a rule, can the effects of it be observed; and even then, probably, not by ourselves.

"Yes, but is there really growth?" you ask. "If I look back over these last twenty years or so, I don't see that I'm much different, and what difference there is can't, I'm afraid, in some directions be regarded as an improvement. How am I to trace, how am I to assess, the progress

I have made? You tell me not to trust my feelings; what other index can I find of my spiritual condition? Ought I to find that as the years go on my temptations grow fewer, grow weaker? Or that the temptations are the same, but I yield to them less? Or should I look round and see if I can catch myself doing unselfish actions which I probably shouldn't have done twenty years ago? It would strengthen my faith in the Holy Eucharist, if I could only watch the Holy Eucharist making a difference, from year to year, in my own life."

For goodness' sake don't talk like that. I'm sure we aren't meant to think of the grace of holy communion as something which can be gauged and weighed up in a balance and written down in the form of a debit and credit account. Do let us get it into our heads that holy communion is an intimacy with Jesus Christ, and that if we do our best to throw our hearts open to his Sacred Heart, there is bound to be an influence passing from him into us. It is the law of friendship.

Iron sharpens iron, says the wise man, and friend shapes friend. Literally the words run, "Iron sharpens iron, and friend sharpens the face of friend", but that is simply the Hebrew way of putting things. What it means, evidently, is that your friendship with So-and-so inevitably knocks you into a particular shape, just as one piece of iron knocks another into a particular shape if you hit them against one another. Inevitably, not as the result of any deliberate attempt on the part of either to influence the other, but simply as the result of daily contact. And of course, speaking of human friendships, I think the wise man had this in mind, that either affects the other equally; it's not like sharpening a pencil, which leaves the knife just as it was. But when we are speaking about the friendship of Jesus Christ, of course it is different. Nothing about us can influence him, there is nothing in him that needs to be influenced. If you come to think of it, I suppose he was the only person who ever came across our blessed Lady without being the better for it. . . . No, the influence is all on one side.

But on our side, shall we doubt the influence is there? How well we know it in ordinary life, the unconsciously received influence of friend on friend! The schoolgirl who adopts the handwriting of her favourite schoolmistress, the young man who picks up all the catch-words and tricks of speech that are used in his fiancée's family, and so on. And as we know, it cuts much deeper than that; nothing can inspire us, nothing can drag us down, like our friendships; and we aren't conscious of it happening. Do we doubt that an influence equally unconscious, and far stronger, attaches to the daily intimacy of Jesus Christ?

Jesus Christ, the same yesterday, today and for ever; that intimacy binds up our days in a gracious unity. We have changed so much, you and I; made so many false starts, picked up so many friends and drifted away from them; am I, are you, the same person as twenty years ago? Yes, it is the same now as then; you and I, now as then, are the unworthy friends of Jesus Christ.

19

FIRST AND LAST COMMUNIONS

What Jesus Christ was yesterday, and is today, he remains for ever.— Hebrews 13. 8.

In the doctrine about the presence of our Lord in the Holy Eucharist, we admit a single exception to a law of science. We admit there is something we come across in our experience which can communicate energy without losing energy in itself. Jesus Christ, the same yesterday, today, and for ever. When he moved on our earth, we know that a power went forth from him which influenced even the material conditions of things around him. When the woman who had an issue of blood came behind and touched his garment, he knew within himself (so the gospel puts it) that virtue had gone out of him. But we cannot suppose that this meant any diminution of the spiritual energies which informed his incarnate nature; the source of those energies was divine. And, since he has ascended into heaven, he has not withdrawn his incarnate presence from the natural order; he has only altered the manner of it. His body born of Mary, his blood shed on Calvary, remain present substantially on our altars under the forms of bread and wine; and thus from the heart of his material creation he continues to radiate that life-giving influence which was his in the days of his humiliation. Here then, once more, you have an energy which continually diffuses itself and never grows less. As the bush which Moses saw in the wilderness burned continually but was never consumed, so our Lord's body and blood, present to us in their substance, not in those accidents which are subject to physical laws of growth and decay, are inexhaustible in their perpetual operation.

Yesterday, today, and for ever—cast your mind back to the first

Mass on the first Maundy Thursday. What the apostles received, what Peter, what Judas received, was not something other than you and I receive, centuries afterwards. True, every circumstance of history conspired to make that occasion memorable and unique. They were being houselled, as no man was ever houselled since, by the very hands of Incarnate God. It was a viaticum, his viaticum, not theirs; deriving its efficacy from a meritorious cause, his Passion, which was not yet in existence. It was the transition, perhaps as yet only dimly appreciated, from the bloody sacrifices of the old law to the one bloodless sacrifice of the new. But it was the same sacrament which you and I receive; with the same virtue, the same effects. It availed no more to sanctify Peter or to condemn Judas, than it avails to sanctify, or to condemn, you and me.

Yesterday, today, and for ever—cast your mind forward to the last Mass that will ever be said on earth. We find it even more difficult thus to transport ourselves into the future; there will be so many novelties, we feel, that we can form no idea of at present. It goes without saying that the Christian liturgy, already so venerable, is less likely than anything else to be modified by the hand of time. Yes, it will be the same in all essentials; but how are we to think of the priest, for example? A Chinaman, perhaps, or a New Zealand native. The language in which the vernacular prayers are said will be a language, perhaps, which the human race has not yet invented. The architecture of the church may be of a kind we can imagine as little as the holy apostles, say, could have imagined Westminster Abbey. The feast celebrated on that occasion may be the feast of some saint who will not be born for many years yet. Yes, it is only a dim picture to our minds—and now, think what it will mean. That Mass will be the world's viaticum; this perishable creation, or our experience of it at least, will have no tomorrow. Nay, if we may dare to put it so, that Mass will be the viaticum of the holy Mass itself; it will never be needed again, for we shall have advanced from faith to sight, from shadows and images into the truth. Ite, Missa est, the priest will say, and there will never be Mass again. And yet, in the consecration of that last Mass the body and blood of our Lord Jesus Christ will be no more and no less present, no more and no less powerful in its effects, than in the Mass you are hearing just now, or in that first Mass of the first Maundy Thursday. That divine energy will remain inexhaustible, when all the wheels of creation threaten to run down.

We have taken a glance at the first page and at the last page of eucharistic history. We stand—where? Somewhere in between, with little right to judge how far we are removed from the later point.

Only, there are certain periods in history, and this is one of them, when we are more than ordinarily conscious of great changes happening and threatening in human affairs. It may be that a new and better world-order is coming to the birth. But we are more immediately conscious of something else; of failing energies (so it would appear) in those institutions which we thought were unalterable and undying. Is the principle of democracy to disappear? Will the British Empire survive? Will Europe continue to hold her own against those Eastern civilizations which hitherto she has defied? Some even doubt whether there are not signs of failing energy about the human genius itself; whether the race of great men is not dying out, and leaving the stage of history to pinchbeck figures that successfully attract the limelight. . . . No loss of power, perhaps, but a redistribution of it and a deconcentration of it, as if the second law of thermodynamics were at work on our human destinies too. In a world of shifting values, there is one fixed point on which our hearts can rest, one fixed star by which our intellects can be guided; it is the personal presence of our Lord on earth, yesterday, today, and as long as earth endures.

Do these long horizons frighten and baffle our imaginations? Then let us remember that each of our individual lives has its own eucharistic history too; can look back to its first communion, look forward to its last.

Your first communion—I am assuming that you were a Catholic from birth—was given you when you were something quite different; I had almost said somebody quite different, from what you are today. That small boy in an Eton collar, that small girl in white, is already so much a thing of yesterday that you almost wonder whether your life is indeed linked, by conscious continuity, with its own past; you scarcely feel concerned to defend your childhood's behaviour, to recall your childhood's thoughts. But it *was* you, at a different stage in the making; the guilt of those tiny sins, the merit of those tiny sacrifices, still live on your record. When you knelt, for the first time, at the communion rail, how different it all was from your communions now! The act, staled since by repetition, was for that child something entirely new and portentously solemn. The eye of faith was clearer, for all experience was fresh to you, and most information came by hearsay, so that you had hardly learned to puzzle over the mysteries of faith. And, with your character still half-formed, you had no legacy of sinful habits to make you unsure of yourself, doubtful of your loyalty to him who came to dwell in you.

You were different, yes; but the gift received that day was no other than the gift you receive now; no more and no less powerful to breed and to nourish the seed of sanctity in you. You received Jesus Christ, the same yesterday, and today, and for ever.

Your last communion—I am assuming that, by God's grace, you will end your life faithful to his service, and that you will leave it fortified by his sacraments. In some ways, your last communion will be like your first. I mean, that the choice of time will not be yours; that other people will be making all the arrangements for you, and that your part will be one of consent rather than one of active co-operation. Your attention, too, will be apt to wander; not this time, from the exuberance of life, but from the weakening of the mortal powers which the approach of death brings with it. In other ways, there will be a great difference between that child that was you and the old man, the middle-aged man, the young man, perhaps, that you will be. That clear faith of the child will not be yours; you will wish that it was, that it might lighten for you the transition from time into eternity. That clear conscience of childhood will not be yours; you will have to look back on many sins indifferently matched by contrition, on many opportunities wasted, many days mis-spent. You will feel, perhaps, for the first time, under that shadow, what holy communion really means, what all your communions ought to have meant and did not mean to you, since that hush of childish anticipation in which our Lord first came to you. But he, remember, will be the same; he will offer to you, at a moment when the richest gift in the world is no longer worth having, a gift surpassing all the riches of the world, himself. He who was yours yesterday, who is yours today, will offer himself then to be yours for ever.

Our natural powers, let us make no mistake about it, are subject to the same law I was alluding to just now; as life goes on, there is a dissipation of energy, a deconcentration of effort. Youth will fling itself into any ambition, however trumpery, as if with a lifetime's ardour; we burn for a cause, or live for an ambition, as if nothing else mattered. As we grow older, our minds broaden and our activities widen; we are no longer so one-sided in our enthusiasms. That is a gain; yes; but at the same time there is a loss of power; we no longer grasp our certitudes so clearly, bring such freshness to the pursuit of our ideals. But the supernatural habit of charity which the Blessed Sacrament implants and breeds in us escapes this law of impermanence; it has the unaging quality of that divine source it springs from. What greater blessing can I wish you, then, for this feast of yours, than that you should learn to make each communion with your first and your last communion before your minds; your first, that you may labour to recover those lost fervours; your last, that you may study to be found now as you would fain be found then, detached from earth and winged for your flight into eternity? The love which our divine Guest shows for us in this sacrament never alters, never wearies; shall we let it be said of us, as the years go on, that his love is the same, and ours has changed? May he rather grant us grace to receive him always as children in our simplicity, as dying men in the utter abandonment of ourselves to him.

20

PITY FOR THE MULTITUDE

I am moved with pity for the multitude; it is three days now since they have been in attendance on me, and they have nothing to eat.—Matthew 15. 32.

THE miracle of the five thousand is so familiar to us, that the miracle of the four thousand, which was performed soon after-wards, makes no clear impression on the mind. "We have heard all that before", we say to ourselves; "it is just the same story, only the statistics were different." But we are wrong; the whole situation is different. On that earlier occasion, the people who accompanied our Lord to the further side of the lake had only had a day's outing; nor had they gone far afield—it would still have been possible for them to buy food in the neighbouring villages. This time, the need is more urgent; crowds of people have followed him right out into the desert, and the scanty provisions they brought with them are already ex-hausted. The disciples, this time, do not pretend to have any solution of the difficulty. And our Lord looks round him, and is moved with pity for the multitude.

I am *moved* with pity—the translators, most of them, have missed a point here. "I am sorry for the crowd", or some such phrase as that, does not do justice to the original. For the verb used, a comparatively rare one, implies a sort of physical discomfort in the speaker; he experiences that sick longing which is sometimes evoked in us by the spectacle of human tragedy. We take no credit to ourselves for our sensibility; we want to do something about it merely by way of relieving our own feelings. And our Lord bears testimony, I think, to the completeness of his own humanity when he makes use of such a phrase; he professes himself, as it were, "got down" by the sight of all these people, invalids, many of them, faint for want of food. His divine beneficence is called into play by a natural feeling of revulsion which links him to our common humanity.

I am moved with pity *for the multitude*; his compassion, because it was human, was spontaneous; because it was divine, was on the grand scale. We find our hearts go out in compassion towards this or that victim of poverty or distress; when a whole crowd of people is affected, our sympathy—I mean our instinctive sympathy—grows fainter, just where it should have been redoubled; if a whole sub-continent is ravaged by pestilence or famine, we put our hands in our pockets, but we are too unimaginative to feel the tragedy. With our Lord, it is not so; he has been dealing with them one by one, these three days past, the blind, the dumb, the lame, the palsied, the possessed; and now, contemplating them *en masse*, he is as conscious as ever of their common need; he has pity on the multitude. His own bodily constitution was no different from ours, and for three days he has been hard at work, virtue going out of him with each miraculous operation; he must have been hungry. But he does not think of himself; he has pity on the multitude.

It is three days now since they have been in attendance on me—oh, it was their own fault. They should have waited till he came back from his travels, met him in Galilee, where he could have dealt with them at leisure. But no, the mere rumour of his coming has sent them flocking out into the desert, regardless of the embarrassments that will result. They have been inconsiderate, as men are commonly inconsiderate when their need is great. And how hard it is to be patient with inconsiderateness of this sort; how readily we excuse ourselves with the reflection, "Really they have no right to expect so much of me". But our Lord does not talk like that; he feels, in a sense, responsible for the predicament in which these people find themselves; it is through their attendance upon his movements that they find themselves so hungry now. Granted that they were swayed by self-interest, some of them in quest of health, others mere sight-seers, full of curiosity, it was nevertheless a kind of rudimentary faith that brought them so far from their homes; it is out of such material that his Church, later on, will be recruited. He is moved with pity—it makes him feel uncomfortable, that followers of his should be faint with exhaustion, just because they were his followers.

Corpus Christi Day reminds us that our Lord has ascended into heaven in his sacred humanity; it is superior, now, to all the accidents of mortality, but the gracious character of it remains complete. He is still in touch with us, his followers, through the power of his eucharistic life; and still, as in that desert place beyond the Lake of Galilee, he has pity on the multitude, all those thronging millions who crowd, so unworthily, about his table. Oh, to be sure, we have not forgotten that the divine nature is full of mercy; we cannot doubt that somehow, in God, all those perfections exist which we recognize as perfections in man. But God's ways are so difficult for us to understand; "I will show pity", he says, "on those whom I pity, I will show mercy where I am merciful"; only an insight into his long-term plans would enable us to comprehend the unequal distribution—so it seems to us—of his favours. We are more at home—put it in that way—in the contemplation of our Lord's Sacred Heart, still human, and still feeling for us in human fashion. We still crowd about him, like those Galileans, without shame or embarrassment, almost inconsiderately, crying out, "Don't forget *me*, Lord! My needs are so pressing; don't forget me!"

And still, in his eucharistic life, he pities us, makes allowances for us. Lest we should be in any doubt of that, he has given us proof of it in our lifetime, by the increased considerateness of holy Church for our human weaknesses. Those of us whose Catholic memories go back over forty-five years can remember what it used to be like going to communion, perhaps, eight times in the year, and even so, how full of anxiety and of scruple! Were we certain that we had really repented of our sins? That this or that fault in us was a venial, not a mortal sin? That we had really given proper time to our preparation, that the distractions which thronged about us on our way to the altar were really involuntary? And then a saintly Pope, the tenth Pius, was filled with the spirit of his Master, and said, like his Master, "I am moved with pity for the multitude." For the multitude—for us work-a-day Christians, so painfully numerous, who fall short, all the time, of the Christian ideal. We were hungry for spiritual nourishment in a desert world, a world that had largely forgotten God, fallen in love with the pitiable illusion of human progress, and St Pius taught us that frequent and daily communion was not to be thought of as a rare privilege of the cloister, as the prize, jealously granted, for a life of uninterrupted devotion in God's service. It was to be our talisman against every-day temptations, our salve for every-day shortcomings. How natural it seems now; what a stir it created then!

Time has moved on since; and from the first it was clear that this ideal of frequent and daily communion offered its advantages only to the few. Schoolchildren could readily avail themselves of it, and old

L

people who had retired, and that rapidly diminishing part of the population which lived in comparative leisure, cushioned by domestic help. But what of all the people who scrambled off, morning by morning, at the last moment, to work; what of nurses in hospitals, soldiers in barracks, and all those others who could not command their own time? To these, the eucharistic fast was still a difficulty not easily surmounted; for these even on feast days, and for some of them even on Sundays, there was neither time nor opportunity to approach the altar, without heroic sacrifice. And now, only the other day, the Holy Father has spoken again in Christ's name, "I am moved with pity for the multitude." The multitude—it was never the Church's wish that only a select few should meet at the common table; it was meant for all alike. And if the conditions under which we live and work interfere with the gathering of ourselves together, then the discipline of an earlier age must be relaxed; not for her to set limits to the compassion of Jesus Christ.

That compassion, mediated through his Church, meets us half way; and shall we do nothing to welcome it? In mere gratitude, we are bound to avail ourselves of these new opportunities. Perhaps you have been content, for years past, to fulfil your paschal duties, and do no more or very little more about it; awkward working hours, distance from a church, uncertain health made it so difficult for you. The reason is gone now, and will you persist in the ungracious habit? Was the reason, after all, only an excuse?

Another thing. When going to communion meant getting up before breakfast, it seemed to create the right atmosphere. Assoiled by sleep from the distractions of yesterday, surrounded by the peaceful influences of early morning, we went out to receive the Christ who was born of a Virgin and at midnight rose at early dawn from a virgin tomb. Our cares, our passions, were in a manner sealed off; we were at leisure for holy thoughts. Let it not be supposed that the Church, when she allows us to approach the altar later in the day after a brief discipline of fasting, cares nothing about this recollectedness of which we are speaking, which used to come to us so naturally. Always we must avoid scruple; but we should be more careful than we were in old days to make a good preparation for holy communion, isolating our minds as far as possible from the day's solicitudes, and asking the Holy Spirit to make a home in us worthy of Christ's coming. It may be we shall not make a great success of it, but the effort must be there.

On all the multitudes who come to receive him, on all the multitudes who neglect him, may Christ have pity.

21

ONE BODY[1]

For we, being many, are one bread, one body, all that partake of Christ.—
I Corinthians 10. 17.

THIS congregation, boundas it is by the title of its church to be a special focus of the eucharistic cult, is privileged to observe the devotion of the Forty Hours at the very time when the Church in general is celebrating the Corpus Christi feast. It is well to ask ourselves, therefore, what we mean by this devotion, and for what special purpose it was ordained. There is no time, and there is no need, in which the exposition of our Lord's body over the altar would not be efficacious in exciting the affections of Christian people. But when we celebrate the Forty Hours, we do it for a special purpose, and that purpose becomes evident the moment we consider the ceremonies which constitute it. Nobody who thinks about his prayers at all can have failed to ask himself, Why is it that the Mass on the second day of the Forty Hours is a Mass for Peace? And the answer is supplied by the very documents which first regularized and standardized this devotion. It was instituted in order to secure concord among Christian princes, and safety from that Turkish menace which still, even in the sixteenth century, disturbed the tranquillity of Christendom.

You will not accuse me, then, of speaking beside the mark if I preach to you about the Blessed Sacrament under one title which a popular hymn has made familiar to us, as the sacrament of peace. More especially, because only next month the Eucharistic Congress is to take place in a country of our own speech, and one separated from us only by a few miles of sea; a country from which many of us trace, at least in part, our parentage, to which all of us owe, at least in part, the preservation of the faith in these islands. And the Eucharistic Congress, although its first object is to kindle the devotion of the faithful towards the divine mysteries, has this incidental quality—that it is the only assemblage of Catholic people from every corner of the world which takes place at fixed intervals under the patronage of a Legate from the Holy See. For one brief week the city so honoured, whether it be Sydney, or Chicago, or Dublin, becomes an image on earth of

[1] This sermon was preached at Corpus Christi Church, Maiden Lane, on the Feast of Corpus Christi, 1932.

that heavenly city which the apostle saw in his vision: "the glory of God hath enlightened it, and the Lamb is the lamp thereof; and the nations shall walk in the light of it, and the kings of the earth shall bring their glory and honour into it."[1] The nations, the kings of the earth; there, rather than at Geneva, rather than at Ottawa, is the centre of the world for the time being, and the focus of the world's peace.

"Peace I leave with you; my peace I give unto you; not as the world giveth, give I unto you"[2]—that is our Lord's promise. How is it that the world gives us peace, or tries to give us peace; and why is that effort unsatisfying? Partly, of course, because peace in the true sense, in the Christian sense, is a threefold gift, and the world only offers us one third of it. True peace means peace with God, peace within ourselves, and peace with one another. I think it is probably true that the world at this moment is more genuinely anxious for the maintenance of peace between nations than it has ever been in all its history; nor should we do well to belittle or to deride the efforts made, even by those who differ deeply from us in fundamental opinions, to secure an object so dear to the heart of Christ. But, if the last irrevocable treaty were signed, and the last cruiser scrapped, and the last gun melted down, would that be peace? Peace in a world that for the most part either forgets God, or openly defies him? Peace in a world where human hearts, emancipating themselves from every moral tie, are carried to and fro by their passions, and win from the gratification of them only discontent? For the war within our own intellects, for the war within our own wills, the world has no solution to offer; hold congresses at every town in Switzerland, and our hearts will still be a battleground, for God made them for himself, and they can find no rest until they find rest in him.

But that is not the whole difficulty. Even when it offers us peace between nations, the world is uncertain whether it will be able to implement its promises, because its present mood is only the mood of an age, and it will pass. I do not doubt the sincerity of those who are working in our time for disarmament and for the increase of national goodwill. But their task is being made easy for them by factors which are not constant factors in human thought. Citizens are over-taxed, and disarmament appeals because it means less taxation. Rulers are alarmed by revolutionary movements, and revolutionary movements find their opportunity when a nation is under arms. Besides, we are still under the influence of reaction from the experiences of the last war, like men caught by the backwash of a current. All that means

[1] Apocalypse 21. 23.   [2] John 15. 27.

that at this moment we want peace; shall we be wanting peace fifty years hence? Only if we find some deeper, some stronger motive for cultivating it. And the Catholic Church, if she can rise to the opportunity that is offered, has a stronger motive to propound than any other. *Caritas Christi urget nos:*[1] the fellowship of Catholics all over the world ought to be enough to give the world peace. It has not succeeded in doing so hitherto; that is not the fault of the Church; it is our fault, the fault of Catholics who have not been Catholic enough.

You will say that world politics are on too vast a scale to engage the active loyalties of undistinguished citizens like ourselves. Be it so; let us admit that charity begins at home. Do we, even within the narrow limits of our own parish, our own neighbourhood, our own immediate circle of friends, avail ourselves of the grace offered us in this sacrament of peace; do we consider, as much as we ought to consider, whether our communions are having the effect on our lives they ought to have, in helping us to live at peace with those around us? You see, I think that is an aspect of eucharistic doctrine which was very prominent in the first age of the Church, but is nowadays very little mentioned; too little mentioned. That is not altogether surprising. When the Church was yet small, and scattered, and persecuted, there was a kind of natural freemasonry among its members which gave them a feeling of solidarity, though even then, even in the lifetime of the apostles, there were schisms and jealousies—you see St Paul trying, with a noble impatience, to extinguish them. In the Middle Ages, when Christendom still preserved a single set of traditions, and those traditions were threatened by a solid block of Mahomedan culture in the East, it was still possible to rouse the common conscience of Europe, at least in defence of the Holy Places. But in our own day, when the society in which we live is so little Catholic, so largely even un-Christian, it is not surprising if Catholic sympathies fail to find a rallying-point. The *philadelphia*, the love of the brotherhood which St Peter and St Paul preached, is not, in our day, the self-evident thing it was at the time when St Peter and St Paul preached it.

It is the teaching of the fathers, that the very elements used in the celebration of the holy mysteries are themselves symbolical of that unity which is part of their sacramental effect. A loaf of bread is so many ears of corn; they have lost their identity now, they are indistinguishable, because they have passed into the unity of a single product. A bottle of wine is the juice of so many grapes, separate once, but now merged, still more evidently than the ears of corn, into a

[1] 2 Corinthians 5. 14.

single fluid essence. And as the offerings are, so ought the congregation to be which makes those offerings, one single whole, compact of a number of separate units. That is definitely stated in the secret prayer of today's Mass: "In thy mercy, O Lord, we beseech thee, grant to thy Church the gifts of unity and peace, which are mystically signified by the gifts we offer up." And it is the meaning, surely, of the text which I read to you just now: "We, being many, are one bread, one body, all that partake of Christ." Think of yourself as flying in an aeroplane over the great open-air Mass at the Eucharistic Congress. You mount higher and higher, and as you mount you can no longer see separate people, only groups of people; higher still, and even the groups of people begin to grow into one another; and at last, if visibility serves, you see the whole of that vast congregation as a single dark speck. That is the true view of a Catholic congregation. It is one bread, offering itself in the Mass to Christ. Representatives, maybe, of every nation under heaven; but one bread in Christ.

And when the miracle of transubstantiation has happened, then not less but more the sacred elements become a sacrament to us of our common union in Christ. For here, beyond the furthest reach of our earth-bound imaginations, the accidents of bread and wine inhere in a substance not their own, the very substance of our Lord's body and blood. The whiteness of the bread inhering in his body; its taste, inhering in his body; its size, shape, chemical properties inhering in his body; they have all lost the old focus in which they were united, and have become united in a new focus instead, the body of Christ. Is not that to remind us, that all our natural friendships and ties and loyalties ought to be supernaturalized when we partake of this holy gift, transmuted into one single supernatural solidarity, the union of Christian people, through Christ, in Christ? Husband and wife, one now in Christ; mother and child, one now in Christ; friends, school-fellows, neighbours, guild-members, one now in Christ.

Oughtn't we to think of that sometimes, you and I, when we go to communion? We are so accustomed to think of our communions as a transaction between our blessed Lord and our own souls, quite private, quite separate, with all the rest of the world shut off from us by the intimacy of that greeting. You are so accustomed to think of that one Host in the ciborium which you are going to receive; your Host, the one in which our Lord is waiting to give himself to you. All that is quite legitimate, quite good theology. Only, oughtn't we sometimes to remember that there is another side to it; that what is contained in the ciborium is not many Christs but one; one Christ, waiting to give himself to a whole congregation, give all of himself to each that each may be one with all? Remember, too, that when we receive the sacred Host we are receiving the blood of Christ, sharing in that true loving-cup which he shared with his disciples before he went out to drain, alone, the chalice of his agony. We all know the famous picture of St John at Ephesus, giving holy communion to our blessed Lady. When we think of that, let us remember that even such love as theirs only found its perfection when it was cemented, not with the memory of Christ dying on the cross, but by the gift of Christ living in the Holy Eucharist.

This unity is there, is real; it only remains for us to make it our own by corresponding with the grace given us, too often neglected. If we would only try to realize our membership in Christ, then perhaps, little by little, bickerings in families would begin to disappear, and then feuds in parishes, and then jealousies between parish and parish, between diocese and diocese; until at last—who knows?—nations themselves might catch the infection of the movement, and the Catholics of Europe, nay, of the whole world, would interpose themselves as a solid barrier against any disturbance of the world's peace. Certainly those of us who go to Dublin next month ought to pray, not for England only, nor for Ireland only, but for a world wanting guidance, wanting unity, wanting charity, wanting self-sacrifice. Let us pray for all the intentions commended to us lately by the tender heart of our Holy Father, so wide in its sympathies, so sensitive to the needs of our time; here before Jesus in the Blessed Sacrament, that his Sacred Heart, no less wide in its embrace, no less tender in its complete humanity, may weld our divided prayers together in the crucible of his divine charity, and offer them before God, a sweet-smelling sacrifice and a propitiation for the sins of the whole world.

22

BREAD AND WINE

Whatsoever the Lord pleased, he hath done in heaven and in earth.—
Psalm 134. 6.

MOST of us, I suppose, when we are celebrating some mystery of our holy religion, prefer to contemplate it simply as it presents itself to the tranquil eye of faith, and to forget, for the time being, the echoes of theological controversy and the niceties of theological definition. But I am venturing this morning to consider as briefly as I can, and to put as simply as I can, the theology of the Holy Eucharist. So much dust has been raised in the press lately, through no fault of ours, over the word transubstantiation, that we shall do well, just now, to have this doctrine clearly before our minds, and to be able, even, to present it in some sort of way if we are questioned about it by our Protestant friends.

Let us approach the subject in this way—we know something of what our Lord could do, and something of what our Lord did, from the records of his life which have been left to us in the holy gospels. And the mention of bread and wine, the elements from which the Blessed Sacrament is consecrated, naturally recalls to us two of the greatest miracles he performed while he was with us on earth, the miracle by which he changed water into wine at Cana of Galilee,[1] and the miracle by which he multiplied five loaves so as to feed five thousand men beside the lake of Genesareth.[2] Let us see what he did on those occasions, and then see whether it throws any light on what he does, day by day, through the hands of his priests, in the Blessed Sacrament of the altar.

Let's take the miracle of Cana first. Our Lord *changed* water into wine; he didn't annihilate water, and then create wine. It is, of course, within the power of almighty God both to create and to annihilate what he has created. But he didn't do that; it would have been easier, perhaps, for our limited intelligence if he had. The servants at the wedding feast didn't look down and find that the water had mysteriously disappeared from the water-pots, didn't look down a moment later, and find that the pots had suddenly filled up with wine. No, St John refers to Cana of Galilee as the place where Jesus *made* water wine; he actually altered something which was there into something else. That which had previously been water was now wine. How do you conceive that? How do you picture that to yourself?

Well, you say, now that you put it like that, it's not very easy. Let us see, how would this do? You know the old line of Crashaw, perhaps the most ingenious line in Latin poetry, *Nympha pudica Deum vidit, et erubuit*[3]—the shame-faced water saw its Lord, and blushed. The water blushed—isn't that perhaps the best way of describing it? The colour of the water was changed, so that it looked red instead of colourless. The taste of the water was changed, so that it resembled the

---

[1] John, ch. 2.　　　　　　　　　　　　　　　　[2] John, ch. 6.
[3] Richard Crashaw, *Epigrammata Sacra*, "Aquae in Vinum Versae".

taste of wine, and of good wine. The medical properties of the water changed, so that it had that power of quickening the heart's motion which belongs to fermented drink. It had, therefore, all the effects, gave, therefore, all the impression, of wine. But it was water all the same; the thing which was there after the miracle was the same thing which was there before the miracle—water; only the divine power had altered its natural properties so as to meet the needs of the situation. Yes, that would be it.

May I make two comments on that explanation you have just given? The first is that in giving it you have recognized the difference between substance and accidents. You have declared, in unphilosophical language, that in the miracle at Cana of Galilee the substance remained the same, while the accidents were changed; it was a miracle of trans-accidentation. In the second place, you have turned the miracle into a trick. It was not really wine the guests drank, it was water which had the properties of wine; and the Evangelist is wrong in speaking of the water as having *become* wine, wrong in saying that our Lord *made* water wine. No, it will not do; what happened at Cana of Galilee was a total change; the water, both in respect of its accidents and in respect of its substance, was turned into wine; became what was needed.

What happens, then, in the miracle of the Holy Eucharist? Our Lord does not do, what you expected him to do at Cana of Galilee, change both accidents and substance at once. He changes the substance without changing the accidents. He changes bread into his flesh, wine into his blood. The colour remains, and the taste, and all the physical effects and all the outward determinations of bread and wine. Just as you thought that at Cana of Galilee what the guests received was something which *was* water but had the outward properties of wine, so in the Blessed Sacrament what is received is something which has the outward properties of bread and wine, but *is* Christ. There is no trickery here, no appeal to fallacious outward appearance; on the contrary, it is our sense-experience which remains undisturbed; what is changed is the substance, that which the thing is, that which makes it what it is in the sight of the Creator who called it into existence. God, who can create and can annihilate, can also change this into that; in the Blessed Sacrament it is his will that the change should be supra-sensible, and that the substance which is truly present should be only seen, only tasted, by faith.

I must apologize if I pause for a moment to consider a criticism recently made by a bishop of the Anglican Communion. He made, if you remember, the blasphemous suggestion that a consecrated Host
LX

should be subjected to chemical analysis, to see whether it would produce any reactions different from those produced by an unconsecrated wafer. It is, of course, a curious assumption that the forms of chemical analysis known to modern Science are necessarily capable of penetrating the innermost secrets of physical reality. But I need hardly point out to you that however far Science may progress in the direction of reading that riddle, it is not possible that it should ever arrive at the point of separating accidents from their substance, since the distinction here, albeit real, is a metaphysical and not a physical distinction. Whatever tests Science proposes must necessarily report, in the long run, to our senses; such are their terms of reference. Whereas the change that takes place in transubstantiation is, as I have said, suprasensible, and cannot submit to the award of any physical test whatever.

But now, we have only mastered half our problem. The miracle of transubstantiation does not merely mean that one substance is changed into another. It is not simply that the substance of bread and wine is turned into the substance of flesh and blood. The bread is changed into a particular body, the body which was born of Mary at Bethlehem. The wine is changed not merely into blood but into the very blood which was spilt for our redemption on Calvary. How is it that an unlimited quantity of material substance—all the hosts that have ever been consecrated since the first Maundy Thursday, all the hosts that ever will be consecrated until the last judgment—can be changed into a limited quantity of material substance, the body and blood of Christ?

To get our ideas clear about that, let us turn our attention to the other miracle I mentioned, that of the five thousand. This, you will notice, is the exact correlative of the miracle at Cana of Galilee. For there both the substance and the accidents of the water were changed into those of wine; nothing remained unaltered, except the quantity of matter present. The jar which had hitherto contained two or three firkins of water now contained two or three firkins of wine, no more and no less. Whereas in the miracle of the five thousand the substance and the accidents alike remain unaltered; bread and fishes it was, bread and fishes it remains. But the quantity has changed; a moment ago it lay in a schoolboy's satchel, a morning's meal for his healthy appetite; now, five thousand men eat and are satisfied, and the fragments of the meal fill twelve baskets. In the one case there is change without multiplication; in the other multiplication without change.

Once again, then, we see what God could have done, if he had willed to do it. Just as he could have changed every host in the world into his own body, visible to our sight and sensible to our touch; so, if he would, he could have multiplied that sacred body, substance and accidents alike; so that it should suffice for every altar in the world until the end of time. But, here again, he has not done what he might have done. He has multiplied only the substance, not the accidents, of his body and blood in this sacrament—or, to speak more truly, there has been no multiplication at all. For extension in space is, as much as colour or taste or touch, one of the accidents which inhere in the substance of a thing, not part of the substance; the substance itself has no parts or magnitude, belonging as it does to the suprasensible order. It is not *part* of the substance of our Lord's body, but the whole of it, that is conveyed by each Host in that ciborium behind me.

Our Lord, then, seems to have performed these two miracles with the special purpose of confirming our faith in the Blessed Sacrament. He would have us say to ourselves, "Yes, this is a wonderful miracle that he does in the Mass, to change the substance of bread and wine into the substance of his own body and blood, so that this body and blood is conveyed to the millions of the faithful by all the million Hosts of the world. But, after all, he did still more evident miracles while he lived amongst us, turned the substance and accidents of water into the substance and accidents of wine; multiplied the substance and accidents of five loaves of bread to feed a hungry multitude." And, since he has thus attached a kind of sacramental significance to these two particular miracles, I wonder if it is fanciful to try and read, in these miracles, a lesson about the way in which he wants his marvellous sacrament to be used, about the place he wants it to take in our lives?

I should like, quite briefly, to draw your attention to three points. The first is this, that our Lord means his sacrament to be a thing for ordinary use, and also a thing for special occasions. When he fed the five thousand, he was intent on merely sustaining life; some of them certainly, though perhaps not all of them, would have fainted by the way if they had lacked this nourishment. So our Lord means the Holy Eucharist to be the constant food, and even if we will the daily food of our souls; he doesn't mean it to be *merely* a thing for great occasions. And at the same time, the miracle at Cana of Galilee is meant to show us that the Holy Eucharist *is* a thing for special occasions too. Our Lord did one of his two great sacramental miracles to grace a wedding feast; and every great feast, such as this, calls us to communion, and calls for a specially devout and a specially well prepared communion.

And the second point is this, that both the miracle of the five thousand and the miracle of Cana have the same social character. A picnic in the open-air, the same food handed round from each man to his neighbour—how it draws us together and makes us feel our human interdependence, our common heritage of daily toil and daily food! A wedding feast—how it diffuses, if only for the moment, the happiness of two human beings over the crowd of friends who collect to do them honour and to wish them joy! So the sacrament of Holy Eucharist is meant to have a social value—a social value to which, I am afraid, we Catholics are sometimes less alive than our Protestant neighbours. We think of receiving holy communion as a solitary act which only affects ourselves; if others are receiving it at the same time, that is only to save the priest trouble. . . . That is not, you know, the way in which our Lord meant us, or the way in which the Church means us, to look upon holy communion. It is a sacramental assertion of that bond of fellowship which unites all the faithful, which should unite them, alas, more closely and more sensibly than it does. As the bread is made from hundreds of ears ground in the same mill, as the wine is made from hundreds of grapes trodden in the wine-press, so we, being many, are one in Christ; we become one body among ourselves through our incorporation into him.

And one last point; both in the miracle of the five thousand and in the miracle of Cana our Lord leaves something to his human assistants. "Give ye them to eat", he says to his disciples; it is in their hands and as the result of their ministry that the wants of his people will be miraculously satisfied. "Fill the waterpots with water", he says to the servants at Cana, and they fill them up to the brim—if they had drawn less water before the miracle happened, you see, there would have been less wine at the end of it. So in this most august sacrament of his risen and ascended body and blood, although the grace of it and the honour which it does to us so far surpass all our human hopes and deserving, he does ask for our co-operation; he does invite us to correspond, by our own devotion, with the grace we receive, does reward us in proportion as he finds in our hearts those good dispositions which he asks of us. May this sacrament be the constant food of our earthly pilgrimage, and comfort our souls for their last passage through the valley of death.

23

PROPE EST VERBUM[1]

Lord, trouble not thyself, for I am not worthy that thou shouldest enter under my roof; for which cause neither did I think myself worthy to come to thee; but say the word, and my servant shall be healed.—Luke 7. 6-7.

THOSE familiar words, *Domine non sum dignus*, familiar to us whenever we hear Mass or approach to receive holy communion, are worth studying in their original context. Like many of the scriptural formulas which have been enshrined in the liturgy of the Church, they tend to become staled for us by repetition; and it is well that they should recover their freshness, now and again, by being examined in the light of the occasion on which they were first spoken. There was a centurion, a Gentile, clearly, but well disposed towards the Jewish religion, if not actually a proselyte, who had gone so far as to build a synagogue for his Jewish neighbours. We are not to think of him as some dashing young officer, the son of rich parents; he was only a sergeant, a sergeant-major at the best, not probably of very much education or of very great wealth. He had a servant who was on the point of death; and the rulers of the synagogue he had built willingly undertook to go and secure for him, in his need, the miraculous help of the new prophet who had come out of Galilee. And they besought our Lord earnestly, saying, "He is worthy that thou shouldest do this for him." He is worthy that thou shouldest do this for him—how typical that utterance is of the well-meaning busybodies who try to get things done in this world! "You are busy, of course, but this is really an exceptional case; he is a very useful person, and a kindness done to him might have important effects on the progress of religion in our district." Our Lord smiled, perhaps, and went with them.

And the centurion, whose worthiness has been so insisted on by his neighbours, sends a message to protest his own unworthiness. He has thought better of his original request; what right has he to monopolize, even for a moment, the attention of this prophet whom the multitudes throng to see? Lord, I am not worthy that you should come to my house; I did not even think myself worthy to come into your presence. All I ask of your charity is that you should heal my servant; you will be

[1] Romans 10. 8.

able to do that, surely, by a word spoken at a distance. I also, he says, am a man subject to authority, having soldiers under me, and I say to one, Go, and he goeth, and to another Come, and he cometh, and to my servant, Do this, and he doth it. You see, our centurion has the military mind; you might almost say that he has the red-tape mind of the War Office. He is accustomed to receiving his orders from the military tribune, who receive orders from the *legatus legionis*. And the centurion, in his turn, delegates those orders to others. Is there a malefactor to be hunted down, a desert fort to be garrisoned, a party of brigands to be pursued? He does not undertake such minor duties himself; he gives a command to his inferior officers, and leaves them to carry out the commission and report. Surely it will be the same with this mysterious prophet? He has angels at his command, who will do his bidding at a word; what need, then, for his personal presence, who is so much needed elsewhere? Trouble not thyself—do not *bother*, it is a slang term he uses—just give the order, and it will be all right. We are both invested with authority; we understand one another, you and I.

Our Lord consents; rewarding, thereby, his faith, rebuking thereby the want of faith shown by those who came to plead for him. These Israelites, who ought to have known better; who must have read in their scriptures how Eliseus had cured Naaman of the leprosy without even coming downstairs to interview him[1]—they can think of no way in which health could be restored to the sick man unless our Lord can exorcize the disease by the virtue of his bodily presence. But this poor Gentile, with his rough military metaphors, his blunt, straightforward way of looking at things, has shown himself more adept at theology than they. If you talked to him about *actio in distans*, he would have no idea what you meant. But he can understand that the power which can heal all sicknesses is not tied down by conditions of time and space.

He had the faith that did not need the reassurance of actual, personal contact. That faith, as our Lord himself implied, is a rare one; and accordingly it was our Lord's habit, when he performed his miracles, not merely to perform them in person, but to reinforce the lesson cf them (where it was possible) by physical contact. So we read that when he healed the deaf and dumb man he put his fingers into his ears, and spat, and touched his tongue; because words had no power to reach him, he would reassure him by a gesture. He knew how difficult it was for the hesitating soul to make an act of faith—such an act of faith as he ordinarily required from those he purposed to heal—unless it could say

[1] 4 Kings, ch. 5.

to itself: "He has come to me; he has come, bringing with him his miraculous powers of healing, to exercise them on me."

And if it was difficult for the men of our Lord's own day to exercise faith without physical presence and physical contact, how difficult it is for us, all these centuries afterwards, to bring our spiritual diseases to him, unless he is physically present, is physically in contact with ourselves. There are two really staggering affirmations which the Christian religion involves, compared with which all its other doctrines are easy to assimilate. One is this: God cares for everybody. And the other is this: God cares for me.

You pass through the streets as you go to your daily work, and see all those thousands of your fellow beings—faces hardened by money-getting, faces impudent with the affectation of vice, faces vacant with frivolity, faces lined with despair—and it seems to you impossible that each one of these faces, with so little recognition in it of a divine vocation or of eternal destiny, can yet represent a soul for which God cares. And yet he does care, if theology is to mean anything; cares for this one as he cares for Zacchaeus,[1] cares for that one as he cared for Mary Magdalen, cares for that one as he cared for the rich young man,[2] cares for that one as he cared for the penitent thief. All these millions of human souls, and he cares for each, thirsts for each. And then suddenly you think of your own soul, only one among all those millions, and among all those millions so little distinguished by really vivid faith, by really generous love, by real intimacy with the things of eternity; can it really be, you ask yourself, that he cares for me? Just that little circle of friends he had while he lived on earth, just that handful of Jews, his fellow countrymen; for them, perhaps, he did care, did think of them when he prayed on the mountain-side or agonized in Gethsemani. But did that human regard of his extend now to all the souls existing now, all those millions, and among those millions does it extend to me?

That is the doubt, the scruple, which the Blessed Sacrament sets aside for us. The Blessed Sacrament, in the perpetuity of its institution and in the universality of its application, visualizes for us, makes imaginable for us, the perpetuity and the universality of the divine love. It was not enough for our Lord that he should become incarnate as man, that the whole fullness of the Godhead should dwell in a human form, should become, for a time, a little baby on a human mother's breast. That the God who made all things and upholds all things by the word of his power should become part of his own creation, should confine himself

[1] Luke, ch. 19.   [2] Matthew, ch. 19.

within the conditions of time and space, for our sakes, so as to bring himself close to us, put himself within our reach—that was not enough. If he was to live the life of an ordinary man, he must be like all other natural objects present only in one place, absent from all other points in space; his immediate presence must be confined and his immediate attention must be concentrated on a particular set of people; that would not do. And again, if he was to live the life of an ordinary man, that life must come to an end; his presence on earth would be limited to a particular period of history. It would be possible for the blind man by the roadside to hear from the multitudes the joyful tidings, "Jesus of Nazareth passes by"; but it would only be possible for one or two blind men here and there, within one limited orbit of the world's circumference; and moreover, at one definite period in history, never again. We, living nineteen centuries after the time of the emperor Tiberius, living far away at the end of the next Continent, should never be able to cry "Jesus of Nazareth passes by" in our turn. The merciful effects of the Incarnation might be applied to the needs of our souls, but we should never be able to feel, in this life, that the Son of God had come close to us too, so far away, so many centuries later. To kindle our love with any consciousness of his near presence, the Incarnation was not enough.

To secure that further object, the Incarnation of our Lord was at once perpetuated and universalized in the sacrament of the Holy Eucharist. Wherever there was a priest to celebrate the holy mysteries, there should be Bethlehem, and there Calvary. The ciborium and the monstrance should be for us to the last end of time that manger in the stable where Christ was born, that home whither he bade his first disciples come to see where he dwelt, that boat which bore him across the lake of Galilee, that tomb where he was buried, that cenacle where he showed himself glorified; everywhere and at all times it should be possible for men to say, "Christ is here". With a prouder boast than the Jews of old, Christians should be able to cry out, "What other nation is there so great, that hath its God approaching so near to it?"[1] Oh see, within a creature's hand the vast Creator deigns to be, reposing infant-like as though on Joseph's arm, or Mary's knee[2]—all that we should be able to say, as we gathered around the tabernacle and saw the monstrance lifted above our heads.

But even that was not enough. If that had been all, if there had been Mass, and Benediction, and processions of the Blessed Sacrament, we

---

[1] Deuteronomy 4.7.
[2] From Fr Faber's Hymn to the Blessed Sacrament, "Jesus, my Lord, my God, my All."

should be able to say, "See how near *our* God *is* to us", but we should not be able to say, "See how near *my* God is to *me*". And because he cares for each of us, not merely for all of us as a body, but for each of us as a lonely individual soul, he devised for us this still more merciful dispensation—he would come to us, singling us out for his visitation, in holy communion. When almighty God perpetuated the mystery of the Incarnation in the mystery of the Holy Eucharist, then his love radiated outwards, like the ripples that spread themselves from edge to edge of a sheet of calm water when a stone has been thrown into the middle of it. But when he saw fit to localize and individualize this mystery of the Holy Eucharist in the mystery of communion, then his love soared over us, like an eagle that sweeps down in narrower and ever narrower circles above its prey, searching for and singling out your soul and mine for the bestowal of its gifts. He comes close to us, gives himself to us, incorporates himself with us, makes himself part of us in order that we may make ourselves part of him; the divine Lover will be content with nothing less than that.

Your Host, the Host you received this morning—in that disc of matter the miracle of transubstantiation was performed, just for you. He came and dwelt there, just for you; as the whole of the sun's glorious face is repeated in every puddle by the roadside, so in every single consecrated Host the whole substance of Christ's glorified body subsists, and with it his soul and his divinity; when a hundred Hosts are consecrated, it is not one miracle that is performed, but a hundred miracles; and one was for you. When you realize that admirable condescension, that God made that one piece of bread become his own body and blood for your sake, then, perhaps, you will shrink back, and cry out with the centurion: "No, no, not that! I am not worthy that thou shouldest come under my roof, I who am only a creature, only one among so many million of creatures, and that one so marred by imperfections, so stained with sin. A countless host of angels waits about thy throne, speeds this way and that to do thy bidding; send one of these, Lord, to give me the grace I need for this day, the strength I need to conquer these temptations; do not trouble thyself, Master, to come to me."

But he will not have that, now. "I will come and heal him", that is the method which, infinitely condescending, he has decreed for our sanctification. No secondary agent, no intermediary, shall communicate to us the influence our souls need; he will come to us himself. How he must love us, to want to do that! How resolute he must be that nothing on his side should be wanting, that no loophole of excuse should be given us for refusing what he offers, when he brings it us himself! And we so blind, we so hesitating, we so neglectful; we so unwilling to give ourselves wholly to him who thus gives himself wholly to us! May he triumph over our unworthiness, and over those faint-hearted scruples that make an excuse of our unworthiness, come into our souls and overmaster them and transform them into his likeness and incorporate them utterly with himself, that henceforth we may live no more, but he in us, the food, the health, the energy of our souls.

24

NOVUM PASCHA NOVAE LEGIS[1]

Lord, give us always this bread.—John 6. 34.

IT is impossible for Christian people to read the story of that miracle by which our Lord multiplied five loaves to feed five thousand people without being reminded of the Blessed Sacrament. But it is well that we should remind ourselves precisely what is the relation between the miracle and the sacrament. You will find rationalist critics today, who, in their eagerness to discredit the whole supernatural element in the gospels, will tell you that the story of the five thousand is nothing more or less than that of a sacrament which has been falsely represented as a miracle. Our Lord, they will tell you, taking his five thousand followers apart, initiated them into the mystery of a sacrificial meal, dividing up five loaves among the multitude in a symbolic manner; and the story grew up afterwards—of course, it was only a mistake— that the tiny morsels of bread which these communicants received had been endowed with supernatural efficacy to satisfy their bodily hunger. Now, that idea that the feeding of the five thousand was a sacrament, not a miracle, is doubly false. The event is recorded in all four Evangelists, and in each of them, even in St John, it is the miraculous element in the story that is emphasized above all else. It is hard to see why we should have been told about the twelve baskets of fragments otherwise. And meanwhile, no evangelist suggests that the meal in question had any sort of sacramental character; all alike take it for

[1] From the Sequence of the Mass of Corpus Christi, *Lauda Sion*.

granted that the primary purpose of the miracle was to satisfy a common physical need.

It was a miracle, not a sacrament, and yet it was a miracle which was designed to prepare the way for a sacrament, and make the difficulties of sacramental doctrine easier for our weak faith. There are two mysteries above all that stagger human belief in the doctrine of the Holy Eucharist. One is that something can be changed into something else; that bread can become flesh, and wine can become blood. The other is that the human flesh and blood which Christ took from his blessed Mother can be multiplied so as to feed, day by day, millions of the faithful. And in either case our Lord has given us something much better than an explanation, he has given us proof. Do you find it difficult, he says, to believe that the wine in the chalice becomes my blood, through a change which affects its substance? See me, then, at Cana of Galilee, change not the substance only of water, but substance and accidents together, water itself, into wine! Do you find it difficult to believe that my one human body can, by the multiplication of its substance, become present in all the myriad hosts of the world? Then see me, by the Lake of Galilee, multiply not the substance only of bread, but substance and accidents together, bread itself, until five thousand people eat of five loaves, and are satisfied! In either case, he proves by a visible miracle his power to work that invisible miracle which will take place in this church half an hour from now.

But this miracle had a further educative value. It marked at once the resemblances and the differences between the old covenant, the covenant which almighty God made with the Jews, and the new covenant which came into force with the Christian Church. Under the old dispensation, God chose out for himself an Assembly—or a Church, it is all the same word—to be his chosen people. He led them for long years through a wilderness till at last they arrived at Canaan, the promised land. Under the new dispensation he chose out for himself a Church—or an Assembly, it is all the same word—and promised to lead them through the wilderness of this transitory world into the rest which he had prepared for them beyond the gates of death. His old people, the Jews, needed material food on their material pilgrimage through the desert;[1] he gave them manna from heaven. His new people, the Christian Church, will need spiritual food on its spiritual pilgrimage; he gives it that bread from heaven which is his own body.

The miracle of the five thousand, then, is an intermediate stage between the gift of manna in the wilderness and the gift of our Lord's

[1] Exodus 16. 31-35.

own body and blood in the Holy Eucharist. It is to correct the ideas which these Jewish followers of his have formed as to what they are to expect when they pray for heavenly food. As a more perfect type of the Blessed Sacrament, the multiplication of bread for the five thousand is at once compared with, and contrasted with the gift of manna to the Israelites. Let me give you three points which bring out the comparison, and three points which bring out the contrast.

First, then, for the comparison. The manna in the wilderness was given to be food for the wilderness, and to be daily food. During forty years, the supply of manna never failed, but during all that time it had to be gathered daily, it must not be laid aside and kept. So here in the wilderness beyond the sea of Galilee, our Lord gives the multitude only what they need to support them in the wilderness; they take nothing home with them. And in the same way the Holy Eucharist is the daily bread of our pilgrimage. When we have passed through the gates of death and reached, please God, the land of our expectation, we shall have no more need of signs and sacraments; there is no need for communion in heaven. But until that time, the Holy Eucharist may be, if we will, should be, if we have the opportunity, our daily food; renewing in us from day to day the image of our Lord's charity. The day's food for the day's march—that is what holy communion is meant to be.

Next, in the story of the miracle you must notice the words "they did *all* eat". It was a common meal for our Lord's followers—five thousand of them this time, only four thousand a little later, when (as St John tells us) many of his disciples left him because they could not understand his doctrine. It is a common meal, to partake of it is a sign of membership. Under the old covenant, to partake of the manna was a bond which united those pilgrims in the wilderness: "they did all eat", says St Paul, "the same spiritual food". And for us Christians the Holy Eucharist is a bond which at once attests and promotes our Christian unity. As the one loaf of bread is ground from so many different ears of corn, so we, individuals distinct from one another, become one body when we receive holy communion, incorporated into Jesus Christ. To be a partaker of the one altar is the test, the pledge, the bond of our Christian fellowship.

They did all eat, the Gospel says, and were filled. And the disciples, we are told, distributed to them "as much as they would". So it was with the children of Israel in the desert; they did not take up, each of them, the same amount; each man took up an amount exactly proportioned to the needs of his household. "They gathered one more, another less: neither had he more that had gathered more, nor did he find less that had provided less"; under the divine direction, each man satisfied his own needs, and satisfied them exactly. The same, surely, is true of the spiritual nourishment which we derive from the Holy Eucharist. The same sacred Host which will support an ordinary workaday Christian like you and me through the dull, daily round of his lukewarm pieties would suffice, if a saint received it instead, to inspire his incessant prayer, his heroic mortifications. God gives his grace in fullest measure where he finds empty vessels to receive it. All ate and all were filled, but each was filled in proportion as he hungered for the food given him—so it is, day by day, at the communion rails.

The day's food for the day's march, the bond of fellowship, sufficiency proportioned to the needs of each—such was the manna in the desert, such was the bread miraculously multiplied, such is the gift which we receive in holy communion. And now for the contrast. The Israelites in the wilderness found the manna, indeed, lying close about their encampment, but still they must go out and gather it by their own exertions. So, when the multitudes were hungry after they had listened to our Lord's preaching, the apostles would have had them shift for themselves: "Send them away, that going into the next villages and towns, they may buy themselves food to eat". Our Lord will not consent to that: "Give *you* them to eat". He is making provision, surely, for the administration of his great sacrament; under the new covenant grace shall be brought to our very doors. Measure, Christians, the effort which it costs you to frequent the altar by comparison with the worth of that gift, or with the condescension which bestows it; and will you not be ashamed of the little generosity shewn on your part? "I am the Lord God; open thy mouth wide, and I will fill it."[1]

And yet at the same time there is this difference; under the old dispensation man could do nothing for himself, must remain a mere pensioner on the divine goodness, contributing nothing to his own support. Man restored by grace under the new dispensation is dignified with the privilege of offering something to God as well as receiving from him. "Give you them to eat." True enough that all we can do is infinitely little; whence can a man provide bread, here in the wilderness? And yet there is something we can do: "How many loaves have you?" Only very little we can do, but it is something, and that something God condescends to want. Just five loaves, stored away by an anxious mother in a schoolboy's satchel; that was all the human help our Lord asked when he fed the five thousand; but it was something. So, in the sacrament of his body and blood, our Lord does ask us to

[1] Psalm 53. 11.

provide something, only common, material things, only his everyday gifts of bread and wine, but we are to contribute our human share to his banquet. And so it is with the sacramental effects of the Holy Eucharist; it is not meant, like baptism, to create good dispositions in us; rather to multiply and transform the trembling faith, the lukewarm charity it finds there. Whence shall we—whence? Why, from the little we have; he will do the rest.

And finally, one more contrast—under the new dispensation the miracle does not stop short with the bare satisfaction of our needs; grace overflows its measure. The manna, if the children of Israel did not make use of it, melted with the noonday sun; it is not so in Galilee. "Gather up the fragments that remain, lest they be lost. They gathered up therefore and filled twelve baskets with the fragments." So in the sacrament of Holy Eucharist, although it would far exceed all our deserts if he only gave himself to be our food, our Lord will redouble his condescension by remaining with us, to be adored in the monstrance or in the tabernacle; he is not content to satisfy our hunger, he spoils us, whenever we address our prayers at the altar, with the crumbs of his grace. O princely benefactor, whose very gleanings are a harvest! May he, who so mercifully sustains us on our pilgrimage with that heavenly food which is his body broken and his blood shed for us, bring us safely to his land of promise, where we shall see him no longer under sacramental veils, but face to face, satisfied with the plenteousness of his house for ever.

25

THE GREAT SUPPER

And the Lord said to the servant: Go out into the highways and hedges, and compel them to come in.—Luke 14. 23.

THE parable from which these words are taken seems either to have been used, with certain changes of detail, upon two separate occasions, or else to have been a long parable of which two different summaries have been preserved to us. It does not matter much which of those two explanations is the true one; it is certain that by comparing the story of the marriage feast in St Matthew[1] with the story of the

[1] Matthew, ch. 22.

great supper in St Luke we can get a composite picture which contains
no element of inconsistency. A man of wealth made a great supper;
think of him if you will as a king who was celebrating the occasion of
his son's wedding. The first invitation was accepted—the parable
clearly implies it—by a number of guests, and the preparations were
made accordingly. It was only when the actual summons came, telling
of the day and hour, to guests who had already accepted the invitation,
that they began to change their minds. They treated the servants who
brought the message with a treasonable discourtesy, and excused themselves from attendance on a variety of different grounds; a variety of
excuses, but all alike failed at the last moment to avail themselves of the
opportunity. The fatlings and the beeves are killed and in readiness; the
preparations for the banquet are complete, only—only there are no
guests. Nothing but rows of empty tables in response to the king's
summons. What is to be done? There is nothing for it but to send out
into the streets and lanes of the city, the highways and hedges of the
countryside, and bring in the poor, the lame, the halt, and the blind,
and fill up the vacant seats with guests less favoured, guests who cannot
afford to refuse such generosity.

It is not difficult to see, it cannot, even when the parable was first
uttered, have been difficult to see, what our Lord was hinting at. The
guests who first accept the invitation, and then disappoint their host at
the last moment—who can they be but the Jews, the Pharisees in
particular, to whom our Lord is speaking? God has planned a great
banquet for them—all the spiritual riches of the Church, if they will
have them. And that banquet is also a wedding feast; for its origin and
its inspiration is that ineffable union between God's nature and man's
which took place at the Incarnation. That hope of redemption the
Jewish people have made their own; they have looked forward to it
through long centuries of unique and providential history. And now
the moment of destiny has arrived; the preaching of our Lord and his
apostles tells them that all things are now ready; the Church of the new
covenant waits for them; they have only to come. And the invited
guests revoke the acceptance they have given. Worldliness, in one form
or another, has killed their appetite for the celestial delicacies so long
promised to them, and with one consent they begin to make excuse.
What remains to be done? What remains, but that almighty God
should send out his neglected summons to the Gentile world instead,
and recall the Gentiles, poor, blind, crippled, after all those centuries
of wandering away from him, to enter into the inheritance which his
own chosen people has refused?

The highways and the hedges, the streets and lanes of the city, the poor and the lame and the blind—that means you and me. Who were we, what were we, as God foresaw our lives in his inscrutable providence, that he should call us into the fellowship of his holy Catholic Church? There was nothing in ourselves that could attract him; there was no claim we could make upon his consideration; there was no added glory that our homage or our gratitude could bring to him, our Creator; we were creatures, and fallen. It was not simply that we were homeless, ever since we were banished from our appointed Paradise; we were helpless too, groping in the dark with limbs that could scarcely carry us. His creatures, and his fallen creatures, God called us to himself; in utter condescension, in generosity for which we can never make return. He has made us children of his Church, and has set before us a banquet of spiritual delights, which is also a marriage feast.

Picture to yourself the rows of hungry tramps and beggars and pavement-artists, mystified, whirled off their feet, by the sudden imperious invitation, yet with no choice left to them—compelled to come in, as they range themselves about the rich man's supper-table. Twenty minutes ago, a soup-kitchen would have seemed a Paradise to them; they would have picked a crust of bread out of the gutter; and now they are sitting down before splendid dishes, at tables loaded with the things they have never seen except in shop windows. It is the Embankment turned loose at the Guildhall. That means you and me, when we go to communion. *O res mirabilis, manducat Dominum pauper, servus, et humilis!*[1] Earth-born creatures, with no rights or titles of our own; sold into slavery by the sin that was our undoing, and, though ransomed by grace, still miserably poor, destitute of all spiritual resources we can call our own—what do we ask for? Grace just to keep us going. What comes to us in return? Grace that can make saints of us, if we will. We went out into the streets to look for a meal, and we were swept out of the streets into a banquet. And more than a banquet —a marriage feast. For as, by the Incarnation, the Church becomes the mystical bride of Christ; so in the sacrament of holy communion the Christian soul is espoused to Christ. That which she desired, she holds in her embrace. For, whatever be our worldliness, all our hunger, did we but know it, is for nothing less than God; and nothing less than God is given to us when we receive the nourishment of our souls.

"They went their way, one to his farm, and another to his merchandise. . . . I have bought a piece of ground, I have bought a yoke

[1] From the hymn of St Thomas Aquinas, "Sacris Solemniis".

of oxen, I pray thee hold me excused. . . . I have married a wife, and therefore I cannot come." Still, all around us, those voices are to be heard: the world's children, in their fancied security, their fancied self-sufficiency, delighting in the latest toy, the latest acquisition, find themselves too busy to accept the invitation of God's holy Church. Let us not think of them today, as we meet, children of the Catholic Church, around our family table and give thanks for this, our intimate food. But what if we, to whom daily opportunity is given of satisfying our spiritual appetite, of gratifying our souls' longing for God, make excuses in our turn; if we, spell-bound by our trumpery occupations, hear God's invitation to the sacrament of his body and blood, and ask him to hold us excused? Is not that as if the beggars in the hedgerows and at the street corners were to refuse the call to the king's supper—refuse it, for other aims whose worthlessness we acknowledge? What if the tramps in the parable had made their excuses too? That is what we do, if we absent ourselves from the marriage-supper of Christ.

And yet, there is something worse than that. Only in St Matthew do we find the terrible sequel to the story—how one of the guests came in without troubling to put on the wedding-garment that had been provided for him, and was found so by the king as he came to visit his guests, and at once cast into the outer darkness. It's a very old postscript, this, to the story. Our Lord's parables are sometimes concerned with individual people, sometimes with whole groups of people; this is the only instance I know in which one of his parables begins with groups of people and then suddenly comes down to an individual. We should have expected to find that a whole section of the beggars had come in without their wedding-garments; instead, it is only one man—one man; why is that?

I don't know if it is just a fancy, but the explanation which I always suspect is that there was one man among our Lord's audience to whose conscience he wished to make a special and a last appeal. Judas Iscariot, although he had not yet betaken himself to the chief priests and made his infamous bargain, was, it may well be, already a traitor in heart; at least his future treachery was already known to him who knew all things. In a few days, he was to sit at the supper-table with the Master he was pledged to betray; most probably he was actually to receive, with that black purpose in his heart, that very body and blood which he had sold for thirty pieces of silver. Called by grace not only to be a member, but to be an apostle of the Church, he had already lost, or was soon to lose, the wedding-garment of charity which the Bride-groom's own hands had given him. A last warning, to bring him to his knees, if he will, before it is too late—surely that is how Judas must have heard the story. "Confess, Judas! Confess now, while there is still time! He has seen your heart already; he is only waiting for your confidence." That is the voice which Judas hears, and hearing does not heed.

Only one among all the guests in the story; please God, it is not often that the table of Christ is profaned by a sacrilegious communion. But when it is so profaned; when, for some unworthy end, the sinner who knows himself to be in mortal sin dares to partake of the marriage-feast, then he makes the choice of Judas and deserves Judas' punishment. Let him not console himself with comfortable Protestant doctrines about the nature of our Lord's presence in the Holy Eucharist; he knows better in his heart. He knows that the very body born of Mary, the very blood spilt on Calvary, are there; that he, who comes to the faithful as their food and their victim, comes to the sinner as his judge. The King passes down between the rows of his guests; his eye is all-penetrating, the guilty wretch cannot hide his nakedness or make answer to his condemnation; speechless, he goes out with Judas into the darkness he has made his own.

Let us thank God, then, on this glorious feast of Corpus Domini, for the unearned generosity with which he has called us to himself, for the abounding riches of what he gives us in this sacrament, for the amazing condescension of the manner in which that gift is bestowed. And let us offer reparation to him, with full hearts, for all the outrages and indignities by which his sacramental presence is profaned, wittingly or unwittingly, by the careless or by the impious; and pray that everywhere his Sacred Heart may be praised, adored, and loved in the holy sacrament of the altar until the last end of time.

You especially, who are of this congregation, should be eager thus to honour the sacred mysteries. Other parishes have some patron saint to honour, some other mystery to commemorate; your Patron is the prisoner of the tabernacle. Other parishes have relics to carry in procession, dead members of the body their saint once wore in life; your reliquary is the monstrance, your relic the living body of our Saviour Jesus Christ. You then, who worship in this church, ought to be a special guard of honour to the Blessed Sacrament; in this church, visits ought to be more frequent, Masses better attended, communions more fervent than in any neighbouring parish; yours is a royal borough. God bless the priests who minister and you who worship here, and make you abound more and more in love and gratitude for his unspeakable gift.

26

A PRIEST FOR EVER

I am with you all days.—Matthew 28. 20

SET before your minds, as you have seen it in a hundred pictures, on a hundred pious cards, the figure of Jesus Christ holding the sacred Host and the chalice in his hands. Think, for a moment, of the paradox which that involves—the figure of our Lord at the last supper. You see before you what seems to be the form of a man; that man is Jesus Christ, his body, his blood, his manhood, his divinity. You also see before you what seems to represent a round disc of bread. That which looks like bread is also Jesus Christ, his body, his blood, his manhood, his divinity. Jesus Christ, then, holds himself in his hands. Host and banquet, priest and victim, are one.

There's more to it than that. We are accustomed to think of the body and blood of Christ as we receive it in holy communion, not merely as the body and blood that drew life from Mary, but as the body broken and the blood shed for us on Calvary. Now, in that first communion which our Lord gave to his apostles on the first Maundy Thursday, he gave to them the same precious gift, exactly the same, as he gave to us this morning. Yet, when he stood in the upper room, and broke the bread and divided the cup among the friends from whom he was parting, the sacrifice of Calvary had not yet happened. The bread of angels has not yet been ground in the mill, the wine of salvation has not yet been trodden in the wine-press, yet here, in the first Eucharist, that bread and that cup are being blessed, and received, and desecrated. The whole Christ gives the whole Christ; the living Christ gives the living Christ; the victim who has not yet been immolated gives the victim that already avails. *O admirabile commercium!*[1]

What does that mean, except that the sacrifice of Christ, although it was effected in the world of sense and under the conditions of time, is yet in its own nature spiritual and eternal? As the merits of that sacrifice could avail to deliver our Lady from all taint of sin at the instant of her conception, so they could avail to effect the miracle of transubstantiation before the sacrifice itself was enacted. And if the merits of his death lived already, before he died, how much more

[1] Opening words of the antiphon for the *Magnificat* (Vespers, Feast of the Circumcision).

easily do we understand that they live on now, after his resurrection! The crucifixion happened at a particular moment in time; the pain of Calvary, the humiliation of Calvary, the agony of Calvary have ceased. It is never repeated, but that is because it has no need to be repeated; it continues, it lives. Every time a priest goes to the altar—he continues the sacrifice which Christ offered in the hour of his Passion.

The priest continues it—or rather, Christ continues it through his priest. It was not only at the last supper that our Lord in person gave his own body and blood with his own hands. In the Passion itself he is, all the time, the principal agent; he was offered because he willed it. He neglected his own opportunities for defence at his trial; he consented to carry his own cross, co-operating, as it were, in the greatest injustice of history; while he hung on the cross, the angel legions were about him, hand on scabbard, ready to interfere and to rescue him, but he waved them back; and at the last, when he laid down his life, he laid it down of his own will, at a moment of his own choosing; no man could take his life from him, he laid it down. Always, *Christus Patiens* is also *Christus Agens*: always, Christ the victim is also Christ the priest. And wherever the bloodless sacrifice is offered in the whole world, whenever the bloodless sacrifice is offered to the last end of time, it is Christ continuing on earth the work he began on earth, our reconciliation with the Father. He lies upon the altar, as he lay stretched out on the cross on Good Friday. Yet he stands at the altar, as he stood in the upper room on Holy Thursday. Operating through the consecrated hands of his unworthy priest, Christ himself blesses the bread and transforms it, and breaks, and offers, and distributes that which he has transformed.

But in the Blessed Sacrament we have more than a continuation of what happened on Maundy Thursday, more than a continuation of what happened on Good Friday: it is a continuation of our Lord's whole life. He came into the world for three ends, to be, to suffer, and to do. To be amongst us men, to make us, through his participation in our nature, participators in his, to bring heaven down to earth, Emmanuel, God with us—that is already something. And it is that divine condescension which is manifested to us in the thirty years of our Lord's hidden life, and most characteristically in the manger at Bethlehem. To suffer for men: to take upon himself, as the head of our fallen race, the sins that we could not expiate; to offer a divine victim in satisfaction to the divine justice; that was more. And it is that divine humiliation which is manifested to us in the whole of our Lord's

Passion, and most characteristically on the cross of Calvary. To go about amongst men doing good: to heal the sick, give sight to the blind, to cast out the evil spirits, to raise the dead; to comfort the mourner and to rescue the souls lost in sin—that was to set the crown on the mercy of his Incarnation. And it is that divine fecundity of charity which is manifested to us in the three years of the ministry, wherever his feet trod, whenever human needs claimed and human hearts welcomed him.

And each of those three ends of our Lord's Incarnation has its analogue in the theology of the Eucharist. The Blessed Sacrament itself is the continuation of Bethlehem, is an eternal Nativity. As the Word was made flesh at the Incarnation, so that he might pitch his tabernacle amongst men, so in the mere consecration of the Holy Eucharist bread is made flesh, made that same flesh, in order that his tabernacle may remain among us to the end of time. The holy Mass is the continuation of Calvary; as he pleaded before the Father in the days of his humiliation for the forgiveness of our sins, so now, glorified, yet under the veil of humble appearances, he pleads. And when holy communion is administered to the faithful, it is the continuation of that long and laborious ministry through which the Son of Man went about to do good. His feet cannot tire now, as they tired on the roads of Galilee; his spirit cannot glow with human anger or melt into human tears. But still, as he goes about in the person of his priest administering to the faithful, through his own body and blood, the virtue that can only come from him; giving strength to our weakness, sight to our blindness, vigour and life to our dead devotion, his earthly ministry goes on.

First, then, the Blessed Sacrament, in the tabernacle or in the monstrance, is the continuation of Bethlehem. Still, as in the days when he lived retired with Mary and his foster-father, he delights to lie hidden; only faith can penetrate the veils that surround him. As once the human form that belonged to his human nature shrouded his Godhead, so now Godhead and manhood alike are shrouded under the forms of common things. As once he waited in the stable of a wayside inn for souls enlightened by faith to come and do him homage, so now in back streets and behind cloistered doorways you will find admission to his presence. And as he waited, not only for the adoration of his servants, but for the jeers and the blasphemies of his persecutors, so now in his sacramental presence he is patient of outrage and of sacrilege—outrage deliberate or indeliberate, our carelessness in church, our indevout communions, among the rest. For his delight is to be with the sons of men; those thirty-three years he spent as man in our midst were not a prodigy, isolated and apart; rather they were the characteristic expression in time and in history of the eternal charity that *will* draw near to us, *will* rule in men's hearts, though it be to rule amongst his enemies, *will* come to his own, though his own do not receive him. And as the Incarnation is the historical expression of that eternal tendency, so the Holy Eucharist is its sacramental expression. Let it not be thought strange or unworthy that bread and wine, mute and material things, should be the vehicle of such grace. The condescension lies not in that, but in his willingness to come and meet us at all on our own ground, Creator revealing himself to creature through the creature's medium of sense. That was the beginning of his condescension, when he became man; it is only the proper and (if we may so take Love for granted) the natural continuation of that beginning, when "within a creature's hand the vast Creator deigns to be, reposing infant-like, as though on Joseph's arm or Mary's knee"[1]—Emmanuel, God with us.

But our Lord did not come to earth simply in order to *exist* as Man. There was an end for his existence as man, and that end to suffer and to be sacrificed. The Atonement is the primary purpose of the Incarnation; the road that begins at Bethlehem leads to Calvary. So in his chief sacrament our Lord becomes present, not simply for the sake of being present, but in order that being present he may be offered up. In what sense? How can the Mass be a sacrifice, if Calvary is a sacrifice complete for all time? Only once the agony and the betrayal, only once the scourging and the injustice, only once the nails, and the crown, and the spear. One drop of that blood spilt might have saved the world from all its transgressions, how much more that long pageant of pain! "And now the matchless deed's achieved, determined, dared, and done"[2]—anything else, surely, that goes by the name of sacrifice must be no more than a shadow and a pale reflex of this!

But no. Mystically, yet none the less really, the immolation as well as the oblation of the spotless Victim takes place whenever the priest goes to the altar. It is not repeated, it is continued. Though in his own nature he be immortal, immutable, impassible, our Lord is still from day to day mystically born and slain and offered; and every such offering has in itself an infinite satisfactory value, won by that sacrifice of Calvary from which it derives. Not a repetition, but a continuation. We might use, very roughly, this analogy to bring the matter clearly before our minds. A piece of music, written years ago, was a complete

---

[1] From Fr William Faber's Hymn to the Blessed Sacrament, "Jesus, my Lord, my God, my All".

[2] Christopher Smart, "A Song to David".

work of art when the composer's hand left, once for all, the paper on which it was copied. Yet, year by year and day by day, those same harmonies are awaked whenever the piece of music is performed. Each performance is not a repetition, but a continuation of that single act by which the composer first brought it into being. So the Mass does not add to Calvary, does not multiply Calvary; it is Calvary, sacramentally multiplied. And in it, the true priest is still our Lord himself, though he makes use of a human agent to repeat the mystic words and to perform the sacramental gestures. The Mass is not the priest doing what Christ did; it is Christ continuing what Christ began.

Our Lord came to be and to suffer; he also came to do. He went about doing good. When we receive communion, we are made partakers of that same virtue which flowed from the incarnate Christ. We are reminded of that every time we go to communion by the words the priest says when he holds up the Host to our view. "Lord, I am not worthy that thou shouldst enter under my roof, but speak the word only, and my soul shall be healed." They are an echo of the words of that centurion who came to ask help from our Lord when his servant lay sick to death.[1] "I will come and heal him" is our Lord's answer, and the centurion expostulates; cannot the word that will bring healing be spoken from afar? What need of a visible presence or a personal contact to effect the mighty works of the Omnipotent? But the common practice of our Lord in his miracles is a continuous rebuke to that attitude. He will go to find the sufferer, he will touch, he will anoint, he will speak to him—why? Because he chooses so to condescend to our service. He could have healed the sick, cleansed the leper, raised the dead, without coming to earth at all; yet he came to earth to do it. He could communicate the grace which we receive through his body and blood without any sacramental medium; yet he makes himself present on our altars to do it. Is not this a God to serve?

Are we therefore going to say to ourselves every Easter: "There, that's all right for another year"? Look back a year or two: are you going to communion now as often as you did then? Jesus Christ offers himself to you as he did a year ago, two years ago. He has no less love for you, and you, believe me, have no less need of him. Your soul is no less than it was the object of his burning zeal: claims it no less, although it deserves it no more. Can it be that he has remained constant, and you have changed? That he means less to you, not because his loving gifts

[1] Luke 7. 6.

are fewer now, but because you are slower to make use of them? Every morning there's a ciborium in the tabernacle, with so many Hosts in it, one for each of you. Think for a moment of your Host, the one that will be given to you, if you will come for it. In that Host, Jesus Christ himself waits for you. Sometimes you may not feel, sometimes, alas, you may not be, in a fit state to receive so tremendous a gift; but ... that you should be there, kneeling in your place, others going up to receive, and from some indolence, some indifference, you should leave that one Host in the ciborium! Surely that is strange?

Every Benediction is Bethlehem. Every Mass is Calvary. Every communion is Christ going about to do good. "When thou dost celebrate or hear Mass, it ought to seem to thee as great, as strange, as joyful a thing as if on this very day Christ were descending into the Womb of the Virgin and becoming Man, or hanging upon the Cross, were suffering and dying for mankind's salvation."[1] It ought to seem so: does it?

27

WORDS OF LIFE

Then Jesus said to the twelve, Will you also go away? And Simon Peter answered him, Lord, to whom shall we go? Thou hast the words of eternal life.—John 6. 69.

WHEN our Lord fed the five thousand in the wilderness, it was, I suppose, a demonstration in force of the little Church which he had mustered round him in Galilee. Probably, in Galilee, it was the high water mark of his evangelistic success. And St John tells us in this passage that after the miracle many of his disciples went back, and walked no more with him; it was then that the ebb of his popularity began. The other gospels do not explicitly mention this fact; but you can infer it from them quite unmistakably. On the next occasion when our Lord held a rally, as we should call it, of his followers, there were only four thousand who went out with him across the lake into the desert. Four thousand instead of five thousand, a loss of twenty per cent. That is strange, isn't it? You would have thought that after so

---

[1] *Imitation of Christ*, Book IV, ch. 2, 6.

staggering a demonstration of his command over the forces of nature, his movement would have become more, not less popular. It is St John who supplies us with the reason. After the miracle of the five thousand, our Lord's teaching became more intimate, more explicit, about the doctrine of the Holy Eucharist. He told them that the true bread from heaven was his own flesh; that he who ate of that bread should live for ever, and so on. When our Lord bestows on us great privileges, it is his custom to make great demands of us in return. And when the faith of his followers had been strengthened by seeing the most wonderful of his miracles take place before their eyes, so strengthened that you would have thought it impossible it should ever be disturbed thenceforward, he made demands upon it. He demanded belief, even then, in the doctrine of the Holy Eucharist. And that was too much for some of them. This is a hard saying, they complained; who can hear it? And they went back, and walked no more with him.

Then Jesus said to the twelve, Will you also go away? Our Lord never asked questions because he wanted to know the answer. He asks them whether they will be loyal to him or not; and yet the moment after he shows that he can foresee what will become of them. "Have I not chosen you twelve?" he asks, "and one of you is a devil." Judas, perhaps just then beginning the series of petty thefts that was to lead to his downfall, and flattering himself that nobody could possibly know about it; and yet our Lord sees more than that; sees the traitor's bargain, and the rope, and the suicide's end. He knows the answer; why then does he ask? He is not asking a question; he is throwing out a challenge. He is proving their loyalty, and giving them the opportunity to assert it. One by one those thousand half-hearted supporters of his have drifted away out of sight, back to the world they had left for him—conventional phrases of gratitude, perhaps, on their lips, telling him that it has all been a very interesting experience, and that they have derived a great deal of spiritual comfort from his teaching; but they are going away, they will not walk with him any more. And as he looks sadly after them, he will use their defection as a lesson to school the loyalty of his own favoured friends. Half ironically, half pathetically, he turns to them and asks, Will you also go away?

Simon Peter answered, and with him all the apostles answered, Lord, to whom shall we go? Thou hast the words of eternal life. To go away is to go somewhere else, to sit at the feet of some other teacher, to kindle with some other enthusiasm, to find some fresh orientation for our life's ambitions. How should we do that? We have been to another teacher, we have sat at the feet of John the Baptist, and he pointed us to

M

you. We have had our youthful enthusiasms, and outlived them; one of us at least has been a Zealot, a Jewish nationalist, sworn to uphold the movement which was to deliver our country from the empire of Rome. What became of it? He learned better; learned that there was only one hope Israel waited for, the Messias, only one deliverance it needed, deliverance from its sins. That Messias, that Deliverer, he found in you. We have had, some of us have had, personal ambitions; tried to make a fortune for ourselves by heaping up ill-gotten gains. And then we saw that it was a thankless task, trying to lay up treasure on earth; we looked for a leader who would give us unselfish ambitions, a cause greater than ourselves to strive for, and that leader we found in you. For you, the latest of our loyalties and the final goal of our quest, we have abandoned all the things we cared for; and now would you have us go away from you? To whom shall we go? You have the words of eternal life; have they lost their charm for human ears, or we the capacity to receive them?

People do go away from the Catholic Church. With the other Christianities, the line of division is perhaps not so clearly marked; there are millions of our fellow countrymen who could not tell you, simply could not tell you, whether they are in any real sense members of the Church of England. But the Catholic system, infinitely patient, infinitely gentle as it is to the consciences of waverers, has sharper edges, and people who lose direct contact with it are more tempted to react against it. You have almost certainly heard of some-one, probably enough you have known someone, within the circle of your immediate acquaintance, who has fallen away from the faith which is in Christ. He married a Protestant, and his wife's family bullied him into apostasy for the sake of the children. Or he moved into some place which was far from a Catholic church, and so fell into neglect of the sacraments, and in the end drifted away altogether. Or he made a career for himself, rose in the social scale, and in leaving behind him the other associations of his early life, managed to leave his religion along with them. And the news of such a defection as that, even when there were circumstances to explain it, is—confess it—a tiny blow to your faith; a very gentle tap to test the stability of your own spiritual foundations. He always seemed such a good Catholic; was at school with you, worked side by side with you; what a dreadful thing! I hope (you say to yourself) I shall never be tempted in that way. Another's apostasy has cast a chill of loneliness over you.

If any such doubt of yourself ever creeps into your mind, then imagine, the next time you go to communion, that your Lord coming to you in the Holy Eucharist holds himself back for a moment from your lips, and asks, Wilt thou also go away? Others, whose childhood was not less sheltered by religious influences, others, whose lives seemed not less clearly marked by the traces of a heavenly guidance, have forgotten their allegiance and denied me before men; wilt thou also go away? No man knows the force of another's temptations; the doubts, the difficulties, which perplexed one soul yesterday may perplex another tomorrow; wilt thou also go away?

And the answer? The answer is the voice of Peter, the voice of the apostles, the voice of the universal Church: Lord, to whom shall we go? If we turn away from him, we must go somewhere else—where else? We can only give up his revelation for some revelation more satisfying than his. We can only abandon the Catholic Church for some spiritual home which is more of a home than the Catholic Church. We can only despise his sacraments if we are in a position to compare them with other sources of inspiration which promise more comfort in this life, more hope in the world to come. Where are we to find such a revelation, such a spiritual home, such sources of inspiration? Nowhere; there is no other system in the world which dares even to claim what the Catholic Church claims. Are we to abandon the Catholic faith for something *less* than the Catholic faith?

Do not be afraid, for a moment, to look over that giddy edge and to imagine what it would be like, for you, to lose faith in your religion. Oh, no doubt there would be a momentary satisfaction, to the more indolent part of your nature, to find an easing of that sense of struggle which we Catholics always feel, though we may feel it only at the back of our minds, living as we do in the midst of a culture which is not ours, a culture which does not understand ours. And we might, for the time being, find an outlet for our energies, a centre for our energies, a centre for our enthusiasm, in some other movement, political or philanthropic; it would carry us along with it while youth lasted, while the excitement of it lasted. But the whole structure and fabric of our life would be gone. We should have no standards to judge by, no light to walk by, no hope to live by. We see all that, and we draw back our feet, shuddering, from the edge. We cannot contemplate the thought of walking no more with Jesus. To whom shall we go? He has the words of eternal life.

But still he holds himself back from us; this Guest who comes to us in the Holy Eucharist; he has not finished, yet, with his challenge, he wants to try our loyalty still further. His friendship, we have found, is something we cannot do without. It is not the mere routine of living that would make it impossible for us, please God, to abandon our religion; it is not merely that we cling obstinately to a set of opinions because they are *our* opinions; it not a mere sentimental attachment, such as fades and dies down with the passing of the years. Habit and head and heart, they have all something to say to it; but the anchorhold of our religion is something deeper than that, something that affects the whole of us, not a part of us. If, then, the religion of Christ is something we could not do without, how is it that most of us use it so little, live it so little? Is it meant to be like a jewel so precious that, for fear of robbery, it can never see the light of day?

We are puzzled over the attitude of lapsed Catholics; oughtn't we really be more puzzled by the attitude of slack Catholics? The people who have the faith, to whom the faith, apparently, means so little? All the staggering assertions of Catholic doctrine about what the Holy Eucharist is, a real change of the substance of bread and wine into the substance of our Lord's body and blood, all that they accept. The embarrassing regulations which the Church imposes upon us, that we should go to Mass every Sunday, that we should purify our consciences and receive holy communion at Easter time, all that they comply with; or, even if they fall short of it, they admit that they are in the wrong when they do so; they are content to carry a burdened conscience. The mystery they believe, the burden they accept; but the consolations of the Holy Eucharist, the privileges conferred on us in the Holy Eucharist, seem to mean nothing to them at all. They still walk with Christ, but they walk with him, as it were, at a distance, in embarrassed silence, instead of throwing themselves upon the enjoyment of his companionship. "Did not our hearts burn within us", asks the two disciples on Easter evening, "while he talked with us on the way?"[1] But these hearts walk with him and remain cold; how is it that they remain cold?

The natural body of our Lord, the body born of Mary, is given to us in the Holy Eucharist to be, among other things, the bond of fellowship which unites us as members of his mystical body, the Church. And when some unhappy soul forsakes that fellowship, the doctrine of the Holy Eucharist, because it is so dear, because it is so central to us, is commonly the first doctrine which it learns to disown, and to blaspheme. Let us, then, gathered in the Church of the Blessed Sacrament, on the feast of the Holy Sacrament, in the presence of the Blessed Sacrament, offer reparation to our divine Lord for the treachery of those unworthy followers of his, in England and in all parts of the world, who have

[1] Luke 24. 32.

gone back and walk no more with him; let us offer reparation especially
for the insults with which these his rebellious children assail him, in the
Sacrament of the altar. And, while we do that, let us offer reparation
too for the little love which is shown him even by the souls that have
not forsaken him; for the little love we ourselves show him, when we
receive him so coldly, so indevoutly, in our own communions.
He asks us, from his throne in the monstrance, whether we too will
go away. Let us resolve, by his grace, to draw all the nearer to him, to
walk all the closer at his side, worshipping not less devoutly with the
four thousand than with the five thousand. For he has the words of
eternal life, without which man must remain for ever disconsolate,
and the world waste itself, over shadows, lost in its wilderness.

28

THE HIDDEN GOD

Verily thou art a God that hidest thyself.—Isaias 45. 15.

GOD hides himself in his creation. That sounds an extraordinary
thing to say; for it is in his creation that God reveals himself.
The works of his hands manifest him to us, as the unoriginated cause
without which they had never been; as the uncommunicated impulse
which kindles their sluggish pulses into life; as the necessary being
which underprops the caducity of their paste-board existence; as the
supreme perfection which their varying degrees of excellence imply,
by approximating to it; as the mind which marshals them in that
deliberate order which our minds find there, but cannot put there.
Yet, so revealing himself to those who patiently seek for him, from
those who indolently ignore the message he conceals himself. Our first
parents, when they had sinned, hid from God's face amidst the trees of
the garden, took refuge in the creature to find an escape from the
Creator. And to this day the soul that is chained to earth by selfishness
or frivolity loses itself in creatures, cannot look above them or beyond
them because it will not. Man has the fatal power of not thinking.
So God allows himself to be blasphemed by those who deny his

existence; he, whose very essence is to exist. From millions of mankind he hides the very principle of his nature.

God hides himself in his government of the world, in the process of history. The Jews knew that; their bewilderment over it runs through the whole of the Old Testament like a plaintive refrain: "Why standest thou so far off, O Lord, and hidest thy face in the needful time of trouble?"[1] Dominated as they were by the notion of strict justice, of an exact proportion between sin and suffering as punishment for sin, they were baffled by the spectacle of a world in which they, God's chosen people, were condemned to defeat and to captivity, while the bloodthirsty heathen flourished. And we too, after all these centuries, are not exempt from the same misgivings. Have not we seen Catholic nations go under in the struggle for survival; laborious edifices of Catholic life and culture demolished at a blow? Or, if we turn to individual lives whose history is known to us, do we find the most devoted and unselfish characters of our acquaintance rewarded, in this world, with prosperity? Do we find that scheming wickedness always defeats its own ends? In our own lives, less obscure to us in the hidden springs of their conduct, can we pretend that it is always our most earnest prayers which have been answered, always the actions that were performed with the purest motives that have brought us happiness? We know that it is not so; God will not make the riddle of existence as easy for us as that. He hides himself; bids his sun shine upon the evil and the good; sends rain upon the just and the unjust.[2]

The time came, in God's mercy, when he would make a fuller revelation of himself to man. Now at last, we thought, all would be plain; there can be no more concealment, when God himself comes down to live amongst his creatures. Under whatever conditions he takes human nature upon himself, conscious divinity cannot but shine through. If we thought that, we were doomed to disappointment. He came, and the world missed the portents of his coming. The stars could not keep the secret, they blurted it out to the wise men, their cronies; the angels could not keep the secret, they sang it to the shepherds over the fields of Bethlehem. But the world, the world of fashion and intelligence, was looking the other way. What, after all, was there for it to see? A baby, crying at its mother's breast; a boy working in a carpenter's shop; a street-corner orator, producing a nine-days' wonder among the fisher-folk at Capharnaum; a discredited popular leader, ignominiously put to death; a corpse lying in a tomb —and this was God! He rose again, but in doing so he showed himself

---

[1] Psalm 9B. 1.   [2] Matthew 5. 45.

to none but a handful of chosen witnesses; the world looked to find him, and he was gone. Would you know that Jesus Christ is divine? Then see how he imitates, in his humanity, the reticence of the God who created the world and left it to forget him, the God who rules the world, yet rules it imperceptibly; and recognize, in the masterpiece of his Incarnation, the touch of the same artist's brush.

The hidden God, whom so many have looked for and have not found; the hidden God, whose presence, even in our best times of prayer, is so fugitive, that we reach only the ante-chamber which he, the Master of the house, has just left—did we think, that when he came to live on earth afresh in his greatest sacrament it would be easy for us to discover him? No, in the Holy Eucharist he repeats and surpasses the mystery in which all our knowledge of his being is involved. No longer content to hide *behind* his creation, he hides *in* his creation. He conceals from us, this time, not merely the principle on which his favours are distributed, but the very knowledge whether his favours have been bestowed or not. And he gives himself afresh into the hands of men, not with the obedience of a human will but, if we may dare to say so, with the mechanical compliance which we expect of material things—gives himself, not merely as a servant but as an instrument, to be used by us and for us. Let me draw that out a little more in detail.

God hides himself in his creation, in the sense that you cannot read in it the evidence to prove his existence unless you will use your reason to do so. If you will use it, reason points to God as surely as the compass to the magnetic pole. But where he hides himself in the Holy Eucharist, reason gives us no indication at all. It can tell us, what the senses cannot tell us, that there is an underlying reality which sustains, in natural objects, those outward appearances which impress themselves on our senses. But, that when the priest has spoken the words of consecration that underlying reality is withdrawn from the appearances of bread and wine, that the reality of Christ's body and blood becomes present instead—over all that reason has no message to give us; nothing, here, will point to God's presence except the divining-wand of faith. Here, then, more than ever, he exposes himself to the mocking incredulity of the profane.

God hides himself in his government of the world, in the sense that he does not, ordinarily, allow us to see which are his chosen friends by singling them out for his special favours. But he does show us, by common experience, what harm can flow from the misuse of his creatures, when we indulge in them wrongly. In the Holy Eucharist, he does not do even that. We know that the Holy Eucharist is a sun which fosters supernatural life in those who receive it worthily, rain which gives them growth; is a sun which dries up life in the soul which receives it unworthily, rain which brings with it only corruption. But all this is hidden from our eyes; you cannot tell whether the gift brought death or life to the communicant who knelt next to you this morning. In his operation, as in his presence, God hides himself here more effectively than ever.

And if, in his Incarnation, God stooped towards us and condescended to our level by uniting his divine nature with a human nature, which, though created, was yet created in his own image, possessing intellect and will, how much lower he stoops, how much more he condescends, when he hides himself in the Holy Eucharist, veiled under the forms of material, insensible things! If in his Incarnation he gave himself up into the hands of men, allowed them to overpower and control his movements, how much more generously does he give himself in the Holy Eucharist, putting himself into the priest's hands and exposing himself to outrage from his enemies! In food and drink, dumb ministers of our human satisfaction, he finds the most secure hiding-place of all.

If, then, this secrecy is characteristic of God's dealings with us, what account, what explanation are we to give of it? Two purposes, at least, it manifestly fulfils. It demands of us an exercise of faith; and it inspires us with an example of resignation.

An exercise of faith—we are apt to be a little impatient when we are told that; just as we are a little impatient when we are told that hard work is good for us because it braces the mind, or that suffering has a purpose because it softens the heart. But that is because we do not understand what faith means. We think of it as a kind of second best, a substitute, a jury-mast, with which we have to be content when reason fails us. But faith, if you come to think of it, is something very much more than that. Considered as an intellectual process, it is inferior to reason, because it gives us no better than a dim and reflected light. But if you consider it as a gift infused by God, it is something higher than reason, because it breathes the air of a supernatural world which lies beyond all our experience. Your lamp may be brighter than the uncertain glimmerings of dawn; but those glimmerings are the foretaste, the reflected brightness of the daylight which is to come. So faith, less luminous to our minds than reason, is the foretaste of that fuller knowledge which we shall enjoy, please God, in heaven. And faith lives on mystery; that is its proper food; without mystery it can only languish. All those candles, then, in the sanctuary, all that gleam of polished metal, shed upon the sacred Host not light, but darkness; the more they make its outward appearance visible, the more they conceal its inner reality. In that darkness our faith moves, and grasps and welcomes its opportunity.

And this hidden God who challenges our faith teaches us at the same time, by his example, to obliterate ourselves, to annihilate ourselves, as he, so far as may be possible, obliterates himself, annihilates himself here. He gives himself, unresisting, into our hands; we are to give ourselves unresisting into his hands, without struggle, without reservations, without misgiving. "You are dead", St Paul says, "and your life is hidden with Christ in God";[1] the inner reality of our souls is to be something different from anything the world sees; behind the mask of our daily cares and preoccupations there is to be some other foundation for our lives, a continual aspiration towards God and desire for his presence. And this aspiration of ours is to transform and divinize us; "I live", St Paul says again, "yet now not I, but Christ liveth in me."[2] As in the Holy Eucharist the body and blood of Christ replace, sacramentally, the substance of the bread and wine, so in our lives, mystically, God's indwelling presence is to replace and supersede the self in us, which is always striving with him for the mastery; we are to be Christ-bearers, vehicles of Christ, nothing more. And just as his presence in the Eucharist is such, that when the sacred species are moved or broken Christ himself is not moved or broken, so this inner life of ours is to make us indifferent to all the outward happenings which affect our earthly fortunes; good or evil chance will affect only the outer fringes of our experience, not ourselves. We shall be hidden men, as befits those who do service to the hidden God.

God hides himself; it is by that sign that we are to recognize him. Look up, then, Christian hearts, and see God enthroned in the monstrance; for here, hidden more than anywhere else, more than anywhere else he is revealed.

[1] Colossians 3. 3.   [2] Galatians 2. 20.

MX

29

THE MIRROR OF CONSCIENCE[1]

It is given to us, all alike, to catch the glory of the Lord as in a mirror, and so we become transfigured into the same likeness.—2 Corinthians 3. 18.

THERE is one moment during the Mass, just about the *Domine non sum dignus*, when the priest, if he is not careful, catches sight of his own features reflected in the paten, as he bends down over it. I've always felt that this rather unwelcome experience had the makings of a sermon in it.

You see, at that moment the priest has no eyes except for the sacred Host. The management of his eyes, all through the Mass, is carefully prescribed by rubric, in such a way as to guard him from distraction. Roughly speaking, you may say that they should be focused, all the time, on one or other of these things, the book, the cross above the altar, the sacred elements, and the floor. And if the priest keeps to that principle, he almost forgets the rest of his surroundings, except in so far as the banging and bashing and coughing and dropping of pennies in the background keeps him reminded of them. Then, just at that sacred moment, an alien thing intrudes upon his thoughts, the sight of his own features. At the same time, it is the kind of distraction he can make good use of. Because he will do well to consider the contrast between what he sees on the paten, and what he meant (and was meant) to see there. He looked there to catch sight of a sinless Victim; he caught sight, instead, of a sinful priest. *Domine, non sum dignus*—how can *this* be worthy to receive *that*?

And now, let me suggest that the sacred Host, in its own way, is a mirror; is a kind of supernatural looking-glass which (as is the way with supernatural things) does just the opposite of what we should expect it to do. You sometimes look in the looking-glass, don't you? It's not a habit I want to encourage; it's a painful exercise for some of us, and a dangerous exercise for others. But, from time to time, the state of our hair or one thing and another makes it necessary that we should. Now, what is it that you see? You see another girl doing her hair, and finding out how to do it by looking at you. And the odd thing is this, that you have complete control over that other girl's movements; you

[1] This sermon was preached to convent school girls.

can impose your will on her. If you make a face, she has to make the same face; if you dodge to one side, she has to dodge to one side; if you scratch your nose, she has to scratch her nose, too. And you are exactly alike, except for one rather important point of difference. Put it in this way; if your father or mother turned up while you were doing your hair, and the nuns asked, "Which of these two girls would you rather have sent home for the holidays?", there would be no difficulty about the answer. The answer would be, "I'd rather have this one, if you don't mind, because this one's real. The other one looks just the same, but she wouldn't do as well, because she isn't real." That's the point about your reflection; it's got everything you've got except reality.

Now, if you come to think of it, with the Blessed Sacrament it is just the other way round; it is just the opposite of a reflection in the looking-glass. Our Lord saw his own image sometimes. He saw it in our Lady's eyes, when he looked up at them from his cradle. He saw it in the waters of Jordan, when he went down into them to be baptized. He saw it miraculously reflected in St Veronica's handkerchief, on the way to his crucifixion. But what he saw then wasn't real. It looked like himself, but it wasn't himself. It was just the other way when he stood by the table at the last supper, and said, "This is my body". His eyes were fixed on something that didn't look like himself but *was* himself. It looked like an ordinary piece of bread; but the reality wasn't just a piece of bread. The reality was something more real than that. It was himself, who is reality. What looked like a piece of bread was, you see, a kind of supernatural mirror—not reflecting, as other mirrors do, the appearance without the reality; it reflected the reality without the appearance.

That, then, is what you see when the priest lifts his hands over his head at the time of the Consecration. You see a supernatural mirror, which, instead of presenting the appearance of our Lord to your eyes, presents the reality of our Lord to your mind. And you mustn't be stupid about it, and say, "I wish he would present the reality to my eyes; then I should find it so much easier to think about him at Mass". Because the reality is something which can't be presented to your eyes, it can only be represented to your mind. When you see your face in the glass, you see something which is less real than it looks. When you see the sacred Host, you see something which is more real than it looks. That's the difference.

It would be easy to point out other ways in which the Blessed Sacrament reminds us of a mirror. There's this for instance—suppose you break a looking-glass. I hope you won't, because they say it is an unlucky thing to do, and I'm sure the nuns would make you feel that you had done something unlucky if you did. But if you break a looking-glass, that other girl hasn't disappeared; on the contrary, she has multiplied. Look in any of the broken pieces, and that other girl is still there. At least, she isn't there really, because there never was any other girl really; but the whole appearance has reproduced itself in each broken piece, though it remains just as unreal as before. Now, suppose that the priest is afraid, at communion time, that there won't be enough Hosts to go round; what does he do? He breaks each Host in two. And if you receive half a Host, what do you receive? Half Christ? No, the whole of Christ. The reality has reproduced itself in each broken fragment, the whole reality, and it remains real as ever.

But there's another way in which the Blessed Sacrament can remind us of a mirror, which is more important to what I'm suggesting this afternoon. I was saying, if you remember, that when you look in the looking-glass, what you see there is something which you can influence; it moves when you move, smiles when you smile, looks grave when you look grave—in a word, it models itself on you. When you look at the sacred Host, it is just the other way round. What you see there is not something which you can influence; it is something which can influence you. You've often been told, I expect, what a striking difference there is between the ordinary food you eat, and that heavenly food which is given you in the Blessed Sacrament. When you eat ordinary food, you turn it into yourself. When you eat the body of Christ, he turns you into himself. And in the same way, this mirror of the Blessed Sacrament works in the opposite way from the ordinary mirror. It is not for you to dictate to Jesus Christ what he is to do: you are to let him dictate to you. He is not to model himself on you, you are to model yourself on him. When you look at Jesus in the Blessed Sacrament, say to him, Dear Jesus, I want to imitate you in the same way as my reflection in the looking-glass imitates me. I want to imitate you promptly, and exactly, and persistently, just as my reflection in the looking-glass imitates me.

Imitating Jesus Christ—that's an easy thing to say, but perhaps you complain that it's rather a vague kind of ambition. Well, let's get closer to the idea of the thing. Let's have a look, alternately, at two different mirrors; the mirror of the Blessed Sacrament, which reflects the life Jesus Christ lived on earth, and the mirror of conscience, which reflects (perhaps rather more mistily than it ought to) the life which you and I are living. First of all, let's concentrate on the point I've been making already—that the Blessed Sacrament is something which conceals the reality it contains, which *looks* much less important than it really is. You see, in that respect, it's a perfect mirror of our Lord's own earthly life. All the time, remember, our Lord was concealing his own Godhead, going about the world looking like an ordinary man, talking like an ordinary man, and, what is more, a poor working man; he was born in a stable, and brought up in a carpenter's shop. He would have nothing to do with rank or privilege. And then, when he began to show that his powers were something more than human, look how he kept on trying to hush it up! He cast out the devils, and then enjoined them not to tell anyone about it; he did the same with some of his most remarkable cures; "Go thy way, and tell no man". And his best friends were the apostles, who were, in those days, rather stupid people; they didn't in the least appreciate him. His own relations thought he was mad, and tried to put him under restraint. And even when he was crucified, he wasn't crucified alone, with all the dignity of martyrdom. No, he would have a thief on each side, so that the careless passer-by who didn't bother to read the title on the cross would say, "Another of those thieves, I suppose". Could anything be more unobtrusive than the way in which God went about the world as man?

Yes, and now let's take a look at the mirror of conscience. Do we go about the world always trying to make as little of ourselves as possible? Are we quite indifferent, whether the world at large thinks us important people or not? Do we say to ourselves, "After all, what does it matter?", when our friends don't seem to appreciate us? Do we try to hide away our good qualities, our kind actions—don't we sometimes rather try to draw attention to them? Do we allow ourselves to be misjudged—don't we even, sometimes, try to put a better colour on our own record than it really deserves? Aren't we ashamed of being seen in the company of people whom we regard as inferior to ourselves? One sometimes hears it said of a person, "He's so completely careless of appearances"; if you come to think of it, there's nobody that could be said of with more truth than our blessed Lord. So careless of appearances while he lived on earth, and now, when he comes to us in the Blessed Sacrament, coming to us under appearances of bread and wine—he doesn't mind about appearances, you see, as long as the reality is there. And we—how often, with us, it is just the other way!

And then, remember what we were saying about the whole of Christ being present in each particle, when the Host is divided. That, you see, is our Lord's great impartiality; he will give himself alike to each. Our Lord never liked the idea of favouritism. Even when he was told that his blessed Mother and his brethren wanted to see him, he replied in that strange phrase, Whosoever doeth the will of my Father that is in heaven, he is my brother and sister and mother. And when Salome wanted to secure the two best places in his kingdom for her sons, James and John, he would do nothing about it; "to sit on my right hand and my left is not mine to give".[1] He is for everybody; he will be the same for everybody, if only they will come to him. Your Host at Mass is just like everybody's else's Host, and it contains the same tremendous reality which everybody else's Host contains. The beggar, when he goes to communion, is on a level with the prince. And now, refer to the mirror of conscience again, and see if we haven't something to learn from our Lord here, something to learn from the Blessed Sacrament here. How difficult it is, not to favouritize; not to treat the people we like with a little more kindness than the people we don't like; to make rather more allowance for their failings, pay rather more attention to their interests! With most of us, there's room here for imitating our Lord more than we do.

And then, there's this to be considered; although our Lord is really present in the Holy Eucharist, he is present in such a way that he cannot be exposed to physical injury. If, for example, by some unfortunate piece of carelessness, the Hosts in the tabernacle were left too long and allowed to corrupt, our Lord's presence, we know, would be withdrawn from them. And that, I think, is a parable of his whole life on earth; living so close to men, and yet so detached from earthly needs. He needs food, yes, but he will not be in any hurry about it, "My meat is to do the will of him who sent me".[2] He is on board a vessel in imminent danger of shipwreck, and he lies down to sleep.[3] And he is always free to go where he is wanted; "I will come and heal him",[4] "Let us go into Judaea again"—he makes up his mind on the spur of the moment, has no plans. This detachment of his from worldly comforts, from the routine of habit, is a thing we all need, and most of us haven't got it. We all need it, and perhaps especially in these days, when the future of everything is so uncertain. It may easily happen to any of you, that she will find herself, when she grows up, much poorer than she expected to be, that the career she was working for is, for some reason, denied her, that the circumstances of her life will be much more uncomfortable, much more unsettled, than she ever guessed they would be. And that will turn you into a discontented and disillusioned person, unless you can get our Lord to give you that spirit of detachment which was his.

Lord, I am not worthy—I am so full of shams and pretences. Speak

[1] Matthew 20. 26.   [2] John 4. 34.   [3] Matthew 8. 24.   [4] Luke 7. 25.

the word only, and my soul shall be healed; I shall learn to be more careless of appearances. Lord, I am not worthy—I am so blinded by fondness and prejudice. Speak the word only, and I shall know how to give my best to everybody, as you did, as you do. Lord, I am not worthy—I am so tied to earthly comforts, to worldly plans. Speak the word only, and I shall learn to be detached, as you were, as you are, from all the things of sense.

30

BREAD FROM HEAVEN

Labour not for the meat which perisheth, but for that meat which endureth unto everlasting life.—John 6. 27.

IT is a curious point about our Lord's teaching, or about that part of it at any rate which has been preserved for us by St John, that he is always treating the things of earth, the material things of sense which are familiar to us, as unreal, as mere shadows and appearances, while the true realities, of which these earthly things are but copies, are in heaven. It is our habit to think the other way; to assume that our own flesh and blood, our food and drink and all the comforts we enjoy, are solid realities; heaven is something distant and shadowy—we believe that we shall be happy if we attain to it, but we cannot imagine how, because it all seems so remote from this real world of our experience. We could understand it easily enough if our Lord said, "You see the water in that well? Divine grace is something like that, has the same clearness, the same refreshing qualities, the same power of diffusing itself, that water has." But he doesn't say that; when he talks to the woman of Samaria, he says, "If thou knewest the gift of God, and who it is that saith to thee, Give me to drink, thou wouldst perhaps have asked of him, and he would have given thee living water."[1] Living water. This water in Jacob's well, which people come so far to fetch, is only dead water after all; the real water, the living water, is the grace of God from heaven. And the purest water in the world, he seems to tell us, is only a shadow, an inferior copy, of the living stream which flows through the city of God. Always, to him, it is the earthly things

[1] John 4. 10.

that are shams, the heavenly things that are the realities. It is as if he could not accustom himself, in spite of that perfect humanity which he took upon himself at the Incarnation, to look upon things from our human point of view. Grace does not remind him of a draught of water; a draught of water reminds him of grace.

So it is when he refers to himself as the true vine.[1] He doesn't point to the vine, and tell us that the closeness of union which binds him to us and ourselves to him is something like the closeness of union which binds the vine to its branches, and its branches to the vine. No, he looks at it the other way round. You see that vine? he says. That is not a real vine. All the vines you may see spreading down like a curtain over some hillside in France—they are not real vines, they are only shams, copies of a reality which exists somewhere else. And that reality is his mystical body, the Church. We shall never understand the mystery of organic growth, of that inner principle which bids the same tree put forth, year after year, fruits of its own kind, until we get to heaven and experience, with our Lady and the saints, the reality of that union which binds us to him, that unction which flows from him to us. And we shall never understand the mystery of water, the secret of its pervasive passage through the earth, of its welling up to reach its own level, of its necessity to animal life, until we get to heaven and know what grace means, how, all our lives through, it has been following us and intertwining itself with the experience of daily life, and achieving its work in us, and satisfying the needs of our souls. When we know what the Church is, we shall begin to understand the vine; when we know what grace is, we shall begin to understand water. It is only in heaven that we shall appreciate those satisfying realities, of which we perceive the echoes and the shadows here on earth.

And so it is above all with this great chapter of St John, the sixth chapter, in which, after the miracle of the five thousand, our Lord talks to his disciples about the manna which was sent to the Israelites in the wilderness. "Thou didst give them bread from heaven",[2] the Psalmist wrote, thinking of that wonderful morning in the desert when the hosts of Israel awoke from sleep to find the earth around them white, as with dew, with the strange food that was to be the strengthening of their pilgrimage. But that wasn't really bread from heaven, our Lord says; not the true bread from heaven. And even your experience just now, he implies, when the five loaves were miraculously multiplied so as to satisfy five thousand hungry men—that was not real bread I gave you, not the true bread. I am the bread of life. I am the

[1] John, ch. 15.   [2] Psalm 77, 24; 104. 40.

living bread which came down from heaven. My flesh is real meat; my blood is really drink. All the most palatable food which can tempt your earthly appetites is only a sham, a shadow, a copy of the true bread, mysteriously to be communicated to my faithful followers, which is myself. And once again, not till we reach heaven and understand there what it was that the sacrament of Holy Eucharist has been doing for us all the time, building up our spiritual strength and satisfying our spiritual needs, shall we begin to understand that ordinary process, so familiar in common life, by which the food we eat builds up and strengthens our material bodies.

Let me put it this way, so as to make my point clear. We think of God, don't we, as first of all designing bread for our use, and then, when he came to earth, instituting the Blessed Sacrament under the form of bread so as to remind us of our earthly food? But that wasn't really how it happened. Before he made the world, almighty God foresaw the need for the Incarnation, and decreed the institution of the Holy Eucharist for the benefit of our souls. And he gave us bread, the common bread we eat, to prepare the way for the Holy Eucharist, to be like the Holy Eucharist, to remind us of the Holy Eucharist when it came. Whenever we eat bread, if we really want to see things as they are, we ought to be reminded of the Blessed Sacrament.

A world of shadows, a world of shams—how difficult it would have been to preach that doctrine, in England, forty or fifty years ago! When we supplied the whole world from our factories, and took toll of it twice over, by exporting what we had manufactured! When colonies, newly opened up, seemed to hold out unlimited prospect of riches to the adventurous; when income tax was less than a shilling in the pound, when railway shares seemed like a gold-mine; when British credit seemed a thing as immovable as the laws of nature, and British influence feared no jealousy abroad, no disaffection in the Dominions. Look about you, as you pass through once prosperous suburbs, or peep between the railings of the parks that fringe our country roads, and see the great houses men built for themselves in those days, with the secure confidence of handing them down to a grateful posterity. Oh, there was poverty, there was misery; but all that was being taken in hand, was to be eliminated almost at once; universal education and a little town-planning would put an end to that. How peaceful they were, those grandfathers of ours, in their possessions; how eagerly they pulled down their barns to build greater, and told themselves that they had much substance laid up for many years! "We don't want to fight, but by jingo if we do—we've got the ships, we've got the men, we've got the money, too";[1] so ran our popular sentiment in 1878, only a little over fifty years ago.

And now? "Your fathers", our Lord says to the Jews, "did eat manna, and are dead." More highly privileged than any other nation on earth, they found their daily needs supplied without any effort on their part; they had only to look round them and to gather in their daily bread, the bread of angels. And yet, it was only their earthly needs that bread supplied. In the course of time they died, and their bones lay white in the wilderness, white as the manna which fell around their tents while they still had need of it. Might he not say to us, too, "Your fathers did eat manna"? He gave them abundance of material riches; they were the envy of the world. And now they are dead, and they have not even left to us their prosperity, the comfortable certainties which they enjoyed in life. We, their descendants, find our legislators hurrying to and fro—and in the shooting season—to balance the budget, to save the pound. The pound sterling, which used to be as solid a fact as the sun in the sky, had to be saved! And we look about us nervously, wondering what is going to be taxed next, whose salary is going to be cut next. Nor is it ourselves only that have felt the pinch; Australia has had its crisis, Germany has had its crisis, the United States have their unemployment problem, far worse than ours. And we look at the houses our grandfathers built, now advertised hopelessly for sale, or left untenanted because their owners cannot afford to live in them, and ask ourselves what has happened.

And what has happened? Has there been a great drought, a wholesale destruction of crops by flood or by blight? Why no, there is more food in the world than we know what to do with. "Thou hast put gladness in my heart", says the Psalmist, "since their corn and wine and oil increased."[2] But when our corn and wine and oil increase, it gives us no gladness; we burn the unwanted stocks of grain, we block up the oil-wells, for fear of over-production. What has happened? Nothing that we can see, nothing that we can blame. Our own laws of supply and demand, based on the desire of every man to get as rich as he can as quick as he can, have caught us in their toils; we are the prisoners of our own machine, and we cannot get out of it. Tell me, did we not do well to say that this is an unreal world we live in? A world in which mere abstractions, like the laws of supply and demand, can bring men to the verge of starvation, when there is food ready for them to eat, being burned because no price can be got for it?

---

[1] G. W. Hunt, "We don't want to fight". (Music hall song.)
[2] Psalm 4. 7-8.

If thou knewest the gift of God! If we could only see the realities of the other world as they! God grant that this glimpse he has just given us of the hollowness and unreality of our own may enlighten us a little, may make us begin to understand how much it is we miss when we neglect the sacraments, or treat them carelessly and approach them without preparation and without reverence. That heavenly dole, proportioned to the needs of each, freely given, and despised by its recipients, God help us all, because it is given freely. Remember, it is very easy for us, in critical times like these, to become all the more attached to worldly advantages and to material comforts, because we see them ready to slip between our fingers; to plunge ourselves feverishly into the enjoyment of the moment, in the hope of shaking off the black load of care that lurks at the back of our minds. But that is not the lesson God means us to read in our present distress. He means us to draw all the closer to him, as the worldly prosperity that made us forget him is taken away from us; to throw ourselves all the more lovingly into his arms, as we see our prospects more uncertain, and our labours less profitable. Come to me, all you that labour and are burdened; it was not to one age, or to the inhabitants of one country, that that loving invitation was issued. He calls us away from a world of shadows into a world of realities; from the perplexities of our earthly citizenship to a city which has foundations whose builder and maker is God.

31

THE DIVINE SACRIFICE

I live, now not I, but Christ liveth in me.—Galatians 2. 20

TODAY a special circumstance marks out our observance of the Corpus Christi festival. The priest who is singing the Mass is singing Mass for the first time, fresh from his ordination on Sunday. And it is an instinct among faithful Christians—not a rule, prescribed by authority, not a doctrine set down in text-books, but one of those instincts which bloom self-sown, from the soil of Christian piety—that we should make much of a newly-ordained priest; kiss his hands while the oil still glistens on them, obtain his blessing before that ceremony is staled by usage. A virtue and an influence must hang, we feel, about the first sacerdotal acts which the neophyte performs. We can quote Gospel precedent; our Lord would be born of a virgin, he would be buried in a tomb wherein man was never yet laid, and when he rode into Jerusalem before his Passion, the beast that carried him should be a beast no man had ever ridden before; and does not he too delight in the fresh fervour of a priest newly ordained! Does not he pardon us if, for once, our thoughts stray from the sacrifice to him who offers it! Today, then, because the whole institution of the priesthood is so closely bound up with the Mass and with the Eucharist, I do not hesitate to make the institution of the priesthood my subject. Today's feast, after all, is but the echo of Maundy Thursday—Maundy Thursday, with all its sorrow turned into gladness. And what our Lord did at the last supper, he accompanied with the words "Do this"; it was not only the first Mass but the first ordination.

When God created sun and moon and stars, and the earth with all its delicate beauty, its intricate workmanship, he pronounced it very good; and the sons of God shouted for joy at the birth of this new creation. But within the material universe itself there was no answering cry of recognition. True, the stars in their courses, the mysterious alternation of light and darkness, the orderly process of the seasons, showed forth the glory of him who ordained them; true, the living things could enjoy some confused pleasures of memory and of hope, and in doing so rendered continually a kind of unconscious praise to their Creator. But amid all that wealth of multitudinous life there was no conscious response given, no reasonable homage. So God took of the slime of the earth, and made man; breathed into his nostrils the breath of life, and man became a living soul. Man was to be the priest of creation, was to praise God on behalf of those mute, material things, with a mind that could reason and a voice to express its reasonings. The priest of creation; the instrument through which the chorus of its gratitude should thrill and become vocal at last.

Centuries later, we have no means of knowing how many centuries later, God breathed into the face of man once more. "When he had said this, he breathed on them, and said, Receive ye the Holy Ghost."[1] When he had rested on the seventh day after the stupendous achievement of the natural creation, God made man to be its priest. When he rose on the third day after resting from the labours of his Passion, Incarnate God set the crown on his work of redemption by instituting the Christian priesthood. It was a fresh act of creation, no less amazing

[1] John 20. 22.

in its results than that other; for the powers which the Christian priesthood enjoys exceed the natural powers of man no less significantly than man's natural powers exceed those of the brute beasts. The world, fallen and redeemed, was to be reconciled to God by the ministry of the priest—a representative man, chosen out among his fellows to be their spokesman and God's ambassador. Sanctified by his office, he was to intercede for his sinful brethren, to come between them and God's anger, offering sacrifice in their name.

True, there was nothing unheard of in that. For centuries before our Lord came priests had been offering sacrifice to God; among the Jews, in obedience to the light of an imperfect revelation, among the Gentiles, from a sort of blind instinct which warned them that atonement for sin, could it only be achieved, was the first step towards communion with God. But all those old sacrifices were no better than a frantic appeal, a despairing gesture. The blood of bulls and goats could not take away sin;[1] and the priests who offered them were themselves encompassed with infirmities; sinful men themselves, they could not bear the petitions of the people into God's presence as having the right to enter it. Our Lord came, to be at once a sinless Victim and a sinless Priest. Priest and Victim, he offered his own death to be the sufficient atonement for a world's transgressions. When the first Adam received the breath of life, this material universe was elevated into a fresh state of communion with God. When the second Adam gave back that same breath of life into his Father's hands, our guilty race was restored to the divine favour. Ruined long since by Adam's fault, the world could cry once more, *Habemus Pontificem*.

It would have been possible, it might even have seemed natural, that our Lord, when he achieved our redemption, should apply thenceforward the virtue and the effects of that redemption to human souls without any kind of priestly ministry to aid his purpose. Many who value the name of Christian still find it reasonable to believe that he did so; the priesthood, they will tell you, was an institution which belonged to a former age of imperfect revelation; when the mercy of God shone out to us in the face of Jesus Christ, the need for all ceremonies and sacraments was done away. But it is not so that the courtesy of our Lord Jesus Christ treats us. When he turned water into wine at Cana of Galilee, he used no word, no touch, no gesture, to claim the miracle as his own. "Fill the water-pots with water. . . . Draw out now, and bear it to the governor of the feast"[2]—the miraculous transformation should take its effect between the hands of the

---

[1] Hebrews 10. 4.   [2] John 2. 8.

servants who were ministering to the guests; they should have the apparent credit for it. And so it was when he multiplied the loaves in the wilderness. He gave the loaves and fishes to the disciples to distribute; it was in their hands, it seems, that the multiplication took place. It is part of his courtesy that he should thus associate human agents with himself, then when most he manifests his superhuman powers. Their obedience to his command shall be the immediate occasion of those prodigies whose operation, in the last resort, can only come from him.

So it is, then, with his new priesthood. Not only when he gives us, under the forms of bread and wine, his own body and blood to be our food; in all the sacraments he is the true author, the true fountain of grace, yet he will suffer a human ministry to intervene—"Receive ye the Holy Ghost;[1] whose sins ye shall remit, they are remitted unto them, and whose sins ye shall retain they are retained". But most, and most characteristically, in the sacrament of Holy Eucharist. When a priest baptizes or absolves, he stands there, sits there, only to unseal the fountains of grace in answer to the faith and penitence which knock to receive them. But when he stands at the altar the priest does something more; he takes upon himself the person of Christ, re-enacting in his name the ceremony which he performed on the night before his Passion. A priest clad in the sacred vestments (says the author of the *Imitation*) is the vice-gerent of Christ himself.[2] He uses our Lord's own words, identifies himself with the offering which our Lord continually makes before the Father of his own body and blood. How is it that men can be found with the assurance, with the presumption, to do that?

The difficulty is solved for us by one golden phrase of St John Chrysostom's. "When you see a priest offering the sacrifice", he says, "do not think as if it were *he* that is doing this; it is the hand of Christ, invisibly stretched forth." The hand of Christ invisibly stretched forth —that is the image we must conjure up if we are to think of the Mass as what it really is. The philosopher Aristotle, in defining the position of a slave, uses the words, "A slave is a living tool". And that is what a priest is, a living tool of Jesus Christ. He lends his hands to be Christ's hands, his voice to be Christ's voice, his thoughts to be Christ's thoughts; there is, there should be, nothing of himself in it from first to last, except where the Church graciously permits him to dwell for a moment in silence on his own special intentions, for the good estate of the living and the dead. Those who are not of our religion are puzzled

---

[1] John 20. 22.   [2] *Imitation of Christ*, Book IV, ch. 5.

sometimes, or even scandalized, by witnessing the ceremonies of the Mass; it is all, they say, so mechanical. But you see, it *ought* to be mechanical. They are watching, not a man, but a living tool; it turns this way and that, bends, straightens itself, gesticulates, all in obedience to a preconceived order—Christ's order, not ours. The Mass is best said—we Catholics know it—when it is said so that you do not notice how it is said; we do not expect eccentricities from a tool, the tool of Christ.

That notion is not a mere fancy; the Church herself is at pains to emphasize it in the ordination rite. If you have witnessed the ceremonies of an ordination, you will have seen the ordination candidates stretched out at their full length face downwards, like corpses, like dummies, while the solemn chant of the litany rolls over their heads. They are waiting there like dead things, for the Holy Spirit to come and quicken them into a new form of life; as Adam's body waited, slime of the earth, for the informing touch of the Creator's hand to quicken him into a living soul. They are yielding their bodies to Christ to be his instruments, as completely as if they had no life, no volition of their own. And even when they have risen from the ground, you will see their hands being tied together with purificators, in token that they are the captives of Jesus Christ, his slaves, to drive and control as he wills. "I live, now not I, but Christ liveth in me"—that is the protestation which these ceremonies make on behalf of the newly-ordained priest. No life of his own, no liberty of his own; henceforth he is Christ's.

Whenever the holy mysteries are celebrated, Christ is doubly present at the altar; present in the sacrifice, and present in the priest. Still, as in the cenacle, both gift and giver are himself. In the sacrifice, as we know, he is present after a special sacramental manner; the outward forms of bread and wine inhere in, are held together by, an underlying reality which is the very substance of his own body and blood. He is present in the actions of the priest not physically but mystically, taking them into himself and making them his own. "I live, now not I, but Christ liveth in me"; that should be the reflection of every priest every time he goes to the altar; in no other confidence could he dare to use the words he uses, to handle that which he handles. But with that thought comes, or should come, a further reflection—this identification of my voice, my thoughts, my will with Christ, is it meant to take effect only for one short half-hour of the day, when I put on the sacred vestments of my calling? Is it not rather his demand that my will, my intentions, my judgments should be made one with his, not for half an hour of the day but for twenty-four hours? To one who remembers that, vocation to the priesthood is hedged about with no ordinary terrors. Dare we priests believe that Christ lives in us?

Our brethren of the laity often complain of the priests they get; I wonder, does it ever occur to them to pray for better? When the Ember seasons come round, how many people remember to pray for the priests who are being ordained? We pile the sanctuary with flowers, we make it a blaze of candles; but there is something else needed far more than lights or flowers for God's honour, that the hearts of his priests should be made a fit habitation for himself. Of his priests? Not of his priests only, but our own hearts, too. When he comes to us in communion, he comes, not to bring some transient influence, but that he may live, more and more, in us. In the miracle of transubstantiation, the substance of his creatures is really, physically replaced by the substance of his own body. And the effect of the Sacrament in you should conform to the same model; your self, your will, should die more and more, be replaced more and more by himself, by his will; choosing for you, operating in you, sanctifying your thoughts and inspiring your actions, the centre and heart of your being. Today is your patronal feast. If this church were dedicated to some martyr or confessor, I would be urging you to imitate his actions, to be like him But since this church takes its title from the Blessed Sacrament, I will urge you rather to be like the Blessed Sacrament; to let Christ live in you, to let him make you the abiding dwelling-place of his presence. May he grant that blessing both to priests and people, that his life may grow more and more in them, absorb them more and more into himself; till at last in that heavenly temple where sacrifice and sacrament are done away, we shall see him as he is, and worship him as he ought to be worshipped.

VIII

FEASTS AND SEASONS OF THE YEAR

I

ADVENT[1]

The light shines in darkness, a darkness which was not able to master it.
—John 1. 5.

DURING these last days of Advent, the Church gives us a series of antiphons to the *Magnificat*, drawing attention to, and adding special urgency to, that sense of expectation which closes in on us as the great feast draws near. They address our blessed Lord under various titles, given to him by the old Jewish prophets before the world was saved. Now he is the Branch that grows, suddenly and belatedly, from the trunk of Jesse, from the royal dynasty of Israel, hardly more than a memory in the great lumber-room of the past. Now he is the Key of David, the providentially designed instrument which fits into the lock of our sad human experience, the one instrument that can provide the answer to all our puzzles, give freedom to all our inhibited aspirations. But the metaphor under which we greet him this evening, the 21st of December, is perhaps the most encouraging of all, because it is the simplest and the most primitive of all. "O Day-star, radiance from the eternal Light, Sun-rise that is the world's amending, come and enlighten us as we sit here in darkness, under the shadow of death."

Everybody knows, even those of us who have lived most unadventurously, what it is to plod on, for miles it seems, eagerly straining your eyes towards the lights that, somehow, mean home. How difficult it is, when you are doing that to judge distances! In the pitch darkness, it might be a couple of miles to your destination, it might be a few hundred yards—you cannot tell. So it was, I think, with the Hebrew prophets, as they looked forward to the redemption of their people. They could not have told you, within a hundred years, within five hundred years, when it was the deliverance would come. They only knew that, some time, the stock of David would burgeon anew; some time, a key would be found to fit the door of their prison house; some time, the light that only showed, now, like a will-o'-the-wisp on the horizon would broaden out, at last, into the perfect day.

This attitude of expectation is one which the Church wants to encourage in us, her children, permanently. She sees it as an essential

---

[1] A sermon broadcast from the London Oratory on Sunday, 21 December 1947.

part of our Christian drill that we should still be looking forward; getting on for two thousand years, now, since the first Christmas Day came and went, and we must still be looking forward. So she encourages us, during Advent, to take the shepherd-folk for our guides, and imagine ourselves travelling with them, at dead of night, straining our eyes towards that chink of light which streams out, we know, from the cave of Bethlehem. Nearer, nearer we come, with the four Sundays of Advent for milestones on our journey, and at last we are in sight of the end; "Do not be afraid", we tell one another on the morning of this twenty-first day of December, "on the fifth day our Lord will come to you"; and then in the evening we make our prayer to him as the Day-star, the flush of Christmas dawn already to be seen, just faintly, in the eastern sky. Tense with expectation, we are to mark off the days till Christmas, just as children at school mark off the days that are still left before the end of term. So soon, now, we shall push open the door, and kneel there, among the lamp-light and the shadows, to greet the miracle of a divine birth.

Yes, you say, I fully admit that this is a beautiful bit of drama. The Church never fails in her instinct for drama. But what, exactly, is the motive behind it all? You tell me the Church wants to encourage an attitude of expectation—expectation, of what? No doubt, in the first days of Christianity, men looked forward to the prospect of our Lord's second coming in judgment; looked forward to it eagerly, because they were tired of a world which persecuted them; looked forward to it anxiously, because they thought of it as something which was going to happen quite soon. That attitude, for some reason, is no longer ours. We know, of course, that the world has got to come to an end some day; we know that when it does the whole history of it will be reviewed at a final judgment. But we don't (for whatever reason) take it for granted that this final catastrophe is just round the corner. When we pray, "Thy kingdom come", we don't mean we want the world to come to an end. We mean, commonly, that we look forward to a time in which the world as we know it will have caught something of the spirit of Christ, when there will be some kind of peace between nations, when there will be some kind of justice done between man and man. We should be ready to keep Advent with a will if we really felt, year after year, that this reign of right was coming nearer and nearer to us. But is it? And is it a good plan that the Church should screw us up, just before Christmas-time, into this attitude of expectancy, when the thing we all want to expect is the thing that never happens?

I know. It's horrible. Nearly twenty centuries, during which the

Sermon on the Mount has been on the statute-book of the human heart, and *this* is all we have to show for it. I don't suppose there has been a Christmas since 1913 when we haven't felt inclined to say, "Well, surely this must be the turning-point; we shall be starting on the up-grade now". And it never came. Every year the mute appeal of Bethlehem, the adoration in Mary's eyes, and the divine Infant stretching forth his hands to a people that refuses obedience! What wonder if we grow weary, in our day, of that magnificent confidence which the Hebrew prophets felt about the future, and feel more in tune with the complaint of the royal cynic—was not he, too, inspired? "That which has been is that which shall be, that which has been done is that which shall be done, and there is nothing new, here under the sun."[1] Pick up the paper any morning, and read how the British Government has ordered a census of all the Jews in Palestine, how a new comet has appeared in southern skies, of unwonted brilliance, unpredicted by the astronomers, and you find yourself asking, "Has Bethlehem really happened? Does anything really happen? Or is the world merely a machine racing round, is history nothing more than a pattern for ever repeating itself?"

Yes; it is time we went back to my text. "The light shines in darkness, a darkness which was not able to master it." Shines, not shone; it may be, nearly a century had passed since the first Christmas Day, when those words were written, and still there was no rift in the clouds. The darkness was not able to master it; what does that mean? To overpower it? Or to understand, to assimilate it? We shall never know; perhaps St John was thinking of both meanings. Perhaps he meant us to see the world as permanently a battle-ground in the struggle between light and darkness, either setting off and showing up the other. On the one hand, darkness cannot take in, cannot assimilate the light. There is that in human nature, a nature wounded by the Fall, and redeemed now but not rectified, which will hold its own to the end of time. And always human nature in the mass will be like a carica-ture, that emphasizes the ugly features of a subject by writing them large; men in crowds will be more impatient, more cruel, more acquisitive than men considered as individuals. Perhaps—we do not know—there will always be shadows, as well as light, around the cave of Bethlehem.

Equally true, and perhaps more importantly true, is the other side of the picture. Darkness cannot overpower, cannot restrain the light. Once Christmas has happened, once we have been allowed to get

---

[1] Ecclesiastes 1. 9.

Bethlehem's angle on the world, things can never be the same again; we may try to live down that revelation, but we shall not forget it. It has been said, and wisely: "Even to make darkness visible, some light is needed. We are only discontented with ourselves when we are struggling to be better than ourselves." If we find the world hideous, do not let us forget to thank God for that illumination which enables us to see its hideousness, for every rush-light that guides our way through darkness, a darkness which it cannot dispel.

And don't let us forget that the same principle holds true of our own personal lives. So many of us, when Christmas comes round, feel as if we had not the courage to present ourself at the crib; it shames us with its poverty—we are so creature-loving; shames us with its humility—we are so full of injured pride; shames us with its faith— we are so full of hesitations and evasions. Why is it still dawn with us; why have we never grown up into the perfect day? As long as you have the grace to be thus discontented with yourself, take courage; all is not lost. No need to despair of any soul, except the soul which despairs of itself. Those deep shadows which chequer the recesses of your conscience are proof that the light is still there. There is head-room in the cave of Bethlehem for everybody who knows how to stoop.

2

THE CROWDED INN[1]

WAS I a very uninquisitive child, or were my early curiosities sternly repressed? It is certain that whenever I sit down to read even the simplest story in the Bible, a crowd of questionings, of the Sir-please-Sir-Sir-why-did-he-do-that-Sir? order come flocking into my mind. Let me unburden myself of the difficulties which present themselves on a re-reading of the most familiar story in the world, that of Bethlehem; let me try, with Lagrange and H. V. Morton and the Dictionary of the Bible at my elbow, to find the solutions of them. I don't mean the census of Quirinius and all that; a barren topic fit for scholars. I mean the minor details which affect the human (and perhaps the divine) interest of the narrative.

There was a census, anyhow, and St Joseph was bound to go up to

[1] A Christmas meditation published in *The Tablet*, 21 December 1940.

Bethlehem and be enrolled there. Apparently this enrolment by clans was a normal thing under the Roman Empire; in Egypt, for example. (It may be that St Joseph had only lately set up his business at Nazareth, and belonged to Bethlehem before that; this would explain why St Matthew, 2. 23, writes as if he had made a new departure when he settled down at Nazareth after the flight into Egypt.) But was St Joseph bound to appear on a special day? (It was not the England of 1940, remember.) If he was not bound to appear on a special day, why did he choose a moment when our Lady's time was so close at hand? Nobody seems to ask this question. I think he *wanted* our Lord to be born at Bethlehem; had those angels let him into the secret? Or was it a sense of the fitness of things, characteristic of the "just man", that made him think of it? If he wanted our Lord to be born at Bethlehem, we can see why he took our Lady with him, whether or not she, too, had to be enrolled, as St Luke seems to imply. St Joseph's branch of the family had come down in the world, but he retained, perhaps, some of the instincts of that aristocratic class which prefers to have births registered at the old place; none of your London nursing-homes.

But if he had friends, or even relations, in Bethlehem, why must he depend (rashly, as it proved) on the hospitality of the local *khan*? Here my authors encourage me to believe that our pictures of the scene have all been wrong, the truculent inn-keeper insisting that it is out of the question, every sofa is occupied as it is. The *diversorium*, they say, was probably not an inn at all; it was the upper half of a private house, built, as Bethlehem's houses were, in two storeys. There would be an underground cave where the beasts were kept, and living-rooms over the top. You did not, in those days, offer the underground shelter to the stray guest as a delicate attention; it was not 1940. But the people of the house, if they were acquaintances of St Joseph's, were not over-considerate acquaintances; the Holy Family were not, after all, the sort of people who minded very much about appearances. Glory be to God, if you moved some of the beasts out, why wouldn't they get on well enough down below? It may have been only a temporary arrangement; when the wise men came (Matthew 2. 11), Mother and Child were in "the house", perhaps in the house proper.

Why was there such a crowd? If you assume that the census had to be taken on one single day, the question is answered easily enough. But, as I say, I find it difficult to believe red-tape had come to its own, *Augusto imperante*. If a census is taken house by house, as they are today, the whole thing must be done by midnight on one single night (I know a young lady who was born twenty-five minutes too late to qualify for a ration-book). But if you are registering by genealogy, things can be done on a more leisurely system. I am inclined to think it was a providential accident that Bethlehem—or perhaps one particular house in Bethlehem—was overcrowded on the night when God came to what was his own, and they who were his own gave him no welcome.

So the world was reborn. "She wrapped him in swaddling-clothes, and laid him in a manger."[1] When I first heard the story, I took it as a matter of course that our Lord was wrapped up in this uncomfortable fashion because his parents were too poor to buy baby-clothes. Nobody explained to me that it is an experience we have all passed through. And my authors encouraged me in the misconception for all the world as if they shared it. "*All meanly* wrapped in swathing bands, and in a manger laid." (St Cyprian had the same idea, probably owing to the use of the word *panni*, which means strips of cloth, but often tattered cloth.) And I used to imagine that the shepherds were to recognize our Lord, among all the babies of Bethlehem, because he was so poorly dressed. Actually, the swaddling-clothes served to identify him as quite recently born. It was only the manger, as far as we know, and the stable itself that marked him out as born in poverty.

Why were the shepherds staying up, all of them, all night, in a kind of mass-meeting? To be sure, in Arcadia the shepherds are always meeting and talking, but that is Arcadia. In real life, would they not be more likely to separate, and keep their flocks separate? Or, if they were together, would not one watch and the rest go to sleep? Mr Morton is full of answers to these questions. "The shepherds at Bethlehem were, no doubt, men keeping guard over a sacrificial flock from the well-known Migdal Eder, the Watch-tower of the Flock." And again, "Early one morning I saw an extraordinary sight not far from Bethlehem. Two shepherds had evidently spent the night with their flocks in a cave. The sheep were all mixed together, and the time had come for the shepherds to go in different directions. One of the shepherds stood some distance from the sheep and began to call. First one, then another, then four or five animals ran towards him; and so on till he had counted his whole flock." He calleth his own sheep by name—that was how they sorted them out. And no doubt they were together in some kind of communal fold, with its own appointed custodian; "to him the porter openeth" suggests that you sometimes left your flock under his care. But Mr Morton assures us that the Palestinian shepherd never leaves his flock "even when they are driven into a cave or a sheep-fold for the night". Of such were these shepherds,

[1] Luke 2. 7.

until a superior attraction conquered their principles. . . . Did they then "leave their flocks a-feeding in tempest, storm and wind"? Think of the wolves; these, surely, were not mere hirelings. No, they left them safe in a fold, with the porter as well as the dogs to look after them. Or perhaps, as Père Lagrange says, "they were encamped in tents; they were not sitting about on a hill side".

"An angel of the Lord stood by them."[1] I have always pictured that scene (doubtless under the influence of some forgotten Bible print) as if the angel stayed hovering in the air, after the manner of those Doré angels which distress the imagination by having wings, but apparently not using them. In fact, the angel stood by them; "came upon them" says the Jacobean Bible, perhaps rightly, for the Greek word is always used by St Luke of unexpected interruptions. Douai, however, is a safer guide when you want to understand the meaning of the angelic announcement. The good tidings of great joy were not—explicitly— for all people, but for all *the* people; that of the Jews, commonly as opposed to the Gentiles. And, as we know, the celestial hymn did not promise peace on earth, good-will to men, but peace on earth to men of good-will—probably, that is, to the men God approves of. No, it was an announcement made to Jews, of Jewish interest; it is only with the wise men that the Gentile world comes into the picture.

They came with haste—half an hour's journey, if tradition is right, climbing between six and seven hundred feet. How they found the Child is a curiosity of mine which my authors do not gratify. The wise men found the house because the star seemed to them to be directly over it; I suppose they had their own astrological principles for determining that. But the shepherds could only ask at dead of night, under open windows. Plainly they had providence on their side. Anyhow, they found their way to the cave, and there, according to our version, "understood of the word that had been spoken to them concerning this child".[2] This curiously meaningless phrase comes from an odd mistranslation in the Latin; in fact, they *made known* the angels' message. It was this added testimony to her Son's origin and destiny that our Lady treasured up, making conjecture of it in her heart.

But what I really want to know is, what happened to the shepherds afterwards? The wise men have their legend, but the shepherds go back to the homely obscurity from which they came. There were no shepherds, as far as we know, among the apostles, to match the fishermen. I expect they found their way all right; *nobis post hoc exilium ostende—* one wants the shepherds to complete the setting of that picture.

[1] Luke 2. 9.   [2] Luke 2. 17.

N

3

THE BIRTH OF OUR LORD[1]

CHRISTMAS is a return to our origins. We make a holiday of it, only
if we have the strength of mind to creep up the nursery stairs again,
and pretend that we never came down them. So I will not apologize,
on Christmas afternoon, for taking you back to the origins of our race;
to those nursery stories which form the preface to the oldest book in
the world, a book whose curtain goes up on a time when the world
was not. They are out of favour nowadays, those old stories from the
book of Genesis; we are half-ashamed of them, and do not like to be
seen taking them out and looking at them; so it was with our nursery
toys, when we had outgrown them. But, make what you will of those
stories, deprive them as you will of their authority by representing
them as a patchwork made up from older legends still, you cannot get
away, altogether, from the spell of those remembered phrases, so apt
to enshrine the primitive. There shall be no controversy; we will leave
out the story of creation and the story of Paradise; the door of that
fairyland shall be closed and the scientists mount guard over it with
their flaming swords. The phrase I want to recall to you is the first
utterance of fallen humanity; it is when Eve says, "I have gotten a man
from the Lord".[2]

In some forlorn cave, remote of access, fenced about from the wild
beasts, the first human mother gave birth to the first human child.
"Cain", she called him, the "acquisition"; she felt enriched. Sentence
of death might have been passed on herself and the partner of her disobedience; they had made shipwreck of their stupendous venture;
within a few years, for all they knew, human life would become
extinct on the planet, and it would be given back to the jungle and to
the white ants. But no, here was something saved from the wreck;
here was a fresh representative to whom the torch of humanity could
be handed on. "Unto us a child is born, unto us a man is given";
the raw material of that Christmas anthem rang through the primeval
forest, with a presage of our immortal hope.

Trace the line of Eve's posterity down, down through the uncharted
centuries, till the index finger of your observation quivers and stands

---

[1] A sermon broadcast on the B.B.C. Third Programme, 25 December 1950.
[2] Genesis 4. 1.

still at a point roughly nineteen hundred and fifty years ago. The same picture of Mother and Child is repeated; even the setting is unaltered, we are still in a cave. This time, the picture is a familiar one; thousands of artists have tried to make it their masterpiece; in a million churches, all over Christendom, the same pattern of Mother and Child is repeated, backed by a crude décor of brown paper and ivy-leaves. And our first thought is—perhaps the very sameness of this constant repetition has put it into our heads—our first thought is that this is just like any other human birth. If the Mother gazes down with rapt adoration at the Child, holds him forward, as if to attract our adoration too, is not that exactly what you see when you visit an ordinary human nursery? And of course we are right. The young mother who can say, with her first ancestress, "I have gotten a man from the Lord", does look upon it as a kind of theophany; this is a miracle; this particular thing has never happened before. And of course she is right. All that is visible here, that tiny body, has come from her; has come through her from the common stock-pot of matter that we can measure and analyse. Even the life that beats there—how can we be certain that it does not simply derive from that mysterious reservoir of life which so extends and reproduces itself? Was not Eve called the mother of all living? And yet we know that because this tiny thing is a human being, it is linked to an immortal soul, to whose cravings, as yet, it is powerless to give expression. This is indeed an acquisition, not to the mother or the father only, but the common treasure-house of the human race; a new thing has come into existence. Unto us a child is born, a body that came from us. Unto us a son is given, a soul that derives neither from father nor mother, but comes direct from God.

No, the first thing we have got to realize about Christmas, if we are to understand its message at all, is that this birth is just like any other human birth. We keep our birthdays, we visit the birth-places of great men, but birth, after all, is only a stage in a process. And the child who was born at Bethlehem had, for nine months, been carried in the womb at Nazareth, just like any other child; this is our guarantee that, although God, he was yet truly man. God did not deceive us by taking on the mere appearance of humanity, after the fashion of the old heathen fairy-stories, he *became* man; that was the leverage, if we may put it in very crude terms, through which the work of our redemption was effected. And, very curiously, this is one of the lessons which the Church found it particularly hard to teach. The early heretics were not people who denied our Lord's Godhead; almost without exception, they were people who denied his manhood. They could believe that

God came to earth; they could not believe that he was human enough to be born, or to die. That primitive heresy re-awoke in the Middle Ages, lasted up to the time of the Reformation and beyond it. Perhaps that is why the Middle Ages gave us the Christmas crib. As we kneel before the crib, the first thing we have got to get into our heads is just that, the human reality of it all; God is actually here, among his creatures. The ox and the ass are represented in the stable, not merely to emphasize the humility in which Jesus Christ came to earth, the poverty of his surroundings. No, they are meant to give us a comfortable sense of earthliness, almost of earthiness; on this first Christmas Day even the poor relations of the human family must be asked in, or the party would not be complete. Unto *us* a Child is born; it is not simply that God will come close to us, that he will stand at our side, to help us fight against the limitations which hamper us, Eve's children; he will become one of ourselves, become part of us.

But when we have said that, when we have said that it was just like any other human birth, we have to add, "Of course, it wasn't actually like any other birth that ever happened". Nor are we ashamed of the paradox; when we are tracing the history of God made man, our very terms of reference are paradoxical. This was like no other human birth, because the Mother in the cave, this time, was and remains a pure virgin. Of that truth, Christian thought never lost sight even for a moment, be the temptation what it might. Obviously, in the first ages the temptation must have been very strong. As we are reminding ourselves just now, the first heretics denied that Jesus Christ was truly man; it was only a phantom that was born—appeared to be born— of the Virgin Mary; that suffered—appeared to suffer—under Pontius Pilate. It would have been understandable enough, if orthodox Christian thought had recoiled to the other extreme; had soft-pedalled, if not actually abandoned, the doctrine of the miraculous birth, in its anxiety to insist that this was the human Son of a human Mother. But always Christian people had the instinct that your theology was safe when your opponents accused you of holding two doctrines that flatly contradicted one another. You were most likely to be right. They saw the Mother in the cave, but never did their steady view lose sight of the Virgin.

And so you take your second look at the Christmas crib, and realize that your first view was wrong; or rather, was wholly incomplete. When you first looked at it, it seemed such a beautiful picture of motherhood—that and nothing more. "I have gotten a man from the Lord"—it was the old cry of Eve, repeated, as if by race-memory, down the centuries. And now it had reached its crucial expression;

this particular cave at Bethlehem would be remembered as the birth-place of the greatest man who ever lived. And then . . . do you know what it is to go into a room, and gradually, not all at once, but gradu-ally, get the feeling that there is a secret about, and everybody in the room is in the secret except you? It is a joke, perhaps, which is being played on you; and you look about uneasily, trying to find the clue to what is wrong, and yet not liking to seem as if you suspected any-thing. There is something of that impression, don't you think, about our second look at the Christmas crib. Everybody is keeping so quiet; the shepherds seem to come in on tip-toe, the ass and the ox are just lying there, not feeding, the angels seem to be standing at attention, waiting for something to happen. And then you take another look at the centre of the group, and you notice at once what you ought to have noticed before. A mother? But this is only a girl! It's not just a question of age, it's a question of atmosphere; they are playing a trick on you, it's a girl dressed up, in childish make-believe, as a young mother. . . . And then you remember that there is no room, here, for make-believe. It is the mystery of the virgin birth.

Do not imagine that the Christian reverence for virginity is just a prudish running away from the facts of sex. If we pass over the facts of sex in silence, it is not because we think them disgusting, but because we think them too holy to be mentioned in common talk. If the Fathers of the Church, from the earliest times, insisted on the virginity of God's Mother, it was not because they wanted to pay her a compli-ment, by ascribing to her a well-known Christian virtue; rather, it was the other way about. They learned to reverence virginity because they had seen it in the Mother of God; because they had seen it in the stable of Bethlehem, and could not forget the experience. What they had seen there was an innocence which spoke to them of renewal. This other woman in the cave had brought them back to Paradise.

Christmas Day is a birthday just like any other; it is a birthday quite unlike any other; and no wonder, for it is the birthday of all of us. Go back for a moment to that first woman in the cave; when she cried out, "I have gotten a man from the Lord", it was *our* birthday in a sense. The long history of woman's child-bearing had begun; the process had been set in motion which was to give existence, all those centuries afterwards, to you and me. Eve, the mother of life; and yet, what thing was it she had given birth to, when she boasted that she had gotten a man? What was the acquisition she had won for us? She had borne the first man, and in doing so she had borne the first murderer. He came into the world to bring death, death to his own brother.

And that natural life which our first mother bequeathed to us is, after all, only a life in death; sons of Eve, we are brothers to Cain and Abel, the villain and the victim of the first human tragedy.

Now turn back to that other cave, that other woman; what acquisition is hers? "I have come", he tells us, "that they may have life."[1] The first-born among many brethren, St Paul calls him; our elder brother, who has brought us supernatural life. Under the old law, the first-born son belonged by right (like all first-fruits) to God; in theory, his life was forfeit; in theory, he died that the rest might live. Not in theory but in fact, the cardinal fact of history, the Child who was born at Bethlehem died that the rest of us might live. To St John, that is the lesson of the virgin birth. Jesus Christ came to us, not in the order of nature; it was not the men of his own race who benefited principally by his birth, "Those who were his own gave him no welcome; but all those who did welcome him, he empowered to become the children of God, all those who believe in his name; their birth came, not from human stock, not from nature's will or man's, but from God".[2] On Christmas Day a whole supernatural family came to birth; virgin-born, because regeneration has brought back to them their lost innocence.

I repeat, we make a holiday of Christmas only if we have the strength of mind to creep up the nursery stairs again, and pretend that we never came down them. And that is what we are doing when we pay our visit to the Christmas crib. We are going back to the nursery where life, supernatural life, first dawned for us; trying to recapture some breath of our own first innocence, as we look at the girl Mother, and the divine Infant, and the manger which was all the cradle he had. It is difficult, at first, to get acclimatized to its atmosphere; everything is so quiet, so secret; the world is so remote; you feel as if there were a conspiracy afoot to keep you out of it. But this is where you belong; you, too, have been born into the family of grace, and this is the cradle of it. Unto *us* a Child is born, to restore something of childhood, year by year, even to the most jaded, even to the most sophisticated, even to the most disillusioned of us.

[1] John 10. 10.   [2] John 1. 11-13.

4

"OSTENDE"[1]

THERE is nothing irreverent, I think, in comparing man's search for God to a game of hide-and-seek. A child's games with its father, all the skill and foresight on the one side, all the romance and excitement on the other! When you read in the Old Testament about almighty God making a covenant with men, your sense of the fitness of things is outraged; how is it possible, considering what he is, that he should make a bi-lateral treaty with us, involving reciprocal duties? But a father plays shop with his children, he with his own income, they with nothing but the pocket-money he allows them; and what complicated transactions take place, in make-believe! And so it is with this game of hide-and-seek, that goes on all through the centuries, that goes on in every man's life from the cradle to the grave.

Why is it that God, who so loves us, makes himself so distant from us, so difficult to find? Dare we say it?—it is part of the rules of the game. He will make himself difficult to find, so that when we do find him, the shock of triumph may be something unexampled in our experience. Why does man, whose heart is made for God, and cannot find rest until it finds rest in him, yet spend long days, long years of his life, may be, trying to run away from God, to avoid his scrutiny? Once more, it is part of the rules of the game; not that we should hide from him, but that we should be able to hide from him.

When the child hides from its father, the hiding-place may be fairly obvious, but the father can always make as if he didn't see. But when it is the father's turn, he always hides himself a little too well; children are always a little more stupid over their games than we expect them to be, pass and repass the place of concealment with unseeing eyes. It is part of the conventions, therefore, that the child does not start out on its search alone; hand in hand, along with it, goes the mother, ready to drop broad hints about the best places to look in; ready, in the last resort, to draw aside the curtain, to open the cupboard door, and reveal the thrilling secret. Almost always, the child's mother-wit has to be helped out by a mother's wits. . . .

And the book of Proverbs will give us a hint here. It describes the wisdom of God, under the figure of a woman, standing beside him

---

[1] A Christmas meditation published in *The Tablet*, 25 December 1948.

during his work of creation, planning how the mountains shall rise, how the rivers shall flow, how the ocean shall keep its appointed limits. Then, quite without warning, comes that extraordinary verse, "I (the divine Wisdom) was at his side, playing continually in his presence, playing in this world of his, because it is my delight to be with the sons of men".[1] Playing—there is no getting out of it, that is the only possible meaning of the word used in the Hebrew text. When man appears on the scene, that Wisdom which has hitherto been the majestic architect of creation becomes man's playmate; joins with him in the game. And what other game, than man's search for God, impossible but for the Wisdom God himself inspires! If he did not help us a little, we should have no chance; we are so outmatched, the game would be all on his side if he did not, somehow, help us a little.

In the history of our race, it was man first that hid himself from God. We know the story; Adam and his wife hid themselves among the trees of the garden. "The woman thou gavest me"—you gave her to be a help-meet, to look after me, to restrain me, and she has been no help here. No resource for Adam in the mother-wit of Mother Eve; she has only dragged him down, and cowers there beside him, ineffectively ambushed, to avoid the scrutiny of a God. Man began it; man issued the challenge; and thenceforward, through long centuries, he was like a frightened child feeling its way alone through the darkness, racked by a thousand causeless terrors, searching for the God who had left so many proofs of his presence, but remained always hidden from sight. "Show us the Father, and it is enough"[2]—yes, but the Wisdom God had bestowed on us was only a rushlight in the darkness, not a mother to draw aside the curtain and tell us, "See, he is here!"

And then, in the fullness of time, God changed his hiding-place. Suddenly, while all was quiet around, with the deep stillness of a winter night, he came and hid in a little country town, came and hid in a manger, came and hid in the form of man. Not quite so silently but he betrayed himself; just a movement among the stars, just the brush of angels' wings, was enough to raise the hue and cry among a few searchers, shepherd folk with their keen ears, stargazers with their sharp eyes. And so the hunt started afresh: Tell us, where is he born, the King of the Jews? The question, repeated to one passer-by after another, begins to sound like the chorus of some children's game. What, this tumble-down house in a back street, this draughty cellar underneath it —it's no good looking in there! He wouldn't hide in a place like that! And then the door opens, and a woman stands there, a finger pressed

<hr />

[1] Proverbs 8. 30-31.   [2] John 14.8.

to her lips; our Mother, come out to help in the search. "Yes, he's in there; but come in quietly; he's asleep." The God who does not dwell in temples made with hands, asleep in there! The God who neither sleeps nor slumbers, watching over Israel, in there asleep!

Et Jesum, benedictum fructum ventris, tui ostende.[1]

5

THE SHEPHERDS AT THE CRIB[2]

IT is becoming fashionable to trace patterns in the narrative of Holy Scripture; nor are we of the Old Guard loth to take a hand in it, always on the understanding that it was divine Providence, not the ingenuity of the sacred writer, that devised those patterns in the first instance. That shepherds and shepherding weave such a pattern through both Testaments, nobody will be inclined to dispute; they fill a whole column in Cruden, while "herdmen" can only muster half a dozen references by contrast. Jacob meeting Rachel at the well; Jacob's experiment—let us hope it was an allegory—in eugenics; Moses feeding the flock of his father-in-law, when he came across the burning bush; David leaving his sheep in the wilderness, to have a glimpse of the battle; Ezechiel reprimanding the Jewish leaders under the image of unfaithful shepherds, who left the flock untended, unfed, undoctored; Zachary's mysterious allusion to the rival shepherds, and the wounds in the clasped hands—at every turn the pastoral metaphor greets you. It gives you no sense of surprise, when you turn the Gospel pages, and read about the hundredth sheep that was lost, about the good Shepherd who calls his own sheep by name, about St Peter's pastoral commission; when St Paul reminds the presbyters to watch over the flock Christ bought with his blood, or St Peter writes about the chief Shepherd, who is the Shepherd of souls.

Christian tradition took over, naturally enough, the same symbolism. We may still see the representation of the good Shepherd in the Catacombs, and the *Pastor* of Hermas enjoyed such early credit that it narrowly escaped inclusion among the books of inspired Scripture.

[1] From the *Salve Regina*.
[2] A Christmas meditation published in *The Tablet*, 20 December 1952.

The word "pastoral" acquired a new and gracious significance, designating the outward relations of the clergy. The shepherd's life symbolizes, and has often been the preparation for, a life devoted to the care of souls.

The shepherd's career is one of solitude; poor David has to miss all the excitement of the prophet's arrival, because he is the fag of the family, and is out minding the sheep. The sheep graze away from the haunts of men, on the short grass of the wilderness. And solitude, notoriously, is the seed-ground of revelation; the call came to Moses like that, came to Amos, "I was but tending sheep when the Lord took me into his service";[1] John Damascene gives you the same picture of St Joachim. The shepherd lives hard, and very close to nature; "burning heat by day, and biting frost by nights, till my eyelids lost the power of sleep—thus it was (says Jacob) that I spent twenty years in thy service". He must be supposed to learn the trick of incessant watchfulness, with all the privations it entails—no bad preparation for the Christian ministry. And he will learn, at the same time, a sense of responsibility; he takes command of the flock, but not in his own name. No employer wants men like those shepherds of Israel who fed themselves instead of the flock; nor even men who will stick to the strict letter of their contract, making good any ordinary damage but drawing the line at wolves; the shepherd's ideal is service without ownership. Such qualities, we must suppose, belonged to the shepherds of Bethlehem, who gathered round the crib on Christmas Day—love of solitude, patient vigilance, a strong sense of responsibility in a position of trust.

Or not? Use the language of literary criticism, and all at once the word "pastoral" has taken on a startlingly different colour. Pastoral theology and pastoral poetry, what have they in common except, perhaps, a note of simplicity? Not that classical antiquity was unfamiliar with the kind of symbolism we have been discussing; a king in Homer was the shepherd of his people, and that "shepherd properly so called" whom we meet in the first book of the *Republic* has something of a New Testament quality. But in the decadent days of the third century B.C., in the relaxing airs of Sicily, Theocritus gave birth to a new literary tradition, destined to colour the whole mind of Europe. Shepherds (and *a fortiori* shepherdesses) were people who lived in delightful simplicity, far from the pomp of courts and the alarms of war. They lay about in the shade, regaling one another with tunes on the Pan-pipe, and making love to one another with more fervour than constancy. These Arcadian shepherds by no means display the qualities catalogued above.

[1] Amos 7. 14.

Solitude? They were for ever chattering; and when you thought you were alone, there was Galatea throwing apples at you, and making tracks for the willows after taking good care that you saw her. Vigilance? You were ready to act as judge in a piping contest when you knew perfectly well that the lambs ought to have been folded by now. Responsibility? You did not gravely resent the suggestion that you milked your master's goats on your own account. Virgil caught up the theme for the Augustans, Spenser for the Elizabethans; it flowed over into the art of Watteau and Fragonard, and came to a tragic end with Marie Antoinette. Arcady, tenanted by shepherds, was synonymous with a return of the Golden Age, with the enjoyment, here on earth, of uninterrupted happiness.

To which pattern should we cut our figures for the Christmas crib? Go to some modern representation of it, with pretensions to accuracy, and your shepherd will be an old man in a burnous, gnarled and weather-beaten, blowing on his nails as he offers a lamb to the Lamb of God. Amos, you would think, or Zachary, carved from the stern granite of the Old Testament. Kneel before one of those baroque panoramas, imported long since from Naples or Venice, and you will identify your shepherd among a crowd of irrelevant onlookers; he is a mere boy, in doublet and hose, with bagpipes over his arm; if any sheep came in with him, he has forgotten about them. Tityrus it is, beyond a doubt; his eyes are wide with wonder: *"Deus, deus ille, Menalca!"*[1]—the old tag will serve. But he has not forgotten his music; indeed, he looks ready to burst into a song, probably beginning with the word "Ut-hoy". Which of the two figures are we to choose? No hope of matching them in combination.

No question of it, if we would go in for archaeological correctness, our shepherd must be a Jew. "To you and to all the people" was what the angel said, not "to all people"; we Gentiles do not really come upon the scene before the Epiphany. But when our Lord came, there had to be a Preparation of the Gentiles, as well as a Preparation of the Jews; and it reaches a point, as we all know, in Virgil's fourth eclogue. Let us have Tityrus there, fresh from Arcady; he will help us to pretend that the Age of Innocence really has come again, on such a night. Tomorrow we shall be reminded that we are still in a fallen world; the *priscae vestigia fraudis* are still with us; but just for tonight let us pretend that the crib is a new Ark—*altera quae vehat Argo*—to float us above the inundation. Just for tonight, let there be no talk of vigilance or of victims; only calm, and renewed hope, and the magic airs of Arcady.

[1] Virgil, Eclogue V, 64.

6

THE EFFECT OF CHRISTMAS[1]

WHAT would the world be like, if Christmas hadn't happened?
If you put that question as a theological question, obviously
we have no means of answering it. We may guess, indeed, that God
in his great mercy would not have allowed the human race to go on
in a state of obstinate rebellion; he would have devised some other
means for counteracting the effects of Adam's fault. But we cannot
pretend to guess what means he would have used; theology is difficult
enough as it is, without puzzling our heads over imaginary difficulties.
So when I ask the question, "What would the world be like if Christmas
hadn't happened?", I must be understood as referring to the world of
our common experience; the sort of way we live, the sort of way we
treat one another, the sort of behaviour we expect of one another.
How would everything be different, in this year 1953, if we had no
year One to date it from—if the world were still waiting to be redeemed? If the picture of a dark stable on a snowy night, a working
man and his wife, and a Baby lying in the straw among the beasts
meant nothing to us?

We always think, nowadays, in terms of politics; so let us ask, first
of all, what difference Christmas has made to our social institutions.
A great change has taken place, two thousand years past, in our notions
of justice, freedom, and human kindness which we vaguely describe
as "progress"; how much of all that really springs from, really took its
main impetus from, the teaching of Christ? St Paul, in that casual,
incidental manner of his, gives you a blue-print of what the Christian
idea ought to do in the way of altering our human values. He writes to
the Galatians, "All you who have been baptized in Christ's name have
put on the person of Christ; no more Jew or Gentile, no more slave and
freeman, no more male and female, you are all one person in Jesus
Christ".[2] In so far as the Gospel succeeded in imposing itself on the
pagan world which surrounded it, the barrier which divided race from
race, nation from nation, was due to disappear. And at the same time
the dignity of human nature would be asserted; all men would stand
on the same footing, instead of being divided up into two classes, a class
of rulers and a class of slaves. And woman (St Paul tells us elsewhere),
although she was the last to be created and the first to fall into sin, is

---

[1] A sermon broadcast on the B.B.C. Home Programme, 29 December 1953.
[2] Galatians 3. 27-28.

to find her salvation in the great Child-bearing;[2] after the events of Christmas Day, she can never be thought of as a mere chattel for man's use; she is a free being, apt for partnership with man.

I suppose if a pagan of St Paul's time could come back to earth, almost the first thing that would strike him about our modern civilization would be the disappearance of slavery. Whatever inequalities there still are in human society, however much human liberty is still abridged in some countries, it is no longer possible for one man to belong to another, to be beaten or maimed or killed at his pleasure. St Paul, to be sure, did not preach a revolt of slaves against their masters; he told them to obey. The pagan world in which they lived was, to the first Christians, a hostile environment from which they must do their best to escape, not a society which they had to permeate and reform. Our Lord's promise that he would return in judgment seemed to them, probably, as if it were due to be fulfilled almost at once; it was not for them to put things to rights in a world-order which was soon to be dissolved. It was only by slow degrees, and with notable set-backs, that St Paul's vision of "no more slave and freeman" came on to the statute-book. Even in the eighteenth century, when emancipation was already in the air, so great a Christian as George Whitefield could own slaves, and could defend the system. But as and when the reform came about, it was the Christian tradition that moved men's consciences. At the back of their minds was the picture of a cold stable in the darkness of midnight, and God taking upon himself the nature of a slave for our sakes.

When the shepherds go back to their flocks, we have not finished with the story of Christmas. Their place at the crib is taken by the three wise men from the east; and Christian piety has always emphasized one significant point about their coming. The birth of a Saviour was not for the Jewish people only, it was for the whole world; all mankind became brothers when God became man. Always, in defiance of the probabilities, one of the three kinds is represented as a native African; there should be no doubt that the Church was world-wide. The brotherhood of man—could the Christian religion ever have achieved it? Will it ever be achieved? At least let it be said that Christendom has never abandoned that idea, has fought for it, time and again, in face of man's obstinate tendency towards nationalism. The fact of international brotherhood seems as far off from us as ever; but God forgive us, if among Christian people the will is not there.

And now for St Paul's third point, the position of women. Was he

[2] 1 Timothy 2. 13-15.

right in thinking that the great Child-bearing would make a difference here? Let me be allowed to cite a witness who will not be accused of any tenderness for Christian sentiment. Lecky, in his *History of Rationalism*, writes as follows: "The world is governed by its ideals, and seldom or never has there been one which has exercised a more salutary influence than the medieval conception of the blessed Virgin. For the first time woman was elevated to her rightful position, and the sanctity of weakness was recognized as well as the sanctity of sorrow. No longer the slave or toy of man, no longer associated only with ideas of degradation and sensuality, woman rose, in the person of the Virgin Mother, into a new sphere, and became the object of a reverential homage of which antiquity had no conception." No Christian, I think, would have anything to add to such testimony as that.

We have been speaking of what Christmas has meant to humanity in the gross, the mark which it has left on the society in which we live. That isn't everything. We want to know what mark it has left on individual human lives; man for man, how do we compare with people who lived two thousand years ago, and had no Christmas to lend them inspiration? Once again, we are not going to talk theology; we are not going to discuss the Christian faith or the Christian hope as such. But are there any personal qualities which the old pagans didn't know about or didn't care about much, which we value today? Qualities we are not, perhaps, conscious of possessing; but we would like to possess them, and we admire them as seen in others, because they remind us of Christmas Day?

I think you can say that there are three qualities, I won't say which have been made known to us, but which show up in a new light, as the result of the Christian revelation: humility, charity, and purity. They are all words derived from the Latin; but if a Roman of Julius Caesar's time could come back to earth, I don't think we could mention them to him without finding ourselves at cross purposes.

Humility—if you look up that word in the Latin dictionary, you will get a surprise. You will find that it means "lowness, meanness, insignificance, littleness of mind, baseness, abjectness", and it has no other sense until you come on to the Christian authors. And yet how instinctively we recognize the worth of it today, even those of us who wouldn't call ourselves in any sense Christians! To be sure, there are all sorts of inferior substitutes for it which owe little or nothing to the influence of Bethlehem; there is the mock modesty which prompts us to underrate our own achievements simply as a matter of good manners; we don't want to make a bad impression of boastfulness on the people we meet. There is the calculating, affected humility of Uriah Heep; you demean yourself before important people because you know which side your bread is buttered. But real humility, how it shines when it catches the light! The man who can take an affront and feel it is no more than he deserves; who takes it for granted that his successful rival was the better candidate; who can work to other men's plans when they run contrary to his own advice, the advice which was not asked for, or went unregarded—how we admire such a man, even when we think that he carries his good qualities to a fault! And the reason for our admiration—the historical reason for our admiration —is because we have been told about a God who for us men and for our salvation came down from heaven, and took upon himself the nature of a slave for our sakes.

And charity—if you look that up in the Latin dictionary, you find that it means affection for your family or your close friends. How should it mean anything more, to people who hadn't read the parable of the good Samaritan? Once again, not everything that is done in the name of charity is real charity. There is the ostentatiousness which likes to see its name on a subscription-list; there is the love of interference which is ever eager to manage other people's lives for them. But, when you have made all allowances for that, charity towards complete strangers has become a habit with us. It has filled the world with hospitals and orphanages and almshouses, all because of Bethlehem; there was no name for such things before Jesus Christ came. Because Jesus Christ came to redeem us when we were strangers who had no claim on him, brought redemption to everybody far and near, we too, even you and I, are ashamed to button up our pockets.

And then—purity. The Romans, of course, use the word often enough, but I don't think they meant any more by it than cleanness of body; no one seems to have bothered much about purity of mind. And yet our Lord tells us that all sins, even the sins of sense, take their origin in the mind. How hard it is, nowadays, to persuade people that there is such a thing as purity! They get it mixed up with mere ignorance about sex; or with prudery, that loves the sensation of being shocked; or with the morbid horror of sex which is found, sometimes, in ill-adjusted natures. But there is such a thing as real purity, which sees the facts of life as they are, and has too much sense of the rich, living thing marriage is, of the bright, delicate thing virginity is, to sully either with brooding thoughts, or with sniggering jocularity. That, too, we owe to Bethlehem; to the memory of that virgin motherhood which saved us all.

All that we owe to Christmas. Whatever difference it may have made in our behaviour, as compared with that of our pagan forefathers, it has altered the standards of behaviour which we reverence and desire. I have not attempted to prove that this change is a change for the better; nor yet that it is something we can never go back on. In the last few years, a new word has been added to the English vocabulary; the word "post-Christian". Those who make use of it mean to imply that there is, after all, nothing final about the Christian culture which has served us these last nineteen centuries—it may be only a phase, a passing phase, in the development of human thought. Well, they have a right to their opinion. Only, let us not flatter ourselves with the expectation that the world is going to find a new religion to replace it. In proportion as the world grows weary of its Christian hope, the alternative is materialism, of a type with which we are already familiar—that and nothing else. Its experience of Christianity has been like a great love, the love of a lifetime, never to be repeated; we are immunized against the supernatural. No new voice which speaks to us in the name of religion will have any appeal for us, if it does not bring us back to the stable at Bethlehem—there to humble our pride, and enlarge our charity, and deepen our sense of reverence with the sight of a dazzling purity.

7

THE DIVINE NAME[1]

Everything in heaven and on earth must bend the knee before the name of Jesus.—Philippians 2. 10.

"WHAT'S in a name?" the poet asks:[2] but when he has said that, we know that he hasn't said everything. There is, somehow, a sort of magic about names; it does not come as a surprise, when St Paul tells us that the name of Jesus is high above every name:[3] or when hymns of the holy Name, litanies of the holy Name, figure in the devotional life of Christendom. In antiquity, a kind of superstition about the use of the right name is part of man's approach to the super-

---

[1] A sermon broadcast from St Augustine's Church, High Wycombe, on 26 August 1956.
[2] Shakespeare, *Romeo and Juliet*.   [3] Philippians 2. 10.

natural. The Greeks and Romans, when they said their prayers, would address some god or goddess by a whole string of alternative titles, for fear of missing out the particular title which would be appropriate, and therefore operative, on this particular occasion. That is why our Lord tells us not to "use many phrases, like the heathens";[1] we are to begin simply, "Our Father, who art in heaven", and leave it at that.

The Jewish people had no such childish hesitations. But for them, too, the divine Name was a thing of mastery and of mystery—the name revealed to Moses at the burning bush, HE WHO IS. A thing of mastery; the name of God and the power of God were intimately connected in their minds; "our help", they told themselves, "is in the name of the Lord",[2] as if somehow those two syllables were a talisman, ensuring them against defeat. And a thing of mystery; "the great God", they would say, "whose habitation is eternity, whose name is holy".[3] And our blessed Lady herself, true to the instinct of her race, would not thank God for the privileges he had showered on her without making the same acknowledgment: "He whose name is holy has wrought for me his wonders."[4] The divine Name, a thing to be kept apart, to be mentioned in whispers; so influential was it, so expressive of the very being of God.

To the Christians of the first age, the name of Jesus could have no such mysterious associations. It was a name in common use, the Greek equivalent of Josue; St Paul had a friend called Jesus who was with him when he was a prisoner at Rome. From the first, it was recognized as a name of mastery; we even hear of magicians at Ephesus trying to exorcize a victim of diabolical possession, with the formula, "I conjure you in the name of Jesus, the name that is preached by Paul".[5] But the name did not often stand in isolation; much more commonly, the New Testament authors refer to our Lord under his full title of "Jesus Christ"; and liturgy, as we know, has preserved that tradition; nor does either word, in the writings of the Fathers, seem to be thought of as more evocative than the other. And then suddenly, in the Middle Ages, something happens: preachers like St Bernard and St Bernardine of Siena begin to single out the holy name of Jesus for special veneration. But observe that their instinct is not the instinct of the primitive Church; they no longer approach the subject with a sense of awe, but with a sense of intimacy. The holy Name is no longer something that terrifies them, but something that makes them feel at home.

---

[1] Matthew 6. 7.   [2] Psalm 123. 8.   [3] Isaias 57. 15.
[4] Luke 1. 49.   [5] Acts 19. 13.

You see, the use of a personal name has a fresh kind of magic about it, which we didn't mention just now; it creates familiarity. How decisively it marks a stage, even in a casual friendship, when two people begin, without effort and without embarrassment, to call one another by their Christian names! And when we fall in love, and all our experience takes on a sharper edge, and little things mean much to us, there is one Christian name in the world which casts a spell over eye or ear when we see it written on the page of a book, or overhear it mentioned in conversation; we are thrilled by the mere encounter of it. And it was with this sense of personal romance that people like St Bernard invested the holy name of Jesus. "Nor voice can sing, nor heart can frame, Nor can the memory find, A sweeter sound than thy blest name. . . ." The personal name evokes, in a special way, the personality of its wearer. And it is no longer to us, as it was to the Jews, a name of unapproachable majesty—"no name in all the world so terrible". It produces in us a sudden lightening of the heart, because we are in love.

Curiously, you find the same thing about the Christianity which was separated from us by the Reformation. In the Book of Common Prayer, and in the writings of those Anglican divines whose piety was nourished upon the Book of Common Prayer, you don't find the name of Jesus singled out for special veneration; you don't find it even in a more popular work like the *Pilgrim's Progress*. It was the Evangelical movement which began with the Wesleys, two centuries after the Reformation, that restored the balance. "How sweet the name of Jesus sounds in a believer's ear"—that hymn was written by John Newton, the friend of Cowper. The Evangelical Movement, which has done so much to form the character of English religion, would be unrecognizable without that tender devotion towards the person of our Lord which finds its natural expression in the use of his human name.

But we are sometimes asked—indeed, we may sometimes be tempted to ask ourselves—whether this devotion to the holy Name is altogether a healthy development. It has been criticized by non-Christians; you will remember Thomas Huxley's indignant outburst: "The power that made the stars and the tiger to be called by a pet name!" And Christians, too, have had their doubts about it. After all, isn't there something presumptuous about isolating the humanness of our Lord Jesus Christ in this way, and treating him as if he were a friend sitting in the room with you, who would look up at the sound of his name? True, he is everywhere present, but he is present as God—the God who created us, the God who will judge us. Have we a right to leave all that majesty of his out of account, and treat him with familiarity, instead of falling down at his feet?

We have just read from the *Imitation of Christ*, a work generally recognized as safe spirituality, both by Catholics and their neighbours. In the second book of it, you will find the holy Name standing by itself fifty times in the course of some thirty pages; you will find a whole chapter about what the author calls "familiar friendship with Jesus". There are souls—that is the long and the short of it—there are souls whose characteristic approach to the unseen is personal romance, with our Incarnate Lord for its object; so real to them, that the very mention of his name sets them off day-dreaming into eternity. You will find nothing like it in any other religion; you may take Mahomet for your prophet, Buddha for your teacher—only Jesus invites you to be his friend. This attitude is one which the Church does not impose on us; that is not her way; but she sanctions it for us, when she encourages devotion to the holy Name. And I think she means us to envy such people, not to criticize them: the people who never lose their childhood's instinct of turning to Jesus Christ as a Friend close at hand. It is not inconsistent with great gifts of the mind; it is not obscured by heavy responsibilities, and arduous labours. It shone out, I think, in that churchman who has just been laid to rest, mourned by all the Catholics of the English-speaking world: a great leader, a great administrator, but above all, a great lover of Jesus Christ. May the soul of Bernard, Cardinal Griffin, through the mercy of God rest in peace.

For souls like this, it is as if the Resurrection had happened, but not the Ascension; still he stands beside them in the garden, and calls them by the way; still, as they sit at table, he comes to them, breaking through the closed barriers of the centuries; still, on the mountain side, they hear his voice asking, "Do you love me?"

What's in a name? Just that much; a name which was as common as yours or mine is, nineteen hundred years ago.

8

THE AGONY OF OUR LORD

*I will not now speak much with you; for the prince of this world cometh, and in me he hath not anything. But that the world may know that I love the Father, and as the Father hath given me commandment, so do I. Arise, let us go hence.—*John 14. 30.

S⊤ LUKE, in concluding his description of our Lord's temptation, uses a phrase which he does nothing to explain elsewhere. "All the temptation being ended", he writes, "the devil departed from him for a time."[1] For a time—that means that the Devil came back; when did he come back? The explanation, surely, is given us not by St Luke, but by St John, in the words I have just quoted. After the last supper, our Lord rises and goes to the garden of Gethsemani; and his explanation of this action is, he will not say much more just then, because the prince of this world is coming; he is pleading, it seems, an appointment. Some commentators try to explain "the prince of this world" as referring to Judas; but it is difficult to see what, in that case, is the application of the words, "in me he hath not anything". Our Lord was going out to meet, not merely Judas, but Judas' master; that old enemy of his who "has nothing in me" in the sense that he can find no echo to his whispered suggestions of evil. "Watch and pray, lest ye enter into temptation"[2]—that was said because, in that moon-lit garden, the spirits of evil were abroad. After the third temptation, angels came to our Lord and ministered to him; during his Agony, there appeared to him an angel from heaven, comforting him—we do not read anywhere else of such angelic ministry. Is it not clear, then, that there was a fourth temptation, which came not at the beginning but at the end of our Lord's ministry, on the very eve of his death? Let us consider that fourth temptation in its turn.

Our Lord's Agony, like his temptation in the wilderness, is difficult to understand, and for the same reasons. What reality could there be, we are inclined to ask, in a struggle at the end of which our Lord's human will formed the resolve to die, if from the first that human will was confirmed in goodness, so that any deflection of it from the will of his heavenly Father was unthinkable? Much can be said to weaken the force of that old difficulty; but when all has been said, we have

[1] Luke 4. 13.   [2] Matthew 26. 41.

reached no complete explanation; we must be content to acknowledge the presence of mystery, where God made man, made perfect man, consents to undergo for us the battle of his soul. Only this is clear, that as in the wilderness the Devil had power to work on his mind by external suggestion, so in the garden he had power to work on his mind by an internal suggestion; and that suggestion was, that he could escape, if he would, the ordeal of his Passion.

It would have been possible to do so, not only by supernatural but by natural means. There was no reason why our Lord should have stayed in Jerusalem that one night of the week, instead of going out to sleep at Bethany. There was no reason why, having gone unmolested as far as Gethsemani, he should not have gone further, and hidden himself from his pursuers under cover of darkness. No reason, I mean, which made it physically impossible for him to do so; he did not do so. because he had a motive for acting otherwise. *Oblatus est quia ipse voluit*, he was offered because he willed it; from first to last the story of our Lord's Passion is the story of a man who was resolved to die. He stood his ground; and not only that, but, as if to show that he was rejecting the alternative of flight, he even made a gesture of self-defence. He encouraged Peter to take two swords with him, and did not even forbid the use of them till the first blow had been struck; why was that? Surely for the same reason that he would not disown, in Pilate's judg-ment-hall, the title of King, though it was evident that such a claim was the one thing which would possibly induce Pilate to condemn him. He claimed a kingdom, though it were not of this world; and in defence of that kingdom he allowed one blow to be struck, as a kind of token resistance. He had come to bring a sword on the earth; he was issuing a challenge to all its institutions, to its kings and its govern-ments. He would not, therefore, be content to stand his ground; he would make a gesture of resistance, lest he should be acquitted as a harmless creature who could be allowed to go free. He was not that; he was the world's enemy, and the world should know it.

When our Lord knelt in Gethsemani, and the sweat poured from him, index of the struggle within, like the spray that rises when the force of the tempest beats against an immovable rock—what was it urged him, in that hour, to escape from it all, to put away the cup of his Passion? Merely the love of life which, human creatures as we are, beats so strong in all of us? No doubt in him, as in all of us, nature recoiled at the prospect of dissolution; who shall say how far that clinging to life is mental, how far merely physical? At any rate, he was completely man; and he would not be exempt from any pull of nature that had not sin in it. But it is well to remember that there were other motives, less self-regarding and (we cannot but suspect) more powerful, which contributed to his reluctance. If he was to die, he was to die through the treachery of a friend, the familiar friend whom he trusted, who had eaten bread with him but a few hours before. If he was to die, it meant that he must die rejected by his own people, the people whom he had so often striven to gather, as a hen gathers her chickens under her wings, and they would not. To avert that double tragedy, the tragedy of Judas and the tragedy of the Jewish people, would he not be justified—so Satan will have whispered to him during his Agony—in taking refuge under the shadow of the olive trees before it was too late; setting out, before it was too late, on that short journey which would bring him within the hour to the friendly lights of Bethany? All that, surely, he had to go through as part of his conflict; and if his superior will decided in favour of remaining at his post, it was because in conformity with the divine will he had to be loyal to his mission at all costs. He had come into the world, so he told Pilate, to bear witness to the truth. And truth has a right to be told; that is its nature; it has that compelling power over minds. Though Judas and the chief priests might make it the opportunity for sealing their own damnation, he must remain where he was.

We have considered, under the heading of the second temptation, how the Church is sometimes criticized for her want of courage, because she does not seek a direct issue with the tyrannical rulers of the modern age; force a conflict with them by forbidding their Catholic subjects to take any part as citizens in states so misgoverned. Curiously, another charge is often launched against the Church, which is exactly the opposite; and it is often launched by the same people. That charge is, that the Church is always interfering in secular matters which are beyond her province. If that is not so, men ask us, how is it that she is continually getting into trouble with the secular power, all over Europe, all over the world? Surely it cannot be an accident that your Church is always reckoned as a political force, whereas other religious bodies are allowed to go their own way, unmolested by the civil authorities? To be sure, that charge has not been brought against us so confidently of late, since the Orthodox clergy were singled out for persecution in Russia, and the Lutherans in Germany. But it is still brought against us, even in our own country: "Why cannot you be content to be a purely spiritual body? Why is it that you always interfere?"

Now, this accusation is in great measure unjustified; but it would be a long business to examine, in full, a favourite thesis of anti-clericalism.

It is true in any case, and we are the first to admit it, that it is not always easy to delimit the exact provinces of the secular and the ecclesiastical power; nor are we prepared to trust the secular power with the demarcation of them. And it is true that the Church could live much more quietly, avoid an infinity of clashes and persecutions, if she would consent to abate her claim on one or two points, constant sources of friction with unsympathetic governments. If only we would be content, for example, to hand over the teaching of children to the State, so far as their general education is concerned, and instil religious knowledge into them somehow else, not in school buildings, not in school hours! If only the Church would be content to have her own laws about marriage and various moral questions, for her own loyal adherents, and not expect them to be adopted as the laws of the country! If only she would keep out of the way, live her own life and let other people live theirs! What a difference it would make to the peace of the world!

On such points as these, it is well known, the Church is prepared to make the best of the situation, if an unfriendly state resists her influence; but always it is under protest. She believes that she has inherited from her divine Master a commission to act as the teacher and guardian of a moral order; she is a city set on a hill, and her light must not be hidden under a bushel. She could purchase for herself an inglorious peace by shutting herself up in the sacristy; but that is not how she interprets her commission. Nor is it only that she could purchase peace for herself; she could, humanly speaking, prevent many blasphemies and even formal apostasies, if she would sit quiet and let the politicians have their own way. Is she justified, we feel inclined to ask, in going out of her way to arouse prejudice by sticking so obstinately to her rights, when that involves peril to the immortal souls of her less docile subjects, who fall away from her membership and give up the practice of religion because they cannot live at peace with her? She knows that; it is part of the sacrifice she has to make; as it was part of our Lord's sacrifice, when he knelt there in the garden, to see Judas and Caiphas losing their souls because of him. But for her, too, truth is truth, and has a right to be told. She cannot alter the conditions of her witness.

The temptations of our Lord are the temptations of his servants individually. We Catholics, like the Church, are called upon to bear witness to our faith; we too are forbidden to hide our light under a bushel. You see, the Christian's life is not meant to be a comfortable one. And part of the disability which belongs to our position as Christians is this—that we live in a world which is very far indeed from understanding our religion, and very far indeed from liking what it understands of it. That means conflict; not in the sense of noisy argument, or bitter remarks passed on both sides, but a permanent want of touch, want of sympathy, between us and our neighbours; as Catholics, we are ugly ducklings in Protestant England, and it is no use trying to disguise it. There is, then, a fresh temptation to worldliness which we have to face, in addition to the others we have been speaking of; I mean the temptation to lie low about it as far as possible, run away from the subject of religion when it crops up in conversation, talk about the Church in a rather detached and dispassionate way, as if we only half belonged to it. I do not say there is anything positively sinful in that attitude; only, it is running away from the cross.

Don't, please, imagine me to be suggesting that we ought all to go about roped with Lourdes medals and badges, boring our friends with long accounts of Catholic services and Catholic preachers, and leaving a C.T.S. tract in the hall whenever we go out to afternoon tea. Very little good is done, probably, whatever your denomination may be, by giving your friends the impression that you are (what one has to call) professionally religious. There are people a little like that, and I don't want to say a word to encourage them to further efforts. But with most of us it is rather the other way round. We suffer from a natural tendency to human respect, feel shy when our religion is mentioned; if we are caught going to church on a week-day we pretend we were going to the hairdresser; if we are fasting we put it down to slimming, and so on. Now, in matters of that kind it is very difficult to give any general advice; you have to know the person you are dealing with and the Protestant friends of the person you are dealing with before you can advise about what is generally known as "shoving religion down people's throats". And of course it is a problem in social tact which continually arises; arises every day almost in certain households, where husband and wife belong to different religions. You promised, when you married, that you would neglect no reasonable opportunity of securing the other party's conversion; you feel scrupulous, sometimes, about whether you are not doing too much. Obviously, there, no general rule is possible.

But there is one thing we can all do, according as God has given us the brains for it—know our religion. As a matter of fact, I am afraid there are certain Catholics who almost make a point of not knowing more about their religion than they can help, for fear of being called upon to defend curious doctrines or explain curious practices, and being made to feel fools over it. That is running away from your Cross. The whole Church of God, you see, is a Catholic Evidence Guild in a sense; we are not meant, all of us, to get up at street corners and explain the faith to the casual passer-by; but we are all meant to be able to give a reasonable account of it, when Protestants misrepresent it or when they ask us questions about it with a genuine desire to learn. People always complain, young people specially, that they were not taught Christian doctrine at school. It would be more modest as well as more accurate to say that they did not learn Christian doctrine at school. But if that is the fact, whoever was in fault, it is high time that they began to learn something about their religion now. There are plenty of books, plenty of reviews, which will help you to bring your knowledge of religion up to the same level as your knowledge on general subjects, to become a really instructed Catholic.

It is so easy to get a name for broad-mindedness and good-fellowship by setting out to be a Catholic with a difference, half-agreeing with all the prejudices of your Protestant friends, making out that you are really paying rather a compliment to our holy religion by belonging to it; you who take it all so very calmly, so far removed from bigotry or fanaticism. But that is not the right way to be a Catholic. The right way to be a Catholic is to feel yourself, all the time, a member of the Church Militant, a limb, living with the life of the whole, sharing its well-being and its discomforts, belonging to it, not talking as if it belonged to you. The right way to be a Catholic is to be associated with the essential activity of the Church, through prayer for the triumph of the truth and the conversion of sinners; as our Lord was when he kept his last appointment in Gethsemani, tempted, once more, by the prince of the powers of darkness.

The prayer which seems most appropriate to what I have been trying to say to you is the prayer which forms the ninth chapter in the fourth book of the *Imitation of Christ*. Here it is, in part:

"Lord, with sincere purpose of heart I offer myself to you now, to be your servant for ever, always in attendance on you, a continual sacrifice made in your honour. Me too accept, when you accept this sacred offering of your own Body, that cost you so much; I make it to you now, in the presence of your Angels, who stand about me all unseen.

"Lord, I offer you all the sins and faults I have committed in your sight, and in the sight of your holy Angels, from the first day when sin I could, right up to this hour. I offer them on this altar of atonement, to be set alight and burned to nothing, all of them, in the fire of your love. And I offer you all that is good in me, so little of it and so imperfect, asking you to patch it together and make it holy; asking you to take pleasure in it and make it welcome and lead it on to something better; asking you to bring me at last to a happy and holy end, even a midget creature, lazy and useless, such as I am.

"And I offer to you the earnest prayers of good people everywhere; the needs of parent and friend, of brother and sister, of all I love. For those, too, I would pray most heartily and make amends, that have caused me any hurt or pain, or spoken ill of me; and for all those whom any word or deed of mine, willingly or unwillingly, has pained, put out, injured, or led astray; to all alike pardon the sin, pardon the wrong done to our fellow men. Have mercy on us, Lord, and make us worthy to have the using of your grace, and win through to life everlasting."

9

THE TRIAL[1]

The high priest asked him and said to him, Art thou the Christ, the Son of the blessed God? And Jesus said to him, I am. Then the high priest, rending his garments, saith, What need we any further witnesses? You have heard the blasphemy.—Mark 14. 61.

JESUS of Nazareth, the Son of Mary, claimed to be the eternal Son of God. His acts were deliberately calculated to identify him with the promised Messias. I have urged that his words, when he is (as it were) taken off his guard, are the words of a God speaking in the outward form of man. I have urged that the hints which he let fall in his parables and in the comparisons he used are proper to conscious divinity. I have urged that his silence, and the silence which he imposed on others, during his lifetime, is even more eloquent testimony to his divine origin than act, or word, or hint. And now we are left to consider the closing scenes of his natural life, during which that strange silence of his finds its culmination, and is broken at last.

Throughout the whole of his process, his silence forced itself upon the notice of his accusers. "He held his peace and answered nothing",

[1] A sermon preached at Our Lady of Victories, Kensington, in 1921.

says St Mark of the trial before the high priest.[1] "Herod", says St Luke, "questioned him in many words. But he answered him nothing." "Pilate saith to him" (this is St Matthew), "Dost thou not hear how great testimonies they allege against thee? And he answered him never a word, so that the governor wondered exceedingly."[2] That silence at his judgment is the crown of a life of silence; we must guess his riddle, he will not tell us. Surely, surely, you can see what he means from the very accusations these bewildered hirelings of witnesses are making against him. "Destroy this temple, and I will raise it up again in three days"[3]—cannot you see that he speaks of himself? The judges sit there baffled, and the secret which love pierced long since, when Peter made his confession, hate still cannot master. Notice that the whole trial leads up to the high priest's question, and the whole issue depends upon it; his patience worn out at last, he turns to the prisoner, and adjures him by the living God to tell them whether he claims to be—what? A prophet? A reformer? A national leader? A disturber of the public peace? A king, lineally descended from David? None of these things agitate, or could agitate, such an audience as this. But— does he claim to be the Christ? Does he claim to be the Son of the blessed God?

And this answer? We will give the critics every consideration; we will go to their pet document, their primitive document, the Gospel of St Mark. And Jesus said to him, "I am".[4] The same utterance that once went in thunder down the slopes of Sinai, now breaks the silence of the judgment-hall. St Luke supplies us with the commentary: "If I tell you, you will not believe me; and if I question you, you will not answer me".[5] The time has gone by when they might have unravelled his secret for themselves, and fallen at his feet with the Prince of the Apostles; now it is too late. God defend us all from that dreadful statute of limitations which he sets upon his graces! That all-seeing eye, from which no human heart can hold its secret, has read at a glance those shrivelled souls opposite, and found them confirmed in evil; no need, then, for further mystery; he may disclose himself. And at the disclosure, the high priest rends the garments of his now usurped authority, and the hall rings with the cries of "Blasphemy". The word is passed round to such as can best rule by their arts the sympathies of the mob; the matter is settled now: only a little brow-beating, to silence the scruples of an ineffective governor, and the carpenter who claimed to be a God will be hurried to his death.

[1] Mark 14. 61.   [2] Matthew 28. 13, 14.   [3] John 2. 19.
[4] Mark 14. 62.   [5] Luke 22. 67-68.

But stay! What voice is this that breaks through their clamour with demands for reversal of the verdict and reprieve? Breathless, uneasy, yet confident of a just contention, still hugging his precious pile of documents, rushes in—the higher critic. "Stop, stop", he cries; "let me explain—it is all a ghastly mistake. Your witnesses have misunderstood, or, perhaps, wilfully misrepresented the facts; the prisoner you see before you never blasphemed. He calls himself the Christ; that is, the Messias—a general title for the great national hero who is to arise and deliver Israel from its foreign rulers; it is not the Scriptures, but a particular interpretation of the Scriptures, which invests that promised Deliverer with circumstances of divinity. He claims to be the Messias, that is, to usher in a new dispensation, a fuller self-revelation of God to Man; you must not hold him responsible for all the theological associations which the use of such language may conjure up for you. True, he goes on to call himself the Son of God; but then, we are all sons of God. Not one of us but claims God for his Father, however far we have strayed from him, by whatever infidelities we have offended him. This man, then, your prisoner, claims God for his Father by the common right of humanity. Only, there are degrees of sonship: each of us, in proportion as he has realized the fact of God's Fatherhood, and made its lesson his own by practising and by preaching the law of human brotherhood, appropriates to himself in a special sense the title of Son. Believe me, sirs, this man is nearer to God than you know. You Pharisees, with all your heroic loyalty to the traditions of your race; you Sadducees, with your broad-minded appreciation of modern tendencies and a civilization other than your own; you Scribes, with all industrious learning in the letter of the Old Testament —there is something you have all missed, and this man has found it. Do not be misled by his use of sonorous titles, by the Oriental imagery in which he pictures to you the terrors of a future judgment: recognize in him, as I do, a heaven-sent teacher who has received divine illumination—may we not even call it inspiration?—in a very special degree, though he be not different in kind from the clay of our common fashioning. To kill him is to make a hero of him, perhaps (such is popular superstition) deify him. Forget your scruples, reverence him as a Master, and let him go in peace."

So pleaded the higher critic before that tribunal of hate, and I confess that, hideous as are the faces of the judges in their cruelty, I find something noble in their scorn. What? Bring this sorry apology before a court so impanelled? On a question of fact they might disagree, did disagree until the prisoner made his own avowal. But on a question of law, cannot those scribes, who have pored till their sight failed over the sacred documents, be trusted to determine whether "Son of God" be a blasphemous title or no? Granted that the Pharisees were blinded by hatred, it was not a Pharisee but a Sadducee who rent his clothes, and cried, "What need of further witnesses?" The high priest, as the enemy of the Pharisees, had rejoiced, perhaps, at those diatribes against hypocrisy and formalism which had left the withers of his own caste unwrung: is it for nothing that he has been suddenly turned from an impartial judge into a fanatical accuser? Is it nothing to the critics that such a man should grow white with anger at the bare mention of the Christ? The court will take no cognizance of such a halting defence, nor does the prisoner need it. Believe me, the vacillations of Pilate were no less futile; and Peter, when he thrice denied his Lord, did him no greater disservice.

He stands there patient, not needing our interference. He stands his trial not only before the Jews, his contemporaries, but before all generations of men; judge him they must, misjudge him they may, if they will. Only you must accept his own definition of the issue, not seek to flatter him with half divine titles, too high praise for a madman, too cold homage for a God. He claims, not merely to defy death or to despise it, but to have conquered it. "Destroy this temple", he says (and we did not need St John to tell us that he referred to his own body), "and in three days I will raise it up."[1] He means, "God will raise it up"; he means "My heavenly Father will raise it up"? No; "*I* will raise it up." The challenge is a perfectly straightforward one: only St John records the actual occasion which produced it; but the witnesses at the trial have preserved the fact for us, and the leaders of the Jews believed those witnesses: "Sir, we have remembered that that seducer said, while he was yet alive, after three days I will rise again."[2] Now, if Jesus of Nazareth claimed to be a king, or a popular leader, or a prophet, or a reformer, that challenge is meaningless. It is a business-like challenge only because he claimed to be God. "Kill me", he says, "and, if I am only human, you will be rid of me; if I am more than human, you will perforce acknowledge the justice of the test." You may call him a seducer, or you may hail him as God; in either case, the story of the Gospel will take rank as a tragedy. But tell us that there was never any challenge, never was any test, and that only a pale phantom left the garden tomb on Easter morning—then you have left us neither a tragedy nor a theology; you have only spoiled a story.

You will tell me, perhaps, that the tragedy of the Passion seems to

[1] John 2. 19.   [2] Mark 27. 63.

you all the more real as a tragedy, if you are allowed to suppose that the chief actor in it was really helpless; could not, if he would, have defended himself. "Surely", you say, "if it is really true that he who was crucified on Calvary hung there of his own free will, making, at every moment of his three hours, a deliberate choice of death; if he parted from his mother only for two short days of absence, comforted the penitent thief against ultimate terrors he himself could not experience; gave way in his weariness to a desolation which came short of despair—then you have made a fine pageant of Calvary, but the human interest is gone. For me (you say) the true pathos of the situation, the element in it that challenges and provokes my tears, is that utter helplessness and hopelessness which your God-man could neither bring upon himself nor feel. It is enough for me that a man who lived generously for what he believed to be his mission died heroically for what he believed to be the truth. Is not this enough (you ask) to bow a man's knee in homage to that divine inspiration which could make so noble a thing of our weak humanity? God forgive me if I lack altogether the instinct of reverence, but it seems to me that your story, though it be moving, is neither a very remarkable, nor a very new one. Word for word, step for step, the story of Jesus of Nazareth seems, by your way of it, to be the story of Savonarola, and I had as soon say my prayers to Savonarola as to your Christ."

But if that God-man we Catholics worship did truly walk the earth, if the Immutable grew to manhood, and the Impassible suffered, and the Immortal died, then I say that to me the three hours on Calvary are more, not less, of a tragedy for the divine personality, that is veiled and unveiled in their passing. If there are really angel legions that stood all about, hand on scabbard, ready to interfere in that history at a single word from the Hero of it—a word which was never given; then there is no detail in the story, no circumstance that invests it whether of Jewish hate or of Roman scorn, that does not become alive with irony—and what is tragedy, if it be not irony? A visionary hated, an innocent man misjudged, an unbefriended victim done to death— that is an old story, a story of every day. But, God rejected by his own people! Eternal Justice arraigned before a human tribunal! The Author of life sighing out the last breath of a human soul! Tell us, if you will, that it is only a story, and we children to believe in it; only do not try to tell it us without the point!

He sat, and sits, in judgment upon the men that have made themselves his judges. His sentence will be pronounced when the time has gone by for regret, or reconsideration or excuse. He will divide us into two classes, only two—those who confessed, and those who denied him. He will point us to one of two destinies, only two—to be confessed or to be denied before his Father in heaven. Judge honestly, then, for to him all hearts are open; judge anxiously, for it is you who will sustain the sentence.

10

HOLY SATURDAY[1]

He went and preached to the spirits who lay in prison.—1 Peter 3. 19.

After the Mass of Holy Saturday, when you are sitting in your room, perhaps with some favourite book in front of you, there is a sudden knock at the door. "Come in", you shout cheerily, half turning to greet the visitor. The door is opened by a priest in cotta and stole, who, after a brief Latin salutation, sprinkles the treasured volume liberally with holy water, and withdraws. What sacred thoughts ought to be ours on this occasion?

For myself, I like to think of some old patriarch in Limbo, King David, let us say, waiting, through long centuries of twilight for his permit to enter heaven. Waiting, not under the stroke of divine chastisement, but with a patience beyond all our imagining; alone there, with his memories and his hopes, like a watchman waiting for the dawn. The Spirit of Christ is in him, making known to him the sufferings which Christ's cause brings with it, and the glory that crowns them; when is it to be? And how is the time of it to be recognized? All at once, the door of his prison swings open, and in a blaze of light he sees the figure so often, in his poetic imaginings, ah, how dimly foreshadowed, the martyred Christ, wounds shining on hands and feet! Christ is risen, and David, waking up after his likeness, finds there everlasting content.

Does prudence, does piety demand of us that we should think of our Lord's Passion as having availed a few, only a very few, of the men who died before him? That was not what medieval writers meant when they talked about the harrowing of hell. They meant that a vast

---

[1] An Easter meditation published in *The Tablet*, 12 April 1952.

army of souls, we cannot tell how multitudinous, escaped in that hour from the grip in which the Devil seemed to hold them. And indeed, in this very passage from which I quoted, St Peter gives a curious description of these souls to whom our Lord preached the message of his Resurrection. "Long before, they had refused belief . . . in the days of Noe."[1] It was not merely, as you might have expected, Noe and Sem and Cham and Japhet, with their wives, survivors of a drowned world, that rose to acclaim the risen Christ. No, even in the days of general corruption before the deluge, there were souls, strange to think of it, that belonged to him. Their mortal natures paid the penalty in men's eyes, but in the sight of God their spirits were to live on. And so it was, doubtless, with all the great catastrophes that overtook mankind before the coming of our redemption. Always a proportion of the victims, by some merciful dispensation whose nature we cannot guess, had escaped hell, had achieved the title to an immortal destiny. They only waited for Easter Day when, in their prison, the imprisoned Christ would come to them, and they would refuse belief no longer.

You and I, maybe, after death, will find ourselves in the twilight state known as purgatory. Saved (please God) by faith in the risen Christ, we shall not yet be partakers in the glory of his Resurrection. Preachers who discuss the conditions of that intermediate state are apt to lay stress on the severity of the divine punishments. They may be right; it is a fearful thing to fall into the hands of the living God. Only, I dare to hope that the severity of it will be relieved by something we had no right to expect, something we had never been told about, the influence of our blessed Lord's passing, on Easter Eve, through the place of departed spirits. The holy water still glistens on your table when the priest has come and gone; what if our Lord, on that first Holy Saturday, blessed it once for all with a lustration which time can never efface? I like to think of purgatory, however long and however dreary it be, as consoled in some measure by the consciousness that *he* has been there before us; as a process of passing onwards from room to room, always with the sense that the presence of one we love has only just been withdrawn. Not strong enough, yet, to follow him out into the sunlight, we shall follow him eagerly through the dark. Is that fanciful?

At least let me say this; I think we do well, at Easter-tide, to remember our dead. No, do not exclaim that I am a kill-joy, clouding your festival with sad thoughts. True, it is life, not death, that is uppermost in our thoughts; the spring air; the crisp, clean associations of the Easter

---

[1] 1 Peter 3. 20.

liturgy, heal the mind with hopes of renewal. But consider, when you see our Lord represented as rising from the tomb with a banner in his hand, it is the symbol of a military penetration; he, the Victor, in rolling back the stone has made a breach in the enemy's lines, for what? So that the army of his redeemed may pour through at his heels. Or, if you will use St Paul's metaphor, his is the first birth out of death; he has opened the barren womb of extinction, not for himself only but so as to be the first-born of many brethren. *Vidi aquam*—our Lord's Resurrection is the opening of the springs; the full river has yet to flow. It broadens out, reaches its fulfilment, in ours.

To be sure, our bodies must await the day of judgment, buried in their native earth; only himself and his blessed Mother escape altogether from the primal curse. But heaven, from hour to hour, is being peopled with the *spirits* of just men made perfect, like the hedgerows yonder, that are silently bursting into bud. And shall we give no thought to those other spirits that are still in prison, thwarted growths, the Gardener bestowed such pains on? Now, when the very air seems charged with paschal grace, it is but common charity that we should want to share it with them; now, while the spring grass is fresh over their graves, it is but seasonable that the memory of them should be renewed. More souls, this Easter morning, looking up to see the stone rolled away from their dungeon door, and a risen Master standing there in the daylight to welcome them: "Rise up, rise up quickly, and come with me! Winter is over now, the rain has passed by."[1]

And can we, in these times, mention the very word "prison" without being reminded of other souls, still in the flesh, tens of thousands of them, held in a captivity which makes purgatory itself seem a welcome thought? Christian souls—have they still means to reckon the calendar of Christendom? If so, you may picture them exchanging today, half ironically, the familiar greeting, "Christ is risen." *Pro afflictis et captivis* —how full of meaning those words sound in war-time, how lightly they cross our lips when our tiny corner of the world is at peace! Let us pray for them, too, bishops and priests and lay folk, forgotten heroes of Christendom; victims of that faith which you and I wear on our sleeves. . . . Then, with slower step, but with undiminished courage, let us go back to keep the feast of our redemption.

[1] Canticle of Canticles 2. 11.

O

II

THE GUARDED TOMB

O N either March the 20th or March the 27th, 1,905 years ago, it seems that a handful of soldiers, probably Roman soldiers, were on guard outside a tomb on the outskirts of Jerusalem. The tomb was freshly made, but it had been diverted from its original purpose, whatever that was. The body of a Galilean teacher, who had been crucified by the Roman Governor's orders, had been hastily put there two days before. No more elaborate burial had been possible at the time, because it was the Paschal sabbath, and no manual work might be done. Two Jewish gentlemen had carried out this burial, apparently by themselves; but their action had been witnessed by some women, who were followers of the dead prophet. A very heavy stone had been rolled against the door of the grave, which was carved out of the natural rock; a stone light enough for two men to put in position, but too heavy for three women to move out of its position again. It was a natural precaution, at a time and in a country where robbing of graves was not unknown. But the soldiers were posted there as a very special precaution; because some words used by the dead man, not long before, had suggested to the authorities that he believed himself capable of rising again from the dead.

As events turned out, the precaution was of no great value. Early in the morning an earthquake shock, the second in two days, was felt in Jerusalem; and it may be that, through some fault in the ground, it was felt with especial violence just where the tomb was. We read in the papers last week that the Church of the Holy Sepulchre, raised long afterwards on this site, has just been closed for repairs, because an earthquake which took place last October has damaged the structure. The soldiers came back to the city in alarm; and some of them made a report to those who had given them their orders. The report was, that when the shock was felt the stone had rolled away from the door of the sepulchre, and an angel had appeared to them, sitting on the stone, dazzling white in the uncertain light of very early dawn. We do not know whether the Jewish authorities believed this story; but they held it was part of prudence to hush the matter up, and bribed the soldiers to say that they had fallen asleep, and that while they were asleep the body of the Galilean prophet had been stolen away by his disciples. It has been pointed out long ago that their story was not very cleverly

concocted; for if the soldiers were really asleep, how could they tell
who had stolen the body, or whether it had been stolen at all? But it
was the best that could be managed, and this story was still current
among the Jews, it appears, years afterwards. The gospel which tells
us all this was probably, unlike the other gospels, written in Judaea;
and it may well have preserved the inner history, long kept secret, of
what the soldiers saw, and why, at dawn, the tomb was left unguarded.

Unguarded it evidently was. It must have been quite soon after the
soldiers left that some five women came to visit the tomb and anoint
the body, a tribute which they had not been able to pay on the Friday
evening. It was still dark, but only with the dusk of twilight; they would
not have left the city in pitch darkness. They were expecting to have
difficulty about moving the stone; and their first surprise was when
they, too, found it rolled away from its place. One of the women,
and perhaps the most active spirit among them, she whom we call
Mary Magdalen, was so much excited or alarmed by this that she
went back at once to report the occurrence to the dead man's disciples.
The rest of the women, however, remained at the tomb, and saw very
much more. What was it they saw?

They reported afterwards, like the soldiers, that they had had a
"vision of angels". Two men stood by them in shining garments and,
this time, had speech with them. To be more accurate, it looks as if
one of the two had been outside the tomb, where the soldiers had seen
him earlier, while the other was inside, and not visible till you had
entered. The evidence on these points of detail is not exactly clear.
True evidence very seldom is. Bribe a handful of soldiers, and they will
spread the same lie all over Jerusalem. Take three women to the tomb,
none of them expecting to find anything unusual, and you will have to
piece the story together for yourself. One will have seen two angels,
another can only swear to the presence of a single angel; this witness
was conscious of the angel first and the empty tomb afterwards, that
one will have got the order of her impressions confused. But their
evidence is quite clear in its main outlines; whether of their own
accord or because the angels invited them to do so, they went into the
tomb, looked for the body, and found that it was not there.

The angels had given them a message; they were to tell the disciples
of the prophet that he had risen from the dead, and that they were to go
back to Galilee, the part of the country to which they belonged;
there, far away from the scene of these recent disturbances, they would
meet him again. The women hastened away on this errand, and said
nothing to anybody on the way. Why is this detail mentioned?

Probably because, on the way, they met two of the disciples in question, without accosting them. By now, you see, Mary Magdalen will have reached Jerusalem, with her story that the grave-door was lying open —so far, that is all the news she has. Two of the disciples, Peter and John, set out, running, to verify the truth of her statement; their first thought may have been that the tomb had been robbed. But if they passed, on their way, the rest of the women, no conversation was exchanged between them; that is the point. They came to the sepulchre not knowing what they were to find there, except that the stone would be rolled away. Mary Magdalen followed the two disciples, presumably at a distance.

One of the two disciples, John, has left us his own story of the event. Both he and Peter went into the tomb, and verified the absence of the body. They noticed something else, still more remarkable. The body had been wrapped in a winding-sheet, and a napkin had been wound round the head. These were found, apparently, still in position, as if the body had passed through them without disturbing them. John tells us that the sight was enough to carry conviction to his own mind; from that moment he believed that he who was dead had risen again. No angels appeared to them, and they went back as they had come.

So far, it will be noticed, the direct evidence about the body of Jesus of Nazareth is purely negative; you have the consistent story of a disappearance, but no story of an appearance. And so far, it is well to observe, the evidence never seems to have been refuted, or even contradicted. We have seen what was the official story put about in Jerusalem; it tried to provide an explanation of the disappearance, as if the fact were beyond denial. Fifty days afterwards one of the dead man's disciples made a speech before a large crowd of people in Jerusalem itself, and treated the fact of the empty tomb as a generally admitted fact on which you could base your arguments. And years later Paul of Tarsus, in his trial before King Herod Agrippa, shows the same confidence: he is persuaded, he says, that the events about which he has been talking—they included the Resurrection—are well known to the king; "for these things were not done in a corner".[1] The empty tomb, in fact, must have been visited by many others besides the friends of the dead prophet. It will have been a nine days' wonder; and King Herod, who would have been six years old at the time, would remember the echoes of it.

But we hear no more in our records about the negative evidence, because at this point the positive evidence begins. Mary Magdalen

[1] Acts 26. 26.

stood by the tomb weeping after the two disciples had gone; weeping, because she evidently thought that somebody had taken her Master's body away. It might be the authorities, it might be his enemies, it might be common robbers—it did not matter to her, she had come out with her ointments to do honour to the dead man's memory, and now it is too late; that is all she thinks about. She looks into the tomb (for the first time, apparently), and sees an angel sitting there, as the other women had, some time back. Before she has time to answer the angel's mysterious greeting, a shadow (I suppose) passes over the door; she looks round, and sees somebody standing behind her. Perhaps it will be the gardener; she will ask if he knows anything about her loss. And the rest of the story is told in two words of dialogue; "Mary . . . Master!" In such a short compass is the script of the world's greatest drama comprised.

The other women will by now have been on their return journey to the tomb, after delivering their message. Perhaps by this time they had rejoined Mary Magdalen, and shared her experience; if not, it must have been soon afterwards that they, too, met their risen Master and clung to his feet. These first rumours of an appearance were not believed by the other disciples, who waited for confirmation of the news. And it was not till the evening or late afternoon that it came. The dead prophet appeared, living, to Peter, that one of his disciples whom he had appointed to be the leader of the others, strengthening their faith. Curiously, no details have been preserved to us of this interview. But Peter described it, fourteen or fifteen years afterwards, to Paul of Tarsus; and Paul of Tarsus, writing ten years later again to the Christians in Corinth,[1] refers to it as if it were the main plank in the platform he used in preaching the Gospel message.

It must have been shortly before or shortly after this that he, whose body men looked for vainly in the sepulchre, appeared again to two of his followers, as they were walking out to a village seven or eight miles from Jerusalem. For whatever reason, they did not recognize him till the very last moment, although he walked for some way with them and shared their evening meal. Like Mary Magdalen, they found a difficulty in recognizing him. Why, we do not know; but do not let us be told that the appearance was, therefore, an hallucination. It was as far as possible the exact opposite. An hallucination makes us mistake a stranger for a friend; this inhibition of which we are speaking, whatever it was, made people mistake, at first, their Friend for a stranger. The two friends went back to Jerusalem, to the upper room in which,

[1] 1 Corinthians 15. 5.

as usual, the followers of the Crucified were assembled; the doors were locked, for fear of hostile action by the Jewish authorities. While they were describing their experience, the Master himself appeared suddenly in their midst; quieted their fears; ate and drank with them to convince them that it was no mere phantom shape they saw.

Those are the events of the first Easter Day, collected from six different sources, of which all except one seem to have been compiled in their present shape within forty years of the events which they describe. What are we going to make of them? We are the jury, as it were, which must sit in inquest, age after age, on the events recorded; and yet, are we the jury, or is it we who are on our trial? Anyhow, the Christian submission is this—that the events I have described, coupled with a set of similar events spread over a period of forty days, coupled with the inferences which we may draw from the behaviour of the dead prophet's followers, immediately afterwards, coupled with a living tradition which has been handed down, from that century to this, by a body of men singularly tenacious of tradition, establishes the supernatural character of the mission with which Jesus of Nazareth went about the world nineteen hundred years ago. If you dissent from that finding, then it is for you to decide at what point you will dissent from it. Will you doubt the authenticity of the documents? Or the veracity of their authors? Or the good faith of the witnesses on whom those authors relied? Or, if you do not doubt the facts themselves, will you doubt the philosophical construction which has been put upon the facts?

In a talk due to last twenty minutes, which are nearly up, I cannot try to meet all those positions. I am only concerned now to challenge one of them; to meet the contentions of the people who say, "Oh, yes, there is no doubt the documents are authentic; no doubt that those who compiled them were, in the main, conscientious; no doubt that the witnesses on whom they depended, simple people and evidently people of good will, were doing their best to describe what they heard and saw. Only, of course, there must be some mistake, because miracles don't happen." There must be some mistake; yes, no doubt. Only, what mistake can it possibly have been?

Take the story of the empty tomb by itself. Could you have circumstantial evidence more complete? The body had disappeared; is there any possible motive to assign for its removal by any human agent using natural means? There is absolutely none. Even if you refuse to believe that the Jews took special precautions to keep the tomb safe, you must still recognize that the story of their doing so is true to life. It was in their interest to keep the body, and to be able at any moment to produce it, should any claim be made that Jesus of Nazareth had risen from the dead. If they removed it from the grave, why did they not produce it afterwards? Nor had Pilate, the Roman Governor, any reason for wishing to smuggle away the body of the man he had crucified; its presence might conceivably lead to rioting and disturbance, but its disappearance was far more likely to have that effect. The women cannot have stolen it, for they were not strong enough to move away the stone, let alone to overpower a military guard. Did the guard, then, desert their posts, and some other human agent remove the body before the women came? That was the only possibility which presented itself to Mary Magdalen. Could Joseph of Arimathea have carried it away, or Nicodemus? But, in that event, why did not the agent who had removed the body give any sign, afterwards, of what he had done? If he were friendly disposed towards the disciples, to the disciples; if he were ill disposed, to the Jews? And, whatever their motives, why did they leave the winding-sheet and the napkin lying there, instead of taking the body as it lay? The presence of the grave-clothes is also fatal to the theory, which has (I believe) been suggested, that the body was buried deeper in the ground as the result of the earthquake.

No, if you are going to give a merely natural account of the whole story, the account which was first given still holds the field—I mean, that there was deliberate fraud on the part of the disciples, who wanted to give the impression that their Master had risen from the dead. What you have to decide is, whether such a notion is consistent with the behaviour of those same people two days before, at the crucifixion, running away and leaving their Master to face his persecutors alone, and with the behaviour of those same people, in the years which followed, suffering imprisonment and dying in support of a story which they had made up to deceive the public. I wonder, did they?

12

THE RISEN CHRIST[1]

There is nothing new under the sun.—Ecclesiastes 1. 9.
Behold, I make all things new.—Apocalypse 31. 5.

WHEN Easter comes, the Church delights to remind herself of that newness which is in the risen Christ. On Holy Saturday morning, a new spark must be struck from the flint, to light a new set of candles and lamps; new holy water must be blessed, and a new font; fresh cloths are spread on the altars, and the tabernacle itself, on Easter morning, is full of freshly consecrated Hosts. We are beginning all over again, making all things new. And we have a right to do so, for in the order of grace there is perpetual novelty. In the order of nature there is perpetual affectation of novelty, which never comes to anything; there is nothing new, the wise man reminds us, under the sun, however much, at the moment, things look different. Whereas in the order of grace there is no change apparent, but in truth it is a perpetual spring, inexhaustible in its fecundity.

On the first Easter Day it must have looked to Pontius Pilate, for example, as if he really had contrived to make a fresh start. The latest of the revolutionary leaders—if he was really a revolutionary leader— was now out of the way. An example had been made of him, and his crucifixion had passed off without incident. The rulers themselves had disowned him; the people had clamoured for his blood. Really, it looked as if at last this stubborn, rebellious people were beginning to take the Roman point of view, to think imperially. What if he, Pontius Pilate, should go down to history as the man who effected a new orientation in Romano-Jewish relations? And Herod, too—by the mere gesture of recognizing his jurisdiction over this unpopular agitator, he had appealed to the man's vanity, and differences of long standing had been settled. A new atmosphere had been created—so, perhaps, he wrote home in his next dispatch.

Meanwhile, the impression of our Lord's own friends about his Resurrection was not, at first, that any epoch-making change had occurred, but rather that everything was, and was going to be, just as it had been before. St Mary Magdalen meets him in the garden, and clings to his feet exactly as she had clung to them in Bethany, less than

[1] An Easter meditation published in *The Tablet*, 8 April 1939.

a week ago. With our Lady, the faithful apostles once more entertain him in the cenacle, where they had entertained him three days earlier; he still eats and drinks with them, and the very gesture he makes in breaking bread is a familiar one. When they are commanded to wait for him in Galilee, they occupy the time by going back to their old craft of fishing, for all the world as if they had never been called away from the nets. Everything is the same—how wonderful! It is as if the crucifixion had never happened.

Pilate's impression was exactly wrong; soon afterwards he was recalled to Rome, in extreme unpopularity, and within a generation Jerusalem was destroyed. In the natural order, our Lord's crucifixion made no difference, heralded no new departure, whatever. Meanwhile, in the supernatural order, where his own friends were concerned, it had made all the difference, constituted a turning point in the history of creation. Those patriarchs who rose from their graves with him could have borne witness to that. Adam had seen the sentence of eternal death, that his own sin had deserved, reversed. Noe had seen Golgotha as Ararat, the cross as a new ark to save the human race from destruction. Abraham had seen a greater than Isaac sacrificed, Jacob had seen a Son more beloved than Joseph rescued from the pit; Moses understood now what the Paschal Lamb meant, and what deliverance he was fore-shadowing, when he led the children of Israel through the Red Sea. King David knew now why he had been inspired to prophesy "thou wilt not suffer thy holy One to see corruption",[1] and Daniel saw the time of his great vision fulfilled.

> Prophets and kings desired it long,
> And died before the sight;

the trustees of an older covenant, they guessed what a momentous event was taking place when the Temple veil was rent, and the earthquake summoned them from their graves to glory. The old covenant was at an end, all was made new.

Since then, as before, the world has shifted its fashions from age to age; and men in each age have hailed the novelty as a decisive novelty, and told themselves that the old, bad state of things could never happen again. We hardly need to be reminded of that, who have lived through the last fifteen years. During that time, most of the great countries of the world have announced a complete break with the past; there has been a proletarian revolution here, and a national resurrection there, and a new deal somewhere else; and all the nations have decided to

[1] Psalm 10. 15

sink their differences once and for all, several times over, and we have
said good-bye again and again to war, and rivalry, and poverty, and
persecution, only to meet them again at the turning of the next street.
Have all things become new? Mind, I am not saying that everything
goes from bad to worse; I am not even concerned to deny that, in
certain ways, the world has changed, and is changing, for the better.
But the change is a gradual one; these sudden new departures, these
much-advertised attempts to break with the past—do they really break
with the past, or are they not a revival of the past in modern dress?
Vanity of vanities, saith the preacher; there is no new thing under
the sun.

And if there is one institution in the world which, by common
consent of its friends and foes, is rooted in the past, indifferent, when it is
not hostile, to this feverish propaganda of innovation all around it,
it is the Catholic Church. During the last three days we have been
assisting at ceremonies which have plunged us back into our Christian
past; ceremonies which in part, I suppose, have come down to us almost
from the catacombs. We have heard the Church, as she prayed over us,
suddenly breaking away from the Latin which is her native tongue and
take refuge in Greek, like a very old man who, in his second childhood,
remembers the language of his youth; we have heard snatches of chants
long disused, seen the survivals of ceremonies which belong to an
older world than ours. Still, obstinately, the Church takes refuge in
her remote past while she announces to us complacently: "Christ is
risen; all things are made new."

So much her friends admit; her enemies are not slow to add that she
herself is nothing better than a cumbrous survival, an institution, once
great, that has outlived its usefulness, ripe for the scrap-heap. Kept
going, who knows how? Partly from sentimental loyalty, partly from
the force of long habit, but . . . an anachronism. Men have been saying
that for four hundred years; even earlier than that, it must have seemed
to many that her days were numbered. "Still doomed to death, but
fated not to die",[1] the Catholic Church has survived one hundred
crucifixions by one hundred resurrections; and those who know her
best know that she does not merely continue to exist; she lives. Her
vitality is profound, witnessed from age to age not by revolutions or
new deals, but by the fresh shoots of devotion and charity which she
puts forth continually, age after age. It is always spring with her, hers
is a perpetual youth; she has but to remember the three words, "Christ

---

[1] John Dryden, *The Hind and the Panther*, 8, "And doom'd to death, though fated not
to die".

is risen", and with the very sound of them, all things are made new.

That spring, that youth, belong as of right, not only to the Church at large, but to the life of the individual Christian. There are so many occasions in life, aren't there, when we say to ourselves, "Now I really shall be able to make a new start"? We leave school; of course, all our troubles will disappear now. We go into business; now the world shall see what we are made of. We get married; that, evidently, is going to be the turning-point of our lives. We rise to a position of responsibility; now, our chance has come. We grow rich, and have more opportunities of leisure; at last our true nature will have the opportunity to develop. We retire from active work; now, with old age to mellow us, we can live as we would wish to die. Yes, but tell me, is there really all that difference between one stage and the next?

But in the life of grace, ah, if we could only see it, there is a perpetual burgeoning of new life, not merely from one Easter to another, from one retreat to another, but with every worthy reception of the sacraments. Perpetual spring, perpetual renovation of our natures, if we could only catch the hour of grace, utilize it, make it our own. Whatever you are, and at whatever time of life you are, that possibility of spiritual renewal is with you no less surely than if you were a boy at school again, or just leaving school to make your way in the world. Christ is risen; those tidings can neither lose their force with age, nor be staled by repetition; Christ is risen, and life, for the Christian, is always new.

13

THE CORNER-STONE[1]

The very stone which the builders rejected has become the chief stone at the corner; this is the Lord's doing, and it is marvellous in our eyes.—Psalm 117. 22.

WHAT is immortality? To that question, there are three possible answers. You may give the word its literal meaning, and say that a man is immortal only if the living consciousness, which till then has been the subject of experience in and through the body, continues to be the subject of experience, even when it has lost contact with the

[1] A sermon preached at Ampleforth College, at Pontifical High Mass on Easter Sunday, 1952.

body. Or you may take refuge in metaphor, and say that a man is immortal as long as he is publicly remembered; why should he want to go on being conscious? Praise, though it falls on deaf ears, was the reward he worked for, and yonder solid statue in the public gardens, not some disembodied wraith, is the true heir of his identity! Or you may refine upon the point, and say that all men are immortal, because each of us leaves some influence on the world in passing through it. The parent is reproduced in the child; not less surely, the teacher is reproduced in his pupils, the patriot in the mind of his fellow citizens, the founder of some movement in that movement's success.

> I need not be missed, if another succeed me
> To reap down those fields which in spring I have sown;
> He who ploughed and who sowed is not missed by the reaper;
> He is only remembered by what he has done.

A man lives on if his work lives on; not otherwise.

When he rose on Easter Day, our Lord Jesus Christ achieved this threefold immortality. As a matter of literal historical fact, he is alive and lives for evermore. He, more than any man who ever passed through the world, is remembered; his image is so familiar to our sight, his praise so common in our mouths, that his memory suffers more from inadvertence than from oblivion. And his influence is not merely the inspiration which men derive from a life nobly lived, that makes them want to imitate it. That is true in the natural order, but there is more than that; in the supernatural order he is himself the fountain of every grace we receive. "He is that head whose body is the Church; it begins with him, since his was the first birth out of death";[1] as surely as we derive our nature from Adam, we derive our supernature from Jesus Christ.

And the Church, because she draws her inner life from his Resurrection, is always rising from apparent death; repeats, in her history, the life-cycle he went through in the womb of earth long ago. It seems to be a law of the Church's development that always, or almost always, she should enjoy peace in certain parts of the world, and in others suffer occultation. The just (so the wise man tells us) "will shine out unconquerable as the sparks which break out, now here, now there, among the stubble";[2] always the embers are trodden out here, to blaze up elsewhere into flame. A hundred and fifty years—we have enjoyed peace so long, been so long accustomed to sympathize with the helpless position of Catholics in other parts of the world, that we

---

[1] Colossians 1. 18.   [2] Wisdom 3. 7.

forget the two centuries during which it was our turn to suffer for the faith. It is like a child's nightmare, instinct in the memory; and perhaps it is as well that we should forget—no one was ever the worse for forgetting an injury. But there are moments of commemoration and retrospect when our minds are forced back into the past; when we cannot choose but remember how we, in God's providence, found our way out of the catacombs, a hundred and fifty years ago.

"The very stone which the builders rejected"—whatever else is uncertain about English history this at least is certain, that the men who built modern England rejected what had always been, what is still to us, the corner-stone of the commonwealth, Catholic unity. All through the centuries when England rose to power, there was one subject of unquestioning agreement among our fellow citizens; there must be no truckling to the persecuted minority which held by the old ways. A mere historical accident, the French Revolution and the Terror, changed, almost imperceptibly, the English habit of thought. And then—then you have to imagine a little, straggling procession of gentlemen in tightly-buttoned frock-coats infiltrating from the Continent into the home of their ancestors; the inquisitive spectator was informed that these were the monks from Dieulouard. Displaced persons, without a passport, they could not very well be refused admission; they were allowed to drift about from pillar to post, subsisting on the charity of the Catholic gentry, until at last—it was their fifth attempt at finding a resting-place—they settled down at Ampleforth, a hundred and fifty years ago. Remote in the isolation of the Yorkshire wolds, it was hardly to be feared that they would ever affect the main currents of English life.

"The very stone which the builders rejected has become the chief stone at the corner"; it would be easy to improve the occasion by reminding you how much the Catholic body stands for now, in the life of England—the same body which looked so pathetic, so contemptible, in the days of the French Revolution. It would be easy to indulge my sense of affection and gratitude towards this great Abbey, which has given me so kindly a welcome any time in these last thirty years, by insisting on the part which it has played, and is playing, in that revival of the old religion. It would be attractive to speculate why that achievement has been so recent, why the development of its resources, and the growth of its influence, belong to the last fifty, rather than the last hundred and fifty years. After all, fifty years ago the praises of God were sung in this chapel by a choir of only fifteen monks. But all that would strike a false note in our rejoicings, and is besides unnecessary; *si monumentum requiris, circumspice.* As you wander round the buildings, and exchange old memories, you will have much to say of the human agents who have been responsible for it all; "this", you will reflect, "was Abbot Smith's doing . . . and this was Abbot Matthews' doing . . . and this was Father Bede's doing". But here, at the heart of our celebrations, we forget all that; "This is the Lord's doing, and it is marvellous in our eyes".

Assuredly neither Ampleforth, nor the men who built up Ampleforth, need any recommendation to you. "You yourselves", they will cry out with St Paul, "are the letter we carry about with us, written in our hearts, for all to recognize and to read."[1] The measure of their success, at least so far as the School is concerned, is you, and you, and you. When they enlarged the boundaries and quickened the energies of the School which had once been a mere alumnate, they set before themselves—all schoolmasters do—a type which they wanted to realize; what was it? Not, I think, that of the English gentleman who happens to be a Catholic. If Ampleforth should ever come to breed polished, sophisticated men of the world, to whom, by the way, you must not talk about religion, because they have a "thing" about it— then it will not be doing what it set out to do. Ampleforth will be doing what it set out to do as long as it breeds Christians, living with the risen life of Christ, bearing easily, not brandishing their religion, retaining that love of the Mass, that confidence in our blessed Lady, which they had during their schooldays, ready for death. Whatever else Ampleforth taught you was extras.

Christ, our Master, was dead, and is alive, and lives for evermore. That inexhaustible vitality of his has borne fruit in the resurgence of Benedictine life among us; may it bear fruit in our own lives, breathe spring into our hearts, and make us faithful witnesses of his risen power.

14

THE TRIUMPH OF LIFE[2]

"LIFE and death", says the Easter Sequence, "have met in wondrous combat." But indeed the combat had been in progress for long centuries, ever since man sinned and lost his paradise; still continues in

---

[1] 2 Corinthians 3. 2.
[2] An Easter meditation published in *The Tablet*, 31 March 1945.

appearance, though now in a kind of masquerade. Year after year, the spring came bringing new life to field and hedgerow; year after year autumn swallowed up that new life in death. Which was the victor? Life could not preserve the individual; the leaves came every year, but not the leaves of last year; flowers blossomed, but to replace, not to revive, the glories of the past. Death could not conquer the type; nature, with stubborn tenacity, quickened the face of the world anew. And so it was if you took a longer basis of measurement. The oak that had stood the tempests of five hundred winters must give way at last, and death could boast that nothing in creation was eternal. Yet, from that parent stock, fresh trees had grown to maturity; life could boast that nothing in creation was really destroyed. It was a perpetually drawn battle; life in death and death in life were facts equally certain— which of the two was the real key to the history of the universe?

Of that contest, man was the sole spectator; in that contest, man was uniquely interested. His mortal body seemed to prove him one with the nature which perished and decayed; generations of men succeeded one another, like the generations of beasts, and found in that undying succession, that continual preservation of the type, a pale reflex of immortality. But the mind of man could not content itself with these narrow horizons; each human body was but an instance of the type, but each human mind was essentially an individual; it was half of creation, with all the rest of the world for its counterpart, the spectator of time and existence. Which part of man, then, was man's true self? Did the mind die with the body, or did the body somehow live on with the mind; or was death a divorce, complete and final, between the two partners; and if so, into what sort of shadowy existence did the mind enter, remote, surely, from all its experience hitherto? That question was one which the human race had debated for centuries, with agonized indecision. Even the heathens could not resign themselves altogether to extinction; some of the wisest of their philosophers preached the immortality of the soul, and the obscure cults of the underworld kept the same hope alive among the vulgar. Even the Jews, favoured children of the divine oracles, could not be sure which side they would take in the controversy; the Pharisee believed, the Sadducee doubted; but on the whole their thoughts were more centred in the family, in the preservation of the type, than in any promise of individual survival. So in men's hearts, as in Creation around them, the secular struggle between life and death went on, it seemed interminably.

At last came One who saw that conflict with level eyes, and faced the future with untroubled brow. He had power, he said, to lay down his life, and power to take it again. No fear of human violence assailed him; when the Galileans would have cast him down from the top of a hill, he passed securely through their midst; when the Jews took up stones to kill him, he withdrew, miraculously it seems, from their malice. Then, at a time he himself had predicted, making all his arrangements with leisurely forethought, and comforting his friends against the trial that was in store for them, he went to his death voluntarily, chose it as his destiny. Deliberately he allowed himself to fall into the hands of his enemies, yet through no weariness of life; deliberately he allowed them to misjudge and condemn him, yet through no sentiment of pride or obstinacy; deliberately he yielded up his Spirit into his Father's hands, with full consciousness, and before the hour when physical death might be expected to supervene. In three days, he had told his persecutors, that mortal body which they had laboured to demolish would be built anew, a temple not made with hands, sublimated alive for evermore. And on the third day he left his tomb empty.

With that action he broke the spell that had chained humanity so long. Immediately after his death, his followers began to spread through the world, living a life of self-discipline and, where need arose, of heroic self-sacrifice, in the unquestioning hope that they, too, would be counted worthy of this Resurrection which they had seen and handled in his flesh. He did not simply convince men that he had risen; he convinced them that they would rise. That change of the body from a passible to a glorious state, which they admired as a portent in him, they looked forward to as a common experience for themselves, did they but become, through faith and through the mystery of the Holy Eucharist, concorporate with him.

He died that he might institute such means of grace; he died that he might obliterate the curse of sin under which our race laboured; he died that he might encourage us to follow heroically in his footsteps; he died that we might learn how intimate a place suffering has in the economy of our existence here. He died also, that he might assume for our sakes, while he was yet on earth, that Resurrection body whose true home and medium of activity is elsewhere; we should see with our eyes, and our hands should handle, the Word of Life.

15

BELIEF[1]

Thou hast learned to believe, Thomas, because thou hast seen me. Blessed are those who have not seen, and yet have learned to believe.—John 20. 29.

WHEN you read in the newspaper of some momentous decision taken, which, for a moment, fills the headlines; when you glance down the column to see what comment has been made on it by public men and by political observers, at home and abroad; the question often suggests itself, What will be the verdict of history about all this? The verdict of history—that was the important thing, the really important thing, on Easter Day all those centuries ago, when Easter Day first earned its title. A Man had died, with the formalities of a legal execution after a trial in which the evidence had broken down, and the judge had disclaimed responsibility for the sentence. What jury was now to sit on the case, and give the verdict of history? The dead Man had appointed them himself, a jury of twelve, good men and true, you would have thought; common folk, such as have a right to sit on juries, a fisherman here, a toll-collector there. He made a prophecy, and invited them to judge him, invited the world to judge him, according as the prophecy came true or not; he would rise from the dead. One of them, alas, was neither a good man nor a true; he vacated his post, a traitor and a suicide. It was not possible to impanel a fresh jury; only the dead Man's nearest friends were competent to make a decision. The eleven survivors are left to make their report. There, then, they sit, in the upper room, a place haunted by memories, charged with emotion. Had the dead Man risen again? Only one of them claims to have seen him; the rest have nothing to go upon except the empty tomb, and some rather confusing hearsay evidence. Their deliberations are cut short when, suddenly, behind locked doors, they see the dead Man standing in their midst.

No difficulty remains now; there can be only one verdict. He who was dead, is alive; he is our Lord and our God—that is the message they will publish to the world. And then—perhaps only after he has gone, a sudden thought occurs to them. They were not, after all, in full session when he came; one of them had been absent; Thomas, for what reason we don't know, had been absent. Well, it is a pity; but

[1] A broadcast sermon.

after all it won't make much difference. Thomas can hardly refuse to go by the vote of the majority, when he has the evidence of all his colleagues, without exception, to sway his judgment. They crowd round Thomas when he returns, with the confident cry, "We have seen the Lord!"

They had reckoned without their man. Thomas, as we know from his record, was loyal to a fault; had been the first to suggest that they should all go and die with their Master. But he was one of those people who will always ask the inconvenient question. One of those hard-headed, you might almost say bullet-headed, people who give so much trouble on juries and on committees of every sort by refusing to take the majority view until they, personally, are satisfied. He has been chosen to be an eye-witness, vouching personally for every event in the life of Jesus of Nazareth. And he was not an eye-witness of this appearance in the upper room; it will not do. How can they be certain it was really their Master they saw? What tests did they make? "Until I have seen the mark of the nails on his hands, until I have put my finger into the mark of the nails, and put my hand into his side, you will never make me believe."

That it was all providentially ordained, one apostle being absent, and that one Thomas, with his bulldog way of looking at things, is beyond question. "Our Faith", says St Gregory, "owes more to the faithlessness of Thomas than to the faithfulness of all the other apostles put together."[1] Because Thomas doubted, our Lord appeared a second time in the upper room; because Thomas doubted, they were privileged to see, and to touch if they would, the indelible scars of Calvary. "What our own eyes have seen of him, what it was that met our gaze, and the touch of our hands"[2]—so John wrote, long afterwards, with that unforgettable scene for his inspiration. In a moment, the verdict of the jury became unanimous; Thomas could cry out "My Lord and my God!" with the rest. Only, there is a postscript. "Thou hast learned to believe, Thomas, because thou hast seen me. Blessed are those who have not seen, and believe all the same." For our sakes, it was a good thing that Thomas doubted. But for himself, he had come short of the ideal, he had missed an opportunity; surely we are meant to see that. In however insignificant a degree, he was at fault. He had all the record of our Lord's life and teaching in front of him; he had the unanimous testimony of those others, his tried companions in arms, and yet . . . some pride, some wilful obstinacy, some chagrin, perhaps, at having been left out when this experience was granted to the rest,

---

[1] St Gregory, Homil. 26 *in Evang.*   [2] 1 John 1. 1.

made him withhold his assent. "I *will not* believe"; mysteriously, it is possible to withhold your assent by an act of the will. He *ought* to have capitulated.

Our Lord doesn't complain. Our Lord wasn't like us; he didn't go about after his Resurrection finding fault and saying "I told you so"; he looked forward to the future. He looked down the centuries at people like you and me, who had no chance of seeing him in his incarnate state, and yet do manage to cry out, "My Lord and my God"; and he said, "What lucky people you are!" When he started out on his ministry, you remember, he gave us the eight Beatitudes, "Blessed are the patient, blessed are the merciful, blessed are the peace-makers", and so on. And now, when he is just going to leave us for heaven, he pronounces a last beatitude, "Blessed are those who haven't seen, and believe all the same." To call a person "blessed" is a form of congratulation; it is as if we had acquired some treasure, been singled out for some honour. We are lucky people: luckier, it would seem, than St Thomas, because he saw.

Our Lord, as we know, was fond of paradox; and this congratulation of his does seem rather unexpected. Earlier on, he said to his apostles, "There have been many prophets and just men who have longed to see what you see, and never saw it";[1] we understand well enough what he means by saying "Blessed are your eyes" in *that* connection. To see our Lord in the flesh, to hear his gracious accents, to feel the touch of his hand—what an opportunity it was that they had, and we have missed! But that is not his last word on the subject. He singles out people like you and me for a special congratulation; because we have not seen? No, but because, not having seen, we believe.

Faith, not anything else, is the definition of a Christian. Even when our salvation was in the bud, the blessed Virgin was greeted by her cousin Elizabeth in the words, "Blessed art thou for thy believing";[2] and from then onwards, all through the New Testament, it dominates the picture. Are Christians, then, in general the victims of credulity, people who will believe anything? Or are they people of normally critical instincts, who, from a sentimental prejudice, make a single departure from their principles by consenting to believe in Jesus Christ? That is how some of our neighbours think of us; it seems natural to them when Easter Day falls on All Fools' Day. But we do not admit the imputation, in either form. We are prepared to argue the truth of the Resurrection from a multitude of converging evidence; argue it as plain fact, as a piece of ascertainable history.

[1] Matthew 13. 17.   [2] Luke 1. 45.

What, then, they ask, is this "gift of faith" you talk about? What can be the use of it, what can be the need for it, except to fill a gap; to make you believe something which you would otherwise admit to be incredible? Nothing of the sort; faith is a gift which fortifies us in holding fast to a belief which we know to be true, when we are tempted to lose sight of it. Our minds are not electronic machines; they are human instruments, with the weaknesses of humanity. True, the evidence of our senses, and the general agreement of human opinion, have a certain power of compelling belief. But when evidence comes to us by hearsay; when a promise, or a warning, or an assurance comes to us on the word of somebody else, however good reason we have for trusting him—then it is possible to withhold our assent; to say, with Thomas, "I *will* not believe".

"Our faith", St John says in today's epistle, "*that* is the triumphant principle which triumphs over the world."[1] The world around us, so unfriendly to every instinct of religion, so full of cruelty and hypocrisy, so tone-deaf to the music of eternity—how it gets us down, makes us wonder if it's worth while going on! And, within ourselves, the continual secret revolt of our nature against the claim God makes on our lives—we find ourselves half dreading, half hoping, that the cord will snap, and we too shall become materialists like everybody else. If only (we say to ourselves) I could see some divine interference in the course of history, some startling answer to prayer in my own life! If we could see . . . yes, if we could see! But our Lord says, "Blessed are those who have not seen, and believe all the same."

16

THE ASCENSION[2]

We can claim a great high priest, and one who passed right up through the heavens, Jesus, the Son of God.—Hebrews 4. 14.

CENTURIES ago, when the men of science were not provided with precision instruments, our whole view of the universe was earthbound; the stars looked small, and close to us, and friendly, and you

[1] 1 John 5. 4.
[2] A sermon broadcast from the London Oratory on 13 May 1956.

could debate, in all seriousness, whether the sky was not a dome of crystal. It was easy for the artist, in those days, to represent the whole mystery of our Lord's Ascension into heaven as a single piece of composition. There, on a grassy slope at the bottom of the picture, were the apostles, all kneeling, all looking in the air; above them spread a light barrier of fleecy cloud; and above that again was the figure of our Lord, still carrying the banner of his Resurrection, making his way upwards towards the jewelled throne on which the eternal Father was seen awaiting him. But for that barrier of cloud, you felt, the whole process would have been visible to human eyes; heaven was as close as that, just up in the air. It was a wonder, on a fine day, you did not catch some glimpse of it.

Today, the men of science have educated us, and we can no longer feel at home in the cosy fairy-land of medieval thought. We know what it is to climb above the clouds, and the intense dreariness of that upper air in which the world seems far behind you, and you are not nearer heaven. Nor have we reached the end of it; already men are working out programmes of interplanetary travel. Beyond these stars, with which we see ourselves, before long, on visiting terms, stretch remote areas of which the solar system is only a neglected corner. And (we say to ourselves) if Jesus of Nazareth really started out from some mountain in Palestine, to make his way up, up beyond the furthest star, how many light-years must his journey have taken? Can we be sure that he has reached heaven yet? We turn away from the mystery with baffled minds. We can still contemplate, devoutly enough, the manner of our Lord's coming to earth; the Christmas crib has not lost its appeal, after all these centuries. But, the manner of his leaving it—we cannot contemplate that without a hundred distracting speculations.

But, of course, we were wrong all the time. Wrong, I mean, if we supposed that that old picture of a throne balanced somewhere in the sky was an accurate picture of what happened at our Lord's Ascension. The upper half of it was only symbol, only metaphor. Almighty God is not really to be imagined as a human figure sitting on a throne; he hasn't really got a right hand to beckon us with, a crown to offer us. Even when we talk of our Lord as going "up" to his Father's throne, we are using human language where human language doesn't apply; "up" in the literal sense of the word simply means "away from the centre of the earth". And even "going" means moving from one point in space to another; can we be certain that the conditions of space obtain in the supernatural world? That cloud in the middle of the picture was not merely a stray vapour, hiding the Incarnate from our sight. It was a barrier of mystery, making it impossible to follow the further stages of his progress even with the imagination. We can tell ourselves, using our nursery language of sight and sense, that Jesus Christ is now sitting at the right hand of his Father. But it is only symbol, only metaphor.

And yet we know that our symbol, our metaphor, enshrines, though it does not express, the truth. And we, widowed now for nineteen centuries by the loss of that Master whose presence was so gracious, whose voice was so reassuring, are nevertheless enriched by his loss. Whatever else is true, we know that a human nature, like ours and therefore representative of ours, has penetrated behind the last barrier, has crossed the last threshold, which separates the human from the divine. And because we are one in and with him, his achievement is ours; St Paul does not hesitate to describe Christian people as here and now "enthroned above the heavens, in Christ Jesus". You and I, already enthroned in heaven; that is hard to believe, hard to understand. How shall we put it to ourselves?

The apostle tries to make it easier for us by writing the words I quoted to you just now, "We can claim a great high priest, and one who has passed right up through the heavens, Jesus, the Son of God". He was writing for the benefit of his Jewish fellow countrymen, and he uses terms which will be familiar to them. Under the old dispensation, one part of the tabernacle, and afterwards of the temple, was curtained off in darkness to serve as the innermost shrine, the holiest place of all. Only once in the year was the curtain drawn aside, only once in the year did any human foot tread there, and that was on the day of Atonement, when the high priest, after doing sacrifice, went in there and sprinkled the blood of the victim, to make amends for his own faults, and those of the people. Just so, our Lord offered the perfect sacrifice of his own death; and as he did so, the veil that hung between the most holy place and the rest of the temple was torn, we read, from top to bottom. The fact was symbolic of the occasion. For our Lord, having offered the perfect sacrifice, ascended into heaven, tore aside the veil of mystery that hangs between earth and heaven, went, once for all, into his Father's presence to make atonement for your sins and mine.

To us, they seem remote and shadowy, these comparisons drawn from the rites of yesterday. Shall we, instead, think of our Lord's Ascension in terms of the Christian sacrifice? Think of him as the priest going up to the altar, going up, going away from us. The very psalm which the priest says on this occasion would be appropriate, wouldn't it, on our Lord's lips instead? "O God, sustain my cause, give me redress; save me from a treacherous foe"[1]—he is appealing against the infamous miscarriage of justice which condemned him, taking it up to a higher court, to be reversed at the bar of eternal justice. "Thou, O God, art all my strength; why hast thou cast me off?"—why, they are almost the very words he uttered on his cross. "The light of thy presence, the fulfilment of thy promise, let these be my escort, bringing me safe to thy holy mountain, to the tabernacle where thou dwellest"[2] —the Son of Man has found no rest on earth; the Son of God must go home. Think of our Lord, in his Ascension, as the priest climbing the altar steps; going up, going away from us, and yet not exactly leaving us behind. No, in a sense he takes us with him; takes our sins with him, to ask forgiveness of them, takes our needs with him, to plead them before God, takes with him, above all, our offering of love.

Our High Priest, we call him, for it is the business of a priest to mediate between man and God; and no one could do that perfectly except he who is both God and Man. And it is his humanness that we chiefly remember, when we think about the mystery of his Ascension; if I may quote once more from the Epistle to the Hebrews, "It is not as if our high priest was incapable of feeling for us in our humiliations; he has been through every trial, fashioned as we are, only sinless".[3] Since he went up into heaven, a cloud has concealed him from our sight; it has not concealed us from his. He knows our individual needs, and can feel for them, because he has had such needs himself. Oh, it is foolish of us, no doubt, to ask for sympathy in that way; we know, of course, that the divine nature is all-merciful—how else could it be divine? But somehow it makes it easier for us to focus our minds on the lovingness of God, if we can tell ourselves that Jesus Christ is in the bosom of the Father—Jesus Christ, who rested his head, at the last supper, on the bosom of a human friend. He has known all our trials, borne all the weaknesses that are a true part of our nature, been helpless in Mary's arms, hung desolate on the cross. "Gall and wormwood", we say to him with Jeremias, "gall and wormwood, keep all this well in memory",[4] and our gall and wormwood becomes less bitter to us, because we know that he remembers.

Since the Ascension, we have found it easier to realize the love of God, because it is mirrored for us in the human sympathy of Jesus Christ. But there is something else—since the Ascension, it has been easier for us to imagine heaven as a desirable goal. Try as we will, the

---

[1] Psalm 42. 1.   [2] *Ibid.*, 3.   [3] Hebrews 4. 15.
[4] Lamentations 3. 19.

idea of heaven eludes us. Are we to think of it as a place, from which every element of unhappiness is excluded? But we know how much our love of places is conditioned by moods and sentiments, by the desire for change, by association and by history! Or are we to think of it as a state? But then, how are we to think of a state except in terms of selfish enjoyment? Or should we look forward to being reunited with those we have loved? But how frail they are, these earthly bonds; how time impairs them! No, when we have tried everything, we shall find no better window on eternity than St Paul's formula, "to depart and be with Christ". If he has left us, and gone to heaven, it is so that we may no longer be disconcerted by the barrier of cloud that stands between us and it. We are not concerned to "go" here or there, to be in this or that state of existence. We want to find him.

So little, and so much it is given us to know about the ascended Christ.

17

PENTECOST[1]

FEW topics recur more regularly in conversation, few provide so much common material for discussion, few are so barren of any conclusion at the end of the evening, as the old question whether ghost stories are true or not. And there is an explanation which never fails to turn up and be considered, the explanation which was preferred, I believe, by Mgr Benson, a man who all his life took the keenest possible interest in the occult. It is this—that when some scene has taken place at a given spot, which is accompanied by very strong human emotions, a murder for example, or a suicide, the material surroundings of that spot become charged, as it were, impregnated with those stored-up emotions, as an electric battery is charged with electricity; and when a sufficiently psychic person comes along, or comes along on the proper anniversary, so that the external conditions of the original event repeat themselves, these stored-up impressions are communicated to his or her mind from the material surroundings themselves.

The material surroundings of the places in which we have been

[1] Sermon preached at Ampleforth Abbey and published in its *Ampleforth Journal*, May 1948.

through any violent emotional crisis possess the power of carrying us back into the past, of impressing upon our minds an echo, as it were, of the feelings we experienced long ago. More especially, I think, when the experience was an uncomfortable one. The place where you had a violent quarrel, or had to go through some very embarrassing interview; the place where you parted from a friend, as it proved, your last parting; the place where you received some sudden shock of bad news —how unforgettable are the memories which linger in such places as those; how easily the emotions once experienced there reconstruct themselves in the imagination! Even years after the original occurrence, you will feel a blush mounting to your cheeks, or a lump rising in your throat, from mere unconscious association with something which happened in the past.

If you come to think of it, there must have been one set of people in the history of the world for whom one particular room must have had associations so crowded and so vivid that they must have felt as if they had been familiar with the place for a lifetime, instead of a couple of months. The set of people I refer to were the apostles and those others, we do not know how numerous, who remained close followers of our Lord during his lifetime and threw in their lot with his Mother and his friends after the crucifixion. And the room in question must have been the upper room, the cenacle, as Christian piety names it, which was the chief focus of Christian history from the time when our Lord ate his last Passover till the time when the Holy Spirit came down on the day of Pentecost. Think of the mental pictures that room suggested to them, the mental pictures that distracted, if any did distract, the prayer in which they waited for the gift of the Holy Ghost.

For them, surely, the cenacle was a haunted room. They could remember how they first came into it, six weeks back; their spirits already overcast with the foreboding of tragedy. "With desire have I desired to eat this pasch with you before I suffer"[1]—such were the words with which their Master prefaced the meal, and struck, from the first, the note of parting. Then, almost immediately, he warned them that one of their own number, one of his chosen friends, would betray him. There is nothing, I suppose, more unsettling to man's whole being than the sudden discovery of treachery in his fellow man. To learn that some friend whose character you have taken for granted, to whom you have unbosomed yourself without reserve, on whom you have relied without hesitation, was really all the time something other than you thought him—that is an experience which of itself seems to

[1] Luke 22. 15.

turn the whole world upside down for you, challenges all your judgments and calls for a revision of all your sentiments. And more poignant still must have been the uncertainty; to know, though it were only for an hour, that one of their number was a traitor without knowing which; to feel that a confidence reposed even in Peter, even in the beloved disciple, might prove to be a confidence misplaced—that will have increased the tumult of their spirits. And, worst of all, that terrible whisper of doubt in the heart of each one, a doubt of his own ultimate loyalty, his constancy in the face of persecution, that dictated to each the shamefaced question, "Lord, is it I?"[1]

Meanwhile our Lord has risen from table, and girded himself with a towel; he is passing from one to another, offering to wash their feet. He is foreshadowing to them the sacramental remission of sins; that they cannot understand now, though they will understand it hereafter. They only realize that this ceremonial purification must be the prelude to some rite more holy and solemn than the paschal rite on which they are already engaged. And, sure enough, almost before their questionings have had time to die down, their Master is standing at the table, and has uttered the words that echo through Christendom from day to day, "Take, eat, this is my body. . . . This chalice is the New Testament in my blood."[2]

In that same room, I suppose, they reassembled an hour later, panic-stricken fugitives. They have seen the Son of Man taken by his enemies; seen it, and escaped with their lives. Yes, they are all there, James and John the sons of Zebedee, who boasted that they could drink the chalice of their Master and share his baptism of blood, there they are, in hiding. Thomas, who inspired his fellow apostles to accompany their Master on that fatal journey with a cry of despairing courage, "Let us also go, that we may die with him",[3] there he is, in hiding. They avoid one another's eyes, beaten men, not daring to accuse each other, every man knowing his own guilt. The only sorry boast of their party is Simon Peter; he at least followed at a distance, and, though it was too late to help, waited at least to see what would happen . . . And then the door opens, and Peter too joins them, his cheeks furrowed with tears, and the tale of their defection is complete.

In that same room they met again, three nights afterwards. The bitterness of the crucifixion lies behind them, and through the twilight of their doubt come flashes of hope. The sepulchre has been found empty, that is certain, and he who lay there has been seen, if the stories are true, in the garden, seen on the road to Emmaus. There will be

---

[1] Matthew 26. 22.   [2] *Ibid.*, 26. 28.   [3] John 11. 16.

trouble over this before long; the rulers of the Jews will find out their hiding-place and put them to the question; best keep the doors locked, for the present anyhow. And suddenly, through those locked doors, passes a figure that is well known to them; is it their Master himself? Or is it a spirit? He shows them his hands, he offers them his side to touch; he gives them his peace and his pardon, he sends them out in his Father's name; he commissions them to forgive sins. Twice in that same room they had proof unmistakable that he who died had risen again.

A room haunted with memories—through that door did Judas slink out into the night, so short a time since; on that table the consecrated chalice reposed; through that window they listened to the shouts of "Crucify him"; that floor had been trodden by impassible feet. It was in these surroundings that the Holy Ghost visited his people on the day of Pentecost. The inspiration he brought was to be something new, something altogether new in the world's history, yet it was to be based upon and rooted in memories of the past; "when he, the Spirit of truth, is come, he will teach you all things, and bring all things to your remembrance, whatsoever I have said unto you".[1] The scene of their inspiration for the future was to be a scene enriched by past experience.

Inspiration and experience, how seldom they go hand in hand! How old a complaint it is, *Si jeunesse savait, si vieillesse pouvait*;[2] if youth had the experience, or age the inspiration! And it is so with the religions of the world; look where you will outside the Catholic Church, and you will find that all religions suffer from one defect or the other. The religions of the East have, many of them, an immemorial antiquity, but they have no instinct which urges them forward, no initiative, no vital power of self-adaptation. The new religions which we invent for ourselves in the West are full of urge and initiative when they begin their careers; they dazzle the eye for their novelty, but they have no roots in experience, and therefore they do not last; in a century the wine has run out of them the effervescence is evaporated. But the Catholic Church, founded by the holy apostles with all the experience of Holy Week and Easter behind them, with all the possibilities of Pentecost in front of them, derived from the fact that the perpetual miracle of her unageing youth. In those six weeks before Pentecost the apostles had already lived through, as it were, the whole cycle of Church history; there was nothing callow, nothing tentative, nothing inexperienced about their methods from the very first. And, because she was born old, the Church remains ever young. That is why men

[1] John 14. 16.   [2] Henri Estienne, *Les Prémices*, Epigramme cxci.

fear her and hate her; they are conscious, even when they are furthest from believing in her claims, that she is neither new nor old, but eternal. She retains the memory of the cenacle and of the catacombs, yet for her Pentecost is continually repeating itself, making all things new. May the Holy Ghost who descended this day guide her and us in these disillusioned times, as in that first joyful dawn of her history.

18

THE MESSAGE OF THE CENACLE[1]

ALL through the Old Testament is the idea of God's Spirit as pervading the whole of nature; "The Spirit of the Lord fills the whole world, and that which containeth all things hath knowledge of the voice". And the medieval attitude—we have somehow rather lost sight of it—was to accept that point of view about the response of creation to God. "Thou", sang Adam of St Victor, "all things fillest, all things lovest, planets guidest, heaven movest, yet unmoved dost persevere." The love which bound the Father to the Son overflowed into created things, and made them, too, aspire lovingly to God.

If we have rather lost sight of that mystical notion, at least we are not allowed to forget that the Holy Spirit, long before our Lord came into the world, was active in the minds of men. "Who spoke by the prophets"—we are not going to cut ourselves adrift altogether from that Jewish Church which bore the Christian Church in its womb. The prophets under the old dispensation were Spirit-filled, were filled with the same Spirit as the apostles under the new. And when it says "the prophets", let us not make the mistake of picturing to ourselves exactly sixteen people in white beards, four of them labelled major prophets and twelve of them labelled minor prophets. It is a very easy thing, from the circumstances of our early education, for us Catholics to become label-minded, list-minded; all those lists, for example, at the end of the catechism! So many fruits of the Holy Ghost, so many ways of sharing in another's sin, everything wrapped up in silver paper and handed to you on a plate with parsley round it—we *must* beware of getting into the habit of drawing hard and fast lines all the time.

[1] A Whit Sunday meditation published in *The Tablet*, 27 May 1950.

No, when we say that the Holy Spirit spoke by the prophets, we ought to be thinking about Elias and Eliseus and a crowd of others who are mentioned by name, and a crowd of others who are not mentioned by name, and a much larger crowd of people who are not mentioned at all. The point is that all through the history of the Jewish people the Holy Spirit was at work, making vocal and putting on record the loving reaction of the Jewish mind to the loving God who had chosen out for himself one nation among all the nations in the world.

And did it happen only among the Jews? Do you not think that all the guesses which the heathen made about the divine nature and about human needs, Plato's guesses, Virgil's guesses, were evoked from them, less distinctly, less surely, but not less really, by the operation of the same Spirit? The human mind, a surging mass of undigested ideas, was being played upon, all the time, by chance beams of divine illumination, so that the heathen too could make, however imperfectly, their response. God did not leave himself without a witness; all the learning of all the ages, though it might be clothed in fantastic forms sometimes was part of this great rhythm, this great melody, which the Holy Spirit continued to play, even on the most unpromising instruments. So we read about the divine wisdom in the Book of Proverbs: "I made play before him all the while, made play in this world of dust, with the sons of Adam for my play-fellows".[1] Do not let us be content to label history, or the history of human thought, "sacred" and "profane", and leave it at that. That same divine goodness, which overflowed when the work of creation began, overflowed from sacred into profane channels; even among the heathen, not quite knowing how, not quite knowing why, men turned to God and made some guesses, at least, which were worth making.

And then comes Pentecost; at Pentecost, what happened? Why, that huge flow which had been dissipated, if it isn't irreverent to put it like that, among so many shallow channels, was canalized into a single stream; that irresistible force which hitherto had only produced faint echoes here and there, was compressed into a single narrow compass; and the result was a kind of flood, a kind of explosion. And yet the process follows the same lines as before. What is the point of all that long list of names from ancient geography which we hear read out on Whit Sunday? And why was it that the people from Elam and the parts of Libya about Cyrene had to be addressed each in his own tongue, each in the native dialect which he probably knew well enough as a child, but by now had almost forgotten? All these people could under-

[1] Proverbs 8. 30-31.

stand Greek; why did the apostles not talk to them in Greek? The answer is, surely, that the whole setting of the occasion was sacramental. It was fitting that the pilgrims at Jerusalem, that first Whit Sunday, should be addressed in all the different languages of the world, because they represented all the different peoples of the world. You are meant to see them as a motley crowd, gathered from all the nations under heaven, surging to and fro about these narrow streets, the rudimentary, unformed material of the Catholic Church, a mass waiting for Mind to energize and organize it. And once more the Spirit of God is moving over the waters, ready to fashion, at last, an adequate instrument which will express the chorus of creation's praise; the Catholic Church.

When St Peter began his speech on the day of Pentecost, he began with a quotation from the prophet Joel, about God pouring out his Spirit upon all mankind. And that quotation starts with the words, "It shall come to pass in the last days".[1] Why "in the last days"? The world didn't come to an end at Pentecost, it has been going on century after century ever since. It is the sort of thing that is always holding you up if you take the trouble to read the New Testament at all carefully; there are constant references to the Christian dispensation, which seem to imply that it is only the fag-end of the world's history, "in the last times", "when the fulfilment of time had come", and so on. What is the meaning of language like that? I think we are meant to see the Christian dispensation, not as the fag-end of the world's history at all, but as the final bursting into flower of something which, all through history, has been in the bud. Or, if I may go back to the rather daring metaphor I used just now, the Christian Church is the detonation of that explosive for which a train has been prepared through the centuries. Everything that happened before the day of Pentecost was a kind of rehearsal of what was due to happen on the day of Pentecost. However many centuries may elapse between the redemption of the world and the end of the world, we lump them all together as "the last times". Because these are the times of fulfilment; that influence which the Holy Spirit exercised hitherto in a general, impartial sort of way, picking out here and there a mouthpiece suited to his ends, he now exercises within a delimited sphere, under agreed conditions, with calculable results. If I may put it very crudely, let me say this; that in our human experience a spirit does not function normally without a body to which it is attached, of which it is the coefficient, the counterpart. And until the Christian Church came into existence, the mystical body of Christ, the Holy Spirit had not, within created existence, a

[1] Joel 2. 28.

body which was his natural self-expression. Now he has. "The wind blows where it will, and thou canst hear the sound of it, but knowest nothing of the way it came or the way it goes"[1]—that was the whole truth, when our Lord spoke. The activities of the Holy Spirit were altogether unconfined, altogether incalculable. Now, he has a body in which and through which his activities are normally mediated. The dove which had no rest for the soles of its feet has now localized its presence in the ark of Christ's Church.

Baptism, the sacraments, the life of grace—it has all been brought within our human compass; this or that exterior action we perform, and the invisible assistance of the Holy Spirit infallibly accompanies those actions; we *know*, for example, that his gifts are bestowed where the sacrament of confirmation is bestowed, although there is no sound of a rushing mighty wind, although there are no tongues of fire parting this way and that, although no miraculous gifts of utterance follow and attest the divine descent. That is the fourth mood of the melody; dare we say it? The captive dove; the response of humanity to its creator regularized, regimented, expressing itself through forms of liturgy and by means of outward tokens. It is a very impoverished Christian life which seeks to attain union with God in entire isolation from the company of its fellow Christians. And it is our characteristic privilege, as Catholics, to enjoy the certainty of belonging to a Spirit-filled, Spirit-actuated body; if we remain in its unity, if we function as its members, we know that the life of the Spirit is effortlessly, imperceptibly expressing itself in each part of the body, and therefore in us.

And at all times the influence of the Holy Spirit in our lives should be manifested as a completion and a response. We must not expect it to make itself felt in sudden, unaccountable illuminations, in outpourings of consolation and of sensible love. Such experiences are, perhaps, less beyond the reach of the average Christian than the average Christian is disposed to imagine. But we have no right to expect them, and no reason to find fault either with God or with ourselves if they don't come; if they come but rarely; if they come and go, in a rhythm whose rise and fall is inexplicable to us. We must not expect, surely, that the operations of divine grace in us shall take place, normally at least, on the level of consciousness. As you read this, physical changes are passing over you of which you are wholly unconscious; your hair, your nails are growing at this moment. Why not spiritual changes too? "The wind breathes where it will, and thou canst hear the sound of it, but knowest nothing of the way it came or the way it goes"; the Holy

[1] John 3. 8.

Spirit is not like some egotistic genius, determined that his interference should be recognized and acknowledged wherever it is brought to bear. He is quite content that his inspirations should seem, to us, bright ideas of our own; that his shaping of our characters should be unaccompanied by any glow of feeling, such as might indicate the source whence it comes. The pattern he weaves in us is something contained in, not something super-added to, the common fabric of our lives.

But because he will work thus imperceptibly, that is no reason why he should pretend he is not there, behave as if we were the masters of our own destiny, and needed no impulse from without. We shall be happier about the decisions we make, and gain from that a sense of confidence which will help to justify our decisions, if we make a practice of appealing for his unseen, unfelt influence at every cross-roads of our lives, even the most insignificant. Our prayer will be less anxious and less restive, if we learn to abandon both the objects of it and the methods of it more and more to his discretion. We shall be the heirs of Pentecost in proportion as we are devotees of the cenacle.

19

THE BIRTH OF THE CHURCH[1]

But there are also many other things which Jesus did, which if they were written every one, the world itself, I think, would not be able to contain the books that should be written.—John 21. 25.
The former treatise I made, O Theophilus, of all the things which Jesus began to do and to teach, until the day on which he was taken up.—Acts 1. 1.

THOSE two verses come immediately next to one another in the Bible, and they present, surely, a very curious contrast. St John, it seems, in concluding his gospel, is overwhelmed with the sense that he has used very little out of the possible material at his disposal; "there are many other things which Jesus did". St Luke, on the other hand, not merely treats his gospel as an account of all that Jesus did and taught; his phrase is, "all that Jesus began to do and to teach", as if even that all were only the beginning of a story, the preface of his

---

[1] A Whit Sunday meditation published in *The Tablet*, 11 May 1940.

next volume. Jesus began—what does he mean? Surely, if ever a complete and perfect life was lived, it was the life which began with Christmas and finished with the Ascension! He who lived it claimed for it such completeness: "I have finished the work which thou gavest me to do",[1] and again, when the last struggle of all is over, "It is consummated".[2] How is it then that St Luke, sitting down to describe the missionary labours of the apostles and birth-pangs of the infant Church, brushes aside this unique achievement of their divine Master as if it were so much pioneer work, destined to be outdone and over-shadowed by the events that followed?

And yet there it is, in the Bible; Jesus began. If all that he did were written down, the world itself would not contain the books that should be written. He cured so many that were sick, and we never hear about them in detail. He preached in so many towns and villages, and today their very names are obliterated. So many questions his bewildered followers must have brought to him; so many words of warning or of encouragement he must have spoken to them; so many converts must have hailed, and followed, and forsaken him; so many fatigues and disappointments must have attended his mission—and the record of it has never reached our day. And yet, this was only a beginning. Some-how, the history of the Church which St Luke sets forth in the Acts is not a mere epilogue, not even a mere sequel to the history of her Founder. It is Part II of the same volume. Jesus began, in his earthly life; why then, Jesus went on, after he had ascended into heaven. In what sense? Are we to suppose that our Lord himself, even after his Ascension, still labours, still suffers, on our behalf? That, although he no longer shares our transitory world, our mortal flesh, he still feels the stab of disappointment when his chosen friends betray him; still agonizes, as in Gethsemani, with regret for the failures of his servants, with anxiety for their future? That the blasphemies men hurl at him sting now, as they stung when he stood in the judgment-hall; that the taunts men utter, reproaching him with his powerlessness to save, are bitter now as when he hung on Calvary?

That, of course, is inconceivable. In the heaven where he reigns there can be no sorrow, no fear, no anxiety now, even for the servants he has ransomed, still less for him who ransomed them. You may say that his Sacred Heart pities, for pity is an activity of the emotions. You may not say that it suffers; it has suffered once for all. Only once the mocking and the rejection, only once the crown, and the nails, and the spear. Once for all, in that perfect life lived amongst men, in that atoning

[1] John 17. 4.   [2] John 19. 30.

P

death dedicated for men, incarnate God suffered and entered into his rest. The incalculable merits by which he won our redemption were the fruit of thirty years, three years, three days, three hours: that further effort should add to them is neither needful nor thinkable.

That life of suffering is not, cannot be continued; and yet we are told, Jesus began. What then, are we to suppose that he began, and what he began others finished? That the life he lived, the death he died, were valuable precisely because they inspired others to imitate his example. and carry on the work which he had left unfinished? That the merits which the sacrifice of Calvary brought into the treasury of divine mercy on our behalf, were only an instalment, only the opening of an account? That it was left to us to pay off that account gradually, through the centuries, by human merits, less precious indeed, but not less necessary to our salvation than his own?

This suggestion is as blasphemous as the other. That life, that death, were a model indeed to be imitated, but a model that can never be approached. The merits of that sacrifice were not unique only, but all-sufficing. That work to need supplementing with man's assistance which was sealed by the blood of Christ!

No; our Lord in his mortal life began a work which was not finished when he ascended into heaven. He does not suffer, he does not labour now. And yet, it must be he who continues the work which he began; no human postscript could add to its value or enhance its efficacy. How is it, then, that he continues the work which his Ascension interrupted? For there is none that can continue it, save he.

The answer to that is the mystery of Pentecost. Pentecost commemorates the birth of the Church, and the birth of the Church is the second birth of Christ.

Think of our Lady, as she was when the Angel Gabriel came to her at the Annunciation. The world all around lay overwhelmed by the deluge of sin; the Holy Spirit, like the dove that could find no rest for her feet when the waters were over the face of the earth, could find no lodgment among the souls of men, save here. Or, if you will, here was Gedeon's fleece, that alone, in a world of drought, was visited by the dew in the morning. Hers was the one heart that could be the accomplice of that momentous inspiration. Her virginity defied the assaults of sin, a fortress, locked safely against all human approach, yielding entrance only to the King. In devout expectation, scarce knowing what she was to expect, she waited until the angelic message came to her. And with that, the Holy Spirit overshadowed her, and in fullness of time she gave birth to the Christ.

Are we not to see, in the cenacle at Jerusalem, where our Lady herself, with the apostles and those other faithful souls, waited for the day of Pentecost to be fulfilled, an image of that immaculate Mother whom the angel saluted at Nazareth? Those thirty-three years have come and gone, during which incarnate God walked on earth; and what is there to show for it in the end? A hundred and twenty souls waiting for the fulfilment of his promise. Others there may have been, perhaps, in Galilee, a faithful heart here and there which still cherished the memory of the Masters who had been taken away from the earth. But this was all the nucleus left for the operation of the Holy Ghost, a hundred and twenty souls! All around, the world still went on its way, incredulous and unredeemed. But here the locked doors that keep the world at bay, and will open only to the touch of a divine hand, symbolize afresh the virginity of the blessed Mother. In devout expectation, scarce knowing what they are to expect, they wait until the time appointed by the providence of God. And with that, the Holy Ghost overshadows them; and in a moment, Christ is born anew; this time in his mystical body, which is the Catholic Church.

Only, this time the life which has come to the birth is animated, not by a human Spirit, but by the Holy Ghost himself. At his Incarnation our Lord would become fully Man; would take, therefore, not a human body, but a human spirit also, which he could restore into his Father's hands as he hung on the cross. But when he takes to himself this mystical body of his, the Spirit which is its life is nothing other than the Third Person of the Blessed Trinity. "That they may be one", our Lord prayed, "even as thou and I, Father, are one";[1] how is it, by what bond is it, that the Father and the eternal Word are one? The Holy Spirit is himself the Love that proceeds from and unites them both. And, that his Church might be one even as he is one with the Father, Christ would not be content to quicken that mystical body of his that was born in the cenacle by some transient influence of grace. The very love which unites the Godhead should be the life that beat in his Church.

And so the life of Christ's mystical body took its origin. In it, he does not repeat what he did in his mortal life; he continues what he began in his mortal life. The merits which he won for us by his mortal life are transmitted to us through our membership in his mystical life. The sacrifice which was made once for all on Calvary is not repeated, cannot be repeated, in time. But the sacrifice of Calvary echoes down the ages whenever the Mass is said and whenever the tabernacle is

[1] John 17. 21.

opened; Christ on the altar is continuing what Christ on Calvary began.

So, too, the Church in her teaching office does not arrive, does not hope to arrive, at a fuller revelation than the Revelation which was made to her once for all by the lips of incarnate Truth. It is only that her privilege of inerrancy enables her to interpret for every age the doctrine once for all delivered to her; what Christ began in Peter's boat, he continues from the slopes of the seven hills. And even the lives of the saints, in which Christendom mirrors the life of its Founder, the fortitude of the martyrs, the mortifications of confessors, the purity of virgins, in what power were they sustained, but the power which his own merits have bequeathed to his mystical body? In the life of Father Pio, or St John Bosco, or St Teresa of Lisieux, Christ in our generation is continuing what Christ in his own generation began.

He breathed on them, and said, "Receive ye the Holy Ghost".[1] The action was theandric,[2] had sacramental efficacy; one sigh of the Incarnate has set the world tingling with a divine influence till the end of time. Shall we doubt that, because his operations are signalized no longer by the rushing of a whirlwind or by visible tongues of fire? Our bodies are the temples of the Holy Ghost; in each of us he would find his cenacle; in each of us he would renew his Pentecost. Only, have we locked the doors of our hearts to secure him welcome? Only, have we waited for him, that he should find us ready for his inspirations when he came?

20

THE HEART OF CHRIST[3]

It was God's good pleasure to let all completeness dwell in him.—Colossians 1. 19.

RATHER more than three hundred years ago, a book came out in London under the title, "The Heart of Christ in Heaven towards sinners on earth; or, A Treatise demonstrating the gracious disposition and tender affection of Christ in His human Nature, now in glory,

---

[1] John 20. 22. [2] Of or pertaining to both God and man.
[3] A sermon preached at St John's Church, Chorlton-cum-Hardy, Manchester, on 17 June 1956.

unto His members, under all sorts of infirmities, either of sin or misery."[1] You would have made certain, after reading so much, that it had been produced by one of that little band of exiles who practised the old religion overseas, and smuggled in books as best they would, by way of keeping it alive here in England. You would have been wrong; it was written by Thomas Goodwin, a distinguished Congregationalist minister who attended Oliver Cromwell on his deathbed. You may read more, if you will, about that very remarkable man in Mr Watkin's book, *Poets and Mystics*.[2] I only mention it here to show that devotion to the Sacred Heart of Jesus Christ, commonly thought of as a Popish superstition from the middle of the seventeenth century, is in fact a form of piety which can commend itself to all Christians.

And yet, when some visitor, not of our faith, comes into a church like this in the month of June, he is commonly repelled by the statue he sees at the end of the nave, opposite the Madonna, marked out at this time of the year, by flowers set round it and candles burning in front of it. Not just because of the flowers and the candles; not just because of the statue itself—though that is often enough executed in poor taste, the features insipid, the mark of the wound in the pierced side crudely realistic. No, it's the whole history of the thing that makes no appeal to him—a nun having a vision about our Lord showing her the wound, and talking about "the Heart which loves so much, and is loved so little in return"; what is this but sentimentalism, and a kind of sentimentalism which we despise even among our fellow men? After all, is there any position more undignified than that of the rejected lover who cannot keep the thing to himself, but must needs go about exposing his wounded feelings for all the world to see, inviting our sympathy because he is unloved? Yet that is the figure under which the divine Love represents itself, in the devotion of the Sacred Heart.

But remember that this is the language in which, all through the Old Testament, almighty God refers to the apostasies of the Jewish people. The covenant which he made with the Israelites when he brought them out of Egypt was a kind of marriage contract, engaging both sides to fidelity; and when they turn to the worship of idolatrous gods, he appeals to it. "And thou", he says through Jeremias, "and thou with many lovers hast played the wanton; come back to me, and thou shalt find welcome."[3] This is pleading language, and it is a God who pleads.

As we know, when the Old Testament talks like that it is using a metaphor; the Old Testament is full of metaphors. When it talks about

---

[1] London, 1642.   [2] London, 1953, pp. 56-69.   [3] Jeremias 3. 14.

God raising his hand, stretching out his arm, keeping a watchful eye over his friends, giving a ready ear to their prayers, we are not to suppose that he, who is pure Spirit, has hands or arms or eyes or ears like ourselves. And so it is when he describes himself as a jealous lover; he means that if he were a man like ourselves, this is how the infidelity of his friends would affect him.

If he were a man—and then, in the fullness of time, he did become a man like ourselves; he trod our earth, and was subject, as Man, to the play of emotions; wept and rejoiced, was indignant, and felt fear. The metaphors had come true at last; God Incarnate really saw with human eyes, stretched out a human hand to save. And he was accessible, like ourselves, to those gusts of feeling which *we* find it so difficult to control. "Jesus, looking round about on them with anger"[1]—when an injury was done to the honour of his Father in heaven, he flared up. "At that time, Jesus was filled with gladness"—the success of his first missionaries gave him the same feeling which comes to you and me when good news reaches us. "Jesus wept"[2]—the tragedy of a friend's death drew from him its tribute of natural tears.

And he did not hide from us his disappointments. "Jerusalem, Jerusalem, still murdering the prophets, and stoning the messengers that are sent to thee, how often have I been ready to gather thy children together, and thou didst refuse it!"[3] How often—he looks back over the sad record of Jewish history; the authentic accents of a divine Person pierce through the veil of his humanity; here is God weeping with human eyes over the pent-up sorrows of a human heart.

And that is the real meaning of the Sacred Heart devotion; it translates the divine Nature into human terms for us. When all is said and done, we find it hard, don't we, to get God into our mind-picture? His glory dazzles us; we are confused by the thought of the enormous gulf which lies between him and his creatures. We know that his Providence extends over all his works; he caters even for the sparrows, and yet . . . he is so great, and we are so small! Even our sins—just an unkind word said about a neighbour, and we tell ourselves that we have offended God; think of the scale of the thing, our little lapse, and his infinite existence, put side by side! And then we think of the Sacred Heart, and all at once the thing becomes vivid to us. Jesus Christ in heaven, taking an interest in our tiny needs, as he took an interest in so many tiny needs on earth. Jesus Christ hurt by our sins, as he was hurt by so many slights and disappointments up and down the villages of Galilee. The echoes of our prayer no longer seem to die away in infinite

[1] Mark 3. 5.   [2] John 11. 35.   [3] Matthew 23. 37.

distance; they strike a chord in the Sacred Heart, and become vocal to us, real to us.

And if our critics still object that we are too sentimental over our devotions in this month of June; that we single out one particular side of our Lord's character, represent him too insistently in one particular attitude, one of mercy, and tenderness, and welcome, let us remind them that it is just these qualities in the divine Nature which we find it most difficult to believe in; here, most of all, we need a diagram in flesh and blood to convince us. How can God, so upright a Judge, be merciful? How can he, who is without passion, be tender to us? How can he, who has no need of human companionship, welcome us? It is these qualities that we rejoice to see mirrored in the Sacred Heart. But that is not all.

The statues, the holy pictures represent our Lord in one particular attitude, as he revealed himself to Sister Margaret Mary; an attitude of tender abasement, of mournful pleading with mankind. And, as I say, people from outside who come into our churches look at it and are scandalized. Is this all your Christ, they ask, this weak, womanish figure, in a posture of sentimental appeal? Is your religion all sugary sweetness, all variations on a minor key? Has it stopped still with the seventeenth century; has it no message for today? And to that we answer, No, you have got it all wrong. The Sacred Heart is the treasury of *all* those splendid qualities with which a perfect life was lived; is the repository of *all* those noble thoughts which mankind still venerate in the gospels. It was the Sacred Heart that burned with anger when the traders were driven out of the temple; it was the Sacred Heart that loved the rich young man, yet would not spare him; it was the Sacred Heart that defied Pilate in his own judgment-hall. It is strong and stern and enduring; it hates prevarications and pretences. The perfect flowering of a human life, not on this occasion or that, but all through, all the time, the utter sacrifice of a human will—*that* is what the Sacred Heart means, and there is no picture, no statue on earth that can portray its infinite beauty.

21

THE FIRE OF LOVE

I am come to cast fire on the earth; and what will I but that it be kindled?—
Luke 12. 49.

FIRE! What sound is there more terrifying to human ears? Not that, I suppose, there is a very large number of deaths from fire every year; not that, in London at any rate, the ravages caused by fire are often widespread or important. But there is, even in the smallest conflagration, an element of uncertainty, a threat of unlimited danger, which makes the hearts of the boldest stop for a moment. You see the flames suddenly leap up as they catch a window-frame or a curtain, and imagination allows you to see that on a large scale. You realize that with every moment of its duration the flames grow terribly in volume; fire breeds fire, communicates itself to all that stands in its way—everything yields before it, and in yielding becomes a traitor, deserts to the enemy, helps to spread the danger and increase the panic. What will happen if it is allowed to go on another half-hour, another hour, unchecked? Will it not be too late for anything to be done at all but leave the whole building to perish? Imagination runs riot at the thought of what might happen; and I suppose we all catch an echo of that feeling of alarm when, above the roar of London traffic, we hear the unmistakable clanging of the firemen's bell.

Fire—I suppose that is at the root of our fear of it—is insatiable; food only increases its appetite; the more it has devoured, the more hungrily it ravens. It is not surprising, then, that it serves human language with a hundred metaphors, stands for type of any violent passion or any sudden agitation which threatens peace of mind in the society or the individual. In the old Greek story, Hecuba the Queen of Troy dreamt that she had given birth to a fire-brand; and the son who was born to her at that time was the reckless Paris, who through his treachery and his lawless love brought war on his country and destruction upon his native city. One man could be pointed out as the source of that universal ruin, just as one match or one spark may be pointed out as the insignificant cause that set a whole factory or a whole warehouse ablaze, just as the smouldering embers of a camp fire may set the forest for miles around roaring in sheets of flame. No wonder the legend called Paris a firebrand.

Now, when the Holy Spirit overshadowed our blessed Lady, and she became the virgin Mother of Incarnate God, she too had brought a fire into the world. "I am come to cast fire on the earth", our Lord says, "and what will I but that it be kindled?" "Beware", said Moses to the people of Israel in his last charge to them, "beware lest thou ever forget the covenant of the Lord thy God which he hath made with thee . . . because the Lord thy God is a consuming fire, a jealous God."[1] A jealous God—he claims everything from his creatures, will not be content that they should rest and find their satisfaction in anything less than himself. A consuming fire—so tyrannous is his love for us whom his own hands have made that when he reveals himself, all that is base in us and all that is unworthy in us—and how much is there in us which is not base and unworthy?—must needs shrink and shrivel away before his presence. "Which of you can dwell with devouring fire?" asks Isaias, "Which of you shall dwell with everlasting burnings?"[2] Man in the presence of his Maker is as stubble ready to be burnt up by the fire —that is the terrified conviction of the Hebrew prophets.

And with the Incarnation, what happened? That consuming fire of Godhead, before the breath of which, we had thought, everything that is human must shrivel and melt away, was brought into the most close and intimate union conceivable with a human nature. But that human nature was endowed with every perfection of which human nature is capable; there was no base dross in it to be purged away even by the searching flame of a divine presence; it was true metal all through. What wonder, then, that the human heart of Jesus of Nazareth, like metal that is perfectly tempered and needs no more refining, should have become as it were a glowing mass, white-hot with the influence of divine love? And what wonder, if a white-hot mass of metal scorches and kindles all around it no less than flame itself, that the Sacred Heart of Jesus should not only glow with the divine love, but kindle with that same influence all that comes within its reach? The fire he came to send on the earth was none other than the fire of love which penetrated and informed his own sacred humanity.

During the thirty years of his hidden life, according to the inscrutable counsel of God, this fire of divine love burned without seeking to kindle what lay around it; isolated in the sacred home at Nazareth, it lived to God alone. But when in the fullness of time the three years of the public ministry began, then its influence must needs burst forth and set the world ablaze. Do you remember how the two disciples who met our Lord on the road to Emmaus after his Resurrection failed, at first,

[1] Deuteronomy 4. 23, 24.   [2] Isaias 23. 14.

to recognize him, until he made himself known to them in the breaking of bread; and their wondering afterwards how they could have been so blind as not to know who it was? "Did not our hearts *burn* within us", they said, "as he walked with us by the way?"[1] Their hearts burned within them, they ought to have recognized him then. That was, it seems, the effect which our blessed Lord's company had on those who were with him, unless pride and obstinate prejudice threw a sort of fireproof curtain round them—the flame of love that burned in the Sacred Heart communicated itself to the hearts of others; theirs glowed too, they knew not why, from the contagion of its proximity.

And when, at the end of the public ministry, our Lord suffered for us on his cross, then indeed the heart that so burned with charity became a crucible, turning all the sufferings and injuries inflicted upon it into rich incense; then the conflagration which he had brought upon the earth passed all power of human malice to control or extinguish it. Many waters cannot quench love—those impious hands that would have put an end to our Lord's influence by persecuting him to the death achieved, instead, the very opposite—the flames of his love rose all the higher for their efforts to combat it.

> My faultless breast the furnace is,
> The fuel, wounding thorns,
> Love is the fire, and sighs the smoke,
> The ashes, shames and scorns;
> The fuel Justice layeth on,
> And Mercy blows the coals,
> The metal in this furnace wrought
> Are men's defiled souls.[2]

The Sacred Heart of Jesus, in that hour of its human tragedy, began to draw all hearts towards itself, to melt and transfuse them with its own ardour of charity.

So he died and rose and ascended into heaven; it might have looked, to the outward view, as if it were all over; the Jews his enemies might congratulate themselves, flatter themselves with the fancy that they had extinguished the conflagration which menaced the security of their pride. But no, the fire was only smouldering; it had not died out. It smouldered still in a few human hearts—not more, perhaps, than a hundred and twenty, this glow of love which they had caught from their close intimacy with the Master who had left them. It only needed a wind to fan those embers into life. And with the day of Pentecost the

---

[1] Luke 24. 32.   [2] Blessed Robert Southwell, "The Burning Babe".

Holy Ghost came down, a rushing mighty wind, and tongues of visible fire lighted upon their heads as they sat in the upper room, the symbol of that inward fire which his visitation fanned into pure flame. "The just shall shine", says the Book of Wisdom, "and shall run to and fro like sparks among the stubble."[1] So the flame that was kindled in the upper room swept through Jerusalem—three thousand souls that day, five thousand souls the next, brought under the influence of the holocaust of love which had been offered for them on Calvary. They continued daily, this multitude of believers, in the breaking of bread; the heart of Jesus in the Holy Eucharist fed the flame within them and made them in their turn missionaries for the faith they had received. The fire was spreading, and the malice of the Jews looked on helplessly, unable to quench the infectious fervour that had set their city ablaze.

What need to follow the history of that conflagration further? Still, all down the centuries, the love that burns in the Sacred Heart has found in men's hearts fresh fuel to catch its flame. Again and again, through the centuries, men have prophesied that the Christian faith was doomed: "the superstition", they say to one another, "cannot last much longer; the blaze has lasted so many centuries; in time it must burn itself out". They do not understand that though the flame of charity in our imperfect human souls seems here to mount, there to die down as the Spirit, blowing where he will, fans it or lets it smoulder, the heart of the blaze is something that glows white-hot with a heat which never varies and can never spend itself. The heart of all this conflagration in the world which we call the Christian religion is the Sacred Heart of Jesus Christ, still white-hot with the interpenetrating glow which the Godhead communicates to it, inextinguishable and indefectible as the Being of God himself. Let them try to quench the flames, they will rise higher; let them wait to see the end of the conflagration, and it will burst out with fresh vigour where they least expected it. Our Lord Jesus Christ came to cast a fire on the earth; and what was his will but that it should be kindled? And what is his will, no human effort can gainsay.

As for us Christians, we will draw near to it. Oh, we are very cautious about it, some of us; we only just want to warm ourselves a little, we don't want to get scorched with the flames. Or are we really Christians, when we calculate like that? Are we really Christians, when we think that the fire of divine love which beats in the Sacred Heart can destroy anything in us, except that base dross in our natures, that worldliness, that selfishness, that pride of the human spirit, which as

[1] Wisdom 3. 7.

Christians we should want to see purged away? It was not so that the
saints understood the invitation of the Sacred Heart; they would not
come near it hesitatingly and with calculation, as if to warm their
hands at it. Rather, they would plunge themselves into that abyss of
fire, to be refined of all that was unworthy, to be melted and moulded
according to God's plan, to become, themselves, glowing reflections
of its heat to kindle the cold hearts of their fellow men.

Let us think what it is we want this divine flame of the Sacred Heart
to do for us when we draw near to it, as we do draw near to it every
time we receive our Lord in the Holy Eucharist. We want, as I say, to be
purged, to be refined. "I offer to thee, Lord", says the *Imitation of
Christ*, "all the sins and offences which I have ever committed since
the day when I could first sin even to this hour, that thou wouldest
burn and consume them with the fire of thy charity."[1] And the
burning away of our sins, remember, is not a process quite external
to ourselves, although the sins lie in the past and have already been
forgiven by the sacrament of penance. Their influence lives on in our
lives, more, probably, than we know; the affection we still retain for
them and for the occasions of them is still a part of our character; a
part of our character, it may be, which we rather admire, or other
people admire in us. But it is these stains of our sins that we must offer
courageously to be burned and seared away by the white-hot charity
of the Sacred Heart, if we are really in earnest about it. Remember,
we have purgatory to look forward to, and it is these stains of our
earthly conversation which will then have to be refined away by the
fire that burns from without, if we have not already consumed them
through the influence of the divine fire that burns within.

That, then, is the first effect we are to pray for, when we draw near
this furnace of love, the heart of Jesus in the Holy Eucharist—that the
dross of our sinfulness may be purged away. And the next is that we
ourselves may grow hot, red-hot, white-hot, from that contact. You
see, it is the nature of this mysterious thing we call fire to reproduce
itself; the effect of a live coal on a dead coal is to make it like itself,
red-hot. So it is with the divine love; we want to be so transformed with
it that we shall become in some measure like Jesus Christ. It would be
true to say, of course, that in proportion as our hearts are more
enflamed with the love of God we become more like God. But, you
see, that tells us so little. We can form only such distant ideas, abstract,
negative sort of ideas, about what God is like, that it would be a
hopeless model to set before ourselves if we said, "I want to be like

[1] *Imitation of Christ*, Book IV, ch. 9.

God". But to say, "I want to be like Jesus Christ"—that is a very different matter. Jesus Christ has lived as Man on earth, and the record of his gracious sayings and doings is still left with us. To say "make our hearts like thy most Sacred Heart" does convey a definite idea to our minds, because we can read in the holy gospels how that most Sacred Heart was wrung with the wilfulness and the injustice and the ingratitude of men, and still loved them and prayed for their pardon. That then is the second effect we pray for when we draw near the Sacred Heart, that our hearts may become like it, as flame is kindled from flame.

And the third effect we shall pray for is that we, too, in our turn, may be able to set light to other hearts, even colder than ours, as the glow of the divine flame diffuses itself more and more through our own. In nature, those substances which conduct heat not only absorb it into themselves but pass it on to their surroundings. And so it is with the love of God. Nobody, says St Augustine, can kindle others until he is himself ablaze. It's true, of course, that in the Providence of God the good which is done by a man or by a mission, the amount of conversation achieved, is out of all proportion to what we should have expected. God is not tied down by his human instruments. But for all that, if we want to bring others to the faith, if we want to reclaim others from lives of sin, if we want to bring up our children in the love of God, then the first thing is to burn red-hot with the love of God ourselves. And then, if it be his will, we shall be able to pass the conflagration on.

May our Lord Jesus Christ kindle and evermore keep alive in our hearts the flame of charity which his most Sacred Heart has sent upon the earth.

22

SAINTS PETER AND PAUL[1]

Afterwards, when Cephas came to Antioch, I made an open stand against him.—Galatians 2. 11.

ON the feast of SS. Peter and Paul, the Church, almost embarrassingly prodigal with her store of memories, invites us to think, at one and the same time, about two great heroes who died in her service.

[1] A sermon preached at the Church of Our Most Holy Redeemer and St Thomas More, Chelsea, on the Feast of SS. Peter and Paul, 29 June 1947.

Two great constellations of sanctity, which the telescope of pious meditation finds it difficult to take in with one sweep.

At the time when the two apostles met face to face at Antioch, the Church had still to decide the question, how much of the Jewish law Gentile converts must be expected to obey. And to St Paul's mind, the attitude of his brother apostle seemed a betrayal. St Peter was blowing hot and cold; it was a kind of hypocrisy—he calls it as much—to eat at the Gentile table one day, at the Jewish table the next. Prince of the apostles he might be, but all the more fatal would be his bad example, all the more important it was to put him right. . . . Are we shocked at his boldness? Do we tell ourselves that was hardly the way to speak to the Pope? Well, St Paul had the advantage of being a saint; and if it comes to that, St Catherine of Siena offered fairly outspoken advice to the Pope in her day. Nor, I think, could the most hardened theologian have maintained that St Peter was concerned, at the moment, to interpret the mind of the Church, or to legislate for posterity. He was simply doing his best to solve an awkward social problem; and all we read in the Acts make it clear that he was on St Paul's side in the Jewish-Gentile controversy. The protest—so much, I think, we can infer from St Paul's language—was effective; there were no bones broken, and the Vicar of Christ, not for the first or the last time in history, accepted correction. Like Innocent XI over the condemnation of Molinos, he was content to say "I have been wrong".

No, there is nothing distressing to the Christian conscience, either in the fact that St Paul should have disagreed with St Peter, or in the fact that St Peter should have been on the wrong side. Nor is it historically accurate to think of St Peter as a man wedded to old ways of thought, over-anxious about what other people would think; the account given of him in the Acts of the Apostles is enough to prove the contrary. But we may, if we will, concentrate our attention upon this particular scene in the lives of two great princes of the Church, and trace in it the age-long conflict between two forces in the history of the Church. Let us not call them two contrary, rather two complementary forces, the resultant of which is the well-being of the Catholic community. One is the tendency to strike out on new lines, try new experiments, assert, wherever it may be lawfully asserted, the principle of freedom. The other is a jealous regard for tradition, for established precedent; a reluctance to be stampeded by the fashion of the moment, to barter away, for some momentary advantage, a long inheritance of accumulated wisdom. Call them, if you will, the Liberal and the Conservative tendency; but do not forget that those words have modern associations which will confuse our thought, if we are not careful in the use of them.

I shall be told that the Catholic Church is not alone in feeling, century after century, the strain of that conflict. It is all around us; in a changing world, all our debates can easily be summed up under the formula, "Is it wiser to go forward, or to protect what we have?" But we Catholics, it must be remembered, cannot approach these questions so lightly, or with such free hands, as our neighbours. It is the first business of the Church to safeguard a deposit of revealed truth handed down to her, for all time, by a divine Founder; let her prove false to that trust, and the Church unchurches herself. Accordingly, our instinct as Catholics is conservative; the danger is always that we shall take our stand against new departures merely because they are new departures, and it is not difficult for our critics to represent us, at every turn, as worshippers of the past, enemies of all liberty and of all enlightenment. What a lot of trouble it would save, if things were as simple as all that! But you and I know that things are not as simple as all that. Inside the Church as well as out of it, with larger issues at stake, and therefore with more anxious sense of responsibility, the question is discussed, "Is it wiser to go forward, or to protect what we have?"

Our attitude, at first sight, is not always consistent; the pendulum swings now this way, now that. A hundred years ago, when Pius IX was reigning, it looked as if the Church had declared war on freedom, and it was widely believed that she had done so. If you read a document like Pope Pius IX's Syllabus of Errors, or even some of Newman's writings at the same period, you will find Liberalism referred to as if it were a kind of sin. Even a matter of forty years ago, when Modernism was in the air, to describe yourselves as a Liberal Catholic would have exposed you to the most lively suspicions. How is it that today you find both in France and in Italy, and not only in France and Italy, political parties which are republican and progressive, manned by Catholic statesmen, and appealing to Catholic principle, which seem to flourish unrebuked? Would Pope Pius IX, you wonder, have received M. Bidault or Signor de Gasperi in audience? And yet the contradiction is only apparent, not real. What has happened in the last hundred years is not that *we* have changed, but that the world has changed about us. Yesterday, the morbid element in human thought was in revolt against authority; today, it is in revolt against liberty. Today, as yesterday, the Church throws her weight into the opposite scale. Rest assured that we shall get no credit for it; we shall be told that we are only manoeuvring for position, that our democratic professions are only hypocrisy. But for ourselves, to whom the Church is a supernatural family, not an international conspiracy, the reflection is worth making, that after nineteen centuries of existence she is still young, still making experiments. We are the fellow citizens both of St Peter and of St Paul.

Shall we remember to pray all the more earnestly for the Holy Father, in troubled times like these? If our critics were right, if the Vicar of Christ had no other office to perform than to be a drag on the wheels of history, forbidding this, repressing that, fulminating endless decrees against everybody who did something which had not been done before, said something which had not been said before, how unlaborious a life he might lead, how unexacting! But it is not so, and it has never been so; in our day, perhaps more than ever, the Popes have a wider and nobler conception of the duty they have undertaken; they will give the world positive guidance, they will initiate, they will spur us to action. They will not be content to criticize (no difficult matter) the false standards they see prevailing in an exhausted and disillusioned world. They will set before it, instead, the pattern of a Christian world-order, of a civilization penetrated with, and expressing, the mind of Christ. And if we are to be worthy, you and I, of those great pontificates under which the divine mercy has privileged us to live, we must not be content, either, with a merely negative Catholicism which forbids us to do this, discourages us from doing that, shuts us up in ourselves and reduces the Christian life to a treadmill routine of avoiding sin. We must react generously, and if need be heroically, to the conditions of our age, of a world which enjoys a precarious, and, if we fail in our duty, an ignoble peace. That is the lesson which the feast of St Peter and St Paul should have for times like ours; they bear the sword, as well as the keys, they were princes of the Church because they sealed their witness by martyrdom. They beckon us to glorious thrones, but through a hard apostolate. If they disagreed once, it was long ago; they have but one voice now, and it bids us go forward.

23

THE FISHERMAN[1]

We have laboured all the night and have taken nothing, but at thy word I will let down the net.—Luke 5. 5.

WE heard these words read in the Gospel only a few Sundays ago; we heard the full account of how St Peter, whose feast we are celebrating today, was called to his apostleship. Our Lord is passing along the lake shore, and wants to preach to the crowds. Preaching in the open air, you know, isn't such an easy thing as it looks. If your voice is to carry and to last out, you want to arrange your congregation as far as possible between you and something else; a wall or something of that kind, which will keep in the sound instead of letting it lose itself all over the countryside. And the best background you can possibly have is a cliff or a sloping beach, such as our Lord must have found, easily enough, by the side of the Lake of Galilee. But there's this difficulty about it—that a large crowd listening to a speaker always tends to edge forwards, the people at the back straining to hear better. And if you are standing with your back to the sea, talking to a crowd like that, you are being edged back yourself all the time towards the sea. Our Lord saw all that; and since he always preferred to use natural means where natural means were forthcoming, he found a practical way out of the difficulty. He climbed on to a boat, and stood on the raised stern of it, as if on a pulpit, and spoke to his audience from there. And the boat he chose was Simon Peter's.

Why he chose St Peter's boat, rather than that of St James and St John who were close by, I can't say. It is very odd, isn't it; a very curious coincidence, isn't it, that if one of the apostles is singled out for mention above the others it is always St Peter? However, that may have been an accident; perhaps his boat was the handiest for the purpose. Only it was a fortunate kind of an accident; there it is, our Lord stands preaching in St Peter's boat; and it is not surprising that later ages, looking back with the eyes of faith over centuries of history to that first dawn of the Gospel preaching, have seen a mystical appropriateness in the arrangement. Peter's boat by the Lake of Galilee, or Peter's Chair at Rome—what difference does it make? From one as from the other Incarnate Truth spoke, and speaks.

[1] A sermon published in *The Tablet*, 24 June 1939.

And when the sermon is over, our Lord seems to make an apology for turning the boat into a pulpit for so long, and perhaps interfering with the fishermen's work as he does so. He turns to St Peter, and suggests that he should put out and try his hand at fishing. Now, in the ordinary way there seems to be no hope in that suggestion; Peter has toiled all night and caught nothing. He has no reason to think that the great Preacher who has been his passenger that morning has any special knowledge of fishing or of the weather. If there was any chance, Peter should know. But Peter has been listening to the sermon. And already something tells him that this Man, who speaks to the crowds as one having authority, is worth obeying without asking questions. It is all against his professional instincts; "nevertheless, at thy word, I will let down the net."

And the net is let down, and the catch, as you will remember, exceeded anything Peter could ever have dreamed of. What do you think happened, exactly, when that miracle took place? I mean, did our Lord then and there create the fish which came into the net? Or were the fish swimming about elsewhere in the lake, and did he attract them to the spot? Or were the fish there all the time in the ordinary course of nature; and was there nothing miraculous about it except our Lord's miraculous knowledge of their presence? Well, I think we should all say that the first of those explanations is too elaborate; we don't want to multiply miracles without necessity. But the third, I think, is equally too simple; our Lord, surely, did more than merely know that the fish were there. Why else did the miracle make such an impression? "Peter was astonished", says the Gospel, "and all that were with him, at the draught of fishes, and so also were James and John." That means, clearly, that, even apart from the unfavourable conditions, the catch itself was one you could not have met with, by any natural means, in those waters. Our Lord didn't merely know that the fish were there, in a position to be caught. He brought the fish there, into a position where St Peter could catch them.

Imagine yourself, gifted with some supernatural insight, looking down under the depths of the dark lake that morning. You can see all that moves beneath the waters as clearly as if Genesareth were a vast aquarium. And you can see the fishes moving about here and there in silver shoals, intent upon their silly fish business. How they dart about this way and that, with an important little flourish of the tail! And yet the sudden dashes they make seem, after all, to lead nowhere. Sometimes food attracts them, more often something which turns out to be quite uneatable; sometimes the throwing of a stone disturbs them, more often the passing of a harmless shadow. What are they all thinking about, down there? What are the aims, the delights, the tremors, that agitate the fish world below you? So much you can see for yourself, any time you will look into some clear pool in the Thames. But that morning, under the Lake of Genesareth, something else was happening. All of a sudden, a little group of fishes here and there detaches itself from a shoal; and all these turn in one and the same direction, at one and the same moment, towards a particular corner of the lake, and all swim away together. No natural need, no natural alarm, accounts for this unanimous tendency; drawn by an unseen force, they forget their favourite pools and the overhanging rocks that sheltered them, and all head one way. The Lord of Nature has bid them come.

Those are you and me, those fish. All the souls that have been brought into the Church of Christ all through the centuries have been brought there because they were drawn by the grace of Christ, not for any other reason. Without grace, our lives, if we could see them in the true perspective, are all haphazard and purposeless, like the movements of the fish in the lake we were thinking about just now. We play about, in love with our own shadows, darting here and there at our pleasure, excited by a thousand perishable hopes, a thousand imaginary alarms; so brisk, so bustling, so self-important. In the midst of all that, a force that was not of nature drew us, we knew not why, we knew not whither. Drew us into the net the Church had spread for us; yes, it is Peter spreads the net, but it is Christ who draws the fish into it. From our Lady downwards, no soul ever attained the means of salvation unless it were drawn by the grace of Jesus Christ.

When the miracle was all over, our Lord explained the meaning of it to his apostles. From henceforth, he said, you will be catching men. Our vocation as Christians does not starve or supersede our natural characters, it directs them and consecrates them to the service of God. Peter is a fisherman; very well, then, a fisherman let him remain; only in future let him fish for men. Why did our Lord number so many fishermen among his twelve apostles? Fishermen, after all, have not a very good reputation for telling the truth; and some of them are idle natures into the bargain. What is the quality our Lord saw in them? One thing, I think, which he prized especially in those who were to be his apostles; an indomitable patience. "In your patience", he says to them, "you shall win souls."[1] They have toiled all night and have caught nothing; weary hours of waiting, in the hope that the grey light of dawn will bring sport—and it has brought none. What, put

[1] Luke 21. 19.

out to sea again under the burning sun of midday, when the very hull of the boat must cast shadows that will scare away the fish to right and left? Yes; "at thy word I will let down the net". There is no limit to Peter's optimism and Peter's endurance, so long as he is following his Master's orders. It is in that patience that he won, and wins, men's souls.

How she has waited, the Church of Christ, all down the centuries, and with how little regard to the maxims of human prudence and human skill! Not seizing her opportunity here and there, where circumstances seemed favourable; not trimming her sails to every passing breeze, but patiently issuing her invitation, and leaving grace to do its work. How many hopes she has seen fail, over how many apostasies has she wept; how she has seen the fashions of the world change about her, old creeds die down and new creeds replace them, the folly of yesterday turned into the wisdom of today! Should she not by now have become hardened and cynical, her pity for mankind turned into a weary scorn, her ambitious hopes into the dogged persistency of despair? We might have expected it, but we were wrong. What if, here and there, she has toiled long and caught little for her Master? Still at his word she will let down the net; until his grace, bound by no law of proportion to human effort, brings her good fishing again. Despise her as you will, criticize her as you will, but do her the justice to admit that the patience of the fisherman is hers.

Will you forgive me if I leave you with this indomitable patience of St Peter as the lesson of St Peter's feast? A trite lesson, perhaps, but a difficult lesson to learn, and in these times especially. After all, we do live—it is time we admitted it to ourselves—in days of great discouragement. Those who are just growing to manhood or womanhood, in a world that seems so shut to honest effort, they will feel it most. We have toiled all night and taken nothing; do we not, inevitably, repeat that complaint as we look around us? Our civilization, so laboriously built up, the fruit of so much noble endeavour—and now it is threatened with collapse by forces not under our direction, perhaps not under our control. The British Empire, so great in its conception, say what you will of it, so wonderfully preserved and organized—and now it is beginning to show signs of breaking up. The Great War, fought and won, so we told ourselves, to save Europe and bring her peace and prosperity—and now we are clinging to peace despairingly, while prosperity has vanished. Have we not toiled through the night, and taken nothing? That sense of public discouragement reflects itself in our individual lives, weighs upon our spirits more than we know, and is making of us disappointed men and women. The indomitable patience I speak of is, believe me, a gift which we all need, or shall need before long.

Don't let us imagine that patience means a tame acceptance of the inevitable, sitting down with folded hands and hoping that somehow better times will turn up. It means action, bestirring ourselves and making the best of things; doing God's will, not merely submitting to it. At thy word I will let down the net; we are to attempt what seems hopeless, what seems hopeless, when we know it is God's will, whether he has made it known to us through conscience, or through revelation, or through the outward circumstances of our lives. As long as we are sure that we are obeying him; that no pride of ours, no neglect, no timidity, no human respect, is preventing us from finding out what his will is.

We are disheartened, perhaps, over material things; times are less prosperous, and we have to make the best of an income smaller than the income we were accustomed to; some of us can find no work to do, and feel the pinch of poverty nearer to the bone. Some of us are disheartened over spiritual difficulties, temptations against which we have long fought, it seems unsuccessfully, or dryness in prayer, or perpetually falling short of the standard we had set before ourselves. Some of us are disappointed over favours denied to us in prayer; all the harder to endure because those prayers were not selfishly offered, but for the needs of others; there is a son who is turning out badly, there is a friend's conversion we have long hoped for, there is an invalid for whose sufferings we asked relief. The temptation (in any case) is to throw up our hands in despair; to tell ourselves that we have done enough, and that we shall be running our heads up against a brick wall if we try to persevere; we have toiled all the night, and have taken nothing; very well, we will toil no more. That is where we want to remember the great "but" of St Peter's utterance; "but" at thy word I will let down the net. Casting all your care upon him, for he hath care of you[1]; so St Peter wrote when he was an old man, and in prison, and the Church for which he had laboured so hard was being assailed by bitter persecution; he had learned his lesson, that day by the Lake of Galilee, long ago.

---

[1] 1 Peter 5. 7.

24

THE PRECIOUS BLOOD: I

*He has proved his love for us, by washing us clean from our sins in his own
blood.*—Apocalypse 1. 5.

IN all language, I suppose, the pouring out of one's blood is taken as a
symbol of generous self-giving. When the Prime Minister told us
he had nothing to offer us but blood and sweat and tears,[1] he uses an
image all the world understood. To the Jewish people, blood had a
special significance; it made you think of an animal victim ceremonially
offered in order to procure, for the worshipper, release from a sentence
of death. The escape from Egypt was a kind of race-memory branded
on their consciousness; and when the first-born of Egypt were killed,
the Israelites had secured their homes from the visit of the Destroying
Angel—how? By sprinkling their door-posts with the blood of the
paschal lamb. So, too, with those sprinklings which were mentioned
in the passage from the Hebrews I have just read to you. They identified the people as ceremonially associated with the sacrifice of that
victim from which the blood came; to it their sins had been ceremonially transferred, and by its death they were ceremonially purified.

Christian thought, from its very beginnings, interpreted those old
Jewish sacrifices as the type, the foreshowing, of the atonement made
for our sins by Jesus Christ on the cross. We were all sinners, and our
sins had offered the eternal Justice of God an immeasurable affront.
What amends could we make? Why, none that would be worth
having; the creature cannot make amends to its Creator, the finite to
the Infinite. Jesus Christ, God and Man, came to offer amends on our
behalf. And he, in order to make amends in full, in order to exhibit,
in terms of human conflict, the issues that were at stake between God's
Justice and man's sinfulness, would suffer a shameful death. His blood
flowed under the lash, the thorns, the nails, the lance; he hung there, a
Victim for his people. And it is not wonderful if Christian writers
borrowed the language and the imagery of the old Jewish sacrifices to
interpret what had happened. The blood is the life; here you could
reckon, in concrete terms, what he gave up for us who gave up his life
for us. "The blood of Jesus Christ his Son makes us clean from all

---

[1] The reference is to Sir Winston Churchill's now-famous speech in the House of
Commons on 13 May, 1940.

sin."[1] And, as if that were not definite enough, you get the text I have quoted from the Apocalypse, "By washing us clean from our sins in his own blood".

Christian piety has seized on that verse, and treated it, it must be confessed, with startling realism. In the hymn which was sung just now the words occur, "There the fainting spirit Drinks of life her fill; There, as in a fountain, Laves herself at will".[2] Is that the language only of Catholic, only of Italian piety? No, a fellow countryman of our own, no less a poet than William Cowper, will echo the same sentiment for you:

> There is a fountain filled with blood,
> Drawn from Emmanuel's veins;
> And sinners, plunged beneath that flood,
> Lose all their guilty stains.[3]

It is our own Evangelical poets, Evangelical preachers, who have made us familiar with the idea of being "washed in the blood of the Lamb".[4] And it is a familiarity which, in some minds, has induced contempt. "What a mawkish thing this Christianity is", they tell us, "and in what miserable taste! First of all you want us to believe that almighty God, instead of punishing human creatures for all the abominable things they have done, is content to regard Jesus Christ, by a kind of legal fiction, as the guilty person, and inflict all the punishment on him. Then, with your morbid interest in sin and suffering, you concentrate all our attention on the unfortunate affair of his death, instead of allowing us to draw inspiration from his very remarkable and noble life. Then, to give your artists and poets opportunity for a lot of crude imagery, you represent his death in terms of blood. Then, as if that wasn't enough, you tell us to come and bathe in his blood, with other disgusting metaphors of the same kind. Can you wonder that people of common sense, people of taste, prefer not to go to church, when they know it will mean being treated to barbarous language of this kind, more suited to the worship of Mithras than to that of Christ?"

Well, keep calm for a moment. Let us take the points one by one. First (if I may begin at the end), let me explain this: it is probably true that the Bible does not refer to being washed in our Lord's blood at all. In the passage of the Apocalypse from which I took my text, there is a variation of reading in the manuscripts. It is only a matter of one letter; but a good many of the manuscripts give you "ransomed us with

---

[1] John 1. 7.
[2] From the hymn, "Glory be to Jesus", tr. Rev. E. Caswall.
[3] *Olney Hymns*, 15.   [4] Apocalypse 7. 14.

his blood" instead of "washed us in his blood", and that is probably what St John wrote. Anybody is quite at liberty, then, to say that he personally doesn't like this metaphor, and thinks it overstrained and vulgar. Is it possible for good religion to produce bad art? That is a very difficult question to decide. But this is certain; that if men are going to be associated together as members of a Church, they will have to make allowances for one another. You can't expect A and B to have exactly the same preferences in art and literature; A will be impressed by what B thinks vulgar. And if you are inclined to hold out for your own point of view about this, read the fourteenth chapter of St Paul's Epistle to the Romans, in some translation which makes it clear what he is talking about.

Meanwhile, as I say, I think St John wrote "ransomed", not "washed". Again and again, in the Old Testament, you get the idea of God *redeeming* his people; that is, buying them for himself, buying them in for himself. And it was natural for Christians to think of our Lord as redeeming his Church, buying it for himself, to be his very own. The price he paid was his blood; and with his blood, too, he marked his own people, as a shepherd marks his own sheep with some characteristic dye. That, surely, was the point of the sprinkling with blood under the old law; it did not precisely wash you from your sins, it marked you out as belonging to a separate, to a privileged community. Blood symbolized not so much purification as redemption.

But then, why blood? Why so much emphasis on the death? Surely the life of our Lord had a significance of its own; he came to earth to live, not simply to die. Here, I think, we want to make the doctrine plainer than it is in many people's minds. The life of our Lord on earth might have been a sufficient atonement for our sins, had God so willed, even if he had not crowned it by a death on the cross. If he had seen fit to ascend into heaven again, when he was still a little child in his Mother's arms at Bethlehem, our redemption might still have been achieved. What made amends for our sins was not precisely his death, but that generous offering of himself to his eternal Father which began with Bethlehem and only ended on Calvary. If we use his blood as the symbol of that life-long generosity which redeemed us, it is only because the cross was the supreme test, the crucial experiment, which gave that generosity its perfect outward manifestation.

The objection remains, that almighty God seems to have neglected the obvious interests of justice in allowing the sacrifice of our Lord's will—his, not ours—to make amends for the guilt of our sins—ours, not his. Can A, we ask, really and literally atone for something which

B has done? Yes, but in asking that, don't we perhaps forget that, in redeeming mankind, our Lord somehow—in a way we shall never understand—identified himself with it? Under the old law the *go'el*, the redeemed, was not just the first person who came along. If a piece of property had to be disposed of the next of kin had the first right of buying it, and no other claim could be looked at until he had waived his rights; you get that very clearly set out in the last chapter of the Book of Ruth. And our Lord, in becoming Man, became something very much more than our next of kin; he became the head of the whole human race; he lived his life, died his death, of perfect sacrifice, not as our substitute, but as our representative. Ah, you say, but once more, that is only a kind of legal fiction. I wonder: can we be so certain of that? Do we not impoverish the whole Christian idea, if we try to interpret the relation between divine and human things in terms merely legal? When we say that our Lord identified himself with us, became the head of the human race, is that just a metaphor?

Meanwhile, the doctrine of the Precious Blood certainly means this, for Catholic and for Protestant alike—it means that you and I had something done for us which we could never have done for ourselves. Deny that doctrine, obscure that doctrine, and you have fatally altered the whole content of the Christian message. The love of God, St John tells us, resides not in our showing any love for God, but in his showing his love for us first, when he sent out his Son to be an atonement for our sins. Forget that, and you have forgotten to be a Christian.

25

THE PRECIOUS BLOOD: II[1]

Unless blood is shed, there is no remission of sins.—Hebrews 9. 22.

COULD our Lord Jesus Christ have redeemed the world without suffering a violent death? It is certain that he could. To be sure, we are accustomed to think of our redemption in terms of Calvary. To you, who worship in this Church of the Holy Redeemer, the word

[1] A sermon preached at the Church of Our Most Holy Redeemer and St Thomas More, Chelsea, on the Feast of the Precious Blood, 22 July 1956.

itself conjures up the thought of your own high altar, surmounted by
that huge picture of a suffering Christ. But, if you come to think of it,
a redeemer is not necessarily one who suffers. By force of language, a
redeemer is simply one who buys in something over which he has the
first claim. Some piece of property is to be sold, but his application to
purchase it has a right to be considered before anybody else's. True, he
must pay the price; but the real point of the word is not simply that
he is buying something; he is buying back something which is his own.

Our Lord Jesus Christ redeemed the world; it was his own. How,
then, had it passed out of his possession? Through the Fall. When he
came to earth, he found the human race in a mood of baffled despair.
The heathen, to be sure, had no doctrine of the Fall in their theology;
but the fact of the Fall was painfully evident to them in their daily
moral experience. They found themselves continually false to their
own high instincts, knowing what they ought to do and doing the
opposite. Unredeemed humanity, whenever its mind turned inwards
in some moment of reflection, laboured under a sense of guilt. Every
catastrophe of nature, every public calamity, deepened the feeling that,
somehow, we had to get right with God.

And the commonest way, the most characteristic way, in which the
pagans tried to do that was by sacrifice. Some instinct told them that
they could only make reparation for their guilt by the killing of a
victim on behalf of the city or the tribe that had sinned. Sometimes it
was a human victim they offered; more often it was a dumb beast,
doing duty, we may suppose, by a kind of legal fiction for the human
victim who was allowed to escape. But always blood must be shed;
the blood was the life, and without shedding of blood there was no
remission of sins. Nor, in this matter, did God's ancient people, the
Jews, differ from their heathen neighbours. They were more highly
privileged; by a progressive revelation through the centuries, God had
taught them more about his nature and his purposes for mankind. But
still he was content that they should honour him with sacrifices; the
blood of bulls and of goats was still being spilt in the temple courts at
the time when our Lord came; they, too, knew no better way of
atoning for sin.

And then our Lord came, to tell us what it was all about. Like a
schoolmaster, who explains to his pupils in one stroke where it was
they were right and where it was they were wrong, he would draw
for us, on the blackboard of history, the true pattern of sacrifice.
He came to redeem us, to claim us as his own. It was through him, the
Second Person of the Blessed Trinity, that the worlds were made; and

when we had unmade our world through sin, it was he who came to recondition it for us. He did that by becoming, himself, Man; he took our nature upon him, and thereby took us, as it were, into partnership with himself. In our name, in expiation of our guilt, he offered to his heavenly Father the perfect sacrifice of a life lived utterly in accordance with the divine will. Nothing more was needed than that; how should it be? Our love for God, yours and mine, is only like a spark in touchwood; dying down here, breaking out again there, smouldering all the while, but never bursting into flame. Our Lord's love for his heavenly Father was not like that; it was like a sheet of flame, uniform and indivisible, all through his lifetime. A continuous sacrifice; accepted on behalf of Man, because he was Man; infinite in its value, because he was God. At whatever moment his life had terminated, that sacrifice would have been sufficient to offset the long history of human rebellion. You remember how the blessed Virgin and St Joseph lost him when he was twelve years old, and found him, afterwards, in the temple? If they had never found him, if he had gone back, there and then, to the heaven which was his Father's, the world would still have been redeemed.

But he was not content to do that; Incarnate charity was not content with that. He would be obedient right up to the point of death, and that death should be on a cross. It was no accident that he came into conflict with the world around him. He chose that world; chose the moment and the place of his coming to earth, chose the nation that was to reject him, and the friend who was to betray him, so as to crown and seal his obedience with death. St Paul does not hesitate to say that Jesus Christ was placarded for us on the cross; hung up there like an advertisement to compel the attention of all who passed by. We were to see that love has no limits; we were to see, in the dearness of the price paid to atone for it, the measure of our guilt. "To ransom thee, I left a throne, Weeds of mortality put on, Nor gems, nor gold, thy surety stood, But, as thou seest, this my blood."

The blood is the life, and the divine will was that remission of our sins should not be granted us without shedding of blood. And that, accordingly, has been the visible symbol under which we think of our redemption; we were saved by the blood of Christ. It is a curious reflection that, if medical science had developed nineteen hundred years ago as it has developed today, Christian piety would have found an image, taken from the practice of medicine, ready to its hand. Today, it is quite a common thing to be able to say, in literal fact, that you have given your blood for somebody else. As it is, we have grown accustomed to a more violent, and, some would say, a less gracious metaphor. St John, at the beginning of his Apocalypse, refers to our Lord as one "who has proved his love for us by washing us clean from our sins in his own blood".[1]

It is not surprising that the Christianity of the Reformation, with its strong insistence on the doctrine of the Atonement, should have fastened on that language and made it familiar to us. For us Catholics, the Precious Blood is proposed as a special subject of meditation during this month of July, and for us, too, the same symbolism does duty. Read a Catholic poet like Crashaw, and you will find him referring to "that blood, whose least drops sovereign be To wash my worlds of sin from me". Read an Evangelical poet like Cowper, and you will find him preaching the same doctrine; "The dying thief rejoiced to see That fountain in his day, And there may I, as vile as he, Wash all my sins away".[2] St John's metaphor has become a commonplace of Christian devotion.

Do you still find it crude, over-strained, unacceptable? Be it so, we are not tied to any particular form of imagery which the piety of a past age has bequeathed to us. Only, in this month of July, we do well to remember the bitter Passion of our Lord, and that giving of his life-blood which sealed it, and seals us through it. A price was paid to redeem you[3] (St Paul says); and because the price paid was so high, because the world itself was not worthy of such a ransom, we must go on reiterating, blindly and uncomprehendingly, our gratitude. Moreover, because the price paid for us was so high, no price can be too high which is demanded of us by our loyalty to Christ, though it should be death itself. To be always generous with God, to go on and on giving him of our best in spite of weariness and disillusionment, to despise soft options, and interpret our duty in terms of love, not in terms of mere justice, to be ready if we might to give him more than he asks of us, ready if that were possible to give him more than he deserves of us—that is the meaning of our devotion to the Precious Blood; may his grace make us worthy of it.

---

[1] Apocalypse 1. 5.   [2] *Olney Hymns.*   [3] 1 Corinthians 7. 23.

MOUNT CARMEL[1]

Thy head is like Carmel.—Canticle of Canticles 7. 5.

OUR blessed Lady is the link between the Old Testament and the New. Take a bird's-eye view of the Old Testament, and what is the process it describes? The process by which, man once fallen and standing in need of a redeemer, almighty God chose out, providentially, the race, the tribe, the family, from which that redeemer was to spring. Abraham called out from amongst his kindred and his father's house; Isaac chosen, the child of promise; Jacob chosen, not Esau, not the elder, not the world's candidate, but God's candidate; Judah chosen from among the twelve tribes of Israel, the house of Jesse singled out from all the tribe of Judah; and of Jesse's twelve sons, so promising, so likely-looking, God took the last of all, the one who had almost been forgotten because he was left at home looking after the sheep, King David. In two separate streams, the blood of David came down to Zorobabel, the hero of Israel's return from captivity. After that, it will have crossed and recrossed; we cannot even tell for certain the name of St Joseph's father; nor do we know in what relationship St Joseph stood to his espoused wife. We only know that somehow, through cadet branches, that royal lineage came down to the second Eve, and the cycle of Old Testament history was complete. To what had the divine promises looked forward? To David, the man after God's own heart? To Solomon, wisest and most powerful of princes? To Zorobabel, the deliverer of his people? No, to one village girl, a shepherd's daughter and a carpenter's bride. The work of selection is accomplished, and mankind stands ready for its redeemer.

And as she is the culmination of the Old Testament, so Christian devotion has found, in the Old Testament, titles and symbols everywhere that can be referred to her. She is the second Eve; in her the serpent's head is crushed. She is the new Ark of our salvation, ready to re-people the world with the seed of grace. She is Jacob's ladder, by which our prayers go up, and graces come down upon us in return. Her virginity is the bush which Moses saw, burning ever, yet never consumed. She is the Ark of the new covenant, where God keeps tryst

[1] A sermon preached at the Church of Our Lady of Mount Carmel and St Simon Stock, Church Street, Kensington, London, on the Feast of Our Lady of Mount Carmel, 16 July 1937.

with man. She is Gideon's fleece, wet with the dew of heaven when all around was dry. She is the King's daughter of whom David sang, and the faithful Sulamite of the Canticles, and Respha, the daughter of Aia, weeping for her sons that were crucified. She is the Rod of Jesse, and the well of living waters, and the gate shut up, save only for the prince. Daughter and Crown of the Old Testament, what wonder if patriarchs, and kings, and prophets spoke of her?

Among all the titles which our blessed Lady bears, there is but one which recalls to us that connection of hers with our pre-Christian past; she is Our Lady of Mount Carmel. Among all the religious congregations which claim her as the chief patroness of their institute, there is but one which looks back beyond her own lifetime; the Carmelite Order. We are not going to knock, this morning, at the reluctant doors of history, to know exactly what became of Mount Carmel between the time when Elias silenced and slew the prophets of Baal, and the time when the Crusader Berchtold took his vows there, two thousand years later. We only know for certain that the place has at all times been a seat of worship and of religious awe. We only know for certain that our medieval forefathers, when they visited the Holy Land at the time of the Crusades, found in Mount Carmel a predestined and, as it were, a remembered home. The flowers, perhaps—for in all Palestine there is no place for wild flowers, we are told, like Mount Carmel—reminded them of European hedgerows. Or perhaps the very lie of the promontory, that seemed to stretch out its arms westwards, as if it would spread to Spain, and to France, and to England, the influence and the blessings of the Holy Land, may have seemed a parable to them. It is certain that on those flowering slopes, where it still has its home, the institute was cradled; and that those blessings did radiate westward, those flowers were transplanted to other gardens—at Aylesford, at Avila, or at Lisieux.

"Thy head is like Carmel"—what did the village lover mean, trying to woo his Sulamite away from King Solomon's court, back to the fields and villages where he had been her first love—why does he say her head is like Mount Carmel? We cannot be answerable for a lover's fancy; perhaps there was something in the proud carriage of her head, not like those other demure slaves of the harem, that recalled to him the bold sweep of the hills, as they frowned down over the plain of Esdraelon. Anyhow, his poetical conceit has outlived the ages, and will last for ever in the liturgy of the Church. For us, there must be some connection to be traced between this solitary headland of the Palestinian coast and her who has placed her name and her sanctuary there. Let us indulge, for a minute or two, in a lecture on geography, and see if it will not give us some clue to the parable for which we seek.

Carmel is a spur, the same in formation with the great hills of Judaea and Galilee, but separated from them by a great plain and by a much lower range of hills. An eccentricity like that in a mountain range carries one's mind back to the past, to those remote ages when, with strange convulsions of nature, the earth came to possess its present contour lines. These hills that seem piled up accidentally have their roots in history; and if one of them appears at a distance from the main range, that is due to some fault in the intervening ground. So it is with Mount Carmel, a solitary outcrop of the everlasting hills that stand round about Jerusalem; surrounded as it is by valleys and plains, its very isolation makes it the more impressive. Immortal eyes have rested on that sight. "These things do not change", writes a recent traveller, "and (Jesus Christ) must have known these rocks and these hills. Looking back, the great plain stretching to the sky and the outward thrust spur of Carmel are intensely significant."

And we know that if Carmel is a solitary outcrop of those old hills, our blessed Lady was, in something the same way, a solitary throwback to the innocence of her first parents. Rising suddenly above the grovelling level to which Adam's fault had reduced our common human clay, she challenges heaven in the lonely isolation of her purity; all other sanctities must seem but petty eminences compared to this. Our tainted nature's solitary boast, she recalls to us, across all those centuries, the first beginning of our race, and the privileges that went with it. When our Lord Jesus Christ looked across the plain from his home at Nazareth, he could see, beyond the plain that lay parched at his feet, the cool heights of Carmel against the sunset. When our Lord Jesus Christ looked at the world his hands had made, and saw, for he could see, all the passions of greed and lust and envy that ruled in the hearts of his fellow men, he could see one heart that was fresh with the freshness of the world's springtime, and that was his blessed Mother's. Her head was like Carmel, towering in its spiritual stature above the world which knew her so little.

And Carmel has had its effect upon history. All along the plain by the sea shore, from Gaza in the south to Sidon in the north, the armies of the conquerors could march unimpeded; by the way of Egypt, the way of the sea; except at one point. At one point they must turn and go aside; where the great ridge of Carmel juts out right across the sea plain, leaving only a dangerously narrow strip of shore beneath it. Here, then, the conquerors must turn inland, across the Plain of

Esdraelon; and it became one of the great battle-grounds of the world. It was the scene of great events in the history of Israel; here Balac scattered the hosts of Sisera; here Gideon with his three hundred routed the Madianites; here Saul and Jonathan fell in their last fight against the Philistines. But it was the theatre, too, of world victories and world defeats. It is the meeting-place of east, north, and south. Here, in the days of King Josias, the empires of Babylon and Egypt met in conflict; here, returning from his conquest of Egypt, the Persian Cambyses met his death. Over that plain the Romans built a huge permanent camp; over that plain rose the last fortress defended by the Crusaders. Through that plain Napoleon marched on his way to southern adventures; through that plain the Turks retreated when the last rout of the central empires began. And we shall hear of it again, for it is the Plain of Armageddon. All through these centuries Carmel, in its beautiful isolation, has looked down on the changing panorama of human history.

And all through the centuries our Lady looks down, in pity and in protest, upon the world whose warring passions pass her by. She holds the secret of the Incarnation, the message which men learn so hardly, and are so quick to forget; she cries out to them in the *Magnificat*, wisdom lifting up her voice in the streets, and they will not hear. "O children, how long will you love childishness, and fools covet those things which are hurtful unto themselves? . . . You have despised all my counsel. . . . But he that shall hear me shall rest without terror, and shall enjoy abundance, without fear of evils."[1] She told us, so long ago, that God would scatter the proud in the conceit of their heart, would put down the mighty from their seat, and exalt the humble; and we go on playing our foolish games, pretending that we are out of earshot of our Mother's voice.

And there is a third point about the position of Mount Carmel—it looks as if it was deliberately meant to be a kind of watch-tower, looking out seawards. Take the merest glance at a map of Palestine, and the first thing that will strike you about it is the long, straight coast-line, only broken at one point—where Carmel boldly juts out into the western sea. The range itself runs from east to west, as if it were a kind of link or hyphen between the self-contained world of Palestine and the blue Mediterranean, with its civilizations and its problems, its possibilities of adventure. It was used, no doubt, as a watch-tower at all times; and few stories in the Old Testament have a stranger thrill about them than the story of Elias' observation from it,

[1] Proverbs, ch. 9.

on the day when he overcame the prophets of Baal, after seven years of drought. "Elias went up to the top of Mount Carmel, and casting himself down upon the earth put his face between his knees. And he said to his servant, Go up, and look toward the sea. And he went up and looked and said, There is nothing. And again he said to him, Return seven times. And at the seventh time, behold, a little cloud arose out of the sea, like a man's foot. And he said, Go up and say to Achab, Prepare thy chariot and go down, lest the rain prevent thee."[1] A natural watch-tower, looking out towards the stormy West.

And our blessed Lady does not only recall to us, as the second Eve, our past; does not only encourage us, as the destroyer of all the heresies, amid the jarring voices of the present; she points forward to the future. There is a dark sea we have all to cross, remote from this comfortable world of our experience, opening up new dangers, and wider horizons. Over that sea the calm eyes of our blessed Lady look out, foreseeing the difficulties of our passage. And it was to the order of Mount Carmel that she gave the holy scapular, to be a life-belt in that sea, a talisman amid those unseen perils. She is not content to be our Mother in this world; she will care for us and see us into the next.

Reverend Fathers, yours is no common boast, no light responsibility. Other congregations—it was only to be expected—have been cradled amid the high hills; at Subiaco or Manresa, on Monte Alverno or Monte Amiato. Our Lord has said to us, "You are the light of the world; a city set on a hill cannot be hid".[2] And if these other congregations must look to it, lest they should be unworthy of the high places that gave them birth, what of you, whose origins connect you with memories so multitudinous and so ancient, with the hill whose name was on our blessed Lady's lips, when she taught her divine Child his first lessons? We will pray for you, then, we others, that you may be worthy of your vocation; that you may go before God in the spirit and power of Elias; in these days of unrest, to turn the hearts of the fathers unto the children; in these days of scepticism, to turn the incredulous to the wisdom of the just; to prepare unto the Lord a perfect people, for the praise and glory of his holy name. Amen.

---

[1] 3 Kings 18. 42.　　　　　　　　　　[2] Matthew 5. 14.

27

THE ASSUMPTION[1]

A cave Jeremias found there, in which he set down tabernacle and ark and incense-altar, and stopped up the entrance behind him. There were some that followed; no time they lost in coming up to mark the spot, but find it they could not.—2 Machabees 2. 5-6.
After this, God's heavenly temple was thrown open, and the ark of the covenant was plain to view, standing in his temple.—Apocalypse 11. 19.

THE Son of God came to earth to turn our hearts away from earth, Godwards. The material world in which we live was, by his way of it, something immaterial; it didn't matter. We were not to be always worrying about our clothes being shabby, or wondering where our next meal was to come from; the God who fed the sparrows and clothed the lilies would see to all that. We were not to resent the injuries done to us by our neighbours; the aggressor was welcome to have a slap at the other cheek, and when he took away our greatcoat he was to find that we had left our coat inside it. Life itself, the life we know, was a thing of little value; it was a cheap bargain, if we lost life here to attain the life hereafter. There was a supernatural world, interpenetrating, at a higher level, the world of our experience; it had its own laws, the only rule we were to live by, its own prizes, which alone were worth the winning. All that he tried to teach us; and we, intent on our own petty squabbles, our sordid struggle for existence, cold-shouldered him at first, and then silenced his protest with a cross.

His answer was to rise from the dead; and then, for forty days in the world's history, that supernatural life which he had preached to us flourished and functioned under the conditions of earth. A privileged few saw, with mortal eyes, the comings and goings of immortality, touched with their hands the impalpable. For forty days; then, as if earth were too frail a vessel to contain the mystery, the tension was suddenly relaxed. He vanished behind a cloud; the door of the supernatural shut behind him, and we were left to the contemplation of this material world, drab and barren as ever.

What was the first thing the apostles saw when they returned from the mount of the Ascension to the upper room? "Together with Mary" —is it only an accident that the Mother of God is mentioned just here,

[1] A sermon broadcast from Buckfast Abbey, Devon, on the Feast of Our Lady's Assumption, 15 August 1954.

by name, and nowhere else outside the gospels? The Incarnate Word
had left us, as silently as he came to us, leaving no trace behind him of
his passage through time. No trace? At least, in the person of his blessed
Mother, he had bequeathed to us a keepsake, a memory. She was bone
of his bone, flesh of his flesh, the new Eve of the new Adam. That body
of hers, still part of the material order of things, had housed and suckled
God. As long as she lived, there would still be a link, a golden link,
between this lower earth and Paradise. As long as she lived; and even if
it was God's will that she, Eve's daughter, should undergo the death
that was Eve's penalty, the penalty she had never incurred, her mortal
remains would still be left with us, an echo from the past, an influence
on our lives. We men, since we are body and soul, do honour even to
the lifeless bodies which have housed the dead; Napoleon rests in the
Invalides, Lenin at Moscow. The day would come when there would be
pilgrimages from all over the world to the shrines of Peter and Paul
at Rome, of James at Compostela. Was it not reasonable to hope that
somewhere, at Jerusalem, perhaps, or at Ephesus, we should be
privileged to venerate the mortal remains of her through whom salvation came to us? Or perhaps at Bethlehem, Bethlehem-Ephrata, this
new Ark of God would rest, as the ark rested of old; "And now, at
Ephrata, we have heard tidings of what we looked for"[1]—the old
tag from the Psalms should still ring true.

God disposed otherwise. Jewish tradition recorded that when
Jerusalem was destroyed by the armies of Babylon, the prophet
Jeremias took the ark of God away from the city, and buried it in some
secret cleft of the rock; it was never seen again. Never again, except by
St John, in his vision on the isle of Patmos; he saw the ark of God,
but in heaven. And so it was with this new Ark of God, the virgin
body that had been his resting-place. When and where she passed away
from this earth, or in what manner, nobody can tell us for certain.
But we know where she is. When Elias was carried up into heaven,
the sons of the prophets at Jericho asked Eliseus if they might go out in
search of him; "it may be", they said, "the spirit of the Lord has
carried him off and left him on some hill-top or in some cleft of the
valleys." He consented grudgingly, and when they returned from their
fruitless errand, greeted them with the words; "Did I not tell you not
to send?"[2] So it is with the body of the blessed Virgin: nowhere in
Christendom will you hear the rumour of it. So many churches, all
over the world, eagerly claiming to possess the relics of this or that
saint; who shall tell us whether John the Baptist sleeps at Amiens, or at

[1] Psalm 131. 6.   [2] 4 Kings 2. 16, 18.

Rome? But never of our Lady; and if any of us still hoped to find that inestimable treasure, the Holy Father has called off the search, only the other day. We know where her body is; it is in heaven.

Of course, we knew it all along. For myself, I have never doubted the doctrine of the Assumption since I heard it preached forty-four years ago, in an Anglican church over at Plymouth. You see, we get it all wrong about body and soul, simply because our minds are dominated by matter. We think it the most natural thing in the world that soul and body should be separated after death; that the body should remain on earth and the soul go to heaven, once it is purged and assoiled. But it isn't a natural thing at all; soul and body were made for one another, and the temporary divorce between them is something out of the way, something extraordinary, occasioned by the Fall. In our blessed Lady, not born under the star of that defeat, human nature was perfectly integrated; body and soul belonged to one another, as one day, please God, yours and mine will.

Long ago, in those fields of Bethlehem, Ruth had gleaned in the footsteps of her beloved; and he, secretly, had given charge to the reapers to drop handfuls of corn on purpose, so that she might fill her bosom the sooner. So he, whose reapers are the angels, would leave for his blessed Mother a special portion of those graces that were to enrich mankind. The child-bearing which brought, to us others, redemption from the fault of our first parents should bring, to her, exemption; the empty tomb, which assures us that our bodies will rise at the judgment, was for her the earnest of an immediate resurrection; Christ the first-fruits, and who should glean them, but she? For that, heaven is the richer, earth the poorer. We can go to Lourdes, and offer adoration in the place where her feet stood; we cannot press with our lips some precious reliquary containing the hand that swaddled Christ. In a world so dominated by matter, in which matter itself seems to carry the seeds of its own destruction, there is no material object left that can link our destinies with hers.

And yet, is the loss all loss? When the dogma of the Assumption was defined a friend of mine, a very intelligent Mohammedan, congratulated me on the gesture which the Holy Father had made; a gesture (said he) against materialism. And I think he was right. When our Lord took his blessed Mother, soul and body, into heaven, he did honour to the poor clay of which our human bodies are fashioned. It was the first step towards reconciling all things in heaven and earth to his eternal Father, towards making all things new. "The whole of nature", St Paul tells us, "groans in a common travail all the while. And not only do we see that, but we ourselves do the same; we ourselves, although we have already begun to reap our spiritual harvest, groan in our hearts, waiting for that adoption which is the ransoming of our bodies from their slavery."[1] That transformation of our material bodies to which we look forward one day has been accomplished—we know it now for certain—in her.

When the Son of God came to earth, he came to turn our hearts away from earth, Godwards. And as the traveller, shading his eyes while he contemplates some long vista of scenery, searches about for a human figure that will give him the scale of those distant surroundings, so we, with dazzled eyes looking Godwards, identify and welcome one purely human figure, close to his throne. One ship has rounded the headland, one destiny is achieved, one human perfection exists. And as we watch it, we see God clearer, see God greater, through this masterpiece of his dealings with mankind.

28

CHRIST THE KING[2]

ANY new departure in the discipline or the liturgy of the Catholic Church tends to be accepted, almost at once, as a legacy from immemorial antiquity. Probably most people think of this feast, the Feast of the Kingship of Christ, that is if they think of it at all, as something that has always been there, like Trinity Sunday, or even All Saints' Day. As a matter of fact, it is only eleven years old; it was established by the present Holy Father[3] in the year of jubilee, 1925. And that means, when you can look back over nineteen centuries of Christendom, that a feast like this is still, as the journalists say, in the news. It isn't a sort of curious survival, over which liturgiologists debate with incredible heat whether it was invented in the seventh century or only as late as the ninth, and what, in any case, it was all about. It is something which relates to an actual situation, the actual situation in which we live. So I do not think there is any harm in considering the question what the Kingship of Christ means, and the further question, why the feast which commemorates it came into existence at the actual moment when it did.

[1] Romans 8. 22-3.
[2] A meditation published in *The Tablet*, 24 October 1936.
[3] Pius XI, 1922-1939.

After all, if you come to think of it, some explanation is needed. The fact that our blessed Lord claimed, while he was on earth, and ought to receive, now that he is in heaven, the honours due to a royal dignity was not a fact which it took nineteen centuries to discover. It was not a fact which daring thinkers have ever assailed with doubts; I don't suppose anybody who ever used the name of Christian, however heretical his beliefs might be in other directions, has ever challenged the sentiment, Christ is King. No, when he instituted that feast the Holy Father was only giving expression to a fact universally recognized among Christians; and it follows that he must have had some special reason for emphasizing that fact, or he wouldn't have interfered with the calendar at all. Just so, within recent years we have seen two feasts revived in the liturgy of the universal Church which do not commemorate new or controverted doctrines; the feast of the Holy Family, and the feast of our Lady's Maternity. Nobody ever doubted that there was a Holy Family, or that our Lady was a Mother. The point, evidently, of reviving those feasts was to counteract, in this particular age, the growing neglect of family life; to exalt, in this particular age, the slighted dignity of motherhood.

Well, that consideration leads to an obvious difficulty. Are we to suppose, by parity of reasoning, that the Holy Father instituted this feast of the Kingship of Christ because he thought that monarchy was an institution which did not receive sufficient reverence in these times? And if he thought so, was it after all very tactful of him to say so? It is true that the Spanish revolution hadn't happened at the time of which we are speaking; but it was pretty clear, all the same, that the monarchical principle was not in the ascendant. Did he mean that he would like to see Austria or Hungary, or both, restore the dynasty of the Hapsburgs? All such suggestions are obviously untrue; to be assured of that, you have only to reflect that the present Holy Father has done his best to detach Catholicism in France from the cause of Royalism, when he condemned the Action Française.

Still less is the Kingship of Christ meant to suggest that the Pope, as the Vicar of Christ, is a kind of super-king, with running rights over all the constitutions of the world, or even of the Catholic world. Catholic theology has always held, even in times when it was far more difficult to distinguish the spiritual and the temporal spheres than it is now, that the spiritual and temporal spheres are entirely separate; and that the secular authority in any country, whether it be monarchical or not, has the same right to govern as the ecclesiastical. It is extraordinary how people outside the Church, and even unreflecting people inside the Church, get that point wrong. They imagine that because the authority of the Pope is higher than the authority of a king—which it clearly is, because it belongs to the supernatural, not merely to the natural order—therefore the Pope claims to control the activities of all earthly rulers. At the last presidential election but one in the United States, the Democrat candidate was a Catholic, Al Smith. And at that time people really wrote and talked, I suppose they really thought, as if a Catholic President would have to ring up Rome every morning after breakfast, not Rome, N.Y., but Rome, Italy, and take his orders from the Vatican like the cook. People's minds have got so accustomed to the idea of churches which are purely national in their outlook, that they cannot conceive the idea of a supra-national Church which is not for ever interfering in politics. When we say that, there's no need to disguise the fact that conflicts do often arise between the Catholic and the civil authorities in a country, simply because in practice the delimitation between the secular and the spiritual spheres is so hard to achieve perfectly. But it's the *theory* of the thing that is in question; and in theory the kingship of Christ is not a doctrine which impairs in any way the rights of secular sovereigns. You may add, that Pope Pius XI is the last man in the world who would wish to make it appear so.

The claim made, then, is to a sovereignty in spiritual things. Let us look at the Gospel to see in what sense our Lord makes that claim himself, and infer from that the mind of his Church on the subject. Our Lord's words, remember, were spoken at a solemn moment, and when he was under oath (so to speak) before a judicial interrogation. The charge preferred against him, the only charge of which a Roman judge is likely to take cognizance, is that he represents himself as being a king. In all probability, he can save his life by denying it. Does he deny it? He does not. "Thou sayest that I am a king"—that, of course, is a Hebrew way of answering in the affirmative; the idiom is exactly the same which you get in modern American slang—"You said it". Then he goes on to explain the sense in which the charge is true. He is a king, but his kingdom is not "*of* this world". Does he mean "My kingdom *does not belong* to this world; it will only be realized in a future life"? No, you can't get that from the Greek. The sense of the Greek words is, "My kingdom does not *arise out of* this world. The means, that is to say, by which it is to be established are not the means which you associate with revolutionary movements; if they were, I should not be standing here, my friends would have rescued me. My kingdom does not arise out of this world, and yet even in this world, even where I stand before you a helpless prisoner, I do claim, here and now, to be a king."

A king, then, in what sense and by what right? Because, he says, "I have come into the world for one express purpose, to bear witness to the truth. And truth, once it is rightly apprehended, has a compelling power over men's hearts; they must needs assert and defend what they know to be the truth, or they would lose their birthright as men. Everyone who is of the truth hears my voice; everyone who makes truth his starting-point, has a true background to his life, and a true spring of motive for his actions, necessarily becomes a subject of my kingdom. You have no reason to fear, so far as I am concerned, an armed rising against the Roman Government. But my servants are going to conquer the Roman Empire; they must, inevitably, because it is founded upon a religion, and that religion is a lie. Those who are of the truth will extend, because they must extend, their influence; and as the truth establishes itself in men's hearts your lie will crumble, and your pagan empire will crumble with it. The Roman discipline has conquered the world by force of arms; the Christian discipline is to conquer the world by the compelling power of its own reasonableness, and the infectious influence which its divine origin guarantees."

Christendom has before now taken up arms in its own defence; or even in a pathetic attempt to recover the Holy Places. Christian princes, before now, have tried to spread the faith at the point of the sword, always, or nearly always, with disastrous results for religion. But the substantial victories of the Church have lain, always, in the sphere of the human conscience. Christ has reigned, not in the councils of nations, but in men's hearts. If every country in the world professed the Catholic religion, set up religious emblems in its market places and voted special honours, special privileges, special revenues to the clergy—that would not be the reign of Christ on earth. It would not be the reign of Christ on earth if the homage which men paid to religion was merely external, merely political; if they treated the emblems of Christianity merely as an ancestral tradition they were proud of, and a convenient rallying-point for civic sentiment, no more. Christ will reign in the world only where, only in so far as, he rules in human hearts.

That brings us back to the question, "Why did the Holy Father want to commemorate, by a special feast, a doctrine so uncontroversial?" Why was the moment ripe, did he suppose, for that particular lesson? I think perhaps it is easier to understand that if you remember who the Holy Father is. He does not belong to the ordinary tradition of ecclesiastical Rome. Until he was sixty, he was known as a librarian and a scholar; he lived in an international and, I think you may say, an interdenominational world of scholarship. He is, for example, the only Pope since the Reformation and long before it who knows what Oxford looks like, except from pictures. He was librarian at Milan; a friend of mine reading recently at the Ambrosian library came across a slip of paper in a book with some MS. notes on it, signed "A. Ratti". Quite suddenly at the age of sixty he was sent out as nuncio to Poland —to all that there was of Poland, when the Russian Revolution had already happened, and the war was not yet over. The story is that he was chosen for that post because he was the only priest in the Church of Christ who was thought capable of learning Polish in a fortnight. His position lasted on after the war; and he was in Warsaw at what was probably the most thrilling moment of history since Versailles; the moment at which the Red Armies swept through Polish territory and were at the very gates of the capital, which seemed doomed to fall. The Government was preparing to leave; it was suggested to the embassies that they should leave, too; nobody was quite certain what to expect of Bolshevism in its moment of military triumph. Mgr Ratti insisted on staying; the American, Italian and Danish envoys—no others—remained to follow his example and share his fate. He saw, on the feast of the Assumption, Pilsudski and Weygand roll back the Bolshevist armies from the gates of Warsaw in defeat.

Then, almost immediately, just when he seemed the only man who could comb out the tangle of Eastern European politics, he was recalled to Italy and made Cardinal Archbishop of Milan. It was under his very eyes that all the early struggles between the Italian Communists and the growing strength of the Fascists took place, within the walls of his own cathedral city. He had not held that position for a year when he was summoned to Rome for the conclave after the death of Benedict XV; and from that conclave he never returned. He would never climb in the Alps, he would never poke about in the Bodleian, again.

In the course of that providential career he had seen more than it is given to most Popes to see. His background was a background of European culture; and circumstances had suddenly thrust under his eyes, after his sixtieth year, vivid impressions of that struggle between two great forces in Europe, nationalism and international socialism, which the rest of the world hardly suspected as yet. When he was crowned Pope, he insisted on giving his blessing to the world from the balcony of St Peter's, a thing no Pope had done since the loss of the temporal power. Even so early, he had made up his mind that the

QX

Papacy must come out of its retirement, and make itself felt as a moral force in the world. And I think he introduced this feast of the Kingship of Christ with the same idea in view. He saw that the minds of men, of young men especially, all over Europe, would be caught by a wave of conflicting loyalties, which would drown the voice of conscience, and produce everywhere unscrupulous wars between class and class, the threat of equally unscrupulous wars between nations. To save the world, if he could, from that frenzy of reckless idealism, he would recall it to the contemplation of a very simple truth. The truth, I mean, that the claim of Christ comes first, before the claims of party, before the claims of nationality. *Pax Christi in regno Christi;* peace and justice were duties which man owed to God more elementary than any duties to his fellow men. All that, before the conflict between the Church and Fascism, before the revolution in Spain, before the name of Hitler had ever been set up in the type-room of a foreign newspaper. The institution of this feast was not a gesture of clericalism against anti-clericalism, still less a gesture of authoritarianism against democracy. It was a gesture of Christian truth against a world which was on the point of going mad with political propaganda.

It affects us, you say, very little. True, we have seen little in our own country of political violence; and probably we are on the whole less caught by political loyalties than any other nation in the world. But we do not know what a day or an hour may bring forth. It may yet be important for men to be reminded in England, in our lifetime, that the claim of the divine law upon the human conscience comes before anything else.

29

ALL SAINTS[1]

There are many who will come from the east and the west, and will take their places in the kingdom of God with Abraham and Isaac and Jacob.—Matthew 8. 11.

TODAY is All Saints' Day, and I thought it would be a good thing if we talked, first of all about saints, and then about all saints, and then about All Saints' Day; by the time we've done that, we shall have more or less covered the ground. It sounds as if it were going to be a

---

[1] A sermon preached in the boys' chapel at All Hallows, Shepton Mallet, Somerset, on All Saints' Day, 1950.

long sermon, but it won't be really, as long as you sit fairly still and
don't shuffle or snuffle or fidget; if you start doing that I don't know
what may happen. First of all, what *is* a saint?

In the very earliest ages of the Church, it was the fashion to describe
all Christian people as "saints", although I daresay Christian people
were a mixed lot, even then. If St Paul had written a letter to you, he
would have addressed it to "the saints at Cranmore". Nowadays, we
don't do that; if your mamma were to send you a letter addressed to
"Saint John Smith" (or whatever your name happens to be) the head-
master would probably return it to the post office, with the comment
"Not known here". You see, words keep on changing their meaning.
It's just the same with the word "scholar". A scholar used to mean
somebody who went to school; and of course you go to school; but
it would be pretty silly to call you a scholar, when you will go on
thinking that the ablative of *mensa* is *mensarum*. And in the same way
it would be pretty silly to call you a saint when you will go on—all
right, we'll leave that part out. A scholar nowadays means somebody
who is terribly brainy; and a saint nowadays means somebody who is a
very special friend of God, and always does what God wants him to do,
and the Church accordingly decides to call him "Saint" so-and-so
ever afterwards.

Well, what exactly is it that you've got to do in order to be a saint?
The first thing is, to be dead. When I say that, for heaven's sake don't
get me wrong; don't imagine that the saints were all people who lived
ages and ages ago, and wore long beards and dressing-gowns like the
pictures in the stained-glass windows. No, there are people alive at this
moment who do just the sort of things the saints have always done.
There's Padre Pio, for example, a Capuchin priest in the south of
Italy; he only sleeps about three hours every night and spends nearly
all day hearing confessions; and when he says Mass it takes him nearly
two hours to get through it, because he gets so overcome with devotion
that he can't go on. You might think that would make people want to
go to some other Mass, but no, they all crowd to Padre Pio's. He says
it at four o'clock in the morning, and at four o'clock every morning
there's a queue outside the church waiting to fight their way in and
hear Padre Pio's Mass, because they know what a holy man he is. I
know what I'm talking about, because one of you has a brother, and
several more of you have a cousin, who went to see Padre Pio only
about a fortnight ago. Just imagine how holy a priest must be, to make
one's brother want to get up at four in the morning and hear his Mass!
And Padre Pio is just as alive as you or me.

No, when I say that you can't be a saint until you're dead, I mean that the Church isn't going to be rash enough to call you a saint until you are dead. And there's a perfectly good reason for that; there always is a perfectly good reason for these things. The Church never calls anybody a saint while he's alive, for fear that he should stop being a saint and go to the bad, and then where should we all be? Rather over four hundred years ago, when the Reformation started, a king of England wrote a very clever book to show how wrong Martin Luther was, and what nonsense the Reformers were talking. And the Pope was so delighted that he called him the Defender of the Faith, and said that all his successors could use that title, which is why you find "Fid. Def." written on English coins to this day. But it was a good thing the Pope didn't decide to make a saint of him, because of course that king was Henry VIII, who afterwards destroyed all the monasteries and killed St Thomas More and St John Fisher and married six wives and cut most of their heads off; so it would have been rather awkward if Henry VIII had been a saint, wouldn't it? No, the Church is too clever for that; she waits till you're in your coffin, and then she says, now, let's see, what kind of person was he?

And what kind of person have you got to be before the Church says, "That was a saint, that was"? Why, you've got to be absolutely eaten up with the love of God; that's the only thing which matters. Our prevailing idea of the saints is that they were people who made themselves very uncomfortable; they wore hair shirts and slept on broken bottles when they slept at all, and generally laid themselves out to give themselves a bad time. St Francis Borgia, when he had to take a pill, always used to suck it, which was rather missing the point of a pill. But all that, you see, was only by the way; if the saints seemed to enjoy suffering, whether it was the suffering they couldn't avoid, or the suffering they took upon themselves, it was only because they could think of no better way to prove their love for God. There was a boy at school with me, a great tough boy, who was called out in class by the science master and told to stand there holding a platinum dish in each hand; and when either of the dishes felt at all hot, he was to put it down immediately—it was some sort of scientific experiment, you see. Well, this boy went on standing there and standing there and swearing that both the dishes were stone cold, till at last the master had to send him back to his place, and there was rather a snigger all round because it looked as if the experiment hadn't come off very well. But about five minutes later the boy had to get leave to go to the infirmary, with an enormous hole burnt in his hand. Because really one of the dishes had been scalding hot all the time, but he thought it would be a good way to rag the master if he pretended it wasn't. There are all sorts of morals to that story, but the one I want to mention here is simply this—that boy made himself extremely uncomfortable, just as the saints are apt to do, but he wasn't a saint. He wasn't a saint, because he didn't do it for the love of God; he only did it to pull a school-master's leg, which is quite a different thing. So you see what I mean when I say that the point about the saints is not the sufferings which they underwent, but the consuming love of God which made them do it.

That's two things you need if you are to become a saint; you want to have a consuming love of God, and you want to be already dead. And there's a third thing which the Church ordinarily demands—that you should do miracles; either you must perform miracles in your life-time, or miracles must be performed through your prayers after you are dead. The Church, as I say, needn't insist on that, but she ordinarily does, and for this reason. God means the saints, these very special people whom we call saints nowadays, to be an unmistakable proof of the Christian religion; they are to be beacon-lights to the world. And because he means them to show up like that, he doesn't take any risks. They aren't just very good people; the whole of their lives is lived on the supernatural plane, and the supernatural keeps on breaking through. "You are the light of the world", our Lord says to them; "a city cannot be hidden if it is built on a mountain top."[1] You might think it rather unnecessary to have a tower here on the top of Cranmore; surely it's high enough without that? Yes, but all over the country, and especially down here in Somerset, you will find that people do put down towers and monuments on the top of high hills, as if to draw attention to them. People looking at them from a long distance off must be able to say, "That is Cranmore". And so, when a soul reaches really high up in the following of Jesus Christ, God adds a kind of finishing touch —the power of doing miracles; then everybody will be able to say, without fear of contradiction, "That was a saint".

Well, that's what saints are, and now, what about all saints? Why does the Church want us to get excited about them? Well, I suppose the reason is that we are all apt to specialize too much, to concentrate too much, in our devotions; there are one or two saints we like specially or feel specially interested in them, and we tend to let the others go. There's our blessed Lady, of course, and the saints we're named after, and the ones we think are useful in getting us what we

[1] Matthew 5. 14.

want, and then there are some who just attract us by the stories we hear about them. October is such a good month for saints, starting off with St Teresa of Lisieux, the Little Flower, whom we all want to be on good terms with, and then going on to St Francis, who has somehow managed to be everybody's saint. And there is one I'm very fond of, St John Cantius, whose feast comes on 20 October. I think I must tell you about him, because his story is so charming. He was a schoolmaster of sorts, and his favourite way of spending the holidays was to go off on a pilgrimage to Rome, not just in the Holy Year, but any old year. But he was rather an absent-minded sort of person—schoolmasters are sometimes, it comes of being so clever—and also, being a saint, he was very liable to give away all his money to the first tramp he met. So when he went off they used to sew a number of gold coins into the lining of his cloak, to make sure that he would always have enough money to come back by the beginning of term. And on one of these journeys he met some robbers, who demanded his money. St John Cantius emptied out his pocket, which probably contained about two-pence half-penny, and said he was so very, very sorry he hadn't got any more. Whereupon the robbers beat him and threw him in the ditch, and went off grumbling. And St John picked himself up, and shook himself, and started out on his journey again, and then . . . then quite suddenly he remembered those gold pieces which were sewn up in his cloak, and he'd told the robbers he hadn't any money; he'd told a lie! So the next thing that happened was that the robbers heard a great hallooing behind them, and there was St John Cantius chasing down the hill after them at top speed, shouting, "Stop, stop, it's all right; I have got money, lots of it, after all!" Well, they were sportsmen, and they gave him back his twopence half-penny, and it was all right. That kind of saint sticks out from the others and makes one wish one knew more about him.

But the Church, you see, doesn't want us to be entirely wrapped up in a handful of saints of our own choosing. There's nothing wrong about picking and choosing; God made them different from each other so that we could have our pick. But it was God who made them all, and made them what they were, and it would be disrespectful of us to take no notice of any of them except a handful. So, once a year, the Church tells us to think about all the blessed saints in heaven. And she chooses, I think, an excellent day for it; the first day of November, when the year has definitely turned to autumn, and the leaves have fallen, and the weather is for the most part rather depressing, either wetter or colder than we quite want it to be. Because it is then that we like staying indoors, and sitting at the fireside, if there's one to sit by; and there's a kind of snug feeling about coming in out of the misty twilight and drawing the curtains across the windows, which helps us to think about the saints in heaven, so snug there, with all the painful struggles of their earthly life behind them. To be sure, it is nice to be out on a November afternoon; but it is still nicer to come in at the end of the afternoon, and shut the world out from us. And the saints are happy, even in this world, in spite of all their uncomfortable goings on. But happier still when they leave this world, and draw the curtains of heaven round them. Our Lord talks about them sitting down to table in the kingdom of heaven, with Abraham and Isaac and Jacob; that's what the words mean—we are to think of heaven as a great comfortable family meal, where everybody has his allotted place, and there is no starvation corner.

Only, let us always remember that the curtains of heaven are transparent curtains. Not in the sense that you and I can look in; ah, if only we could! What a world of good it would do us! No, but the saints can look out; they can see you and me still ploughing our way through the mud and the darkness of this earthly existence, feeling our way with difficulty and falling, every now and again, into the ditch. And they can help us; not only because the light of their example shines down on us, and makes it easier, sometimes, to see what we ought to do. They can help us with their prayers, strong prayers, wise prayers, when ours are so feeble and so blind. When you look out on a November evening, and see the sky all studded with stars, think of those innumerable saints in heaven, all ready to help you; and all rather pleased with Cranmore, because Cranmore is dedicated to All Hallows.

30

ALL SOULS[1]

A MATTER of more than three hundred years ago there was a small conspiracy of Catholic gentlemen in the Midlands against the Government in power—a Government whose hands were red with the blood of martyrs. At the same time, an unfortunate fellow, of no

[1] A meditation for All Souls' Day published in *The Westminster Cathedral Chronicle*, November 1935.

great education, signed a confession that he had been storing up barrels of gunpowder in the neighbourhood of the Houses of Parliament with a view to blowing them up. They did not do what we should do nowadays, send him to a lunatic asylum; they put him on the rack, and it was after a long time on the rack, when his poor fingers could scarcely trace his own signature, that he signed the confession in question. Let us, indeed, remember it. But today, people don't seem to remember November 5 as much as they did. We are all getting so broadminded. We're getting so broadminded that some of us wouldn't much mind if Parliament *was* blown up nowadays. Still, there are worse things than being broadminded; by all means let us forget poor old Guy Fawkes.

But we mustn't forget the bonfire! Don't let us allow November to be ushered in without the bonfire, the natural sacrament of the dying year. The dying year, mark you, not the dead year. The year lies dead in January, under its shroud of white and its pall of black skies; but November is a transition stage between the golden glories of its maturity and the silver fineries of its funeral. And because the year is drawing to its end, we occupy ourselves in tidying up. Those leaves, whose violent emerald colour we welcomed so when they first sprang in March; those leaves, that made such a riot of restfulness over us and around us in the summer; those leaves, that autumn showed us beautiful even in decay, a golden ceiling over our heads till they fell, a golden carpet under our feet when they were fallen; they have lost, now, even the splendours of their maturity; they lie brown and damp underfoot, an unwelcome reminder of our decay. Sweep them up, then, and carry them to the bonfire. For the year is passing, and we must tidy up.

Most of us, I suppose, when we were small, didn't care much for tidying up—at least, if we were brought up to put away our toys on Saturday night. It gave a chill finality to the end of the week—almost a premonition of death, that last, solemn Saturday night when all our toys have to be put away. We scoured the room half-heartedly, working under orders; and, when the last dragoon had been restored to his long-lost charger, and the last elephant had folded its reluctant legs into the Noah's Ark, we turned away with a sense of duty done, indeed, but a sense, too, of regret at the law that will not let our games last for ever. But the bonfire in November, at the great tidying-up of the year—that was a very different matter! Here was rich, pungent smoke rising, it is true, from a heap of refuse, but how satisfying to the nostrils! How it invited us to rush, breathlessly, through its fragrant eddies. And there was always the chance that you might find a potato or two somewhere, to roast on the embers. That tidying-up was worth having.

People are always telling us that our Christian festivals and fasts are only heathen festivals and fasts that have survived with altered names and altered ceremonies; but I take comfort sometimes in the fact that our All Souls' Day, anyhow, is in bonfire month, in November. The ancients, too, had their Day of the Dead; but the Romans and Greeks, at least, the only ancient peoples for whom I can answer, celebrated it in February, and very naturally. For in February the year is dead; bare trees and sighing winds make us think of our end and the short time of our earthly passage. But that is not our Christian tradition. We think of our dead in November, the tidying-up of the year. For, when death separates us from the toys of earth, our souls are still such that there is a work of tidying-up to do. And, as St Paul warns us, that process can only be effected "so as by fire". There are still the leaves to be burnt.

Do you remember how our blessed Lord, when the time had come to pronounce his final sentence of rejection against his ancient people, the Jews, went up to a fig-tree outside the walls of Jerusalem, and cursed it so that it withered away? He did so, because for all its fair show of leaves it had borne no fruit. And yet the time was not the time for figs; nor could he have been deceived in his expectations who knew all things. The miracle by which he caused the fig-tree to wither was a parable and a warning; a parable of the life that wastes all its effort in fruitless activities, and is content to show nothing for itself but fair pretences. Such was our Lord's condemnation of the formalism into which the Jewish religion had sunk; such will be his condemnation of the soul that has no more to offer him when he comes to it in judgment. But that is final rejection; there is a more merciful sentence than that. "Every branch in me that beareth not fruit, he will take away . . . if any one abide not in me, he shall be cast forth as a branch and shall wither; and they shall gather him up and cast him into the fire, and he burneth"—that is the eternal reprobation of hell. But "every one that beareth fruit, he will purge it, that it may bring forth more fruit".[1]

"He will purge it"—that is a process which all of our lives need, except hers who was conceived without sin. And some of us have a great part of our purgation in this life; the saints, above all, that after their death they may come into God's presence the sooner. All through the New Testament you will find suffering recognized as the condition

[1] John 15. 2, 6.

of admission to glory: "We must, through many tribulations, enter the kingdom of God",[1] "if we suffer with him, that we may also be glorified with him",[2] "if you be without chastisement, whereof all are partakers, then are you bastards and not sons",[3] and so on. Suffering, as we see it in this world, must be the wiping out of a debt; otherwise we should go mad with thinking of it, so unevenly distributed. If some of us have to suffer so much more than most of us, there must be compensation for that in the world to come. If you will not grant me that, then I will go out into the street with the atheists and rail at my God. That is our great comfort in this world; if some of us suffer so much more than most of us, there is compensation for it in another world. But—that picture has another side to it. If most of us suffer so much less than some of us, there is compensation for that in another world. You and I, how little we have suffered, how much we have sinned! Oh, I know, there are the indulgences. But indulgences aren't everything. Purgatory didn't shut down, you know, when the holy rosary was invented, or when our Lady appeared at Lourdes. We still have to suffer in the spirit for earth's inequalities have to be tidied up.

And there, of course, our Protestant friend commonly parts company with us. He is no longer concerned, like the Protestant of a century ago, to deny the existence of an intermediate state altogether. "Oh, no", he will tell you, "I believe in purgatory right enough. I quite see that, whatever happens to the saints, ordinary humdrum sinners like you and me can't expect to pass, at the moment of death, straight from those earthly defilements which had become a part of our nature into the presence of the all-holy God. There must, no doubt, be some intervening stage by which we are educated to heaven; by which eyes accustomed to the darkness of sin are gradually trained to the dazzling light of glory. But that does not mean a time of suffering; only a time of apprenticeship, of probation. Probation, that is the word, rather than purgation." But does not St Paul speak of the fire that will try every man's work, of what sort it is?[4] It's true, St Paul does, but that is because in the passage from which I have quoted, he is combining two pictures, that of judgment and that of purgatory; that of the light which will make manifest and that of the fire which will cleanse. But don't tell me that St Paul wasn't thinking of purgation here. If any man's work shall be burned—that means more than a light which reveals; it means the refiner's fire, purifying the true metal by burning away the base alloy with which it has become united. Call it probation

[1] Acts 14. 21.
[2] Romans 8. 17.
[3] Hebrews 12. 8.
[4] 1 Corinthians 3. 13.

if you will, but it is not the probation of the sieve, it is the probation of the bonfire.

"Well, then", pursues our critic, "call it purgation if you will; but to purify is not the same thing as to punish. Granted that our souls need, after death, not testing merely or educating, but actually cleansing, need that cleansing be a painful thing for us? Cannot almighty God wash away the stains from his guilty creatures without making them suffer afresh after all the suffering they have experienced here?" Well, all I can say is that that idea of purgatory seems to me simply immoral. What? Are we to think of sin as something merely external to us, a sort of coating with which our souls are overlaid, so that it can be removed by some merely external process of scrubbing? I could quote you a heathen poet who knew better than that. Sin has become part of us, wrought, through our own fault, into our very being. And when God purifies a soul from its sinful attachments in this world, he does it by suffering: "Thou hast refined us even as silver is refined",[1] "the trial of your faith, which is far more precious than gold which is refined in the fire"[2]—why did Jesus Christ have to suffer for our sins? And if it is by suffering that our souls are refined in this world, why not in the next? If some of us suffer more than most of us in this world, most of us have got to suffer more than some of us in the next. It's no good talking about purgatory as if it were a mangle; it's not a mangle, it's a bonfire. What it burns, true enough, is not us but our sins; yet, if you would burn away the dross from an alloy, must you not melt the metal as you do it? It is our sins that need burning, but we shall suffer in the process. If any man's work shall be burned, he shall suffer loss, but he himself shall be saved, "yet so as by fire".

"If any man build upon this foundation, gold, silver, precious stones, wood, hay, stubble: every man's work shall be made manifest. . . ."[3] How much of what we build in this life, on the foundation laid in us by baptism, is of the enduring, and how much of the perishable sort? We are apt, I think, to deceive ourselves about this, because of a natural instinct of charity towards the dead. We have said so much about them behind their backs while they lived; so much that was spiteful, and harsh, and unnecessary, that we try instinctively to make up to them for it when they are gone. When we are thinking of dead friends, don't we usually find that all the faults we had to accuse them of vanish into the background, the little foibles, the defects of birth and upbringing; and the souls of the departed, lit up by that haze of gracious reminiscence, lose the shadows that stood out so boldly when

[1] Zacharias 9. 13.   [2] 1 Peter 1. 7.   [3] 1 Corinthians 3. 12.

we criticized them in life? How kind they were to us all the time, how good-hearted, how pardonable in their follies, how admirable in their rugged sternness! Oh, yes, I know; we do think of the dead like that. Shall we suppose that one of us dies tonight; what will the rest of us be saying of him tomorrow? "People often said he was selfish, and, of course, he was a little self-centred, those introspective people always are. But I remember once, in an illness I had, what kind offices he showered on me. . . . A little wild in his youth, yes, but think what temptations he had, and what poor chances! He made good afterwards, anyhow. . . . A sharp tongue? Yes, but he never meant any harm; he said a thing now and again that wounded, but it was always in the utmost good humour. . . . Oh, a fine character, take it one way and another; I wish I had his chances of heaven." So we speak, vying with one another to make amends to the poor corpse for all the criticisms we have made in years past. And, meanwhile, that soul has stood on its trial, and is expiating, in purgatory, the stains of its conversation here.

Would you learn to pass a true judgment on that soul? Look into your own heart, and read its story there. See, with your own conscience to bear witness against you, what hay and wood and stubble you have built upon the foundation of sanctifying grace Christ laid in your life, how many useless leaves encumber the branches of your vineyard, and mar the promise of its fruit. Tell me this—how much of what the world praises, of what the world finds attractive in you, is to be put down, when you judge the matter calmly and soberly, to three imperfect or even sinful motives—vainglory, worldly respect, respect of persons? Your epitaph in friends' mouths will tell how you worked restlessly, unceasingly, in some cause you had at heart, with no hope of worldly reward or even worldly recognition; how in time of sorrow you controlled yourself, and would not let your feelings be betrayed by any change in your outward demeanour; how you struggled with, and overcame, some deeply-rooted defect in your character—ask yourself, how much of that was due to vainglory? How often, when you longed to give way under the strain and confess yourself beaten, no supernatural motive, no unselfish motive even, but sheer pride forbade you to confess yourself unequal to the task you had undertaken. Will that look like silver in purgatory? Or hay?

Your epitaph will go on to say how regular you were at early Mass, how faithful a visitor at the tabernacle and at the confessional; how high your name stood on subscription lists, how modestly you declined all tributes of praise, how charitable was your language, how edifying your behaviour. Ask yourself, how much of that was worldly respect? How often would it have been a disappointment had no human eye been there to mark your acts of devotion? How often was a hasty word or a rash deed checked, not by any thought of eternity, but by the mere consciousness that you had a character to live up to? Not a sin, exactly, but still, an imperfection. Will that look like gold in purgatory? Or like stubble?

And then, your little acts of kindness! The trouble you took over So-and-So's conversion, the patience with which you helped So-and-So through that long time of temptation, those bitter months of anxiety, the smiles and the presents with which you brightened the lives of little children, the ready tact, the unfailing sympathy. . . . How much of that was respect of persons? How many of those touching incidents would never have happened, how much of that gentle demeanour would have been exchanged for irritation or for indifference, if the recipient of your kindness had been someone you hardly knew and hardly cared to know, somebody who got on your nerves and rubbed you up the wrong way? It's hardly even an imperfection, perhaps, but still it's an inferior motive. Will that look like precious stone in purgatory? Or like wood?

Have I drawn for you too dark a picture of human nature in its imperfections? If so, it is because I doubt if we think often enough, or seriously enough, about our purgatory. What refreshment it is when we can turn from the contemplation of our own characters, with their imperfect motives, their confused issues, their vanities and their pettinesses, to the sight of a man who goes through the world with one single ambition, to promote the glory of God. There may be foibles and mannerisms about such a life, but they will be all on the surface; directly you ask yourself, "What is this man getting at?" you are forced to reply, "He is out for the greater glory of God, nothing else".

3 1

PURGATORY[1]

IT is curious to note how our foolish modern catchwords contrive, now and again, to open a sudden window on our serious thoughts. Not long ago, you heard people saying (without meaning anything by it), "Where do we go from here?" If you translate that into old-fashioned English, it sounds like a quotation from the Bible, "Whither do we go hence?" And that is the problem which, more than any other except the existence of a supernatural world in general, has exercised the human mind at all times. What happens to us after death?

I am not going to discuss the subject from the philosophical point of view. It is, indeed, an uncommonly interesting question, how we can attach any meaning to the statement, "The soul is destroyed at death", since destruction means, in our experience, that a thing is resolved into its parts, and the soul, being immaterial, has no parts to be dissolved into. But these academic discussions have, for most of us, something of the quality of winter sunshine; they communicate light without warmth, and leave us shivering. I mean to assume as genuine the findings of Christian tradition about our future state, and attempt, if I may put it that way, to get them more in focus. Our picture of the other world is so blurred, its outlines are so confused. That is inevitable; partly because there is no subject on which Christian tradition is so reticent, partly because we are forced to use terms and ideas drawn from everyday experience, and it is evident that they do not quite apply. It is like playing Wagner on a tooth-comb.

The mistake we are tempted to make, do make in our moments of idle thinking, is to suppose that eternal life merely means going on living. That, naturally enough, was what the pagans thought, when they dreamed that there was some possibility of a life after death. There is an epigram in the *Greek Anthology*, often quoted for its beauty, in which the poet says to his dead friend, "Once, a morning star, you shone among the living; now you shine, an evening star, among the dead." You see, it has the marmoreal finality of a Greek epigram about it, but it has also something of a marmoreal flatness. We are back where we were; nothing has happened. So, in Virgil's *Aeneid*, the heroes of Elysium are found looking after their horses and chariots: "The same

[1] A sermon published as an Introduction to *God's Threshold, Purgatory*, by Marie René-Bazin (Clonmore and Reynolds, 1957).

grateful task that was ever theirs, to feed their sleek horses, is theirs still, now that earth has covered them."[1] Do we, children of a later age, look forward to an eternity spent in washing down the car? But it is the same mistake we are making, if we think of eternal life as the mere continuation of living. We unconsciously compare the experience of a future life to that of waking up after an operation; waking up to breakfast and the morning paper. And, of course, if we think of survival after death in those terms, it becomes an open question for some of us whether we want to survive or not. The unpleasant thing is the experience of dying; if we could avoid that, many of us would be content to go on living, even in an atomic age. But when we have once been put to all this inconvenience, would we be sure that we wanted to come back again and go on living, more or less as before? I do not see how the question, if you feel like that, admits of solution.

But eternal life is not that sort of thing at all. When our Lord said he had come that we might have life, and might have it more abundantly, he clearly did not mean that he was going to introduce, into our humdrum, day-to-day existence, more *joie de vivre*. The "life" which he came to bring—we have to call it "life", because that is the nearest thing to it we know—belongs to a different order of existence. It has its own avenues of experience, its own range of faculties, its own proper activities. And it will find its true medium only in heaven. True, that life is in us now, implanted by baptism. But we are not yet in a position to enjoy it, in the sense of savouring its possibilities. We are, if I may put it so, embryonic citizens of heaven, borne at present in the womb of matter and of time. And that is why we are foolish if we try to project our present experience into a future life, and say, "I hope we shall be able to do this, I hope we shall be allowed to do that, in heaven". We are like the child in Stevenson's poem, who said:

> When I am grown to man's estate
> I shall be very proud and great,
> And tell the other girls and boys
> Not to meddle with my toys.[2]

To wake up after death is not like waking up, after an operation, from the life of today to the life of tomorrow. It is like waking up from a dream world into a world, hitherto unexperienced, of realities. We are not to think of the soul as a star which is going to shine there

---

[1] Virgil, *Aeneid* VI, 653-5.
[2] R. L. Stevenson, *A Child's Garden of Verses*, XII, "Looking forward".

because it can no longer shine here. Henry Vaughan has said the last word about that:

> If a star were confined into a tomb,
> Her captive flames must still burn there;
> But when the hand that locked her up gives room,
> She'll shine through all the sphere.

"Into a tomb"; we shall never begin to understand heaven until we realize that it *is* life, and our life here, by comparison, is not.

Sometimes, in moments of dejection, we pick up some pious book and read about going to heaven, and reigning there in glory, and enjoying everlasting happiness; and the effect is not to raise our spirits but to put us out of temper with the whole Christian doctrine of a future life. Is it not only too obvious that the tradition of the Church has projected our experiences in this life on to the screen of eternity? But when we feel like that, we are forgetting that heaven is the substance, earth the shadow, and these inadequate phrases of ours are inadequate simply because we have no colours to dip our paint-brush into. They are like those shaded lines by which heraldry represents colours—red represented by upright lines, blue by horizontal lines, and so on. Just so these phrases of ours stand, all of them, for a reality which we have no means of expressing.

When we talk about "going" to heaven, we do not think of a future life as necessarily conforming to the conditions of space as we know it, like the literal-minded theologians in old days who discussed whether hell was, or was not, larger than Italy. But we get as near as we can to the truth, in describing a change of state necessarily unimaginable to us. As for "glory", it has an old-fashioned ring nowadays; and, indeed, if the truth must be told, the idea of dressing up in our best clothes and taking part in a triumphal ceremony afflicts us with a slight sense of *malaise*. But if we have at all mastered our Lord's teaching, we cannot doubt that in a re-fashioned existence there will be a complete reversal of our worldly values; that worth will shine out in its own colours, showing the darkest tomb as the hiding place of the brightest star.

And happiness? There at least our expectations are unambiguous. Happiness, as we know, is something quite distinct from pleasure; pleasure is associated with this or that gratification of this or that particular need in our natures, whereas happiness, the feeling of overall contentment, depends on such a multitude of contributing factors that you cannot pin it down to a single experience, or to a single moment.

Because it is so elusive, so fugitive a thing on earth, we know what we mean when we cherish the hope of finding it in heaven. Only, because our life in heaven will be a new life, not a mere continuation of this, our happiness, we must suppose, will be of a quality which, in this world, even the mystics have hardly dreamed of. And it has always been the instinct of Christian people—although so little is said about it in the New Testament—that it will be a shared happiness. It seems incredible that our lives here should be so interwoven, if we were destined to be solitary units in the world to come.

But always, when we are thinking about heaven, St Paul's description of it rebukes the exuberance of our imagination: "things no eye has seen" (the painters have missed it), no ear has heard (even the musicians have made a mess of it), no human heart has conceived—our ideas, however abstruse, however poetic, are inadequate, must be inadequate, to the supernatural reality; not by their intensity, but in their very quality, the joys of heaven elude us. And perhaps, when we have sadly admitted this incapacity of ours, a scruple assails us: How can I, this very second-rate, unilluminated person I know myself to be, ever become the subject of such a sublime experience? Understand me, I am not speaking of scruples about our eternal salvation. Scruples of that kind have been felt even by people of great holiness; we know that it is possible to miss everlasting life, and that without the grace of Christ we shall miss it. No, I am speaking now simply of the difficulty we sometimes have in imagining ourselves as possible candidates for the kingdom of heaven, just because we are so ordinary. Here am I, sitting in my flat reading a novel; can it be I who will be clothed with immortality? Nature, they say, does nothing by leaps and bounds; the caterpillar does not turn all at once into a butterfly. Is there no process of graduation, of slow acclimatization, which will turn me from this kind of soul into that?

If you accept the full teaching of the Church—I am perhaps speaking to some who do not, but they must pardon me for parting company with them here—if you accept the full teaching of the Church, these scruples will be sublimated for you by the doctrine of purgatory. We have, most of us, a despairing sense of inadequacy when we contemplate the holiness of God's saints, and compare our own record with it; we have, many of us, a feeling almost of envy when we visit people, or hear of people, whose life seems nothing better than one long round of suffering. Why is it that this discipline of suffering has fallen so little on us, who need it so greatly? If I may use a modern phrase, we are appalled at the differential. It straightens things out for us, if we believe that after death we shall go through a period of waiting and of discipline before we can become what we long to be, yet almost fear to be—perfect souls.

So, all through the month of November, we have been remembering in our prayers the needs of the faithful departed; the holy souls, we call them, but we mean that they are not quite holy enough. What picture are we to form of those needs? We shall not find, I think, even in Dante, much aid to the imagination. But we can, perhaps, get some glimpse of what it all means if we concentrate our attention on the ancient prayer which the Church uses in this connection: "Grant them, O Lord, eternal rest, and may perpetual light shine upon them".

It seems, at first sight, an exacting demand. Light and rest are both primary needs of our natures; but in the usual way when we need rest we draw the curtains. I suppose we are meant to see the interlude between earth and heaven under the image of an uneasy night between two stretches of daylight. Just as the cares of yesterday haunt us with their echoes and deny us sleep, so we can think of the soul which has left this world full of imperfections as longing for the echoes of those imperfections to die down in it, and restore its nature to equilibrium. And just as the mounting light of day seems to heal us, we cannot tell why, after a sleepless night—first the pale streaks, then the growing distinction between light and shadow, and at last the sun—so we may imagine the light of heaven, in some dim reflection, dawning on and into those immortal spirits which have still their heaven to attain. An interlude in which yesterday is forgotten, and tomorrow, somehow, grows gradually more real.

You still find them childish, these analogies by which we try to realize the world beyond? Well, we are only children, all of us, hoping to grow up one day into the stature of the perfect man in Jesus Christ. And perhaps, if we are found worthy to do that, we shall see that these guesses of childhood were not altogether misleading; we shall smile at them, but we shall not disown them.

32

THE IMMACULATE CONCEPTION[1]

"WHAT things soever were written", says St Paul, "were written for our learning, that, through patience and the comfort of the scriptures, we might have hope."[2] They needed hope, the nation of the Jews, during those long centuries before the Redeemer came. Was there ever a people whose history was, to all outward appearance, such a long series of tragedies and of disappointments? But all through their darkest times they had a hope to cling to; a hope founded in the promises made to them and to their forefathers that one day redemption would come to them. Of what form that redemption would take they had, I suppose, no clear notion; few of them, certainly, can have anticipated the form which it actually took. But they lived by their promises.

How often we read in the Gospels, in the Gospel of St Matthew especially, which was evidently written for the Jews, the words "that it might be fulfilled which was spoken by the prophet"! In St Matthew's Gospel alone you will find that the Old Testament is quoted on more than a hundred occasions, nearly four times, on an average, to every chapter. When we come across those quotations we pass over them lightly, taking them for granted; we suppose they can have no interest for us now. But it was not so in the early Church; it was almost the first object of Christian writers to prove that our Lord's life fulfilled, in every detail, the prophecies which had been made about it by men of old; to convince the Jews that here, and nowhere else, lay the consummation of those hopes which they had cherished through the centuries. If the prophets had foretold that a virgin would conceive and bear a Son; that a Messias would come out of Egypt, that the kings of the East would find their way to worship him, that he would be a man of sorrows and acquainted with grief, that he would heal the sick and preach to the poor, that he would come into his own city riding on an ass, that he would be rejected, set at nought, and murdered at last by those he came to save—all those references were jealously treasured up by Christian writers and turned into a sort of scrap-book; a store-house of evidence to prove the divine mission of Christ. We tend to forget that; but we do ill to forget it; for in truth it is still

---

[1] A meditation published in *The Tablet*, 9 December 1939.
[2] Romans 15. 4.

one of the most impressive arguments you can find in the defence of our holy religion. And the Church does not want us to forget it; so once a year, and at the very beginning of the year, she recalls it to our minds.

She takes the Scripture portion of Matins from the prophecy of Isaias, who is rich beyond all the prophets in his references to the coming of a Messias; and for a week before Christmas the antiphons of *Magnificat* at Vespers hail the advent of Christ under titles taken expressly from the Old Testament. Here, she says, is what the Jews were told to expect, and here is what actually happened; compare the two, and see how deliberately God prepared the way for his Son's coming, and made it easy for his own people, if they would recognize him when he came.

One of these antiphons speaks of our Lord as the Root of Jesse. But indeed, if you will look at the text just cited from Isaias, and at the comments which the fathers of the Church have made upon that text, you will see that to speak so is to confuse the metaphor slightly. There shall come forth a rod out of the Root of Jesse, and a flower shall rise out of his root. The sign towards which the prophet points is not the root itself, but a rod, a fresh green sapling, which is to arise out of the root, and the flower which this green sapling is to bear. Some of the fathers identify the root with our Lady, the rod and the flower with Jesus Christ. But their more common sense is that the root of Jesse is the old kingdom of Juda, the old dynasty of David; the rod which springs from it is our blessed Lady, and the flower which springs from the rod is Jesus Christ.

The Root of Jesse, the old dynasty of Juda—what meaning has it for us now, the history of those old kings we read of? Their wars and their treaties, their pieties and their apostasies, their defeats and their rebellions? The wicked Ahab, the devout Jodias, what mark have they left on the world, either of them, what ripple on the surface of history? They were so many years old when they began to reign, they reigned so many years, their mother's name was so-and-so, they did that which was good or that which was evil in the sight of the Lord; they fought and intrigued and took their pleasures.

> Till in due time, one by one,
> Some lives that came to nothing, some with deeds as well undone,
> Death stepped tacitly and took them where they never see the sun.

And what became, even, of their sovereignty? Did it grow into a great world empire; did it rise, century after century, to fresh heights of achievement? Why no; it is a melancholy story of slow decline; it reaches its fulfilment when the king of Babylon leads away first Israel and then Juda into captivity, destroys the holy city and the temple of God. Oh, yes, a remnant returns later on; but how poor a remnant, struggling pitiably against neighbours that are always too strong for it. And, soon after that return, the family of King David disappears from history; other heroes must achieve for God's people whatever deliverance can yet be achieved. By the time of our Lord's coming, we find the Jews a mere subject nation, a tiny dependency on the Syrian coast-line, of the vast empire of Rome. And their royal family? Why, the very name of it seems extinguished. What has become of the old stock of Jesse? Effete, surely, and condemned to eternal barrenness; we are not likely to hear of it again.

Yes, the old trunk, gnarled and withered, no more life in it now. And yet it is from that trunk that a single, slender branch is to come forth, a woman named Mary, of the house and lineage of David. She, in her virgin innocence, is to dare a man's winter with the promise of God's spring; she, by the miracle of her spotless motherhood, is to bear the one blossom that is to redeem our barren creation, and make it burst into flower. The old root, the old trunk, have little meaning for us now. Jesse, and David the son of Jesse, are figures very far removed from us by the centuries, and the earthly dynasty which sprang from them is no more to us than other great memories in the lumber-room of the past. But because from that stock our Lady came to us, and because through her our Lord traces all the kinship he has with earth, Jesse and David, the son of Jesse, are not forgotten. Their root lingers in grateful remembrance, through that divine afterthought which its failing energies produced.

The feast of our Lady's Immaculate Conception is the promise and the earnest of Christmas Day; our salvation is already in the bud. As the first green shoot heralds the approach of spring, in a world that is frost-bound and seems dead, so in a world of great sinfulness and of utter despair that spotless conception heralds the restoration of man's innocence. As the shoot gives unfailing promise of the flower which is to spring from it, the Immaculate Conception gives unfailing promise of the Virgin Birth. Life had come into the world again. And it grew there unmarked by human eyes. No angels sang over the hills to celebrate it; no shepherds left their shepherding to come and see; no wise men were beckoned by the stars to witness that prodigy. And yet the first Advent had begun. Our Lady, you see, is the consummation of the Old Testament; with her, the cycle of history begins anew. When God created the first Adam, he made his preparations beforehand; he fashioned a paradise ready for him to dwell in. And when he restored our nature in the second Adam, once more there was a preparation to be made beforehand. He fashioned a Paradise for the second Adam to dwell in, and that Paradise was the body and soul of our blessed Lady, immune from the taint of sin which was the legacy of Adam's curse. It was winter still in all the world around, but in the quiet home where St Anne gave birth to her daughter, spring had begun.

Man's winter, God's spring; the living branch growing from the dead root; for that, year by year, we Christians give thanks to God when Advent comes round. It is something that has happened once for all; we look for no further redemption, no fresh revelation, however many centuries are to roll over this earth before the skies crack above us and our Lord comes again in judgment.

33

PRAYER [1]

Dust and ashes though I be, I have taken it upon me to speak to my Lord, and speak I will.—Genesis 18. 27.

W HAT are we doing, you and I, when we say our prayers? If I may give you a very simple comparison, by way of clearing the ground, let me suggest that we are making an aside to the audience. If you have ever acted in amateur theatricals, you have probably come across that stage direction when you were learning your part, "so-and-so (aside, to audience)". The rest of the company had to pretend not to notice what you were doing, and you came forward to the footlights, put your hand (probably) to your mouth, and said, "He little knows that he is my long-lost brother"—or something of that kind. For once you gave up the pretence—it was only a pretence—that you were talking to your fellow actors, people dressed up in strange clothes and supporting imaginary characters, like yourself; you were talking, instead to the real people who sat before you in the dark, listening.

[1] A sermon broadcast from the Church of St Philip Neri, Arundel, on 27 September 1953.

It did not need an actor and a dramatist like Shakespeare to tell us that "all the world's a stage, and all the men and women only players".[1] We have felt it for ourselves, coming away from some party at which we had spent the whole evening in talking to a lot of strangers; "How unreal the whole thing is!" we said to ourselves. "Coming away from it is like coming away from the theatre." And of course we were right; the whole of life is like that. When you are acting on the stage, nothing seems real to you at the moment except the brilliantly lighted space of a few square yards in which you are standing; beyond that, there is nothing but a great darkness which seems mere emptiness. But out in that darkness are the real people, the people for whose benefit you are acting; it is their applause, not the applause of your fellow actors, you are out to win. When, into that darkness, you speak your aside, you are for once talking to real people. And that is what prayer is; it means using your powers of speech and thought and will so as to put yourself in communication with that real world which looks all dark to us, the supernatural world, instead of wasting them on chattering to the other mummers in the show.

There is an obvious difference. When the actor went up to the footlights and said, "He little guesses that he is my long-lost brother", he was telling the audience something they didn't know. But when we say our prayers, we don't tell God anything which he doesn't know; our sins are all stale news to him, our needs are something that goes without saying. If a human being who had been brought up, were that possible, without any notion of religion at all, were to see you kneeling down by the side of your bed whispering into the counterpane, he would think you were a lunatic. Why is it that we talk about "saying" our prayers? Why don't we always—as we do sometimes, just *think* our prayers instead of saying them? When you come to look at it, you have to admit that you go through this business of moving your lips in prayer not because God needs it, or because our blessed Lady and the saints need it; it's because you need it. You like to be sure of yourself; you like to go to bed feeling that you've said your prayers—if you merely thought your prayers, you would be afraid that you might have gone to bed thinking that you'd thought them.

But, of course, you won't have satisfied the curiosity of your atheist friend when you have explained all that. "Even if your lips aren't moving", he says, "you kneel there shaping ideas in your mind, about how grateful you are to God, how sorry you are for your sins, how

[1] Shakespeare, *As You Like It*, II, vii.

badly you want this or that blessing which it is in his power to bestow. Why should he want you, why should he expect you, to do all that? He knows what you need better than you do yourself; if he sees that it is good for you, surely he will give it to you without being asked for it?" Well, we shall have more to say about that later. For the present, what we want to make clear is that prayer doesn't necessarily mean asking for things. We Christians believe that, as a matter of fact, God does grant us special favours in answer to our petitions. But even if he didn't, it would still be possible to pray, and it would still be our duty to pray, and we should still want to pray. Because prayer in its essence is not asking God for things, it is simply talking to God. We talk to him, and somehow the mention of our needs, and of our friends' needs, keeps on coming in.

Our critic, I need hardly say, won't be disposed to let us get away with that. When we say we are "talking to God", aren't we after all using a metaphor? Aren't we simply "putting on an act" when we shut ourselves off from human company, and go down on our knees, and tell ourselves that we want to be alone with God and talk to him? When two human beings talk to one another, there is a constant intercourse of ideas; news and gossip are exchanged, either side communicates something of its own appreciations, its own enthusiasms, to the other, and each in this way gets to know the other better. But in prayer, what exchange of thought can there be? Unless God sees fit to give me a supernatural revelation, do I rise from my knees knowing any more about him than I did when my prayer began? And he—he knows all about me already; there is nothing new I can tell him about myself. Isn't it, then, an abuse of language when we describe prayer as "talking to God"?

It is easy to put up a debating answer to that difficulty. Even in the common affairs of human life, the things which go without saying do sometimes have to be said. The man who makes you a generous present can have little doubt that you feel grateful; all the same, it is customary to tell him so. And when you have trodden on a lady's dress, it is easy for her to conjecture that you feel sorry about it, but civility demands that your sorrow shall be expressed in words. And shall we never go out of our way to thank the Giver of all gifts, to beg pardon of the God whom all offences offend? But that is only a debating answer; partly because it would cut down the province of prayer to a formal minimum, and partly for a more intimate reason. Some of the people who have lived closest to God *have* found that, in proportion as they got to know him, their prayer became simplified;

was able to dispense with words, and even to dispense with thoughts
—or at least with consecutive, clearly articulated thoughts. The French
peasant who was asked what was going on when he sat praying before
the tabernacle, and replied, "I look at him, and he looks at me", had
evidently got the secret of it. A mere clinging of the soul to God, to a
God not represented to the mind by images, but veiled in a darkness
which is yet luminous to the eye of faith; without any multiplicity of
acts, so that one mystic was able to declare she never said anything in
her prayer except the word "Yes"—that is prayer, and prayer of a very
high order; perhaps of the highest order. And did we say there was no
talk without the interchange of ideas? Perhaps not, in ordinary human
conversation. But our conversation is in heaven.

What, then, of ourselves, whose prayer is so very unsimplified, so
full of images? And not merely of pious images, but of memories and
regrets and day-dreams, that spring out of our prayers and constantly
distract them? Are we simply wasting our time by chattering to
almighty God, instead of keeping silence in his presence? I don't think
we ought to take quite such a low view of our performance. The
thoughts which run through our minds when we are on our knees,
even the most unsanctified of them, may not be essential to our prayer,
but they are the natural accompaniment of it. Straws, if you will,
floating on the stream; or, better, motes dancing in the sunlight, which
give substance and body to the beams of it. As you kneel there, you
register some resolution for the better ordering of your life; you resign
yourself to the heavenly will in some emergency that lies ahead; you
recall to yourself the needs of some friend, too long churlishly forgotten; you repose in the contemplation of some favourite mystery,
the thought of some saint whose patronage you dare to claim—and all
these are symbols, in which your desire for closer intimacy with God
clothes itself and takes shape. The things of common life are transformed, like motes lit up in the sunbeam, by being taken up into your
prayer. Just so, the hundred unimportant pieces of gossip which fill up
a lover's letter are transformed, to the eye that reads them, because they
are the symbols of his love. Only, this time, it is for ourselves that the
transformation takes place; what these symbols of ours look like to God,
we cannot tell; we cannot tell what anything looks like to God.

At the same time, we have to remind ourselves that prayer is not
simply an attitude or an exercise on our part. It means talking to God;
turning away from the patter which we human beings exchange in
common life, and addressing yourself to an all-seeing and all-hearing
audience, out there in the dark. But that is not all; prayer means asking

R

for things, and getting them. Petition, to be sure, is not the essence of prayer; the model of all Christian prayer is the Our Father, and of the Our Father less than fifty per cent is petition. Our petitions, viewed in themselves, are of secondary importance; they are only the symbols by which we express our utter dependence upon God, our utter confidence in him. Any such symbol will do; a boy praying for a new scooter may pray just as well as a mother praying for the safety of her child. But that is not all; God, in his wisdom, has annexed some of his blessings, we do not know in what manner or in what measure, to our confidence and our patience in asking for them. He wanted us to pray, and he knew some of us would be slack about it; he wanted us Christian people to be good neighbours, and so he established this gracious bond of prayer by which we are united to one another, and to Holy Church. Ask, and you shall receive; he doesn't want us to puzzle our heads over the machinery of it all, he wants us to go to him like children, not ashamed to tell him what we have set our hearts on. Only, at the back of it all, the object of prayer is not to make God want what we want, it is to make us want what God wants—in his will lies our peace.

IX

ST PAUL'S GOSPEL*

* This series of Lenten conferences, preached at Westminster Cathedral in Lent 1950, was first published in *St Paul's Gospel* (1953).

THE PAULINE APPROACH

Our beloved brother Paul, with the wisdom God has granted him, has written you a letter.—2 Peter 3. 15.

WHEN you have been looking at a child's picture-book, it may have occurred to you to wonder, before now, how the printer ever managed to transfer those brightly-coloured illustrations from the block to the paper. The process, of course, is not a simple one; in reality, there are three processes, and the page you are looking at has been three times through the press, receiving successively its tints of red, yellow and blue. So it is, if you come to think of it, about the knowledge you and I have of the basic facts of our religion; three different layers of evidence have been superimposed, one on the next. First, there is tradition. The earliest Christians learnt their faith by word of mouth; you and I, if God had so ordered our destiny, might still, after all these centuries, be learning our faith by word of mouth. Next, there are the holy Gospels; an account of our Lord's life deliberately composed, for your information and mine, by men who had witnessed the events of it, or had lived so close to first-hand witnesses that the question of tradition hardly comes in. And finally, in the remaining books of the New Testament, you have a set of documents, mostly in the form of letters, written during the lifetime of men who had seen our Lord. They don't set out to give us a course of religious instruction, but they are all the better as evidence for that. We learn from such writers in the course of conversation (as it were) how Christian people lived and thought in that first age, an age lit up by the afterglow of our Lord's own life on earth.

Leave out the four Gospels, and most of the New Testament comes to us from the mind of one man, St Paul. I say "from the mind" not "from the hand", because St Paul didn't usually write, he dictated. And you can trace his influence, no doubt, in the writings of other men who derived their inspiration from him. The Acts of the Apostles was written, not by St Paul, but by his friend St Luke; yet I think it is clear that St Paul must have encouraged him to write it, and supplied him with a good deal of his material. What shall we say of the Epistle to the Hebrews? The Church holds by the tradition that it was, in some sense, the work of St Paul, but the style of it differs noticeably from that of his acknowledged Epistles. Must we suppose that, this time, he wrote with his own hand, wrote carefully, as a man writes when he is working out a thesis, instead of blurting out the thoughts of his pregnant mind, as he did to the stenographer? Or is it possible that he drew up a skeleton of the things he wanted said, and left some trusted disciple, Silvanus or another, to clothe it in his own words? Be that as it may, for our present purposes we will not use either the Acts of the Apostles or the Epistle to the Hebrews except here and there, by way of illustration. We build up our picture of St Paul's gospel from those vivid, personal letters of his, thrown off in the heat of the moment to the Christians in Rome, Corinth, Galatia, Ephesus, Philippi, Colossae, Thessalonica, and to one or two of his immediate friends.

I want to study St Paul's letters in isolation, forgetting for the moment that we have any Christian tradition, any Gospel narrative, to supplement them. So, I imagine, you might get the printer to give you a pull-off of that childish picture all in blue, with the yellows and the reds left out. I want you to see what an admirable blue-print you can get, even so, of the Christian world-picture, simply from listening to what St Paul has to tell us. It is rather like listening to one side of a telephone conversation; we can only guess, as we go along, what the people at the other end of the wire have been saying. Our pattern will be all built up out of bits and pieces, just fragments of talk overheard, sparks struck from the anvil of forgotten controversies, and problems that have no meaning for us now. But we shall see, already, the outlines of our Christian world-picture etched in for us, and with a firm hand, by a man who is not thinking about us or our difficulties; he is just talking to his friends.

It is an extraordinary thing, if you come to think of it, how the account of our Lord which you get in the Gospels dovetails in with the account of him you get in the Epistles. Not in the sense that the two accounts agree; that would be natural, that would be commonplace; rather in the sense that they disagree. I don't mean that they contradict one another; I mean that the things on which St Paul concentrates his attention are things upon which, apparently, the evangelists do not concentrate attention, and vice versa. After all, ask anybody in the world who has heard of Jesus Christ to tell you what kind of man he was. You will be told, at once, that Jesus Christ went about the world doing good, healing the sick, giving sight to the blind, and so on.

There is no word of that in St Paul; with him, the whole of our Lord's earthly biography passes unnoticed. Watch him, for example, when he is recommending to the Philippians the virtue of humility.[1] You would expect him to remind them how our Lord was born in a stable, his mother a peasant; how he lived as a poor man, how he died as a common criminal. But it isn't, you find, our Lord's behaviour as man that he appeals to for his illustration; it is the condescension of our Lord in becoming man at all. Always he misses the opportunity of telling us a story, the story of the greatest man who ever lived.

Again, think how much space is occupied in all the Gospels by long extracts from what our Lord said. Very probably, even before the Gospels were written, there were collections of such sayings handed on to the faithful by word of mouth. How often does St Paul quote the words of his Master? In the Epistles, never; only once in a speech recorded in the Acts, and then it is a saying which the Gospels haven't preserved for us at all.[2] Think of it, here was the whole Sermon on the Mount at his disposal; here was St Luke at his elbow, writing our Lord's biography, and never once does St Paul reinforce his own authority by pointing to the things Christ said! What a lot of our Lord's teaching was devoted to showing the Jews they could no longer claim a monopoly of the divine mercies; they had got to make room for the Gentiles in the new kingdom! Parables which evidently pointed to that and nothing else, like the labourers in the vineyard and the prodigal son—all that was a subject on which St Paul felt and wrote furiously; all through the Galatians and the Romans he is talking about nothing else. But he never quotes our Lord as having said anything on the subject; never borrows an illustration, even, from our Lord's teaching. He must have known; and yet, somehow, the two streams of Christian tradition don't overflow into one another. Merely as a matter of literary curiosity, and quite apart from any bearing it has on religion, I should say that this lack of interdependence between the Gospels and the Epistles is a fascinating circumstance, a baffling circumstance.

If we want to understand what St Paul's approach to the matter was, I think we have to concentrate our attention on a passage in the second Epistle to the Corinthians.[3] "Christ died for us all", he writes, "so that being alive should no longer mean living with our own life, but with his life, who died for us and has risen again. And therefore, henceforward, we do not think of anybody in a merely human fashion; even if we used to think of Christ in a human fashion, we do so no longer.

[1] Philippians 2. 5 ff.   [2] Acts 20. 35.   [3] 5. 15-17.

It follows, in fact, that when a man has become a new creature in Christ, his old life has disappeared, everything has become new about him." The interpretation of that passage is neither easy nor certain, but I think the kind of thing St Paul means is this. It is for the beginner, for the man who is still finding his way into the Church, to study the proofs of our Lord's divine mission, the miracles, the fulfilments of prophecy; it is for the beginner to learn by heart, if he will, our Lord's recorded sayings. But all that is to know Christ after a human fashion, to treat him as a man who once lived but now is dead, the subject of a biography. Once you have learned to accept Christ, and to be united with him by baptism, everything becomes different; he who was once a dead hero is now a living friend. Difficult for us, after all these centuries, to think in those terms; we have to treasure up the least crumbs of information we can get about Jesus of Nazareth—it all happened so long ago. But in St Paul's time it was different; the Ascension had only happened the other day; the airs of grace were all about you; why should you go back over the past?

Some instinct of that kind it must have been, I think, which made St Paul and the other New Testament writers strike out a line for themselves, instead of constantly quoting our Lord, constantly appealing to his example, as we should have expected them to do. The evangelists, you see, were so very much on their good behaviour; they were determined to tell a plain story, not dotting the i's or crossing the t's, leaving it to the reader to form his own conclusions. Every scene must be described just as it appeared to the people who saw it happen; there was to be no improving the occasion, no morals drawn, no theological footnotes. Their readers were to see the hero of the Gospels as a man among other men, who lived and died at a given moment in history. All that he was, but for St Paul that was not the point. The point was that our Lord was alive; that he lived on in his mystical body, the Church. When they met on the road to Damascus, our Lord said, "Why dost thou persecute me?" and that me remained in St Paul's thought as the keynote of all his theology.

No, they were not to think of Christ after a human fashion. His nature was divine; if all things came from the eternal Father, they came from him through Christ; and that "through" denoted, not a less ultimate responsibility, but somehow a more intimate relation. He was the elder Brother of all created things, and it was suitable that when God determined to reconcile his rebel world to himself, Christ should be the focus in which all creation should be at once resumed and renewed. His nature was divine, but the incommunicable privileges of

Godhead were not allowed to detain him;[1] somehow, he took upon himself the nature of man, accepted all its inadequacies, shouldered all its responsibilities. He, our elder Brother, our Representative, became our Victim, the Representative of our sin; hung upon the cross, and, as if by the shock of that unparalleled encounter, shattered all the barriers that had existed till then[2]—the barrier between God and man, the barrier between life and death, the barrier between Jew and Gentile. He died, and in his death mankind, as mystically associated with him, died too, so that the old debt incurred by Adam's sin was cancelled.[3] He rose again, and thereby acquired a second title to the headship of the human race; he was the elder Brother of all risen men.[4] The life into which he rose was not a force that quickened his natural body merely; it quickened to birth a new, mystical body of his, the Church. In the power of that life the individual Christian becomes supernaturally alive; dead to sin, dead to the fetters of the old legal observance, he lives now in Christ, lives to God.[5] Baptism, his initiation into his Master's death and Resurrection, leaves him, as it were, tongue-tied and gasping for breath, while the Holy Spirit within him cries out, "Father, Father", to claim the promise of adoption.[6] Meanwhile, the Church as a whole is Christ's building, in which we all inhere, is Christ's bride, inspiring and prescribing sanctity, is Christ's body, of which we are cells. Our whole life now is Christ-conditioned, he is the medium in which we exist, the air we breathe; all our nature is summed up, all our activities are given supernatural play, in him.

That is St Paul's programme; and perhaps it is not to be wondered at if he passes over in silence the details of a biography, whose total effect so reverberate with theological significance. The Incarnation, for St Paul, did not mean primarily that God had become *a* man; it meant primarily that God had become *man*, had infected the human race, as it were, with his divinity. "The Life of Christ" is a phrase which suggests to you and me a book on a shelf, a book by Père Didon or Archbishop Goodier. For St Paul, the phrase had no such meaning; or anyhow, that was not the meaning which leaped to the mind. The life of Christ was to him an energy that radiated all about him, was the very breath he drew in with his lungs.

Do you know what it is to meet some great man, or even some interesting personality that arrests you, and to go away quite forgetting how he was dressed or even what he looked like, because the inspiration of what he was saying riveted you at the time, so that you were uncon-

---

[1] Philippians 2. 6. [2] Ephesians 2. 15. [3] Romans 6. 6.
[4] Colossians 1. 18. [5] Romans 6. 10. [6] Galatians 4. 6.

scious of anything else? And afterwards, even what he said hardly
remains in the memory; what exactly *did* he say? All you know is that
a kind of glow pervades you, a kind of clarity that reveals your own
thoughts to you, as the result of what passed. It is the man's personality
that haunts you, something too subtle and too elusive to admit of
analysis, something beyond the play of features or the sound of speech;
the man himself has cast a kind of spell on you. Something like that
happened to St Paul, I suppose, but in an infinitely higher degree, after
his experience on the road to Damascus. The shock passed off, the
blindness was cured; but always the interior sight of the apostle was
dazzled by the memory of that interview. Stories about Christ, things
Christ said, repeat them by all means, but St Paul wanted something
more than that; he wanted Christ.

St Ignatius put it on record that, even if no documents of the Christian
religion remained, he would have been prepared to die for the faith,
in the light of what our Lord had made known to him at Manresa.
And St Paul was in the same category.

There is, I think, something providential about this attitude of the
New Testament writers. Because St Paul contrives to fill in for us,
like the blue plate which the printer superimposes on the red, our
picture of what our Lord was like, I think there is, about the synoptic
Gospels, a kind of deliberate objectiveness which sometimes makes it
hard to understand the way in which their story develops. Why did
the apostles leave their nets and start out without a word, when our
Lord said "Follow me"? What was the magic of voice or look that
drew them away, in those early days when no miracles had yet been
done, when the campaign of preaching had not yet been opened?
Something escapes us in their narrative; what we call, in the loose
sense, "personality". The tremendous impact which his force of
character made on people—do you remember how, according to
St John, his captors in the garden went back and fell to the ground
when he said, "I am Jesus of Nazareth"? All that is difficult to realize
in the synoptist account. It becomes easier to realize when you watch
the effect it had on St Paul; how, after that interview on the Damascus
road, he saw Christ in everyone, Christ in everything; nothing but
Christ.

Meanwhile, let us not be betrayed, even for one unguarded moment,
into suggesting that St Paul's gospel was different from anybody else's
gospel. There was no imputation which he would have met with a
more vigorous protest; that we know, because the imputation was in
fact made by rival teachers in his own day, anxious to undermine his

influence. Always he described his teaching as a tradition, something which he is handing on; beset with missionary problems, he will yet find time, not once or twice, to go back to Jerusalem and confer with those who were apostles before him; "Was it possible", he asks, "that the course I had taken was useless?"[1] No, we shall hear nothing from St Paul that is not in accord with the full stream of Christian theology. Only divine truth is rich enough to admit of different angles of human approach. Grace does not destroy nature, it perfects nature; something of the human genius remains, and the pure gold of revelation is not always minted in the same workshop. And St Paul's was no ordinary mind; sensitive, yet fearless, logical, yet poetic, infinitely tender with the scruples of others, yet unflinching in its honesty. A delicate instrument, it will interpret the melody of Christian thought in its own way. We must listen patiently, allowing him his own choice of language, not trying to fix on his words a meaning which has since become technical, not allowing our minds to be disturbed by the echoes of later controversy. You must come to St Paul with fresh eyes if you are to feel his magic.

2

ST PAUL AND THE OLD TESTAMENT

All that is an allegory. The two women stand for the two dispensations; Agar stands for the old dispensation, which brings up its children to bondage, the dispensation which comes to us from Mount Sinai.—Galatians 4. 24.

EVERY year, on the fourth Sunday of Lent, the Epistle at Mass consists of an elaborate allegory, in which St Paul contrasts Sara with Agar, Isaac with Ismael, something (it is not clear what) with Mount Sinai, and the earthly with the heavenly Jerusalem. Every year, the faithful listen with an air of polite detachment, evidently feeling that they cannot be expected to understand what all this is about. It is this business of the overheard telephone conversation once more; the Galatians, no doubt, had a clue to St Paul's meaning which we haven't. . . . Yes, but, before you say that, think. Who were the Galatians? Heathens quite recently converted; it was only a year or two, perhaps

[1] Galatians 2. 2.

only a month or two, since they had mistaken St Barnabas for Jupiter, and St Paul for Mercury. Now, Jewish missionaries were trying to persuade them that, in order to be good Christians, they must adopt the law of Moses. What an extraordinary thing that these people, quite stupid country people, Gentile by birth, heathen by education, should be expected to know all about Agar, all about Mount Sinai, and not only to know about them, but to understand the mystical significance of them, when you and I can't make head or tail of it!

There is only one possible explanation of it; and that is that St Paul, when he instructed enquirers in the faith, told them a great deal about the Old Testament, or at least about the books of Genesis and Exodus. Even if they were Gentiles, to whom the sacred books of the Jews meant nothing, they had got to learn about the old dispensation first, before they could see the new dispensation in its right context, against its right background. Poor stupid slaves from Galatia had got to be taken all through the family history of Abraham and the patriarchs before they got on to the part about Jesus Christ. That is perhaps why, in writing to these same Galatians, St Paul refers to the ordinances of the Jewish law as "those old schoolroom tasks";[1] the Jewish background of the Christian revelation is something that must be laboriously learnt, like the Gender Rhymes, like the Rule of Three; it is a preliminary grind which you have got to get through before your education proper really begins. It might seem dull, but there was no help for it; you must be properly grounded before you could master your subject, and the groundwork of the Christian religion was the story of the Old Testament, which the poor Gentiles had never heard of.

How then does St Paul look back on it, the panorama of history, and the pattern which his own race had woven through it? As a mirror, I think, which reflects the mysteries of the new dispensation, but reflects them, you might almost say, back to front. Most of us, when we were younger, have tried to cheat the hours of some long railway journey by kneeling up on the seat and watching the scenery flash past, telegraph poles and fields and distant hills, in the looking-glass. Then, when you had got thoroughly accustomed to the rhythm of its movement, you would turn round suddenly and look out of the window at the real scenery, flashing past in the opposite direction. St Paul's view of history is rather like that; he looks back over history and sees the world not merely as bad but as going from bad to worse; that terrible passage in the first chapter of the Romans is meant, evidently, to be a picture of contemporary manners. And the coming of

<hr>

[1] Galatians 4. 9.

Christ meant, for him, that all that process had gone into reverse; with the coming of Christ, history was repeating itself, but repeating itself just the other way round.

He saw our Lord as the second Adam, the Adam who rose, the Adam who restored us, as contrasted with the Adam who fell, the Adam who ruined us. A familiar consideration; but how many times is it mentioned in the Gospels? There is no allusion, from end to end of the Gospels, to the Fall of Man. Adam is only twice mentioned in the New Testament, outside St Paul's Epistles, and both times merely in passing. How much St Paul was following the lines of current Jewish interpretation, when he laid such stress on the Fall, we cannot be certain; but the references to it in the Old Testament, outside the second chapter of Genesis, are meagre and inconclusive. The tradition of the Church would beyond doubt have preserved for us, in any case, the doctrine of the Fall, and some account of how it dovetails in with the doctrine of our Redemption. But, so far as Scripture is concerned, you may say it was St Paul alone, under the prompting of the Holy Spirit, who gave the Fall of Adam the place it has in Christian theology.

St Paul saw the Old and New Testaments as a series of parallel columns; he tells us as much in that passage from the Galatians which I gave you as my text. And the list begins quite simply, "Adam equals Christ". We must see Adam as the head of the human race by physical descent, as summing up in his own person the whole experience of humanity; then we shall begin to understand how Christ is the head of the human race by spiritual adoption, and how he sums up in his own person the whole experience of his Church. Because Adam was the head of the human race, the guilt of his transgression transferred itself automatically to his descendants. Oh, no doubt they were sinners too; nobody was more certain than St Paul about the corruption of heathen humanity. But he does not think of them, in this connection, as imitating and therefore sharing the sin of Adam. He is speaking of transgression; and where there is transgression there must be a direct commandment to transgress; after the Fall, until the law of Moses came, there was no such direct law issued to mankind, and yet mankind had to bear Adam's punishment. Death reigned; physical death, at once the symbol and the sequel of spiritual inanition. The status of guilt incurred by Adam's transgression lived on in us, his descendants in the natural order.[1]

The obverse of that medal is not difficult to read. Sprung from Adam by physical descent, we acquire the status of guilty men; incorporated

[1] Romans 5. 12-14.

into Christ by spiritual adoption, we acquire the status of men reprieved; that is what it means, to be justified. And as it is not, primarily, anything we do that makes guilty men of us, but mere birth from Adam, so it is not anything we do that justifies us, but mere re-birth in Christ. To become the second Adam, it was only necessary for our Lord to come to earth as man; he "took birth from a woman, so as to make us sons by adoption".[1] It is in that sense, probably, that we should understand an obscure passage in the first Epistle to Timothy, where St Paul, after alluding to the sin of Eve, tells us that "woman will find her salvation in the child-bearing";[2] almost certainly, our Lady's child-bearing is meant. More commonly, it is our Lord's death and resurrection that are represented as the gate of the new life which comes to us; mystically associated with our Lord, we die with him and rise again with him. But always St Paul will keep to his chosen symbolism; baptism does not remind him, as it reminds St Peter, of Noe coming out of his ark to repeople the world, does not chiefly remind him, as it reminds the Church on Holy Saturday, of Moses crossing the Red Sea at the head of a redeemed people. No, mankind begins with Adam, who became, as Scripture tells us, a living soul; it is fulfilled in the Adam who has become a lifegiving spirit. In a garden the second Adam, like the first, awakes to life.

Meanwhile, there is a gulf of history to be bridged, between man's fall and man's redemption. Something, surely, happened, something of far-reaching importance to mankind, when God gave his law to Moses on Mount Sinai. We are accustomed to think of Mount Sinai as a partial revelation, and perhaps St Paul might have used the same language; "the Jews", he writes, "had the words of God entrusted to them"[3] although it is doubtful whether "promises" would not be a better rendering than "words". But St Paul thinks in terms of redemption, not of revelation; and where redemption is concerned he will not allow the Mosaic covenant even the dignity of a half-way house. Ever since Adam's fall, the ambition of man was to be justified; that is, to get rid of the sentence of outlawry imposed on him, and to be once more what Adam had been, *persona grata* with God. Towards the achieving of that ambition, the law of Moses has not brought us one step nearer; not a single step.

No, if anything the law left us worse off than we were before. "It was brought in", St Paul tells the Galatians, "to make room for transgression."[4] What does that mean? Why, surely this; that the sins

---

[1] Galatians 4. 4.   [2] 2. 15.
[3] Romans 3. 2.   [4] Galatians 3. 19.

committed between the time of Adam and the time of Moses were not, strictly speaking, transgressions, because (as we have seen) there was no direct law to transgress. With Moses, God's law was expressly promulgated to mankind, and every sin after that was a transgression; nobody could plead that he didn't know he was doing wrong, because here was God's law in black and white to tell him that he was doing wrong. God's purpose, as always, was beneficent; by thus throwing our sins into relief, he made us more eager than ever for the coming of our redemption. But the law didn't help us to get nearer to God, because we all immediately started disobeying it, just as if it wasn't there. The Psalm describes almighty God as looking down from heaven to see if he could find a single innocent man; but no, there is nobody who reflects, and searches for God, all alike are on the wrong course[1]—it was a moral which you could illustrate abundantly, at every period, from the writings of the prophets. The Jews, who had received the law, were nevertheless continually disobeying it. That means, evidently, that the law showed us what was the right thing to do, without bringing us the grace which would enable us to do it; revelation without illumination. To prove his point, St Paul gives you in the Romans that terrible chapter which describes the soul, unbefriended by grace, seeing at every turn what is the right thing to do, and doing just the opposite. "The sense of sin, with the law's ban for its foothold, caught me unawares, and by that means killed me. . . . It is not the good my will prefers, but the evil my will disapproves, that I find myself doing. . . . Pitiable creature that I am, who is to set me free from a nature thus doomed to death?"[2] The law didn't justify us; it found us sinners, and left us not only sinners but transgressors; that is the long and short of it.

Not that there is anything wrong with the law; it is holy and just and good.[3] Notice, once again, a difference between the Gospels and the writings of St Paul. The Jews of our Lord's time had elaborated the law into a complicated system of taboos which made it unnecessarily burdensome; and our Lord denounced the Pharisees, in terms familar to all of us, for the pedantry and the legalism of it. Nothing easier than for St Paul to have taken up the same point in writing to the Romans or to the Galatians. But he does not attempt to take any such advantage of his opponents; he will yield to none in his respect for the law, only —only the law was a temporary dispensation, meant to last until our redemption came, and no longer. By way of emphasizing the fact that it was only something temporary, something secondary, St Paul makes

[1] Romans 3. 11; Psalm 13. 2.   [2] Romans 7. 11, 15, 24.
[3] Romans 7.12.

use of a tradition, evidently common among the Jews, although you find no trace of it in the Old Testament, that the law was given to Moses, not directly by God himself, but by the holy angels, using one of their number as a spokesman.[1] The law itself was not God's solemn covenant with man; it was only a sort of codicil, added afterwards to regulate the terms of it.

What, then, was God's solemn covenant with man? The promise made, long before, to Abraham. The prophets when they appealed to the divine fidelity, rested their claim chiefly on the promises made to King David; you will only find Abraham mentioned about seven times in the whole of their writings. But the older tradition survived; both in the *Magnificat* and in the *Benedictus* Abraham is the name of destiny. A series of prophecies had been made to him, of which the most far-reaching was, that in his posterity all the nations of the world should find a blessing. We must not lay too much stress on the actual form of the words. To say that all mankind will bless themselves in the name of Abraham's posterity does not mean more, necessarily, than that it will be used in formulas of benediction: "May the Lord bless thee as he blessed the seed of Abraham". But it was the tradition of the race that a more solemn assurance was involved; the remote issue of a homeless desert chief was, somehow, to acquire a world-significance. And had it, St Paul asks?[2] For a time it might have seemed as if the promise were being fulfilled, when Solomon's empire bridged the land-passage between east and west, receiving in its coffers the tribute of east and west alike. But all that was a thing of the remote past; the balance of the world had shifted, empires had changed hands, and the Jewish race was a despised, a scattered minority of mankind.

And now, with a stroke of the pen, St Paul sweeps away the whole edifice of Jewish privilege. Abraham believed God, and it was reckoned virtue in him; when was that? Before any law had been promulgated on Sinai, before the rite of circumcision had been enjoined, before the birth, even, of Isaac.[3] It follows that the true descendants of Abraham are not those who claim his physical parentage, but those who share his faith. Carrying the war into the enemy's country, St Paul goes back to Ismael, the eldest son of Abraham, but born out of wedlock. And he allegorizes the whole story; Ismael, the natural son, serves for a type of physical descent, of outward observance, of the old covenant generally; Isaac, the child of promise, stands for a type of spiritual sonship, of interior religion, of the new covenant which was given to

---

[1] Galatians 3. 19.   [2] Romans 4. 14.

[3] Romans 4. 10.

us in Jesus Christ.[1] St Paul has told us elsewhere that what is first in order of importance comes last in order of time;[2] man's body is created first, his soul afterwards. So it is here; Isaac, the late-born, who is despised by Ismael, and is none the less Abraham's heir—we are to see, in him, the image of the Christian Church, later in time than the synagogue, derided by the synagogue, and yet the final repository of God's mercies, the true explanation of his mysterious dealings with mankind, all those centuries ago.

And then, as if the lesson hadn't been made plain enough, the same situation repeats itself in Isaac's family as in Abraham's. Two brothers again; both, this time, born in wedlock; but Esau is the elder, Esau is his father's favourite, Esau is the world's choice, and Esau is rejected. How the Jews had relished that story, contrasting their own future greatness with the rude barbarism of their desert neighbours, the Edomites! But no, says St Paul, the contrast foreshadowed in the book of Genesis was not a contrast between two rival nations, both descended from Isaac. It was a contrast between two orders, the natural and the spiritual order; between those older things, the law of Moses, the pride of the Jews in their ancestry, and the newer thing that had come to pass, the birth of the Christian Church. Physically descended from Jacob, the Jewish people, like Esau, were being excluded from the promise of divine mercy—or say, rather, they were excluding themselves from it, by their obstinate rejection of Christ.[3] Useless to ask, why God should allow such blindness to fall on them; you might as well ask why he allowed Pharao to harden his heart—indispensable prelude to the triumph of the Exodus. It is a mistake to read that ninth chapter of the Romans as if it were an essay on predestination and free will. St Paul is not thinking about all that; he is thinking about the rejection of the Jews, his fellow countrymen, so melancholy to witness, so difficult to understand.[4]

Always it is like that with St Paul; you cannot make any allusion to the Old Testament without his transposing it into a fresh key, restating it in terms of the New. Even the sins of Israel in the desert were recorded, he says, as a warning to us; to us, in whom history has reached its fulfilment.[5] Not a mirage, those old promises, but a mirror for Christian souls. I don't mean that St Paul had to invent all this for himself; our Lord, during those forty days after his Resurrection, went back to Moses (we are told) and the whole line of prophets, interpreting the words used of himself by the Scriptures. All I want to suggest is that

[1] Galatians 4. 21 ff.   [2] 1 Corinthians 15. 46.   [3] Romans 9. 9 ff.
[4] Ibid., 14 ff.   [5] 1 Corinthians 10. 1 ff.

St Paul fills in for us the outline which the Gospels have left indistinct; what *did* it mean, in the long run, that providential history of the Jewish people? St Paul can tell us; the Old Testament is a great overture, introducing beforehand all the motifs of the New.

3

ST PAUL AND CHRIST'S DIVINITY

He is the true likeness of the God we cannot see; his is that first birth which precedes every act of creation.—Colossians 1. 15.

WHEN a man gets hold of a new idea, or rather, is got hold of by a new idea, which throws him off his balance and reinterprets the world for him, it may have any one of three effects on his daily conversation, and on his published writings. He may keep silent about it, except when he is in specially congenial company; he may have the feeling that this idea is so much too big for him, he will only spoil it if he tries to put it into his own words; people will take it up wrong, and be offended by it, or people will misunderstand it, and exaggerate it, and vulgarize it; far best, when the general public is listening, to hush it up. Or the effect may be just the opposite; he may be so full of his subject that he cannot resist bringing it up on any and every occasion; always he is wanting to buttonhole people and tell them about it, argue about it. Or, finally, it may become, from the first, part of the background of his mind, something which he takes for granted, and takes it for granted that everybody else takes it for granted too. He does not drag it in, does not harp on it, it seems to crop up naturally; it makes itself known in casual allusions, in the unconscious overtones of his thought. Now, which of those three effects did his conversion have on St Paul?

Rather unexpectedly, neither the first nor the second, but the third. The more you read his Epistles, the more (I think) you get the impression that the mysteries of Christian theology are neither a difficult topic which he is anxious to avoid, nor the professed subject of his teaching, but his whole mental background, which keeps on showing whether he means it to or not.

It would have been so easy to understand, if St Paul, writing when he did, writing for the sort of people who were going to hear his letter read out, had felt inclined to soft-pedal the note of dogma. After all, who were these people? Mostly, you would imagine, rather stupid people, many of them slaves, nearly all of them pagans till yesterday. As pagans, they had worshipped a whole pantheon; it had been hard enough to make them believe there was only one God—wouldn't the doctrine of the Trinity be rather confusing to them? As pagans, they had offered incense to the memory of dead emperors, deified now, the neuropath Tiberius, the madman Caligula—would they be able to see the point of the Incarnation? Wouldn't it be safer to tell them stories about the life of Jesus? But no, St Paul would spare them nothing. Contrariwise, if you *were* going to mention dogma, you would be inclined to rub it in, with a lot of simplification and a lot of repetition: "Remember, three Persons, the Father, the Son, and the Holy Ghost" — staccato echoes of the classroom. But no, that is not St Paul's method either. He treats his converts as if they had been instructed as well as you or I—better than some of us; he will refer to the august mysteries of the Faith in an almost casual way; as if everybody, naturally, would understand all about *that*; he alludes to these things not because the gutter-snipes of Philippi will need to be told about them, but because they happen, for the moment, to throw light on his argument; a mere reference, a mere allusion, and he passes on to something else. How strange it seems to us! And perhaps rather humiliating.

The doctrine of the Trinity—how little your attention is drawn to it as you read through the first three Gospels! Only at the last moment, when our Lord is making ready to ascend into heaven, does he explain to his apostles that they are to baptize in the name of the Father and of the Son and of the Holy Ghost. With St Paul it is quite otherwise; he doesn't insist on the doctrine, but it keeps on cropping up. It's not merely that he closes an Epistle with a formula of blessing which includes the threefold invocation.[1] What is much more significant is the way his thought travels back, unbidden, to the subject we half expected him to avoid. He is telling the Corinthians that they ought not to quarrel about the importance of this or that spiritual endowment; after all, he says, all alike are the gift of the same Spirit. And then he adds, quite unnecessarily as it seems, "just as there are different kinds of service, but it is the same Lord we serve, and different manifestations of power, though it is the same God who manifests his power everywhere in all of us".[2] He is not out to tell us anything about the Trinity,

---

[1] 2 Corinthians 13. 13.   [2] 1 Corinthians 12. 5, 6.

you see, but there is a kind of Trinitarian groove in his mind which carries it on from one divine Person to another.

So it is when he has been talking to the Romans about the call of the Gentiles; he breaks out into praise of God's inscrutable wisdom, and once again there must be a threefold division: "All things find in him their origin, their impulse, and their goal".[1] All things come *from* him; that is the turn of phrase St Paul regularly uses for the divine Word. All things aspire *to* him; that is less natural and more difficult. But I think St Paul sees creation as an outward echo of that divine life which is shared by the three Persons of the Trinity. The Holy Spirit is that love by which the cycle of the divine life returns upon itself; and the love which goes back to God from his creatures is therefore, as it were, his province; not because it is specially directed to him, but because he inspires and energizes it.

So it is again when St Paul is trying to promote a spirit of unity among his converts at Ephesus. You are one body, he writes, with a single Spirit, each of you, when he was called, called in a single hope; and then, after this threefold appeal to the Holy Spirit, there must be a threefold appeal to the second Person of the Trinity, "with the same Lord, the same faith, the same baptism". And next, there ought to be a threefold appeal to God the Father; only St Paul is carried away, poetry as so often getting the better of logic, and finishes up with a fresh Trinitarian formula: "who is above all, pervades all, and lives in all".[2] This time, we will not examine his choice of words; spend too much attention on the details of what St Paul says, and you get left behind; the majestic sweep of his argument has passed you by. Enough to have satisfied ourselves that the doctrine of the Blessed Trinity is always close to the surface of St Paul's thought. If for no other reason, because that is the starting-point from which he approaches the doctrine of the Incarnation.

I said just now that we are to think of God's creation as an echo, an extension (if that word may be cautiously used) of his own divine life. The eternal act of generation by which the Father begets the divine Word is the model and as it were the impetus of that external activity by which he creates things outside himself. And so, even before we have begun to talk about the Incarnation at all, it is natural for us to think of the divine Word as in some sense the medium by which we approach the Godhead. "For us", St Paul says, "there is only one God, the Father who is the origin of all things, and the end of our being; only one Lord, Jesus Christ, the creator of all things, and our way to

---

[1] Romans 11. 3.   [2] Ephesians 4. 4 ff.

him".[1] In the same sense, the Epistle to the Hebrews tells us that it was through his Son God created this world of time; "without him", adds St John, "nothing came that has come to be". Somehow, by some title we cannot hope to understand, the divine Word is to be thought of as the link between God and his creatures.

That notion St Paul has worked out for us in one passage which startles us by its richness and firmness of expression; will startle us still more if we remember that the Christian religion was only about thirty years old—how rapidly its thought had crystallized! St Paul is writing to the Church at Colossae, threatened with an invasion of that heresy which afterwards gave the Church so much trouble under the name of Gnosticism. The starting-point of the Gnostic is this: The world we see about us is such a hotch-potch of good and evil, you cannot possibly attribute the creation of it to one God, and a God who is infinitely good. No, you can only account for the facts by supposing that a whole unseen world of angels exists, much higher than ourselves but not enjoying the perfections of divine Wisdom; between them, as the resultant of ill-balanced forces, these must have produced the world as we know it. Easy to see that such a doctrine did not look altogether unlike Christian doctrine; easy to see that it had attractions for the mind of a Christian who, till yesterday, had worshipped a whole multitude of gods. In recalling the Colossians to the right tradition of theology, St Paul is concerned to point out that no responsibility for the acts of creation can rest with any being outside the Godhead itself. Angels and men and all the rest of creation are the direct work of God, and in some special sense of the divine Word. Among all the short-comings of the Gnostic system this especially challenges his attention; it denies the unique position of the second Person of the Blessed Trinity as the sole intermediary between things human and things divine.

With that in view, St Paul gives us a well-known description of the Son of God, as he exists independently of his human nature, independently of the work of redemption. "He is the true likeness of the God we cannot see; his is that first birth which precedes every act of creation. Yes, in him all created things took their being, heavenly and earthly, visible and invisible; what are thrones and dominions, what are princedoms and powers? They were all created in him and for him; he takes precedency of all, and in him all subsist."[2] He is the true likeness of the God we cannot see—the Epistle to the Hebrews puts that in another way by saying that he is "the radiance of his Father's splendour, and the full expression of his being".[3] Perhaps the least misleading of all

[1] 1 Corinthians 8. 6.   [2] Colossians 1. 15.   [3] Hebrews 1. 3.

the images by which we try to understand the divine nature is that of the artist. Every artist will tell you that he is trying to express himself, yet when he has done his best he will acknowledge that he has failed; he did not express himself fully. He tried to put himself into his work, but only a little of it, he feels, is really there. But God the Father, in the eternal generation of his Son, does express himself fully; for once, the likeness is adequate to the original, and is one with it. Of that eternal act, the creation of all things visible and invisible is only a kind of echo, only a kind of ripple; but to that tenuous extent it reflects the divine paternity. That is why, St Paul tells us, creation stands in a special relation, or rather in a special series of relations, to the eternal Son of God. It comes to be *through* him; he communicates to it the impulse which gives it birth. It exists *in* him; he is the medium which gives it coherency. It exists *for* him; he is the end towards which all its imperfect efforts aspire. He is, in a sense, the elder Brother of every created thing; not that he ranks with them in a series, but they lay claim like him, only under a very different title, to a divine parentage. Even if we had never sinned, and needed no redemption, there would be something in our very position as creatures which would draw us closer to him.

Having said that, St Paul has said enough for his immediate purposes. He has warned the angel-worshippers at Colossae that they are cheating the divine Word of the honour due to him, as being the sole inter-mediary (if such a word can be used) in the work of creation. But when he has reached that point, he digresses; it would not be St Paul if he did not digress. He goes on at once from the work of creation to the work of redemption, and insists that the divine Word himself is the sole intermediary between God and man, here too. Only, this time, as incarnate; a close parallel is drawn between Christ as Creator and Christ as Redeemer, with a repetition of the actual words used. "He too is that head whose body is the Church; it begins with him, since his was the first birth out of death; thus in every way the primacy was to become his. It was God's good pleasure to let all completeness dwell in him, and through him to win back all things, whether on earth or in heaven, into union with himself."[1] The eternal generation of the divine Word is the first echo, as it were, which breaks the mysterious silence of heaven. And the Resurrection of Jesus Christ is the first echo which breaks the silence after the long sleep of death which has gone on undisturbed since Adam fell. Christ as God stood in a vague relation to all his creatures as in some sense their elder Brother; Christ as Man

[1] Colossians 1. 18 ff.

stands in a definite relation to them as the Head, the clan Chief in whom and with whom the whole clan is mystically united; all creation is summed up in him. Nothing henceforward is complete without him; everything lives, with a new life now, in him; he, the centre of their being, is now also the magnet which draws them back towards him. To him, whether as God or as Man, both priority and primacy belong.

We sometimes wonder why a single Person of the Blessed Trinity, and the second Person rather than the first or the third, should have brought us salvation. St Paul, to be sure, has no doubt that this, like every other divine act, is fundamentally the act of all three Persons at once; "God was in Christ, reconciling the world to himself",[1] and by "God" St Paul evidently means God the Father, except where the context makes such an interpretation unnatural. But for St Paul, as for St John, there was a clear appropriateness about the redemptive mission of the divine Word; he who had made should remake us. And he will not begin to tell us the story of Christmas Day by taking us to our Lady's home at Nazareth, or to the stable at Bethlehem. Like St John, he will begin at the other end; or rather, he will begin at the beginning. Its starting-point shall be a prologue in heaven.

And then, from that height, he swoops down suddenly to earth. He has assessed for us the meaning of the Incarnation in a passage we all know almost by heart, a famous passage in his Epistle to the Philippians. "His nature is, from the first, divine, and yet he did not see, in the rank of Godhead, a prize to be coveted; he dispossessed himself, and took the nature of a slave, fashioned in the likeness of men, and presenting himself to us in human form."[2] There is metaphor, of course, in the terms St Paul uses; you cannot refer to such a subject without the use of metaphor. And I think you may say the picture St Paul has in his mind is that of a young prince who is determined to win the hearts of his subjects. Born in the purple, he is not dazzled by the pomp of royalty; he is prepared to lay all that aside. He cannot cease to be what he is, but he can voluntarily reduce himself to a condition in which the outward signs of royalty are forgone. And then the metaphor breaks down, as all metaphors must break down when you are referring to such a subject. The divine Word really took upon himself the nature of man, he, whose inalienable possession is the nature of God. If he came to us in human likeness, in human form, he was not practising a deception on our simplicity; he was man.

So he came to us. We have seen what man's position had been since Adam had fallen, how the fulfilment of the promises lingered, and

[1] 2 Corinthians 5. 19.   [2] Philippians 2. 6.

the world seemed only to go from bad to worse; how the law was given, with no other result than to convict us more clearly of the guilt it could do nothing to remove. In that darkest hour the dawn came, as we are reminded in the thrilling Epistle for the second Mass on Christmas Day: "We, after all, were once like the rest of them, the dupes of error . . . our lives full of meanness and of envy, hateful, and hating one another. Then the kindness of God, our Saviour, dawned on us, his great love for man. He saved us, and it was not thanks to anything we had done for our own justification; in accordance with his own merciful design he saved us."[1] All that happened in the interval had made no difference; we toiled away at our schoolroom tasks "till the appointed time came. Then God sent out his Son on a mission to us. He took birth from a woman, took birth as a subject of the law, so as to ransom those who were subject to the law, and make us sons by adoption".[2] Born of a woman—yes, he was of our own flesh and blood, he had been through all the stages of human growth. Born under the law— yes, he had a historical context, belonged to a particular race, shared the culture of one particular countryside. St Paul knows how to come down to bedrock after all, to a particular cradle in a particular cave. But behind that, what a background of providential design! He will not be satisfied until he has taken us back to the very origins.

4

ST PAUL AND CHRIST'S HUMANITY

No question of it, it is a great mystery we worship.—1 Timothy 3. 16.

WHEN we talk about the life and death of our Lord Jesus Christ, we are using words in a special way. The word "life-and-death" ought, if I may put it in that way, to be connected by hyphens; the two facts are intimately connected—indeed, you might almost say that you have a single fact there, viewed under two different aspects. Our Lord's death wasn't just the crown of his life; it was the bud of his life bursting into flower. Let me explain that phrase a little.

When somebody writes a book called "The Life and Death of Lord Nelson", he is writing about two separate subjects. He is writing the

---

[1] Titus 3. 3 ff.　　　　　　　　　　　　　　[2] Galatians 4. 4.

life of a great admiral, who saved England. He is also writing about the death of a brave seaman who fell in battle. Oh, to be sure, Nelson's end was an appropriate one, from the spectacular, from the dramatic point of view. A poet could not have improved on the facts. But Nelson's life would have been that of a great admiral, even if he had lived as long as the Duke of Wellington. And Nelson's death would have been that of a brave seaman, if he had been a simple foremast hand. Whereas in our Lord's case we know that he came to earth to die. Most of us have seen that picture of Holman Hunt's, which represents our Lord in the carpenter's shop at Nazareth, when some chance arrangement of shadows has marked the wall behind him, where he stands with outstretched arms, in the figure of a cross. I don't know whether that picture is good art, but it is good theology. Our Lord's whole life is explained and is orientated by the death he foresees.

Because the two things are so closely connected, you will find a certain difference, I will not say of opinion but of emphasis, between Christian theologians. To some, his atoning death is the only reason, as far as we know, why he came into the world at all. The affront which our sins offered to God was infinite, and if full satisfaction was to be made for it, that could only be done by a divine Victim; so the second Person of the Blessed Trinity became man and suffered, in our stead, the penalty we had deserved. That explains the Incarnation; what more could you want? Others have laid more stress on Bethlehem, and less on Calvary; the mere fact of God taking manhood upon him was enough of itself to heal and restore our fallen nature. They have considered it probable that there would have been an Incarnation, even if there had been no Fall.

Very roughly, you may say that the division is, as so often, a division between east and west; that it is the Latin Fathers who lay so much emphasis on the Atonement, the Greek Fathers who are more interested in the Incarnation. Very roughly, you may say that the party of the Atonement interprets the result of the Fall under a legal metaphor; the balance of the divine justice has been disturbed, and there must be compensation before it is adjusted. Whereas the party of the Incarnation interprets the result of the Fall in organic terms; human nature has been fatally wounded, and it can only be restored by being grafted somehow into the divine nature; it is something like a transfusion of blood. Very roughly, you may say that one party takes its cue from our Lord's own account of his mission, "the Son of Man came to give his life as a ransom for the lives of many";[1] the other takes its cue from that other

[1] Matthew 20. 28.

account which our Lord gave, "I have come so that they may have life, and have it more abundantly".[1]

So the stream of Christian tradition is divided, though only, as I say, as a matter of emphasis. On which side does St Paul come down? Which party claims his support?

It would be impossible to deny that St Paul describes the work of our salvation, sometimes, under legal metaphors. You cannot, after all, speak of redemption, as St Paul often does, without using a legal metaphor. In the Old Testament almighty God is often described as redeeming his people, in a sense which generally passes over our heads. The Jewish law was very careful about hereditary titles to landed property, and if a piece of ground was up for sale, there was always somebody who had the first claim to be the purchaser, because he was the head of the family to which it originally belonged. Only if he could not or would not buy it might it be sold to a stranger; you get that prominently mentioned in the book of Ruth. In the mind of the Hebrew prophets, ever since their deliverance from Egypt, Israel belonged specially to God, by a kind of hereditary right; and when Israel was conquered by its enemies, when its people went into exile, it meant that God's ancient inheritance was (so to speak) up for sale. Surely then he, as having the first claim upon it, would buy in this precious possession of his, instead of letting it go to strangers! That sense of the word passes over into the New Testament, and when Zachary blesses the God of Israel for having visited his people and wrought their redemption, that sense will have been uppermost in his mind. And quite possibly St Paul, too, has it in mind when he writes to the Galatians about God sending his Son into the world to buy up those who were subject to the law;[2] salvation was offered first to the Jews, because God had proprietary rights over them as his own people.

But it is not merely in this vague sense of proprietorship that Jesus Christ is said to redeem us. "A great price was paid to ransom you", St Paul writes to the Corinthians, and again, "A price was paid to redeem you";[3] here, perhaps, he is thinking of slaves being set at liberty, and drawing special attention to the fact that this can only be done by the payment of a ransom. What ransom it was that was paid to deliver us from the bondage of sin is a matter that admits of no doubt; the price paid for our liberty was a human life.

The idea of a life being given up by way of ransom was, of course, familiar to Jewish thought; it entered into the whole philosophy of sacrifice. Our Lord himself, as the first-born Son of his Mother, had

---

[1] John 10. 10.   [2] Galatians 4. 5.   [3] 1 Corinthians 6. 20; 7. 23.

to be redeemed by the slaughter of a turtle-dove, or two young pigeons. And he himself, as we saw just now, told us that the Son of Man came to give his life as a ransom for the lives of many—instead of many, if you insist on the full flavour of the word. St Paul does not imitate that turn of speech; he doesn't say that our Lord gave up his life in our stead, only that he gave it up on our behalf—perhaps a significant variation of language. We have reminded ourselves that, in St Paul's language, Christ incarnate is the elder Brother of humanity; what a temptation for him to point to the position of the first-born in Jewish law! In theory, the first-born of every man or beast was forfeit as a sacrifice to almighty God. In theory, then, you may say that the eldest son of a family gave up his life as a ransom for the lives of the rest; how apt a parallel that would have been! But nowhere does St Paul's language suggest it; he avoids, for the most part, the idea of a substituted Victim. Although he once refers to our Lord as a paschal Victim,[1] offered on our behalf, he never uses the word "lamb"; it is St John and St Peter who tell us about the Lamb of God. Why that is, perhaps we shall see later.

At the same time, you cannot deny that the death of our Lord Jesus Christ is central to St Paul's theology. He is always for drawing attention to the cross; he will make his boast of nothing else, however much the Jews shrink, however much the Gentiles mock, at the sight of its ignominy. Indeed, I think you can say that to St Paul the cross suggested, not so much the idea of suffering, as the idea of publicity. He tells the Galatians that Christ has been advertised to them, hanging on a cross;[2] and later in the same Epistle he says that through it the world has been crucified to him, and he to the world;[3] it was a kind of legal instrument, setting it on record that the world has nothing to do with Paul, that Paul has nothing to do with the world, in future. Yes, a legal instrument; St Paul is never afraid of talking lawyer's language. And above all the cross is a document which sets on record the establishment of peace between God and man, like those old cairns and pillars which the patriarchs used to raise when they wanted to make a covenant. God's forgiveness means that he cancelled the deed which excluded us, the decree made to our prejudice, swept it out of the way, by nailing it to his cross[4]—the cross, you see, is still the notice-board of the new covenant. A covenant of peace; it was through the cross that he abolished all feuds, including the old feud between Jew and Gentile; "both sides, united in a single body, he would reconcile to God through

---

[1] 1 Corinthians 5. 7.
[2] Galatians 3. 1. [3] *Ibid.*, 4. 14. [4] Colossians 2. 14.

his cross".[1] It was a legal instrument; you must not preach the Gospel with devices of human rhetoric, for that would be cancelling—it is the plain meaning of the word—cancelling the cross of Christ.[2]

That notion perhaps throws light on a very curious phrase used in the Epistle to the Colossians, about "making peace through the blood of his cross".[3] It is all very well to say that it simply means "his blood shed on the cross"; but if St Paul simply meant that, it would have been easy to say that. Surely he means us to have before our eyes the picture of a cross stained with blood; surely he means us to connect it with the picture you get in the Epistle to the Hebrews, of Moses sprinkling the book with blood when he founded the old covenant.[4] Either testament was sealed with blood; the old, when Moses sprinkled the document which enshrined it, the new, when those red drops trickled down the upright wooden beam. The new covenant has the cross for its parchment, blood for its ink.

I don't mean to suggest that St Paul's thought was in any way out of harmony with our traditional Catholic doctrine of the Atonement; that he didn't look upon our Lord's death as the payment of a ransom, didn't see a foreshadowing of it in the Old Testament sacrifices. No, when Easter came round he would write to the Corinthians about Christ our paschal Victim,[5] and in his farewell speech to the elders of Ephesus he would refer to the Church as that flock which God won for himself at the price of his own blood.[6] But that way of talking wasn't habitual with him; possibly because the old sacrifices always suggested to him the idea of substitution. Even when you offered sacrifice for a fault committed, and laid your hands on the head of the victim by way of transferring your guilt from yourself to it, that was only a kind of legal ceremony; the fact remained that you had committed a fault, and it was the goat, not you, that suffered for it. Now, we understand very little about the mystery of our redemption, and it isn't unnatural that we should represent it to ourselves as a transaction of that kind. God consented to treat our Lord's death as an expiation for our fault, although the suffering, and the acceptance of suffering, were not ours but his. The reason, I think, why St Paul didn't use that language was because it didn't match his outlook on the Incarnation. The Incarnation effected a mystical union between Christ and his Church which made it misleading to talk as if our Lord were one thing and his Church another. He didn't suffer instead of a guilty race; he identified himself,

[1] Ephesians 2. 16.   [2] 1 Corinthians 1. 17.
[3] Colossians 1. 20.   [4] Hebrews 9. 19.
[5] 1 Corinthians 5. 7.   [6] Acts 20. 28.

not by a legal fiction, but by a real (though mystical) union, with a guilty race, and suffered as its representative.

All through the Epistle to the Galatians, especially, this idea seems to be pressing on the mind of the apostle, the identification of Christ with the Christian. He, Paul, has no longer any life of his own, it is Christ that lives in him; with Christ he hangs on the cross,[1] so that the world is crucified to him, and he to the world;[2] he bears on his body the scars of the crucified.[3] And this intimate indwelling is not for a privileged few, it is general to the Christian community; the apostle feels something like the pains of childbirth while he waits for Christ to be fully formed in his spiritual children.[4] It is only a matter of development; already, it seems, they are Christ in embryo. "All you who have been baptized in Christ's name have put on the person of Christ; no more Jew or Gentile, no more slave and freeman, no more male and female; you are all one person in Jesus Christ."[5]

Bethlehem means Christ born in man, and man re-born in Christ. Calvary means that mankind has died in the person of Christ, it means also that Christ has died in the name of mankind; not instead of us, as our substitute, but in our name as our representative. He identified himself with us; I do not know where you can get clearer evidence of St Paul's view in this matter than a passage in his second letter to the Corinthians, where he argues thus: "If one man died on behalf of all, then all thereby became dead men".[6] If he had written "instead of all", the argument would be nonsense; if one man dies instead of another, like Sidney Carton in the *Tale of Two Cities*, then we infer that the other man remains alive. But St Paul does not think of Christ as dying *for* us in that sense; rather as dying in the capacity of our representative, so that when he died we died with him. For St Paul, Christ did not die in order that we might live; he died in order that we might die. In what sense, we shall see in a moment.

It was not, then, by a kind of legal fiction that the sufferings of Jesus Christ, his, not ours, were allowed to count as reparation for our sins, ours, not his. It was in virtue of a mystical union with mankind that he was qualified to act as mankind's representative. And in this mystical sense you can even say that our guilt was transferred to him. At least it is difficult to read any other meaning into that curious verse of the Galatian Epistle, where St Paul writes: "Those who take their stand on the law are all under a curse. . . . From this curse invoked by the law Christ has ransomed us, by himself becoming, for our sakes, an accursed

---

[1] Galatians 2. 20.   [2] *Ibid.*, 6. 14.   [3] *Ibid.*, 6. 17.
[4] *Ibid.*, 4. 19.   [5] *Ibid.*, 3. 27, 28.   [6] 2 Corinthians 5. 14.

thing."[1] There is a rather far-fetched allusion, here, to a text in Deuteronomy; we need not go into the details of all that; the fact remains that St Paul is prepared to describe our Lord as becoming "an accursed thing". And in writing to the Corinthians he uses an even more startling phrase: "Christ never knew sin, and God made him into sin for us, so that in him we might be turned into the holiness of God."[2] Christ never knew sin—oh, it is all right, St Paul is not being heretical. It was impossible that our Lord should feel, personally, the consciousness of guilt. Yet our Lord had so identified himself with us, that what hung on the cross was, to the mystic's view, a load of guilt. To be sure, the Hebrew language made it easier for St Paul to talk like that; in Hebrew, the word for "sin" can also be used to mean "a victim for sin". But the underlying sense of what St Paul says is plain enough; our Lord for our sakes became sin, so that through him we might become innocence. It is not enough to think of the cross, like the hymn *Vexilla regis*, as a pair of scales with our sin on one side and our Lord's sacrifice on the other. We are to think of the cross as a pillory, upon which he who summed up the whole of humanity summed up the whole guilt of humanity, hung there as a kind of impersonation of guilt, and by the destruction of his body destroyed the body of our sin.

We think of our Lord's death as the meritorious cause of our deliverance from guilt; we say, "Christ died in order that we might arise again from the death of sin". St Paul, usually though not always, thinks of Christ's death as the exemplary cause of our deliverance from guilt; he says, "Christ died, and with him and in him we died to our sins; Christ rose again, and with him and in him we rose again to a new life of innocence." When he says "We died to our sins", he is using language with which we are unfamiliar, but after all, as he points out, it is the language of common life. Death cancels all obligations; and we, who were debtors under the law, and bankrupt debtors, because we were bound to keep the law and we couldn't, escaped from our obligations by dying with Christ. We are dead, and our life is hidden with Christ in God; our creditor, the law of Moses, cannot get at us now.

Well, we haven't yet answered the question we set out to answer: Which school of Christian thinkers did St Paul belong to? Did he see the Incarnation as something important in itself, or as something important because of what it led up to—the Atonement? If you had put the question in that way, I don't think he would have known what to answer; because to him the Atonement was part of the Incarnation,

---

[1] Galatians 3. 10, 13.   [2] 2 Corinthians 5. 21.

one aspect of it, one mood of it, not to be isolated in contrast with the rest· "All I know", he would have told you, "is that when Jesus Christ became man, you and I were somehow mystically identified with him. His life, not just by the circumstances of it but by the whole purpose and dedication of it, led up to his death on the cross. And when he died, you and I, mystically identified with him, became dead to our old life of sin and disobedience; we were buried with him, and rose again with him into a new life, in which God is our sun and Christ is the air we breathe. Was it the Incarnation, or the Atonement, that did that? I cannot tell; all I know is that my life is 'the faith I have in the Son of God, who loved me, and gave himself for me'."[1]

5

ST PAUL ON THE MYSTICAL BODY

May he be glorified in the Church, and in Christ Jesus.—Ephesians 3. 21.

THE words I quoted to you at the end of my last sermon were a favourite text with the old-fashioned evangelicals, "the Son of God, who loved me, and gave himself for me". The reason is not far to seek; for the evangelical, everything depends on an inner conviction that Jesus Christ has died for him personally, and this text was the ideal expression of it. What they omitted to tell us is that it stands alone in St Paul's writings; everywhere else, I think, he insists that Christ died for us, gave himself for us.

The point I am making is that St Paul is, if ever a man was, a churchman. St Peter, curiously, doesn't use the word "church" in his Epistles at all; St Paul uses it more than sixty times—in fact, if you are reading him in the Vulgate, you will find that the word occurs almost on every page. But it is not merely that he often has occasion to mention the Church; more than once he seems to mention it where you would have thought there was no occasion to do so at all. In those words, for example, which I gave you just now as my text, why was it necessary for him, if he wanted to end up the chapter with a doxology, to phrase it in this extraordinary way? "May he be glorified in the Church, and

[1] Galatians 2. 20.

in Christ Jesus"—as if the Church took rank with her Incarnate
Master as one of the organs of God's praise; nay, took first rank, with
her Incarnate Master second? It bothered the copyists, and some of
them left out the word "and". If you look in the Authorized Version
you will find, "to him be glory *in* the Church *by* Christ Jesus"—it has
even altered the preposition. But there is no doubt that ours was the
true reading, "in the Church and in Christ Jesus". St Paul's mind is so
occupied with the thought of the Church, God's splendid tapestry of
Jew and Gentile, that he can think of nothing else for the moment, and
for once the Person of Jesus Christ comes in as a kind of afterthought.

Our Lord doesn't seem to have talked much about his Church; his
favourite way of describing the Christian commonwealth was "the
kingdom of God" or "the kingdom of heaven". But on two occasions,
at least, he did talk about the "Church", and the memory it will have
called up in the minds of his disciples was the assembly, the "gathering
together" of his ancient people the Jews, when he brought them out of
Egypt into Chanaan. In old days, God had chosen a particular nation
to be his assembly; now he, Jesus Christ, would have an assembly of
his own, no longer merely national in its membership. When the
apostles took to preaching the Gospel in Greek, they didn't call this
new assembly a "gathering together", because that word "synagogue"
had already been appropriated by the Jews. They called it the ecclesia,
the "outcalling" of Christ. This was evidently, from the first, the
technical way of describing the Christian body, and for the most part
the New Testament authors use it in a severely technical sense. They
don't seem to get excited about it; it is merely a convenient way of
describing, either the total number of Christians in some particular
area, or the total number of Christians in the world. Three times out
of four, the word "congregation" would answer just as well. Strange,
that our Lord's defiant utterance, "On this rock I will build my church",
finds no echo, for example, in the Acts of the Apostles! No, I am
wrong, there is one. "Keep watch, then, over God's church, in which
the Holy Spirit has made you bishops; you are to be the shepherds of
that flock which he won for himself at the price of his own blood."[1]
But it comes in a speech reported verbatim, and the speaker is St Paul.

For St Paul, especially when he is writing to the Ephesians and to the
Colossians, the Church is a mysterious entity with a life of its own,
something much more than the sum of its members. He calls it, for
example, the "pillar and foundation upon which the truth rests";[2]
already, in that dawn of believing, heresy begins to threaten, and the

[1] Acts 20. 28.   [2] 1 Timothy 3. 15.

appeal from it is made, not precisely to the apostles who still lived, but to the *Ecclesia Docens*, human in her membership, and yet wiser than ourselves. But that is a solitary reference, late in his career. For the most part, he is lyrical about the Church, not as the touchstone of truth, but as the focus of unity. We Christians are one in Christ, and the Church is both ideally the expression of that unity, and in practice the arena for realizing it.

Oh, I know, St Paul will talk to you about "the churches" of Asia or "the churches" of Macedonia, in a way that is apt to make you think of them as so many independent units, vaguely federated. But even as he does that, if you will look more closely at the context, St Paul is deliberately over-riding these local boundaries. He is appealing to the various "churches" to subscribe to a charity of his; a fund he is raising to help the impoverished "church" at Jerusalem. And if you will read the eighth and ninth chapters of his second Epistle to the Corinthians, you will see what importance he attached to it, and why. "The administration of this public service", he says, "does more than supply the needs of the saints; it yields, besides, a rich harvest of thanksgiving in the name of the Lord. . . . They will intercede, too, on your behalf, as the abundant measure of grace which God bestows on you warms their hearts towards you."[1] This very practical form of intercourse was the best way, he saw, of knitting together the hearts of Christian people who live remote from one another; he calls it "the communion",[2] calls it by that sacred name by which, already, men referred to participation in the Holy Eucharist. That was what St Paul thought of second collections.

For him, there was one Church, and its unity was diffused everywhere, like the air we breathe. He is not content to talk about "the church" in this or that town; he will talk about "the church" in so-and-so's household[3]—the little group of Christian slaves, perhaps not always with a Christian master, who met to say their prayers together were a cross-section of Christendom, a little microcosm in which the Church was represented, as the sun may be reflected in a puddle. The Church itself was a glorious reconciliation of human differences; in it there was neither Jew nor Gentile, neither slave nor freeman, neither barbarian nor Scythian, neither male nor female, all were one person in Christ.[4] And each family, in the same way, had its differences to be reconciled; "I call upon thee, Evodia, and I call upon thee, Syntyche, to make common cause in the Lord."[5] Who were

---

[1] 2 Corinthians 9. 12, 14.   [2] *Ibid.*, 8. 4; 9. 13.   [3] Cf. Romans 16. 5.
[4] Galatians 3. 28.   [5] Philippians 4. 2.

S

they? We don't know; we don't even know whether Evodia was male or female—perhaps St Paul didn't; but their bickerings were not to go on. And in the same way, he will put an end to rivalries in this or that congregation; everybody is to do his own job, and not be envious of the next man. How small-minded they were, even those first Christians! But St Paul is not discouraged by it; here is an excellent opportunity, he thinks, for realizing on a small scale the glorious comprehensiveness of Christ's Church.

How does he think of that Church, seen in its full extension? Three metaphors he has for it, all familiar enough, but all worth looking into. For him, it is the bride of Christ; it is the building of which Christ is corner stone; it is the body of which Christ is head.

It is not a matter for surprise that St Paul should have pictured the relations between Christ and his Church under the image of man and wife. The Church was the people of Christ, exactly as the Synagogue was the people of God; and it is a commonplace, when you are reading the Old Testament prophets, to find Israel referred to as the bride of his youth, false to him now. "And thou with many lovers hast played the wanton", so runs the appeal of Jeremias, "yet come back to me, the Lord says, and thou shalt find welcome."[1] No wonder that St Paul should employ the same kind of metaphor: "My jealousy on your behalf is the jealousy of God himself; I have betrothed you to Christ, so that no other but he should claim you, his bride without spot; and now I am anxious about you".[2] And so, in writing to the Ephesians, he represents our Lord himself as showing his love for the Church by giving up his life for it, so that he might summon it into his presence, the Church in all its beauty; it was to be holy, it was to be spotless. All that we should expect; it is what follows, in this Ephesian passage, that makes us rub our eyes.

It is very characteristic of St Paul that he is not setting out to read the Ephesians a lesson in his doctrine of the Church. No, the Church comes in merely by way of illustration; what he is setting out to do is to make the husbands at Ephesus treat their wives less selfishly! But he is not content to say, "Christ treated his bride the Church so lovingly, you men ought to treat your wives lovingly, in imitation of him". He says, apparently, that a man ought to be a good husband merely from self-interest; after all, the wife is part of her husband just as the Church is part of Christ. "That is how a man ought to love his wife, as if she were his own body; in loving his wife, a man is but loving himself. And so it is with Christ and his Church; we are limbs of his body, flesh

[1] Jeremias 3. 1.   [2] 2 Corinthians 11. 2.

and bone, we belong to him. That is why a man will leave his father and mother and will cling to his wife, and the two will become one flesh. Yes, those words are a high mystery, and I am applying them here to Christ and his Church."[1]

Useless, perhaps, to ask St Paul which is the premiss from which he starts, which is the conclusion he reaches. Is he telling us that man and wife are one thing, therefore Christ and his Church are one thing? Or is he telling us that Christ and his Church are one thing, therefore man and wife ought to be one thing? I doubt if you can hold St Paul down to a syllogism like that. Rather, he sees the two truths simultaneously, either mirrored in the other. Either truth is mystical, although in the case of the husband there is a moral application; the grace of the sacrament, here as elsewhere, has to be lived up to. What concerns us, is that our mystical union with Christ is essentially a corporate one; St Paul has betrothed the Corinthians to Christ not as so many brides (the language of a later mysticism) but as a single bride; it is in and through our identification with the Church that we are identified with Christ.

The point is still more clearly emphasized by an alternative image which the apostle gives us in this same letter to the Ephesians, that of a spiritual building. "Apostles and prophets are the foundation on which you were built, and the chief corner-stone of it is Jesus Christ himself. In him the whole fabric is bound together, as it grows into a temple, dedicated to the Lord; in him you too are being built in with the rest, so that God may find in you a dwelling-place for his Spirit."[2] Two minor difficulties occur to the reader, neither of which has great importance for our present purposes. Are the prophets in question the prophets of the Old Testament? More probably those of the New; not in the sense that they were ever recognized as taking rank, merely as prophets, in the hierarchy of the Church, but in their capacity as preachers; "he who prophesies", we are told elsewhere, "builds up the church".[3] Again, does the "foundation of the apostles" mean a foundation consisting of the apostles, or a foundation which the apostles laid, as in the third chapter of the first Corinthian letter?[4] I doubt very much if St Paul stopped to ask himself which of the two he meant.

The metaphor is a common one; St Peter uses it,[5] perhaps with some memory of Caesarea Philippi. St Paul, in writing to the Ephesians, has a particular application for it; he has been talking, all through the chapter, about the vocation of the Gentiles, and he represents Christ as

[1] Ephesians 5. 28, 29, 30-32.   [2] Ephesians 2. 20-22.
[3] 1 Corinthians 14. 4.   [4] *Ibid.*, 3. 10.   [5] 1 Peter 2. 4.

the corner-stone, *lapis angularis qui facis utraque unum*[1]; in him Jew and Gentile, hitherto distinct, meet and are bound into one. The key-word of the passage is a word which only occurs in one other place in Greek literature; "the whole fabric is bound together"—perhaps we ought to say "is dove-tailed together", if we want a vivid translation. The apparently ill-assorted people fitting in together after all—that was how St Paul saw the ideal Christian congregation, each man following his own aptitudes and doing his own job without, somehow, feeling inclined to criticize the way the other man was doing his. And so it is here, on a larger scale; Jew and Gentile, why shouldn't they mix in Christ? Why shouldn't different nations, different cultures, each have their own contribution to make for the perfecting of Christ's building? All that, perhaps, St Paul would have developed; even, perhaps, developed the other side of it, as it is developed in the hymn *Caelestis urbs*[2]; the shaping, the fashioning of each stone, *fabri polita malleo*, which has to be done before it fits into its right niche, the retrenchment of personality which we call mortification. . . . But he doesn't develop all that; and if he doesn't, I think it is because he didn't like taking his metaphor from stones and mortar; they were dead things merely superimposed on one another, and St Paul liked to think of Christian people as living things, growing out of one another.

Living things, growing out of one another—so, in his Epistle to the Romans, he compares the fusion of Jew and Gentile in the Church not to a feat of architecture, but to a feat of gardening. They are not two walls, meeting at a common angle, they are two growths of olive, one wild, one fruit-bearing, and the wild growth of the Gentiles is grafted into the fruitful Jewish stock.[3] That was well enough, but he would go deeper yet. I said just now that the word which I translated "dove-tailed" only occurs twice in Greek literature. It does; once in Ephesians 2. 21, and once in Ephesians 4. 16. In this latter passage he takes the same word and deliberately grafts it on to an organic metaphor. It is as if he were saying "Dove-tailed, yes; I told you just now that we were dove-tailed into one another like different parts of a building. But really it is a closer union than that; we are dove-tailed into one another like different parts of the human body." So it is that you get that magnificent passage in which he tells us that we are to grow up, through charity, into a due proportion with Christ, who is our head. How good his metaphors are! Because of course a child's head is out

[1] From the "Great Antiphon" for 22 December, *O Rex Gentium*.
[2] Hymn of the Office for the Dedication of a Church.
[3] Romans 11. 17 ff.

of proportion, it is waiting for the rest of the body to grow up and match it; so Christ and we. "On him all the body depends; it is organized and unified by each contact with the source which supplies it; and thus, each limb receiving the active power it needs, it achieves its natural growth, building itself up (he is betrayed into the old, discarded image again)—building itself up through charity."

He is not really happy, you see, about his doctrine of the Church until he has expressed it in terms of the mystical body. As our Lord had a natural body, which must be swaddled and suckled by our Lady at Bethlehem, so he has a mystical body which must take shape and receive nourishment and so grow up into the perfect thing he wants it to be. This image is the same, yet not the same, as our Lord's own image of the True Vine.[1] The same, because there too you get the sense of an intimate connection; the branch does not depend upon its parent stock more wholly than we depend on our incorporation into Christ; does not perish more surely if it is lopped off than we do if, most miserably, we allow ourselves to be separated from him. And yet not the same, for our Lord is thinking only of our relations with him, not of our relations with one another. Each of the people to whom he is speaking—and they, remember, were the great princes of his Church —is only a twig, you can hardly call it a branch, of the one Vine; the Vine, all of it except the twigs, is himself. All that tells you the truth about our union with Christ; it does not tell you the full truth about our union in Christ. For St Paul, Christ is the head, and we are members of the body, depending not only upon him but upon one another, as the members of a human body do. "The body, after all, consists not of one organ but of many; if the foot should say, I am not the hand, and therefore I do not belong to the body, does it belong to the body any the less for that? There was to be no want of unity in the body; all the different parts of it were to make each other's welfare their common care. If one part is suffering, all the rest suffer with it; if one part is treated with honour, all the rest find pleasure in it. And you are Christ's body, organs of it depending on each other."[2] One with Christ, and one in Christ; the doctrine of the mystical body will not be summed up under any formula which falls short of that.

We have said that Christ grows in his mystical body; no need, then, to suppose that all these high-sounding phrases which St Paul uses about the Church refer to a collection of saints already made perfect. To be sure, he calls all Christian folk "saints"; it is his way; he sees us not as we are but as we ought to be. These "saints" had to be warned

[1] John 15. 1-6.   [2] 1 Corinthians 12. 14 ff.

against fornication, against thieving, against bitter schisms; it is the Church we know. We are not impeccable, not confirmed in grace, he tells us, any more than the Jewish people, God's church in the desert.[1] But we are Christ's bride; shall we mar that beauty? We are Christ's body; shall that unity go for nothing?

6

ST PAUL ON THE RISEN LIFE OF THE CHRISTIAN

You, by baptism, have been united with his burial; united, too, with his resurrection, through your faith in that exercise of power by which God raised him from the dead.—Colossians 2. 12.

WE HAVE seen how St Paul loves to dwell on the union, the self-identification, of Christ with his Church. The Church is his body, "the completion of him who everywhere and in all things is complete"[2]—nothing less than that paradox will content St Paul. The humanity of our blessed Lord is the most absolute achievement in God's creation; you cannot think of it but as a thing utterly complete in itself. And yet, if you look at the whole question from another angle, the sacred humanity would be incomplete without us; it was for our sakes he came down from heaven, and if, *per impossibile*, nobody from our blessed Lady downwards had believed in him or accepted the gift of salvation from him, the purpose of the Incarnation would have remained unrealized. St Paul is very fond of this word "completion", and it may be true that he was using, in an orthodox sense, the language of those heretics whose false teaching was a danger to the Church at Colossae. But I sometimes wonder whether it may not have suggested to him, besides, a familiar image. St Paul came from Tarsus, a place of ships and seamen; less than a century before, it had been the great centre of piracy in the Mediterranean. And the Greeks talked about "completing" a ship where we should talk of "manning" a ship; described the crew of a ship as its "completion". Did he, perhaps, at the back of his mind, think of the sacred humanity as a ship, an ark, which would have meant nothing if there had been no crew to sail it?

[1] 1 Corinthians 10. 12.   [2] Ephesians 1. 23.

On the other side, hard as it may be to think of ourselves as the completing of Christ's nature, there is no difficulty whatever in realizing that he is the completion of ours. "In Christ", says the apostle, "the whole plenitude of Deity is embodied, and in him you find your completion. . . . You, by baptism, have been united to his burial, united, too, with his resurrection."[1] Man's nature, ever since the Fall, incapable of achieving his clear destiny, conscious, however dimly, of the desire to please God, yet with no apparatus for doing it—how could anything be so manifestly incomplete? Compare him, if you will, to a ship bound for some distant port, with no complement of sailors to man her. . . . You would almost expect to find St Paul comparing Christian baptism with the rescue of Noe and his sons in the ark. But he doesn't; it is St Peter who does that.[2] For St Paul, the type of baptism is the people of Israel, led out from its Egyptian bondage through the Red Sea.

That analogy will have been in the minds of Christian people from the first; it could hardly be otherwise. Our Lord suffered death at the time of the great Jewish feast; evidently he meant us to understand that he was being sacrificed for us as our Paschal Victim, meant us to understand that the escape of Israel from Egypt by way of the Red Sea was a type of Christian baptism, cutting us off, as if by a wall of water, from our dead past. The hymn *Exultet*, which we sing on Holy Saturday, a hymn that in its whole inspiration takes you right back to the very beginnings of Christendom, is full of that imagery. "This night, long ago, thou didst rescue the sons of Israel, our fathers, out of Egypt, over the Red Sea bidding them pass dry-shod; none but this, with pillar of cloud to enlighten it, shadow of man's sin could purge away." So we bless the candle that is the type of our Lord himself, that will be dipped into the new font, and make it pregnant with the power of spiritual re-birth. All that, or at least the doctrinal kernel of all that, St Paul knew about; we learn as much from a casual reference, a single word of one of his letters—how prodigal he is of unexploited allusion, throwing out a significant word to us, and passing on!

He is warning the Corinthians that it is a fatal error to presume on one's grace; you must co-operate with it energetically; he who thinks he stands firmly should beware of a fall. And he illustrates that by recalling the infidelities of the Jewish people in the wilderness; they (he says) could sin and did sin in spite of the great graces bestowed on them. Had they not been saved from the pursuit of their enemies by the cloud that overhung their camp, by the waters of the Red Sea

[1] Colossians 2. 10, 12.   [2] I Peter 3. 20.

which closed behind them? Only he does not use that phrase, "saved from the pursuit of their enemies"; his words are, "All alike, in the cloud and in the sea, were baptized into Moses' fellowship".[1] What he means, evidently, is that Christian baptism, intimately connected with our Lord's Resurrection and with the feast of our Lord's Resurrection, is the fulfilment of a type; it puts a distance between us and our sins, isolates us in the close unity of Christian fellowship; we too are like men who have escaped from bondage, rallied now under a divine leadership. On all that background of his thought the apostle just lifts, as it were, the corner of a curtain when, almost absent-mindedly, he calls the crossing of the Red Sea a baptism.

But of course, from his point of view, the type is only a feeble image, it doesn't do justice to the situation. The Israelites, when they escaped from Egypt, escaped with their lives; it is not so with Christian baptism. To be baptized is to undergo a mystical death, in union with our Lord's death on the cross, a mystical burial in union with his burial, a mystical resurrection in union with his resurrection. We have been taken up into Christ's death, "in our baptism, we have been buried with him, died like him, that so, just as Christ was raised up by his Father's power from the dead, we too might live and move in a new kind of existence". We are grafted into a new stock; "our former nature has been crucified with him, and the living power of our guilt destroyed, so that we are the slaves of sin no longer. Guilt makes no more claim on a man who is dead."[2] Do not ask St Paul whether this mystical death sets us free from the old law, or sets us free from guilt; it is the same process—the burden we carried when we were still unregenerate was that of an obligation we could not meet; the law and our sinfulness played into one another's hands, were the upper and nether millstone which ground us between them. Now it is all right; we are dead, and death cancels all obligations. Elsewhere, pressing his imagery still more boldly, he tells us that we are dead, and our life is hidden away with Christ in God;[3] we take refuge from our pursuers, and our hiding-place is a tomb.

Not that St Paul is unacquainted with that other and more familiar imagery which describes baptism as washing us clean from our sins; "he saved us with the cleansing power which gives us new birth".[4] But that is not his favourite way of talking; and, I think, for two reasons. Washing is something external to ourselves, we get rid of something on the surface that was never really part of us; whereas the

---

[1] 1 Corinthians 10. 2.   [2] Romans 6. 6, 7.
[3] Colossians 3. 3.   [4] Titus 3. 5.

grace of baptism goes down to the very roots of our nature, restores us to a new kind of existence. And washing is a process we may repeat as often as we will; baptism is not like that, it is a single, crucial moment like the moment of death. Dead, buried, and risen with Christ, that is our state, when we have been baptized. We must not imagine, when St Paul uses a legal metaphor about death cancelling all claims, that he looks on this baptism-death as a mere legal fiction. No, we must think of ourselves as dead to sin, and alive with a life that looks towards God.[1] New life, for St Paul, does not mean merely new habits of living, turning over a new leaf. It means that a new principle of life altogether has been implanted in us; it is as if God were repeating that act by which he breathed life into the dumb clay of his creature Adam, long ago in Paradise.

There are passages in which you will find the apostle pressing this notion still further, as if the change which takes place in us at baptism were something more, even, than a death and a rising again; as if it involved the annihilation of the thing we once were, and the creation of a fresh human being altogether. "Circumcision means nothing", he tells the Galatians, "and the want of it means nothing; when a man is in Christ Jesus, there has been a new creation."[2] And so, in a passage I have already quoted, he insists that our old self has been crucified with Christ.[3] Of course, by a metaphor, you may talk of a man's old self and his new self when he has undergone any considerable change of heart. But St Paul seems to mean more than that; does he mean (we are tempted to ask) that the regeneration which comes to us with baptism undoes all the effects of the Fall, that we no longer feel the sting of concupiscence, that we are sealed, irresistibly and automatically, for heaven? But no, that is not what he is telling us. On the contrary, in these very passages where he insists so strongly on the catastrophic effects of the new birth, he is pleading with us to live up to it and be worthy of it. "You must be quit, now, of the old self whose way of life you remember, the self that wasted its aim on false dreams. . . . You must be quit of the old self, and the habits that went with it; you must be clothed in the new self, that is being refitted all the time for closer knowledge, so that the image of the God who created it is its pattern."[4] He tells us that we have got to get rid of the old self, not that we are rid of it. The doctrine of the new birth is not an all-clear signal to tell us that the struggle with sin is all over. It is a call to arms, bidding us enter on the struggle, because at last we have a chance of victory.

[1] Romans 6. 11.   [2] Galatians 6. 15.   [3] Romans 6. 6.
[4] Ephesians 4. 22; Colossians 3. 9.

"You must not make your bodily powers over to sin. . . . Sin will not be able to play the master over you any longer; you serve grace now, not the law."[1]

You serve grace now, not the law—that means, evidently and most importantly, a better chance in the struggle; the law does but set before us a high standard, which we despair of achieving, grace enables us. But something else, I think, is implied. When you serve the law, you serve it, inevitably, in a legal spirit, unwillingly, grudgingly, according to the letter. When you serve free grace, you serve it in a spirit of freedom; you enter (as we say) into the spirit of it, co-operate, gladly and generously, with its designs for you. That contrast between doing God's will because you want to is more explicitly set forth elsewhere. When the Jews were rescued from their bondage in Egypt, they emerged (you might almost say) from one bondage into another; they were God's slaves now instead of Pharao's, obeying him, if they obeyed him at all, blindly, unquestioningly, as they obeyed Pharao. But when the grace of Jesus Christ came to us, it was no longer, this time, a mere change of masters. "The spirit you have now received is not, as of old, a spirit of slavery, to govern you by fear; it is the spirit of adoption, which makes us cry out Abba, Father!"[2] It is the same principle which our Lord himself had taught, though with a slightly different emphasis, when he told his apostles, "I do not speak of you now as my servants; a servant is one who does not understand what his master is about, whereas I have made known to you all that my Father has told me, and so I have called you my friends".[3] If the practice of the Christian religion seems to you and me something uncommonly like drudgery, that is our fault; it was not meant to be. The only really Christian attitude is to obey God with the dutifulness of loving sons, is to follow Christ with the loyalty of devoted friends.

With baptism, we escape from the sense of mere law-abidingness which afflicted us under the old covenant, a dull, negative thing, and become conscious of an active principle working in us instead. What is this active principle? Nothing other than the Holy Spirit; where the Lord's Spirit is, there is liberty.[4] We have not, after all, finished the story when we have reminded ourselves that Christ died and was buried, and rose again from the dead. The natural corollary of our Lord's rising from the dead is his Ascension. He went down to the lower regions of earth; and he who so went down is no other than he who has gone up, high above all the heavens, to fill creation with his

---

[1] Romans 6. 13, 14.   [2] Romans 8. 15.
[3] John 15. 5.   [4] 2 Corinthians 3. 17.

presence. He has given gifts to men—so one of the psalms had prophesied, in the version of it which St Paul knew; Pentecost, in its turn, is the corollary of the Ascension.[1] And now he, who fills all things with his presence, has poured out the love of God in our hearts by the Holy Spirit, whom we have received. Confirmation, in those days when so many catechumens were grown men, followed close on baptism, just as Pentecost followed close on the Resurrection. "We too, all of us, have been baptized into a single body by the power of a single Spirit, . . . we have all been given to drink at a single source, the one Spirit"—you have two processes there, but they are complementary; how should a body exist without breath in it? We are to live by the Spirit as naturally (I had almost said, as unconsciously) as our physical bodies live by the breath we breathe.

To live by the Spirit, as, in ideal at least, Christians should, is sometimes referred to as "walking about in the Spirit";[2] strolling about at our pleasure (that is the notion of the Hebrew metaphor), taking our ease, "finding ourselves" in that element. Sometimes it is referred to as being "led about" by the Spirit, as if the responsibility for every decision was taken out of our hands, so instinctively do we respond to the least touch of the divine guidance.[3] That is why, as we were reminding ourselves just now, the new covenant of grace is a covenant of freedom. The life of the spirit, St Paul tells us, has appetites of its own, diametrically opposed to the appetites of unregenerate nature and therefore, ideally, excluding them.[4] A combat the Christian life may be at any level; if we find it a conflict, that is because it is being lived at a low level—the reign of the Spirit in us is incomplete.

I say, ideally; it is quite evident that even in St Paul's day there could be, and there was, maladjustment in Christian lives. All through his letters to the Corinthians, that is his chief anxiety; the exceptional gifts of the Holy Spirit—less exceptional then than now—such as prophecy, healing of sickness, speaking with unknown tongues, abounded at Corinth; but where were those other qualities, gifts of the Holy Spirit no less, that made for the building up of the Church, the spirit of discipline, the spirit of humility, above all, the spirit of charity?[5] This doubt on the apostle's part will account for the way in which he always includes in his list of spiritual gifts various aptitudes which have nothing of the abnormal, nothing of the sensational about them; there is a charisma of preaching the word, a charisma of teaching, a charisma, even, of financial administration.[6] Any quality, he insists, which makes us

---

[1] Ephesians 4. 8-10.   [2] Galatians 5. 16.   [3] Romans 8. 14.
[4] Galatians 5. 18 ff.   [5] I Corinthians 12. 31.   [6] *Ibid.*, 12. 28; Ephesians 4. 11.

useful members of the Church is bestowed upon us by that same Spirit who enables us to prophesy, to speak with tongues. The craving for powers which are unusual, which are apparently supernatural, is for St Paul a kind of vulgarity.

It is perhaps possible to trace the same warning when he tells us that "the Spirit comes to the aid of our weakness; when we do not know what prayer to offer, to pray as we ought, the Spirit himself intercedes for us, with groans beyond all utterance".[1] He does not mean that the groans are indescribable, but that they find no outlet in words. More impressive, to him, than all the outcry of prophet and glossolalist was that inner, silent experience of the mystic who feels that the business of prayer is being taken out of his own hands, that the Holy Spirit is praying in him.

"Abba, Father"—why does St Paul say that? Why does he give you the title first in Aramaic and then in Greek? He does it twice over; the Galatians, too, are reminded that God has sent out the Spirit of his Son into our hearts, crying out in us, Abba, Father.[2] Is he consciously quoting from St Mark's account of Gethsemani, where alone (perhaps by way of an editorial note) the Aramaic word is given and then translated? If so, it is the only verbal quotation from the Gospels in St Paul's writings. Or is it possible that the first two words of the Paternoster were pronounced, in the first age of the Church, bilingually, just as we still talk Greek and then translate it into Latin when we recite the Reproaches on Good Friday? Nobody can tell you. But when St Paul uses little touches like that, one thing emerges about him clearly, the very thing I have been trying to emphasize all through this course of sermons—that he is an authentic, independent witness, agreeing always with the Gospels, yet never quoting the Gospels or referring to the Gospels. He has preserved for us, concurrently with them yet independently of them, the same tradition of Christian teaching which has come down across all these centuries to you and me; only, he tapped it at the source. When he wrote, Christian theology had not been standardized in technical terms; consequently, the presentation of it you get in St Paul's writings has something individual about it, something of himself in it; and the same can be said of the images which are his favourite images. But always, as he told the Corinthians, the message he hands on to us is the message which was handed on to him.[3] Original, if ever a human mind was, the mind of Paul has been surrendered to Christ's service.

[1] Romans 8. 26.　　　　[2] Romans 8. 15; Galatians 4. 6.
[3] 1 Corinthians 15. 3.

INDEX